Writing the Journey

Essays, Stories, and Poems on Travel

David Espey
University of Pennsylvania

PEARSON
Longman

New York   San Francisco   Boston
London   Toronto   Sydney   Tokyo   Singapore   Madrid
Mexico City   Munich   Paris   Cape Town   Hong Kong   Montreal

Vice President and Editor-in-Chief: Joseph P. Terry
Managing Editor: Erika Berg
Development Editor: Barbara Santoro
Executive Marketing Manager: Ann Stypuloski
Production Coordinator: Shafiena Ghani
Project Coordination, Text Design, and Electronic Page Makeup: Dianne Hall
Cover Design Manager: Wendy Ann Fredericks
Cover Designer: Joseph DePinho
Cover Photo: Stuart Redler/Image Bank/Getty Images, Inc.
Manufacturing Buyer: Lucy Hebard
Printer and Binder: R. R. Donnelley & Sons Co., Harrisonburg
Cover Printer: Coral Graphics Services

For permission to use copyrighted material, grateful acknowledgment is made to the copyright holders on pp. 427–432, which are hereby made part of this copyright page.

Library of Congress Cataloging-in-Publication Data

CIP data is on file with the Library of Congress.

Please visit our Website at http://www.ablongman.com

ISBN 0-321-19816-6

12345678910–DOH–07060504

For Molly, Claire, and Dan, fellow travelers.

CONTENTS

II Passages: Destinations and Encounters

III Issues: Tourism and Exile

IV Home: Memory and Return

PREFACE

"The literature of travel is gigantic;
it has a thousand faces and forms."

Percy G. Adams,
Travel Literature and the Evolution of the Novel

As one of the oldest and most persistent forms in storytelling, the journey pervades literature. The critic Northrup Frye has remarked that the imaginative journey is "the one formula that is never exhausted." The purpose of this anthology is to provide a selection of modern travel writing for use in writing and literature courses. It offers a diversity of travel writing within a broad thematic framework of expectation, departure, passage, and return. The anthology draws on the richness of travel as a literary subject. It relates travel to the very process of reading; to the imaginative worlds of adventure, romance, and myth; and to the education and transformation of the traveler, writer, and reader. The various selections expand the concept of travel to such different activities as quest, pilgrimage, migration, escape, discovery, tourism, exile, and wandering and, ultimately, to the meaning of "home."

The enormity of travel as a literary topic is both inspiring and daunting. Over the centuries, travel writing has been one of the most popular and best-selling forms of literature. In the last 25 years, it has enjoyed renewed popularity as the travel industry itself flourishes and more people take to the road. "To travel is not to be at home," says contemporary traveler and writer Jonathan Raban, providing a simple but ambitious definition as well as a place to begin and end. In this sense everyone travels—leaving home is a universal rite of passage.

This book is designed for use in any of the following kinds of courses. The anthology is appropriate for composition courses because it focuses primarily on the essay and non-fiction, and it defines travel as a broadly humanistic subject encompassing such universal topics as searching for identity, undergoing rites of passage, experiencing cross-cultural encounters, and enlarging one's sense of the world. Since most of the selections are first-person narratives varying greatly in voice, setting, and subject matter, the anthology would also be an ideal text for creative non-fiction courses. For literature courses that focus on travel as a primary theme, *Writing the Journey* provides an archetypal framework of travel as an activity first imagined, then experienced, then subjected to analysis and reflection.

Approach and Organization

Keeping in mind the need to furnish some general thematic order within a pattern of organization broad enough to adapt to the differing aims of composition, creative non-fiction, and literature courses, I have arranged the readings to reflect the form that journeys often take. The general introduction sets forth an archetypal scheme of travel: first—curiosity, desire, and expectation; next—departure, passage, and encounter; and ultimately—return, remembrance, and reflection. The selections in the first section, "Beginnings: Motives and Expectations," consider how language, literature, and culture shape the imaginative desire to travel. The second part, "Passages: Destinations and Encounters," focuses on the material realities of travel and the varieties of individual experience. The social problems and questions raised by both voluntary and involuntary travel are the subject of the third section, "Issues: Tourism and Exile." The final part, "Home: Memory and Return," concerns the relation of travel to memory and identity and ends at home, where the anthology begins.

In addition to the general introduction, each of the four parts has an introduction that explains the major concepts and the common themes shared by the selections in that section. Every selection, in turn, is introduced by a brief commentary that summarizes the writer's experience as a traveler and the ways that the major themes of the section—beginnings, passages, issues, and home—are reflected in the particular selection.

Within each part, the selections are arranged to complement and inform each other's themes, make good pairings, and show a progression in thought about each section topic. Specifically, in Part I, the writers start by thinking about travel, then imagining journeys and departing; in Part II, the focus moves from how one travels to the places visited and the people encountered. Part III contrasts the experiences of privileged travelers (the tourists) to the travails of less fortunate travelers in difficult or hostile surroundings. In Part IV, the writers first consider how travel changes their feelings about specific homes they have known, and then they move to more abstract reflections on the very idea of home.

Travelers use the works of their predecessors as a kind of map for their own journeys; as they travel and then write, they carry on a kind of dialogue with other travelers and writers. This dialogue is suggested by the arrangement of the readings in this anthology and their relation to each other.

Selections

Selections were chosen according to two principles: that they would be interesting and accessible to students and that they would each represent some significant part of the vast spectrum of writing about travel. Taking the many cultural meanings of travel into account, the writer and reader may conceive of travel in such different forms as pilgrimage, spiritual quest, romance, adventure, exploration, scientific discovery, educational tour, escape, field trip, entertainment, vacation, migration, and nomadism. These kinds of travel are usually undertaken voluntarily by the traveler. Involuntary travel—displacement by social or natural catastrophes like war, political oppression, or poverty—provides a very different viewpoint on the experience of traveling; therefore, examples of writing by exiles, refugees, and the homeless are also included. Literature arising from both voluntary and involuntary travel often raises questions about ethnicity, class, race, gender, nature, the environment, and political and economic power; the selections touch on many of these various issues and points of view.

As a form of creative non-fiction, travel writing roams the borders between the realms of desire and actuality, the imaginative and the factual. Fictional journeys inspire real ones; real journeys in turn become the material for fiction. It's hard to separate the two. The term *travel writing* usually indicates non-fiction accounts written by travelers about journeys they have made. This kind of writing makes up the majority of the anthology. The broader term *literature of travel* can designate any writing in which travel is the primary subject: folklore, fiction, poetry, memoir, essay, journalism, drama, film script, song. These various forms of travel literature borrow from each other.

Pedagogical Features

This book includes the following beneficial features for both instructors and students:

- An **accessible organization** that presents the broad and complex category of travel writing in a clear pattern reflecting the individual dynamics of travel: expectation and departure, passage and encounter, and return.
- A **general introduction** as well as **thematic introductions** to each of the four sections. The general introduction provides an overview of travel literature, and the thematic introductions suggest ways to relate the individual selections to each other and to the larger, underlying ideas of the section.

- Brief but **informative headnotes** to each selection, with comments on each writer as traveler and the relation of each selection to the themes of the section.
- **Selections** that relate travel to a multitude of issues, including self-discovery, identity, gender, race, ethnicity, nationality, political conflict, border crossing, diaspora, tourism, the environment, transience, exile, and home.
- **Appendix:** An annotated **list of films** in which travel is a major theme or activity. Since travel is visually dramatic by nature, movies provide an ideal medium to supplement the printed page.

Please visit <www.english.upenn.edu/~despey> for suggestions on ways to use the anthology in class, related reading, a bibliography of critical writing on travel literature, and links to other sources and sites on travel.

Acknowledgments

I would like to thank members of the International Society for Travel Writing and the MLA Discussion Group on Travel Literature for their many contributions to the study of travel literature and their infectious passion for travel writing. The staff of Van Pelt Library at the University of Pennsylvania has been generous with study space and enormously helpful with bibliographic advice. I am very grateful to Erika Berg for suggesting and nurturing this anthology and to Barbara Santoro for her sound editorial advice. Chrysta Meadowbrooke was very helpful with copyediting. Special thanks to my colleague Paul Fussell for his work in making the study of travel writing a respected pursuit within the discipline of literary studies. The support of my wife Molly has made this project a delight.

I would also like to thank those professors around the country who reviewed this text in its many stages of development: David Beach, George Mason University; Keith Comer, Idaho State University; Sandra Jamieson, Drew University; Karla Saari Kitalong, University of Central Florida; Brian Kitely, University of Denver; Philip Krummich, Morehead State University; Alan McKenzie, Purdue University; Jeffrey Melton, Auburn University; David Porter, University of Michigan; Alison Russell, Xavier University; James Schramer, Youngstown State University; Karen Silva, Johnson and Wales University; Mary Beth Simmons, Villanova University; Jon Volkmer, Ursinus College; and Jill Weinberger, Central Connecticut State University.

DAVID ESPEY

INTRODUCTION

"Departures evoke the earliest separations of childhood; passage, those experiences of earlier flight and physical freedom; arrivals, the magic of return to beginnings and achievement of coherence."

Eric Leed, The Mind of the Traveler

Everyone travels in some manner; everyone leaves home and encounters an external world. The universality of travel as an experience makes it a rich theme and subject under which to gather a variety of literary examples. One usually thinks of travel as a voluntary and often leisure activity. This kind of travel, from study abroad to mountain trekking to tropical cruises, is a privilege. Many travelers, however, are forced from home by natural or social catastrophes such as war or famine. Exiles, refugees, and the homeless can be considered travelers, and accounts of their experiences constitute one kind of travel writing. The world could be divided into people who can afford to travel voluntarily, for their own enjoyment or education, and those who cannot. Cultural critic James Clifford offers another way to categorize travel: it can be viewed negatively as "transience, superficiality, tourism, exile, and rootlessness" or positively as "exploration, research, escape, transforming encounter."

Using the journey as an organizing structure, travel writers can include many kinds of material. Travel writing is a miscellany, a mixture of impression, reportage, opinion, autobiography, and memoir. The terms *outer journey* and *inner journey* provide a way to distinguish between travelers' more objective focus on the places and people they encounter and the more subjective focus on their own thoughts and feelings. Travelers emphasizing the outer journey might comment on the geography, history and archaeology, climate, botany, and zoology

1

of a certain place; they could discuss culture, politics, or national characteristics in the context of their adventures. Travel writers can also focus on their inner journeys, on introspective matters of mood, memory, identity, belief, self, and home as they are affected by travel.

Travel is often a means of education and a process of discovery, a way of exploring the world outside of home and expanding one's experience and knowledge. The eighteenth-century critic, Dr. Samuel Johnson, pronounced with his usual directness: "The use of traveling is to regulate imagination by reality, and instead of thinking about how things may be, see them as they are." The literature of travel derives from the realities of experience, journeys over the surface of the earth, encounters with real places and living people. Thus in travel literature, one finds a strong concern for the factual. At the same time, travelers' tales have been marked by exaggeration and fantasy. Returning from strange and unknown places, travelers often faced eager but gullible audiences. From the beginning, travelers' tales have been rooted both in material reality and the realm of the imagination.

Travel and Tourism

Travel writing has a close but uneasy relationship with the travel industry and the business of advising on sightseeing, hotels, and restaurants. Travel writing often gets confused with the guidebook industry. Indeed, popular guidebook companies like *Lonely Planet* now publish travel writing in addition to guidebooks, further compounding the two. Novelist and travel writer Bruce Chatwin once remarked that he wanted his books placed next to Chaucer on bookstore shelves, but they ended up next to *Czechoslovakia on $20 a Day*. Chatwin even refused a cash prize for the Thomas Cook Travel Book Award because he considered *The Songlines*, his narrative about Australia, to be a novel rather than a travel book. Like Paul Theroux, he simply preferred to be called a writer rather than a travel writer. In his introduction to *The Best American Travel Writing, 2001*, Theroux attempts a definition of travel writing by explaining what it is not:

> Travel writing these days seems to be many things; but in my opinion it is not what usually passes for travel writing. It is not a first-class seat on an airplane, not a week of wine tasting on the Rhine, not a weekend in a luxury hotel. It is not a survey of expensive brunch menus, a search for the perfect margarita, or a roundup of the best health spas in the Southwest. In short, it is not about vacations or holidays, not an adjunct to the public relations industry. Travel writing is certainly not an overedited, reader-friendly text bowdlerized by fact checkers, published with a layout of breathtaking photographs—and heretically, travel writing is not necessarily tasteful, perhaps not even factual, and seldom about pleasure.

In myths, epics, and romances, travel demanded heroic endeavors and brought about a transformation in the travelers. Thus travel as a literary subject carries with it a tradition of challenge, ordeal, and illumination that is often at odds with the spirit of leisure, enjoyment, and entertainment now promoted by the publicity of mass tourism. Since the establishment of the paid vacation as a worker's benefit, travel has been looked upon as an activity like play, to be distinguished from work. Travel writers, on the other hand, insist that travel is work, but they often remark how travel is like being a child again. A traveler in a foreign country can feel innocent and vulnerable, like a child. At the same time, travel can renew a sense of delight in the world and a freshness of perception. But childlike wonder and a feeling of play do not make travel a superficial or inconsequential activity. As Henry David Thoreau said, "True and sincere traveling is not a pastime, but it is as serious as the grave, or any part of the human journey."

Travel can be an intensely individual pursuit, often an escape from the constrictions of a traveler's own society or community. At the same time, travel—whether by individual or group—is a social act, a source of encounters between peoples of different nationalities and cultures. The experience of travel draws travelers out of themselves and thrusts them into communities and social situations quite different from what they have known.

Though on the surface it may seem unrelated to home, travel complicates the meaning of "home." The distinction between "home" (where travel originates) and "not home" (where travel takes place) seems clear enough but can be ambiguous. As we grow, our notion of home expands from house and family to neighborhood, community, city, state, country, continent, hemisphere, or planet. In the movie about the damaged spacecraft, *Apollo 13*, the astronauts look wistfully through the porthole at the far-away globe and wonder if they will ever get back home to earth.

Travel can make one appreciative as well as critical of home. In a global and multicultural society, people can have attachments to a number of homes. Home may be a state of mind, a memory, or a center of perpetual routes of outward and returning movement. The literature of travel often implies that an understanding of home (and the self formed by the home) can be attained only after one journeys away from home and returns. Thus travel, which often begins in a need to escape the confines of home, may end with a new appreciation and understanding of home and its meaning to the traveler.

Overview of This Text

The obvious challenge in putting together a collection of this nature is the sheer volume of literature about travel. Every literate culture and era has produced its travelers and travel tales, and the continuing expansion of mass travel has encouraged an ever-increasing audience for writing about travel. This anthology of non-fiction, with a few selections of fiction and poetry, offers a number of literary perspectives on modern travel, but it is not meant to be a survey, either historically or geographically. No travel anthology can include everyone's favorite travel writer. The selections reflect the generic nature of travel writing. Since travel is also a frequent theme of fiction and poetry, examples of both genres are included, especially for comparison with the non-fiction pieces. Given the breadth and complexity of travel as a literary subject, most of the selections could fit easily into more than one part of the collection. Students can question how the various essays, stories, and poems relate to each other and how the individual experiences of travelers raise questions about the behavior of societies and groups. The anthology is limited, with a few exceptions, to English-speaking writers, but the framework provides for the inclusion of many different voices and perspectives. Instructors can use this anthology in combination with full-length works of travel literature and reading lists for courses of their own design.

Beginnings: Motives and Expectations

INTRODUCTION

"I had long seen clearly that a great part of the pleasure of travel . . . is rooted . . . in dissatisfaction with home and family. When one first catches sight of the sea, crosses the ocean, and experiences as realities cities and lands which for so long had been distant, unattainable things of desire—one feels oneself like a hero who has performed deeds of improbable greatness."

Sigmund Freud, A *Disturbance of Memory on the Acropolis*

Motives for travel can be as varied as boredom, restlessness, impulse to escape, curiosity, yearning for adventure, and desire for knowledge. Travelers often lack full consciousness of their motives. They are simply seized by an urge to go away and see the world in a different perspective. Regardless of motive, however, travel is commonly viewed as a leisure activity, a form of recreation, a break from domestic routines.

In human prehistory, however, travel *was* the domestic routine. Humans were first nomadic hunters and gatherers of food before they settled in fixed, agricultural communities. Human history has been a narrative of perpetual movement, a conflict between the desire to remain rooted and the necessity of seeking a better place to dwell. Thus, some regard the impulse to travel as atavistic, a willed return to the nomadic spirit of our ancestral past.

In contrast to this nomadic spirit is the ancient myth of the Garden of Eden, so central to Judeo-Christian culture. The myth reverses the nomadic-to-settled sequence of human history. Adam and Eve are exiled from their garden home and condemned to wander. This story exerts a powerful influence on the literature of travel. Travelers dream of finding a perfect, Eden-like place—a paradise on earth. In the words of novelist and travel writer D. H. Lawrence, who wandered through Europe, North and South America, and Australia, "We travel, perhaps, with an absurd and secret hope . . . of running up a little creek and landing in the Garden of Eden."

Philosophers and writers have looked upon human existence as a journey and have viewed life as a matter of following a moral path or spiritual way. The most common metaphor in literature for the life of a people or an individual is the journey—the movement through time and space toward some end. Mythical journeys can transcend death. In fact, many cultures, notably the ancient

Egyptians, envisioned the afterlife as a further journey; the dead were buried with provisions for travel—food, clothing, weapons, horses, even sailing vessels. It is as if travel were life itself, and the journey after death the promise of renewed life. As the French philosopher Blaise Pascal observed in his *Pensees*, "Our nature lies in movement; complete calm is death."

Among the most important things travelers carry in their minds (and often in their luggage) are the books of those who have gone before them. Travelers' motives, itineraries, and experiences are shaped by reading about the journeys of earlier writers who have followed similar routes. Accounts of travel inspire readers to take to the road or the sea, then write of journeys themselves. The literature that travelers have read inevitably colors the world they encounter outside the pages of a book. For instance, Joseph Conrad made his own journey to the Congo and wrote about it first in a journal, then as fiction in *Heart of Darkness*. That tale itself draws on earlier epic journeys like Homer's *Odyssey* and Dante's *Inferno* and accounts of real African travels like Henry Stanley's search for David Livingstone. Conrad's novel in turn has influenced many modern novels and travel books about sub-Saharan Africa.

Epics, poems, novels, and travel narratives have all served as guidebooks for travelers. Through those books, travelers "read" the world of their own travels, then echo that literature as they represent in their own writing what they encounter. Many travel books literally follow in the footsteps of earlier narratives. For example, Jonathan Raban, whose book about going down the Mississippi River is excerpted in this section, started thinking about the journey as a child when he read Mark Twain's novel *The Adventures of Huckleberry Finn*. While traveling on the Mississippi, Raban constantly thought of Mark Twain and often saw the landscape through the pages of Twain's books.

Though the direction of the traveler's journey is forward in space and time, the expectations of the journey are often influenced by an idealized past, childhood memories, the voices of earlier writers, and the patterns of stories and myths. Memories of childhood reading are especially powerful for sowing the seeds of travel. Indeed, the very act of reading for a child (and for adults as well) can be a kind of transport, an imagined version of travel. A staple of children's literature is the imaginative journey: consider *Where the Wild Things Are*, *Treasure Island*, and *The Wizard of Oz*. Countless fairy tales dramatize the perils and rewards of the journey away from home: "Snow White," "Hansel and Gretel," and "Little Red Riding Hood." For children limited to the world of home, reading is like traveling, and many of the writers in Part I describe how the seeds of their journeys were sown by childhood reading.

Leaving home to go on a journey is a rite of passage familiar in children's literature, recalled in childhood memoir and autobiography. Such narratives celebrate the early impulses of one of the most powerful motives for travel: escape from the confinements of home and desire for independence. Many writers also see the act of travel as rebellious and subversive, as well as adventurous and instructive.

Joseph Campbell's *The Hero with a Thousand Faces* links folklore and children's literature with myth in their fundamental pattern of the hero's journey outward to adventure and illumination, then homeward to tell the tale. Campbell sees travel as a transcendental and heroic activity yielding wisdom and transformation.

In his book, *The Tourist: A New Theory of the Leisure Class*, Dean MacCannell traces the idea of the journey as a quest for meaning and identity from the first epics through human history to the present:

> Self discovery through a complex and sometimes arduous search for an absolute Other is a basic theme of our civilization, a theme supporting an enormous literature: Odysseus, Aeneas, the Diaspora, Chaucer, Christopher Columbus, *Pilgrim's Progress*, Jules Verne, Western ethnography, Mao's Long March. This theme does not just thread our way through our literature and our history. It grows and develops, arriving at a kind of final flowering in modernity. What begins as the proper activity of a *hero* (Alexander the Great) develops into the goal of a socially organized *group* (the Crusaders), into the mark of status of an entire social *class* (the Grand Tour of the British "gentleman"), eventually becoming *universal experience* (the tourist).

Homer's epic *The Odyssey* has become a kind of model for travel books in general; the very word *odyssey* denotes an arduous and meaningful journey. Significantly, the hero Odysseus makes the journey, but his wife Penelope stays home and awaits his return. This pattern of men venturing out into the world while women are confined to home can be seen in travel literature from ancient to modern times. Over the centuries, the literature of travel has been dominated by men; there were comparatively fewer women travel writers. In recent decades, however, that perspective has changed. Increasing numbers of women have written of their travels and rediscovered neglected works by women travelers from previous centuries.

The selections in Part I begin with N. Scott Momaday's retracing of the "way," the culture and the migration route as well as the mythology of his Native American ancestors. Momaday's memoir of his people's journey introduces many of the major themes and issues of travel: our human origins as nomads, the mythic pattern of the journey to give shape and form to human existence, the transformation of culture brought about by the acquisition of a new form of transportation (for the Kiowa, the horse), the importance of memory and a rediscovery of the past as motives for travel, and the quest for a spiritual home. Robert Frost's two poems express both the impulse to travel and the tendency to see one's life as a journey. Eric Leed surveys the historical structure of travel narratives from the first epic to the present day, and Salman Rushdie considers the literary heritage behind the spirit of adventure in travel. The children's poems by Robert Louis Stevenson exemplify how the seeds of the desire to travel are planted in childhood and the experience of reading. The genius of maps and their relation to travel is the subject of Paul Theroux's essay, and the excerpts from books by Erika Warmbrunn and Sara Wheeler acknowledge the inspiration of maps for their projected journeys.

Keats's sonnet is one of the best-known expressions of reading as vicarious travel. Inspired by childhood reading, Jonathan Raban traces the origins of his own Mississippi journey to his memories of the fictional Huckleberry Finn. Susan Rich's poem associates the fragrance of gasoline with childhood and the perpetual excitement of travel. Mary Morris combines her own early visions of travel with her mother's dreams in spite of the legacy of home-bound women in life and literature. The confinements of childhood and segregation color the associations of bell hooks and Richard Wright with travel. The selections by Harry Dean and John Masefield express an adolescent restlessness and urge to set out. In prose and in poetry respectively, Alain de Boton and Philip Larkin explore expectations versus the realities of travel, and Francis Bacon sets forth a prescription for travel. Bruce Chatwin speculates on the links between travel and literature in oral maps and myths of Australian aborigines. Geographic isolation is behind the travel urge of contemporary Australians like Tony Wheeler. Finally, Elizabeth Bishop poses poetic questions about the enigmatic motives for travel.

Overall, the selections in this section provide insight into each writer's motives for and expectations of travel. Readers of this anthology should look for the sources of each writer's desire to travel. The patterns of earlier stories and myths shape not only the actual journeys but also the ways that travelers write and think about travel. Many of the selections can be read and discussed in pairs: Raban and Stevenson on travel and the child's imagination, hooks and Wright on race and constraint, Momaday and Chatwin on ancestral myth and travel. The selections by Leed, Theroux, and Morris contain general observations about historical patterns, literary genres, maps as metaphors, and gender that can be linked to many of the individual experiences of travel in the other selections.

N. SCOTT MOMADAY

(1934–)

N. Scott Momaday earned a Ph.D. in English literature from Stanford, but his interests turned to the myth and history of his people. He received the Pulitzer Prize for his novel, *House Made of Dawn* (1969), which drew upon the traditions of Navajo, Pueblo, and Kiowa peoples. Momaday has also written poetry and a memoir, *The Names* (1976). He sought to understand his Kiowa ancestors by following the route they had taken centuries ago as they migrated from the northern Rocky Mountains to the plains of what is now Oklahoma. The resulting book, *The Way to Rainy Mountain* (1969), recreates the experience of the Kiowa people through fragments of myth, history, and memory.

In the excerpt from the book that follows, Momaday uses the image of the path or way as a metaphor for the history and culture of an entire people. He returns to the home territory of his nomadic forbearers and reenacts the story of the Kiowas' migration by retracing their long journey himself and attempting to see the world as they saw it. His trip links beginnings and endings, past and present.

From *The Way to Rainy Mountain*

Prologue

The journey began one day long ago on the edge of the northern Plains. It was carried on over a course of many generations and many hundreds of miles. In the end there were many things to remember, to dwell upon and talk about.

"You know, everything had to begin. . . ." For the Kiowas the beginning was a struggle for existence in the bleak northern mountains. It was there, they say, that they entered the world through a hollow log. The end, too, was a struggle, and it was lost. The young Plains culture of the Kiowas withered and died like grass that is burned in the prairie wind. There came a day like destiny; in every direction, as far as the eye could see, carrion lay out in the land. The buffalo was the animal representation of the sun, the essential and sacrificial victim of the Sun Dance. When the wild herds were destroyed, so too was the will of the Kiowa people; there was nothing to sustain them in spirit. But these are idle recollections, the mean and ordinary agonies of human history. The interim was a time of great adventure and nobility and fulfillment.

Tai-me came to the Kiowas in a vision born of suffering and despair. "Take me with you," Tai-me said, "and I will give you whatever you want." And it was so. The great adventure of the Kiowas was a going forth into the heart of the continent. They began a long migration from the headwaters of the Yellowstone River eastward to the Black Hills and south to the Wichita Mountains. Along the way they acquired horses, the religion of the Plains, a love and possession of the open land. Their nomadic soul was set free. In alliance with the Comanches they held dominion in the southern Plains for a hundred years. In the course of that long migration they had come of age as a people. They had conceived a good idea of themselves; they had dared to imagine and determine who they were.

In one sense, then, the way to Rainy Mountain is preeminently the history of an idea, man's idea of himself, and it has old and essential being in language. The verbal tradition by which it has been preserved has suffered a deterioration in time. What remains is fragmentary: mythology, legend, lore, and hearsay—and of course the idea itself, as crucial and complete as it ever was. That is the miracle.

The journey herein recalled continues to be made anew each time the miracle comes to mind, for that is peculiarly the right and responsibility of the imagination. It is a whole journey, intricate with motion and meaning; and it is made with the whole memory, that experience of the mind which is legendary as well as historical, personal as well as cultural. And the journey is an evocation of three things in particular: a landscape that is incomparable, a time that is gone forever, and the human spirit, which endures. The imaginative experience and the historical express equally the traditions of man's reality. Finally, then, the journey recalled is among other things the revelation of one way in which these traditions are conceived, developed, and interfused in the human mind. There are on the way to Rainy Mountain many landmarks, many journeys in the one. From the beginning the migration of the Kiowas was an expression of the human spirit, and that expression is most truly made in terms of wonder and delight: "There were many people, and oh, it was beautiful. That was the beginning of the Sun Dance. It was all for Tai-me, you know, and it was a long time ago."

Introduction

A single knoll rises out of the plain in Oklahoma, north and west of the Wichita Range. For my people, the Kiowas, it is an old landmark, and they gave it the name Rainy Mountain. The hardest weather in the world is there. Winter brings blizzards, hot tornadic winds arise in the spring, and in summer the prairie is an anvil's edge. The grass turns brittle and brown, and it cracks beneath your feet. There are green belts along the rivers and creeks, linear groves of hickory and pecan, willow and witch hazel. At a distance in July or August the steaming foliage seems almost to writhe in fire. Great green and yellow grasshoppers are everywhere in the tall grass, popping up like corn to sting the flesh, and tortoises crawl about on the red earth, going nowhere in the plenty of time. Loneliness is an aspect of the land. All things in the plain are isolate; there is no confusion of objects in the eye, but one hill or one tree or one man. To look upon that landscape in the early morning, with the sun at your back, is to lose the sense of proportion. Your imagination comes to life, and this, you think, is where Creation was begun.

I returned to Rainy Mountain in July. My grandmother had died in the spring, and I wanted to be at her grave. She had lived to be very old and at last infirm. Her only living daughter was with her when she died, and I was told that in death her face was that of a child.

I like to think of her as a child. When she was born, the Kiowas were living the last great moment of their history. For more than a hundred years they had controlled the open range from the Smoky Hill River to the Red, from the headwaters of the Canadian to the fork of the Arkansas and Cimarron. In alliance with the Comanches, they had ruled the whole of the southern Plains. War was their sacred business, and they were among the finest horsemen the world has ever known. But warfare for the Kiowas was preeminently a matter of disposition rather than of survival, and they never understood the grim, unrelenting advance of the U.S. Cavalry. When at last, divided and ill-provisioned, they were driven onto the Staked Plains in the cold rains of autumn, they fell into panic. In Palo Duro Canyon they abandoned their crucial stores to pillage and had nothing then but their lives. In order to save themselves, they surrendered to the soldiers at Fort Sill and were imprisoned in the old stone corral that now stands as a military museum. My grandmother was spared the humiliation of those high gray walls by eight or ten years, but she must have known from birth the affliction of defeat, the dark brooding of old warriors.

Her name was Aho, and she belonged to the last culture to evolve in North America. Her forebears came down from the high country in western Montana nearly three centuries ago. They were a mountain people, a mysterious tribe of hunters whose language has never been positively classified in any major group. In the late seventeenth century they began a long migration to the south and east. It was a journey toward the dawn, and it led to a golden age. Along the way the Kiowas were befriended by the Crows, who gave them the culture and religion of the Plains. They acquired horses, and their ancient nomadic spirit was suddenly free of the ground. They acquired Tai-me, the sacred Sun Dance doll, from that moment the object and symbol of their worship, and so shared in the divinity of the sun. Not least, they acquired the sense of destiny, therefore courage and pride. When they entered upon the southern Plains they had been transformed. No longer were they slaves to the simple necessity of survival; they were a lordly and dangerous society of fighters and thieves, hunters and priests of the sun. According to their origin myth, they entered the world through a hollow log. From one point of view, their migration was the fruit of an old prophecy, for indeed they emerged from a sunless world.

Although my grandmother lived out her long life in the shadow of Rainy Mountain, the immense landscape of the continental interior lay like memory in her blood. She could tell of the Crows, whom she had never seen, and of the Black Hills, where she had never been. I wanted to see in reality what she had seen more perfectly in the mind's eye, and traveled fifteen hundred miles to begin my pilgrimage.

Yellowstone, it seemed to me, was the top of the world, a region of deep lakes and dark timber, canyons and waterfalls. But, beautiful as it is, one might have the sense of confinement there. The skyline in all directions is close at hand, the high wall of the woods and deep cleavages of shade. There is a perfect freedom in the mountains, but it belongs to the eagle and the elk, the badger and the bear. The Kiowas reckoned their stature by the distance they could see, and they were bent and blind in the wilderness.

Descending eastward, the highland meadows are a stairway to the plain. In July the inland slope of the Rockies is luxuriant with flax and buckwheat, stonecrop and larkspur. The earth unfolds and the limit of the land recedes. Clusters of trees, and animals grazing far in the distance, cause the vision to reach away and wonder to build upon the mind. The sun follows a longer course in the day, and the sky is immense beyond all comparison. The great billowing clouds that sail upon it are shadows that move upon the grain like water, dividing light. Farther down, in the land of the Crows and Blackfeet, the plain is yellow. Sweet clover takes hold of the hills and bends upon itself to cover and seal the soil. There the Kiowas paused on their way; they had come to the place where they must change their lives. The sun is at home on the plains. Precisely there does it have the certain character of a god. When the Kiowas came to the land of the Crows, they could see the dark lees of the hills at dawn across the Bighorn River, the profusion of light on the grain shelves, the oldest deity ranging after the solstices. Not yet would they veer southward to the caldron of the land that lay below; they must wean their blood from the northern winter and hold the mountains a while longer in their view. They bore Tai-me in procession to the east.

A dark mist lay over the Black Hills, and the land was like iron. At the top of a ridge I caught sight of Devil's Tower upthrust against the gray sky as if in the birth of time the core of the earth had broken through its crust and the motion of the world was begun. There are things in nature that engender an awful quiet in the heart of man; Deveil's Tower is one of them. Two centuries ago, because they could not do otherwise, the Kiowas made a legend at the base of the rock. My grandmother said:

Eight children were there at play, seven sisters and their brother. Suddenly the boy was struck dumb; he trembled and began to run upon his hands and feet. His fingers became claws, and his body was covered with fur. Directly there was a bear where the boy had been. The sisters were terrified; they ran, and the bear after them.

They came to the stump of a great tree, and the tree spoke to them. It bade them climb upon it, and as they did so it began to rise into the air. The bear came to kill them, but they were just beyond its reach. It reared against the tree and scored the bark all around with its claws. The seven sisters were borne into the sky, and they became the stars of the Big Dipper.

From that moment, and so long as the legend lives, the Kiowas have kinsmen in the night sky. Whatever they were in the mountains, they could be no more. However tenuous their well-being, however much they had suffered and would suffer again, they had found a way out of the wilderness.

My grandmother had a reverence for the sun, a holy regard that now is all but gone out of mankind. There was a wariness in her, and an ancient awe. She was a Christian in her later years, but she had come a long way about, and she never forgot her birthright. As a child she had been to the Sun Dances; she had taken part in those annual rites, and by them she had learned the restoration of her people in the presence of Tai-me. She was about seven when the last Kiowa Sun Dance was held in 1887 on the Washita River above Rainy Mountain Creek. The buffalo were gone. In order to consummate the ancient sacrifice—to impale the head of a buffalo bull upon the medicine tree—a delegation of old men journeyed into Texas, there to beg and barter for an animal from the Goodnight herd. She was ten when the Kiowas came together for the last time as a living Sun Dance culture. They could find no buffalo; they had to hang an old hide from the sacred tree. Before the dance could begin, a company of soldiers rode out from Fort Sill under orders to disperse the tribe. Forbidden without cause the essential act of their faith, having seen the wild herds slaughtered and left to rot upon the ground, the Kiowas backed away forever from the medicine tree. That was July 20, 1890, at the great bend of the Washita. My grandmother was there. Without bitterness, and for as long as she lived, she bore a vision of deicide.

Now that I can have her only in memory, I see my grandmother in the several postures that were peculiar to her: standing at the wood stove on a winter morning and turning meat in a great iron skillet; sitting at the south window, bent above her beadwork, and afterwards, when her vision failed, looking down for a long time into the folds of her hands; going out upon a cane, very slowly as she did when the weight of age came upon her; praying. I remember her most often at prayer. She made long, rambling prayers out of suffering and hope, having seen many things. I was never sure that I had the right to hear, so exclusive were they of all mere custom and company. The last time I saw her she prayed standing by the side of her bed at night, naked to the waist, the light of a kerosene lamp moving upon her dark skin. Her long, black hair, always drawn and braided in the day, lay upon her shoulders and against her breasts like a shawl. I do not speak Kiowa, and I never understood her prayers, but there was something inherently sad in the sound, some merest hesitation upon the syllables of sorrow. She began in a high and descending pitch, exhausting her breath to silence; then again and again—and always the same intensity of effort, of something that is, and is not, like urgency in the human voice. Transported so in the dancing light among the shadows of her room, she seemed beyond the reach of time. But that was illusion; I think I knew then that I should not see her again.

Houses are like sentinels in the plain, old keepers of the weather watch. There, in a very little while, wood takes on the appearance of great age. All colors wear soon away in the wind and rain, and then the wood is burned gray and the grain appears and the nails turn red with rust. The windowpanes are black and opaque; you imagine there is nothing within, and indeed there are many ghosts, bones given up to the land. They stand here and there against the sky, and you approach them for a longer time than you expect. They belong in the distance; it is their domain.

Once there was a lot of sound in my grandmother's house, a lot of coming and going, feasting and talk. The summers there were full of excitement and reunion. The Kiowas are a summer people; they abide the cold and keep to themselves, but when the season turns and the land becomes warm and vital they cannot hold still; an old love of going returns upon them. The aged visitors who came to my grandmother's house when I was a child were made of lean and leather, and they bore themselves upright. They wore great black hats and bright ample shirts that shook in the wind. They rubbed fat upon their hair and wound their braids with strips of colored cloth. Some of them painted their faces and carried the scars of old and cherished enmities. They were an old council of warlords, come to remind and be reminded of who they were. Their wives and daughters served them well. The women might indulge themselves; gossip was at once the mark and compensation of their servitude. They made loud and elaborate talk among themselves, full of jest and gesture, fright and false alarm. They went abroad in fringed and flowered shawls, bright beadwork and German silver. They were at home in the kitchen, and they prepared meals that were banquets.

There were frequent prayer meetings, and great nocturnal feasts. When I was a child I played with my cousins outside, where the lamplight fell upon the ground and the singing of the old people rose up around us and carried away into the darkness. There were a lot of good things to eat, a lot of laughter and surprise. And afterwards, when the quiet returned, I lay down with my grandmother and could hear the frogs away by the river and feel the motion of the air.

Now there is a funeral silence in the rooms, the endless wake of some final word. The walls have closed in upon my grandmother's house. When I returned to it in mourning, I saw for the first time in my life how small it was. It was late at night, and there was a white moon, nearly full. I sat for a long time on the stone steps by the kitchen door. From there I could see out across the land; I could see the long row of trees by the creek, the low light upon the rolling plains, and the stars of the Big Dipper. Once I looked at the moon and caught sight of a strange thing. A cricket had perched upon the handrail, only a few inches away from me. My line of vision was such that the creature filled the moon like a fossil. It had gone there, I thought, to live and die, for there, of all places, was its small definition made whole and eternal. A warm wind rose up and purled like the longing within me.

The next morning I awoke at dawn and went out on the dirt road to Rainy Mountain. It was already hot, and the grasshoppers began to fill the air. Still, it was early in the morning, and the birds sang out of the shadows. The long yellow grass on the mountain shone in the bright light, and a scissortail hied above the land. There, where it ought to be, at the end of a long and legendary way, was my grandmother's grave. Here and there on the dark stones were ancestral names. Looking back once, I saw the mountain and came away.

[1969]

ROBERT FROST

(1874–1963)

Robert Frost is closely identified with the rural New England where he lived and worked as a farmer, teacher, and writer. With the exception of residing in England with his family from 1912 to 1915, Frost did not travel widely. He spent most of his life in Vermont and Massachusetts. His volumes of poetry won Pulitzer Prizes in four different years between 1923 and 1942, and he received many awards and honors, including an invitation to read at President John F. Kennedy's inauguration.

"The Road Not Taken," one of Frost's best-known works, presents a popular image of individual existence as a journey necessitating a choice between roads to be followed. The poem is often read as a directive for taking the less traveled route—choosing an original or unusual path for one's life. But the speaker may well imply that although the two roads are indeed very different, the routes are in fact similar. The difference may be an imagined one, created by memory. The poem "Away," by contrast, celebrates the impulse to escape settled life by traveling.

"The Road Not Taken"

Two roads diverged in a yellow wood,
And sorry I could not travel both

And be one traveler, long I stood
And looked down one as far as I could
To where it bent in the undergrowth;   5

Then took the other, as just as fair,
And having perhaps the better claim,
Because it was grassy and wanted wear;
Though as for that, the passing there
Had worn them really about the same,   10

And both that morning equally lay
In leaves no step had trodden black.
Oh, I kept the first for another day!
Yet knowing how way leads on to way,
I doubted if I should ever come back.   15

I shall be telling this with a sigh
Somewhere ages and ages hence:
Two roads diverged in a wood, and I—
I took the one less traveled by,
And that has made all the difference.   20

[1915]

"Away!"

Now I out walking
The world desert,
And my shoe and my stocking
Do me no hurt.

I leave behind   5
Good friends in town
Let them get well-wined
And go lie down.

Don't think I leave
For the outer dark   10
Like Adam and Eve
Put out of the Park.

Forget the myth.
There is no one I
Am put out with   15
Or put out by.

Unless I'm wrong
I but obey
The urge of a song:
I'm — bound — away!   20

And I may return
If dissatisfied
With what I learn
From having died.

[1958]

ERIC LEED

(1942–)

In *The Mind of the Traveler: From Gilgamesh to Global Tourism* (1991), Eric Leed traces the cultural history of travel and its representations in folklore and literature. Retired as Professor of History at Florida International University, Leed has also written *No Man's Land: Combat and Identity in World War I* (1979) and *Shores of Discovery: How Expeditionaries Have Constructed the World* (1995).

The following selection, from the introduction to *The Mind of the Traveler*, surveys travel as a universal cultural experience and examines its associations with heroism, suffering, and illumination. Leed again emphasizes the importance of past traditions of travel in shaping the form and meaning of modern journeys.

"For a History of Travel"

From *The Mind of the Traveler*

What gives value to travel is fear. It is the fact that, at a certain moment, when we are so far from our own country . . . we are seized by a vague fear, and the

instinctive desire to go back to the protection of old habits. This is the most obvi-
ous benefit of travel. At that moment we are feverish but also porous, so that
the slightest touch makes us quiver to the depths of our being. . . . This is why
we should not say that we travel for pleasure. There is no pleasure in travelling,
and I look upon it as an occasion for spiritual testing. . . . Pleasure takes us
away from ourselves in the same way that distraction, as in Pascal's use of the
word, takes us away from God. Travel, which is like a greater and graver sci-
ence, brings us back to ourselves.

–Albert Camus, 1963

Travel is a common, frequent, everyday occurrence in our present. In fact, it
is a source of our commonality, as in 1987 over forty million Americans traveled abroad, and many more at home. Comprising less than 5 percent of the
world's population, U.S. citizens accounted for over 25 percent of the world
spending for domestic and international travel—estimated at $2.3 trillion. If
one counts all the California trips and journeys seasonally made, north and
south, it is not merely a metaphor to say America is on the move and connected through mobilities. Travel, in the form of tourism, is becoming increasingly pervasive in our world. By the turn of the millennium, it will be the most
important sector of world trade, surpassing oil, and is currently the second
largest retail industry in the United States. The impression of the commonality of travel is intensified when one includes in the ranks of travelers those
who obviously belong but do not appear in the tourism statistics—business
travelers, nomads, commuters, itinerant laborers, refugees, members of the
armed services, diplomatic personnel, temporary and permanent immigrants.
Indeed, in the first half of the twentieth century, military tourism was a common form of popular mobility and the only form of mass travel the masses
could afford. A 1958 survey by the University of Michigan found that one
adult American out of five had been overseas at some time in their lives, two
out of three with the armed services.[1]

The term *mass tourism* conveys the scale of modern tourist business, the
mass production of journeys, the infinite replication of trips to the point that
even a formerly extraordinary voyage—to Machu Picchu, say, or to the Forbidden City or to Tashkent—has become something rather ordinary, a kind of
norm rather than an escape from the norm. The sheer number of travelers
crowding the terminals, roads, holy and sacred grounds, merchandising marts
and markets alerts us to the fact that we are a society of travelers. In this society the journey is the ordinary way members link their lives and consume a
world of meanings and places.

Though living in an era of mass tourism, the average American tourist is
by no means representative of the masses of Americans. A survey of Americans
traveling abroad in 1986 found that the average overseas tourist had an annual

income of $55,519, was a member of the professional, managerial, or technical class (61 percent of overseas travelers), male (57 percent), forty-four years old, most likely to come from New York or California (46 percent), traveling for pleasure on a holiday (57 percent), was a repeat rather than a first-time traveler (91 percent), booked through a travel agency, traveled economy class (74 percent), and most likely going to one country (68 percent) in Western Europe or to the United Kingdom (60 percent).[2] Indeed, "travel for pleasure" remains as it was through the ages, a mark of success and status, while travel under compulsion of some necessity or in service of need is a mark of commonality and a common fate.

If one broadens the definition of travel to encompass all passage across significant boundaries that separate differing persona, kinds of social relations, activities, then it becomes obvious that travel is much more than common. It is an activity that weaves the fabric of contemporary lives. Very few of us eat, sleep, work, and play in the same place—this would be a definition of confinement and unfreedom. Normally our lives are segmented into places of work, play, privacy, to be joined through territorial passage along the corridors and passsageways, road and rail networks of modern metropolitan areas—those extended "cities" that differ so markedly from ancient cities, like the city of Nejef in Iraq where the twentieth-century adventurer and travel writer Freya Stark once found herself:

> To sit there among the pressed houses, so crowded within the security of their wall that there was scarcely room in front of the mosque for the little stone-flagged square, was to realize what for several thousand years of our history has constituted the feeling of safety, the close-packed enclosure of small cities crammed within walls. Outside are the wilderness, or the neighbouring unfriendly cities, or the raiding deserts; inside the intimacy where strangers or dissenters are watched with fear or anger.[3]

There, in the ancient city, citizens and insiders confront the outside as a world of strangers held at bay with rampart and wall; here, in modern metropolitan corridors, the vast majority of human relations are relations between strangers, who are served by a variety of roads, markets, communicational networks, pathways that constitute our cities. The contrast is sufficiently powerful to draw millions of tourists out of our modernity back into those ancient cities of Mesopotamia, Egypt, ancient Europe, to experience the difference between contained lives and lives lived openly and in passage.

The commonality and familiarity of travel may also be seen in the fact that travel is the most common source of metaphors used to explicate transformations and transitions of all sorts. We draw upon the exprience of human mobility to define the meaning of death (as a "passing") and the structure of life (as a "journey" or pilgrimage); to articulate changes of social and existential conditions in rites of initiation (of "passage"). In their now-classic works, the anthropologists Arnold van Gennep, Victor Turner, and Mircea Eliade have found rites and symbols of passage everywhere and in all periods of human history.[4] If the essence of a metaphor or a symbol is the use of the familiar to grasp the less familiar or ineffable,[5] then the universality of symbols and rites of passage testifies to the sheer normality of the experience of travel.

Travel is as familiar as the experience of the body, the wind, the earth, and this is why at all times and in all places it is a source of reference, a ground of symbols and metaphors, a resource of signification. The anthropologist and historian of religions Mircea Eliade laments the absence of genuine rituals of initiation in modern life and suggests that "modern man has lost all sense of traditional initiation."[6] But perhaps it is only that the reality of passage has replaced the ritual, and the most important transitions we experience are written into our journeys, which make of our lives a procession and spectacle more engrossing and transforming than any ritual could possibly be.

But the point is made: travel is, in contemporary civility, normal and a source of norms. Usually, contemporary lives are connected, segmented, sequenced through journeys—small ordinary journeys of a few miles or larger, extraordinary trips of hundreds and thousands of miles. Contemporary society, as many have noted, is a "mobile" society, but even more than that, it is a society of travelers. We may find in the history of travel the origins, the evolution, the manners, the forms of knowledge characteristic of our present, of this society of travelers. Contemporary life is perhaps unprecedented in the scale, quantity, and global organization of modern journeys, and yet it is clear that travel is not a new human experience. Mobility is the first, prehistorical human condition; sessility (attachment or fixation to one place), a later, historical condition. At the dawn of history, humans were migratory animals. Recorded history—the history of civilization—is a story of mobilities, migrations, settlements, of the adaptation of human groups to place and their integration into topography, the creation of "homes." In order to understand our present, we must understand how mobility has operated historically, in the past, as a force of change, transforming personalities, social landscapes, human topographies, creating a global civilization.

Travel as Experience

Often I feel I go to some distant region of the world to be reminded of who I really am. There is no mystery about why this should be so. Stripped of your ordinary surroundings, your friends, your daily routines . . . you are forced into direct experience. Such direct experience inevitably makes you aware of who it is that is having the experience. That is not always comfortable, but it is always invigorating.

—Michael Crichton, 1988

The sheer familiarity and commonality of territorial passage in the past and the present makes it difficult to understand its effects upon individuals, societies, and cultures: these effects are so often assumed that we feel they require little or no demonstration. Travel is the paradigmatic "experience," the model of a direct and genuine experience, which transforms the person having it. We may see something of the nature of these transformations in the roots of Indo-European languages, where *travel* and *experience* are intimately wedded terms.

The Indo-European root of *experience* is **per* (the asterisk indicates a retro-construction from languages living and dead). **Per* has been construed as "to try," "to test," "to risk"—connotations that persist in the English word *peril*. The earliest connotations of **per* appear in Latin words for "experience": *experior* and *experimentum*, whence the English *experiment*. This conception of "experience" as an ordeal, as a passage through a frame of action that gauges the true dimensions and nature of the person or object passing through it, also describes the most general and ancient conception of the effects of travel upon the traveler. Many of the secondary meanings of **per* refer explicitly to motion: "to cross space," "to reach a goal," "to go out." The connotations of risk and danger implicit in *peril* are also obvious in the Gothic cognates for **per* (in which *p* becomes an *f*): *fern* (far), *fare, fear, ferry*. One of the German words for experience, *Erfahrung,* is from the Old High German *irfaran:* "to travel," "to go out," "to traverse," or "to wander." The deeply rooted assumption that travel is an experience that tests and refines the character of the traveler is demonstrated by the German adjective *bewandert,* which currently means "astute," "skilled," or "clever" but originally (in fifteenth-century texts) meant merely "well traveled."[7]

These crossings of words and meanings reflect one of the first conceptualizations of travel as suffering, a test, an ordeal—meanings explicit in the original English word for travel: *travail.* Implicit is a notion of the transformations of travel as changes that strip, reduce, and waste the passenger. This ostensibly negative sense pervades ancient travel epics, including *The Epic of Gilgamesh,* the first work of Western travel literature (transcribed 1900 B.C.). At every stage of his passage, Gilgamesh is met with the same questions: "Why are your cheeks so starved and your face drawn? Why is despair in your heart and your face like the face of one who has made a long journey; yes, why is your face burned with heat and cold, and why do you come here wandering over the pasture in search of the wind?"[8]

Gilgamesh's journey is a prime example of heroic travel . . . the fatigue, hardship, and danger it entails essentially reduce the character who undertakes it. The young Gilgamesh, who was a king too strong for his city, is sent on a journey as a way of decreasing his excessive appetite for labor, soldiers, and women so as to be compatible with the urban order in which he has originated. His journeys transform him from a predator upon his city into "the shepherd of the city." On his journey, Gilgamesh is, like Odysseus, stripped of his following, of his energies, of his chief companions, and of his ambitions. Ultimately he is brought to the extremity of the world, the Far West, the land of death and immortality. Because he falls asleep during a night in which he must stay awake, Gilgamesh fails to win immortality; and, on the way home, he loses his consolation prize, a rejuvenating plant. But his travels have the desired effect: he is reduced to a level coherent with the precincts of his city, and he is made wise: "This was the man to whom all things were known: this was the king who knew the countries of the world. He was wise, he saw mysteries and knew secret things, he brought us a tale of the days before the flood. He went on a long journey, was weary, worn-out with labour, returning he rested, he engraved on a stone the whole story."[9]

The Ancients and the Moderns: From Suffering to Freedom

*"Here we go, we're all together. . . . What did we do in New York? Let's forgive."
We had all had our spats back there. "That's behind us, merely by miles and inclinations. . . ." We all jumped to the music and agreed. The purity of the road.*
—Jack Kerouac, 1957

Ancient and modern conceptions of the "meaning" of travel are very different, as are their emphases on the transformations effected by a journey. The ancients valued travel as an explication of human fate and necessity; for moderns, it is an expression of freedom and an escape from necessity and purpose. Ancients saw travel as a suffering, even a penance; for moderns, it is a pleasure and a means to pleasure. Ancient epics of travel describe those motions through which individuals, in groups and often armed, confirmed an order of the world and demonstrated their status; travel today is marketed as a means of discovery, of acquiring access to something new, original, and even unexpected.

In general, the ancients most valued the journey as an explication of fate or necessity, as a revelation of those forces that sustain and shape, alter and govern human destinies. The travels narrated in the *Odyssey* and *The Epic of Gilgamesh* are god-decreed and thus not wholly voluntary nor pleasurable. Odysseus wanders on a long, frustrating journey toward home, personified by Penelope, the territorialized and virtuous woman whose exclusion of suitors preserves that home. When Odysseus finally arrives in Ithaca, disguised as a beggar, he thanks the swineherd Eumaeus for his hospitality in terms that adequately express the ancient conception of travel as a driven state of existence, a necessitated, even prophesied suffering: "You have given me rest from the pains and miseries of wandering. To be driven hither and then thither—nothing mortals endure can be worse than that, yet men will bear with such utter wretchedness, will accept such wandering and grief and sorrow for the sake of their accursed bellies."[10]

The sufferings of travel clearly frame and intensify the significance of the heroic traveler's actions. When Odysseus accepts the challenge of the nobles of Sphacteria to compete in their games, he cites the wastings and reductions of travel as factors that will make his victory even more significant: "As you see me now, I am ground down by distress and misery; I have had many trials to endure, fighting my way through hostile warriors and battering waves. Yet nevertheless, despite all sufferings, I will try my fortune in your contests. Your insult rankles and you have roused me."[11] The ability to rise to the new occasion despite the losses and frictions of the journey demonstrates, at the very least, that Odysseus, even though reduced, is still superior to the best efforts of the locals. The rhythm of this epic, the recurrent pattern of phallic self-assertion and exhaustion, of freedom and captivity, suggests that it is a narrative of male potencies deployed in the classical journey.

This emphasis upon travel as a test, as a loss that brings a gain of stature and certainty of self, suggests that the changes of character effected by travel are not so much the introduction of something new into the personality of the traveler as a revelation of something ineradicably present—perhaps courage, perdurance, the ability to endure pain, the persistence of skills and abilities even in a context of fatigue and danger. The transformations of passage are a species of "identification" through action, which adds to the being in motion only a consciousness of the irreducible form and individuality of that being. In the difficult and dangerous journey, the self of the traveler is impoverished and reduced to its essentials, allowing one to see what those essentials are.

In this sense, the heroic journey resembles what the critic and philosopher Kenneth Burke has spoken of as a "fictional death"*—fictional rather than real because death is used as a context for the assertion of an essential and irreducible self; implicitly denied is the reality of death as a dissolution of form and a solvent of identity. The *topos* of the fictional death is prominent in funeral orations, in narrations of epic and heroic journeys as well as in war literature, in which it is frequently assumed that a "true" and genuine self is tried, proven, reduced to its essence by a journey through the valley of death. This *topos*, characteristic of ancient journeys, occurs in modern adventure travels and travels of discovery. Captain James Cook, upon reading the journals of his gentlemen companions, became indignant, believing that they had exaggerated the perils encountered on the around-the-world voyage of the *Endeavour* (1768–71); but he resigned himself to their hyperbole as inevitable:

---

*Personal communication, 1978.

[S]uch are the dispositions of men in general in these voyages that they are seldom content with the hardships and dangers which will naturally occur, but they must add others which hardly ever had existence but in their imaginations, by magnifying the most trifling accidents and circumstances to the greatest hardships, and insurmountable dangers . . . as if the whole merit of the voyage consisted in the dangers and hardships they underwent, or that real ones did not happen often enough to give the mind sufficient anxiety; thus posterity are taught to look upon these voyages as hazardous to the highest degree.[12]

The dangers and fatigues of travel remain today, in some sense, a test of the heroism of the traveler. The great structural anthropologist Claude Lévi-Strauss, who ostensibly despises the mere tourist and the self-promoting adventurer ("adventure has no place in the anthropologist's profession"), nevertheless makes use of the traditional *topos* in gauging the value of what an ethnographer acquires on a voyage to the peripheries. The anthropologist "may endure months of travelling, hardships, and sickening boredom for the purpose of recording (in a few days, or even few hours) a hitherto unknown myth, a new marriage rule or a complete list of clan names."[13] In some sense, hardship, boredom, and physical effort contribute to the value of the rite or myth recorded, and to the stature of the anthropologist among equals.

Indeed, the fatigues and characteristic dangers of the journey may be precisely calibrated and itemized in one's hotel bill. A hotel in the Ecuadorean Amazon advertises, "The hosts try very hard to meet individual interests and provide levels of adventure according to what you feel you are up to—from easy guided walks on marked trails, to strenuous Outward Bound–style overnight hikes through the forest, which make you feel like the real Indiana Jones."[14]

The fatigues of travel, the sufferings of the journey, remain a cause and a measure of the extent to which a traveler is marked and tested by experience, becoming *bewandert*—"skilled" and "wise." It is this factor that distinguishes the mere tourist from the real and genuine traveler, for whom travel is a test rather than a pleasure. This traditional theme persists beneath the modern emphasis upon the pleasures of travel, which in any case do not exist, Albert Camus insists, for those traveling on cheap tickets or with no tickets at all.[15] For the poor contemporary traveler, travel retains its ancient significance and is given value by the fear that makes the individual "porous" and sensitive. However ancient the theme, Camus's emphasis is modern: the fear of the wayfarer, the loss of security implicit in unaccommodated travel is a gain of accessibility and sensitivity to the world. Travel, from the moment of departure, removes those furnishings and mediations that come with a familiar residence. It thus substantiates individuality in its sense of "autonomy," for the self is now separated from a confirming and confining matrix.

Today the very vicissitudes, strippings, and wastings that constituted the ancient sufferings of the traveler are prized as an ascetic, disciplined freedom, as the confirmation of an individuality that encounters directly a world held at bay by the walls and boundaries of one's home. "'Being naked' always has associations of physical liberty, of harmony between the hand and the flower it touches, of a loving understanding between the earth and men who have become freed of human things."[16] The sufferings of travel constitute a simplification of life that enhances the objectivity of a world within which the traveler becomes aware of an irreducible subjectivity, a self. This contemporary conception of the strippings and wastings of travel as a freedom from mediations is only a present appearance of the ancient conception of travel as a penance and a purification which have a morally improving effect upon the traveler. The conception of travel as a penance is as old as the journey of the primal pair, evicted from the Garden for their sins and enjoined to travel and labor as an expiation for those sins. Departure breaks the bonds between the sinner and the site and occasions of the sin. It is a way of leaving trouble behind. This is perhaps the reason travel, as exile, was conceived to be at once punishment and cure, retribution and purification. The stripping away by the frictions of passage of all that is not of the essence of the passenger, the removal of defining associations, of bonds to the world of place—all effect changes in the character of the traveler that are strictly analogous to a cleansing, the reduction of the purified entity to its smallest, truest dimensions.

The penance of travel was also prescribed to the second biblical generation, as Cain was set upon his course of wanderings for his act of fratricide, the act that alienated him from the soil that had defined him and that he had watered with his brother's blood. Denying him any further attachment to the soil, God made wandering Cain's permanent condition: "When you till the ground, it will no longer yield you its wealth. You shall be a vagrant and a wanderer upon the earth." At the same moment, God decreed the sanctity of the wanderer whose travels and exile are his penance and make him sacrosanct, with the "mark of Cain": "So the Lord put a mark on Cain, in order that anyone meeting him should not kill him."[17]

Pilgrimage is the institutionalization of this transformation of travel, a formalization of the notion that travel purifies, cleanses, removes the wanderer from the site of transgressions. This notion is explicit in the charter of Buddhist pilgrimage, the *Aitareya Brahmana*: "There is no happiness for him who does not travel; living in the society of men, the best man often becomes a sinner; for Indra [Vedic deity of rain and thunder] is the friend of the traveler. Therefore wander."[18] Here the loss of travel may be a moral and psychological gain—as was understood by that modern Odysseus, Neil Cassady, fictionalized as Moriarity in Jack Kerouac's epic *On the Road*, who left behind any number of sins in a life spent in passage.[19] In chapter 2, on passage, I will examine the phenomenon noted by Kerouac and generations of travelers: the purity of the road.

Implicit in the conception of travel as a penance and a purge is the assumption that "self" and "place" are integrated realities, and that the self may be changed with change of place. The reductive effects of travel begin with the first term of a journey—departure, a separation requiring one to leave behind much that has previously defined the civil self. This event transforms the passenger into a species not unlike Rousseau's savage man, who has his own forces constantly at his disposal and carries himself "whole and entire" about with him. But such stripping away of defining relations and furnishings of the civil self is often painful, evoking protest, grief, and mourning. Departure is an occasion of human suffering. Though celebrated in modern travel, departure was traditionally undertaken only for the most urgent of motives. These may be explicit or implicit, and they change over time. In chapter 1, I discuss why a particular age places certain motives ahead of others, decreeing the propriety of traveling as a penance, a purification, a test, a liberation, a pleasure, a satisfaction of curiosity. In that chapter, too, I set out the rough but evident historical transition that is the backbone of this work: the transition from the ancient emphasis upon travel as a necessary suffering to the modern emphasis upon travel as an experience of freedom and the gaining of autonomy.

The ancients had no conception of travel as a voluntary and altruistic act. Even ancient tourism, which flourished under the *Pax Romana*, appears to Seneca as a driven state of existence, a distracted wandering:

> This is the reason why men undertake aimless wanderings, travel along distant shores and at one time by sea, at another by land, try to soothe the fickleness of disposition which is always dissatisfied with the present. "Now let us make for Campania: now I am sick of rich cultivation: let us see something of wild regions, let us thread the passes of Brulli and Lucania: yet amid this wilderness one wants something of beauty to relieve our pampered eyes after so long dwelling on savage wastes. Let us seek Tarentum with its famous harbor, its mild winter climate. . . . Let us now return to town; our ears have long missed its shouts and noise: it would be pleasant also to enjoy the sight of human bloodshed." Thus one journey succeeds another, and one sight is changed for another.[20]

The travels of Odysseus, Heracles, and many other ancient heroes were imposed upon them by an external "command"—from a god, a goddess, fate. The identity-defining travels of the medieval knight were, on the other hand, ostensibly voluntary and undertaken to no utilitarian purpose. The chivalric journey, which is the pattern and model for significant modern travel, is essentially self-referential, undertaken to reveal the essential character of the knight as "free," once the essence of nobility but since the seventeenth century considered an attribute of human nature. The voluntariness of departure and the solitude of the knight identified the new concept of adventure; travel became a demonstration of freedom from necessity, the mark of a status above the "commons." This transmutation of the heroic journey into a freely chosen opportunity to demonstrate an identity—as freedom, self-display, and self-discovery—enters into the very definition of a new species of travel characteristic of the postmedieval world: the voyage of discovery and, later, the "scientific" expedition and the travels of curious and recording tourists. The celebration of travel as a demonstration of freedom and means to autonomy becomes the modern *topos*, clearly evident in William Wordsworth's evocation of the condition of the wanderer:

> Whither shall I turn,
> By road or pathway, or through trackless field,
> Up hill or down, or shall some floating thing,
> Upon the river point me out my course?[21]

The very indeterminacy of wandering, which Odysseus found hard to bear, is the source of the freedom the Romantics prized in travel. This association of travel and freedom may be traced to medieval roots, where it was written into law. According to the laws of Henry II, a lord who wished to free his serf had first to declare that intention in a church, a market, or a county court, to bestow a lance and a sword upon his former bondsman, and then take him to a crossroads to show him that "all ways lie open to his feet."[22] These two features—arms and the right of free departure—long remained the distinguishing marks of the status of "free" man. Their opposites—the forbidding of arms or of travel—were the marks of unfreedom. The right to travel had entered into the Western definition of the free autonomous individual whose associations to others are a result of conscious acts of connection, of allegiance and contract.

In Wordsworth and the Romantics, and in modern travels generally, we find divorced those things with which travel had been inextricably wedded in ancient conceptions. Travel became distinguishable from pain and began to be regarded as an intellectual pleasure. Thus, Wordsworth's "Old Man Travelling" is a portrait of "A man who does not move with pain, but moves / with thought."[23]

These factors—the voluntariness of departure, the freedom implicit in the indeterminacies of mobility, the pleasure of travel free from necessity, the notion that travel signifies autonomy and is a means for demonstrating what one "really" is independent of one context or set of defining associations—remain the characteristics of the modern conception of travel. Michael Crichton's explanation of why he travels draws upon these themes:

And I felt a need for rejuvenation, for experiences that would take me away from things I usually did, the life I usually led. In my everyday life, I often felt a stifling awareness of the purpose behind everything I did. Every book I read, every movie I saw, every lunch and dinner I attended seemed to have a reason behind it. From time to time, I felt the urge to do something for no reason at all.

Done "for no reason at all" except to escape a world where all things are a means to an end, travel, in modern circumstances, is prized less as a means of revealing ungovernable forces beyond human control than for providing direct access to a new material and objective world. In the apprehension of that world, the passenger acquires a new awareness of self in the context of a direct experience that "inevitably makes you aware of who it is that is having the experience."[24]

If travel is, as the great African-American writer and folklorist Zora Neale Hurston observed, "the soul of civilization,"[25] then in the history of European travels we may find the soul of the West, its continuities, evolution, permutations. For the history of travel is in crucial ways a history of the West. It recounts the evolution from necessity to freedom, an evolution that gave rise to a new consciousness, the peculiar mentality of the modern traveler.

[1991]

NOTES

1. John B. Lansing et al., *The Travel Market, 1958, 1959–60, 1961–62* (Lansing, Mich.: University of Michigan, Survey Research Center Reprint, 1963).

2. Donald E. Lundberg, *The Tourist Business* (New York: van Nostrand Reinhold, 1990).

3. Freya Stark, *The Journey's Echo* (New York: Ecco Press, 1963), p. 19.

4. See Arnold van Gennep, *The Rites of Passage* (Chicago: University of Chicago Press, 1972); Victor Turner, "Betwixt and Between: The Liminal Period in Rites of Passage," in *Betwixt and Between*, ed. Louise Mahdi, Stephen Foster, and Meredith Little (La Salle, Ill.: Open Court, 1987); and Mircea Eliade, *The Rites and Symbols of Initiation* (New York: Harper Torchbooks, 1965).

5. This is Frederik Barth's definition of metaphor in *Ritual and Knowledge Among the Baktaman of New Guinea* (New Haven: Yale University Press, 1975), p. 204.

6. Eliade, *Rites and Symbols*, p. 134.

7. See Carl D. Buck, *A Dictionary of Selected Synonyms in the Principal Indo-European Languages* (Chicago: University of Chicago Press, 1949); and Alois Walde, *Vergleichendes Worterbuch der Indogermanischen Sprachen*, vol. 2 (Berlin and Leipzig: Walter De Gruyter, 1927).

8. N. K. Sandars, trans., *The Epic of Gilgamesh* (New York: Penguin Books, 1975), p. 103.

9. Ibid., p. 61.

10. Homer, the *Odyssey*, trans. Walter Schewring (Oxford: Oxford University Press, 1980), p. 183.

11. Ibid., p. 89.

12. Captain James Cook, *Journals*, vol. 1, ed. J. C. Beaglehole (London: Hakluyt Society, 1955), p. 461.

13. Claude Lévi-Strauss, *Tristes Tropiques* (New York: Atheneum Press, 1975), p. 17.

14. *Chicago Tribune*, 18 June 1989, sec. 12, p. 6, col. 1.

15. Albert Camus, *Notebooks, 1935–1942* (New York: Alfred A. Knopf, 1963); see pp. 13–14 for epigraph quote on p. 1.

16. Ibid., p. 57.

17. Gen. 4.12, 4.15.

18. Quoted from "Pilgrimage," in *Encyclopedia of Religion and Ethics*, vol. 10, ed. James Hastings (New York: Charles Scribners Sons, 1951), p. 23.

19. Jack Kerouac, *On the Road* (New York: New American Library, 1957); see p. 111 for epigraph quote on p. 7.

20. Seneca, *De Tranquilitas*, chap. 2, trans. Aubrey Stewart, quoted in Caroline Skeel, *Travel in the First Century after Christ* (Cambridge: Cambridge University Press, 1901), pp. 12–13.

21. William Wordsworth, "The Preludes," in *Poetical Works*, vol. 3 (Oxford: Clarendon Press, 1968), pp. 27–30.

22. Quoted in F. W. Maitland and Sir Frederick Pollock, *The History of the English Laws, Before the Time of Edward I*, vol. I (Cambridge: Cambridge University Press, 1968), p. 428.

23. Quoted in George Roppen and Richard Sommer, *Strangers and Pilgrims. An Essay on the Metaphor of the Journey* (Oslo: Norwegian Universities Press, Norwegian Studies in English, no. 11, 1964), p. 116. See also Charles Norton Coe, *Wordsworth and the Literature of Travel* (New York: Bookman Associates, 1953).

24. Michael Crichton, *Travels* (New York: Alfred A. Knopf, 1988), pp. ix, x.

25. Zora Neale Hurston, *Dust Tracks on a Road* (New York: Arno Press and the New York Times, 1969), p. 189.

ROBERT LOUIS STEVENSON

(1854–1894)

Troubled by ill health all his life, Robert Louis Stevenson nevertheless traveled constantly and lived abroad for many years. He moved back and forth from his native Scotland to the south of France, the east and west coasts of America, the South Pacific, and finally the island of Samoa, where he spent his last years. Although he wrote non-fiction about his travels, many readers first encountered Stevenson's fiction and poetry in their childhoods. His novels *Treasure Island* (1883) and *Kidnapped* (1886) introduced generations of young readers to travel and adventure.

A number of the poems in his still-popular collection for children, *A Child's Garden of Verses* (1885), from which the following poems are taken, show how childhood reading excites curiosity about foreign places and generates the desire to travel. One of the charms of travel for adults is that it recreates the sense of childhood wonder at the world. Travel could be considered a form of play for adults, a renewal of the imaginative activities of childhood reading.

"The Land of Story-Books"

At evening, when the lamp is lit,
Around the fire my parents sit;
They sit at home and talk and sing,
And do not play at anything.

Now, with my little gun, I crawl   5
All in the dark along the wall,
And follow round the forest track
Away behind the sofa back.

There, in the night, where none can spy,
All in my hunter's camp I lie,   10
And play at books that I have read
Till it is time to go to bed.

These are the hills, these are the woods,
These are my starry solitudes;
And there the river by whose brink   15
The roaring lions come to drink.

I see the others far away
As if in firelit camp they lay
And I, like to an Indian scout,
Around their party prowled about.   20

So, when my nurse comes in for me,
Home I return across the sea,
And go to bed with backward looks
At my dear land of Story-books.

[1885]

"Travel"

I should like to rise and go
Where the golden apples grow;
Where below another sky
Parrot islands anchored lie,
And, watched by cockatoos and goats,   5
Lonely Crusoes building boats;
Where in sunshine reaching out
Eastern cities, miles about,
Are with mosque and minaret
Among sandy gardens set,   10
And the rich goods from near and far
Hang for sale in the bazaar;
Where the Great Wall round China goes,
And on one side the desert blows,
And with bell and voice and drum,   15
Cities on the other hum;
Where are forests, hot as fire,
Wide as England, tall as a spire,
Full of apes and cocoa-nuts
And the negro hunters' huts;   20
Where the knotty crocodile
Lies and blinks in the Nile,
And the red flamingo flies
Hunting fish before his eyes;
Where in jungles, near and far,   25
Man-devouring tigers are,
Lying close and giving ear
Lest the hunt be drawing near,
Or a comer-by be seen
Swinging in a palanquin;   30
Where among the desert sands
Some deserted city stands,
All its children, sweep and prince,
Grown to manhood ages since,
Not a foot in street or house,   35
Not a stir of child or mouse,
And when kindly falls the night,
In all the town no spark of light.
There I'll come when I'm a man
With a camel caravan;   40

Light a fire in the gloom
Of some dusty dining-room;
See the pictures on the walls,
Heroes, fights and festivals;
And in a corner find the toys   45
Of the old Egyptian boys.

[1885]

SALMAN RUSHDIE

(1947-)

Salman Rushdie moved from India to Pakistan with his Muslim parents shortly after the British ended their empire on the Indian subcontinent and divided the land into two separate countries. Later, Rushdie traveled to England for an education at Rugby School and Cambridge University. A writer who exemplifies the multicultural nature of the English-speaking world, he has described himself as "coming from too many places." Rushdie mixes not only cultures but also history and fantasy in his fiction. His novel *Midnight's Children* (1981), concerning the stories of children like himself born in the year of Indian independence in 1947, won the Booker Prize. *Satanic Verses* (1988) earned him the wrath of the Ayatollah Khomeini, fundamentalist ruler of Iran, who accused Rushdie of committing blasphemy against Islam and pronounced a death sentence upon him. This condemnation forced Rushdie into hiding for several years, but it also increased his fame. Besides fiction and literary criticism, he has written a travel narrative (*The Jaguar's Smile: A Nicaraguan Journey*, 1987).

The following essay from *Imaginary Homelands* (1991) examines how adventure today has lost much of the spiritual significance ascribed to it through literature of the past. Rushdie also points out the economic reality of contemporary adventure—that travelers come from wealthier countries and journey to poorer ones.

"On Adventure"

From *Imaginary Homelands*

'The true adventurer,' wrote O. Henry in *The Green Door*, 'goes forth aimless and uncalculating to meet and greet unknown fate. A fine example was the Prodigal Son—when he started home.'

Among the most remarkable qualities of the words *adventure* and *adventurer* is their capaciousness. Any idea that can encompass the Prodigal Son and Indiana Jones, that finds common ground between the Pilgrim Fathers' voyage to America and the journey of the Darlings with Peter Pan to the Neverland, that suggests a connection between Alice's step through the looking-glass and Crick and Watson's discovery of the double helix of DNA, is clearly one of the most resonant notions in the culture. We often think of adventure as a metaphor of life itself, and not only of life: 'To die,' Peter Pan muses, 'will be an awfully big adventure.'

Closely connected with this version of the idea of adventure are notions of danger, of a journey, of the unknown. And, of course, of heroism: he (or she) who would voyage into the secret night, who would step off the edge of the earth because it is there, must clearly be made of the Right Stuff. Sam Shepard as Chuck Yeager is perhaps a modern archetype of this myth; Huck Finn its antithesis, adventure's anti-hero. Heroic adventure is, typically, an individualist affair. There are of course adventurer-heroes who travelled in groups—Argonauts, Everest climbers, the Magnificent Seven—but the myth more often seems to require the existentialist purity of a single human being pitted against the immensity of the universe, to prefer the lone sailor in the small boat traversing the liquid Andes of Cape Horn to any team effort, to elevate the lone gunman (Clint Eastwood in most of his Western roles) above the Wild Bunch.

Contemporary literary travellers tend, it being an anti-heroic age, to be more Huck than Chuck. Their true ancestors are not, perhaps, so much the wandering heroes of the classical epoch (Jason, Ulysses, unspeakably pious Aeneas) as the *picaros* of the novel. Many of the most appealing pieces of twentieth-century 'travel writing' read very like picaresque novels, offering us the notion of adventure-as-mad-quest. Even Italo Calvino's fictional Marco Polo, in *Invisible Cities,* has a whole series of such quests in mind: he travels through his wondrous cities in search of his past, his future, Venice, memory, and stranger things: 'This is the aim of my explorations: examining the traces of happiness still to be glimpsed. I gauge its short supply.' Such conceits, exquisite and comic, suggest parodies of the ancient myth of the Holy Grail.

To invoke the Grail is to realize that adventure, as it is understood today, has lost a certain high-minded grandeur, and that the loss lies in the area of purpose. Once upon a time the journey, the quest, the adventure was not so much a private, or idiosyncratic, or crazy enterprise as a spiritual labour. The Knights of the Round Table sought the Sangreal in God's name. The *Pilgrim's Progress,* like its Islamic counterpart, Farid-ud-din Attar's *Conference of the Birds,* is an adventure of purification, of winning through to the divine. The voyages of Sindbad the Sailor have been explicated in religio-mystical terms. Like the line of sight in a Gothic cathedral, the adventuring spirit was swept forwards and upwards in the direction of God. This allegorical, transcendent adventuring is, these days, more or less completely defunct.

There are good reasons for feeling relieved that adventure is nowadays the province of the determined, the curious and the idiosyncratic. The adventuring spirit, when ruled by faith or ideology, has not been an entirely Good Thing. The behaviour of the Crusador knights, Spanish conquistadors and the like bears witness to this. Like all important ideas, adventure has a dark side as well as a light. For every Christopher Columbus there is also a Captain Hook, for every lamp-genie there is a fiend. The world of the adventurer contains at least as many mercenary 'soldiers of fortune' as idealistic knights-errant, and for every Vasco da Gama there is also an *Aguirre, Wrath of God*. When the spirit of adventure invades the historical process—when States or their leaders or representatives go adventuring—the results are usually catastrophic. From Genghis Khan to Napoleon and Mussolini, history is littered with examples of what happens when adventurers come to power: disaster, rapine, fire and the sword, Bad Things galore. Adventure and politics are best kept far apart, rather like uranium and plutonium.

On the whole, then, the Candide/Quixote model of adventure seems preferable to older versions. In our increasingly vicarious culture, the adventurers are the people who perform marvels on our behalf. Escaping from their own roots, from the prison of everyday reality, they enable us to experience, if at one remove, something of the exhilaration of the successful jailbreaker. If urban society be a confining chain, then the adventurers are our necessary Houdinis, reminding us that change, difference, strangeness, newness, risk and achievement really do still exist, and can, if we wish, be attained.

This kind of adventuring has become, or so it seems to me, a pretty well exclusively Western phenomenon. Once there was an Ibn Battuta to set against Marco Polo, and even an Islamic empire to likened to the Christian ones. But it's hard to conceive of, say, an Indian Paul Theroux becoming obsessed with the railways of the United States, or a black African Karen Blixen heading for Scandinavia. I offer the theory that adventuring is, these days, by and large a movement that originates in the rich parts of the planet and heads for the poor. Or a journey from the crowded cities towards the empty spaces, which may be another way of saying the same thing. I recently watched a television documentary in which a group of British adolescents on Honda motortrikes roared across the perfection of the Saharan sand-dunes, boasting that the crossing of the Erg had never been done before 'on motorized transport'. I was left with the memory of the bemused courteous faces of the locals they encountered, many of whom had very probably crossed that desert on admittedly non-motorized camels; and I fretted about the ethnocentric narrowness of vision of some who venture forth into the exotic South. To a Saharan nomad, after all, the journey is the point, the shaping fact of existence; arriving at some notional destination—'conquering the desert'—is a kind of fiction, the illusion of an end. Adventures tend to be linear narratives, but in life, as in literature, that's not the only way of seeing things.

As all writers know, you don't have to leave home to embark on an adventure. The poet Basho, in Edward Bond's play *Narrow Road to the Deep North*, returns from his dangerous northward pilgrimage in search of enlightenment, claiming to have found what he sought. And what was enlightenment? 'I saw there was nothing to learn in the deep north . . . You get enlightenment where you are.' Many of the greatest adventurers of our age, Marie Curie, Freud, Marx, Einstein, Proust, Kafka, Emily Dickinson and the rest, didn't travel much further than a laboratory, a library, a consulting room. Adventure may have much to do with the pushing back of frontiers, but few topographical boundaries can rival the frontiers of the mind.

Even in the case of travel-adventures, the best of all are those in which some inner journey, some adventure in the self, is the real point. *Peter Pan* would not be the same if Wendy and the Lost Boys didn't disvcover that they wanted to grow up, that Paradise has to be lost. The real plot of *Moby Dick* takes place inside Ahab; the rest is a fishing trip. And even Quixote, maddest of *picaros*, sees himself ridiculous at last: 'For there are no birds this year in last year's nests. I was mad, but I am sane now.'

So it turns out that Basho is both right and wrong; that the travelling adventurer can, after all, gain knowledge that is not available elsewhere, and then, by living to tell the tale, offer that knowledge to us. Enlightenment is certainly to be had at home, but it's still worth making the long, arduous trip, in spite of the storms and brigands, into the remote fastnesses of the deep north.

[1991]

PAUL THEROUX

(1941–)

Paul Theroux helped revive contemporary interest in travel books by taking the train all the way from London to Japan and back—and then writing *The Great Railway Bazaar: By Train through Asia* (1975). He first went abroad to Africa in the early 1960s as a Peace Corps volunteer in Malawi, then returned to teach privately in Uganda and later Singapore while writing fiction set in these places. Settling with his family in London, he began to alternate trips and travel books with novels and short stories. A prolific writer, he has taken train journeys to Latin America (*The Old Patagonian Express: By Train through the Americas*, 1979) and China (*Riding the Iron Rooster: By Train through China,* 1988). He walked the sea coast of England, Scotland, and Wales (*Kingdom by the Sea: A Journey around Great Britain,* 1983), paddled a kayak about the islands of the South Seas (*The Happy Isles of Oceania: Paddling the Pacific,* 1992), and traveled by rail, bus, and boat around the Mediterranean Sea (*The Pillars of Hercules: A Grand Tour of the Mediterranean,* 1995). He returned to Africa and made his way from Cairo, Egypt, to Capetown, South Africa, for his most recent travel book, *Dark Star* (2003). Among his many novels are *Mosquito Coast* (1982), *Kowloon Tong* (1997), and *Hotel Honolulu* (2001), all set in places where he has traveled.

The selection which follows, "Mapping the World," relates the art of map-making to the history of travel and to the creative imagination. As Theroux points out, maps represent the realities of the physical world. At the same time, they function like metaphors and symbols for the traveler. They excite the imagination in anticipation of travel, and they suggest stories and adventures.

"Mapping the World"

From *Sunrise and Seamonsters*

Cartography, the most aesthetically pleasing of the sciences, draws its power from the greatest of man's gifts—courage, the spirit of inquiry, artistic skill, man's sense of order and design, his understanding of natural laws, and his capacity for singular journeys to the most distant places. They are the brightest attributes and they have made maps one of the most luminous of man's creations.

But map-making also requires the ability to judge the truth of travelers' tales. Although Marco Polo's *Travels* allowed early European cartographers to give place-names and continental configurations to their maps, the book itself contained only a tiny sketch map and had many odd omissions (no Great Wall, no mention of tea). Columbus had the Latin version of 1483 among his belongings on his voyage westward—which was why, in Cuba in 1493, he sent a party of men searching the Cuban hinterland for the Great Khan, and on later voyages believed he was coasting past Indochina (it was Honduras) and about three weeks away from the Ganges. Columbus was not unique in his misapprehension: cartographic ignorance has been universal. There are the many maps of the Abyssinian kingdom of Prester John, and the maps which show California to be an island (this belief persisted throughout the seventeenth century). And it was only seventy or eighty years ago that the Chinese were finally satisfied that the world was round.

"It would seem as though cartography were an instinct implanted in every nation with any claim to civilization," the geographer, Sir Alexander Hosie wrote. He had in mind a map of China, carved in stone, and discovered in the Forest of Tablets at Hsian, the capital of Shensi province. That stone map is dated in the year called *Fou Ch'ang*, 1137, but the Chinese had been making maps for centuries on wood, silk and paper. The Chinese and the Romans were making maps of their respective known worlds at roughly the same time. In 128 BC, Chang Ch'ien, China's first historic traveler, returned home after having covered the immense distance to the Oxus (we know it as the Amu Darya) in Central Asia. Chang reported to the Emperor Wu on what he had seen, and the emperor named the mountains K'un-lun, where the Yellow River rose.

For the next thousand years, China was active—a nation of travelers, warriors, conquerers, traders and, inevitably, map-makers. What was the point of conquering if the subject lands were not then given a shape, and their rivers and households described on maps? The Chinese word for map, *t'u*, also means "plan," "chart" and "drawing." (Our own word *map* has Latin cousins meaning "napkin" and "sheet.") Chinese cartography could be ambitious. P'ei Hsiu (224–271), sometimes called The Father of Chinese Cartography, did a magnificent map of China in eighteen panels ("The Map of the Territory of the Tribute of Yu"), and codified map-making in Six Principles. His First Principle, an enormous contribution to the art, was *fen lu*, the grid system.

P'ei's successor was Chia Tan, whose masterpiece in 801 was "The Map of China and Barbarian Countries Within the Seas." Chia was working in the T'ang Dynasty (618–907), one of the most renowned in Chinese history. It was very much a map-making dynasty—it had imperial ambitions, pursuing a policy of conquest in the west and south. Chia was commissioned to make maps of the conquered territories. Subsequent maps of China for the following few hundred years were based on Chia's ninth century work.

China also exemplifies the way cartography can go into decline. As a nation craves silence and becomes xenophobic and inward-looking, demanding tribute instead of initiating trade, it loses the will to communicate with the world and begins to wither of its own egotism. The Chinese still continued to regard the world as flat and four-square (though they believed the sky to be round). One cannot attribute this to stubborn ignorance; after all, it took Europe a thousand years to accept the notion that the world was round.

Yet all of China's naive geocentricity can be seen in the outrage of the Imperial Court's scrutiny of a Jesuit map in which China was situated in the eastern corner. What was the Middle Kingdom doing on the far right? Father Matteo Ricci cleverly redrew his map by spinning his globe, so to speak, and placing the Celestial empire smack in the middle, with Europe in the distant west. That was in 1602. The Chinese accepted the priest's version of the world—it somewhat resembled their own—but they rejected his spherical projection.

When China lost interest in foreign countries her maps became inaccurate, not to say bizarre. These maps showed European countries and the United States and Africa as tiny islands and sandbars off the Middle Kingdom coast. Even in the mid-nineteenth century Chinese maps depicated the natives of these little islands as monstrous and one-eyed, and some were shown with holes through their stomachs for their convenient carrying on poles. Around the turn of the nineteenth century, the Chinese accepted that the world was round. It is possible, I think, to read in this acceptance of a new map a profound understanding of their place in the world.

Cartography has always required utter truthfulness—it is one of its most appealing features: crooked maps are worse than useless, and nothing dates more quickly than the political map ("German East Africa," "French Indochina," "The Central African Empire," "Jonestown"). But until the recent past, maps have been more than scientific; they have depended on a high level of pictorial art—vivid imagery and lettering—and a style of labeling and a conciseness in description that is literary in the best sense.

Blaeu is the Rembrandt of geography. Most maps, even modern ones, are beautiful—beautiful in colour and contour, and often breathtaking in their completeness. They can tell us everything, and the best ones, from the great periods of trade and exploration—our own is one such period—have always attempted to do this. In 500 BC Anaximander's successor, Hecataeus, made a disc-shaped map—it was a startling illumination. But maps specialize in such surprises.

Consider the Ortelius map of China of 1573—"Regnum Chinae." It is full of fictitious lakes, but it accurately places rivers, mountains, and cities—enough to guide any explorer or trader to his destintion. It also includes the westernmost portion of America ("America Pars") at 180° longitude, and it shows what we know as the Bering Sea. In vivid marginal pictures it tells us about the Far East—the Great Wall is drawn, a Chinese junk is rendered in perfect detail, a man is shown being crucified in Japan for being a Christian and keeping the faith (there is a warning in Latin). In a corner is a Chinese four-wheeled cart, powered by a sail, and this cart (so the inscription tells us) can also be used as a boat. The map is a masterpiece of practicality and imagination.

Cartography has the capacity to open up countries to world trade. For example, throughout most of the nineteenth century it was recognized that a canal was needed in Central America to join the two great oceans. Mexico and most of the Central American countries were exhaustively mapped, and a dozen canals were proposed. These maps expressed hopes, promises and fantasies. On a map by F. Bianconi in 1891, Honduras—which could not have been emptier—is shown as a teeming go-ahead republic. "Railways under construction," it says and you see hundreds and hundreds of miles of track, two lines from coast to coast. Who needs a canal with such trains! In the Mosquito jungle you have the impression of intense cultivation, and mining, and cattle-grazing. Honduras looks blessed—full of sarsparilla and sugar-cane, and iron, zinc, silver and gold. The word "gold" appears on this map sixty-five times, in each spot where it apparently lies in the ground.

There were similar maps of Panama, and of course Panama won out. But a modern map of Honduras shows most of the cartographic detail in this hundred-year-old map to be unfulfilled promises. Anyone who looks at a lot of maps becomes highly suspicious of the designations "Proposed railway," "Road under construction," Projected highway"—with dotted lines; or that other heart-sinker, "Site of proposed Hydro-electric Dam." These are not features which are found only on maps of Third World countries. "The M25 Ring-Road" is shown on some maps of Outer London, though the road has yet to be finished. The most ominous line on a map is the one labelled "Disputed boundary," and it makes one think that there are perhaps fifty versions of the world map, depending on your nationality. Israel has about four different shapes, and on some modern Arab maps it does not exist at all.

The map of the London Underground is by almost any standard a work of art—a squint turns it into late-Mondrian—but it also has great practical value. After ten years of residence in London I still have to consult this map every time I travel by tube: the underground system is too complex for me to hold in my head. The same goes for the New York subway, which is a problem for cartographers—at least three recent attempts have been made to map it so that it can be understood and used by a stranger. None has succeeded. It remains an intimidating map.

The map predates the book (even a fairly ordinary map may contain several books' worth of information). It is the oldest means of information storage, and can present the most subtle facts with great clarity. It is a masterly form of compression, a way of miniaturizing a country or society. Most hill-climbers and perhaps all mountaineers know the thrill at a certain altitude of looking down and recognizing the landscape that is indistinguishable from a map. The only pleasure I take in flying in a jet plane is the experience of matching a coastline or the contour of a river to the corresponding map in my memory. A map can do many things, but I think its chief use is in lessening our fear of foreign parts and helping us anticipate the problems of dislocation. Maps give the world coherence. It seems to me one of man's supreme achievements that he knew the precise shape of every continent and practically every river-vein on earth long before he was able to gaze at them whole from the window of a rocketship.

This sense of map-shapes is so strong it amounts almost to iconography. The cartographer gives features to surfaces, and sometimes these features are resonant. It is easy to see a dependency in the way Sri Lanka seems to linger at the tip of India; Africa looks like one of its own paleolithic skulls; and some countries are, visibly, appendages. Who has looked upon Chile and not seen in it an austere narrowness, or smiled at Delaware, or wondered what Greenland is *for?* The shape of a country may condition our initial attitude towards it, though I don't think any conclusion can be drawn from the fact that Great Britain looks like a boy riding on a pig. And position matters, too. It does not surprise me that the Chinese called their country the Middle Kingdom. It is human to be geocentric. Every country, to its people, is a middle kingdom—zero longitude, where East and West begin. And what a shock it must be for the Pacific islander looking for his country for the first time on a world map, and not finding it, and having to be told that his great island is this tiny dot. The opposite is also remarkable. We have the word of many British people who have spoken of their pride at seeing the Empire verified in pink on a globe.

Maps have also given life to fiction. From *Gulliver's Travels* to *The Lord of the Rings*, novels have contained maps of their mythical lands. Thomas Hardy carefully drew a map so that his readers could understand his Wessex novels, and so did Norman Mailer when he published *The Naked and the Dead*. In these books the map came later, but there is an example of a fantasy map preceding a work of literature. Robert Louis Stevenson wrote,

> . . . I made the map of an island; it was elaborately and (I thought) beautifully coloured: the shape of it took my fancy beyond expression; it contained harbours that pleased me like sonnets; and with the unconsciousness of the predestined, I ticketted my performance *Treasure Island* . . . as I pored over my map of Treasure Island, the future characters in the book began to appear there visibly among imaginary woods; and their brown faces and bright weapons peeped out upon me from unexpected quarters, or they passed to and fro, fighting and hunting treasure. The next thing I knew I had some paper before me and was writing out a list of chapters . . .

I was delighted to find this example for Stevenson's cartographic inspiration, because for two years I worked on a novel—*The Mosquito Coast*—with a map of Central America next to my desk. When I was stuck for an idea, or when I wanted to reassure myself that my fictional settlements really existed, I studied this map.

Most novelists are map conscious, and all great novelists are cartographers. So are all true explorers, and the most intrepid travelers and traders. The real explorer is not the man who is following a map, but the man who is making one.

I do not think that it is profit alone, the desire for financial gain or celebrity, that animates such men. But it is a fact that the most commercial-minded countries have also been the most outward-looking. In the past, there were no trading nations that were not also the dedicated patrons of cartographers. Today, the proudest boast of any commercial enterprise is its illustration, with a map, of its influence and success. All maps are records of discovery; without fresh discoveries no new maps are possible. Our fastidious curiosity and our passionate business sense and even our anxieties have made ours a cartographic age.

Maps reflect the face of the land. They tell us most things but not everything. Long ago, they were shorelines; and then they were riverbanks; and at last they were territories with a million features. But they have always been surfaces figured with routes and suggestions. To the most courageous and imaginative of us, these surfaces are eloquent, showing the way to new discoveries. In a sense, the world was once blank. And the reason cartography made it visible and glowing with detail was because man believed, and rightly, that maps are a legacy that allows other men and future generations to communicate and trade.

A good map is better than a guidebook: it is the ultimate tool of the man who wishes to understand a distant country. It can be merciless in its factuality. It can also tell us things that are unobtainable anywhere else.

About ten and a half years ago, in Singapore, I rented a house—sight unseen—in the English county of Dorsetshire. I had been to England twice, but never to Dorset. The village, South Bowood, was not mentioned in any guidebook. What descriptions I came across were general and unhelpful. After a great deal of reading I still knew absolutely nothing of the place in which I was now committed to spend six months with my wife and two small children. I began to wonder if the place existed.

It was then that I found some Ordnance Survey Maps. The whole of Britain is scrupulously mapped. I had the correct sheet. I located South Bowood: it was a hamlet of about eight houses. Letters and symbols told me there was a public house down the road, and a mailbox, and a public telephone. The post office and school were a mile distant, and the nearest church was at Netherbury; but we would be on a hill, and there were meadows all around us, and footpaths, and not far from us the ruins of an Iron-Age hill fort. The houses were small black squares, and at last, sitting there in the Singapore Library studying the map, I worked out which house would be ours. So I knew exactly where I was going, and all my fears vanished. With this map, I was prepared: without it, I would have been in darkness.

[1981]

ERIKA WARMBRUNN

(1965–)

Erika Warmbrunn left the United States and a job in the theater to bicycle through East Asia. In *Where the Pavement Ends: One Woman's Bicycle Trip through Mongolia, China, and Vietnam* (2001), she recounts her adventures across the empty steppes of Mongolia and down the crowded and dangerous roads of China to her destination in Saigon. Warmbrunn repeatedly encountered what she called "The Seven Questions": "Where are you from? Where are you coming from? Where are you going? Alone? You're not scared? How old are you? Are you married?" In this excerpt we see how the plan for the trip takes shape and how books, maps, and the sense of Mongolia as a metaphor for her own freedom drive her fantasy and fuel her expectations.

From *Where the Pavement Ends*

I wanted to run away. Far away. Drawn by its thriving theater community, I had moved to Seattle after college, ignoring my Russian major to pursue a life in the footlights. Five years later, I knew that I had failed. The only jobs I had had in the theater in two years had been as the interpreter for visiting Russian companies. I was working in a travel bookstore, hiking in the summer and skiing in the winter, but never setting foot inside a theater unless I had a ticket in my hand. I went to auditions and was not called back. I went to work and stared at maps and imagined getting so far away that it would be like starting over again. I had traveled a lot, by some people's standards; by others', I had barely begun. I had made beds in a nursing home in Berlin, tended bar on the French Riviera, and gone to Mass in Krakow because in 1984 the church was the only place open at 5:00 A.M. when the train pulled in. A friend and I had rented bicycles in Ireland, bungee-corded our backpacks to their rear racks, and spent a week tooling around the south coast, making tents out of our rain ponchos and sleeping on the cliffs. I had studied in Moscow, played the heroine in a little movie shot in the Caucasus, and walked out of Georgia into eastern Turkey. But I had never been to South America or Africa or Asia, and to make things new, you have to keep going farther and farther away from what you know.

The bookstore sold maps of Botswana, Delhi, and Antarctica. We sold phrasebooks for Arabic, Swahili, and Tagalog. We sold guides to traveling the French canals by barge, crossing Russia by train, and hiking the Andes. There are very few corners left on this planet where you are not following in everyone else's footsteps. I wanted, once, to trace my own path across a land as yet untrampled by hordes of tourist feet. I want to lose myself in unmapped landscapes and to meet the people who inhabited them. I wanted uncompromising, boundless space, and nature's reminders of how minute a human being is. I wanted the kind of empty, demanding landscape that some people call lifeless or inhospitable and that fills me with a visceral sense of freedom. Mongolia was one of the few countries not in the title of any guidebook we carried. I didn't know much about the vast north Asian land, but I imagined untamed expanses of steppe rolling to the horizon. I imagined puffy white yurts nestled in the middle of nowhere. I imagined hardy little horses running free across desolate stretches of grassland unmarked by the twentieth century. Mongolia sounded like freedom to me.

Four years earlier, in Munich, Germany, on my way to buy a train ticket to France, I had decided, on a whim, to buy a bicycle instead. When I started pedaling, I thought I knew where I was going. I thought I knew France and Germany pretty well, but over the next five weeks, my department-store bicycle's two wheels suddenly opened up the lands' remote corners—the farmhouses, the mountains, the villages where the trains don't stop. So now, as I stared at a map of Asia, I knew that where I wanted to go lay beyond Mongolia's dozen scattered towns and cities. I knew that I wanted to move freely, unconstrained by the routes and schedules of infrequent and unreliable public transportation. But I am not a hard-core cyclist. The charms of intense off-road travail are lost on me. I doubted that a bicycle was the optimal mode of travel in a country three times the size of France with fewer than a thousand kilometers of paved road and not one single bicycle shop. I moved on to a better idea: buy a horse—Mongolia's age-old form of transportation. But staring at that map of Asia, I could not help but see that there, not really so very far away from Mongolia, was Vietnam. White sand beaches, the inevitable mystique borne of war, and, in 1993, the attraction of an until recently inaccessible land. If I got to Mongolia, I might as well keep going. My finger traced a line across the paper, from Russia's Lake Baikal south to Saigon. I had no particular interest in China, never had had, but there it was, smack-dab between the other two, so across China I would go. I had no doubt that a horse was *not* the optimal mode of travel in China and Vietman. A bicycle was.

So I had a plan. Or at least an idea, a fantasy floating around in the back of my mind. Then one day the phone rang and a man I had never met, a friend of a friend, offered me a job as interpreter for his theater's tour to Vladivostok, in Far Eastern Russia. Russia *east* of Siberia. They would be leaving in less than two months. Vladivostok, all things being relative, was just around the corner from Mongolia. This was as close as I was ever going to get for free, but a recent audition had gone well and it was a great part. If I got it, I would not say no, not even for Mongolia. A few evenings later, the phone rang again. They had cast the thin, beautiful blonde who could sing.

I started applying for visas. I started packing my apartment into cardboard boxes. I started bicycle shopping. I knew my trusty road bike was not up to the trip. I knew I needed fat, knobby tires. I knew I needed a frame that would withstand months of brutal abuse. That was all I knew. I tripped into cycle shops and asked, "If you were riding across Mongolia, what would you ride?" It was like a metaphor, "Mongolia." The middle of nowhere. The back of beyond. Someplace far, far away. Nobody thought that I actually meant Mongolia, the country. Almost nobody knew that there still *was* a country called Mongolia, that it was not part of China, that it was not part of Russia, that time and history had not wiped it off the map altogether. I rode bicycles up and down Seattle streets trying to imagine rocky, sandy, muddy grassland. With five weeks to go, I settled on a neon-green mountain bike with the fattest, knobbiest tires in the store and drop handlebars for my weak wrists. I strapped on an odometer and calibrated it to run in kilometers. For the next eight months, a mile would be an irrelevant measurement—all maps, road signs, and directions from passersby would be figured in kilometers, a distance equal to roughly $\frac{5}{8}$ of a mile. I rode my new bicycle home, dubbed her "Greene," and drowned her in a can of automotive primer. Then I put her in a box and got on a plane to Russia.

After three weeks in Vladivostok, the American theater company flew back to California, and Greene and I aimed west toward Irkutsk. As the plane tilted over the vast stretches of southeastern Siberia, I could not believe where I was going. There had been heady days of anticipation and quaking days of terror. One minute, life was unalloyed exhilaration and I was pure courage. I could not wait to be on the road—just me and Greene and the weather and the wonderful, terrifying freedom of never having to be anywhere ever again. The next minute, there was a churning in my stomach. I wanted some really good reason to stop before I started. I wanted to burst into tears and flee home to an easy Seattle summer of baseball games and hiking trips. I knew nothing about Mongolia, and little more about self-sufficient bicycle travel. I was throwing myself at an idea, leaving everything behind and heading blindly into I knew not what. I was running away.

But I was also running toward something. Ahead of me lay the unknowns that are the soul and purpose of a journey. I was completely intimidated, and I was absolutely at peace. I was at the beginning of an adventure: Tomorrow was a mystery, and that mystery was terrifying. It was also the most enticing thing in the world.

[2001]

SARA WHEELER

(1961–)

British writer Sara Wheeler takes the image of a blank map for the title of her travel book on Antarctica. *Terra Incognita* (1998) expresses the continent's identity as the epitome of the unknown. She first became interested in that part of the world while traversing Chile for her earlier book, *Travels in a Thin Country* (1994). To many, the whiteness of Antartica on maps represents the featureless and uncharted nature of the land. For explorers of Antarctica, whiteness becomes a metaphor for the emptiness, as well as the blank slate of imaginative possibilities for the continent. Wheeler has also written a biography of an earlier Antarctic traveler, Apsley Cherry-Garrard, whose 1930 account, *The Worst Journey in the World*, a portion of which appears later in this anthology, details the hardship and suffering of an expedition to the South Pole.

The excerpt that follows is from Wheeler's introduction to her own journey in *Terra Incognita*. The excerpt gives a good idea of a travel writer's thorough intellectual and psychological preparations for the journey as well as the effects of literary and historical tradition in her own expectations.

From *Terra Incognita*

Antarctica left a restless longing in my heart beckoning towards an incomprehensible perfection for ever beyond the reach of mortal man. Its overwhelming beauty touches one so deeply that it is like a wound.
—Edwin Mickleburgh, *Beyond the Frozen Sea*

'It is the last great journey left to man,' Shackleton said. He didn't mean that we all had to pack our crampons and set off, ice axes in hand. For Shackleton, Antarctica was a metaphor as well as an explorer's dream, and he added, 'We all have our own White South.' It is true that for me Antarctica was always a space of the imagination—before, during and after my own journey. No cities, no bank managers, no pram in the hall. Some people think that before the ice came Antarctica was the site of Atlantis, the ancient civilisation which disappeared in a cosmic gulf, but when I went there I learnt that Atlantis is within us.

As I struggled out of stiff sleeping bags over waterbottles, VHF radios, batteries and stray items of scientific paraphernalia stowed alongside me in the epic battle with the big freeze, I didn't think about Atlantis or Shackleton or metaphorical allusions. I thought about how cold I was.

Until I was thirty, my relationship with Antarctica was confined to the biannual reinflation of the globe hanging above my desk, its air valve located in the middle of the mis-shapen white pancake at the bottom. As far as I was aware, the continent was a testing-ground for men with frozen beards to see how dead they could get. Then, in 1991, I travelled several thousand miles through Chile for a book I was writing. As I prodded around in the hinterland of the national psyche I discovered that the country did not come to a stop in Tierra del Fuego. A small triangle was suspended at the bottom of every map. They called it *Antártida chilena* and behaved as if it were their fifty-first state. I had to go down there if I wanted to paint a complete portrait of contemporary Chile, so one day in February I hitched a lift from a blustery Punta Arenas to King George Island, off the tip of the spindly Antarctic peninsula, on an antediluvian Hercules belonging to the Chilean Air Force.

With nothing but Chile on my mind and a carpetbag on my shoulder I climbed down the steps of the plane into the rasping air and shook the bearpaw extended by the hapless wing-commander who had been appointed as my minder. I looked out over the icefields vanishing into the aspirin-white horizon. Above them, a single snow petrel wheeled against the Hockney blue. Much later I climbed a snowhill with a Uruguayan vulcanologist, already feeling that I had found a blank piece of paper. There was no sound on the top of the hill except the occasional tap-tap as the vulcanologist scraped snow into a specimen tin, and as the shadows lengthened on the rippling Southern Ocean I looked beyond the small base in the foreground and thought—that's an ice-desert bigger than Australia. Antarctica is the highest continent, as well as the driest, the coldest and the windiest, and nobody owns it. Seven countries might have 'claimed' a slice for themselves, and there might be almost two hundred little research camps, but the continent is not owned by anyone.

Standing on the edge of the icefield in a wind strong enough to lean on, squinting in the buttery light, it was as if I were seeing the earth for the very first time. I felt less homeless than I have ever felt anywhere, and I knew immediately that I had to return. I sensed that the icefields had something to teach me.

After consorting with Russians, Chinese, Uruguayans and Poles on King George Island and observing how the continent blunts the edges of nationality, I realised that I had found the perfect *tabula rasa*. When I left, wedged into position on the same decrepit Hercules, I wrote *Terra Incognita* on the cover of a virgin notebook.

*   *   *

I discovered that the ancient Greeks had sensed it was there because something had to balance the white bit at the top of the globe. Medieval cartographers had a stab at mapping it and called it *Terra Australis Incognita*, the Unknown Southern Land. For centuries, it seemed, everyone thought it was rich, fertile and populous and that finding it would be like winning the National Lottery. It was Captain Cook, the greatest explorer of all time, who sent the message back to the naval hydrographers fidgeting through the long reign of George III to say no, down here there are no golden fields or burgeoning trees or tall people with flaxen hair. Down here there is only cold hell.

After that most people forgot about it for a while, and when all the other white spaces on the map had been coloured in, they came back to it. The British were especially keen on Antarctica, as they had done Africa and spent much of the nineteenth century fretting over the Arctic. By the time the twentieth century rolled around they were fully engaged in the great quest for the south. For these British people the quest culminated in the central Antarctic myth, that of Captain Scott, a man woven into the fabric of our national culture as tightly as the pattern in a carpet.

Once I had glimpsed it, the Antarctic lodged in my mind's eye and rose unbidden on every horizon. I forced my friends to sit in empty cinemas whenever Charles Frend's 1948 film *Scott of the Antarctic* resurfaced, and we watched John Mills striding across a psychedelic backdrop which made the continent look like a seventies album cover. Shaw had used Antarctica as a metaphor, T. S. Eliot recycled Antarctic material in *The Waste Land*, and I found it in Saul Bellow, Thomas Pynchon, Vaclav Havel, Doris Lessing and Thomas Keneally. When I went to the National Theatre to get away from its blinding light I found that Tony Kushner had set a whole scene of his epic *Angels in America* down there. All places are more than the sum of their physical components, and I saw that Antarctica existed most vividly in the mind. It was a metaphorical landscape, and in an increasingly grubby world it had been romanticised to fulfil a human need for sanctuary. Mythical for centuries, so it remained.

It took two years to organise the journey. During that period I was accepted as the first foreigner on the American National Science Foundation's Antarctic Artists' and Writers' Program. The two years unravelled in a seamless roll of letters, interviews, meetings, conferences on two continents, endless hand-to-mouth freelance work, exhaustive medicals and long walks through the bowels of the Foreign Office in London to get to Polar Regions, which was a long way from anywhere else in the building and the temperature dropped as I approached it. Nobody knows what my dentist and I went through to satisfy the punitive requirements of the U.S. Navy. My tattoo was logged in the Disabilities and Disfigurements section of the British Antarctic Survey's medical records. Three weeks before departure I had to undergo various unpleasant tests to produce documentation that my heart murmur was not one of the uncommon kind likely to stage a rebellion on the ice. The cardiologist in Harley Street who applied himself to this task was Brazilian, and I had made an appointment to collect the results at eight o'clock on the morning after Brazil won the World Cup. I sat taut with tension on the steps outside his elegant practice, clinging helplessly to my dream until he fell at my feet out of the back of a taxi, his tie unknotted, shouting, 'You have the best heart I have ever seen.'

At the British Antarctic Survey pre-deployment conference in Cambridge I was woken each morning by the padding footsteps of a dog-handler in the chilly corridors of Girton College, and the padder and I went running along the river Cam together. On the last night I sat in candlelight under dour oil portraits of tweed-skirted Victorian scholars in the Great Hall, listening to Barry Heywood, the head of BAS, telling us in hushed tones that we were about to experience the time of our lives.

The very next day I picked up the telephone in an institutional room in the vast Xerox Document University in Leesburg, Virginia, at the American Antarctic Program's pre-deployment conference, and a computer-generated voice said, 'Good morning, this is your wake-up call'. Through it all, my dream sustained me.

I sat in Scott's cabin aboard *Discovery* in Dundee and stood in pouring rain on the Eastern Commercial Docks in Grimsby among excitable relatives waiting for the *James Clark Ross* to arrive at the end of its long journey from Antarctica. Week after week Shirley, the obliging information assistant at the Scott Polar Research Institute in Cambridge, unlocked the dust-encrusted basement so I could get at the fiction section, which was hidden behind dented tins of film spools and cardboard boxes of redundant dogfood. At the same institute I worked my way through blubber-splashed pages of leather notebooks inscribed by the men who gave Antarctica a history: reading them all was like looking at an object through the different angles of a glass prism. On assignment in India, I escaped to find the headquarters of the Indian Antarctic Programme in the asphyxiating concrete heartland of New Delhi, and when I walked up to its ramshackle eighth-floor offices, the air-conditioning had just sighed to a stop and a tall secretary in an orange sari was fanning herself in front of a photograph of a pristine snowscape. I drank warm beer outside railway stations in the south of England, waiting to be collected by veteran explorers, long since retired, and later, in their neat homes, liver-spotted hands turned the stiff black pages of cracked photograph albums. In Hampshire I was entertained by Zaz Bergel, granddaughter of Sir Ernest Shackleton, the Antarctic explorer's Antarctic explorer, and when I put on my coat to leave she said, 'Grandfather was much happier there than anywhere else.'

As for the profound appeal of ice on the imagination, I had only to think of the chilly opening line of García Márquez's novel *One Hundred Years of Solitude*: 'Many years later, as he faced the firing squad, Colonel Aureliano Buendia was to remember that distant afternoon when his father took him to discover ice.'

There were psychological preparations too, though these were more difficult. In the Foreword to a seminal book about the opening up of the continent I read: 'Some of the most prominent challenges of polar living fall into the provinces of mind and emotion, rather than muscle and matter.' A man with many years experience on the ice wrote in the same book: 'The Antarctic generally wields a profound effect on personality and character and few men are the same after a stay there.' I wasn't afraid of loneliness; I had learnt that it doesn't arrive on the coat-tails of isolation. All the same, I was apprehensive about where Antarctica would take me, and about seeing my life *sub specie*. Robert Swan, who walked to both Poles, told me that going to either is like watching a child's magic slate wipe away your life as you knew it.

In an academic book on Antarctic psychology I read, 'It is intuitive that life in a confined environment is an adverse experience and may lead to human dysfunction.' A scientist who went south with both Scott and Shackleton coined the phrase 'polar madness', and Admiral Byrd packed two coffins and twelve strait-jackets when he led one of the earliest U.S. Antarctic expeditions. Soon I was familiar with the folklore: the base commander who torched all the buildings in camp, the man who started talking with a lisp, the chef who set to with a meat-cleaver, the Soviet who killed a colleague with an ice axe during a game of chess (to ensure it didn't happen again, the authorities banned chess). One of the earliest behavioural findings in Antarctica was Mullin's discovery of spontaneous trance states, and papers had been written on alterations in consciousness induced by exposure to Antarctic isolation. At the same time it had melted frozen hearts. "At the bottom of this planet', wrote Admiral Byrd, the first man to fly over the South Pole, 'is an enchanaged continent in the sky, pale like a sleeping princess. Sinister and beautiful, she lies in frozen slumber.' 'There, if anywhere,' said another explorer, 'is life worthwhile.'

The people lighting my way had one thing in common. They were all men. It was male territory all right—it was like a gentleman's club, an extension of boarding school and the army. Only the U.S. programme even approaches normality in its ratio of men to women. Alastair Fothergill, who produced the *Life in the Freezer* television series and wrote the accompanying book, told me that for British men, going south was still like going to the pub. I had tea with Sir Edmund Hillary in New Zealand. 'My experience has been', he said between mouthfuls of chocolate cake, 'that the scientific community in the Antarctic regard it as their property and bitterly resent any outsiders venturing there.' Men had been quarrelling over Antarctica since it emerged from the southern mists, perceiving it as another trophy, a particularly meaty beast to be clubbed to death outside the cave. Mike Stroud, who played a Boswellian role to Ranulph Fiennes's Johnson when the pair of them attempted an ambitious trek across the continent, was more honest with me than most of the Frozen Beards. 'Sometimes I think I didn't have time to stop and appreciate it,' he said. "I walked across, but most of the time I was miserable.'

*   *   *

The Antarctic continent is shaped roughly like a cross-section of the human brain, with a grossly misplaced finger tapering towards South America (this is usually shown coming out on the left at the top, depending which way round the map is drawn). More than ninety-nine per cent[1] of this landmass is permanently covered with ice formed by thousands of years of tightly compacted snowfalls. The other 0.4 per cent consists of exposed rock. Like glutinous white icing flowing off a wedding cake, the layer of ice on the surface of Antarctica is slowly but persistently rolling towards the coast, forcing its way between mountains, turning itself into glaciers split by crevasses and inching its way into a floating ice shelf or collapsing into the Southern Ocean. As a result, ice shelves surround the jagged Antarctic coastline. One of them, the Ross Ice Shelf, is larger than France.

The continent consists, broadly speaking, of two geological zones divided by the Transantarctic mountain chain. Greater Antarctica (also known as East Antarctica) is generally thought to be one stable plate. Lesser Antarctica (or West), on the other hand, consists of a lot of smaller, unstable plates—that's why all the volcanoes are in it. Besides the Transantarctics slicing down the middle, mountains form a ring around much of the continent. Beyond these coastal heights, in the interior, topography tends to disappear into thousands of miles of apparently flat ice—the enormous polar plateau. Mountain ranges as high as the Appalchians are hiding under this flat ice. The South Pole, the axis of the earth's rotation, is located in greater Antarctica, on the polar plateau.

For much of the year, Antarctica enjoys total darkness or total daylight. The cusps between the two are short and exciting: it might be eight weeks from the moment the sun makes its first appearance over the horizon to the day it never sets. The summer season, broadly speaking, runs from mid-October to late February.

One of Antarctica's most salient characteristics is that of scale. The continent, one tenth of the earth's land surface, is considerably larger than Europe and one-and-a-half times the size of the United States. It has ninety per cent of the world's ice, and at its deepest, the ice layer is over 15,000 feet thick, pushing the land under it far below sea level. Thousands of cubic miles of ice break off the Antarctic coast each year. It is, on average, three times higher than any other continent. It never rains and rarely snows on most of it, so Antarctica is the driest desert in the world.

Into this land of superlatives I plunged. My plan was to fly in from New Zealand with the Americans in November, just as the austral summer was under way. Their main base is on one of the many hundreds of islands scattered around the Antarctic coast, and from there I could travel to a variety of field camps on the continent itself, perhaps make the Pole for Christmas, and later hook up with the New Zealanders, who were based nearby, and the Ital-

---

1. 99.6 per cent is the latest figure from the BAS/SPRI satellite map.

ians in Victoria Land only a couple of hundred miles away. At the end of January I was going to make my way over to the British Antarcticans, all working on the peninsula, the finger tapering off towards South America. As this was on the other side of the continent, I was obliged to travel back to New Zealand on an American military plane and take a fiendishly roundabout route to the Falklands (so diabolical was it that I ended up back in my own flat in London in the middle) in order to catch a lift on the British Antarctic Survey Dash-7 plane down to the Antarctic Peninsula. I was going to travel with my compatriots for two months, by which time night would have begun its swift descent, and then sail up the peninsula in an ice-strengthened ship and arrive in the Falklands in early April.

In my grandmother's youth a restless spirit would probably have got her as far as Spain, then as exotic as Xanadu. The world has shrunk, and I was able, now, to go to its uttermost part.

By the end of the beginning I understood something, at least. I understood that Scott was right when he endorsed Nansen's exhausted remark, 'The worst part of a polar expedition is over when the preparation has ended and the journey begun.'

When someone asked Jonathan Raban why he was making his journey down the Mississippi, he said he was having a love affair with it. Antarctica was my love affair, and in the south I learnt another way of looking at the world. What I want to do now is take you there. As Shackleton said, 'We all have our own White South,' and I believe that the reach of the imagination extends far beyond the snowfields.

[1998]

JOHN KEATS

(1795–1821)

A major poet of the Romantic period in the first part of the nineteenth century, John Keats left school at age 15 and never learned Greek, a staple of secondary education at the time. Apprenticed to a surgeon, Keats pursued literature on his own and nourished his desire to be a poet. He read Greek in translation, and a version of Homer by the Elizabethan poet George Chapman delighted him. In this sonnet, Keats equates the pleasure of reading to the excitement of exploration, and no one minds the fact that he names Cortez rather than Balboa as the discoverer of the Pacific Ocean. Keats, who suffered from tuberculosis, later traveled to Italy for his health and died in Rome while still a young man. He was close to Homer's Mediterranean, a destination for generations of English travelers who read the classics and sought the spirit of the ancient world by traveling to the landscapes and the ruins of modern Greece and Italy.

"On First Looking into Chapman's Homer"

Much have I travell'd in the realms of gold,
  And many goodly states and kingdoms seen;
  Round many western islands have I been
Which bards in fealty to Apollo hold.
Oft of one wide expanse had I been told   5
  That deep-brow'd Homer ruled as his demesne;
  Yet did I never breathe its pure serene
Till I heard Chapman speak out loud and bold:
Then felt I like some watcher of the skies
  When a new planet swims into his ken;   10
Or like stout Cortez when with eagle eyes
  He star'd at the Pacific—and all his men
  Look'd at each other with a wild surmise—
    Silent, upon a peak in Darien.

[1816]

JONATHAN RABAN

(1942–)

Reading Mark Twain's *The Adventures of Huckleberry Finn* had a powerful effect on Jonathan Raban. In his childhood he dreamt of imitating Twain's young runaway by fleeing his native England, going to America, and taking his own river trip. As an adult Raban acted out his dream, piloted a small boat down the Mississippi from Minnesota to the Gulf of Mexico, and wrote a travel book about the experience (*Old Glory*, 1981). An experienced sailor, Raban has circumnavigated his native country (*Coasting*, 1987) and traced the northwest coast of America to Alaska (*Passage to Juneau: A Sea and Its Meanings*, 1999). He has also edited *The Oxford Book of the Sea* (1992). Raban has gone overland as well, to follow the dreams and disappointments of American settlers on the northern plains (*Hunting Mr. Heartbreak: A Discovery of America*, 1991), and he has traveled in the footsteps of Richard Burton and T. E. Lawrence by exploring Saudi Arabia (*Arabia: A Journey through the Labyrinth*, 1979).

The selection that follows from *Old Glory* recounts how Raban's childhood reading grew into an obsession with the Mississippi River. He also identified the confining atmosphere of rural England with the figure of his father, an observation that supports Freud's premise that travel is an escape from the confines of the family and paternal authority.

"The River"

From *Old Glory*

It is as big and depthless as the sky itself. You can see the curve of the earth on its surface as it stretches away for miles to the far shore. Sunset has turned the water to the color of unripe peaches. There's no wind. Sandbars and wooded islands stand on their exact reflections. The only signs of movement on the water are the lightly scratched lines which run in parallel across it like the scores of a diamond on a windowpane. In the middle distance, the river smokes with toppling pillars of mist which soften the light so that one can almost reach out and take in handfuls of that thickened air.

A fish jumps. The river shatters for a moment, then glazes over. The forest which rims it is a long, looping smudge of charcoal. You could make it by running your thumb along the top edge of the water, smearing in the black pines and bog oaks, breaking briefly to leave a pale little town of painted clapboard houses tumbling from the side of a hill. Somewhere in the picture there is the scissored silhouette of a fisherman from the town, afloat between the islands in his wooden pirogue, a perfectly solitary figure casting into what is left of the sun.

It is called the Mississippi, but it is more an imaginary river than a real one. I had first read *Huckleberry Finn* when I was seven. The picture on its cover, crudely drawn and colored, supplied me with the raw material for an exquisite and recurrent daydream. It showed a boy alone, his face prematurely wizened with experience. (The artist hadn't risked his hand with the difficulties of bringing off a lifelike Nigger Jim.) The sheet of water on which he drifted was immense, an enameled pool of lapis lazuli. Smoke from a half-hidden steamboat hung over an island of Gothic conifers. Cut loose from the world, chewing on his corncob pipe, the boy was blissfully lost in this stillwater paradise.

For days I lay stretched out on the floor of my attic room, trying to bring the river to life from its code of print. It was tough going. Often I found Huck's American dialect as impenetrable as Latin, but even in the most difficult bits I was kept at it by the persistent wink and glimmer of the river. I was living inside the book. Because I was more timid and less sociable than Huck, his and my adventures on the Mississippi tended to diverge. He would sneak off in disguise to forage in a riverside town, or raid a wrecked steamboat; I would stay back on the raft. I laid trotlines for catfish. I floated alone on that unreal blue, watching for "towheads" and "sawyers" as the forest unrolled, a mile or more across the water.

I found the Mississippi in the family atlas. It was a great ink-stained Victorian book, almost as big as I was. "North Africa" and "Italy" had come loose from its binding, from my mother's atempts to keep up with my father's campaigns in the Eighth Army. North America, though, was virgin territory: no one in the family had ever thought the place worth a moment of their curiosity. I looked at the Mississippi, wriggling down the middle of the page, and liked the funny names of the places that it passed through. Just the sounds of Minneapolis . . . Dubuque . . . Hannibal . . . St. Louis . . . Cairo . . . Memphis . . . Natchez . . . Baton Rouge . . . struck a legendary and heroic note to my ear. Our part of England was culpably short of Roman generals, Indians and Egyptian ruins, and these splendid names added even more luster to the marvelous river in my head.

The only real river I knew was hardly more than a brook. It spilled through a tumbledown mill at the bottom of our road, opened into a little trouty pool, then ran on through water meadows over graveled shallows into Fakenham, where it slowed and deepened, gathering strength for the long drift across muddy flatlands to Norwich and the North Sea. All through my Huckleberry Finn summer, I came down to the mill to fish for roach and dace, and if I concentrated really hard, I could see the Mississippi there. First I had to think it twice as wide, then multiply by two, then two again . . . The rooftops of Fakenham went under. I sank roads, farms, church spires, the old German prisoner-of-war camp, Mr. Banham's flour mill. I flooded Norfolk, silvering the landscape like a mirror, leaving just an island here, a dead tree there, to break this lonely, enchanted monotony of water. It was a heady, intensely private vision. I hugged the idea of the huge river to myself. I exulted in the freedom and solitude of being afloat on it in my imagination. . . .

Year by year I added new scraps of detail to the picture. I came across some photographs of the Mississippi in a dog-eared copy of the *National Geographic* in a doctor's waiting room. Like inefficient pornography, they were unsatisfying because they were too meanly explicit. "Towboat *Herman Briggs* at Greenville" and "Madrid Bend, Missouri" gave the river a set of measurements that I didn't at all care for. I didn't want to know that it was a mile and a quarter wide, or that its ruffled water wasn't blue at all but dirty tan. The lovely, immeasurable river in my head was traduced by these artless images, and when the doctor called me in to listen to the noises in my asthmatic chest I felt saved by the bell.

Then I saw a painting by George Caleb Bingham. It showed the Missouri, not the Mississippi, but I recognized it immediately as my river. Its water had a crystalline solidity and smoothness, as if it had been carved from rosy quartz. The river and the sky were one, with cliffs and forest hanging in suspension between them. In the foreground, a ruffianly trapper and his son drifted in a dugout canoe, their pet fox chained to its prow. The water captured their reflections as faithfully as a film. Alone, self-contained, they moved with the river, an integral part of the powerful current of things, afloat on it in exactly the way I had been daydreaming for myself. The French fur trader and his half-caste child joined Huck Finn—the three persons of the trinity which presided over my river.

Crouched under the willow below the mill, I lobbed my baited hook into the pool and watched the water spread. The Mississippi was my best invention; a dream that was always there, like a big friendly room with an open door into which I could wander at will. Once inside it, I was at home. I let the river grow around me until the world consisted of nothing except me and that great comforting gulf of water where catfish rootled and wild fruit hung from the trees on the towhead islands. The river was completely still as the distant shore went inching by. I felt my skin burn in the sun. I smelled sawn timber and blackberries and persimmons. I didn't dare move a muscle for fear of waking from the dream. . . .

I had never quite given up dreaming of the river and still found comfort in the idea of that lovely, glassy sweep of open water. The rivers I fished, on weekend escapes from the city, were always shadowed by another, bigger river, broad and long enough to lose oneself on. Once, I'd actually seen the Mississippi, but it was from the window of a jet thirty thousand feet up, and the river looked as remote and theoretical as the twisty black thread in the family atlas. One sip of a Pan American highball, and it was gone.

Its afterimage lodged obstinately at the back of my head. In London, I had gone stale and dry. I felt that I'd run out of whatever peculiar reserves of moral capital are needed for city life. I couldn't write. For days on end I woke at five, confused and panicky, as the tranquilizers that I'd taken lost their grip. I listened to the jabbering sparrows in the yard and to the restless surf of overnight traffic on the road beyond. I lay clenched, struggling to get to sleep, and found myself thinking of the river, the great good place of my childhood. It was still just visitable. The dream was heavily overgrown now, and there were prohibitive signs and stretches of barbed wire to pass before one could get back to the old spot where the water spread away for miles, then dissolved into sky. Here, already half asleep, I let myself drift out into the current and watched the rising sun loom like a gigantic grapefruit through the mist.

Going down the river turned into an obsessive ritual. I had to relearn the child's trick of switching instantly into an imagined world. Soon I could work the magic with a few bare talismanic symbols—a curling eddy, a reedbed, an island, and a canister of photographer's smoke. It wasn't long before these daily dawn voyages began to suggest a real journey and a book.

The book and the journey would be all of a piece. The plot would be written by the current of the river itself. It would carry me into long deep pools of solitude, and into brushes with society on the shore. Where the river meandered, so would the book, and when the current speeded up into a narrow chute, the book would follow it. Everything would be left to chance. There'd be no advance reservations, no letters of introduction. I would try to be as much like a piece of human driftwood as I could manage. Cast off, let the Mississippi take hold, and trust to whatever adventures or longueurs the river might throw my way. It was a journey that would be random and haphazard; but it would also have the insistent purpose of the river current as it drove southward and seaward to the Gulf of Mexico.

It's hard to make travel arrangements to visit a dream. The voyage I was planning was on a river which existed only in my head. The real Mississippi was an abstraction. I studied it with impatience, feeling that the facts were just so many bits of grit in my vision of a halcyon river. I learned, without enthusiasm, about the construction of the lock-and-dam system. Figures began to swim in my head where the dream ought to be. In 1890, thirty million tons of freight had been carried downriver; in 1979, after a long and catastrophic decline in river trade, business was up again to forty million tons. The Civil War and the coming of the railroads had almost smashed the river as a commercial highway, but the oil crisis of the 1970s had brought the Mississippi back to life. A river barge, I read, "can move 400 tons of grain a mile on a gallon of fuel, compared with only 200 tons for a locomotive"; and a lot of people were now wanting to move a lot of tons of grain, because the United States had raised its quota of grain exports to Russia. So the port of New Orleans was busy with ships carting Midwestern wheat and corn and soybeans off to Murmansk and Archangel. To someone somewhere, I suppose, this kind of information has the ring of industrial poetry; it didn't to me. It was reassuring to find that the river was important again, a central artery linking north and south in a drifting procession of towboats and barge fleets, but I found the details of its renascence grindingly dull. They threatened to contaminate that great, wide-open stretch of level water which was far more actual for me than these tawdry scraps of intelligence from the real world.

I went for long walks by the Thames, following the ebb tide as it ran out through Kew, Chiswick, Barnes, Putney, watching the way it piled against the bridges and came to the boil over deep muddy holes in the river bottom. It was the simple movement of the water that I liked, and its capacity to make the city which surrounded it look precarious and makeshift. The pastel cottages on the bank, with their bookshelves, net curtains, standing lamps and potted plants, stood on the lip of a real and dangerous wilderness. A freak tide, a careless shift in the current, and they could be swept away. The river, as it sluiced past their doorsteps, carried plenty of evidence of its deadliness. There were dead dogs in it, and stoved-in boats, and the occasional bloated human corpse. Once I found the body of a drowned woman. She was spread-eagled on the shore; her coat, of sodden leopard skin, had ridden up over her torso and covered her head. There were runs in her tights. Her boots were very new. At the coroner's inquest on her death, I heard that she'd left a note. It was rambling, disjointed, full of resentment and depression, but it didn't actu-ally say that she intended to kill herself. It seemed rather that she had come to the river without knowing what she was going to do. Perhaps she believed that the mess and tangle of her life would somehow resolve itself if she could put it in perspective beside the bleak placidity of all that drifting water. It was probable, said the coroner, that she'd thrown herself into the river without premeditation; not really meaning to commit suicide, merely trying to assuage her misery and confusion in the comforting void of the Thames. He announced his verdict: death by misadventure.

I felt I understood what had drawn the woman to the river. I wanted to lose myself too. I had no intention of landing up in some small Midwestern city morgue, but I ached to run away from the world for a while, to put myself in the grip of a powerful current which would make my choices for me, to be literally adrift. The woman had gone to the river for solace, and had ended up drowning in it; I was going for much the same motive, but meant to stay afloat.

I hardly gave a thought to the mechanics of the voyage. It was, after all, a dream journey, and like a dream it was supposed to unfold spontaneously without effort on my part. Obviously I would need a craft of some kind, but I knew almost nothing at all about boats. A raft would turn the trip into a piece of quaint playacting; canoes capsized. I vaguely assumed that somewhere at the top end of the river I'd come across a leaky tub with a pair of oars, and cast off in that.

To make the voyage come true, I began to talk about it. At a party in Lon-don I met a man who had seen the Mississippi at St. Louis and had gone on a half-day tourist cruise up the river.

"It was amazingly depressing," he said. "Totally featureless. An awful lot of mud. You couldn't see anything over the top of the banks except dead trees. The only bearable thing about the entire afternoon was the ship's bar. It was full of people getting dead drunk so that they didn't have to look at the sheer bloody boredom of the Mississippi."

"That was just around St. Louis, though."

"Oh, it's all like that, I gather. That's what it's famous for, being very long and very boring. The only reason people ever go on the Mississippi at all is because after you've spent a couple of hours looking at that horrendous bloody river, even a dump like St. Louis starts to look moderately interesting. I think God made the Mississippi as a sort of warning, to prove that things really can be worse than you think."

He had an air of mighty self-satisfaction, having delivered me at a stroke from the lunatic fantasy with which I'd been possessed. Actually, I'd been rather excited by his description of the river. It had given it something of the melodramatic awfulness of a landscape by John Martin, a touch of *Sadek in Search of the Waters of Oblivion* with its dwarfish hominid scrambling into a world of treeless crags and dead seas.

"I suppose you thought you were going to do it in a rowing boat," the man said, snuffling with amusement at the notion. I didn't like the way he had consigned my trip to the past subjunctive tense.

"No, no. I'll have a . . . an outboard motor." I had had one experience with an outboard motor. I had driven myself from one end of a small Scottish loch to the other, where it had coughed and died. It had taken me three hours to row back through a rainstorm.

"You'd get swamped. Or be run down by one of those tow-things. When we were in St. Louis, people were always getting drowned in the river. Went out fishing, never came back, bodies recovered weeks later, or never recovered at all. So bloody common that it hardly ever made the local news."

Some days afterward, I ran into the man again.

"You're not still thinking of going down that river, are you?"

"I've written off about getting a motor."

"It'd cost you a hell of a lot less if you just swallowed a packet of razor blades. According to the Euthanasia Society, putting a plastic bag over your head is pretty much the best way to go." He introduced me to the woman he was with. "He's going to go down the Mississippi in a *dinghy*," he said.

"What a lovely thing to do," she said. "Just like Tom Sawyer—or was that Huckleberry Finn?"

The man smiled with exaggerated patience. It was the smile of a lonely realist stranded in the society of cloud-cuckoos.

[1981]

SUSAN RICH

(1959–)

A former Peace Corps volunteer in the west African country of Niger, Susan Rich has also worked as a human rights educator in Palestine, an electoral monitor in Bosnia, and a program coordinator for Amnesty International.

Images of maps, map-making, and travel abound in her book *The Cartographer's Tongue: Poems of the World* (2000). In the following poem, the sharp smell of gasoline is a childhood memory that becomes for her the essence of travel and her father's spirit. For Rich, travel is an evocation of the paternal presence rather than an escape from it.

"The Scent of Gasoline"

As a child I'd inhale deeply the scent of gasoline,
open the back seat window and lift my chin to the wind.

My life shone with petroleum products:
paint thinner, shoe polish, amber jars of shellac.

High test my father would order   5
and while we checked the mileage chart

fumes would enter our bodies, the lightness
burnishing our capillaries,

investing us with longing
for *Rhode Island, Maine, Vermont.*   10

For my birthday I asked for a sky blue bottle
of cologne, *Eau de Esso;*

but instead he brought me smoky gray glasses,
oven-ware plastic tubs, the *limited time offer* of nostalgia.

What I needed was a burning sense across my skin,   15
gas stains on my scarf.

                                        *

In Gaza City, I found excuses
to frequent the "Gas Palace," the chrome pillars

rinsed in florescent greens and shades of blue.
I loved to watch the arched pumps with their reckless   20

slot machine eyes, their loaded guns.
My friend Ámjad would fill the tank and sing a little to himself—

greet the employees smoking cigarettes
and fixing cars; men who worked extra hours,

their bodies like scraps of metal   25
taking their place among the stars.

I sent my father postcards edged in lighter fluid,
Greetings from Gaza no Quaker State, no bars.

                              *

Why mythologize bitter coffee
and squalid rest rooms?   30

BP for Niger, Senegal, and Mali.
I'd ride my mobilette up to the island,

uncap the tank. And more often times
than not, the sweet liquid would overflow

onto the body of my bike, splash   35
the braceleted knobs of my wrists,

and give the attendant and me
a soft rag of conversation.

A filling station. A place to go
to get filled up.   40

                              *

I miss the flying horse,
the nether worlds of *Gulf* and *Texaco.*

I miss the road maps, key chains, *Rubbermaid* cups;
the belief blossoming behind the words *fill 'er up.*

My father's world is gone now,   45
his body returning to the oil fields underground.

And to conjure him I breathe in
the dangerous, clock the miles to the gallon

before the needle stops traveling backward—falls
unencumbered, empty, lost.   50

                                                            [2000]

MARY MORRIS

(1947–)

Mary Morris has written both fiction and nonfiction inspired by travel. In *Nothing to Declare: Memoirs of a Woman Traveling Alone* (1989), she looks back on an earlier period of her life as an expatriate and traveler in Mexico and Central America. *Wall to Wall: By Rail from Beijing to Berlin* (1991) chronicles her journey on the Trans-Siberian railroad in search of her grandmother's birthplace in eastern Europe. The titles of several of her fictional works—*Bus of Dreams* (1985), *Crossroads* (1987), and *Waiting Room* (1989)—suggest the influence of travel. Morris has also co-edited a collection of women's travel writing, *Maiden Voyages* (1993), and teaches creative writing at Sarah Lawrence College.

In "Women and Journeys," she combines an overview of the constraints faced by women travelers with her own memories and experiences of traveling and writing. Her essay brings together a number of ideas about travel writing introduced earlier in this section: the inspiration of maps, the importance of the traveler's childhood fantasies, the heritage of *The Odyssey* (in the figure of Penelope), the omnipresence of travel in narrative, and the interplay between external realities and the traveler's imagination.

"Women and Journeys: Inner and Outer"

The late John Gardner once said that there are only two plots in all of literature: you go on a journey or the stranger comes to town. Since women have for so many years been denied the journey, we were left with only one plot to our lives—to await the coming of the stranger to town. Indeed, there is no picaresque tradition among women novelists. Women's literature from Jane Austen to Virginia Woolf is mostly a literature about waiting, and usually waiting for love. Denied the freedom to roam outside themselves, women turned inward, into their emotions. As the feminist critic Elaine Showalter puts it: "Denied participation in public life, women were forced to cultivate their feelings and to overvalue romance. Emotions rushed in to fill the vacuum of experience."

For centuries it was frowned upon for women to travel without escort, chaperone, or husband. To journey was to put one at risk not only physically but morally. A little freedom could be a dangerous thing. Erica Jong chose well when she picked the metaphor of fear of flying to depict the tremulous outset of a woman's sexual liberation. The language of sexual initiation is oddly similar to the language of travel. We speak of sexual "exploits" or "adventurers." Both body and globe are objects for exploration and the great "explorers," whether Marco Polo or Don Juan, have traditionally been men.

By contrast, I find it revealing that the bindings in women's corsets were called *stays*. Someone who wore stays wouldn't be going very far. The binding of feet in the Orient or the corseting of the body in the West were ways of restricting women's movement. There is an interesting reference to stays in the letters of Lady Mary Wortley Montagu, who went to Turkey with her husband in 1716. Upon visiting a Turkish bath where the women implored her to undress, Lady Mary wrote, "I was forced at last to open my shirt and shew them my stays; which satisfied them very well for, I saw, they believed I was so locked up in that machine that it was not in my own power to open it, which contrivance they attributed to my husband."

It was my mother who made a traveler out of me, not so much because of the places where she went as because of her yearning to go. She used to buy globes and maps and plan dream journeys she'd never take while her "real life" was ensconced in the PTA, the Girl Scouts, suburban lawn parties, and barbecues. She had many reasons—and sometimes, I think, excuses—for not going anywhere, but her main reason was that my father would not go.

Once, when I was a child, my parents were invited to a Suppressed Desire Ball. You were to come in a costume that depicted your secret wish, your heart's desire, that which you'd always yearned to do or be. My mother went into a kind of trance, then came home one day with blue taffeta, white fishnet gauze, travel posters and brochures, and began to construct the most remarkable costume I've ever seen.

She spent weeks on it. I would go down to the workroom, where she sewed, and she'd say to me, "Where should I put the Taj Mahal? Where should the pyramids go?" On and on, into the night, she pasted and sewed and cursed my father, who it seemed would have no costume at all (though in the end my bald father would win first prize with a toupee his barber lent him).

But it is my mother I remember. The night of the ball, she descended the stairs. On her head sat a tiny, silver rotating globe. Her skirts were the oceans, her body the land, and interlaced between all the layers of tafffeta and fishnet were Paris, Tokyo, Istanbul, Tashkent. Instead of seeing the world, my mother became it.

How do you know if you are a traveler? What are the telltale signs? As with most compulsions—such as being a gambler, a kleptomaniac, or a writer—the obvious proof is that you can't stop. If you are hooked, you are hooked. One sure sign of travelers is their relationship to maps. I cannot say how much of my life I have spent looking at maps, but there is no map I won't stare at and study. I love to measure each detail with my thumb, to see how far I have come, how far I've yet to go. I love maps the way stamp collectors love stamps. Not for their usefulness but rather for the sheer beauty of the object itself. I love to look at a map, even if it is a map of Mars, and figure out where I am going and how I am going to get there, which route I will take. I imagine what adventures might await me even though I know that the journey is never what we plan for; it's what happens between the lines.

I come from the Midwest, from the bluffs along the shores of Lake Michigan. It is not an exotic place, though it is very beautiful. You might stumble on an arrowhead, and there are a few trees, bent and tied to the ground a century before by Indians, which mark trails. But other than that, there is nothing remarkable about the part of the world I come from. Nothing extraordinary ever happened to me in the years that I was growing up—except once.

One day as I was coming home from school, I spotted a bird, larger than myself, sitting in the lower branches of a tree in a wooded area I passed through every day. It was huge and peered down with dark, curious eyes. It appeared weary and a bit confused, surprised to find itself in a tree in the Chicago suburbs, yet it stretched its wings and fluttered them with tremendous dignity. I spent the better part of an afternoon watching until my mother, half crazed, came searching and found me entranced by a bald eagle.

The eagle, off course from its home in the wilderness, had somehow landed in my neighborhood. Though lost, it seemed sure of itself. I wondered then as I wonder now what led it to suburbia, so far away from where its nest should be. At times I have thought it just wanted to get away, to go somewhere else. I knew it would find its way.

It was the first traveler I ever encountered and it made me thirsty to take a trip. Whenever I find myself somewhere I don't think I belong, I remember the confidence of that lost wanderer. I have tried to imitate it.

As a child I had a great capacity for staring into space, and I liked doing this best from the backseat of cars, from the dome car of the Union Pacific Railroad when my family went west in the summer, and later from the windows of buses and trains. And what I liked to do best while in a moving vehicle, staring into a vast expanse of scrub desert or a suburban Chicago landscape was to daydream.

I dreamed I was a pioneer girl, an adventurer, a woman hero. I saw myself as an Indian maiden named White Eagle or Running Deer. I rode a pinto horse with bow and arrow at full gallop and my arrows always went straight to the heart. I was faithkeeper, peacemaker, diviner, matchmaker, sister, interpreter of magical signs. I envisioned myself in wagon trains and tepees, in jungles and exotic desert lands, discovering the flight of owls, blazing trails across virgin land.

Travelers, like writers—and, I suppose I must add, women—are dreamers. Our lives are filled with endless possibility. Like readers of romances, we think that anything can happen to us at any time. We forget that this is not our real life—our life of domestic details, work pressures, attempts and failures at human relations. We keep moving. From anecdote to anecdote, from hope to hope. Our motion is forward, whether by train or daydream. Our sights are always set on the horizon, across moonscapes, vast deserts, unfordable rivers, impenetrable ice peaks.

I never intended to be a travel writer, and it is possible that I'll never write another travel book. I went to Latin America to live in 1978 because I was tired of life in New York and I was weary of my own life as a single woman in America. I felt as if I lived in a foreign land, so I decided to actually live in a foreign land and see if I could figure out what home meant to me.

Though I have always kept journals and made notes, I never set out on the open road thinking I'd write about travel. The only time I did do this—a year and a half ago, when I went around the world, through China, Tibet, and the Soviet Union in search of my ancestral land—it was the kiss of death for me. This trip was hampered by bureaucratic restrictions, the lack of language, Chernobyl, and the fact that I was pregnant at the time, but mainly I think by the fact that I was on assignment for a magazine. Traveling on a magazine assignment I have learned is a little like going to a party intending to fall in love. The moment you go with intent, the chances of true, spontaneous discovery are nil.

My year and a half in Latin America was an entirely different matter from my travels through the Soviet Union. What began as an experience, an adventure, turned into a love affair with a culture, a language, a people, which has continued to the present day. For me the only way to really experience a place is to live there, to go for a long time without the props of everyday life. In Mexico I lived without telephone, radio, television, or people who knew me. I lived without resume, biography, personal history.

As I said, I did not go away intending to write about it, but a time came when I knew I would. Still, writing about Latin America must have been in the back of my head. When I began to write about it some eight years after going there for the first time, I read through my travel journals and found this passage: "What is happening to me here is very strong and I will not leave as I came. Perhaps someday, when I am far away, I will write about it."

I have always kept journals—the essential tool of the dreamer—since I was twelve years old and felt the need to record my secret life. That was the year an important event happened in my town and in my adolescence. It was the year when Gary Niblock, a surfer from the beaches of Southern California, returned to live with his father in the landlocked Midwest. He was the first person I ever met from the fringes of the Empire, and he told me stories of high waves and stretches of white sand, of sea creatures that could devour you with one gulp and tall, blond girls.

He looked down at our surfless great lake and stared with disdain across the Illinois prairie. How could I not love this boy who longed to be elsewhere, who told stories of places I'd never seen. It was that winter of my eighth-grade year, while Gary shivered in misery, snowbound away from his surfboard and wet suit, that I went to Larsen's Stationery Store and purchased a small volume with a key, entitled "My Day and How I Shot It" and recorded my thoughts on the surfer boy I had grown to love.

Since then, I have put everything in my journals that I can. Scenes, strange happenings, conversations, ideas, descriptions, lists of things to do. I've often recorded these entries in a chaotic way I'm sure no one could ever make sense out of. But I cross-reference them and somehow when I go back I manage to recall what I need to recall. For instance, I might write "alfalfa field—Victoria— the psychic of lost dogs" and know immediately, even years later, what I want to say about Victoria who lived in a trailer in an alfalfa field along with her one-eyed, grey and white mutt who runs away, and so on.

I have never been successful trying to write about something soon after it happens to me, which is perhaps another reason why I don't do very well when I am sent away on assignment. It took me eight years to write about Latin America. I understand that Joan Didion wrote her book on El Salvador almost immediately upon returning from there, but that is not how I work. As I tell my students, if you want fuel, you don't throw a live dinosaur into a fire. Instead you let it die its natural death, pile on leaves and soil, let the centuries of memory pile upon it, let experience turn to sediment, and eventually it will be useful fuel for the imaginative fires.

I write in my journals as I travel not because I think that some day something may come of it, but rather because I have always carried on this continuing dialogue with myself. Whenever I actually turn back to my journals and find that my writing draws from the journal entries, I am surprised. I am always surprised when what began as raw experience somehow turns itself into memory, which turns itself into stories or, in the case of my travel memoir, *Nothing to Declare* (1988), into *memoire*.

In 1985 the *New York Times Book Review* listed the best new travel writing for the summer. I was struck by the fact that in the twenty or so best travel books mentioned, not one had been written by a woman. Though never intending to write a travel book, I now began to think seriously about women and travel and how the two relate to questions of self-realization and fulfillment. The great and sudden upsurge in travel writing probably has its roots in a complex restlessness in our culture that has to do with the breakdown of the family, a certain spiritual emptiness in our lives, and a thirst for the unusual. Whatever its sources, the recent interest in travel writing has inspired the recovery of lost travel narratives by women. Isak Dinesen's *Out of Africa* (1937) and Beryl Markham's elegant *West with the Night* (1942) have made it to the best-seller list. Beacon Press, in conjunction with Virago, has launched a reprint series of classic women travel writers, which includes Isabella Bird's remarkable writing about China and Japan, Kate O'Brien on Spain, and Mary Kingsley's *Travels in West Africa* (1897).

Still, many women who traveled and wrote about their adventures did so because of circumstances, not because they went off seeking excitement and intending to write about it. And they wrote about their experiences in a very different way than their male counterparts did. Isak Dinesen went to Africa to marry. Beryl Markham was raised in Africa and taught to fly by her father. As an editorial assistant just out of college, I recall being moved by the journals of a pioneer woman, Mary McClane, who wrote of life in the prairies where she grew up and who speaks of her deep longing that grew out of her loneliness in a way that was plainly sexual. It was, in fact, in reading the journals of Mary McClane that I began to see how women who wrote about their adventures experienced their lives differently than men. Or at least they were able to express what they experienced in a different way—one that, for better or worse, reflected their own inner workings.

Henry Miller says, in his wonderful travel narrative *The Colossus of Maroussi* (1941), that all voyages are accomplished inwardly and that the most difficult are made without moving from the spot. In saying this, he sums up the kind of inner dialogue that women who travel feel. Because of the way women have cultivated their inner lives, a journey often becomes a dialogue between the inner and outer, between our emotional necessity and the reality of the external world. For me, writing and travel have always fed one another. As a writer I have found that what I experience externally I must process internally and what I feel inside I must test on the outside world.

I think something has always held women back, and I'm not sure this is necessarily bad. Women need and want to be connected, to be joined to other human beings. We don't easily go off alone into the wild, to the North Pole or in search of elusive beasts. Most women travel writers until the last fifty years went accompanied. Rebecca West begins *Black Lamb and Grey Falcon* (1941), her enormous tome on Yugoslavia, with a call to her husband who is alseep on a train: "My dear, I know I've inconvenienced you terribly by making you take a holiday now." A few single women like Mary Kingsley, who braved west Africa in the late nineteenth century, had plots for insuring their safety. Wherever Miss Kingsley arrived, the Africans asked where her husband was. She replied, "He is waiting for me, over there," pointing in the direction in which she was traveling. This insured her safe passage.

I have traveled wearing a wedding ring in such places as the Middle East. I am not proud of this fact but in some parts of the world, it helps to appear as if one belongs to a man. For many women, such as my mother, it helps to belong—period. It is not such a bad thing to be connected, but women have paid for their dependency. As a woman, I travel differently than a man. I believe most women do. When I read the classic travel memoirs, I am amazed at how many times women traveled in difficult parts of the world disguised as men. I am also amazed at how often there are sudden gaps in the writing of women travel writers of the previous century where they will say something like "the sailors won't leave me alone" and then leave no journal entry for two weeks. You must read between the lines.

Rape and abduction are realities for women traveling that make us wander differently than men. I have never walked down an unlit street or on a desolate strip of mountain road without some fear in my heart. Anything can happen at any time. It is like a whisper in the back of our brains, but it is there. I don't know if I'll ever just jump in my car and drive across America or walk across north Africa without recalling some of the terrible stories of women traveling that have been told to me. On the other hand, it will not stop me. I seem to have no choice.

From Penelope to the present, women have waited—for a phone call, a date, a proposal, the return of the intrepid man from the sea or war or a business trip. And Penelope, the archetypal waiter, is awaiting the return of the traveler. To wait is to be powerless. Like patients and prisoners women have waited for the freedom to enter the world. Now if we grow weary of waiting, we can walk out the door. The other half of the plots of all literature are now open to us: we can go on a journey, though perhaps a bit warier, more self-conscious than the other half of our species. We can be the stranger who comes to town.

[1992]

BELL HOOKS

(1955–)

bell hooks reflects on travel from the perspective of a black woman who grew up in segregated America and experienced the conflicts and changes of the civil rights and feminist movements. She has produced numerous works of cultural criticism, including *Ain't I a Woman: Black Women and Feminism* (1981); she has also written memoirs (*Wounds of Passion: A Writing Life* and *Bone Black: Memories of Girlhood*, both 1997). She is Distinguished Professor of English at the City University of New York.

The selection here is taken from a talk entitled "Representing Whiteness," which hooks gave at a large international conference in 1990. She looks at travel not as a privileged activity for a political and economically dominant class of people but as an ordeal—an uneasy passage through hostile territory. For her, travel has historical roots in the forced journeys and dislocations of slavery as well as her own childhood in a segregated neighborhood.

From "Representing Whiteness"

Collectively, black people remain rather silent about representations of whiteness in the black imagination. As in the old days of racial segregation where black folks learned to "wear the mask," many of us pretend to be comfortable in the face of whiteness only to turn our backs and give expression to intense levels of discomfort. Especially talked about is the representation of whiteness as terrorizing. Without evoking a simplistic, essentialist "us and them" dichotomy that suggests black folks merely invert stereotypical racist interpretations, so that black becomes synonomous with goodness and white with evil, I want to focus on that representation of whiteness that is not formed in reaction to stereotypes but emerges as a response to the traumatic pain and anguish that remain a consequence of white racist domination, a psychic state that informs and shapes the way black folks "see" whiteness. Stereotypes black folks maintain about white folks, are not the only representations of whiteness in the black imagination. They emerge primarily as responses to white stereotypes of blackness. Speaking about white stereotypes of blackness as engendering a trickle-down process, where there is the projection onto an Other of all that we deny about ourselves, Lorraine Hansberry in *To Be Young, Gifted, and Black* (1969) identifies particular stereotypes about white people that are commonly cited in black communities and urges us not to "celebrate this madness in any direction":

> Is it not "known" in the ghetto that white people, as an entity, are "dirty" (especially white women—who never seem to do their own cleaning); inherently "cruel" (the cold, fierce roots of Europe; who else could put all those people into ovens *scientifically*); "smart" (you really have to hand it to the m.f.'s); and anything *but* cold and passionless (because look who has had to live with little else than their passions in the guise of love and hatred all these centuries)? And so on.

Stereotypes, however inaccurate, are one form of representation. Like fictions, they are created to serve as substitutions, standing in for what is real. They are there not to tell it like it is but to invite and encourage pretense. They are a fantasy, a projection onto the Other that makes them less threatening. Stereotypes abound when there is distance. They are an invention, a pretense that one knows when the steps that would make real knowing possible cannot be taken—are not allowed.

Looking past stereotypes to consider various representations of whiteness in the black imagination, I appeal to memory, to my earliest recollections of ways these issues were raised in black life. Returning to memories of growing up in the social circumstances created by racial apartheid, to all black spaces on the edges of town, I re-inhabit a location where black folks associated whiteness with the terrible, the terrifying, the terrorizing. White people were regarded as terrorists, especially those who dared to enter that segregated space of blackness. As a child I did not know any white people. They were strangers, rarely seen in our neighborhoods. The "official" white men who came across the tracks were there to sell products, Bibles, insurance. They terrorized by economic exploitation. What did I see in the gazes of those white men who crossed our thresholds that made me afraid, that made black children unable to speak? Did they understand at all how strange their whiteness appeared in our living rooms, how threatening? Did they journey across the tracks with the same "adventurous" spirit that other white men carried to Africa, Asia, to those mysterious places they would one day call the third world? Did they come to our houses to meet the Other face to face and enact the colonizer role, dominating us on our own turf? Their presence terrified me. Whatever their mission they looked too much like the unofficial white men who came to enact rituals of terror and torture. As a child, I did not know how to tell them apart, how to ask the "real white people to please stand up." The terror that I felt is one black people have shared. Whites learn about it secondhand. Confessing in *Soul Sister* (1969) that she too began to feel this terror after changing her skin to appear "black" and going to live in the South, Grace Halsell described her altered sense of whiteness:

> Caught in this climate of hate, I am totally terror-stricken, and I search my mind to know why I am fearful of my own people. Yet they no longer seem my people, but rather the "enemy" arrayed in large numbers against me in some hostile territory. . . . My wild heartbeat is a secondhand kind of terror. I know that I cannot possibly experience what *they*, the black people experience. . . .

Black folks raised in the North do not escape this sense of terror. In her autobiography, *Every Good-bye Ain't Gone* (1990), Itabari Njeri begins the narrative of her northern childhood with a memory of southern roots. Traveling south as an adult to investigate the murder of her grandfather by white youth who were drag racing and ran him down in the streets, killing him, Njeri recalls that for many years "the distant and accidental violence that took my grandfather's life could not compete with the psychological terror that began to engulf my own." Ultimately, she begins to link that terror with the history of black people in the United States, seeing it as an imprint carried from the past to the present:

> As I grew older, my grandfather assumed mythic proportions in my imagination. Even in absence, he filled my room like music and watched over me when I was fearful. His fantasized presence diverted thoughts of my father's drunken rages. With age, my fantasizing ceased, the image of my grandfather faded. What lingered was the memory of his caress, the pain of something missing in my life, wrenched away by reckless white youths. I had a growing sense—the beginning of an inevitable comprehension—that this society deals blacks a disproportionate share of pain and denial.

Njeri's journey takes her through the pain and terror of the past, only the memories do not fade. They linger, as does the pain and bitterness: "Against a backdrop of personal loss, against the evidence of history that fills me with a knowledge of the hateful behavior of whites toward blacks, I see the people of Bainbridge. And I cannot trust them. I cannot absolve them." If it is possible to conquer terror through ritual reenactment, that is what Njeri does. She goes back to the scene of the crime, dares to face the enemy. It is this confrontation that forces the terror of history to loosen its grip.

To name that whiteness in the black imagination is often a representation of terror: one must face a palimpsest of written histories that erase and deny, that reinvent the past to make the present vision of racial harmony and pluralism more plausible. To bear the burden of memory one must willingly journey to places long uninhabited, searching the debris of history for traces of the unforgettable, all knowledge of which has been suppressed. Njeri laments in her Prelude that "nobody really knows us"; "So institutionalized is the ignorance of our history, our culture, our everyday existence that, often, we do not even know ourselves." Theorizing black experience, we seek to uncover, restore, as well as to deconstruct, so that new paths, different journeys are possible. Indeed, Edward Said (1983) in "Traveling Theory" argues that theory can "threaten reification, as well as the entire bourgeoise system on which reification depends, with destruction." The call to theorize black experience is constantly challenged and subverted by conservative voices reluctant to move from fixed locations. Said reminds us:

> Theory, in fine, is won as the result of a process that begins when consciousness first experiences its own terrible ossification in the general reification of all things under capitalism; then when consciousness generalizes (or classes) itself as something opposed to other objects, and feels itself as contradiction to (or crisis within) objectification, there emerges a consciousness of change in the status quo; finally, moving toward freedom and fulfill-

ment, consciousness looks ahead to complete self-realization, which is of course the revolutionary process stretching forward in time, perceivable now only as theory or projection.

Traveling, moving into the past, Njeri pieces together fragments. Who does she see staring into the face of a southern white man who was said to be the one? Does the terror in his face mirror the look of the unsuspected black man whose dying history does not name or record? Baldwin wrote that "people are trapped in history and history is trapped in them." There is then only the fantasy of escape, or the promise that what is lost will be found, rediscovered, returned. For black folks, reconstructing an archaeology of memory makes return possible, the journey to a place we can never call home even as we reinhabit it to make sense of present locations. Such journeying cannot be fully encompassed by conventional notions of travel.

Spinning off from Said's essay, James Clifford in "Notes on Travel and Theory" celebrates the idea of journeying, asserting that

> This sense of worldly, "mapped" movement is also why it may be worth holding on to the term "travel," despite its connotations of middle-class "literary," or recreational, journeying, spatial practices long associated with male experiences and virtues. "Travel" suggests, at least, profane activity, following public routes and beaten tracks. How do different populations, classes, and genders travel? What kinds of knowledges, stories, and theories do they produce? A crucial research agenda opens up.

Reading this piece and listening to Clifford talk about theory and travel, I appreciated his efforts to expand the travel/theoretical frontier so that it might be more inclusive, even as I considered that to answer the questions he poses is to propose a deconstruction of the conventional sense of travel, and put alongside it or in its place a theory of the journey that would expose the extent to which holding on to the concept of "travel" as we know it is also a way to hold on to imperialism. For some individuals, clinging to the conventional sense of travel allows them to remain fascinated with imperialism, to write about it seductively, evoking what Renato Rosaldo (1988) aptly calls in *Culture and Truth* "imperialist nostalgia." Significantly, he reminds readers that "even politically progressive North American audiences have enjoyed the elegance of manners governing relations of dominance and subordination between the 'races.' " Theories of travel produced outside conventional borders might want the Journey to become the rubric within which travel as a starting point for discourse is associated with diffferent headings—rites of passage, immigration, enforced migration, relocation, enslavement, homelessness. Travel is not a word that can be easily evoked to talk about the Middle Passage, the Trail of

Tears, the landing of Chinese immigrants at Ellis Island, the forced relocation of Japanese-Americans, the plight of the homeless. Theorizing diverse journeying is crucial to our understanding of any politics of location. As Clifford asserts at the end of his essay: "Theory is always written from some 'where,' and that 'where' is less a place than itineraries: different, concrete histories of dwelling, immigration, exile, migration. These include the migration of third world intellectuals into the metropolitan universities, to pass through or to remain, changed by their travel but marked by places of origin, by peculiar allegiances and alienations."

Listening to Clifford "playfully" evoke a sense of travel, I felt such an evocation would always make it difficult for there to be recognition of an experience of travel that is not about play but is an encounter with terrorism. And it is crucial that we recognize that the hegemony of one experience of travel can make it impossible to articulate another experience and be heard. From certain standpoints, to travel is to encounter the terrorizing force of white supremacy. To tell my "travel" stories, I must name the movement from a racially segregated southern community, from a rural black Baptist origin, to prestigious white university settings, etc. I must be able to speak about what it is like to be leaving Italy after I have given a talk on racism and feminism, hosted by the parliament, only to stand for hours while I am interrogated by white officials who do not have to respond when I inquire as to why the questions they ask me are different from those asked the white people in line before me. Thinking only that I must endure this public questioning, the stares of those around me, because my skin is black, I am startled when I am asked if I speak Arabic, when I am told that women like me receive presents from men without knowing what those presents are. Reminded of another time when I was strip-searched by French officials, who were stopping black people to make sure we were not illegal immigrants and/or terrorists, I think that one fantasy of whiteness is that the threatening Other is always a terrorist. This projection enables many white people to imagine there is no representation of whiteness as terror, as terrorizing. Yet it is this representation of whiteness in the black imagination, first learned in the narrow confines of the poor black rural community, that is sustained by my travels to many different locations.

To travel, I must always move through fear, confront terror. It helps to be able to link this individual experience to the collective journeying of black people, to the Middle Passage, to the mass migration of southern black folks to northern cities in the early part of the twentieth century. Michel Foucault posits memory as a site of resistance suggesting (as Jonathan Arac puts it in his introduction to *Postmodernism and Politics*) that the process of remembering can be a practice which "transforms history from a judgment on the past in the name of a present truth to a 'counter-memory' that combats our current modes of truth and justice, helping us to understand and change the present by placing it in a new relation to the past." It is useful when theorizing black experience to examine the way the concept of "terror" is linked to representations of whiteness.

In the absence of the reality of whiteness, I learned as a child that to be "safe" it was important to recognize the power of whiteness, even to fear it, and to avoid encountering it. There was nothing terrifying about the sharing of this knowledge as survival strategy; the terror was made real only when I journeyed from the black side of town to a predominately white area near my grandmother's house. I had to pass through this area to reach her place. Describing these journeys "across town" in the essay "Homeplace: A Site of Resistance" I remembered:

> It was a movement away from the segregated blackness of our community into a poor white neighborhood. I remember the fear, being scared to walk to Baba's, our grandmother's house, because we would have to pass that terrifying whiteness—those white faces on the porches staring us down with hate. Even when empty or vacant those porches seemed to say *danger*, you do not belong here, you are not safe.
>
> Oh! that feeling of safety, of arrival, of homecoming when we finally reached the edges of her yard, when we could see the soot black face of our grandfather, Daddy Gus, sitting in his chair on the porch, smell his cigar, and rest on his lap. Such a contrast, that feeling of arrival, of homecoming—this sweetness and the bitterness of that journey, that constant reminder of white power and control.

Even though it was a long time ago that I made this journey, associations of whiteness with terror and the terrorizing remain. Even though I live and move in spaces where I am surrounded by whiteness, surrounded, there is no comfort that makes the terrorism disappear. All black people in the United States, irrespective of their class status or politics, live with the possibility that they will be terrorized by whiteness. . . .

[1992]

RICHARD WRIGHT

(1908–1960)

Richard Wright is one of the foremost African-American writers of the twentieth century. Wright tells of his escape from poverty and segregation in his memoir of childhood and adolescence, *Black Boy* (1945). Through learning to read in a society that discouraged education and literacy for black people, Wright was able to imagine the possibility of intellectual as well as social freedom. His flight from Memphis to Chicago, an example of the larger social phenomenon of internal migration by African Americans from the post–Civil War South to the cities of the North, became an odyssey that eventually led to expatriate life in Europe and finally Africa. Among his many works are the acclaimed novel *Native Son* (1940); a travel narrative, *Pagan Spain* (1957); and *Black Power* (1954), his impressions of Africa.

The passage below comes from the end of *Black Boy*, when Wright tells his white boss that he is leaving the South to go to Chicago. If, as Freud argues, travel is an escape from the individual constraints of family and paternal authority, one can imagine the importance of travel for Wright in escaping not merely from a family but from the whole paternal social system of segregation that treated all people of his race essentially as children.

From *Black Boy*

"Boy, you won't like it up there," he said.

"Well, I have to go where my family is, sir," I said.

The other white office workers paused in their tasks and listened. I grew self-conscious, tense.

"It's cold up there," he said.

"Yes, sir. They say it is," I said, keeping my voice in a neutral tone.

He became conscious that I was watching him and he looked away, laughing uneasily to cover his concern and dislike.

"Now, boy," he said banteringly, "don't you go up there and fall into that lake."

"Oh, no, sir," I said, smiling as though there existed the possibility of my falling accidentally into Lake Michigan.

He was serious again, staring at me. I looked at the floor.

"You think you'll do any better up there?" he asked.

"I don't know, sir."

"You seem to've been getting along all right down here," he said.

"Oh, yes, sir. If it wasn't for my mother's going, I'd stay right here and work," I lied as earnestly as possible.

"Well, why not stay? You can send her money," he suggested.

He had trapped me. I knew that staying now would never do. I could not have controlled my relations with the whites if I had remained after having told them that I wanted to go north.

"Well, I want to be with my mother," I said.

"You want to be with your mother," he repeated idly. "Well, Richard, we enjoyed having you with us."

"And I enjoyed working here," I lied.

There was silence; I stood awkwardly, then moved to the door. There was still silence; white faces were looking strangely at me. I went upstairs, feeling like a criminal. The word soon spread through the factory and the white men looked at me with new eyes. They came to me.

"So you're going north, hunh?"

"Yes, sir. My family's taking me with 'em."

"The North's no good for your people, boy."

"I'll try to get along, sir."

"Don't believe all the stories you hear about the North."

"No, sir. I don't.

"You'll come back here where your friends are."

"Well, sir. I don't know."

"How're you going to act up there?"

"Just like I act down here, sir."

"Would you speak to a white girl up there?"

"Oh, no, sir. I'll act there just like I act here."

"Aw, no, you won't. You'll change. Niggers change when they go north."

I wanted to tell him that I was going north precisely to change, but I did not.

"I'll be the same," I said, trying to indicate that I had no imagination whatever.

As I talked I felt that I was acting out a dream. I did not want to lie, yet I had to lie to conceal what I felt. A white censor was standing over me and, like dreams forming a curtain for the safety of sleep, so did my lies form a screen of safety for my living moments.

"Boy, I bet you've been reading too many of them damn books."

"Oh, no, sir."

I made my last errand to the post office, put my bag away, washed my hands, and pulled on my cap. I shot a quick glance about the factory; most of the men were working late. One or two looked up. Mr. Falk, to whom I had returned my library card, gave me a quick, secret smile. I walked to the elevator and rode down with Shorty.

"You lucky bastard," he said bitterly.

"Why do you say that?"

"You saved your goddamn money and now you're gone."

"My problems are just starting," I said.

"You'll never have any problems as hard as the ones you had here," he said.

"I hope not," I said. "But life is tricky."

"Sometimes I get so goddamn mad I want to kill everybody," he spat in a rage.

"You can leave," I said.

"I'll never leave this goddamn South," he railed. "I'm always saying I am, but I won't . . . I'm lazy. I like to sleep too goddamn much. I'll die here. Or maybe they'll kill me."

I stepped from the elevator into the street, half expecting someone to call me back and tell me that it was all a dream, that I was not leaving.

This was the culture from which I sprang. This was the terror from which I fled.

The next day when I was already in full flight—aboard a northward bound train—I could not have accounted, if it had been demanded of me, for all the varied forces that were making me reject the culture that had molded and shaped me. I was leaving without a qualm, without a single backward glance. The face of the South that I had known was hostile and forbidding, and yet out of all the conflicts and the curses, the blows and the anger, the tension and the terror, I had somehow gotten the idea that life could be different, could be lived in a fuller and richer manner. As had happened when I had fled the orphan home, I was now running more away from something than toward something. But that did not matter to me. My mood was: I've got to get away; I can't stay here.

But what was it that always made me feel that way? What was it that made me conscious of possibilities? From where in this southern darkness had I caught a sense of freedom? Why was it that I was able to act upon vaguely felt notions? What was it that made me feel things deeply enough for me to try to order my life by my feelings? The external world of whites and blacks, which was the only world that I had ever known, surely had not evoked in me any belief in myself. The people I had met had advised and demanded submission. What, then, was I after? How dare I consider my feelings superior to the gross environment that sought to claim me?

It had been only through books—at best, no more than vicarious cultural transfusions—that I had managed to keep myself alive in a negatively vital way. Whenever my environment had failed to support or nourish me, I had clutched at books; consequently, my belief in books had risen more out of a sense of desperation than from any abiding conviction of their ultimate value. In a peculiar sense, life had trapped me in a realm of emotional rejection; I had not embraced insurgency through open choice. Existing emotionally on the sheer, thin margin of southern culture, I had felt that nothing short of life itself hung upon each of my actions and decisions; and I had grown used to change, to movement, to making many adjustments.

In the main, my hope was merely a kind of self-defence, a conviction that if I did not leave I would perish, either because of possible violence of others against me, or because of my possible violence against them. The substance of my hope was formless and devoid of any real sense of direction, for in my southern living I had seen no looming landmark by which I could, in a positive sense, guide my daily actions. The shocks of southern living had rendered my personality tender and swollen, tense and volatile, and my flight was more a shunning of external and internal dangers than an attempt to embrace what I felt I wanted.

It had been my accidental reading of fiction and literary criticism that had evoked in me vague glimpses of life's possibilities. Of course, I had never seen or met the men who wrote the books I read, and the kind of world in which they lived was as alien to me as the moon. But what enabled me to overcome my chronic distrust was that these books—written by men like Dreiser, Masters, Mencken, Anderson, and Lewis—seemed defensively critical of the straitened American environment. These writers seemed to feel that America could be shaped nearer to the hearts of those who lived in it. And it was out of these novels and stories and articles, out of the emotional impact of imaginative constructions of heroic or tragic deeds, that I felt touching my face a tinge of warmth from an unseen light; and in my leaving I was groping toward that invisible light, always trying to keep my face so set and turned that I would not lose the hope of its faint promise, using it as my justification for action.

The white South said that it knew "niggers," and I was what the white South called a "nigger." Well, the white South had never known me—never known what I thought, what I felt. The white South said that I had a "place" in life. Well, I had never felt my "place"; or, rather, my deepest instincts had always made me reject the "place" to which the white South had assigned me. It had never occurred to me that I was in any way an inferior being. And no word that I had ever heard fall from the lips of southern white men had ever made me really doubt the worth of my own humanity. True, I had lied. I had stolen. I had struggled to contain my seething anger. I had fought. And it was perhaps a mere accident that I had never killed . . . But in what other ways had the South allowed me to be natural, to be real, to be myself, except in rejection, rebellion, and aggression?

Not only had the southern whites not known me, but, more important still, as I had lived in the South I had not had the chance to learn who I was. The pressure of southern living kept me from being the kind of person that I might have been. I had been what my surroundings had demanded, what my family—conforming to the dictates of the whites above them—had exacted of me, and what the whites had said that I must be. Never being fully able to be myself, I had slowly learned that the South could recognize but a part of a man, could accept but a fragment of his personality, and all the rest—the best and deepest things of heart and mind—were tossed away in blind ignorance and hate.

I was leaving the South to fling myself into the unknown, to meet other situations that would perhaps elicit from me other responses. And if I could meet enough of a different life, then, perhaps, gradually and slowly I might learn who I was, what I might be. I was not leaving the South to forget the South, but so that some day I might understand it, might come to know what its rigors had done to me, to its childen. I fled so that the numbness of my defensive living might thaw out and let me feel the pain—years later and far away—of what living in the South had meant.

Yet, deep down, I knew that I could never really leave the South, for my feelings had already been formed by the South, for there had been slowly instilled into my personality and consciousness, black though I was, the culture of the South. So, in leaving, I was taking a part of the South to transplant in alien soil, to see if it could grow differently, if it could drink of new and cool rains, bend in strange winds, respond to the warmth of other suns, and, perhaps, to bloom . . . And if that miracle ever happened, then I would know that there was yet hope in that southern swamp of despair and violence, that light could emerge even out of the blackest of the southern night. I would know that the South too could overcome its fear, its hate, its cowardice, its heritage of guilt and blood, its burden of anxiety and compulsive cruelty.

With ever watchful eyes and bearing scars, visible and invisible, I headed North, full of a hazy notion that life could be lived with dignity, that the personalities of others should not be violated, that men should be able to confront other men without fear or shame, and that if men were lucky in their living on earth they might win some redeeming meaning for their having struggled and suffered here beneath the stars.

[1945]

HARRY DEAN

(1864–1935)

As a child, Harry Dean was inspired by reading about sea adventures and by listening to visitors' tales of travel. Dean went to sea at an early age, spent a number of years in Africa, and later started a school in California to educate African Americans as seamen. He was a native of Philadelphia and fortunate in his education and upbringing.

In this selection from his memoir, *The Pedro Gorino* (1929), Dean recalls the excitement of the departure and first impressions on shipboard. He also expresses nostalgia for the days of sailing vessels and a pride in the traditions of African-American seafaring.

"I Go to Sea"

From *The Pedro Gorino*

I am an African and proud of it. There is not a drop of white blood in my veins. My ancestors have been sea captains and merchants and I have spent my life on the sea.

My father was a tall, proud, not very religious, but kindly sort of man. My mother was a fine singer and a cultured and idealistic woman. I hope I have proved worthy of them.

While I was still a boy I was given copies of Horace, Homer, Virgil, Petrarch, Shakespeare, Coleridge's "Ancient Mariner," a translation of "The Arabian Chronicles," "Arabian Nights," Colonel George Williams's "History of the Negro," a hand-illumined "Spirit of the Laws," and many others. Mother delighted in training us, and when I was old enough she put me under the tutelage of Fannie Jackson, the great "negro" woman educator, at the Institute for Colored Youth in Philadelphia. Here I was taught grammar, arithmetic, and a foundation in the five natural sciences. Everything theoretical, nothing practical.

I lived such a sheltered life that I became idealistic. I was entirely unaware of the race problem. I knew nothing of the hardships and treacheries of life. We had all the money we needed and I knew nothing of poverty. Since that time I have experienced all the hardships known to man.

Often we had visitors. Major Martin R. Delaney, major in the Union Army during the Civil War; United States Senator Revels, and General Belaski, an escaped rebel officer from Cuba, were among the most frequent. I remember General Belaski in particular. He was as black as pitch and as far across as he was tall. He told me stories of the Cuban Rebellion in his mild voice. "I come from salt water, Sonny, land alive! Should see them islands and the sea a-swishin' on the shore. Should see them black boys, Sonny, creepin' on their bellies through the brush. Guns no good, clothes all ragged, but filled with the spirit and not afraid o' the Devil hisself." It was music to my young ears. I could have listened forever.

Besides these few celebrities there were many fine neighbors, particularly the Mintons, Wares, Fortunes, and Dutrelles, a strange class of people whose history has never been written. They were for the most part of maritime ancestors and had become enmeshed in the devastating American environment only after generations of protest. We kept in close contact with these people, for they were the few who could understand our aims and ideals.

The summer I was twelve we went as usual to our cottage at Atlantic City. I swam in the sea and played on the beaches in the sunshine. Some days my father would let me ride in the little twenty-ton schooners whose business it was to carry any who chose to the horizon and back for twenty-five cents. Suddenly I was crazy to go to sea. The salty tang in the air, the rough sailors, the glamour about boats, the stories of adventure I had heard all through my childhood, filled me with a tremendous urge. I thought of the sea night and day.

On returning to Philadelphia we found my Uncle Silas, an honest-to-goodness sea captain come to stay with us for a few days. He was preparing to make a three-year voyage around the world, aboard his ship Traveler the Second. He was, therefore, a hero. He was a man of splendid physique, rapid in his movements and a true sea captain. He had a terrible stare. I was never sure when he looked at me whether he was angry or not. If he had not been my uncle I should have been afraid of him. But his stories were as rich and fabulous as those of Sinbad the Sailor.

One evening as we sat at supper he said to my father: "John, I can tell by the cut of his jib the boy would make a good sailor. He'd reef and furl in no time and I'd have him boxing the compass and shooting the sun before we got around the Horn. Why not let me take him along?"

It seemed as if whole minutes passed before my father answered and when he did I hung on every word.

"Would you take good care of him, Silas?"

"Bring him back shipshape or my name's not Dean," my uncle answered.

"The sea's a rough place for a boy."

"There's nothing like the sea to test what's in a boy. It would make a man of him, John."

"I'll have to think it out," my father said. "Give me till morning." He seemed worried that evening. Mother cried a little. But with all the thoughtlessness of youth I was hardly aware of their sorrow. It was more miraculous than my Arabian Nights. They must let me go, I knew they would. But why did I have to wait until morning to be sure? My brain was whirling with excitement and emotion.

Morning came at last. I could go. Ah, Christophe, Toussaint l'Ouverture, strong men of my race, were you as exultant in your power as I in mine upon that happy morning! In my imagination I already ruled the seas. I had a fleet of ships, their white sails filled with the wind. But little did I realize the hardships of the sea or the hard life that awaited me. And little did I realize the impotence of a child of twelve.

My uncle and I took a train from Philadelphia and landed at Jersey City late at night. We went from the station to the ferry landing and for the first time I saw the lights of New York. The way they were reflected on the dark waters of the Hudson stays with me all these years. Then aboard the ferry boat. Everywhere there was the bustle of boats, horns blowing, and men calling over the water. Having lived in the quiet city of Philadelphia all my life, I had never seen anything like this wild, tumultuous life. We landed at wooden docks that thronged with rough dirty barefoot boys selling newspapers, sleeping in out-of-the-way corners, fighting for no apparent reason. It was an Irish part of town crowded with sailors and toughs. Uncle Silas pushed and crowded, pulling me along by the hand. We passed along narrow streets and between high brick buildings until we came to Manetta Lane, squalid enough to-day but respectable then. Here we put up for the night with an aunt who made a great fuss over me. "Honey-chile let me give yo' one mo' cake."

The next morning we went down to the harbor and for the first time I saw my uncle's ship, Traveler the Second. I liked the smell of Stockholm tar. The way the sailing vessels floated and bobbed on the water was a mystery. The lines and the rigging of the ship impressed me and set me wondering. I remember the Traveler was a barentine with both square rig and fore-and-aft rig, a mixture of the two types of rigging. She carried studding booms for studding sails that bellied balloon-like on each side so that to those on board and to those who saw her pass, she gave the impression of a sea-gull on the wing. She was very fast under full sail.

There on the docks at New York were sailors from every country. Some of them were dressed in flannel shirts as red as fire. Their great bulging muscles showed through their clothing. Where their sleeves were rolled up their strong brown arms rippled like the surface of water in a breeze. The proportions of these men and their hoarse voices impressed me and made me wish I were as big and strong as they.

Where will you find such men now? Gone are the sailing vessels and gone the men who sailed them. They were a singing, laughing, bunch in port, but let their ship get into rough weather rounding the Horn or off the Cape of Storms, up in the Gulf of Alaska or wherever they were, let the decks get icy and the gale go whistling and moaning through the shrouds, and see if they weren't as true as steel. No grumbling or growling when the bos'n called "All hands ahoy!" They're gone now, but there they were on the dock at New York and aboard the Traveler when I went to sea as a boy.

Sometimes chanties came clearly over the water, one sailor singing a line, the crew answering:

> Haul the bowline, the good ship's a rolling.
> Haul the bowline, the bowline haul.

Then before I could catch more, a dozen voices on the dock laughing and shouting would drown out the singing. "Give a hand there, man."

"An' if the mate ain't seven kinds of Devil I ain't never been in Cork."

"Shet your mouth, Folley. Give a heave on that puncheon."

"Where's Mr. Watson? Oh, Mr. Watson."

It was our men making the racket. They were loading the cargo of hardware, notions, bright cloth, beads and trade goods of all kinds into puncheons, great barrel-like containers as tall as a man. They had been at the work for over a week. The Traveler had made her departure from Boston some two weeks before, dropped anchor at New York and prepared to receive cargo. Uncle Silas had come to Philadelphia to get me, leaving the loading of the vessel in charge of the first mate. We had arrived in New York in time to see the last of that work.

My uncle was talking to the first mate. "We'll muster the men this evening, Mr. Watson. See that they're aboard early. We'll up anchor at dawn." My uncle and I went aboard late that afternoon and made ourselves comfortable in his spacious cabin. What a great man I thought him, with his charts, and sextants, and compasses, his wealth of sea knowledge, and his exciting stories. Aboard ship, however, he had little time to play. His stern expression seldom relaxed into a smile. And although I admired and respected him as did his sailors, I was a little in awe of this dark brown giant whose word was law to so many men. And he was a man to inspire awe, courageous, as every sea captain must be. I found in the days that followed that he was perfectly fearless and would never shorten sail until the docks were at an angle of forty degrees.

At dawn we made our departure from Red Bank. We might have been a phantom ship we moved so gently over the ocean. The pale early morning light flooded the decks of the ship where men moving at their work seemed scarcely men of this world. But as the breeze stiffened and the sun rose higher and the last mist of sleep cleared from before my eyes, I realized that we had put to sea and that my life of adventure had begun. Because of my experiences on the small pleasure schooners I felt myself quite a sailor. The commodious barkentine seemed perfectly safe in my young eyes. Everything was expectation. I wanted to see pirates and buried treasure. I wanted to lead a wild and gallant life. I did not realize how helpless I was or how unprepared for the sea and the hardships of sailors.

The crew was a mixed one. More than half of the men were "negroes." As they worked they sang,

> For seven long years I courted Sally,
> Weigh, roll and go.
> The sweetest flower in all the valley;
> Spend my money on Sally Brown.

How many times I was to hear that and similar songs, filled with the wailing rhythm of the African race. What is it you have lost, what have you left behind, what are you looking for, you unhappy hostages of an alien race?

At Charleston, South Carolina, a colored pilot came out in a small sailing vessel and took us into port. That was the only colored pilot I ever saw in

American waters. I remember my uncle had a lot of trouble in Charleston. There was an argument with a port official of which I caught but little and understood less.

"Ain't no nigguh goin' run this po't," the official shouted.

And my uncle in his quiet cold voice, "I merely asked for clearance papers and the usual civility shown a ship's officer."

Whatever the trouble was, my uncle thought it necessary to admonish the crew not to leave the ship. He told them that the boat was to up anchor the minute the clearance papers were ready. Other crews swarmed all along the water-front, but ours remained aboard the ship sullen and angry. Each man felt that the indignity done the ship was a personal affront.

My uncle and I went ashore, however. I accompanied him everywhere, particularly to the custom house. We were in Charleston over one Sunday. We went to church. The colored people were nice to us, but their dialect was so strange that I could scarcely understand them at times.

At last we got our clearance papers and made our departure. We were no sooner out of the harbor than we ran into severe rain and hail storms. The ship was fighting adverse winds and currents and the hail set up a great tattoo on the deck. I was too young to realize our danger. The excitement was more or less pleasurable to me. That night was an anxious one for the crew and for my uncle.

I could not understand the serious demeanor of the men. None of them would talk or laugh with me. Each hurried about the deck doing his appointed task. Some clambered up the ratlines to reef sails, some pulled and hauled on halyards. The mate's orders and the crew's "Aye, aye, sir!" were carried far out over the water by the storm. I heard their voices as if they had come from a great distance.

Most of the crew were on deck all night. And although my uncle told me to go to my bunk in the cabin and get some sleep I was unable to close my eyes. I was not afraid. But I was aware of a sinister foreboding. I was as if the sailors could sense something terrible and strange, something within the darkness which I could not see or hear or feel with my unaccustomed senses. Of course the weather was dark and stormy with black clouds hurrying across the flattened dome of heaven, but that alone was not enough to account for their actions. Their silence was more expressive than all the rough weather.

Later in the night the rain and hail let up and I got out of my bunk to see how things were going on deck. At the door of the galley sat Johnson, a fine old man who was our cook and steward. He liked me a great deal and always carried on an engaging conversation. Even he was still. He had been sitting there at the door of his galley all night. His pipe had long since gone out. When I spoke to him he would only answer in monosyllables.

The sea was running high and white caps were breaking. The salt spray stung my face. And although I did not realize that we were on a lee shore with a shifting wind and in great danger, I did know that I was lonesome and lost and very homesick. . . .

[1929]

JOHN MASEFIELD

(1878–1967)

John Masefield left his native England at an early age to go to sea, and after several years as a seaman, he turned to writing as a career. "Sea-Fever" was one of the poems in the first volume he published, *Salt-Water Ballads* (1902), and remains his best-known lyric. He wrote fiction, drama, and juvenile literature in addition to a steady output of poetry and several books about World War I. In 1930 he was named Poet Laureate of England.

The poem that follows captures in a few memorable lines the eternal attraction of the sea and the romantic attraction of "the vagrant gypsy life" of the sailor.

"Sea-Fever"

I must down to the seas again, to the lonely sea and the sky,
And all I ask is a tall ship and a star to steer her by,
And the wheel's kick and the wind's song and the white sails shaking,
And a grey mist on the sea's face and a grey dawn breaking.

I must down to the seas again, for the call of the running tide   5
Is a wild call and a clear call that may not be denied;
And all I ask is a windy day with the white clouds flying,
And the flung spray and the blown spume, and the sea-gulls crying.

I must down to the seas again, to the vagrant gypsy life,
To the gull's way and the whale's way where the wind's like a whetted   10
     knife;
And all I ask is a merry yarn from a laughing fellow-rover,
And quiet sleep and a sweet dream when the long trick's over.

[1902]

ALAIN DE BOTON

(1969–)

Alain de Boton is professor of philosophy at the University of London. He has written a novel, *Kiss and Tell* (1996), as well as works on scholarly subjects for a popular audience, including *On Love* (1993), *Romantic Movement: Sex, Shopping, and the Novel* (1995), *How Proust Can Change Your Life* (1997), and *The Consolations of Philosophy* (2000).

In *The Art of Travel* (2002), from which this selection is taken, de Boton combines reflections on the history and culture of travel with his own travel experiences. This account of one reader's desire to travel, kindled by books but quickly extinguished once the reader leaves his study and faces the discomforts of actually taking a train trip, exemplifies just how much the pleasure of travel can depend on imagination and expectation.

From *The Art of Travel*

If our lives are dominated by a search for happiness, then perhaps few activities reveal as much about the dynamics of this quest—in all its ardour and paradoxes—than our travels. They express, however inarticulately, an understanding of what life might be about, outside of the constraints of work and of the struggle for survival. Yet rarely are they considered to present philosophical problems—that is, issues requiring thought beyond the practical. We are inundated with advice on *where* to travel to, but we hear little of *why* and *how* we should go, even though the art of travel seems naturally to sustain a number of questions neither so simple nor so trivial, and whose study might in modest ways contribute to an understanding of what the Greek philosophers beautifully termed *eudaimonia*, or "human flourishing."

3.

One question revolves around the relationship between the anticipation of travel and its reality. I came upon a copy of J. K. Huysmans's novel *A Rebours*, published in 1884, whose effete and misanthropic hero, the aristocratic Duc des Esseintes, anticipated a journey to London and offered in the process an extravagantly pessimistic analysis of the difference between what we imagine about a place and what can occur when we reach it.

Huysmans recounts that the Duc des Esseintes lived alone in a vast villa on the outskirts of Paris. He rarely went anywhere to avoid what he took to be the ugliness and stupidity of others. One afternoon in his youth, he had ventured into a nearby village for a few hours and had felt his detestation of people grow fierce. Since then he had chosen to spend his days alone in bed in his study, reading the classics of literature and moulding acerbic thoughts about humanity. Early one morning, however, the duc surprised himself by experiencing an intense wish to travel to London. The desire came upon him as he sat by the fire reading a volume of Dickens. The book evoked visions of English life, which he contemplated at length and grew increasingly keen to see. Unable to contain his excitement, he ordered his servants to pack his bags, dressed himself in a grey tweed suit, a pair of laced ankle boots, a little bowler hat and a flax-blue Inverness cape and took the next train to Paris. With some time to spare before the departure of the London train, he stopped in at Galignani's English Bookshop on the Rue de Rivoli and there bought a volume of Baedeker's *Guide to London*. He was thrown into delicious reveries by its terse descriptions of the city's attractions. Next he moved on to a nearby wine bar frequented by a largely English clientele. The atmosphere was out of Dickens: he thought of scenes in which Little Dorrit, Dora Copperfield and Tom Pinch's sister Ruth sat in similarly cosy, bright rooms. One patron had Mr Wickfield's white hair and ruddy complexion, combined with the sharp, expressionless features and unfeeling eyes of Mr Tulkinghorn.

Hungry, des Esseintes went next to an English tavern in the Rue d'Amsterdam, near the Gare Saint Lazare. It was dark and smoky inside, with a line of beer pulls along a counter spread with hams as brown as violins and lobsters the colour of red lead. Seated at small wooden tables were robust English-women with boyish faces, teeth as big as palette knives, cheeks as red as apples and long hands and feet. Des Esseintes found a table and ordered some oxtail soup, a smoked haddock, a helping of roast beef and potatoes, a couple of pints of ale and a chunk of Stilton.

But as the moment to board his train approached, along with the chance to turn his dreams of London into reality, des Esseintes was abruptly overcome with lassitude. He thought how wearing it would be actually to make the journey—how he would have to run to the station, fight for a porter, board the train, endure an unfamiliar bed, stand in lines, feel cold and move his fragile frame around the sights that Baedeker had so tersely described— and thus soil his dreams: 'What was the good of moving when a person could travel so wonderfully sitting in a chair? Wasn't he already in London, whose smells, weather, citizens, food, and even cutlery were all about him? What could he expect to find over there except fresh disappointments?' Still seated at his table, he reflected, 'I must have been suffering from some mental aberration to have rejected the visions of my obedient imagination and to have believed like any old ninny that it was necessary, interesting and useful to travel abroad.'

So des Esseintes paid the bill, left the tavern and took the first train back to his villa, along with his trunks, his packages, his portmanteaux, his rugs, his umbrellas and his sticks—and never left home again.

[2002]

PHILIP LARKIN

(1922–1985)

Philip Larkin worked most of his life as head librarian at the University of Hull in England. Educated at Oxford, he published two novels and a volume of essays, but his literary reputation rests on his poetry. *The Less Deceived* (1955), *The Whitsun Weddings* (1964), and *High Windows* (1974) all won British awards for poetry. He was selected to edit *The Oxford Book of 20th Century Verse* (1973), and his own *Collected Poems* were published posthumously in 1988.

Larkin's aversion to travel comes through in the following poem, "Poetry of Departures." Larkin's speaker provides another example of getting excited about travel from reading but then rejecting actual travel because it doesn't meet one's imaginative expectations.

"Poetry of Departures"

Sometimes you hear, fifth-hand,
As epitaph:
He chucked up everything
And just cleared off,
And always the voice will sound   5
Certain you approve
This audacious, purifying,
Elemental move.

And they are right, I think.
We all hate home   10
And having to be there:
I detest my room,
Its specially-chosen junk,

The good books, the good bed,
And my life, in perfect order: 15
So to hear it said

He walked out on the whole crowd
Leaves me flushed and stirred,
Like *Then she undid her dress*
Or *Take that you bastard*;   20
Surely I can, if he did?
And that helps me stay
Sober and industrious.
But I'd go today,

Yes, swagger the nut-strewn roads,   25
Crouch in the fo'c'sle
Stubbly with goodness, if
It weren't so artificial,
Such a deliberate step backwards
To create an object: 30
Books; china; a life
Reprehensibly perfect.

                                            [1954]

FRANCIS BACON
(1521–1626)

Francis Bacon was a statesman, philosopher, and lawyer who exemplified the Renaissance man in his breadth of intellectual interest. The rediscovery in the Renaissance of the culture of ancient Greece and Rome inspired many scholars to travel to the countries of the Mediterranean where classical civilization had flourished. Bacon left Cambridge University as a very young man, preferring the broadening experience of travel to the confining life of a university student. His literary reputation derives from his famous *Essays* (1612) marked by their brevity and epigrammatic style.

    The selection below, "Of Travel," taken from the *Essays*, sets forth a view of travel that became a kind of prescription for the Grand Tour, the traditional journey abroad that was part of an English gentleman's education. Bacon lists the kinds of places and activities that the young traveler, accompanied by his tutor, should seek. It is interesting to examine the other selections in this anthology with Bacon's prescriptions in mind, to see how other travelers may follow or reject his advice. The Grand Tour is a forerunner of contemporary study-abroad programs for undergraduates.

"Of Travel"

From *Essays*

Travel, in the younger sort, is a part of education; in the elder, a part of experience. He that travelleth into a country before he hath some entrance into the language, goeth to school, and not to travel. That young men travel under some tutor, or grave servant, I allow well; so that he be such a one that hath the language, and hath been in the country before; whereby he may be able to tell them what things are worthy to be seen in the country where they go; what acquaintances they are to seek; what exercises or discipline the place yieldeth. For else young men shall go hooded, and look abroad little.

It is a strange thing, that in sea voyages, where there is nothing to be seen but sky and sea, men should make diaries; but in land-travel, wherein so much is to be observed, for the most part they omit it; as if chance were fitter to be registered than observations. Let diaries therefore be brought in use.

The things to be seen and observed are, the courts of princes, especially when they give audience to ambassadors; the courts of justice, while they sit and hear causes; and so of consistories ecclesiastic; the churches and monasteries, with the monuments which are therein extant; the walls and fortifications of cities and towns, and so the havens and harbours; antiquities and ruins; libraries; colleges, disputations, and lectures, where any are; shipping and navies; houses and gardens of state and pleasure, near great cities; armories; arsenals; magazines; exchanges; burses; warehouses; exercises of horsemanship, fencing, training of soldiers, and the like; comedies, such whereunto the better sort of persons do resort; treasuries of jewels and robes; cabinets and rarities; and, to conclude, whatsoever is memorable in the places where they go. After all which the tutors or servants ought to make diligent inquiry. As for triumphs, masks, feasts, weddings, funerals, capital executions, and such shows, men need not be put in mind of them; and yet are they not to be neglected.

If you will have a young man to put his travel into a little room, and in a short time to gather much, this you must do. First as was said, he must have some entrance into the language before he goeth. Then he must have such a servant or tutor as knoweth the country, as was likewise said. Let him carry with him also some card or book describing the country where he travelleth;

which will be a good key to his inquiry. Let him also keep a diary. Let him not stay long in one city or town; more or less as the place deserveth, but not long; nay, when he stayeth in one city or town, let him change his lodging from one end and part of the town to another; which is a great adamant of acquaintance. Let him sequester himself from the company of his countrymen, and diet in such places where there is good company of the nation where he travelleth. Let him upon his removes from one place to another, procure recommendation to some person of quality residing in the place whither he removeth; that he may use his favour in those things he desireth to see or know. Thus he may abridge his travel with much profit.

As for the acquaintance which is to be sought in travel; that which is most of all profitable, is acquaintance with the secretaries and employed men of ambassadors: for so in travelling in one country he shall suck the experience of many. Let him also see and visit eminent persons in all kinds, which are of great name abroad; that he may be able to tell how the life agreeth with the fame. For quarrels, they are with care and discretion to be avoided. They are commonly for mistresses, healths, place, and words. And let a man beware how he keepeth company with choleric and quarrelsome persons; for they will engage him into their own quarrels. When a traveller returneth home, let him not leave the countries where he hath travelled altogether behind him; but maintain a correspondence by letters with those of his acquaintance which are of most worth. And let his travel appear rather in his discourse than in his apparel or gesture; and in his discourse let him be rather advised in his answers, than forward to tell stories; and let it appear that he doth not change his country manners for those of foreign parts; but only prick in some flowers of that he hath learned abroad into the customs of his own country.

[1612]

BRUCE CHATWIN

(1940–1989)

Bruce Chatwin became a lifelong traveler after he temporarily went blind while working in London as an art appraiser. The British-born Chatwin took a trip to Africa to recover, then continued traveling to places like South America and Australia and writing both novels and non-fiction. His travel books, which incorporate elements of fiction, include *In Patagonia* (1977), *What Am I Doing Here?* (1989), and *The Songlines* (1987), from which this selection is taken.

In *The Songlines*, Chatwin visits the Australian Aborigines and studies their nomadic culture. He relates his own nomadic lifestyle, as well as the human impulse to travel, to the nomadic origins of our species, preserved in the culture of the Aborigines. The songlines of the title refer to the Aborigines' tradition of marking the landscape of their continent by composing songs about various places. These songs, preserved in memory, serve as a kind of map to guide the singers as they wander over the harsh terrain of the bush. By singing their way, in effect, across the barren terrain of central Australia, the Aborigines link the primal activity of human migratory travel to the oral tradition of literature. In the selections that follow, Chatwin relates his childhood reading to his interest in Australia. In a series of fragments, he suggests—by analogy and metaphor rather than sustained argument—how the activities of travel and storytelling share deep instinctual roots in our cultural evolution.

From *The Songlines*

In my childhood I never heard the world 'Australia' without calling to mind the fumes of the eucalyptus inhaler and an incessant red country populated by sheep.

My father loved to tell, and we to hear, the story of the Australian sheep-millionaire who strolled into a Rolls-Royce showroom in London; scorned all the smaller models; chose an enormous limousine with a plate-glass panel between the chauffeur and passengers, and added, cockily, as he counted out the cash, 'That'll stop the sheep from breathing down my neck.'

I also knew, from my great-aunt Ruth, that Australia was the country of the Upside-downers. A hole, bored straight through the earth from England, would burst out under their feet.

'Why don't they fall off?' I asked.

'Gravity,' she whispered.

She had in her library a book about the continent, and I would gaze in wonder at pictures of the koala and kookaburra, the platypus and Tasmanian bush-devil, Old Man Kangaroo and Yellow Dog Dingo, and Sydney Harbour Bridge.

But the picture I liked best showed an Aboriginal family on the move. They were lean, angular people and they went about naked. Their skin was very black, not the glitterblack of negroes but matt black, as if the sun had sucked away all possibility of reflection. The man had a long forked beard and carried a spear or two, and a spear-thrower. The woman carried a dilly-bag and a baby at her breast. A small boy strolled beside her—I identified myself with him.

I remember the fantastic homelessness of my first five years. My father was in the Navy, at sea. My mother and I would shuttle back and forth, on the railways of wartime England, on visits to family and friends.

All the frenzied agitation of the times communicated itself to me: the hiss of steam on a fogbound station; the double clu-unk of carriage doors closing; the drone of aircraft, the searchlights, the sirens; the sound of a mouth-organ along a platform of sleeping soldiers.

Home, if we had one, was a solid black suitcase called the Rev-Robe, in which there was a corner for my clothes and my Mickey Mouse gas-mask. I knew that, once the bombs began to fall, I could curl up inside the Rev-Robe, and be safe.

Sometimes, I would stay for months with my two great-aunts, in their terrace house behind the church in Stratford-on-Avon. They were old maids.

Aunt Katie was a painter and had travelled. In Paris she had been to a very louche party at the studio of Mr Kees van Dongen. On Capri she had seen the bowler hat of a Mr Ulyanov that used to bob along the Piccola Marina.

Aunt Ruth had travelled only once in her life, to Flanders, to lay a wreath on a loved one's grave. She had a simple, trusting nature. Her cheeks were pale rose-pink and she could blush as sweetly and innocently as a young girl. She was very deaf, and I would have to yell into her deaf-aid, which looked like a portable radio. At her bedside she kept a photograph of her favourite nephew, my father, gazing calmly from under the patent peak of his naval officer's cap.

The men on my father's side of the family were either solid and sedentary citizens—lawyers, architects, antiquaries—or horizon-struck wanderers who had scattered their bones in every corner of the earth: Cousin Charlie in Patagonia; Uncle Victor in a Yukon gold camp; Uncle Robert in an oriental port; Uncle Desmond, of the long fair hair, who vanished without trace in Paris; Uncle Walter who died, chanting the suras of the Glorious Koran, in a hospital for holy men in Cairo.

Sometimes, I overheard my aunts discussing these blighted destinies; and Aunt Ruth would hug me, as if to forestall my following in their footsteps. Yet, from the way she lingered over such words as 'Xanadu' or 'Samarkand' or the 'wine-dark sea', I think she also felt the trouble of the 'wanderer in her soul'. . .

•   •   •

Aunt Ruth loved reading Shakespeare aloud and, on days when the grass was dry, I would dangle my legs over the riverbank and listen to her reciting, 'If music be the food of love . . . ,' 'The quality of mercy is not strained . . . ,' or 'Full fathom five thy father lies.'

'Full fathom five . . .' upset me terribly because my father was still at sea. I had another recurring dream: that his ship had sunk; that I grew gills and a fishy trail, swam down to join him on the ocean floor, and saw the pearls that had been his bright blue eyes.

A year or two later, as a change from Mr Shakespeare, my aunt would bring an anthology of verse especially chosen for travellers, called *The Open Road.* It had a green buckram binding and a flight of gilded swallows on the cover.

I loved watching swallows. When they arrived in spring, I knew my lungs would soon be free of green phlegm. In autumn, when they sat chattering on the telegraph wires, I could almost count the days until the eucalyptus inhaler.

Inside *The Open Road* there were black and white end-papers in the style of Aubrey Beardsley which showed a bright path twisting through pine woods. One by one, we went through every poem in the book.

We arose and went to Innisfree. We saw the caverns measureless to man. We wandered lonely as a cloud. We tasted all the summer's pride, wept for Lycidas, stood in tears among the alien corn, and listened to the strident, beckoning music of Walt Whitman:

> O Public Road . . .
> You express me better than I can express myself
> You shall be more to me than my poem.

One day, Aunt Ruth told me our surname had once been 'Chettewynde', which meant 'the winding path' in Anglo-Saxon; and the suggestion took root in my head that poetry, my own name and the road were, all three, mysteriously connected.

• • •

I had a presentiment that the 'travelling' phase of my life might be passing. I felt, before the malaise of settlement crept over me, that I should reopen those notebooks. I should set down on paper a résumé of the ideas, quotations and encounters which had amused and obsessed me; and which I hoped would shed light on what is, for me, the question of questions: the nature of human restlessness.

Pascal, in one of his gloomier *pensées*, gave it as his opinion that all our miseries stemmed from a single cause: our inability to remain quietly in a room.

Why, he asked, must a man with sufficient to live on feel drawn to divert himself on long sea voyages? To dwell in another town? To go off in search of a peppercorn? Or go off to war and break skulls?

Later, on further reflection, having discovered the cause of our misfortunes, he wished to understand the reason for them, he found one very good reason: namely, the natural unhappiness of our weak mortal condition; so unhappy that when we gave to it all our attention, nothing could console us.

One thing alone could alleviate our despair, and that was 'distraction' (*divertissement*): yet this was the worst of our misfortunes, for in distraction we were prevented from thinking about ourselves and were gradually brought to ruin.

Could it be, I wondered, that our need for distraction, our mania for the new, was, in essence, an instinctive migratory urge akin to that of birds in autumn?

All the Great Teachers have preached that Man, originally, was a 'wanderer in the scorching and barren wilderness of this world'—the words are those of Dostoevsky's Grand Inquisitor—and that to rediscover his humanity, he must slough off attachments and take to the road.

My two most recent notebooks were crammed with jottings taken in South Africa, where I had examined, at first hand, certain evidence on the origin of our species. What I learned there—together with what I now knew about the Songlines—seemed to confirm the conjecture I had toyed with for so long: that Natural Selection has designed us—from the structure of our brain-cells to the structure of our big toe—for a career of seasonal journeys *on foot* through a blistering land of thorn-scrub or desert.

If this were so; if the desert were 'home'; if our instincts were forged in the desert; to survive the rigours of the desert—then it is easier to understand why greener pastures pall on us; why possessions exhaust us, and why Pascal's imaginary man found his comfortable lodgings a prison.

From the Notebooks

> Our nature lies in movement; complete calm is death.
>
> Pascal, *Pensées*

*

> A study of the Great Malady; horror of home.
>
> Baudelaire, *Journaux Intimes*

*

The most convincing analysts of restlessness were often men who, for one reason or another, were immobilised: Pascal by stomach ailments and migraines, Baudelaire by drugs, St. John of the Cross by the bars of his cell. There are French critics who would claim that Proust, the hermit of the cork-lined room, was the greatest of literary voyagers.

*

The founders of monastic rule were forever devising techniques for quelling wanderlust in their novices. 'A monk out of his cell,' said St. Anthony, 'is like a fish out of water.' Yet Christ and the Apostles *walked* their journeys through the hills of Palestine.

*

What is this strange madness, Petrarch asked of his young secretary, this mania for sleeping each night in a different bed?

*

> What am I doing here?
>> Rimbaud writing home from Ethiopia

* * *

> He who does not travel does not know the value of men.
>> Moorish proverb

* * *

On the night express from Moscow to Kiev, reading Donne's third 'Elegie':

> To live in one land, is captivitie,
> To runne all countries, a wild roguery

*

This life is a hospital in which each sick man is possessed by a desire to change beds. One would prefer to suffer by the stove. Another believes he would recover if he sat by the window.

I think I would be happy in that place I happen not to be, and this question of moving house is the subject of a perpetual dialogue I have with my soul.
>> Baudelaire, 'Any Where Out of this World!'

* * *

In *The Descent of Man* Darwin notes that in certain birds the migratory impulse is stronger than the maternal. A mother will abandon her fledglings in the nest rather than miss her appointment for the long journey south.

* * *

Above all, do not lose your desire to walk: every day I walk myself into a state of well-being and walk away from every illness; I have walked myself into my best thoughts, and I know of no thought so burdensome that one cannot walk away from it . . . but by sitting still, and the more one sits still, the closer one comes to feeling ill . . . Thus if one just keeps on walking, everything will be all right.
>> Soren Kierkegaard, letter to Jette (1847)

*

Solvitur ambulando. 'It is solved by walking.'

* * *

One commonly held delusion is that men are the wanderers and women the guardians of hearth and home. This can, of course, be so. But women, above all, are the guardians of continuity: if the hearth moves, they move with it.

It is the gipsy women who keep their men on the road. Similarly, in the gale-lashed waters of the Cape Horn archipelago, it was the women of the Yaghan Indians who kept their embers alight in the bottom of their bark canoes. The missionary Father Martin Gusinde compared them to the 'Ancient Vestals' or to 'fidgety birds of passage who were happy and inwardly calm only when they were on the move'.

* * *

Useless to ask a wandering man
Advice on the construction of a house.
The work will never come to completion.

After reading this text, from the Chinese *Book of Odes*, I realised the absurdity of trying to write a book on Nomads.

*

Psychiatrists, politicians, tyrants are forever assuring us that the wandering life is an aberrant form of behaviour; a neurosis; a form of unfulfilled sexual longing; a sickness which, in the interests of civilisation, must be suppressed.

Nazi propagandists claimed that gipsies and Jews—peoples with wandering in their genes—could find no place in a stable Reich.

Yet, in the East, they still preserve the once universal concept: that wandering re-establishes the original harmony which once existed between man and the universe.

*

There is no happiness for the man who does not travel. Living in the society of men, the best man becomes a sinner. For Indra is the friend of the traveller. Therefore wander!

Aitareya Brāhmana

*

You cannot travel on the path before you have become the Path itself.

Gautama Buddha

*

Walk on!

His last word to his disciples

*

In Islam, and especially among the Sufi Orders, *siyahat* or 'errance'—the action or rhythm of walking—was used as a technique for dissolving the attachments of the world and allowing men to lose themselves in God.

The aim of a dervish was to become a 'dead man walking': one whose body stays alive on the earth yet whose soul is already in Heaven. A Sufi manual, the

Kashf-al-Mahjub, says that, towards the end of his journey, the dervish becomes the Way not the wayfarer, i.e. a place over which something is passing, not a traveller following his own free will.

*

Arkady, to whom I mentioned this, said it was quite similar to an Aboriginal concept, 'Many men afterwards become country, in that place, Ancestors.'

By spending his whole life walking and singing his Ancestor's Songline, a man eventually became the track, the Ancestor and the song.

[1987]

TONY WHEELER

(1946–)

Tony Wheeler founded the popular *Lonely Planet Travel Guide* series. Wheeler and Lonely Planet have had an enormous influence on contemporary travel and have provided practical information and advice for millions of readers, from backpackers in the Himalayas to gamblers heading for Las Vegas. After his experience of traveling the world on the cheap, Wheeler began publishing the series 30 years ago as a tip sheet for economy-minded travelers. *Lonely Planet* has become one of the leading guidebooks in the English language, with over 700 titles in print, including anthologies of travel writing. Wheeler has written numerous guides in the series and edited many others, for destinations as varied as New Zealand, Sri Lanka, Nepal, and Dublin.

In the essay that follows, Wheeler explains why the geographic and cultural isolation of Australia makes him and his fellow countrymen such inveterate travelers.

"The Aussie Way of Wanderlust"

Terminal Wanderlust: It's one of the conditions of today that Douglas Coupland defined in *Generation X*: a state of being so disconnected to anywhere that everywhere is home, or might just as well be. I reckon I'm infected. I was born in Britain, grew up in Pakistan, the Bahamas, and the United States, with short interludes back in Britain, and now live in Australia, although recently there have been year-long interludes in France and the United States. Even when I am at home I'm typically away traveling for six months each year. So nowhere is really home; almost anywhere could be. Perhaps I can blame my personal wanderlust on my peripatetic upbringing—but could a whole nation get this affliction?

I've spent half a lifetime wondering who goes where, and the results of my surveys may be unscientific but they're certainly conclusive: Australians go everywhere. I scan the hotel registers in towns in Africa, I glance back through visitors' books in churches in southern India, I check who has gone scuba diving with a Red Sea dive operator, I add up who has checked into youth hostels along the Pennine Way in England. Everywhere it's the same story: more Australians than there should be. Come on, there are less than twenty million of them. If there's an Australian on the register there should be three Germans, seven Japanese, fifteen Americans. It's never that way.

One night, after the sound and light show at Chichén Itzá in Mexico, a dozen or so of us were left, sprawled on the grass, talking about Mayans, Mexico, and whatever else you talk about when you're in that great Mayan center. And then about where we'd been and where we were going. Mexico is not an Australian destination. Australia is not only a lot farther south of the border; it's also a dateline to the west, and there aren't lots of cheap flights to Mexico from Australia, as there are from Europe. Australia doesn't have a shared history with Mexico or enjoy constant Mexican influences in everyday life (from Taco Bell to Mexican beer to Mexican politics), as America does.

So why should three of the twelve Chichén Itzá travelers be Australians? Okay, twelve people in front of a Mayan pyramid doesn't make a statistically significant survey; this little nationality count really doesn't count. Except it is, it does. In fact, my home-spun surveys and gut instinct are more than adequately backed up by hard statistics and clear indicators. On measurements ranging from per capital expenditure on international travel to number of passports held relative to population, Australians are always up toward the top of the charts.

Australia, like America, is a wide and varied land, offering plenty to attract the traveler. So why are Americans perfectly content to see America first, to explore their own country with, comparatively speaking, rarely a thought of setting foot abroad, while Australians seem intent on going everywhere before they give their homeland a second glance?

Perhaps the country's wanderlust dates to its European beginnings. Australia's European settlement, like America's, was relatively recent. It's surprisingly similar in other ways too—a pattern of sailing fleets bringing hardy settlers to a lightly populated country where they displaced the native peoples (often violently) and then did very well for themselves. The people on those sailing ships, however, were aboard for entirely different reasons. The new Americans were fleeing Europe, going in search of a new home with no intention of ever looking back. In contrast, Australia's convict settlers were being flung out from Europe, exiled to Australia against their will, with return home always uppermost in their minds. So perhaps that need to leave, that need to hit the road, to go somewhere, anywhere, everywhere, has been in the Australian psyche from the very start.

Or perhaps it's a more modern affliction, a product of modern media and information. Until the last twenty-five years, when an explosion of Australian movies, books, fashion, and music defined for the first time a real Australian culture, the whole country was said to suffer from "cultural cringe," an overwhelming feeling of being culturally second-rate. To make it meant going abroad, because success achieved in Australia, even if it was exactly the same sort of success as one might find in Europe or America, would inevitably be tainted, second best.

As a result, a whole generation of Australians moved to London, turned that city's Earls Court district into "Kangaroo Valley," and ended up behind the steering wheel, driving half the popular culture of Britain. Just look at Rupert Murdoch and his international media grab; it had its takeoff outside Australia, in Britain, and there were plenty of Aussie foot soldiers ready and waiting in Fleet Street to staff his army when the call to arms came. Today the culinary revolution that has swept through London, leading many food critics to opine that the food's better there than in Paris, has partly been led by Australian chefs, who run the kitchens of many of the city's best restaurants.

Or perhaps it's simple mileage that drives Australians to become the world's premier long-term travelers, the "tyranny of distance," as the Australian historian Geoffrey Blainey has called it. Flying to Europe from Australia takes a solid twenty-four hours; even the most direct flight to the U.S. West Coast involves at least twelve hours aloft. To most overseas destinations from Australia, a flight of at least seven or eight hours is a short hop, a mere kangaroo skip for an outward-bound Aussie. When getting anywhere takes that long, there's clearly an incentive to stay away longer; you don't take a weekend in Europe when it takes the whole weekend just to get there.

Accordingly, a year off between education and employment became an Australian norm, like the gentlemanly European tour of the Victorian era. Grab a representative bunch of Australians and a surprising percentage of them will have spent a year or more abroad at some point. In this activity the Australians may have simply been a bit ahead of the game, for today the expression "gap year" has found its way into the English dictionary, to signify the year between school and university when young Brits set out to see the world. Reportedly, even in America, a "blank" year or two on your CV, once looked upon as a sure sign of unreliability and lack of application, is now starting to be seen as a sign of adventurousness and a wider understanding of the outside world.

Or perhaps Australian wanderlust goes further back than modern travel, back beyond the cultural cringe and the tyranny of distance, even back before Captain Cook, the First Fleet of convicts, and the other pioneering Europeans. After all, the term "walkabout" just puts an English spin onto an Aboriginal concept. Right from the beginning, European observers noted the native Australians' tendency to put down tools and head off somewhere else for an indeterminate period of time for inscrutable reasons. Perhaps from the very beginning the whole island continent was deeply infected with Terminal Wanderlust, waiting to be passed on to the next foolish arrivals.

Or perhaps it's the landscape. When first-time visitors ask me where to go in Australia, I always point toward the Outback. Yes, the cities can be beautiful, but there are other beautiful cities in the world. Yes, the Great Barrier Reef is marvelous, but there are other coral reefs. There's only one Outback, and Australians have a strangely passionate but arm's-length affair with it; it's celebrated in every medium, from songs like "Waltzing Matilda" to movies like *Crocodile Dundee* to bookshops full of photographic essays. The passion and the celebrations are, however, edged with caution. The Outback is like an exciting but vaguely dangerous lover who might just roll over and stab you in the back some night. There's always a distance about it, an alien, vaguely unsettling, vaguely feral atmosphere. In fact, you don't really love it; the relationship has a touch of love-hate. The green fields and ordered landscapes of Europe seem infinitely more secure, reliable, and trustworthy.

Or perhaps linking Terminal Wanderlust with Australia overlooks the most glaring example of all: There's a small country slightly to the southeast of Australia—human population about three million, sheep population about twenty times as great—where they really have Terminal Wanderlust bad.

[1997]

ELIZABETH BISHOP

(1911–1979)

American poet Elizabeth Bishop traveled extensively in Europe and South America and lived in Brazil for a number of years. Many of her poems draw upon scenes and landscapes she observed as a traveler. Several of the titles of her volumes of poetry reflect motifs of travel, including *North and South* (1946) and *Questions of Travel* (1965). The subject of geography, both recollected and imagined, also supplied her with images for poems and titles for volumes. Bishop won the Pulitzer Prize for poetry in 1956 and a

National Book Award for her *Collected Poems* in 1969. She also co-edited and translated *An Anthology of Twentieth-Century Brazilian Poetry* (1972).

The poem below, "Questions of Travel," evokes the motion surrounding us in the natural and social worlds; Bishop implies that in traveling, human beings imitate the restless activity of clouds and streams. The poem asks a familiar series of questions about travel, associating it with theater, childishness, and dreams.

"Questions of Travel"

There are too many waterfalls here; the crowded streams
hurry too rapidly down to the sea,
and the pressure of so many clouds on the mountaintops
makes them spill over the sides in soft slow-motion,
turning to waterfalls under our very eyes.   5
—For if those streaks, those mile-long, shiny, tearstains,
aren't waterfalls yet,
in a quick age or so, as ages go here,
they probably will be.
But if the streams and clouds keep travelling, travelling,   10
the mountains look like the hulls of capsized ships,
slime-hung and barnacled.

Think of the long trip home.
Should we have stayed at home and thought of here?
Where should we be today?   15
Is it right to be watching strangers in a play
in this strangest of theatres?
What childishness is it that while there's a breath of life
in our bodies, we are determined to rush
to see the sun the other way around?   20
The tiniest green hummingbird in the world?
To stare at some inexplicable old stonework,
inexplicable and impenetrable,
at any view,
instantly seen and always, always delightful?   25
Oh, must we dream our dreams
and have them, too?
And have we room
for one more folded sunset, still quite warm?

But surely it would have been a pity 30
not to have seen the trees along this road,
really exaggerated in their beauty,
not to have seen them gesturing
like noble pantomimists, robed in pink.
—Not to have had to stop for gas and heard 35
the sad, two-noted, wooden tune
of disparate wooden clogs
carelessly clacking over
a grease-stained filling-station floor.
(In another country the clogs would all be tested. 40
Each pair there would have identical pitch.)
—A pity not to have heard
the other, less primitive music of the fat brown bird
who sings above the broken gasoline pump
in a bamboo church of Jesuit baroque: 45
three towers, five silver crosses.
—Yes, a pity not to have pondered,
blurr'dly and inconclusively,
on what connection can exist for centuries
between the crudest wooden footwear 50
and, careful and finicky,
the whittled fantasies of wooden cages.
—Never to have studied history in
the weak calligraphy of songbirds' cages.
—And never to have had to listen to rain 55
so much like politicians' speeches:
two hours of unrelenting oratory
and then a sudden golden silence
in which the traveller takes a notebook, writes:

"Is it lack of imagination that makes us come 60
to imagined places, not just stay at home?
Or could Pascal have been not entirely right
about just sitting quietly in one's room?

Continent, city, country, society:
the choice is never wide and never free. 65
And here, or there . . . No. Should we have stayed at home,
wherever that may be?"

[1965]

Passages:
Destinations
and Encounters

INTRODUCTION

"The condition of motion produces a structure of experience with its own logic and order, distinct from the logic and order of place."

Eric Leed, *The Mind of the Traveler*

The lands and cultures travelers experience, their means of transport, and the varieties of people they encounter are three material elements of the journey. Where travelers go, how they get there, and whom they meet all furnish the drama and excitement of travel narratives. The way that travelers get around affects their experiences. Whether they walk, ride on horseback, bicycle, hitchhike, drive, sail, kayak, take the train, or fly—the very kind of passage they undertake influences travelers' points of view and helps determine the kinds of adventures that ensue.

Various modes of travel make for very different kinds of travel writing. One sees the landscape through different eyes, depending on how one is journeying. Walking puts one into immediate physical contact with a terrain and slows passage so that all the senses can take in one's surroundings fully. In comparison to walking, travel on a beast of burden quickens the pace: from astride a camel, donkey, or horse, one views the world from a different perspective than does the pedestrian. Sailing vessels and boats separate one from land, change one's sense of contact with the earth, and increase one's awareness of wind and current. Taking public transportation puts one in close contact with natives and fellow travelers. Whether one journeys by oneself or travels in a group can change the tone of travel narratives. Travel writers are generally solitary creatures who journey alone but welcome the intermittent company of others.

Travel writing develops along with the history of transportation; the invention of the railroad and the steamboat increased the comfort, speed, and volume of travel and made mass tourism possible but also changed the perspectives of travel writers. A railroad car insulated the traveler from the world outside, offering both a small society within and a moving panorama from the window. The steamship removed much but not all of the danger and discomfort from trans-oceanic crossings and opened the continents to middle-class tourists. By the mid-1900s, the airplane and the automobile were becoming the primary vehicles of tourism. Air travel began as an adventure; now, travel writers find little inspiration inside the confines of a jetliner and consider airports to be artificial places indistinguishable from one another. By comparison, cars and recreational vehicles still offer a spontaneous itinerary, a freedom of movement, the prospect of the road as adventure.

Perhaps because the industrial revolution made travel more comfortable and accessible for masses of people, travel writers value the experience of solitary travel and the difficulty of earlier modes of transport. For much of human history, travel has been difficult and burdensome; *travel* has the same root as *travail* ("hard work," "toil," "intense pain," "agony"). Contemporary travelers often seek to recreate the ordeals and physical challenges of earlier days by rejecting modern transport in favor of walking, bicycling, hiking, canoeing, kayaking, sailing, or simply taking battered public busses or aging trains in less developed countries. These more basic forms of transportation increase the chance of difficulty and misadventure, provide more opportunity for spontaneous encounters with native inhabitants, and even intensify contact with the natural world—a fact that emphasizes the close ties between travel writing and nature writing.

Travel writing is strongly imbued with a spirit of place. One of the challenges of travel writing is to recreate a place, both in its physical detail and in the emotions it brings about in the mind of the traveler. As Beldon C. Lane observed in *Landscapes of the Sacred*, "The most gifted travel writers have all performed the impossible task of affording entry to the landscape and consciousness of another world."

A desert exudes a different atmosphere than a jungle, a seashore, or a mountain. A traveler's state of mind is affected by the physical qualities of a particular site—the bustle and excitement of a city, for example, as opposed to the tranquility of a remote village. Besides the nature of the place, the manner in which travelers visit a place influences the travel experience and the quality of the encounters with native inhabitants. If travelers merely pass through a region, they may engage only superficially with the inhabitants, compared with the kinds of relationships formed if they linger for a while or even take up residence there.

Interactions with peoples and cultures of other countries have been at the heart of travel writing. Whether its essence is one of hostility, misunderstanding, friendship, or love, the encounter supplies the main dramatic substance of travel writing and some of the richest material for the traveler's reflections. The traveler's knowledge of human nature—and his or her own nature—is enlarged by the experience of travel. In *Travel Writing: The Self and the World*, Casey Blanton remarks that "By the early nineteenth century, travel writing had clearly become a matter of self-discovery as well as a record of the discovery of others."

Overall, the selections in Part II are organized according to their primary emphasis on mode of travel, spirit of place, or nature of encounter with people. Of course, it is difficult to separate the readings according to these elements because all three combine and interact in the experience of travel. The selections begin with deliberate reflections on how one travels, then move more toward contemplation of terrain and landscape and interactions with people and cultures.

Henry David Thoreau, a solitary traveler, focuses on the activity of walking, which he praises as the simplest and oldest form of travel. He values traveling on foot for the way it puts the walker in close contact with the natural world. John Haines's meditations on hiking reiterate the value of walking, but with an increased attention to wilderness. A different self-propelled form of travel, the bicycle, becomes for Fred Strebeigh not merely a way to get around but also a means of cultural encounter with the masses of Chinese people who ride alongside him.

The selections by Jack Kerouac, Will Ferguson, and Peter Chilson center on the worlds of the automobile, but what different worlds they are! For Kerouac, the automobile signifies freedom, escape, and even rebellion. Ferguson finds in hitchhiking that the often private world of Japanese society opens up to him in the interior of their cars, as Japanese drivers welcome him into a kind of domestic space, a momentary home on wheels. Chilson travels the wild roads of Niger in the company of resourceful and often desperate West African taxi drivers who dodge numerous accidents and scrape together a meager living. William Least Heat-Moon explores the back roads of America, not in a car but in a pickup truck rigged with sleeping quarters. Like the other three writers, he looks to find on the open road spontaneous encounters with people whose stories become material for his own narrative.

The railroad has declined from its heyday as the premier form of overland travel but still exerts an appeal on the imagination. Ted Conover drops out of college to experience what it was like to be a hobo, riding the rails in empty freight cars. Truman Capote's account of happy misadventure on a slow train in southern Spain demonstrates how the railroad can lead the traveler into the company and the culture of fellow passengers. The spirit of early aviation is the subject of "Why Do We Fly," an excerpt from Beryl Markham's *West with the Night*, which revisits the world of the African bush pilot, the aviator as adventurer before the age of mass commercial air travel.

A focus on Mexico as place is shared by two very different pieces, D. H. Lawrence's evocation of a rural market day and Anita Desai's comparison of her feelings for Mexico with those for her native India. The mystique of historic Istanbul is at the center of Jan Morris's reflections on Turkish character. Angela Carter moves eastward to Central Asia, where the exotic essence of place is transmuted into fiction. The contrasting terrains of polar ice field and tropical jungle and the states of mind they induce are explored in the pieces by Apsley

Cherry-Garrard and Tim Cahill. In the vastness of Siberia, Colin Thubron finds an enduring human spirit in the midst of the oppressions of climate and history; his fluent Russian is essential both to his survival as a solo traveler in Asiatic Russia and his appreciation of Siberian character.

In two light and comical encounters that yield opposing perceptions about cultural relativity and body size, Mary Roach seems like a giant in the confines of a traditional Japanese hotel, while Todd McEwen feels dwarfed by obese Americans in the Midwest. When travelers make homes in foreign countries and become expatriates, whether temporary or permanent, they become more like insiders. Amitav Ghosh, an Indian who traveled to North Africa to study Arabic, learns by living in a village how home and travel come together in the world of rural Egypt. Mike Tidwell lives and works for two years in a remote region of the Congo; he learns not only the language of the villagers but also the values and beliefs of their culture. He finds that the Congolese look after him as if he is one of their own, but they also expect him to do the same.

Finally, the transformative potential of travel can be seen in the illumination that Malcolm X undergoes on his pilgrimage to Mecca as he discovers how Islam embraces people of all colors. He returns to America a truly changed man with an altered vision about religion and race. This selection from his autobiography brings together the three elements of travel emphasized in this section: the mode of travel—a religious pilgrimage, first by plane and then by foot, a centuries-old tradition modernized but also preserved; the importance of place—Mecca, the desert city that serves as the spiritual home of Islam; and the encounters with others, pilgrims from around the world who changed Malcolm X's perception of the community of Islam.

In contrast to the readings in Part I about the travelers' preconceptions of their journeys, the selections in Part II focus on the actual experiences and material realities of travel. The writers begin with reflections on how particular ways of travel affect their own thoughts and perceptions. Then the atmosphere and spirit of particular places become more the subject of the traveler's attention. Finally, the writers consider more deeply their interactions with the inhabitants of these places and reflect on how these encounters illuminate and even change the travelers themselves.

HENRY DAVID THOREAU

(1817–1862)

Henry David Thoreau often traveled in the American northeast, but he is better known for staying home. He found more than enough to occupy him within a small part of his native New England, and he subsisted famously for a time in a one-room cabin he built by Walden Pond. One might consider Thoreau a hermit, especially since he praised being alone: "I never found the companion that was so companionable as solitude. We are for the most part more lonely when we go abroad among men than when we stay in our chambers." Thoreau traveled vicariously by reading, especially travel literature, though he did produce three travel books of his own, centered on New England: *A Week on the Concord and Merrimac Rivers* (1849), *Cape Cod* (1864), and *The Maine Woods* (1864).

A central figure in American nature writing as well as travel writing, Thoreau was a skilled observer of natural life, and the following essay in praise of walking is also a recommendation to be out of doors in the natural world. As the oldest and most natural form of transportation, walking unites the traditions of travel writing and nature writing through narratives of journeys on foot—hiking, climbing, backpacking, or trekking overland. In his most famous book, *Walden* (1854), Thoreau celebrates the simple pleasures of living close to nature in a cabin near a rural pond.

Thoreau wrote the following selection, taken from his essay "Walking," as a lecture, and it was published in the June 1862 issue of the *Atlantic Monthly*. The second part of the essay, not included here, is entitled "The Wild" and relates the activity of walking to an appreciation of wilderness.

From "Walking"

I have met with but one or two persons in the course of my life who understood the art of Walking, that is, of taking walks—who had a genius, so to speak, for *sauntering*, which word is beautifully derived 'from idle people who roved about the country, in the Middle Ages, and asked charity, under pretense of going *à la Sainte Terre*,' to the Holy Land, till the children exclaimed, 'There goes a *Sainte-Terrer*,' a Saunterer, a Holy-Lander. They who never go to the Holy Land in their walks, as they pretend, are indeed mere idlers and vagabonds; but they who do go there are saunterers in the good sense, such as I mean. Some, however, would derive the word from *sans terre*, without land or a home, which, therefore, in the good sense, will mean, having no particular home, but equally at home everywhere. For this is the secret of successful sauntering. He who sits still in a house all the time may be the greatest vagrant of all; but the saunterer, in the good sense, is no more vagrant than the meandering river, which is all the while sedulously seeking the shortest course to the sea. But I prefer the first, which, indeed, is the most probable derivation. For every walk is a sort of crusade, preached by some Peter the Hermit in us, to go forth and reconquer this Holy Land from the hands of the Infidels.

It is true, we are but faint-hearted crusaders, even the walkers, nowadays, who undertake no persevering, never-ending enterprise. Our expeditions are but tours, and come round again at evening to the old hearth-side from which we set out. Half the walk is but retracing our steps. We should go forth on the shortest walk, perchance, in the spirit of undying adventure, never to return—prepared to send back our embalmed hearts only as relics to our desolate kingdoms. If you are ready to leave father and mother, and brother and sister, and wife and child and friends, and never see them again—if you have paid your debts, and made your will, and settled all your affairs, and are a free man, then you are ready for a walk.

To come down to my own experience, my companion and I, for I sometimes have a companion, take pleasure in fancying ourselves knights of a new, or rather an old, order—not Equestrians or Chevaliers, not Ritters or Riders, but Walkers, a still more ancient and honorable class, I trust. The chivalric and heroic spirit which once belonged to the Rider seems now to reside in, or perchance to have subsided into, the Walker—not the Knight, but Walker, Errant. He is a sort of fourth estate, outside of Church and State and People.

We have felt that we almost alone hereabouts practised this noble art; though, to tell the truth, at least if their own assertions are to be received, most of my townsmen would fain walk sometimes, as I do, but they cannot. No wealth can buy the requisite leisure, freedom, and independence which are the capital in this profession. It comes only by the grace of God. It requires a direct dispensation from Heaven to become a walker. You must be born into the family of the Walkers. *Ambulator nascitur, non fit.* Some of my townsmen, it is true, can remember and have described to me some walks which they took ten years ago, in which they were so blessed as to lose themselves for half an hour in the woods; but I know very well that they have confined themselves to the highway ever since, whatever pretensions they may make to belong to this select class. No doubt they were elevated for a moment as by the reminiscence of a previous state of existence, when even they were foresters and outlaws.

> 'When he came to grene wode,
>   In a mery mornynge,
> There he herde the notes small
>   Of byrdes mery syngynge.

'It is ferre gone, sayd Robyn,
That I was last here;
Me lyste a lytell for to shote
At the donne dere.'

I think that I cannot preserve my health and spirits, unless I spend four hours a day at least—and it is commonly more than that—sauntering through the woods and over the hills and fields, absolutely free from all worldly engagements. You may safely say, A penny for your thoughts, or a thousand pounds. When sometimes I am reminded that the mechanics and shopkeepers stay in their shops not only all the forenoon, but all the afternoon too, sitting with crossed legs, so many of them—as if the legs were made to sit upon, and not to stand or walk upon—I think that they deserve some credit for not having all committed suicide long ago.

I, who cannot stay in my chamber for a single day without acquiring some rust, and when sometimes I have stolen forth for a walk at the eleventh hour, or four o'clock in the afternoon, too late to redeem the day, when the shades of night were already beginning to be mingled with the daylight, have felt as if I had committed some sin to be atoned for—I confess that I am astonished at the power of endurance, to say nothing of the moral insensibility, of my neighbors who confine themselves to shops and offices the whole day for weeks and months, aye, and years almost togther. I know not what manner of stuff they are of—sitting there now at three o'clock in the afternoon, as if it were three o'clock in the morning. Bonaparte may talk of the three-o'clock-in-the-morning courage, but it is nothing to the courage which can sit down cheerfully at this hour in the afternoon over against one's self whom you have known all the morning, to starve out a garrison to whom you are bound by such strong ties of sympathy. I wonder that about this time, or say betwen four and five o'clock in the afternoon, too late for the morning papers and too early for the evening ones, there is not a general explosion heard up and down the street, scattering a legion of antiquated and house-bred notions and whims to the four winds for an airing—and so the evil cure itself.

How womankind, who are confined to the house still more than men, stand it I do not know; but I have ground to suspect that most of them do not *stand* it at all. When, early in a summer afternoon, we have been shaking the dust of the village from the skirts of our garments, making haste past those houses with purely Doric or Gothic fronts, which have such an air of repose about them, my companion whispers that probably about these times their occupants are all gone to bed. Then it is that I appreciate the beauty and the glory of architecture, which itself never turns in, but forever stands out and erect, keeping watch over the slumberers.

No doubt temperament, and, above all, age, have a good deal to do with it. As a man grows older, his ability to sit still and follow indoor occupations increases. He grows vespertinal in his habits as the evening of life approaches, till at last he comes forth only just before sundown, and gets all the walk that he requires in half an hour.

But the walking of which I speak has nothing in it akin to taking exercise, as it is called, as the sick take medicine at stated hours—as the swinging of dumbbells or chairs; but is itself the enterprise and adventure of the day. If you would get exercise, go in search of the springs of life. Think of a man's swinging dumbbells for his health, when those springs are bubbling up in far-off pastures unsought by him!

Moreover, you must walk like a camel, which is said to be the only beast which ruminates when walking. When a traveller asked Wordsworth's servant to show him her master's study, she answered, 'Here is his library, but his study is out of doors.'

Living much out of doors, in the sun and wind, will no doubt produce a certain roughness of character—will cause a thicker cuticle to grow over some of the finer qualities of our nature, as on the face and hands, or as severe manual labor robs the hands of some of their delicacy of touch. So staying in the house, on the other hand, may produce a softness and smoothness, not to say thinness of skin, accompanied by an increased sensibility to certain impressions. Perhaps we should be more susceptible to some influences important to our intellectual and moral growth, if the sun had shone and the wind blown on us a little less; and no doubt it is a nice matter to proportion rightly the thick and thin skin. But methinks that is a scurf that will fall off fast enough—that the natural remedy is to be found in the proportion which the night bears to the day, the winter to the summer, thought to experience. There will be so much the more air and sunshine in our thoughts. The callous palms of the laborer are conversant with finer tissues of self-respect and heroism, whose touch thrills the heart, than the languid fingers of idleness. That is mere sentimentality that lies abed by day and thinks itself white, far from the tan and callus of experience.

When we walk, we naturally go to the fields and woods: what would become of us, if we walked only in a garden or a mall? Even some sects of philosophers have felt the necessity of importing the woods to themselves, since they did not go to the woods. 'They planted groves and walks of Platanes,' where they took *subdiales ambulationes* in porticos open to the air. Of course it is of no use to direct our steps to the woods, if they do not carry us thither. I am alarmed when it happens that I have walked a mile into the woods bodily, without getting there in spirit. In my afternoon walk I would fain forget all my morning occupations and my obligations to society. But it sometimes happens that I cannot easily shake off the village. The thought of some work will run in my head and I am not where my body is—I am out of my senses. In my walks I would fain return to my senses. What business have I in the woods, if I am thinking of something out of the woods? I suspect myself, and cannot help a

shudder, when I find myself so implicated even in what are called good works—
for this may sometimes happen.

My vicinity affords many good walks; and though for so many years I have
walked almost every day, and sometimes for several days together, I have not yet
exhausted them. An absolutely new prospect is a great happiness, and I can still
get this any afternoon. Two or three hours' walking will carry me to as strange a
country as I expect ever to see. A single farmhouse which I had not seen before
is sometimes as good as the dominions of the King of Dahomey. There is in fact
a sort of harmony discoverable between the capabilities of the landscape within
a circle of ten miles' radius, or the limits of an afternoon walk, and the three-
score years and ten of human life. It will never become quite familiar to you.

Nowadays almost all man's improvements, so called, as the building of
houses and the cutting down of the forest and of all large trees, simply deform
the landscape, and make it more and more tame and cheap. A people who
would begin by burning the fences and let the forest stand! I saw the fences half
consumed, their ends lost in the middle of the prairie, and some worldly miser
with a surveyor looking after his bounds, while heaven had taken place around
him, and he did not see the angels going to and fro, but was looking for an old
post-hole in the midst of paradise. I looked again, and saw him standing in the
middle of a boggy Stygian fen, surrounded by devils, and he had found his
bounds without a doubt, three little stones, where a stake had been driven, and
looking nearer, I saw that the Prince of Darkness was his surveyor.

I can easily walk ten, fifteen, twenty, any number of miles, commencing at
my own door, without going by any house, without crossing a road except where
the fox and the mink do: first along by the river, and then the brook, and then
the meadow and the woodside. There are square miles in my vicinity which have
no inhabitant. From many a hill I can see civilization and the abodes of man
afar. The farmers and their works are scarcely more obvious than woodchucks
and their burrows. Man and his affairs, church and state and school, trade and
commerce, and manufactures and agriculture, even politics, the most alarming
of them all—I am pleased to see how little space they occupy in the landscape.
Politics is but a narrow field, and that still narrower highway yonder leads to it.
I sometimes direct the traveller thither. If you would go to the political world,
follow the great road—follow that market-man, keep his dust in your eyes, and it
will lead you straight to it; for it, too, has its place merely, and does not occupy
all space. I pass from it as from a bean-field into the forest, and it is forgotten.
In one half-hour I can walk off to some portion of the earth's surface where a
man does not stand from one year's end to another, and there consequently, politics are not, for they are but as the cigar-smoke of a man.

The village is the place to which the roads tend, a sort of expansion of the
highway, as a lake of a river. It is the body of which roads are the arms and legs—
a trivial or quadrivial place, the thoroughfare and ordinary of travellers. The

word is from the Latin *villa*, which together with *via*, a way, or more anciently *ved* and *vella*, Varro derives from *veho*, to carry, because the villa is the place to and from which things are carried. They who got their living by teaming were said *vellaturam facere*. Hence, too, the Latin word *vilis* and our vile, also *villain*. This suggests what kind of degeneracy villagers are liable to. They are wayworn by the travel that goes by and over them, without travelling themselves.

Some do not walk at all; others walk in the highways; a few walk across lots. Roads are made for horses and men of business. I do not travel in them much, comparatively, because I am not in a hurry to get to any tavern or grocery or livery-stable or depot to which they lead. I am a good horse to travel, but not from choice a roadster. The landscape-painter uses the figures of men to mark a road. He would not make that use of my figure. I walk out into a nature such as the old prophets and poets, Menu, Moses, Homer, Chaucer, walked in. You may name it America, but it is not America; neither Americus Vespucius, nor Columbus, nor the rest were the discoverers of it. There is a truer account of it in mythology than in any history of America, so called, that I have seen.

[1862]

JOHN HAINES

(1924–)

John Haines is one of many modern writers who live and write in the tradition of Thoreau. A native of Michigan, he made a home in the Alaskan wilderness for a number of years. He is primarily a poet, and his books of poetry, among them *Winter News* (1966) and *News from the Glacier* (1982), evoke the world of the north.

The following meditation, from *Living Off the Country: Essays on Poetry and Place* (1981), brings together walking and nature writing in a meditation on the relation between human travel and the movement of elements within the physical universe.

"Moments and Journeys"

From *Living Off the Country: Essays on Poetry and Place*

The movement of things on this earth has always impressed me. There is a reassuring vitality in the annual rise of a river, in the return of the Arctic sun, in the poleward flight of spring migrations, in the seasonal trek of nomadic peoples. A passage from Edwin Muir's autobiography speaks to me of its significance.

> I remember . . . while we were walking one day on the Mönchsberg—a smaller hill on the opposite side of the river—looking down on a green plain that stretched away to the foothills, and watching in the distance people moving along the tiny roads. Why do such things seem enormously important to us? Why, seen from a distance, do the casual journeys of men and women, perhaps going on some trivial errand, take on the appearance of a pilgrimage? I can only explain it by some deep archetypal image in our minds of which we become conscious only at the rare moments when we realize that our own life is a journey. [Edwin Muir, *An Autobiography* (Sommers, Conn.: Seabury, 1968), p. 217].

This seems to me like a good place to begin, not only for its essential truth, but because it awakens in me a whole train of images—images of the journey as I have come to understand it, moments and stages in existence. Many of these go back to the years I lived on my homestead in Alaska. That life itself, part of the soil and weather of the place, seemed to have about it much of the time an aura of deep and lasting significance. I wasn't always aware of this, of course. There were many things to be struggled with from day to day, chores of one sort or another—cabins to be built, crops to looked after, meat to kill, and wood to cut—all of which took a kind of passionate attention. But often when I was able to pause and look up from what I was doing, I caught brief glimpses of a life much older than mine.

Some of these images stand out with great force from the continual coming and going of which they were part—Fred Campbell, the old hunter and miner I had come to know, that lean, brown man of patches and strange fits. He and I and my first wife, Peg, with seven dogs—five of them carrying packs—all went over Buckeye Dome one day in the late summer of 1954. It was a clear, hot day in mid-August, the whole troop of us strung out on the trail. Campbell and his best dog, a yellow bitch named Granny, were in the lead. We were in a hurry, or seemed to be, the dogs pulling us on, straining at their leashes for the first two or three miles, and then, turned loose, just panting along, anxious not to be left behind. We stopped only briefly that morning, to adjust a dog pack and to catch our wind. Out of the close timber with its hot shadows and swarms of mosquitoes, we came into the open sunlight of the dome. The grass and low shrubs on the treeless slopes moved gently in the warm air that came from somewhere south, out of the Gulf of Alaska.

At midday we halted near the top of the dome to look for water among the rocks and to pick blueberries. The dogs, with their packs removed, lay down in the heat, snapping at flies. Buckeye Dome was the high place nearest to home, though it was nearly seven miles by trail from Richardson. It wasn't very high, either—only 3,000 feet—but it rose clear of the surrounding hills. From its summit you could see in any direction, as far west as Fairbanks when the air was clear enough. We saw other high places, landmarks in the distance, pointed out to us and named by Campbell: Banner Dome, Cockscomb, Bull Dome, and others I've forgotten. In the southeast, a towering dust cloud rose from the Delta River. Campbell talked to us of his trails and camps, of years made of such journeys as ours, an entire history told around the figure of one man. We were new to the North and eager to learn all we could. We listened, sucking blueberries from a tin cup.

And then we were on the move again. I can see Campbell in faded jeans and red felt hat, bending over one of the dogs as he tightened a strap, swearing and saying something about the weather, the distance, and himself getting too old to make such a trip. We went off down the steep north slope of the dome in a great rush, through miles of windfalls, following that twisting, root-grown trail of his. Late in the evening, wading the shallows of a small creek, we came tired and bitten to his small cabin on the shore of a lake he had named for himself.

That range of images is linked with another at a later time. By then I had my own team, and with our four dogs we were bound uphill one afternoon in the cool September sunlight to pick cranberries on the long ridge overlooking Redmond Creek. The tall, yellow grass on the partly cleared ridge bent over in the wind that came easily from the west. I walked behind, and I could see, partly hidden by the grass, the figures of the others as they rounded the shoulder of a little hill and stopped to look back toward me. The single human figure there in the sunlight under moving clouds, the dogs with their fur slightly ruffled, seemed the embodiment of an old story.

And somewhere in the great expanse of time that made life in the wilderness so open and unending, other seasons were stations on the journey. Coming across the Tanana River on the midwinter ice, we had three dogs in harness and one young female running loose beside us. We had been three days visiting a neighbor, a trapper living on the far side of the river, and were returning home. Halfway across the river we stopped to rest; the sled was heavy, the dogs were tired and lay down on the ice.

Standing there, leaning on the back of the sled, I knew a vague sense of remoteness and peril. The river ice always seemed a little dangerous, even when it was thick and solid. There were open stretches of clear, blue water, and sometimes large, deep cracks in the ice where the river could be heard running deep and steady. We were heading downriver into a cloudy December evening. Wind came across the ice, pushing a little dry snow, and no other sound—only the vast presence of snow and ice, scattered islands, and the dark crest of Richardson Hill in the distance.

To live by a large river is to be kept in the heart of things. We become involved in its life, the heavy sound of it in the summer as it wears away silt and gravel from its cutbanks, pushing them into sandbars that will be islands in another far off year. Trees are forever tilting over the water, to fall and be washed away, to lodge in a drift pile somewhere downstream. The heavy gray water drags at the roots of willows, spruce, and cotton-woods; sometimes it brings up the trunk of a tree buried in sand a thousand years before, or farther back than that, in the age of ice. The log comes loose from the fine sand, heavy and dripping, still bearing the tunnel marks made by the long dead insects. Salmon come in midsummer, then whitefish, and salmon again in the fall; they are caught in our nets and carried away to be smoked and eaten, to be dried for winter feed. Summer wears away into fall; the sound of the river changes. The water clears and slowly drops; pan ice forms in the eddies. One morning in early winter we wake to a great and sudden silence: the river is frozen.

We stood alone there on the ice that day, two people, four dogs, and a loaded sled, and nothing before us but land and water into Asia. It was time to move on again. I spoke to the dogs and gave the sled a push.

Other days. On a hard-packed trail home from Cabin Creek, I halted the dogs part way up a long hill in scattered spruce. It was a clear evening, not far below zero. Ahead of us, over an open ridge, a full moon stood clear of the land, enormous and yellow in the deep blue of the Arctic evening. I recalled how Billy Melvin, an old miner from the early days at Richardson, had once describd to me a moonrise he had seen, a full moon coming up ahead of him on the trail, "big as a rain barrel." And it was very much like that—an enormous and rusty rain barrel into which I looked, and the far end of the barrel was open. I stood there, thinking it might be possible to go on forever into that snow and yellow light, with no sound but my own breathing, the padding of the dog's feet, and the occasional squeak of the sled runners. The moon whitened and grew smaller; twilight deepened, and we went on to the top of the hill.

What does it take to make a journey? A place to start from, something to leave behind. A road, a trail, or a river. Companions, and something like a destination: a camp, an inn, or another shore. We might imagine a journey with no destination, nothing but the act of going, and with never an arrival. But I think we would always hope to find *something* or *someone*, however unexpected and unprepared for. Seen from a distance or taken part in, all journeys may be the same, and we arrive exactly where we are.

One late summer afternoon, near the road to Denali Park, I watched the figures of three people slowly climb the slope of a mountain in the northeast. The upper part of the mountain was bare of trees, and the small alpine plants there were already red and gold from the early frost. Sunlight came through broken rain clouds and lit up the slope and its three moving figures. They were so far away that I could not tell if they were men or women, but the red jacket worn by one of them stood out brightly in the sun. They climbed higher and higher, bound for a ridge where some large rocks broke through the thin soil. A shadow kept pace with them, slowly darkening the slope below them, as the sun sank behind another mountain in the southwest. I wondered where they were going—perhaps to hunt mountain sheep— or they were climbing to a berry patch they knew. It was late in the day; they would not get back by dark. I watched them as if they were figures in a dream, who bore with them the destiny of the race. They stopped to rest for a while near the skyline, but were soon out of sight beyond the ridge. Sunlight stayed briefly on the high rock summit, and then a rain cloud moved in and hid the mountaintop.

When life is simplified, its essence becomes clearer, and we know our lives as part of some ancient human activity in a time measured not by clocks and calendars but by the turning of a great wheel, the positions of which are not wage-hours, nor days and weeks, but immense stations called Spring, Summer, Autumn, and Winter. I suppose it will seem too obvious to say that this sense of things will be far less apparent to people closed off in the routine of a modern city. I think many peoople must now and then be aware of such moments as I have described, but do not remember them, or attach no special significance to them. They are images that pass quickly from view because there is no place for them in our lives. We are swept along by events we cannot link together in a significant pattern, like a flood of refugees pushed on by the news of a remote disaster. The rush of conflicting impressions keeps away stillness, and it is in stillness that the images arise, as they will, fluently and naturally, when there is nothing to prevent them.

There is the dream journey and the actual life. The two seem to touch now and then, and perhaps when men lived less complicated and distracted lives the two were not separate at all, but continually one thing. I have read somewhere that this was once true for the Yuma Indians who lived along the Colorado River. They dreamed at will, and moved without effort from waking into dreaming life; life and dream were bound together. And in this must be a kind of radiance, a very old and deep assurance that life has continuity and meaning, that things are somehow in place. It is the journey resolved into one endless present.

And the material is all around us. I retain strong images from treks with my stepchildren: of a night seven years ago when we camped on a mountaintop, a night lighted by snow patches and sparks from a windy fire going out. Sleeping on the frozen ground, we heard the sound of an owl from the cold, bare oak trees above us. And there was a summer evening I spent with a small class of schoolchildren near Painted Rock in central California. We had come to learn about Indians. The voices of the children carried over the burned fields under the red glare of that sky, and the rock gave back heat in the dusk like an immense oven. There are ships and trains that pull away, planes that fly into the night; or the single figure of a man crossing an otherwise empty lot. If such moments are not as easily come by, as clear and as resonant as they once were in the wilderness, it may be because they are not so clearly linked to the life that surrounds them and of which they are part. They are present nonetheless, available to imagination, and of the same character.

One December day a few years ago, while on vacation in California, I went with my daughter and a friend to a place called Pool Rock. We drove for a long time over a mountain road, through meadows touched by the first green of the winter rains, and saw few fences or other signs of people. Leaving our car in a small campground at the end of the road, we hiked four miles up a series of canyons and narrow gorges. We lost our way several times but always found it again. A large covey of quail flew up from the chaparral on a slope above us; the tracks of deer and bobcat showed now and then in the sand under our feet. An extraordinary number of coyote droppings scattered along the trail attracted our attention. I poked one of them with a stick, saw that it contained much rabbit fur and bits of bone. There were patches of ice in the streambed, and a few leaves still yellow on the sycamores.

We came to the rock in mid-afternoon, a great sandstone pile rising out of the foothills like a sanctuary or a shrine to which one comes yearly on a pilgrimage. There are places that take on symbolic value to an individual or a tribe, "soul-resting places," a friend of mine has called them. Pool Rock has become that to me, symbolic of that hidden, original life we have done so much to destroy.

We spent an hour or two exploring the rock, a wind and rain-scoured honeycomb stained yellow and rose by a mineral in the sand. Here groups of the Chumash Indians used to come, in that time of year when water could be found in the canyons. They may have come to gather certain foods in season, or to take part in magic rites whose origin and significance are no longer understood. In a small cave at the base of the rock, the stylized figures of headless reptiles, insects, and strange birdmen are painted on the smoke-blackened walls and ceiling. These and some bear paw impressions gouged in the rock, and a few rock mortars used for grinding seeds, are all that is left of a once-flourishing people.

We climbed to the summit of the rock, using the worn footholds made long ago by the Chumash. We drank water from the pool that gave the rock its name, and ate our lunch, sitting quietly in the cool sunlight. And then the wind came up, whipping our lunchbag over the edge of the rock; a storm was moving in from the coast. We left the rock by the way we had come, and hiked down the gorge in the windy, leaf-blown twilight. In the dark, just before the rain, we came to the campground, laughing, speaking of the things we had seen, and strangely happy.

[1981]

Fred Strebeigh

(1951–)

Fred Strebeigh teaches non-fiction writing courses at Yale and has published articles on a variety of subjects in *The New York Times Magazine*, *The New Republic*, *Atlantic Monthly*, and *American Heritage*. He traveled in China in the late 1980s when the democracy movement, which would lead to the massacre in Beijing's Tiananmen Square, was in full flower. Strebeigh found himself caught up in the bicyclists coming to and from political demonstrations. In the United States, bicycles are less numerous than cars, but in China, the "foreign horse" (introduced to China in the late 1800s by an American) is a beast of burden as well as a means of mobility. In a society of bicycle riders—more than 42 million—bicycle traffic jams are commonplace, and bicycle repairmen make more money than professors.

Strebeigh's essay "The Wheels of Freedom," originally written for *Bicycle Magazine*, illustrates how this mode of travel offers freedom of movement to the Chinese and symbolizes political freedom as well.

"The Wheels of Freedom: Bicycles in China"

"Hello." She appeared at my right shoulder, her face inches from mine. We were cycling together, though I had never seen her before. We rode side by side through the city of Beijing, and around us streamed thousands of bicycles with red banners flying. Beijing was in revolt. And as we rode together we broke the law.

I had gone to China with an odd goal: to learn a bit about what the bicycle means to people who live in a country with only a few thousand privately owned cars but some 220 million cycles—vastly more than any other nation. And I had arrived at an odd time.

My first day in China was also the first day of what became known as the Beijing Spring of 1989. As I awoke, students and citizens by the hundreds of thousands were flowing from all over Beijing to Tiananmen Square, the vast plaza at the city's heart, creating the largest spontaneous demonstration in the history of China and perhaps the world. They came on foot and by bus and subway, of course, but mostly they came by bicycle, calling for freedom. (I could see why bicycles are forbidden in the capital of North Korea, China's more repressive neighbor. It's government reportedly fears that bikes give people too much independence.)

Within hours of my arrival in Beijing, bicycles became more crucial than ever. Buses stopped. Subways shut. Taxis struck. But on flowed the bikes of Beijing. Bicyclists carried messages from university to university. Tricyclists rushed round delivering food to demonstrators. Families and schoolmates and couples and commuters smiled and waved as they rode, in twos and threes and throngs.

On my own bicycle, hesitant at first and then lost in the cycling masses, I roamed freely. Daily I rode to Tiananmen Square, with its mood of carnival, its students from all regions, and its uncountable cycles. Bicycles and tricycles became flag holders and tent supporters. They became tea dispensers and cold-drink stands. They became photographers' perches, families' viewing platforms, old men's reading chairs, and children's racing toys.

On my bicycle I also strayed far from Tiananmen, to the quiet corners of the city. Everywhere the bicycle set the rhythm of life. Martial artists rode to practice with swords strapped to their bikes. Women in jet-black business suits pedalled their daughters to school. Boys fished beside parked bicycles at placid lakes. Bakers in white toques headed for work on transport tricycles. Pedalling beside them at their slow pace, I felt at ease and oddly at home. I felt as I had years ago in my small hometown, where automobiles never clogged the streets and where the bicycle offered a mix of peace and freedom.

Riding among the bicycles of Beijing, I began to recognize dozens of China's famous brands: Golden Lion and Mountain River, Plum Flower and Chrysanthemum, Red Flag and Red Cotton, Flying Arrival and Flying Pigeon, Pheasant and Phoenix and Forever. Long and stately bicycles, recalling decades past, they possessed the rake and sheer and grace that today I associate less with cycling than with yachting. I felt as if I were cruising, on the wake of clippers like *Red Jacket* or *Flying Cloud,* in a regatta of tall ships.

Then the Chinese government declared martial law. It forbade citizens to attend the student demonstrations and forbade foreigners, like me, to visit Tiananmen or talk to students. It sent its army in a first push into the city, but citizens peacefully blocked its way. My Chinese hosts (I had been invited to lecture at a couple of universities) warned me to obey the government, and I said I would try.

In the second day under martial law, as I was riding down one of Beijing's leafy boulevards, suddenly a young woman appeared at my shoulder. She said "hello," and we were cycling together.

I had been rolling at Beijing speed, eight miles an hour—in synch with commuters, demonstrators, and vegetable haulers. To catch me she had accelerated, maybe to eight-and-a-half miles an hour.

"What," she wanted to know, did I "think about the students?" She wore tinted glasses, a shy smile in a radiant face, a lab coat—she was a science student, and by law we were forbidden to talk.

"I think what they are doing is very brave," I said, "and very scary." And so we became two petty criminals, riding handlebar-to-handlebar.

We floated together and others floated past. But they travelled fractions of a pedal-turn faster or fractions slower, and we were left alone in talk, our handlebars occasionally nudging each other, in the bizarre intimacy of Beijing cycling. I worried aloud about the Chinese army—now half a mile to our west, still blocked but still pressing towards us. She praised George Washington. We would not have talked so freely in a restaurant or hotel, I realized; police could have demanded our names. But here we were just two bicycles lost in the mass—the most private place in Beijing.

Ahead of us appeared Tiananmen Square, where some of her classmates had been starving themselves in protest and others had been singing "We Shall Overcome." Within moments, she drifted south and I north. Soon I was at the American embassy. They warned me against talking to students.

To stay in Beijing, I decided, was to endanger anyone I met. And so I resolved to travel out from the capital and return later, in order to talk about bicycles in a time of greater calm and, I hoped, greater freedom.

One of the people I most wanted to meet outside Beijing was a student in Sichuan Province named Fang Hui. The year before, she had become the first woman to ride a bicycle from Chengdu, the capital of Sichuan in central China, to Lhasa, the capital of Tibet—bumping for thirteen hunded miles over one of China's worst roads, a sawtooth of rock tracks and mountain passes which reach altitudes above 15,000 feet. In recognition, China honored her as one of the nation's "Ten Brave Young People."

I didn't care much about Fang Hui's honors. I cared more about her motivations, her goals. I guess I expected her to be a hot but somewhat dull athlete, the sort who wins Chinese honors by excelling in volleyball. When we met at her university in Chengdu, where she is a graduate student in English, she surprised me.

As we pedalled through the streets of Chengdu, I asked Fang Hui if she had always been a cyclist. Not really, she said. Before her trip she had not owned a bicycle. The day before departing for Tibet she bought an old, single-speed Arched Eyebrow for 75 yuan ($15). She then taught herself to ride, over a thousand miles of mountains.

I asked how she chose Tibet. She said she had answered a poster advertisement. I was shocked. So, apparently, were the five men, mostly teachers from a local school, who had planned the trip and posted invitations for fellow travellers. Only Fang Hui accepted.

The men doubted she could reach Tibet, perhaps because she looked like a pudgy schoolgirl. Uphill she always rode more slowly than they, falling miles behind. Downhill, because her old bike had wretched brakes, she squeezed its levers with all her strength as the Arched Eyebrow hurtled down pitted roads. "I went very fast," she said. "I felt as if I would become light." At the end of each day of clinging to her brake levers, her hands were so cramped she could not open them.

Eventually, the men admitted that her strength egged them on. "If even a girl can do this," they said, "how shameful for a man to give up."

Fang Hui had not really worried about giving up on the journey, she told me. But, earlier, she had worried about giving up on life. "Before," she said, "yesterday, today, tomorrow were all alike—so dull. What I most wanted was to meet something unexpected."

Not just the road's pain but also its loneliness changed Fang Hui. At remote outposts she would meet soldiers, mere isolated boys, who would write love letters that followed her up the Lhasa road, carried by lone truck drivers. In yet remoter terrain she would ride half a day, she recalled, and "not see a single man. So when I heard a dog bark, it would arouse a tender feeling—a reminder of the human world. When I came back, people all said I had changed. Now I can find something new in every day." And now at night, she added with glee, "sometimes I dream I am riding very fast downhill."

As I rode through Chengdu, sometimes talking with Fang Hui or with other university students and teachers, I began to see that the bicycle offered an escape not just *from* everyday life. It also offered escape within everyday life.

One day as Fang Hui and I rode through a crush of cyclists, a young couple passed us riding two bicycles side-by-side. They rode pedal-to-pedal and almost arm-in-arm. At first the girl rode with her left hand on the boy's right, controlling his hand and handlebar, steering them both. Then he moved his hand to round the small of her back. They reminded me of partners in a waltz.

The boy lowered his hand to the girl's bicycle seat and leaned to her, and as they rode they whispered. In the often-dehumanizing crush of urban China, two bicycles had made space for romance. Fang Hui said that young "lovers" often ride so utterly together, so alone in their world.

Providing such measures of human dignity, one professor told me, was one of the bicycle's gifts to China—and particularly to people like his parents, who were "peasants" (the term in China for all people who work the land). Here in the center of China's richest farmlands, he said, I could watch the bicycle making life less hard. Flower farmers with hollyhocks and asters tied to their bicycles arrived in Chengdu at dawn, flicked down their kickstands on side streets, and began to sell. Farmers' sons strapped saws and other carpenters' tools to their bicycles, rode into the city, and waited at curbside for customers to hire them to build beds or bureaus. In Sichuan's booming "free markets" (free, that is, of government control), geese came to town on the backs of farmers' tricycles, were sold to families for domestic egg laying, and then departed with their wings still flapping, strapped to the buyers' handlebars. Everywhere, cycles kept life rolling.

The professor told me that peasants in his parents' remote village always refer to the bicycle, appreciatively, as the "foreign horse." The government opposes the name, he said, but it helps explain the history of the bicycle in China. The first bicycle arrived in 1886, carrying Thomas Stevens, a young San Franciscan who was completing the first cycling journey around the world. With its huge front wheel and small rear one, his penny-farthing cycle must have looked very foreign but, unlike a good horse, not very practical.

The first practical bicycle to reach China came in 1891, again transporting a round-the-world cyclist. By the early twentieth century, the foreign horse had won the fascination of China's last emperor, the young Puyi, who rode one around his palace, Beijing's "Fobidden City."

Slowly cycling trickled down from the throne toward the masses. By the 1940s China's bicycle factories were producing a vehicle like today's most common model, a viertual twin of England's stately Raleigh Tourist.

In the years before the Chinese revolution of 1949, the professor told me, almost everyone called the bicycle "foreign horse," because "foreign" suggested both "modern" and "admirable." Since peasants carried most goods on their backs, they particularly admired the bicycle. Every peasant longed to shift his burden to the back of a foreign horse—a longing frustrated by high price and short supply.

Then came the revolution of 1949. Hoping to "raise the people's dignity," the professor continued, the young government made two decisions. Happily, in an effort to give wheels to an impoverished population, it encouraged bicycle production, which began doubling and redoubling. But sadly, because the old name suggested blind worship of foreign things, the government banned the lyrical phrase "foreign horse" (which, pronounced yang ma in Chinese, resounds like ringing gong). The government imposed, instead, the unpoetic "self-running cart" (zi xing che in Chinese, which sounds like a dental problem).

Not surprisingly, the cycle's foreign resonance remains. Peasants in remote villages still pedal "foreign horses." And many Chinese factories, seeking a touch of class, still adorn their bicycles with prominent English names: "Forever" or "Light Roadster" or, on the most celebrated of foreign horses, "Flying Pigeon—The All-Steel Bicycle." (When George Bush made his first presidential visit to China, his welcoming gift from the nation was a pair of Flying Pigeons.)

A regional branch of the Flying Pigeon Bicycle Factory lies an hour's ride from the center of Chendu, and one day I was given a tour of its old-style assembly line by Jiang Guoji, the factory's present director—the first ever elected by its workers. He spoke with the ease of a manager whose workers trust his judgment and whose society trusts his product.

Since Jiang Guoji's factory sits in the middle of China's best farmland, he and his co-workers decided to specialize in what Jiang called the "ZA-62" or "Reinforced Flying Pigeon." This bike, which I came to think of as the "Peasant Pigeon," comes with massive tubing, a formidable rack, a second set of forks to hold the front wheels, and—probably unique among Chinese bicycles—a three-year warranty. It contains 68 pounds of steel which, together with some leather and rubber, brings its total weight above 72 pounds—three times that of my average American bike.

Jiang Guoji's factory has raised production steadily, along with all Chinese cycle factories, creating an unprecedented problem. The year before my visit, Chinese bicycle production reached 42 million cycles—dwarfing any other nation's output and, more significantly, overtaking Chinese demand for the first time in history. For years, bicycles had been rationed, and families had longed to own a good one. Now "if a person has money, he can buy," Jiang told me, with a mix of pride and regret—because prices have begun dropping and "bicycle factories have real competition."

In response, Jiang said, he was trying to spur international demand for Peasant Pigeons. Looking for good "propaganda," two years earlier he donated "Peasant Pigeons" to five local riders who wanted to go around the world. Alas, one had been run down by a truck in Pakistan. But the other four were riding on, circling the globe back towards his factory. He expected his 72-pound Pigeons home within a year, still under warranty. (He added that, despite transport costs and import duties, he would gladly sell Peasant Pigeons wholesale in America for less than a dollar a pound.)

All Chinese bicycles—whether sturdy Flying Pigeons or sad Arched Eyebrows—must survive long after their warranties have expired. To help them along, repairmen have set up roadside stands in every city. Entering the business proves simple. A would-be repairman chooses a site, asks the city to license it to him, and lays down his tools. He then puts up his advertisement—a circle of overlapping innertubes, colored black and deep pink, perhaps hung on a tree limb.

Some Chinese portray repairmen in a style that outdoes American caricatures of car mechanics. Most of my Chinese acquaintances knew one repairman they relied on and dozens they distrusted. One university professor insisted that underemployed repairmen scatter tacks to puncture passing tires and inflate profits.

Another professor invited me to meet her revered neighborhood repairman. Since he worked incessantly and had little time for chatter, she devised a ruse to buy time for asking questions: we would take him her Flying Arrival, which had a useless rear brake.

We found him at the back gate of her university beneath a circle of inner-tubes. When my friend arrived, the repairman put aside a Phoenix he was polishing and greeted her as a long-term client. She presented the brake problem. He took a quick look, produced two sets of pliers, loosened a nut, tightened a cable, tensioned a spring and, after 30 seconds of work, handed the bike back to her—fixed. He refused payment. The job was too small. He resumed polishing the Phoenix.

Though her ruse had failed, the professor pressed forward: How did he become a repairman? Three years ago when he was twenty-seven, he told us, he stopped working his family's farm because the land was small and the family had more than enough laborers—including his wife, their three children, his two sisters and two brothers, and their aging parents. He still lives on the farm but commutes three miles to the city on his Forever. He works seven days a week, from 9 A.M. to 8 P.M., except when it rains.

He likes bike repair because it "makes *money*," he said, emphasizing the word as if it were a novelty. Back on the farm, where he hopes never to work again, he "just produced *crops*," which sold for "not-so-much money."

When we asked him how much he made in a month, he told us 800 yuan ($216). The professor gasped. To me she said, quietly, "That's five university professors!" Still, she seemed to believe him. She pointed out to me that he had paid the government's penalty for having three children. The penalty in recent years has run as high as 2,000 yuan ($540), she said, too much for professors—but not for an industrious bike fixer.

As I talked to more repairmen, I saw that their job may be the freest in China. A hard worker needed only a street corner and a few tools. Before his eyes bikes would inevitably break down and, if he was skilled, clients would multiply. Bicycle repair seemed to offer an extension of what the bike itself offered and what so many Chinese sought: modest dignity, new choices, ample freedom.

The farm country outside Chengdu, contrary to the complaints of one peasant-turned-repairman, generates much of the new agricultural wealth enjoyed by the Chinese people. In early June, by train and by bicycle, I travelled to the southern mountains that rim this rich agricultural bowl within Sichuan province. There I was the guest at another university, tucked in verdant hills.

During my stay, one teacher lent me an old "Peasant Pigeon"—one well past its warranty. I rode it daily over farm tracks of rut and rock that would have jolted the nuts off my light American bike. The big Pigeon just bobbed along, high and easy.

One midday while I was exploring narrow paths through emerald-colored rice paddies, two girls whizzed past me, riding double on a black Forever.

Both wore red uniforms and one carried an abacus—students dashng home for lunch.

With me was a professor who was fluent not only in English but also the quite-obscure local dialect. She suggested we follow the students so I could meet a "peasant family."

We travelled through flooded paddies, past water buffaloes, up to a newly built home that stretched around a cement courtyard, and found the older of the two girls talking with her mother next to their vegetable garden. The professor introduced us. Their mother, Mrs. Fang, invited us for tea and introduced her daughters: Liya, third-grader and bicycle passenger, and Jianmei, sixth-grader and bicyclist. Because Jianmei's Forever still had protective wrapping paper on its top bar, as if it had just come from the store, I asked if it was new.

Jianmei, who was gulping down rice in preparation for her afternoon at school, said proudly that she won it just last year. Her mother explained that the family offers their daughters prizes for each year that they sustain grades of 90% or better. In autumn each daughter names a prize she wants, and then for the rest of the school year she tries to win it. In third grade Jianmei won a set of nice clothes; in fourth grade, a golden wristwatch; in fifth grade, the Forever. (I said to the professor, in English, "Are you sure we're talking to *peasants*?")

Mrs. Fang then led us through her tiled kitchen to a room that held, along with awards won by Jianmei for track and basketball, another full-sized bicycle— a cherry-red "Cuckoo," also still wrapped to protect its paint. It was Jianmei's earlier bike. I was astonished; ten years ago here, the professor had told me, only one family in ten could afford even a single bicycle.

Jianmei explained that she wanted the Forever because it was strong and smooth enough to carry her little sister. With it, she rides not just to school but up to the university, off to a nearby temple, even to a town 22 miles away to see the world's largest carved Buddha.

As we walked away from the Fang household—so imbued with work and reward and independence—I said to the professor: "Don't you wish you grew up in a place like that?" A bit later I thought to myself: "I did grow up in a place like that." Riding off to school, studying hard, cycling ten and twenty miles on a whim—this was like being back in sixth grade in my small hometown.

On the same day I talked with the Fang family, stories of the Beijing massacre—of hundreds or perhaps thousands of citizens killed by army troops and tanks—were reaching our remote region. Soon travelers arrived with tales of killing in other provincial cities. Students began to flee our rural campus, fearing the army would next descend on them. I returned to Chengdu.

There, I tried to continue the work I had planned—looking for the city's used bicycle market, avoiding the army troops who had arrived to quell outbursts, gathering statistics on bicycle ownership. But I could not concentrate.

My mind was on Beijing. Finally I decided to return, to what just days before had been the world's most exuberant city.

Again I rode its leafy boulevards, but no excited voice at my shoulder asked what I thought of the students. No banners waved. No people smiled. All faces seemed as if carved, years ago, in soft stone—at once fixed and badly weathered.

Each evening, Beijing television proudly showed the now-barren Tiananmen Square, cleared of all students and, for that matter, all life. Understandably, the TV cameras did not show what people in Beijing had seen: citizens trying to stop tanks by shoving bicycles at them, flatbed tricycles turned into ambulances for slaughtered childen. Less understandably, the cameras often began their pan across the square with an image of a pile of crumpled bicycles.

That odd image haunted me for months, long after I had left China. Only slowly did I realize that the government had chosen that scene precisely. The government cameras wanted to show more than a few crushed machines. They wanted to show crushed dignity, crushed humanity, crushed freedom—so much that the bicycle means in China.

And finally I realized that of course the old men who cling to power in China would want to show off the crumpled bicycles of the young men and women who had called for freedom. How terrifying it must have been to those old men, to see millions of young people cycling toward them—so independent, so alive, so free—all those wheels turning and turning beyond the control of fear or fiat. Of course those old men would want to crush the cycles of the young. For they would know too well that history itself runs in cycles—sometimes foreign horses, sometimes self-running carts, always wheels of change. How sad: Four decades earlier these same old men, seeking to "raise the people's dignity," had set rolling the cycles of modern China. And then, in a few days of a Beijing spring, they sought to crush, all at once, cycles and dignity and change together. They might as easily have sought to stop the circling, round the sun, of earth's revolution. For as each spring comes round, the old fade and the young quicken. And every day throughout China, the wheels of freedom roll.

[1991]

JACK KEROUAC

(1922–1969)

Jack Kerouac was one of the best-known writers of the Beat generation. The term *Beat* has connotations of exhaustion (with contemporary American values of competition and conformity) as well as spiritual enlightenment ("beatific") and emulation of the spontaneous style, or beat, of jazz.

Precursors to the later countercultural movements like the hippies, the Beats rebelled against established traditions of behavior and of writing. Kerouac grew up in Lowell, Massachusetts, and attended Columbia University, which he left to go to sea. From 1943 to 1950, Kerouac hitchhiked around the United States and Mexico, supporting himself with odd jobs.

The selection that follows is taken from *On the Road*, an autobiographical novel about his travels alone and with other Beat figures. Published in 1957, the book helped popularize Beat style and inspire a whole genre of "road books." This selection, and the book in general, describe how driving around the highways and back roads of America becomes a means of rebellion, escape, freedom, and self-discovery.

From *On the Road*

It was drizzling and mysterious at the beginning of our journey. I could see that it was all going to be one big saga of the mist. "Whooee!" yelled Dean. "Here we go!" And he hunched over the wheel and gunned her; he was back in his element, everybody could see that. We were all delighted, we all realized we were leaving confusion and nonsense behind and performing our one and noble function of the time, *move*. And we moved! We flashed past the mysterious white signs in the night somewhere in New Jersey that say SOUTH (with an arrow) and WEST (with an arrow) and took the south one. New Orleans! It burned in our brains. From the dirty snows of "frosty fagtown New York," as Dean called it, all the way to the greeneries and river smells of old New Orleans at the washed-out bottom of America; then west. Ed was in the back seat; Marylou and Dean and I sat in front and had the warmest talk about the goodness and joy of life. Dean suddenly became tender. "Now dammit, look here, all of you, we all must admit that everything is fine and there's no need in the world to worry, and in fact we should realize what it would mean to us to UNDERSTAND that we're not REALLY worried about ANYTHING. Am I right?" We all agreed. "Here we go, we're all together . . . What did we do in New York? Let's forgive." We all had our spats back there. "That's behind us, merely by miles and inclinations. Now we're heading down to New Orleans to dig Old Bull Lee and ain't that going to be kicks and listen will you to this old tenorman blow his top"—he shot up the radio volume till the car shuddered—"and listen to him till the story and put down true relaxation and knowledge."

We all jumped to the music and agreed. The purity of the road. The white line in the middle of the highway unrolled and hugged our left front tire as if glued to our groove. Dean hunched his muscular neck, T-shirted in the winter night, and blasted the car along. He insisted I drive through Baltimore for traffic practice; that was all right; except he and Marylou insisted on steering while they kissed and fooled around. It was crazy; the radio was on full blast. Dean beat drums on the dashboard till a great sag developed in it; I did too. The poor Hudson—the slow boat to China—was receiving her beating.

"Oh man, what kicks!" yelled Dean."Now Marylou, listen really, honey, you know that I'm hotrock capable of everything at the same time and I have unlimited energy—now in San Francisco we must go on living together. I know just the place for you—at the end of the regular chain-gang run—I'll be home just a cut-hair less than every two days and for twelve hours at a stretch, and *man*, you know what we can do in twelve hours, darling. Meanwhile I'll go right on living at Camille's like nothin, see, she won't know. We can work it, we've done it before." It was all right with Marylou, she was really out for Camille's scalp. The understanding had been that Marylou would switch to me in Frisco, but I now began to see they were going to stick and I was going to be left alone on my butt at the other end of the continent. But why think about that when all the golden land's ahead of you and all kinds of unforeseen events wait lurking to surprise you and make you glad you're alive to see?

We arrived in Washington at dawn. It was the day of Harry Truman's inauguration for his second term. Great displays of war might were lined along Pennsylvania Avenue as we rolled by in our battered boat. There were B-29's, PT boats, artillery, all kinds of war material that looked murderous in the snowy grass; the last thing was a regular small ordinary lifeboat that looked pitiful and foolish. Dean slowed down to look at it. He kept shaking his head in awe. "What are these people up to? Harry's sleeping somewhere in this town. . . . Good old Harry. . . . Man from Missouri, as I am. . . . That must be his own boat."

Dean went to sleep in the back seat and Dunkel drove. We gave him specific instructions to take it easy. No sooner were we snoring than he gunned the car up to eighty, bad bearings and all, and not only that but he made a triple pass at a spot where a cop was arguing with a motorist—he was in the fourth lane of a four-lane highway, going the wrong way. Naturally the cop took after us with his siren whining. We were stopped. He told us to follow him to the station house. There was a mean cop in there who took an immediate dislike to Dean; he could smell jail all over him. He sent his cohort outdoors to question Marylou and me privately. They wanted to know how old Marylou was, they were trying to whip up a Mann Act idea. But she had her marriage certificate. Then they took me aside alone and wanted to know who was sleeping with Marylou. "Her husband," I said quite simply. They were curious. Something was fishy. They tried some amateur Sherlocking by asking the same questions twice, expecting us to make a slip. I said, "Those two fellows are going back to work on the railroad in California, this is the short one's wife, and I'm a friend on a two-week vacation from college."

The cop smiled and said, "Yeah? Is this really your own wallet?"

Finally the mean one inside fined Dean twenty-five dollars. We told them we only had forty to go all the way to the Coast; they said that made no difference to them. When Dean protested, the mean cop threatened to take him back to Pennsylvania and slap a special charge on him.

"What charge?"

"Never mind what charge. Don't worry about *that*, wise guy."

We had to give them the twenty-five. But first Ed Dunkel, that culprit, offered to go to jail. Dean considered it. The cop was infuriated; he said, "If you let your partner go to jail I'm taking you back to Pennsylvania right now. You hear that?" All we wanted to do was go. "Another speeding ticket in Virginia and you lose your car," said the mean cop as a parting volley. Dean was red in the face. We drove off silently. It was just like an invitation to steal to take our trip-money away from us. They knew we were broke and had no relatives on the road or to wire to for money. The American police are involved in psychological warfare against those Americans who don't frighten them with imposing papers and threats. It's a Victorian police force; it peers out of musty windows and wants to enquire about everything, and can make crimes if the crimes don't exist to its satisfaction. "Nine lines of crime, one of boredom," said Louis-Ferdinand Céline. Dean was so mad he wanted to come back to Virginia and shoot the cop as soon as he had a gun.

"Pennsylvania!" he scoffed. "I wish I knew what that charge was! Vag, probably; take all my money and charge me vag. Those guys have it so damn easy. They'll out and shoot you if you complain, too." There was nothing to do but get happy with ourselves again and forget about it. When we got through Richmond we began forgetting about it, and soon everything was okay.

Now we had fifteen dollars to go all the way. We'd have to pick up hitchhikers and bum quarters off them for gas. In the Virginia wilderness suddenly we saw a man walking on the road. Dean zoomed to a stop. I looked back and said he was only a bum and probably didn't have a cent.

"We'll just pick him up for kicks!" Dean laughed. The man was a raged, bespectacled mad type, walking along reading a paper-backed muddy book he'd found in a culvert by the road. He got in the car and went right on reading; he was incredibly filthy and covered with scabs. He said his name was Hyman Solomon and that he walked all over the USA, knocking and sometimes kicking at Jewish doors and demanding money: "Give me money to eat, I am a Jew."

He said it worked very well and that it was coming to him. We asked him what he was reading. He didn't know. He didn't bother to look at the title page. He was only looking at the words, as though he had found the real Torah where it belonged, in the wilderness.

"See? See? See?" cackled Dean, poking my ribs. "I told you it was kicks. Everybody's kicks, man!" We carried Solomon all the way to Testament. My brother by now was in his new house on the other side of town. Here we were back on the long, bleak street with the railroad track running down the middle and the sad, sullen Southerners loping in front of hardware stores and five-and-tens.

Solomon said, "I see you people need a little money to continue your journey. You wait for me and I'll go hustle up a few dollars at a Jewish home and I'll go along with you as far as Alabama." Dean was all beside himself with happiness; he and I rushed off to buy bread and cheese spread for a lunch in the car. Marylou and Ed waited in the car. We spent two hours in Testament waiting for Hyman Solomon to show up; he was hustling for his bread somewhere in town, but we couldn't see him. The sun began to grow red and late.

Solomon never showed up so we roared out of Testament. "Now you see, Sal, God does exist, because we keep getting hung-up with this town, no matter what we try to do, and you'll notice the strange Biblical name of it, and that strange Biblical character who made us stop here once more, and all things tied together all over like rain connecting everybody the world over by chain touch. . . ." Dean rattled on like this; he was overjoyed and exuberant. He and I suddenly saw the whole country like an oyster for us to open; and the pearl was there, the pearl was there. Off we roared south. We picked up another hitchhiker. This was a sad young kid who said he had an aunt who owned a grocery store in Dunn, North Carolina, right outside Fayetteville. "When we get there can you bum a buck off her? Right! Fine! Let's go!" We were in Dunn in an hour, at dusk. We drove to where the kid said his aunt had the grocery store. It was a sad little street that deadended at a factory wall. There was a grocery store but there was no aunt. We wondered what the kid was talking about. We asked him how far he was going; he didn't know. It was a big hoax; once upon a time, in some lost back-alley adventure, he had seen the grocery store in Dunn, and it was the first story that popped into his disordered, feverish mind. We bought him a hot dog, but Dean said we couldn't take him along because we neeeded room to sleep and room for hitchhikers who could buy a little gas. This was sad but true. We left him in Dunn at nightfall.

I drove through South Carolina and beyond Macon, Georgia, as Dean, Marylou, and Ed slept. All alone in the night I had my own thoughts and held the car to the white line in the holy road. What was I doing? Where was I going? I'd soon find out. I got dog-tired beyond Macon and woke up Dean to resume. We got out of the car for air and suddenly both of us were stoned with joy to realize that in the darkness all around us was fragrant green grass and the smell of fresh manure and warm waters. "We're in the South! We've left the winter!" Faint daybreak illuminated green shoots by the side of the road. I took a deep breath; a locomotive howled across the darkness, Mobile-bound. So were we. I took off my shirt and exulted. Ten miles down the road Dean drove into a filling station with the motor off, noticed that the attendant was fast asleep at the desk, jumped out, quietly filled the gas tank, saw to it the bell didn't ring, and rolled off like an Arab with a five-dollar tankful of gas for our pilgrimage.

[1957]

TED CONOVER

(1958–)

Ted Conover combines travel writing with documentary journalism. In the tradition of Jack London and countless other writers who took up the life of hobos and riders of the rails, Conover dropped out of college for a while, rode freight trains around the American West, and wrote about his experiences in *Rolling Nowhere* (1984). In his book *Coyotes: A Journey through the Secret World of America's Illegal Aliens* (1987), he traveled the border between Mexico and the United States. He explored the world of prison from the viewpoint of a guard in *Newjack: Guarding Sing-Sing* (2000). As a cab driver in Aspen, Colorado, he observed the lifestyles of the inhabitants of one of America's wealthiest resort communities and then wrote *Whiteout: Lost in Aspen* (1991).

In the passage below, taken from *Rolling Nowhere*, he has just been released from jail, and the brief experience of prison has turned him against a settled life of respectability, comfort, and security.

From *Rolling Nowhere*

The Denver & Rio Grande Western yards: a mythic, imagined place of my childhood. Here the trains that climbed from plains to mountains, winding their way through canyons and tunnels, over passes and trestles like muscular, writhing snakes, were set out uniformly, equidistant, arrow-straight. Here, momentarily, they were in suspended animation, resting from the last trip and getting readied for another. Switch engines pulled apart newly arrived trains, car by car, and remade them into new trains. Brakemen walked their length, connecting the air hoses between each car, and "car knockers"—railroad inspectors—checked the cars for damage. The units, nerve centers of the trains, disconnected themselves for refueling and repairs; when they returned, making the train whole, one knew which way the train was going, and more important, that it was about to leave.

Here, also, was where men boarded the trains, secretly, without benefit of ticket or conductor, in violation of the law. Today, that last part scared me. I sat under a bridge over which an interstate highway ran, and under which tracks led south out of the yard. All the way from downtown, I had painstakingly obeyed the law, crossing only in the crosswalks, obeying DON'T WALK signs as though they, too, had the power of arrest. Yet it was hard, as walking was the thing I most wanted to do in the world—walk and not stop, walk and get out of town, walk and be free.

It took a moment to become reaccustomed to brightness and shade, to wind blowing and clouds coming and going, to a temperature that moved up and down, not holding steady at a deadening sixty degrees. But after my enforced hibernation, I welcomed the outdoors—recklessly, for though I had emerged from jail with my jacket, my bedroll and other survival tools were gone. I didn't know what I would do; but I did know Lonny had been able to make do in circumstances much rougher than my own, and that I should be able to, too.

Yet my exhilaration at being out was undermined by my anger. President nearby or not, people should not be treated that way in America. And compared to what happened to other people, what happened to me was probably nothing. In Dallas, again and again I had heard poor people complaining about police brutality. Why had I always questioned them, assuming the real problem was a lack of respect for policemen?

Possibly worst was that the arrest had interrupted my daydream. The hobo trip, in other words, was in ways a lived-out fantasy. Entering the hobo world, I fancied I had entered a world free of responsibility and unjust authority. And even as the hobo subculture stands as a reproach to the dominant culture, I could reproach academe by doing schoolwork and *enjoying myself.*

But the cops had reminded me that the hobo's life was not a game. I realized I had not predicted the fright of it. Hoboes themselves, I supposed, could treat each other even worse than the cops did. Armed with a new realism, I took long, Treetop-style steps back to the jungle on the Platte, en route to the D & RGW yards. I wanted to say good-bye to Al and Tree.

But they had vanished, along with the dogs and the tarpaulin. A new tramp was there now, making use of the spool table and enjoying a lunch of a few leftover concessionaire's sandwiches. He said he didn't know where Tree and Al had gone, though he had heard from tramps down the river that cops had been there looking for "a real tall guy" the night before. He probably caught out on the "Nighttime Man," I thought to myself.

Earlier that week, on the way back from our dumpster hunt, Al had spied an old sleeping bag stashed in woods adjoining the river. Claiming finder's rights, he had hidden the bag in brush behind the tent. I checked the spot, told the surprised tramp it was mine, and had myself a new bedroll. By commandeering one of several surplus water jugs that littered the site, I had nearly a full complement of gear. I asked the tramp for directions to the Denver & Rio Grande yard, and had hiked there in the hot afternoon sun.

It was not a fun place to be. For company there was only an empty bottle of white port, ant lions beneath the sand, and a thousand FUCK YOU's scratched and painted on the beams of the bridge. FUCK YOU TOO, read one response. It could have been mine.

The yard's tower was tall and prominent, and I didn't dare venture into the yard to gather intelligence on train departures. Finally, though, dusk began to fall, and I scrambled down to ask a passing switchman for directions to a west-bound train. There was one called for soon, he answered quickly, glancing at the tower, and told me what track it was on. I found an empty and, as night fell, left Denver.

The train wound its serpentine way up into the mountains. I planted my feet firmly near the doorway and looked out over the plains, doing an about-face to see out the other door every time the train did a hairpin turn and changed direction. Denver sparkled with the variously colored lights of buildings, houses, and streets, and all of a sudden I felt very sad. Back there were cops and the jail but also, a million times more important, back there was my family. In Jack Kerouac's *On the Road*, which I had read over the summer, I had been struck by the frequent use of the word "sad" to describe almost anything connected with his travels—the "sad highway," the "sad town," the "sad American night." Why, I had wondered, did it have to be sad? Life on the road for me had always been adventuresome, unpredictable, exciting, more fun than sad. But tonight, the sad made sense. It could have been used to describe almost anything around me—the city view, the boxcar, the mountains ahead. It was my sadness, the sadness of moving alone, to destinations unknown. And I realized that night what must be common knowledge among hoboes: it's easier to be on the road when home is something you don't feel too good about, or miss too much.

But as the train climbed higher, and the air grew cooler, I steeled myself. Misgivings about leaving home and friends I had had before. But for now, I had resolved, I had to be tramping. Now I was a son and brother to one family; later, I might be husband and father to another. My own family would depend on me more heavily, and the risks I took would in a way be theirs.

And, of course, I had to tramp sometime, to have my own stories to tell, not those of someone's uncle, or the big kids, or a movie. Even if I didn't return to tell the stories . . . well, long ago I had decided that I'd rather go by falling off a freight into a bottomless gorge than by dying of heat prostration in the Washington, D.C., rush-hour traffic.

Slowly now, the train climbed steeply. Moonlight shone through the box-car doors, illuminating my breath and making the snow-capped mountaintops glow. Already the train had passed through a number of short tunnels, plunging me into darkness and a self-imposed paralysis, for I knew that the slightest imprudent move could send me through the doorway and into oblivion. Soon the train woud pass through one of the longest railroad tunnels on the continent, the six-mile-long Moffat tunnel, which cuts beneath an 11,500-foot high automobile pass and the Continental Divide. The Moffat was one of the Goliaths of the older, railriding boys of my childhood—the black hole of the rails, a dark space seemingly without end. Its blackness was surpassed in awfulness only by the dense accumulation of exhaust fumes inside. The best survival strategy, I had heard, was to place a wet handkerchief over the mouth. Since my bandanna had disappeared with my bedroll, I unbuttoned one of my cuffs, soaked it with water from my bottle, and, using that as my gas mask, suffered only slight dizziness.

The tunnel opened up on the ski area of Winter Park, and suddenly I was back in familiar territory. My family owned a vacation home in the adjacent town, and many times I had cross-country-skied on the railroad right-of-way to get from the house to the ski area. Often, too, I had waited at the crossing I would soon be passing through and marveled at the train, the only one I ever got to see up close.

Soon we chugged through the crossing, to the flash of red lights and the jangling of warning bells. I gazed out the door at the familiar road, with the familiar pines and spruce and, now that the exhaust had blown away, the familiar mountain smell. I thought of jumping off: the embankment was steep, but I could make it. I could take the house key from its hiding place, go inside, and take a shower and lie between warm sheets.

But I turned the other way. There was no such thing as home to hoboes—or if there was, it was only a memory—and I resolved it was time to get the idea out of my mind.

[1984]

WILLIAM LEAST HEAT-MOON

(1939–)

William Least Heat-Moon lost his job as an English professsor about the time his marriage was breaking up. He decided to escape it all and go on the road in a truck he had outfitted as a makeshift camper. In his first book, *Blue Highways* (1981), he writes of the small towns and the people he met while traveling the back roads of the United States (the ones marked in blue on the roadmaps) looking for a sense of history and community in forgotten, out-of-the way places. To his surprise, the book became a best-seller. Following that success, he decided to focus intensely on one small area in the middle of Kansas, criss-crossing Chase County and combining a sense of geography and history with his encounters in *Prairyerth* (1991). His most recent book is a study of Columbus as traveler and explorer, *Columbus in the Americas* (2002).

In the following selection from the first part of *Blue Highways*, Least Heat-Moon demonstrates how the journey outward can also become a search for one's past.

From *Blue Highways*

1

Beware thoughts that come in the night. They aren't turned properly; they come in askew, free of sense and restriction, deriving from the most remote of sources. Take the idea of February 17, a day of canceled expectations, the day I learned my job teaching English was finished because of declining enrollment at the college, the day I called my wife from whom I'd been separated for nine months to give her the news, the day she let slip about her "friend"—Rick or Dick or Chick. Something like that.

That morning, before all the news started hitting the fan, Eddie Short Leaf, who worked a bottomland section of the Missouri River and plowed snow off campus sidewalks, told me if the deep cold didn't break soon the trees would freeze straight through and explode. Indeed.

That night, as I lay wondering whether I would get sleep or explosion, I got the idea instead. A man who couldn't make things go right could at least go. He could quit trying to get out of the way of life. Chuck routine. Live the real jeopardy of circumstance. It was a question of dignity.

The result: on March 19, the last night of winter, I again lay awake in the tangled bed, this time doubting the madness of just walking out on things, doubting the whole plan that would begin at daybreak—to set out on a long (equivalent to half the circumference of the earth), circular trip over the back roads of the United States. Following a circle would give a purpose—to come around again—where taking a straight line would not. And I was going to do it by living out of the back end of a truck. But how to begin a beginning?

A strange sound interrupted my tossing. I went to the window, the cold air against my eyes. At first I saw only starlight. Then they were there. Up in the March blackness, two entwined skeins of snow and blue geese honking north, an undulating W-shaped configuration across the deep sky, white bellies glowing eerily with the reflected light from town, necks stetched northward. Then another flock pulled by who knows what out of the south to breed and remake itself. A new season. Answer: begin by following spring as they did—darkly, with neck stuck out.

2

The vernal equinox came on gray and quiet, a curiously still morning not winter and not spring, as if the cycle paused. Because things go their own way, my daybreak departure turned to a morning departure, then to an afternoon departure. Finally, I climbed into the van, rolled down the window, looked a last time at the rented apartment. From a dead elm sparrow hawks used each year came a high *whee* as the nestlings squealed for more grub. I started the engine. When I returned a season from now—if I did return—those squabs would be gone from the nest.

Accompanied only by a small, gray spider crawling the dashboard (kill a spider and it will rain), I drove into the street, around the corner, through the intersection, over the bridge, onto the highway. I was heading toward those little towns that get on the map—if they get on at all—only because some cartographer has a blank space to fill: Remote, Oregon; Simplicity, Virginia; New Freedom, Pennsylvania; New Hope, Tennessee; Why, Arizona; Whynot, Mississippi. Igo, California (just down the road from Ono), here I come.

3

A pledge: I give this chapter to myself. When done with it, I will shut up about *that* topic.

Call me Least Heat Moon. My father calls himself Heat Moon, my elder brother Little Heat Moon. I, coming last, am therefore Least. It has been a long lesson of a name to learn.

To the Siouan peoples, the Moon of Heat is the seventh month, a time also known as the Blood Moon—I think because of its dusky midsummer color.

I have other names: Buck, once a slur—never mind the predominant Anglo features. Also Bill Trogdon. The Christian names come from a grandfather eight generations back, one William Trogdon, an immigrant Lancashireman living in North Carolina, who was killed by the Tories for providing food to rebel patriots and thereby got his name in volume four of *Makers of America*. Yet to the red way of thinking, a man who makes peace with the new by destroying the old is not to be honored. So I hear.

One summer when Heat Moon and I were walking the ancestral grounds of the Osage near the river of that name in western Missouri, we talked about bloodlines. He said, "Each of the people from anywhere, when you see in them far enough, you find red blood and a red heart. There's a hope."

Nevertheless, a mixed-blood—let his heart be where it may—is a contaminated man who will be trusted by neither red nor white. The attitude goes back to a long history of "perfidious" half-breeds, men who, by their nature, had to choose against one of their bloodlines. As for me, I will choose for heart, for spirit, but never will I choose for blood.

One last word about bloodlines. My wife, a woman of striking mixed-blood features, came from the Cherokee. Our battles, my Cherokee and I, we called the "Indian wars."

For these reasons I named my truck Ghost Dancing, a heavy-handed symbol alluding to ceremonies of the 1890s in which the Plains Indians, wearing cloth shirts they believed rendered them indestructible, danced for the return of warriors, bison, and the fervor of the old life that would sweep away the new. Ghost dances, desperate resurrection rituals, were the dying rattles of a people whose last defense was delusion—about all that remained to them in their futility.

A final detail: on the morning of my departure, I had seen thirty-eight Blood Moons, an age that carries its own madness and futility. With a nearly desperate sense of isolation and a growing suspicion that I lived in an alien land, I took to the open road in search of places where change did not mean ruin and where time and men and deeds connected.

*   *   *

1

What happened next came about because of an obese child eating a Hi-Ho cracker in the back of an overloaded stationwagon. She gave me a baleful stare. As I passed, the driver, an obese woman eating a Hi-Ho, gave me a baleful stare. Ah, genetics! Oh, blood!

Blood. It came to me that I had been generally retracing the migration of my white-blooded clan from North Carolina to Missouri, the clan of a Lancashireman who settled in the Piedmont in the eighteenth century. As a boy, again and again, I had looked at a blurred, sepia photograph of a leaning tombstone deep in the Carolina hills. I had vowed to find the old immigrant miller's grave one day.

Highway 421 became I-85 and whipped me around Winston-Salem and Greensboro. For a few miles I suffered the tyranny of the freeway and watched rear bumpers and truck mudflaps. As soon as I could, I took state 54 to Chapel Hill, a town of trees, where I hoped to come up with a lead on the miller in the university library. All I knew was this: William Trogdon (1715–1783) supplied sundry items to the Carolina militia for several years during the Revolutionary War; finally, Tories led by David Fanning found him watering his horse on Sandy Creek not far from his gristmill and shot him. His sons buried him where he fell. Fanning terrorized the Piedmont through a standard method of shooting any man, white or red, who aided the patriots; and he was known to burn a rebel's home, even with a wife and children inside. Faster than King George, Colonel Fanning turned Carolinians to the cause.

After I'd given up in the library, by pure chance as if an omen, in a bookshop I came across an 1856 map showing a settlement named Sandy Creek east of Asheboro. That night I calculated the odds of finding in the woods a grave nearly two hundred years old. They were lousy.

The next morning I headed back toward Asheboro, past the roads to Snow Camp and Silk Hope, over the Haw River, into pine and deciduous hills of red soil, into Randolph County, past crumbling stone milldams, through fields of winter wheat. Ramseur, a nineteenth-century cotton-mill village secluded in the valley of the Deep River, was the first town in the county I came to. I had to begin somewhere. Hoping for a second clue, I stopped at the library to ask about Sandy Creek. Another long shot. "Of course," the librarian said. "Sandy Creek's at Franklinville. Couple miles west. Flows into Deep River by the spinning mill. Town's just sort of hanging on now. You should talk to Madge in the dry goods across the street. She knows county history better than a turtle knows his shell."

Madge Kivett was out of town, but a clerk took me back across the street to the Water Commissioner, Kermit Pell, who owned the grocery and knew something of local history. In Pell's store you still weighed vegetable seed on a brass counterbalance with little knobbed weights; the butcher's block was so worn in the center you could pour a bucket of water over it and only a pint would run off.

Pell, a graying, abdominous man with Groucho Marx eyebrows, chewed gum and continually took off and put on his spectacles. Sitting in a dugout of ledgers and receipt books, he couldn't reach the phone so I had to hand it to him the six times it rang. Between rings, it took an hour to get this: the miller's isolated grave had been covered by a new hundred-twenty-seven-acre raw water reservoir (the town bought the grave twice when two men claimed ownership— buying was cheaper than court). The old tombstone, broken up by vandals digging in the grave to look for relics, had been moved to the museum; the commissioners transferred a few token spades of dirt and put up a bronze and concrete marker a few feet from the original gravesite. The Asheboro *Courier-Tribune*, in an article dated two years earlier to the day, told of the imperiled grave setting off a hurried archaeological survey to turn up both colonial history and artifacts from a thousand years of Indian camps. The site, the clipping said, "although known to historians, is deep in the wilds of the creek."

"I've got to see it," I said.

"It's a hell of a walk in. You better know what you're doing before you go into that woods. I mean, it's way back in there."

"Can you give me directions?"

"Only one peson I know of could show you—if he would. Noel Jones over in Franklinville might lead you in. Lived along the creek all his life. He's getting on now, but you can ask for him at the mill."

2

Thick muddy water in the ancient millrace of Randolph Mills at Franklinville curled in slow menace like a fat water moccasin waiting for something to come to it. The mill ran on electicity now, and the race was a dead end—what went in didn't come out. Inside, spoked flywheels tall as men spun, rumbling the wavy wooden floors and plankways, but no one was around. It seemed a ghost mill turned by Deep River. I knocked on the crooked pine doors; I tapped on a clouded window and pressed close to see in. On the other side, an old mis-shapen face looked back and made me jump.

"Looking for Noel Jones!" I shouted.

The face vanished and reappeared at a doorway. It said, "Gone home. First street over," and disappeared again. I took the street, asked at a house, and found Jones at the end of the block.

"I know the place you're alookin' for," he said, "but I'm not up to goin' back in there just now. Got a molar agivin' me a deal of misery."

"I understand, but maybe you could describe the way."

He took off his cap and ran his hand over his head. "It's possible to walk in. Not so far you cain't. But directions gonna be hard. Sorry I cain't take you." He put his cap back on. "Tell you what. Get in my truck and I'll show you where to start. It'll keep my mind off this molar. One thing though, you got some work in front of you, son. And not aknowin' the way, well, that's a worry of its own."

In the warm afternoon, we followed a dirt road until it turned into a grassy trail so narrow the brush screeched against the windows. At a small clearing, he stopped. "This is my old family property," he said. "Just down the hill you can see Sandy Crick. The old mill of yours musta been right along there. Let me show you somethin' else."

We walked over to a cabin with only the back wall of logs still standing. Hanging to it was a warped kitchen cabinet lined with layers of newspaper. "July of 'thirty-six on this paper," Jones said. "Used to stick it up to keep wind out of the cracks. Pitiful. But look at the price of shoes."

He pulled a broken coffee cup from the cabinet, scowled, and put it back. "When I was a boy, an old fieldhand lived in this house. He was adyin' of pneumonia one night my daddy took me by, and I watched through the window. Man was out of his mind with fever, and he thrashed in bed. He thought he was aplowin' with his mule, John. 'Come on over, John! Pick it up there, John!' Whole night he and that mule plowed, we heard. Dead by mornin'. My daddy said he worked himself to death that night. Said if he coulda put the plow down, he mighta rested enough to live. Those days, it was hard livin' and no easier dyin'. Took thirteen months a year to grow 'bacca."

We went on through a hump of woods into another clearing where stood several small tobacco sheds with roofs falling in and an old smoke-house.

"These the old curin' barns where they dried the 'bacca. Haven't been used in years, but you can still smell the 'bacca inside." We walked over to one. "Look here. That hearth cover's a Model T hood the blacksmith's touched up with his hammer. Nobody ever heard of junk then. Junk's a modrun invention." We went in the low doorway. Poles that women once strung tobacco on were still in place under the roof.

Jones explained the curing: to "fix the color," leaves hung from cross poles for three days and nights as heat from the fire cured the burley. Skill in getting a good color could mean the difference between loss and profit. In his boyhood he had stayed up all night with the men tending the hearths. "They told stories the night long. Mostly true stories and mostly how troubles come in a thousand shapes."

We walked down the wooded hillside to Sandy Creek Reservoir. "Here musta been your granddaddy's mill. Before the dam, you could walk the length of the crick and hardly see the sun, trees grew so heavy. Animals too. Bobcats, foxes, weasels, deer, wood ducks. Good soil along the crick bottom. That's why Indians took to it. Had all they needed—water, meat, berries, protection."

"It's a big reservoir for such a little town."

"Got dry a few summers back—a real drouth—and the old town reservoir below where the dam is now almost run dry. Some people got scared. But I heard said too—couldn't tell you the truth of it—that there's some awantin' new industry in here. Mills don't produce like they did. Randolph Mills used to spin raw cotton into cloth. All we do today is finish cloth. Bleach, nap, and print patterns on cotton flannel mosly. We're printers now."

He sat on a rock and stared out over the flat, silent water to a bulldozed hill. "I'm not atakin' sides, I'm just atellin' you, but there's people who say there was plenty of water in that old reservoir. They say, 'Who needs a bigger reservoir?'"

"New industry means more people to buy clothes and open savings accounts."

"I mind my own business." He looked toward the dam. "Already a crack in the spillway. Cain't seem to get it fixed. I wouldn't say how long this crick'll say drowned." He got up. "Good fishin' along Sandy. Wasn't lunkers in it, but it was cool in here and the water moved. Now you cain't put as much as a fishin' line from the bank in that lake legally. No swimmin', no nothin'. It's a watchin' lake because that's about all you can do with it."

We walked back up the slope into the woods. Halfway, Jones stopped and edged his shoe into a small depression. "Dried up now, but this used to be a spring where women came to boil their wash clothes in iron pots. One time a woman was here, they say, abeatin' a rug clean with a stick. Had her daughter along. The little girl disappeared, but the woman just figured she was aplayin' hide and seek. The mother was athumpin' her rug when it commenced aturnin' red. She got vexed with the child for hidin' raspberries in the rug. She opened it to wash away the stain and her little girl rolled out. Child was hid in the rug. Woman run off through the woods acryin', 'I bludgeoned my baby! I beat my baby dead!' Next night she come out here to a big oak and hung herself with a bedsheet. That sheet, they say, blowed in the trees until it rotted away. Terrified many a man acomin' through at night."

On the road back, Jones pointed out the trail to start with. "Grave's yonder, dead ahead, but the hills and water is in the way. Woods gets terrible heavy over that first rise, and if you follow the reservoir around, you'll be in water or mud most the way. The grave sits out on a little tip of land about seven feet above the water line."

"I'll try through the woods. Get that molar fixed."

"Gonna have to see a tooth dentist. Stop by tomorrow if you make it. Best you wait 'til mornin', or you'll be wipin' shadows all the way."

3

But I didn't wait until morning. The smell in the pines was sweet, the spring peepers sang, and the trail over the first hill was easy. Whippoorwills ceaselessly cut sharp calls against the early dark, and a screech owl shivered the night. Then the trail disappeared in wiry brush. I began imagining flared nostrils and eyed, coiled things. Trying to step over whatever lay waiting, I took longer strides. Suddenly the woods went silent as if something had muffled it. I kept thinking about turning back, but the sense that the grave was just over the next hill drew me in deeper. Springs trickled to the lake and turned bosky coves to mud and filled the air with a rank, pungent odor. I had to walk around the water, then around the mud—three hundred yards to cross a twenty-foot inlet. Something heavy and running from me mashed off through the brush.

When I was a boy, my mother would try to show the reality of danger by making up newspaper headlines that described the outcome of foolhardy activity. I could hear her: REMAINS OF LONE HIKER FOUND. She would give details from the story: " . . . only the canteen was not eaten."

Common sense said to turn back, but the old sense in the blood was stronger. I compromised: one more cave. It wasn't there. On the ridge above the last cove I went sprawling over something hard. Concrete. Had the grave been open, I'd have fallen into it.

A brass plate indicated that the original grave lay just beyond the shoreline. "Who knows the fate of his bones?" Sir Thomas Browne asked. Whatever was left of the old miller, whatever the red soil and grave robbers and town commissioners had missed, was now under ten feet of Sandy Creek. Even this far back in the fastness, the twentieth century had found him out. Now, the citizens drank from his grave.

I sat so long, the sky cleared and showed all of the moonrise. I tried to imagine the incident here, tried to see the seditious old miller as he lay bleeding to death on the white Piedmont flint, and I wondered whether he knew he was dying for something greater than himself.

The smooth, dark water reflected stars as brilliant points of light—a mirror couldn't have shown a crisper image. I went down to it and washed away the thicket and sweaty dust. In my splashing, I broke the starlight. And then I too drank from the grave.

[1981]

WILL FERGUSON

(1964–)

Will Ferguson left home in Canada to teach English in Japan. Learning Japanese gave him the confidence to attempt the ambitious feat of hitchhiking the length of the country. He chose the season of cherry blossoms, the most festive time in Japan, to make his way from one end of the country to the other, following the blooms from south to north. He suspected that hitchhiking might provide a way to get beyond the formalities of Japanese culture and the obstacles of being a foreigner (*gaijin*). The natives themselves did not think that Japanese drivers would offer him rides, but Ferguson found the opposite to be true. Better yet, the Japanese opened up to him in the privacy of their cars, which he perceived as extensions of their homes.

In this selection from *Hokkaido Highway Blues: Hitchhiking Japan* (1998), Ferguson becomes, for a comic moment, like one of the family, pestered by the Japanese children in the back seat of the car.

From *Hokkaido Highway Blues*

All things considered, there are only two kinds of men in the world—those who stay at home and those who do not. The second are the more interesting.

—Rudyard Kipling, as quoted in *The Honorable Visitors*

His name was Mr. Migita and he was driving a big boat of a car, shiny-black like cobalt and filled with kids. In the front seat was his daughter, a junior-high-school student simply agog at the sight of me, and in the back were his two sons, around seven and five years old.

Mr. Migita asked me where I was going and when I said Cape Sata, he told me I was heading in the wrong direction. He offered to take me back out to the coast, so I crawled in and faced the gaping stares of the two boys. You could tell what they were thinking: Dad's gone mad. It was as though their father had let a large bear into the backseat.

Mr. Migita looked at me in the rearview mirror. "Can you speak Japanese?"

Now, one thing I've noticed about travel writers in Japan is that they tend to reproduce the conversations they have in Japanese as though they spoke the language fluently: "*Why yes, my good man,*" *I said to the chap in perfect Kantō dialect. "I am fully able to converse in your language. Why, what do you think we've been speaking all this time?*" At the same time, any English spoken by the Japanese is presented as being moronically inept. "*You no go Toyko. Tokyo far. Go with car. Faaar!*" After careful consideration, I have decided to follow this time-honored, self-aggrandizing method, even though I speak Japanese in what would best be presented as thick ungrammatical pidgin slang. (Unless noted, all conversations in this book were originally in Japanese. Or at least something that resembles Japanese.)

"Why yes," I said to Mr. Migita in fluent Kantō dialect, "I am fully able to converse in your language."

The younger boy, Hidenori, was becoming suspicious. "Are you American?" No. "Then you're Japanese." No. "Well, if you aren't American and you aren't Japanese, what are you?"

Put like that, I wasn't quite sure. "I'm a *tanuki*," I said, and they burst into peals of laughter.

"You're not a tanuki!"

"Sure I am." Tanuki are creatures of folklore in Japan: raccoon-dogs with huge bellies and gigantic testicles who roam the forests drinking saké and trying to seduce young maidens by passing themselves off as noblemen.

The boys laughed and laughed, the daughter giggled behind her hand, and Mr. Migita eyed me warily from the rearview mirror. Hidenori then asked me with grave sincerity, "Are you really a tanuki?" His older brother biffed him one on the head. "You idiot, of course he's not a tanuki! He's an American." And everyone laughed some more, as the little guy rubbed his head and grinned sheepishly.

"Do you know how tanuki make music?" I asked them.

"Sure!" they yelled. "They use their stomachs like a drum!" Hidenori then proceeded to show me how by punching himself repeatedly in the stomach. "Very good," I said, but he kept on going.

"Ah, that's fine," I said. "You can stop anytime." He continued pummeling himself in the stomach even as his eyes watered. "Come on," I said, and then, slipping into English, "*I get the picture, kid.*"

His eyes widened with an audible *boing.* "English! You speak English! Say something, say something in English."

"*Wayne Newton is the Antichrist.*"

"Wow! What does that mean?"

"It's a poem. Kind of a haiku."

When we reached the coastal highway, Mr. Migita pulled over and told me to wait in the car. (You could tell he was a real Papa; he talked to me the same way he addressed his five-year-old.) He made a call from a pay phone and when he returned he said, "I told my wife we'd be late. We're going to Sata."

The kids cheered and the three of us in the back did the Wave. Mr. Migita then told his daughter to change seats and he moved me up front. I had been promoted.

The highway twisted from one hairpin to another and there I was, sitting right up front like a big person. I swung my feet and watched the palm trees and villages spin by. There are no roads in Sata, just corners joined together. The corners kept coming and coming, and I began to get queasy. I could feel my stomach percolating—never a pleasant sensation—and soon I was threatening to erupt, volcanolike, across Mr. Migita's dashboard. Even in my stupor I realized that throwing up on your host was a bad way to start a relationship, and I fought hard to keep my lunch (pork and rice with a raw egg) from making an unexpected encore. We came to the parking lot just in time, and I bolted from the car and bent over, gulping down fresh air and trying not to faint. The littlest boy came up and punched me in the stomach. "You're not a tanuki!" he said.

"*I'll kill you, you little shit.*"

"Hey," he called to his dad, "he's talking poetry again!"

When my inner ear had stopped spinning like a gyroscope and my stomach had ceased its amusing Spasm Dance, I joined the others at the tunnel. Mr. Migita had paid my entrance fee and there was no way I could talk him out of it.

"You are my guest," he said.

No, I am a freeloader hitching a ride. "Thank you," I said, as I accepted his generosity.

I did manage to decline the squid, however, even though Migita's daughter offered me her last tentacle. Standing at the top of the observation deck overlooking Cape Sata, I told her and her brothers about the mythical, faraway land of Ka-Na-Da, where children didn't have to go to school on Saturday or wear uniforms or even actually learn anything, and they sighed with understandable envy.

"Do you have a gun?" the youngest asked, and his older brother, Toshiya, immediately chimed in, "Yes, did you ever shoot anybody?"

"No," I said. "Only evil Americans shoot people. In Ka-Na-Da everyone lives in peace and harmony."

It sure is great being a Canadian. You get to share all the material benefit of living next door to the United States, yet at the same time you get to act smug and haughty and morally superior. You just can't beat that kind of irresponsibility.

"Tell us more about Ka-Na-Da," said the children, and I obliged.

It was almost dusk when we left Sata. The sun was throwing long shadows across the road, and Mr. Migita had decided that I should come back to Kanoya City and have supper with him and his family. He pulled over to stock up on beer, and while he was gone his daughter leaned up and whispered in my ear, in English so soft I almost missed it. "My name is Kayoko. I am fine. And you?"

She then leaned back in her seat, obviously pleased with herself. Her brothers were dying to know what she had said. "Tell us, tell us!" they demanded, but she held her head high and proud and didn't say a word.

The Migitas lived on the outskirts of Kanoya City, in a two-story apartment block that faced an open field. Mr. Migita's wife welcomed me without batting an eye and, like a conjurer, she produced a full-course meal out of thin air. We nudged our way in around their low dining-room table and the food never stopped coming: raw fish with sinus-clearing horseradish, fried vegetables, noodles, more fish, salad, seaweed, soup, mini-sausages. It became a challenge to see if they could ever fill me up. Mr. Migita kept topping my glass with beer and encouraging my gluttony until finally, bloated like a water balloon, I conceded defeat. Mrs. Migita cleared the table of the wreckage and debris, and her husband and I settled back, sucking on toothpicks like a pair of feudal lords. This may sound sexist and insensitive and politically incorrect—and it is—but I had long since learned that had I offered to wash the dishes, or worse, had I *insisted*, I would only have humiliated Mrs. Migita. And anyway, I'm a lazy git and I was weighed down with forty pounds of excess food at the time.

The kids were doing their homework in front of the television. Which is to say, they were *not* doing their homework, they were watching television. It was clear that my presence had caused a lapse of household rules, and whenever their father absentmindedly looked over at them, they all began to scribble away with feigned studiousness. A sci-fi animation show was moving stiffly across the screen. Everyone in it had huge blue eyes and ridiculous yellow hair and all the fluidity of a comic book being flipped through—*slowly*. Man, I hate Japanese animation. Give me some good live-action drama any day: Ultraman or Godzilla or Mothra. *Oh no! A giant moth!* Those were the classics. But you tell that to kids today and they just don't listen.

This isn't true, of course. Godzilla and Ultraman are still superstars with Japanese children, and with adults as well. Godzilla is always turning up to stomp on Tokyo. The filmmakers churn those movies out like clockwork, and

Tokyo Tower has been destroyed so many times you'd think they'd have given up by now. *Rebuild it? What's the point? Godzilla will just come and knock it over again.*

Sometimes, Godzilla destroys other major metropolii, like Osaka or Nagoya, just for a change of pace, but mainly he sticks to Tokyo. The smaller cities in Japan have compained about this. They're jealous. The citizens of Fukuoka City even went so far as to circulate a petition asking—nay, *begging*—the producers of the Godzilla movies to destroy their fair city in the next movie. Thousands of people signed these petitions and after years of pressure the producers relented and said, "All right, we'll destroy Fukuoka. Quit whining." Everyone in Fukuoka was delighted to hear this. Newspaper headlines boasted GOOD NEWS! GODZILLA TO DESTROY OUR CITY, and when it was later revealed that Godzilla would in fact rampage over all of Kyushu, the entire island was simply delirious with joy.

Mr. Migita eventually did notice what his kids were up to, and they had that immortal parent-child conversation, one so innate I believe it is imbedded right in the DNA. It goes something like this: Hey you kids, turn off the TV, it's bedtime. Just a few minutes more, please, Dad, please. No, you have school tomorrow. But the good part is coming, please, Dad, please. No! I said no, and when I say no I mean no, so the answer is no.

As usual, the children won. The animated characters blew up the planet and everyone was very happy, and the three kids filed off to bed. Mr. Migita and I, meanwhile, were on our sixth bottle of Yebisu Beer. He cleared a space on the table and began spreading out maps like a general planning a campaign.

"You can do it," he said. "But we must chart your way with great care."

We sat up late into the night, he and I, tracing highways with red pens, and with me making copious notes. His wife sat patiently for a while but then, somehow, vanished. All the lights were out., except for the one directly over our table. As Mr. Migita and I sat in the pool of light, hunched over the maps, we really did look like a pair of generals planning a campaign. Or maybe samurai retainers plotting a revenge attack over some obscure point of honor. Or maybe a couple of boys in a tree house drawing a treasure map with lots of skull-and-crossbones and backwards s's. Either way, it was all very serious.

Eventually we came up with a complex course that zigzagged brilliantly across Japan and that made complete sense to us at the time. But the next day and miles away, when I unrolled Mr. Migita's maps, the routes we had marked and the cryptic asides I had jotted down with such conviction were now completely incomprehensible: "Good here, but not overland—highway changes to new one, must check to always see—Do *not* (and here I had underlined the word *not* forcibly several times) cross highway—wait at other places—West instead?—Check as I go."*

---

*This is, I believe, how the Vietnam War was planned: late at night and over a couple of beers. Cambodia—invade?—check as we go."

It was two in the morning by the time Mr. Migita and I finished our cunning plan. We congratulated ourselves heartily and opened another bottle of Yebisu. By this point, he and I were blood brothers and we vowed eternal loyalty and friendship. He rolled up the maps with that careful deliberation people get when they have consumed too much alcohol, and we shook hands. Again. We did that a lot, often in lieu of coherent conversation.

M. Migita straightened himself up and said, with sudden determination, "You are my friend. You do not need to hitchhike. I will give you the money for a train ticket."

I was taken aback. "I'm not hitchhiking because I can't afford a train ticket." Had he offered me food and shelter, because he thought I was broke? He was equally puzzled. If I wasn't short of funds, why was I hitchhiking? Why did I want to go all the way to Hokkaido in the company of strangers?

I assured him that the reason was not financial. Then I told him about Amakusa. For my first two years in Japan I lived in the most beautiful place on earth: the islands of Amakusa, south of Nagasaki. I taught in fishing villages lost in time, in misty coves with weathered temples and unexpected church spires. Amakusa is where the Jesuits of Portugal first landed in Japan, and it was in Amakusa that I first discovered the Power of the Thumb.

It was a discovery borne of necessity. My work involved commuting between fishing villages without a car in an area where the buses apparently ran only on odd-numbered vernal equinoxes. Buses in Amakusa were like UFOs; I heard a lot about them but I never actually saw one. So I began hitching rides from school to school across the islands, much to the consternation of my supervisor. What began as a necessity, soon became something else. It became a way *inside*. The car is an extension of the home, but without any of the prescribed formalities that plague Japan. The hitchhiker in Japan slips in under the defenses, as both guest and travel companion. Bumming rides became its own reward, the journey its own destination.

In this spirit, I had set out for Hokkaido.

Arduous solo travel has a long history in Japan, and I was following in a proud tradition. The mendicant poet Matsuo Bashō wandered the highways of the deep north in the late fifteenth century and wrote a classic travel narrative about it. Three hundred years later an Englishwoman named Lesley Downer retraced his footsteps, and in 1980, Alan Booth *walked* the entire length of Japan, north to south, and wrote a travel narrative of his own. But these are solitary ways to see the country. I didn't want to travel among the Japanese, I wanted to travel with them. I didn't want to walk Japan, as Alan Booth had done, precisely because it is such a lonely, aloof way to travel. Also, it would have involved a lot of walking. Personally, I peferred zipping along in an air-conditioned car. Tromping down a highway all day often put Booth in a sour mood; but when you are constantly prevailing upon the kindness of strangers—

as a hitchhiker must—it keeps you in a positive frame of mind. Call it Zen and the Art of Hitchhiking. The Way of the Lift. The Chrysanthemum and the Thumb. Heady on beer and the sound of my own voice, the aphorisms spilled out unchecked.

"Good-bye, *Gaijin-san*," said the lady of the house, bowing to me from the driveway as her husband and I drove away. "Good-bye and thank you."

There was a time I would have rankled over someone calling me *gaijin-san*. The word *gaijin* means "outsider," and is derived from the term *gai-koku-jin*, "outside-country-person." When the suffix *san* is added to gaijin, it means Mr. Outsider. This was how the lady in Nango referred to me. Most Japanese insist that the word *gaijin* is strictly an abbreviated form with no undertone of racism intended, but they are wrong. Unintentional racism is still racism. Like *gringo*, the word *gaijin* has an edge to it. And when I ask my Japanese friends how they would feel if I were to refer to them in a similarly abbreviated form—*Jap*—their jaws harden and they insist that it is not the same thing at all.

Like most visible minorities living in Japan, I went through a hypersensitive phase. It happens after the initial euphoria has worn off and you realize, "Hey! Everyone is talking about me! And they're looking at me. What do they think I am, some kind of foreigner or something!"

We became Gaijin Detectors. It's like a silent dog whistle. It got so I could detect a whispered, "Look, a gaijin!" across a crowded street, and spin and glare simultaneously at everyone within a fifty-mile radius.

Even when I could understand the language, I ran into problems. The word for the inner altar of a Shinto shrine sounds exactly like gaijin. I remember visiting a shrine in Kyoto and having a tour group come up behind me. The tour guide pointed in my direction and said, "In front of us, you can see the *inner altar*. This *inner altar* is very rare, please be quiet and show respect. No photographs. Flashbulbs can damage the *inner altar*." Except, of course, I didn't hear *inner altar*, I heard *foreigner*. It was a very surreal moment.

Looking back, the biggest culture shock about Japan was not the chopsticks or the raw octopus, it was the shock of discovering that no matter where you go you instantly become the topic of conversation. At first it's an ego boost. You feel like a celebrity. "Sorry, no autographs today, I'm in a hurry." But you soon realize that in Japan foreigners are not so much celebrities as they are objects of curiosity and entertainment. It is a stressful situation, and it has broken better men than me.

And yet it seems so petty when you put it down on paper: They look at you, they laugh when you pass by, they say "Hello!" They say "Foreigner!" They even say, "Hello, Foreigner!" But it's like the Chinese water torture. It slowly wears you down, and this relentless interest has driven many a foreigner from Japan.

It is still fairly mild. I tried to imagine what would happen if the tables were turned. I think of my own hillbilly hometown in northern Canada, and I wonder what kind of greeting the beetle-browed, evolutionarily challenged layabouts at the local tavern would give a lone Japanese backpacker who wandered into their midst.

I stilll hate the word *gaijin* and I stilll hate it when people gawk at me or kids follow, shouting, "Look, a gaijin! A gaijin!" But I have also learned an important distinction, and one that has made all the difference to my sanity. It was explained to me by Mr. Araki, a high-school teacher I once worked with. "Gaijin means outsider. But gaijin-san," he insisted, "is a term of affection." Sure enough, once I started paying closer attention to who was saying *gaijin* and who was saying *gaijin-san*, I discoverd that Mr. Araki was right. *Gaijin* is a label. *Gaijin-san* is a role.

In Japan, people are often referred to not by their name but by the role they play. Mr. Policeman. Mr. Post Office. Mr. Shop Owner. As a foreigner, you in turn play your role as the Resident Gaijin, like the Town Drunk or the Village Idiot. You learn to accept your position, and even take it as an affirmation that you do fit in—albeit in a very unsettled way—and you begin to enjoy Japan much more.

[1998]

PETER CHILSON

(1961–)

Peter Chilson, who teaches in the English Department at Washington State University, served as a Peace Corps Volunteer in Niger, then returned to the West African country with a Fulbright grant to study bush taxis, the makeshift vehicles that ply the single, accident-filled highway of Niger. He recalls in *Riding the Demon: On the Road in West Africa* (1999) that he was fascinated with travel even as a child: "My first memory is of a road." Chilson recounts in his book how people in Niger rely on bush taxis to get around the country. As part of his research, Chilson rode with and befriended some of Niger's long-distance taxi drivers.

In the selection that follows, he comes to appreciate these drivers as "a dashing, reckless male elite, akin to the image of early airplane pilots." Through them, he studies the culture of the road, which is often in Niger a dangerous and chaotic place.

From *Riding the Demon*

The road in Africa is more than a direction, a path to take. After you've paid the passage and taken your seat, the road becomes the very concern, the center of life over every mile, a place where you realize, suddenly, that you have surrendered everything. Even the right to survive. The first time on the road in a bush taxi is like boarding a rickety plane or bus only to find you've been kidnapped, which places every experience that follows in a different, sobering light. For me, the term *bush taxi* became far more than just a road transport term; it became an image of memory and road culture.

After college, in 1985, I went to West Africa, where I was first a Peace Corps English teacher in Niger and then a journalist based in Ivory Coast. I traveled in bush taxis across a dozen countries. The endurance and ingenuity of drivers, mechanics, and passengers—and their curiously fatalistic view of life—frightened and fascinated me. I first rode a bush taxi on my way to my Peace Corps post. The vehicle, so heavily dented that it resembled a crumpled shoebox, was an early Mercedes heavy truck with a cab that looked out over a wide snout. The radiator hung at an angle, as if someone had tacked it to the front of the engine as an afterthought. I could see steel webbing on the tires where the treads had worn away. Someone had refashioned the trailer by cutting window squares in the sides and installing plywood benches for thirty people. But in fact, some fifty passengers sat inside, squeezed onto bench boards that were screwed into metal frames bolted to the floor. Four men were stacking luggage five feet high on the roof—nylon bags, bed frames, mattresses, grain sacks, a bookcase, bundles of sugarcane, chickens in a palm-rope cage. When I paid my fare, the ticket seller at a wooden table must have read something in my face. He smiled and pointed at the bus. "*Taxi de brousse*," he said— It's a bush taxi.

Inside, I sat on a bench with room for five but packed with nine: two old farmers in tattered khaki robes; three delightfully happy, very large women wearing colorful cotton cloth wraps and carrying a baby each; and me, struggling for a space on the aisle. Cultures blended in this vehicle: Fulani men with fine-boned faces and conical hats; women traveling on market business—women I had seen firmly directing the men loading their goods on the roof; Tuareg men in indigo turbans that hid their faces; and Hausa merchants in bright, wide-flowing robes called *boubous* and striped cylindrical caps. I lost track.

After three and a half years, I left West Africa, exhausted, my nerves raw. I was glad for the respite but dissatisfied with my understanding of the place and its effect on me. That alone does not explain why I wanted to go back and once again face fear on the road. There was as well my curiosity about the road culture and the story it had to tell. And there was restlessness: a desire to know better the outposts of my limitations.

In 1990, I began planning my return to Africa. I spent two years working on my French and Hausa, and studying African transport, history, literature, and religion. I pored over maps and interviewed road engineers and historians. I drew up a research proposal and won a Fulbright grant. I gave up my apartment. I made out my will.

In 1992, I landed back in Niger having decided not to travel the entire continent—too difficult to do without inexhaustible time and money. I chose a tighter focus: to filter the road's story and character through the experience of Niger, the African country I know best. Although my story is chronological, it does not follow a steady geographic progression. I made the southeastern city of Zinder my home base, and I traveled many roads over and over again with the same driver, Issoufou Garba. I wanted to get to know one driver well enough to understand his point of view. I detoured occasionally into Nigeria—whose northern regions share much with Niger culturally and geographically—and hitchhiked from Niamey to Abidjan in Ivory Coast, riding in cotton trucks. In Niger, I also traveled with other bush taxi drivers, truckers, road engineers, an anthropologist, Niger's only licensed woman commercial driver, and a customs officer. In my time on the road I sometimes thought of a Sierra Leonian official who years before told me his opinion of Washington, D.C., which he had visited once. "It makes me crazy," he said. "Those damned traffic lights and speed limits."

It isn't that automobiles or the road hold more cultural importance in Africa than in the West, or that accidents there are more gruesome. Somehow the road takes a more dangerous, visceral, and spiritual position in everyday life in Africa. Demons dwell in wrecks strewn about like the carnage of a vainglorious hunt: a minibus upended against a tree as if attempting escape, a blackened truck overturned in a ditch.

Accidents on United States roads attract stares, slow traffic, and are quickly cleared away. On African roads, car wrecks are as common as mile markers. And the remains stay in place for months or years. The violence predates the automobile, tracing its roots to the old Saharan camel caravans that fell under attack by desert nomads, the Tuaregs, and to the destructive itineraries followed by European military missions at the end of the nineteenth century. Those expeditions' pathways often roughly match the motor highways—unintentional monuments to murder and plunder.

The African road is about blood and fear, about the ecstasy of arrival: the relief of finding yourself alive at the end of a journey and the lesser relief of passing unscathed through another army checkpoint. The road is boredom, joy, and terror punctuated by heat in the air and under your feet. The African road is a world of extremes lived out with the punching of a foot against a gas pedal.

As we approached that rising black smoke, I saw a clearer shape: a thick, leaning column like a giant tether to the sky. The driver kept an eye on the smoke and uttered a prayer to himself in Arabic, not his language or mine, but it was a prayer I had heard before and understood: *"Belsfemallah Arahman Arahim"*—a plea for God's protection. Then he struck his chest lightly with his right fist and fell quiet. A moment later, as the plume of smoke got closer, higher, blacker, he mumbled and frowned, shook the index finger of his right hand at the smoke as if he had just identified a thing he'd rather not encounter, and made a sound: *"Yai, yai, yai."*

The next minute we rounded a curve to see five cars backed up behind flames and smoke on the road, as if the asphalt demon itself had reared up to reveal its face. We were just in time to see a burst of flame as part of the petrol load ignited. The sight sickened me, already fatigued by fear. I could feel myself going up in the flames, wishing it would just happen, finally conclude in a spectacular, painless explosion that would turn my life to vapor and end the fear and uncertainty of the road. When I began traveling, I had not expected this risk, this emotion.

As I sat in the shade of that tree, risk consumed my thoughts. I was nauseous, in need of a walk to clear my head but afraid of what I might find lying on the ground: human remains that might have been mine had I left earlier that morning, reminders of the terrible fate that might lay ahead for me. I didn't think to just walk away from the wreck. Clear thought didn't come. All I knew was on that spot of earth, off the road, I felt safe.

Transport in Africa is a free-for-all system so chaotic that few travelers, even Africans, agree on a precise definition of the bush taxi. Consider this broad interpretation: Bush taxis are dangerous, dilapidated, slow, crowded, demoralizing, and suffocating; they are also fast, intimate, exciting, equalizing, and enlightening. They are bowls of human soup, microscope slides of society, mobile windows on the raw cultural, economic, and political vitality of Africa. Most bush taxis are Peugeot or Toyota station wagons, minibuses, or pickups, but big semis and cars of other makes do the job as well: Renaults, Mercedes, Mitsubishis, Hondas. More specifically, bush taxis are private cars rented out to transport goods and people. They are unregulated; they leave when they are full and arrive whenever. Bush taxis are cheap, are used by all levels of society, and are an important means of transporting trade goods. Any automobile can qualify, but most come secondhand from Europe.

Few Africans own cars, and African governments cannot support large transport systems. Bush taxis fill the void, making up most of the rural motor traffic. Much of what is manufactured, smuggled, or grown in Africa passes weekly through vast, seething outdoor car depots—the motor parks—in cities, and through smaller parks in villages. Similar systems exist in many countries where private car owners are comparatively few, from the Middle East to Southeast Asia, from Africa to South America. In other words, those who own cars cash in on them.

I spoke about bush taxis with John Riverson, a civil engineer from Ghana who studies African rural transport for the World Bank, in Washington, D.C.

Riverson views bush taxis as tools of reality. We talked in his cramped office amid shelves of technical reports and photos of road projects.

"There is such a deprivation of transport that people are grateful to have anything that moves," he told me, pointing out that in rural areas most vehicles, government owned or private, serve as bush taxis at some point. Riverson's words called to mind a government ambulance driver in Niger who took on passengers at four dollars a head while delivering medicine to villages in a Land Rover ambulance. Riverson acknowledged the difficulty of defining the bush taxi, but offered this rough guideline: "If we're looking at bush taxis as something identifiable, we're looking at vehicles in the range of three tons' weight"—starting with heavier minibuses, then pickups, station wagons, and sedans. But the number and kinds of vehicles used as bush taxis fluctuate between countries.

Our conversation came down to this: bush taxis are the legacy of an overburdened but vital freelance rural transport network that supports West Africa's economies—a network starved of motor vehicles, spare parts, fuel, mechanics, drivers, and decent roads. Whatever rolls, works.

It occurred to me that the growing crowd on both sides of the wreck was remarkably calm. I hadn't noticed where my fellow passengers had gone, but I realized that only I seemed to be alone. All around me people sat in the shade, sleeping, talking, or eating. Children played and traveling merchants laid out their products on the ground or on small folding wooden tables—clothes, vegetables, cheap jewelry. The scene looked as if all these people, perhaps two hundred by now, were traveling together in one big group. Only small clusters of drivers and a few children paid the burning wreck close attention. This was not a festive crowd, but rather a respectful and patient one that seemed to know better than to argue or complain about something they could not control. Being held up on the road by a calamity was a common event, something not to obsess about but to deal with. Why not sleep or do a little business during the wait?

A man sitting with a woman and a baby a few yards away from me rose to his feet and approached, carrying something wrapped in newspaper. I looked up and smiled, though we had never met.

"Have you got food?" he asked.

"No, I'm not hungry, thank you."

"You will be hungry. You must eat. God knows how long we will be here." He watched me for a moment and then handed me the object in the newspaper. "It's meat, take it."

I was embarrassed but grateful, and I knew better than to refuse a food offering. I shook his hand and took the meat, which turned out to be roasted chicken breast. "Thank you, sir."

"It's nothing, my friend." The man walked back to his family.

In Africa, there are fewer than twenty million motor vehicles to serve 700 million people. The number of cars that actually works is far less. Car accidents in Africa, according to the World Bank, number eight to ten times higher, proportionately, than in developed nations and are a leading cause of death. In Nigeria, home to 90 million people, road accidents consume 2 percent of the gross national product in destroyed vehicles, material, and lives—around 100,000 people injured and ten thousand deaths a year, according to Nigeria's Federal Road Safety Commission. In contrast, in the United States, with its 250 million people and 145 million passenger cars, the figure hovers around forty thousand deaths each year.

Niger has sixteen thousand passenger vehicles and eighteen thousand commercial cars to serve its 9 million people. There are eight thousand miles of roads, two thousand miles of them paved; the rest are packed dirt road and sandy track. Almost 2,000 people are reported injured annually in road accidents; some 300 of them die. Many, many more injuries and deaths go unreported. Niger's national highway, Route Nationale I, absorbs half the carnage on its thousand-mile east-west odyssey from Mali to Chad.[1]

Bad driving, poor road and vehicle maintenance, and chaotic traffic are the primary factors to blame for Africa's road deaths, according to a 1990 World Bank study entitled Transport Policy Issues in Sub-Saharan Africa." The language of this paper employs the wordy bureaucratese of international development documents: "The deterioration of the road networks is causing heavy losses to both the road system itself and to its users and requires urgent action."[2]

On lawless roads the problem is obvious. The human impulse to speed, the desire to get there quickly, takes over. And the bush taxi, more than any other form of transport, rules West Africa's roads.

I have come to know many bush taxi drivers, to like them and sympathize with how they work and live, if not to completely understand their point of view. They see themselves as transporters, honest professionals, survivors forced by circumstances to use guerrilla methods. So, during my travels, I was careful not to express my fears and concerns too bluntly; the drivers do not appreciate hearing about their roguish image. "People think we are irresponsible or thieves," my driver friend Issoufou Garba from Niger once told me. "But they don't understand the difficulty of our work."

---

1. Automobile statistics for Africa and related data were compiled from the *1995 World Almanac*; a World Bank report entitled "The Road Maintenance Initiative," by Steve Carapetis, Hernan Levy, and Terje Wolden (Washington, D.C.: World Bank Economic Development Institute, 1991); and *World Transport Data*, published annually by the International Road Transport Union in Washington, D.C.

2. Hernan Levy and Patrick Malone, "Transport Policy Issues in Sub-Saharan Africa," EDI Policy Seminar Report 9 (Washington, D.C.: World Bank Economic Development Institute, 1988), I.

In the 1980s, bush taxi drivers struck me as a dashing, reckless male elite, akin to the image of early airplane pilots. The drivers worked blindly and intuitively, vulnerable to technology and the will of a hostile environment: sun, wind, sand, demons, darkness, and checkpoint soldiers. Today, the African bush taxi driver still strikes me as a rogue folk hero: adventurous, kind, cruel, and selfless all at once. A bit like the contradictions inherent in the American cowboy myth—the free-spirited, big-hearted soul with a malicious edge. The drivers, too, are struggling to survive.

It was probably half an hour later, though I'm unsure of the passage of time that day. The tanker was still burning fiercely. No police or emergency services had arrived, and they would not before I left that day. I sat and watched without really seeing. *Can I walk to Kaduna?* I asked myself. *Fifty miles. Three days and I'll be there, still alive. I'll just follow the road and sleep in villages.*

The heat made me think again. In March, even the night offers little temperature relief.

My gaze fell on our driver. When we arrived at the accident, he had huddled with other drivers in discussion. But now he was standing alone, as close to the tanker—perhaps fifteen yards away—as the heat would allow. He stood with folded arms and feet planted a little apart. I'm not sure how long he had been standing there, studying the burning wreck. He stood for fifteen minutes more, moving only to shift his weight from one leg to the other. After a while, I realized what he was thinking, and it scared me. I had seen him scouting detour possibilities just after we arrived at the wreck, but the bush was too thick to drive through. Now, I understood that he wanted to challenge the gods.

He turned around, arms swinging with determination, and strode back to the car. This was both a game and a performance to this man, a career opportunity. He understood other drivers were observing him, waiting to see what he would do.

He opened the door and leaned against the roof, looking first at the fire and then around at his audience. He pursed his lips, raised his shoulders and hands, palms skyward, as if he were asking God for help.

He got into the car, moved it onto the road, and backed up a hundred yards or so. And then we heard him yell: "EEEOOOHHWW!" The wheels of the car spit dirt. He shot forward, aiming for the left side of the wreck, which was pulsing with just as much smoke and fire as when we first arrived. He had seen what others had not: that the haze masked a gap between the rear of the wreck and the bush about the width of his Peugeot.

Issoufou Garba, I thought, would never have risked this—a point to his credit. But I found myself glad this driver had tried. I badly wanted to be gone from this scene, and this man was obliging me.

The taxi disappeared into the smoke and reappeared seconds later on the other side of the wreck where the road began a low ascent. It lifted gently out of the curve where the wreck lay and then stopped.

No one cheered when the driver stepped out from behind the wheel and looked around for his passengers. Time was wasting. Nor did he seem to encourage cheering. Maybe he didn't want to taunt the gods any further. He leaned against the roof, braced by the outstretched palm of his left hand. All at once, drivers and passengers scrambled for vehicles, sprinting to make the run themselves. Hundreds of cars, trucks, and buses lined up on both sides of the wreck to take advantage of that small gap. I thought of an hourglass, but with jumping grains of sand fighting and trampling each other from both sides in their efforts to get through the narrow middle before it closed.

I made my way to the car by going through the bush, around the fire and wreckage. Looking back, I saw a fight start between two drivers, a pushing and shouting match. One man threw a punch to the face of the other, who went down. I heard more shouting in several languages, the rhythmic slap of sandals on cement, engines starting, doors slamming, the soft rumble of flames eating gasoline, and, finally, a siren wailing from the south.

We drove away.

[1999]

TRUMAN CAPOTE

(1924–1984)

Truman Capote is best known for his "non-fiction novel" *In Cold Blood* (1965) about a multiple murder. It was made into a film and generated enormous publicity, much of it encouraged by the author himself. Capote has written novels, notably *Other Voices, Other Rooms* (1948) and *Breakfast at Tiffany's* (1958) as well as short stories and essays. Although he moved to Manhattan and became a writer for *The New Yorker* magazine, Capote often drew on memories of his childhood in the American South for his fiction. A lifetime traveler, he once said, "I prefer travel to any other form of entertainment and do not know that I should ever care to be settled in any specific place." In a preface to one of his books, he remarked: "Everything here is factual, which doesn't mean that it is the truth," a statement that could easily be applied to travel writing as a genre.

The essay presented here, from a collection entitled *The Dogs Bark: Public People and Private Places* (1973), captures the pace of life in southern Spain as experienced on a slow train. A collage of vivid impressions and one comical misadventure, the essay has the structure of a short story. Sharing a train compartment with a group of Spaniards, Capote finds that this mode of transportation thrusts him dramatically into the rhythm and spirit of Spanish life.

"A Ride through Spain"

From *The Dogs Bark: Public People and Private Places*

Certainly the train was old. The seats sagged like the jowls of a bulldog, windows were out and strips of adhesive held together those that were left; in the corridor a prowling cat appeared to be hunting mice, and it was not unreasonable to assume his search would be rewarded.

Slowly, as though the engine were harnessed to elderly coolies, we crept out of Granada. The southern sky was as white and burning as a desert; there was one cloud, and it drifted like a traveling oasis.

We were going to Algeciras, a Spanish seaport facing the coast of Africa. In our compartment there was a middle-aged Australian wearing a soiled linen suit; he had tobacco-colored teeth and his fingernails were unsanitary. Presently he informed us that he was a ship's doctor. It seemed curious, there on the dry, dour plains of Spain, to meet someone connected with the sea. Seated next to him there were two women, a mother and daughter. The mother was an over-stuffed, dusty woman with sluggish, disapproving eyes and a faint mustache. The focus for her disapproval fluctuated; first, she eyed me rather strongly because as the sunlight fanned brighter, waves of heat blew through the broken windows and I had removed my jacket—which she considered, perhaps rightly, discourteous. Later on, she took a dislike to the young soldier who also occupied our compartment. The soldier, and the woman's not very discreet daughter, a buxom girl with the scrappy features of a prizefighter, seemed to have agreed to flirt. Whenever the wandering cat appeared at our door, the daughter pretended to be frightened, and the soldier would gallantly shoo the cat into the corridor: this by-play gave them frequent opportunity to touch each other.

The young soldier was one of many on the train. With their tasseled caps set at snappy angles, they hung about in the corridors smoking sweet black cigarettes and laughing confidentially. They seemed to be enjoying themselves, which apparently was wrong of them, for whenever an officer appeared the soldiers would stare fixedly out the windows, as though enraptured by the land-slides of red rock, the olive fields and stern stone mountains. Their officers were dressed for a parade, many ribbons, much brass; and some wore gleaming, improbable swords strapped to their sides. They did not mix with the soldiers, but sat together in a first-class compartment, looking bored and rather like unemployed actors. It was a blessing, I suppose, that something finally happened to give them a chance at rattling their swords.

The compartment directly ahead was taken over by one family; a delicate, attenuated, exceptionally elegant man with a mourning ribbon sewn around his sleeve, and traveling with him, six thin, summery girls, presumably his daughters. They were beautiful, the father and his children, all of them, and in the same way: hair that had a dark shine, lips the color of pimientos, eyes like sherry. The soldiers would glance into their compartment, then look away. It was as if they had seen straight into the sun.

Whenever the train stopped, the man's two youngest daughters would descend from the carriage and stroll under the shade of parasols. They enjoyed many lengthy promenades, for the train spent the greatest part of our journey standing still. No one appeared to be exasperated by this except myself. Several passengers seemed to have friends at every station with whom they could sit around a fountain and gossip long and lazily. One old woman was met by different little groups in a dozen-odd towns—between these encounters she wept with such abandon that the Australian doctor became alarmed: why no, she said, there was nothing he could do, it was just that seeing all her relatives made her so happy.

At each stop cyclones of barefooted women and somewhat naked children ran beside the train sloshing earthen jars of water and furrily squalling *Agua! Agua!* For two pesatas you could buy a whole basket of dark runny figs, and there were trays of curious white-coated candy doughnuts that looked as though they should be eaten by young girls wearing Communion dresses. Toward noon, having collected a bottle of wine, a loaf of bread, a sausage and a cheese, we were prepared for lunch. Our companions in the compartment were hungry, too. Packages were produced, wine uncorked, and for a while there was a pleasant, almost graceful festiveness. The soldier shared a pomegranate with the girl, the Australian told an amusing story, the witch-eyed mother pulled a paper-wrapped fish from between her bosoms and ate it with a glum relish.

Afterward everyone was sleepy; the doctor went so solidly to sleep that a fly meandered undisturbed over his open-mouthed face. Stillness etherized the whole train; in the next compartment the lovely girls leaned loosely, like six exhausted geraniums; even the cat had ceased to prowl, and lay dreaming in the corridor. We had climbed higher, the train moseyed across a plateau of rough yellow wheat, then between the granite walls of deep ravines where wind, moving down from the mountains, quivered in strange, thorny trees. Once, at a parting in the trees, there was something I'd wanted to see, a castle on a hill, and it sat there like a crown.

It was a landscape for bandits. Earlier in the summer, a young Englishman I know (rather, know of) had been motoring through this part of Spain when, on the lonely side of a mountain, his car was surrounded by swarthy scoundrels. They robbed him, then tied him to a tree and ticked his throat with the blade of a knife. I was thinking of this when without preface a spatter of bullet fire strafed the dozy silence.

It was a machine gun. Bullets rained in the trees like the rattle of castanets, and the train, with a wounded creak, slowed to a halt. For a moment there was no sound except the machine gun's cough. Then, "Bandits!" I said in a loud, dreadful voice.

"*Bandidos!*" screamed the daughter.

"*Bandidos!*" echoed her mother, and the terrible word swept through the train like something drummed on a tom-tom. The result was slapstick in a grim key. We collapsed on the floor, one cringing heap of arms and legs. Only the mother seemed to keep her head; standing up, she began systematically to stash away her treasures. She stuck a ring into the buns of her hair and without shame hiked up her skirts and dropped a pearl-studded comb into her bloomers. Like the cryings of birds at twilight, airy twitterings of distress came from the charming girls in the next compartment. In the corridor the officers bumped about yapping orders and knocking into each other.

Suddenly, silence. Outside, there was the murmur of wind in leaves, of voices. Just as the weight of the doctor's body was becoming too much for me, the outer door of our compartment swung open, and a young man stood there. He did not look clever enough to be a bandit.

"*Hay un médico en el tren?*" he said, smiling.

The Australian, removing the pressure of his elbow from my stomach, climbed to his feet. "I'm a doctor," he admitted, dusting himself, "Has someone been wounded?"

"*Si, Señor.* An old man. He is hurt in the head," said the Spaniard, who was not a bandit, alas, merely another passenger. Settling back in our seats, we listened, expressionless with embarrassment, to what had happened. It seemed that for the last several hours an old man had been stealing a ride by clinging to the rear of the train. Just now he'd lost his hold, and a soldier, seeing him fall, had starting firing a machine gun as a signal for the engineer to stop the train.

My only hope was that no one remembered who had first mentioned bandits. They did not seem to. After acquiring a clean shirt of mine which he intended to use as a bandage, the doctor went off to his patient, and the mother, turning her back with sour prudery, reclaimed her pearl comb. Her daughter and the soldier followed after us as we got out of the carriage and strolled under the trees, where many passengers had gathered to discuss the incident.

Two soldiers appeared carrying the old man. My shirt was wrapped around his head. They propped him under a tree and all the women clustered about vying with each other to lend him their rosary; someone brought a bottle of wine, which pleased him more. He seemed quite happy, and moaned a great deal. The childen who had been on the train circled around him, giggling.

We were in a small wood that smelled of oranges. There was a path, and it led to a shaded promontory; from here, one looked across the valley where sweeping stretches of scorched golden grass shivered as though the earth were trembling. Admiring the valley, and the shadowy changes of light on the hills beyond, the six sisters, escorted by their elegant father, sat with their parasols raised above them like guests at a *fête champêtre*.[1] The soldiers moved around them in a vague, ambitious manner; they did not quite dare to approach, though one brash, sassy fellow went to the edge of the promontory and called, "*Yo te quiero mucho.*"[2] The words returned with the hollow sub-music of a perfect echo, and the sisters, blushing, looked more deeply into the valley.

A cloud, somber as the rocky hills, had massed in the sky, and the grass below stirred like the sea before a storm. Someone said he thought it would rain. But no one wanted to go: not the injured man, who was well on his way through a second bottle of wine, nor the children who, having discovered the echo, stood happily caroling into the valley. It was like a party, and we all drifted back to the train as though each of us wished to be the last to leave. The old man, with my shirt like a grand turban on his head, was put into a first-class carriage and several eager ladies were left to attend him.

In our compartment, the dark, dusty mother sat just as we had left her. She had not seen fit to join the party. She gave me a long, glittering look. "*Bandidos,*" she said with a surly, unnecessary vigor.

The train moved away so slowly butterflies blew in and out the windows.

[1946]

BERYL MARKHAM

(1902–1986)

Beryl Markham flew small planes in Africa in the early days of aviation. Though not as famous as Amelia Earhart, she wrote a compelling book about flying, *West with the Night* (1942), from which this excerpt is taken. Today, the uniformity of air service and the sameness of airports merit at best a shrug of annoyance from travel writers and at worst, a diatribe. In its early days, however, air travel was not a form of mass transportation but a challenge to adventuresome aviators who lacked sophisticated instruments and braved capricious weather and the constant threat of mechanical breakdown—the price they paid for the thrill of flight and the unmatched feeling of transcendence.

---

1. fête champêtre An outdoor festival.
2. "Yo te quiero mucho." I want you very much.

The selection "Why Do We Fly?" conveys both the panoramic perspective and the camaraderie experienced by bush pilots as well as the challenges to survival.

"Why Do We Fly?"

From *West with the Night*

If you were to fly over the Russian steppes in the dead of winter after snow had fallen, and you saw beneath you a date palm green as spring against the white of the land, you might carry on for twenty miles or so before the inconguity of a tropical tree rooted in ice struck against your sense of harmony and made you swing round on your course to look again. You would find that the tree was not a date palm or, if it still persisted in being one, that insanity had claimed you for its own.

During the five or ten minutes I had watched the herd of game spread like a barbaric invasion across the plain, I had unconsciously observed, almost in their midst, a pool of water bright as a splinter from a glazier's table.

I knew that the country below, in spite of its drought-resistant grass, was dry during most of the year. I knew that whatever water holes one did find were opaque and brown, stirred by the feet of drinking game. But the water I saw was not brown; it was clear, and it received the sun and turned it back again in strong sharp gleams of light.

Like the date palm on the Russian steppes, this crystal pool in the arid roughness of the Serengetti was not only incongruous, it was impossible. And yet, without the slightest hesitation, I flew over it and beyond it until it was gone from sight and from my thoughts.

There is no twilight in East Africa. Night tramps on the heels of Day with little gallantry and takes the place she lately held, in severe and humourless silence. Sounds of the things that live in the sun are quickly gone—and with them the sounds of roving aeroplanes, if their pilots have learned the lessons there are to learn about night weather, distances that seem never to shrink, and the perfidy of landing fields that look like aerodromes by day, but vanish in darkness.

I watched small shadows creep from the rocks and saw birds in black flocks homeward bound to the scattered bush, and I began to consider my own home and a hot bath and food. Hope always persists beyond reason, and it seemed futile to nurse any longer the expectation of finding Woody with so much of the afternoon already gone. If he were not dead, he would of course light fires by night, but already my fuel was slow, I had no emergency rations—and no sleep.

I had touched my starboard rudder, altering my course east for Nairobi, when the thought first struck me that the shining bit of water I had so calmly flown over was not water at all, but the silvered wings of a Klemm monoplane bright and motionless in the path of the slanting sun.

It was not really a thought, of course, nor even one of those blinding flashes of realization that come so providentially to the harried heroes of fiction. It was no more than a hunch. But where is there a pilot foolhardy enough to ignore his hunches? I am not one. I could never tell where inspiration begins and impulse leaves off. I suppose the answer is in the outcome. If your hunch proves a good one, you were inspired; if it proves bad, you are guilty of yielding to thoughtless impulse.

But before considering any of this, I had already reversed my direction, lost altitude, and opened the throttle again. It was a race with racing shadows, a friendly trial between the sun and me.

As I flew, my hunch became conviction. Nothing in the world, I thought, could have looked so much like reflecting water as the wings of Woody's plane. I remembered how bright those wings had been when last I saw them, freshly painted to shine like silver or stainless steel. Yet they were only of flimsy wood and cloth and hardened glue.

The deception had amused Woody. 'All metal,' he would say, jerking a thumb toward the Klemm; 'all metal, except just the wings and fuselage and prop and little things like that. Everything else is metal—even the engine.'

Even the engine!—as much of a joke to us as to the arrant winds of Equatorial Africa; a toy engine with bustling manner and frantic voice; an hysterical engine, guilty at last perhaps of what, in spite of Woody's jokes and our own, we all had feared.

Now almost certainly guilty, I thought, for there at last was what I hunted—not an incredible pool of water, but, unmistakable this time, the Klemm huddled to earth like a shot bird, not crushed, but lifeless and alone, beside it no fire, not even a stick with a fluttering rag.

I throttled down and banked the Avian in slow, descending circles.

I might have had a pious prayer for Woody on my lips at that moment, but I didn't have. I could only wonder if he had been hurt and taken into a manyatta by some of the Masai Murani, or if, idiotically, he had wandered into the pathless country in search of water and food. I even damned him slightly, I think, because, as I glided to within five hundred feet of the Klemm, I could see that it was unscathed.

There can be a strange confusion of emotions at such a moment. The sudden relief I felt in knowing that at least the craft had not been damaged was, at the same time, blended with a kind of angry disappointment at not finding Woody, perhaps hungry and thirsty, but anyhow alive beside it.

Rule one for forced landings ought to be, 'Don't give up the ship.' Woody of all people should have known this—did know it, of course, but where was he?

Circling again, I saw that in spite of a few pig-holes and scattered rocks, a landing would be possible. About thirty yards from the Klemm there was a natural clearing blanketed with short, tawny grass. From the air I judged the length of the space to be roughly a hundred and fifty yards—not really long enough for a plane without brakes, but long enough with such head wind as there was to check her glide.

I throttled down, allowing just enough revs to prevent the ship from stalling at the slow speed required to land in so small a space. Flattening out and swinging the tail from side to side in order to get what limited vision I could at the ground below and directly ahead, I flew in gently and brought the Avian to earth in a surprisingly smooth run. I made a mental note at the time that the take-off, especially if Woody was aboard, might be a good deal more difficult.

But there was no Woody.

I climbed out, got my dusty and dented water bottle from the locker, and walked over to the Klemm, motionless and still glittering in the late light. I stood in front of her wings and saw no sign of mishap, and heard nothing. There she rested, frail and feminine, against the rough, grey ground, her pretty wings unmarked, her propeller rakishly tilted, her cockpit empty.

There are all kinds of silences and each of them means a different thing. There is the silence that comes with morning in a forest, and this is different from the silence of a sleeping city. There is silence after a rainstorm, and before a rainstorm, and these are not the same. There is the silence of emptiness, the silence of fear, the silence of doubt. There is a certain silence that can emanate from a lifeless object as from a chair lately used, or from a piano with old dust upon its keys, or from anything that has answered to the need of a man, for pleasure or for work. This kind of silence can speak. Its voice may be melancholy, but it is not always so; for the chair may have been left by a laughing child or the last notes of the piano may have been raucous and gay. Whatever the mood or the circumstance, the essence of its quality may linger in the silence that follows. It is a soundless echo.

With the water bottle swinging from my hand on its long leather strap, like an erratic pendulum, I walked around Woody's plane. But even with shadows flooding the earth like slow-moving water and the grass whispering under the half-spent breath of the wind, there was no feeling of gloom or disaster.

The silence that belonged to the slender little craft was, I thought, filled with malice—a silence holding the spirit of wanton mischief, like the quiet smile of a vain woman exultant over a petty and vicious triumph.

I had expected little else of the Klemm, frivolous and inconstant as she was, but I knew suddenly that Woody was not dead. It was not that kind of silence.

I found a path with the grass bent down and little stones scuffed from their hollows, and I followed it past some larger stones into a tangle of thorn trees. I shouted for Woody and got nothing but my own voice for an answer, but when I turned my head to shout again, I saw two boulders leaning together, and in the cleft they made were a pair of legs clothed in grimy work slacks and, beyond the legs, the rest of Woody, face down with his head in the crook of his arm.

I went over to where he was, unscrewed the cap of the water bottle and leaned down and shook him.

'It's Beryl,' I called, and shook him harder. One of the legs moved and then the other. Life being hope, I got hold of his belt and tugged.

Woody began to back out of the cleft of the rocks with a motion irrelevantly reminiscent of the delectable crayfish of the South of France. He was mumbling, and I recalled that men dying of thirst are likely to mumble and that what they want is water. I poured a few drops on the back of his neck as it appeared and got, for my pains, a startled grunt. It was followed by a few of those exquisite words common to the vocabularies of sailors, airplane pilots, and stevedores—and then abruptly Woody was sitting upright on the ground, his face skinny beneath a dirty beard, his lips cinder-dry and split, his eyes red-rimmed and sunk in his cheeks. He was a sick man and he was grinning.

'I resent being treated like a corpse,' he said. 'It's insulting. Is there anything to eat?'

I once knew a man who, at each meeting with a friend, said, 'Well, well—it's a small world after all!' He must be very unhappy now, because, when I last saw him, friends were slipping from his orbit like bees from a jaded flower and his world was becoming lonely and large. But there was truth in his dreary platitude. I have the story of Bishon Singh to prove it and Woody to witness it.

Bishon Singh arrived in a little billow of dust when there was nothing left of the sun but its forehead, and Woody and I had made insincere adieus to the Klemm and were preparing to take off for Nairobi and a doctor—and a new magneto, if one could be had.

'There's a man on a horse,' said Woody.

But it wasn't a man on a horse.

I had helped Woody into the front cockpit of the Avian, and I stood alongside the craft ready to swing her propeller, when the little billow made its entrance into our quasi-heroic scene. Six wagging and tapered ears protruded from the crest of the billow, and they were the ears of three donkeys. Four faces appeared in four halos of prairie dust, and three of these were the faces of Kikuyu boys. The fourth was the face of Bishon Singh, dark, bearded, and sombre.

'You won't believe it,' I said to Woody, 'but that is an Indian I've known from childhood. He worked for years on my father's farm.'

'I'll believe anything you tell me,' said Woody, 'if only you get me out of here.'

'Beru! Beru!' said Bishon Singh, 'or do I dream?'

Bishon Singh is a Sikh and as such he wears his long black hair braided to his long black beard, and together they make a cowl, like a monk's.

His face is small and stern and it peers from the cowl with nimble black eyes. They can be kind, or angry, like other eyes, but I do not think they can be gay. I have never seen them gay.

'Beru!' he said again. 'I do not believe this. This is not Njoro. It is not the farm at Njoro, or the Rongai Valley. It is more than a hundred miles from there—but here you are, tall and grown up, and I am an old man on my way to my Duka with things to sell. But we meet. We meet with all these years behind us. I do not believe it! Walihie Mungu Yango—I do not believe it. God has favoured me!'

'It's a small world,' groaned Woody from the plane.

'Na furie sana ku wanana na wewe,' I said to Bishon Singh in Swahili. 'I am very happy to see you again.'

He was dressed as I had always remembered him—thick army boots, blue puttees, khaki breeches, a ragged leather waistcoat, all of it surmounted by a great turban, wound, as I recalled it, from at least a thousand yards of the finest cotton cloth. As a child, that turban had always intrigued me; there was so much of it and so little of Bishon Singh.

We stood a few yards in front of his three nodding donkeys, each with a silent Kikuyu boy in attendance, and each with an immense load on its back—pots, tin pans, bales of cheap Bombay prints, copper wire to make Masai ear-rings and bracelets. There was even tobacco, and oil for the Murani to use in the braiding of their hair.

There were things made of leather, things of paper, things of celluloid and rubber, all bulging, dangling, and bursting from the great pendulous packs. Here was Commerce, four-footed and halting, slow and patient, unhurried, but sure as tomorrow, beating its way to a counter in the African hinterland.

Bishon Singh raised an arm and included both the Klemm and the Avian in its sweep.

'N'dege!' he said—'the white man's bird! You do not ride on them, Beru?'

'I fly one of them, Bishon Singh.'

I said it sadly, because the old man had pointed with his left arm and I saw that his right was withered and crippled and useless. It had not been like that when I had seen him last.

'So,' he scolded, 'now it has come to this. To walk is not enough. To ride on a horse is not enough. Now people must go from place to place through the air, like a *diki toora*. Nothing but trouble will come of it, Beru. God spits upon such blasphemy.'

'God has spat,' sighed Woody.

'My friend was stranded here,' I said to Bishon Singh, 'his n'dege—the one that shines like a new rupee—is broken. We are going back to Nairobi.'

'Walihie! Walihie! It is over a hundred miles, Beru, and the night is near. I will unpack my donkeys and brew hot tea. It is a long way to Nairobi—even for you who go with the wind.'

'We will be there in less than an hour, Bishon Singh. It would take you as long to build a fire and make the tea.'

I put my hand out and the old Sikh grasped it and held it for a moment very tightly, just as he had often held it some ten years ago when he was still taller than I—even without his fantastic turban. Only then he had used his right hand. He looked down at it now with a smile on his thin lips.

'What was it?' I asked.

'Simba, Beru—lion.' He shrugged. 'One day on the way to Ikoma . . . it makes us like brothers, you and me. Each has been torn by a lion. You remember that time at Kabete when you were a little child?'

'I'll never forget it.'

'Nor I,' said Bishon Singh.

I turned and went forward to the propeller of the Avian and grasped the highest blade with my right hand and nodded to Woody. He sat in the front cockpit ready to switch on.

Bishon Singh moved backward a few steps, close to his Tom Thumb cavalcade. The three donkeys left off their meagre feeding, raised their heads and tilted their ears. The Kikuyu boys stood behind the donkeys and waited. In the dead light the Klemm had lost her brilliance and was only the sad and discredited figure of an aerial Jezebel.

'God will keep you,' said Bishon Singh.

'Good-bye and good fortune!' I called.

'Contact!' roared Woody and I swung the prop.

He lay, at last, on a bed in the small neat shack of the East African Aero Club waiting for food, for a drink—and, I suspect, for sympathy.

'The Klemm is a bitch,' he said. 'No man in his right mind should ever fly a Klemm aeroplane, with a Pobjoy motor, in Africa. You treat her kindly, you nurse her engine, you put silver dope on her wings, and what happens?'

'The magneto goes wrong,' I said.

'It's like a woman with nerves,' said Woody, 'or no conscience, or even an imbecile!'

'Oh, much worse.'

'Why do we fly?' said Woody. 'We could do other things. We could work in offices, or have farms, or get into the Civil Service. We could . . .'

'We could give up flying tomorrow. You could, anyhow. You could walk away from your plane and never put your feet on a rudder bar again. You could forget about weather and night flights and forced landings, and passengers who get airsick, and spare parts that you can't find, and wonderful new ships that you can't buy. You could forget all that and go off somewhere away from Africa and never look at an aerodrome again. You might be a very happy man, so why don't you?'

'I couldn't bear it,' said Woody. 'It would all be so dull.'

'It can be dull anyway.'

'Even with lions tearing you to bits at Kabete?'

'Oh, that was back in my childhood. Some day I'll write a book and you can read about it.'

'God forbid!' said Woody.

[1942]

D. H. LAWRENCE

(1885–1930)

A prolific writer and perpetual traveler, D. H. Lawrence published poetry, plays, short stories, novels, literary criticism, and travel books. His autobiographical novel, *Sons and Lovers* (1913), which drew on his background as a miner's son from the industrial midlands of England, established him as a writer. Subsequent novels, including *The Rainbow* (1915) and *Women in Love* (1920), and especially *Lady Chatterley's Lover* (1928), explored human psychology and sexuality and made his name synonymous with candid literary treatment of love and passion. The latter novel was banned until after his death. Lawrence eloped with Frieda von Richthofen Weekley, and they spent most of their life together in foreign countries. In his long exile, Lawrence was searching for a perfect place, as if he were seeking some earthly Eden. He lived for brief amounts of time in Italy, Ceylon, Australia, New Mexico, Mexico, Germany, Spain, and Italy before dying in southern France of tuberculosis.

Lawrence celebrated the vividness that travel brought to the life of the senses; he wrote three travel books on Italy, as well as *Mornings in Mexico* (1932), from which the following selection, "Market Day," is taken. One of the charms of travel is that it heightens the senses; sounds, smells, colors become more vivid. Lawrence felt that he was living life most fully when he traveled. Markets, especially those in traditional societies, can be vibrant places, full of activity and color, where the energies of commerce envelop both travelers (who usually love to shop) and natives.

"Market Day"

From *Mornings in Mexico*

From the valley villages and from the mountains the peasants and the Indians are coming in with supplies, the road is like a pilgrimage, with the dust in greatest haste, dashing for town. Dark-eared asses with running men, running women, running girls, running lads, twinkling donkeys ambling on fine little feet, under twin baskets with tomatoes and gourds, twin great nets of bubble-shaped jars, twin bundles of neat-cut faggots of wood, neat as bunches of cigarettes, and twin net-sacks of charcoal. Donkeys, mules, on they come, great pannier baskets making a rhythm under the perched woman, great bundles bounding against the sides of the slim-footed animals. A baby donkey trotting naked after its piled-up dam, a white, sandal-footed man following with the silent Indian haste, and a girl running again on light feet.

Onwards, on a strange current of haste. And slowly rowing among the foot-travel, the ox-wagons rolling solid wheels below the high net of the body. Slow oxen, with heads pressed down nosing to the earth, swaying, swaying their great horns as a snake sways itself, the shovel-shaped collar of solid wood pressing down on their necks like a scoop. On, on between the burnt-up turf and the solid, monumental green of the organ cactus. Past the rocks and the floating *palo-blanco* flowers, past the towsled dust of the *mesquite* bushes. While the dust once more, in a greater haste than anyone, comes tall and rapid down the road, overpowering and obscuring all the little people, as in a cataclysm.

They are mostly small people, of the Zapotec race: small men with lifted chests and quick, lifted knees, advancing with heavy energy in the midst of dust. And quiet, small, round-headed women running barefoot, tightening their blue *rebozos* round their shoulders, so often with a baby in the fold. The white cotton clothes of the men so white that their faces are invisible places of darkness under their big hats. Clothed darkness, faces of night, quickly, silently, with inexhaustible energy advancing to the town.

And many of the serranos, the Indians from the hills, wearing their little conical black felt hats, seem capped with night, above the straight white shoulders. Some have come far, walking all yesterday in their little black hats and black-sheathed sandals. To-morrow they will walk back. And their eyes will be just the same, black and bright and wild, in the dark faces. They have no goal, any more than the hawks in the air, and no course to run, any more than the clouds.

The market is a huge roofed-in place. Most extraordinary is the noise that comes out, as you pass along the adjacent street. It is a huge noise, yet you may never notice it. It sounds as if all the ghosts in the world were talking to one another, in ghost-voices, within the darkness of the market structure. It is a noise something like rain, or banana leaves in a wind. The market, full of Indians, dark-faced, silent-footed, hush-spoken, but pressing in in countless numbers. The queer hissing murmurs of the Zapotec *idioma*, among the sounds of Spanish, the quiet, aside-voices of the Mixtecas.

To buy and to sell, but above all, to commingle. In the old world, men make themselves two great excuses for coming together to a centre, and commingling freely in a mixed, unsuspicious host. Market and religion. These alone bring men, unarmed, together since time began. A little load of firewood, a woven blanket, a few eggs and tomatoes are excuse enough of men, women, and children to cross the foot-weary miles of valley and mountain. To buy, to sell, to barter, to exchange. To exchange, above all things, human contact.

That is why they like you to bargain, even if it's only the difference of a centavo. Round the centre of the covered market where there is a basin of water, are the flowers: red, white, pink roses in heaps, many-coloured little carnations, poppies, bits of larkspur, lemon and orange marigolds, buds of madonna lilies, pansies, a few forget-me-nots. They don't bring the tropical flowers. Only the lilies come wild from the hills, and the mauve red orchids.

"How much this bunch of cherry-pie heliotrope?"

"Fifteen centavos."

"Ten."

"Fifteen."

You put back the cherry-pie, and depart. But the woman is quite content. The contact, so short even, brisked her up.

"Pinks?"

"The red one, Señorita? Thirty centavos."

"No. I don't want red ones. The mixed."

"Ah!" The woman seizes a handful of little carnations of all colours, carefully puts them together. "Look, Señorita! No more?"

"No, no more. How much?"

"The same. Thirty centavos."

"It is much."

"No, Señorita, it is not much. Look at this little bunch. It is eight centavos."—Displays a scrappy little bunch. "Come then, twenty-five."

"No! Twenty-two."

"Look!" She gathers up three or four more flowers, and claps them to the bunch. "Two *reales*, Señorita."

It is a bargain. Off you go with multicoloured pinks, and the woman has had one more moment of contact, with a stranger, a perfect stranger. An intermingling of voices, a threading together of different wills. It is life. The centavos are an excuse.

The stalls go off in straight lines, to the right, brilliant vegetables, to the left, bread and sweet buns. Away at the one end, cheese, butter, eggs, chicken, turkeys, meat. At the other, the native-woven blankets and *rebozos*, skirts, shirts, handkerchiefs. Down the far-side, sandals and leather things.

The *sarape* men spy you, and whistle to you like ferocious birds, and call "Señor! Señor! Look!" Then with violence one flings open a dazzling blanket, while another whistles more ear-piercingly still, to make you look at *his* blanket. It is the veritable den of lions and tigers, that spot where the *sarape* men have their blankets piled on the ground. You shake your head, and flee.

To find yourself in the leather avenue.

"Señor! Señor! Look! Huaraches! Very fine, very finely made! Look, Señor!"

The fat leather man jumps up and holds a pair of sandals at one's breast. They are of narrow woven strips of leather, in the newest Paris style, but a style ancient to these natives. You take them in your hand, and look at them quizzically, while the fat wife of the huarache man reiterates, "Very fine work. Very fine. Much work!"

Leather men usually seem to have their wives with them.

"How much?"

"Twenty reales."

"Twenty!"—in a voice of surprise and pained indignation.

"How much do you give?"

You refuse to answer. Instead you put the huaraches to your nose. The huarache man looks at his wife, and they laugh aloud.

"They smell," you say.

"No, Señor, they don't smell!"—and the two go off into fits of laughter.

"Yes, they smell. It is not American leather."

"Yes, Señor, it is American leather. They don't smell, Señor. No, they don't smell." He coaxes you till you wouldn't believe your own nose.

"Yes, they smell."

"How much do you give?"

"Nothing, because they smell."

And you give another sniff, though it is painfully unnecessary. And in spite of your refusal to bid, the man and wife go into fits of laughter to see you painfully sniffing.

You lay down the sandals and shake your head.

"How much do you offer?" reiterates the man, gaily.

You shake your head mournfully, and move away. The leather man and his wife look at one another and go off into another fit of laughter, because you smelt the huaraches, and said they stank.

They did. The natives use human excrement for tanning leather. When Bernal Diaz came with Cortes to the great market-place of Mexico City, in Montezuma's day, he saw the little pots of human excrement in rows for sale, and the leather-makers going round sniffing to see which was the best, before they paid for it. It staggered even a fifteenth-century Spaniard. Yet my leather man and his wife think it screamingly funny that I smell the huaraches before buying them. Everything has its own smell, and the natural smell of huaraches is what it is. You might as well quarrel with an onion for smelling like an onion.

The great press of the quiet natives, some of them bright and clean, many in old rags, the brown flesh showing through the rents in the dirty cotton.

Many wild hillmen, in their little hats of conical black felt, with their wild, staring eyes. And as they cluster round the hat-stall, in a long, long suspense of indecision before they can commit themselves, trying on a new hat, their black hair gleams blue-black, and falls thick and rich over their foreheads, like gleaming bluey-black feathers. And one is reminded again of the blue-haired Buddha, with the lotus at his navel.

But already the fleas are travelling under one's clothing.

Market lasts all day. The native inns are great dreary yards with little sheds, and little rooms around. Some men and families who have come from far, will sleep in one or other of the little stall-like rooms. Many will sleep on the stones, on the earth, round the market, anywhere. But the asses are there by the hundred, crowded in the inn-yards, drooping their ears with the eternal patience of the beast that knows better than any other beast that every road curves round to the same centre of rest, and hither and thither means nothing.

And towards nightfall the dusty road will be thronged with shadowy people and unladen asses and new-laden mules, urging silently into the country again, their backs to the town, glad to get away from the town, to see the cactus and the pleated hills, and the trees that mean a village. In some village they will lie under a tree, or under a wall, and sleep. Then the next day, home.

It is fulfilled, what they came to market for. They have sold and bought. But more than that, they have had their moment of contact and centripetal flow. They have been part of a great stream of men flowing to a centre, to the vortex of the market-place. And here they have felt life concentrate upon them, they have been jammed between the soft hot bodies of strange men come from afar, they have had the sound of stranger's voices in their ears, they have asked and been answered in unaccustomed ways.

There is no goal, and no abiding-place, and nothing is fixed, not even the cathedral towers. The cathedral towers are slowly leaning, seeking the curve of return. As the natives curved in a strong swirl, towards the vortex of the market. Then on a strong swerve of repulsion, curved out and away again, into space.

Nothing but the touch, the spark of contact. That, no more. That, which is most elusive, still the only treasure. Come, and gone, and yet the clue itself.

True, folded up in the handkerchief inside the shirt, are the copper centavos, and maybe a few silver pesos. But these too will disappear as the stars disappear at daybreak, as they are meant to disappear. Everything is meant to disappear. Every curve plunges into the vortex and is lost, re-emerges with a certain relief and takes to the open, and there is lost again.

Only that which is utterly intangible, matters. The contact, the spark of exchange. That which can never be fastened upon, forever gone, forever coming, never to be detained: the spark of contact.

Like the evening star, when it is neither night nor day.

Like the evening star, between the sun and the moon, and swayed by neither of them. The flashing intermediary, the evening star that is seen only at the dividing of the day and night, but then is more wonderful than either.

[1932]

ANITA DESAI

(1937–)

Anita Desai is one of India's most important contemporary novelists. Born of German and Indian parents, she has lived in both India and the West, and she often contrasts the two worlds in the lives of her characters. Her many novels and short stories deal with the psychological and social conflicts of modern Indian families. Three of her novels, *Clear Light of Day* (1980), *In Custody* (1984), and *Fasting, Feasting* (1999) were nominated for the Booker Prize.

In the essay below, "The Sensation of Infinity," Desai brings an Indian sensibility to the landscape and culture of Mexico, a land to which she has frequently returned as a traveler. Travelers inevitably compare their home countries to those they visit; such comparisons are part of the process of relating to a new culture and growing beyond the limitations of national identity. Desai finds something of the spirit of her native country in Mexico. "I have not seriously explored the prehistoric link between the Indians of India and the Indians of the Americas, but I do know that it must exist, because when I am in Mexico, I do not feel a stranger, nor am I regarded as one."

"The Sensation of Infinity"

Why Mexico? I am constantly asked and, packing up my bags to leave the gray, frozen, colorless north, I am as puzzled by the question as people are by the regularity with which I leave for Mexico.

To me, the very name spells everything attractive and enchanting: an ancient name of a land where every stone and rock is old, old and imbued with history, where vistas are endless and the light is so pure it dazzles, like crystal, or flame. Who would not want to leave the dullness of the north, this rawness and sad urban ugliness, for a land where volcanoes rise from the valleys into snow-topped cones, where hills flow outward in waves of lilac and rose and violet all the way up to the horizon, where trees bear golden oranges and lemons as in some romantic ballad and flowers bloom in colors so rich and varied as are not dreamt of in the north?

That is the obvious answer, it seems to me, but since no one I have tried to explain this to seems in the least convinced, I have to go further and admit that of course there is more than the attraction of a perfect climate—the eternal spring that Cortés and the *conquistadores* discovered—or of beautiful scenery and marvelous food for one who spends the workaday life in a northern city, catching a bus and descending into the subway to go to work, returning after dark through streets where no life stirs except for the automobiles hurrying by.

When I give the matter thought (and usually it is a matter of instinct rather than thought), then I realize that being Indian has something to do with the affinity I feel with the land about which I knew nothing till, one bitter New England winter, I could not bear the cold or the dark another day and simply packed my bag and flew to Oaxaca, and on landing at the little airport surrounded by low scrubby hills and flowering bougainvillea and flooded with a light of piercing clarity, I felt like the surrealist André Breton, who said: "I dreamt of Mexico and I am in Mexico. . . . Never before has reality fulfilled with such splendour the promises of dreams." After checking into a hotel, I walked out of the tropical jungle contained in its courtyard, with cages full of squawking parrots, and found a church built of stone, a jacaranda tree blooming against the cobalt sky, and children playing with a ball in the dust and felt an urge, unknown to me before, to go down on my knees and kiss those stones, that dust. Clearly, I had had the experience, albeit in reverse, that Octavio Paz described in *In Light of India* when he wrote, "The strangeness of India brought to mind another strangeness: my own country."

I have visited and loved many places in the world, places I am always happy to see again and of which I have dear memories, but my response to Mexico goes much deeper and was formed much faster—in fact, instantly. I have to put this down to an affinity of the blood, an affinity of race and tribe that I would not normally acknowledge. I have not seriously explored the prehistoric link between the Indians of India and the Indians of the Americas, but I do know it must exist, because when I am in Mexico, I do not feel a stranger, nor am I regarded as one. I feel I know and understand this place without having to have it explained to me. In the north, when I walk down a street and catch glimpses of the lives lived in the closed houses I pass, I am filled with the desolation of finding the streetscape utterly foreign to me, of not knowing what goes on behind the picture windows and the white picket fences, whereas in Mexico, when I see a crowd waiting at a bus stop or clustered around a barrow of food, or when I see a family strolling through a park or old women climbing stairs to a cathedral to light candles there, I know instinctively what they are thinking, what they are talking about, why and how. There is no sense of strangeness, of inscrutability—it is as though I have lived there always.

In a way, I have: India is so similar, the way of life so familiar. Oh, there are obvious differences: Mexicans were all converted to Christianity, Indians were not; Mexicans accepted Spanish ways far more than Indians did British—but, just as in India, one has a constant awareness in Mexico of history being a palimpsest, with layers and layers of time accreting to form the present, each contributing to what life is now. This is the great contrast with the civilizations of the north, where what you see on the surface is what there is beneath. Here, too, is a culture that is not monolithic and undivided but, on the contrary, diverse and manifold. Kaleidoscopically, it is forever presenting different views, different patterns.

There are differences, certainly: The quietness, the silence, of the Mexican is certainly not shared by the Indian. Travelers from D. H. Lawrence to Graham Greene to Sybille Bedford have commented on the ability of the Mexican to remain still, silent, isolated even in a crowd. They have interpreted it as sullenness, stupidity, or danger; I see it differently—as a well of thought that goes down, down deep into history and long experience, reaching to the very heat of things, to an Indian self buried beneath all the centuries of otherness. Very few Indians from India are capable of such silence, such isolation—it has to be acquired and cultivated. Whereas Mexicans escape from it into the cacophony of music, fireworks, and the drunkenness of fiestas with exhausting, even tiresome, frequency, in India, one feels the need to escape from the press of people into solitude, as in meditation.

On my visits to Mexico, I find myself returning to two towns over and over, and they stand in sharp contrast to each other. In certain moods I am drawn to one, in others I am drawn to the other.

One is San Miguel de Allende, a sixteenth-century Spanish colonial town high in the mountains of the Sierra Madre Occidental to the northwest of Mexico City. Climatically speaking, it is "high desert," a zone I had not encountered before: The Himalayan mountains I know are wooded and lush. Here the mountains are sere, with very little growth, low and scrubby, and it is where I discovered how beautiful earth and rock are in themselves, how varied at different times of day: "Untiring games of light, always different and always the same," Octavio Paz wrote, give "the sensation of infinity and pacify the soul." The light is pale, almost opalescent, in the early morning, dun and ochre in the blaze of afternoon, before acquiring violet and rose and indigo tints as the sun sinks over the valley and disappears behind the farthest rim of hills.

The houses are built of the soft pink stone of the region that the desert light turns to rose. All day, bells ring from one cathedral or another, striking the hours and pealing to celebrate a particular occasion. Old women wrapped in shawls climb the stairs with bouquets as tall as themselves of white calla lilies and bloodred gladioli to offer to the gilt images glowing in the flickering candlelight inside. Often the women are accompanied by small children, who continue to play among the pews as they might outside; often even a dog will sink down on the cool stone floor for a little nap, or a young couple, holding hands, will drop in to make a sign of the cross before going out into the sunshine to find themselves an ice cream.

The entire town is given over to the leisurely stroll, and most strolls end up in the little *jardín*, or central plaza, in front of the great pink stone cake of the *parroquia*, the parish church. Low, bushy trees cast an intense shade on the hottest days over the benches where everyone gathers to wait for the day's newspapers to arrive, get their shoes shined to a high gloss, watch children chasing the plump pigeons around, listen to a mariachi band play, and, of course, snack on roasted corn on the cob or ice cream in a hundred flavors, from tequila to tamarind. This is a town where no one wakes to an alarm clock, no one runs; the sun imposes its slow, stately measure, and the body gratefully accepts it. Here one realizes that a city can mold itself to its environment; it need not oppose or destroy its surroundings, as elsewhere.

Pleasant as the *jardín* is in the day, at night it is magical—lamps bloom into light, the daytime bustle disappears like one act of a play giving way to the next, and, on the steps of the *parroquia*, the *estudiantinas* of the local university gather, dressed in the costume of medieval troubadours—flowing black capes and colored ribbons, velvet caps and buckled shoes. They come with their guitars and tambourines to sing old Spanish ballads. When a ring of listeners has gathered—and they tend to be Mexicans, not foreign tourists—the *estudiantinas* lead them up and down the cobbled streets, singing; a little burro trots alongside, carrying a cask of wine to help create the illusion of a medieval and romantic Spanish city under the burning Mexican stars.

Day and night, dark and light. When morning dawns, white egrets rise from the trees in the Parque Juárez, soaring up into the radiant bubble of the sky and drifting away for the day. As evening approaches, they return, descending into the trees where they nest in the spring and raise their fledglings in the summer before migrating for the winter. At the same hour, all the black, glossy grackles settle for the night in great hordes in the trees around the *jardín* with the greatst possible avian cacophony. It might be a chess game played out in the sky by white bird, black bird, changing day for night.

To an even greater extent is one aware of the place of the human being in the natural world in a little town, a village really, to the south of Mexico City and northeast of Cuernavaca, a place called Tepoztlán, nestled against the forested flanks of hills and spilling into the valley below. Although the houses look recent and temporary compared to those of the Spanish colonial towns to the north—really little more than constructions of the local black lava stone or of adobe bricks under sloping tiled roofs—it is actually a far, far older habitation. There are people here who speak no Spanish but only Nahuatl, and the steep roads were laid in pre-Columbian times, according to the design of the Aztec pyramid temple—a steep incline with a level platform, then another steep incline and another level platform, and so on till one reaches the top. At the highest peak, twelve hundred feet above the valley, stands the temple of El Tepozteco, the god of harvest, fertility, and wine, whose festival is celebrated with much dance and drink for three days in the spring (the Dominican friars who brought Christianity to the place found it impossible to dislodge this cult and fabricated a Christian festival to coincide with it, so its rites are conducted within the boundaries of the cathedral grounds). The converts embraced the Christian faith with that inclusiveness so much a mark of Mexican culture, and each of the seven *barrios* of the town—named after the bird, insect, or reptile most common to that area: scorpion, lizard, turtle, for example—has its own church and its own saint, who is venerated with three-day festivals twice a year. As a result, the whole year round, the town resounds with music, dances, and, most deafeningly, fireworks—built into towering *castillos*—that are set off at sunset. On these occasions every house in the *barrio* will open its doors so neighbors and strangers may enter, seat themselves at the long tables laid under the avocado and custard apple trees, and share the food (papayas and mangoes carved into elaborate flowers on sticks, ice cream, tamales, corn on the cob, chili sauce) and hospitality.

Then there is the open market, held twice a week, to which people from surrounding villages have brought their produce and crafts for generations and centuries—fruit and vegetables, grains and spices on Wednesday; arts and crafts (baskets, gourds, pottery, silver, and copperware) on Sunday. If a pig has been slaughtered, its head will be mounted outside; if a goat, then the goat's. As in India, no attempt is made to disguise or obscure.

The Convento Domínico de la Natividad is the still center of all the town's festivities and commerce, its quiet cloisters painted with fading red roses, its refectory with the figures of the Dominican friars who first occupied cells on the upper floor, which have some of the fairest views in all Mexico. Nowadays these rooms house a museum of local lore and galleries that display the work of local and visiting artists.

But one has only to walk a little way down the steep roads radiating from the center to see that the town is little more than a marketplace; most people still live as if they were in the country, their walled compounds guarded by packs of dogs and full of chickens, turkeys, woodpiles, washing troughs, and the coffee bushes that provide the red berries one can smell being roasted over fires and ground early in the morning. In no time at all one is out in the countryside, and the ranches and haciendas of the rich from Cuernavaca and Mexico

City give way to the cornfields, orchards, streams, and forests that have always been there. The roads here are made for horses, burros, and sandaled feet, not automobiles. At dusk one sees shepherds leading their flocks home and farmers carrying machetes back from their fields, and then the land is swallowed up by the dark. The night has enormous depth, and the night sky brilliance; one is very aware that this land gave birth to the legendary Aztec serpent god, Quetzalcoatl. Perhaps it is why artists and writers have always come here—to find the pulse of that creative force.

Perhaps. Perhaps not. What does make Mexico, for me, the perfect environment for a writer is that slow, regular heartbeat of time in a land where it has been beating for a long, long time, through so much history, building up a long, long past into which one may immerse oneself, then reemerge—the same, yet altered, renewed. In the same spirit of contradiction, one can be solitary as a writer must be solitary, on a patio or a veranda with one's books and papers, but whereas in the city this solitude is confining, deadening, here in a Mexican village one is never truly isolated or separated. Birds as tiny as butterflies come by to sip from the flowers around one, butterflies as large as birds swoop regally by, and all around there is the hum of life: the village dogs exchanging threats and insults, the church bells booming, the vendor going by with his bucket of boiled corncobs, the knife sharpener on his bicycle who plays but two melancholy notes on his little pipe, the maid sluicing down the paving stones of the patio or thrashing clothes in the trough, a burro trotting by with a load of firewood, a fountain trickling (and, yes, one must admit, at least six radios blaring in the compounds around) . . . One is not banished from the web of life, one is included. A metaphor, is that not, for art?

[2002]

JAN MORRIS

(1926–)

Jan Morris is probably the only writer who has written travel narratives from the viewpoints of both genders. As James Morris, a native of Wales, she was a member of the Ninth Queen's Royal Lancers during World War II and took part shortly after the war in Edmund Hilary's conquest of Mount Everest. *Conundrum* (1974) relates her sex change operation to her career as a writer and traveler. Jan Morris has been particularly attracted to cities and has written books on Manhattan, Sydney, Hong Kong, Trieste, and Oxford, in addition to collections of articles: *Journeys* (1984), *Locations* (1992), and *Among the Cities* (1985).

In "City of Yok," a selection from the latter book, she combines an evocation of the contemporary Turkish metropolis of Istanbul with a sense of history. She examines both the negative and the positive connotations of the Turkish word *yok*, which symbolizes for her a theme expressing the strength and solidity of Turkish character and the problems of Turkish society. The "sensations of unrest" that Morris felt in Istanbul three decades ago have only increased, given the wars in Iraq and the rise of Islamic fundamentalism. Still, Istanbul remains one of the world's most scenic cities, full of color, energy, and charm. Rather than focusing on the process of journeying, Morris's essay exemplifies travel writing that seeks to articulate the spirit of a place through a series of impressions and encounters.

"City of Yok"
Istanbul, 1978

From *Among the Cities*

The favourite epithet of Istanbul seems to be *yok*. I don't speak Turkish, but *yok* appears to be a sort of general-purpose discouragement, to imply that (for instance) it can't be done, she isn't home, the shop's shut, the train's left, take it or leave it, you can't come this way or there's no good making a fuss about it, that's the way it is. *Yok* (at least in my interpretation) is like *nyet* in Moscow, 'Sorry luv' in London or 'Have a good day' in New York. It expresses at once the good and the bad of Istanbul civic philiosophy: the bad, a certain prohibitive attitude to life, a lack of fizz or obvious hopefulness, a forbidding fatalism and an underlying sense of menace; the good, an immense latent strength, an accumulated toughness and stubbornness, which has enabled Istanbul to keep its personality intact, if not its fabric, through 1,600 years of viciously variable fortune.

Istanbul is a traumatic kind of city. Standing as it does on the frontier between Europe and Asia, it is like a man with a squint, looking east and west at the same time; it is also a northern and a southern city, for immediately above it is the Black Sea, a cold Soviet lake, while almost in sight to the south are the warm waters of the Mediterranean, waters of Homeric myth and yearning.

Contemplating all this one evening, wondering about the meaning of *yok* and looking at the famous view from a high vantage on Galata hill, I found myself peculiarly disturbed by my thoughts. Morbid fancies assailed me, and wherever I looked I seemed to see threatening images. Up the Bosporus towards Russia, a mass of water traffic steamed or loitered between the green, villa-lined shores of the strait, but the ships did not have a cheerful air—they seemed balefully assembled, I thought, like a ragtag invasion fleet. To the south, the Sea of Marmara, which ought to have looked wine-dark and heroic, seemed instead bland, pallid, almost accusatory. Across the inlet of the Golden Horn the ridge of Stamboul, the original core of the city, was crowned in sunset with a splendid nimbus of domes, towers and minarets, but its flanks of hills below seemed to be festering in the shadows, like a maggot heap beneath a throne.

I shook myself free of the obsession, and hurried down the hill for a late tea; but *yok, yok, yok,* the birds seemed to be squawking, as they whirled beady-eyed above my head.

Istanbul leaves many of its visitors similarly unsettled, for it is not an easy place. It is one of the most obsessively fascinating of all cities, but indefinably deadening too; a gorgeous city, but unlovely; courteous, but chill. If you came to it by sea from the south, the classic way to come, you may sense these paradoxes almost from the start. The view from the Marmara is an unforgettable first prospect of a city, but its beauty is somehow unwelcoming. The tremendous skyline stands there, high above the sea, like a covey of watchtowers: one after another along the high Stamboul ridge, the pinnacles seem to be eyeing your approach suspiciously.

For Istanbul does possess, as you can feel from the deck of your ship, the arrogance of the very old: like the rudeness of an aged actor whose prime was long ago, whose powers have failed him but who struts about still in cloak and carnationed buttonhole, snubbing his inferiors. Seen from the sea, Istanbul seems to be sneering from across the confluence of waters, the junction of the Marmara, Bosporus and Golden Horn, which is its *raison d'être,* and all the caiques and motorboats and ferries seem to scuttle past it as though afraid of wounding comments.

It is only when you get closer that you realize the illusion of it, just as you observe, if he leans too close to you on the sofa, the creases of despair around the actor's mouth. Then that proud mass above the water dissolves into something crumblier and shabbier; the watchtowers lose some of their haughty command, the great sea wall of Stamboul is no more than a ruin, and it turns out that the passing boats are taking no notice of the city at all, but are simply impelled to and fro across the waterways, up and down the Golden Horn, zigzagging across the Bosporus, like so many mindless water insects.

For half the civilized world this was once *the* City, the ultimate—Byzantium, Constantinople, the stronghold and repository of all that civilization had retrieved from the wreck of Rome. For the Turks it still is. It is no longer the political capital of Turkey; but it is much the greatest Turkish city: the place where the money is made, the books are written, the place, above all, where the Turks see their own national character most faithfully mirrored or fulfilled. When I put myself into Istanbul's shoes that evening, I felt only some inkling of schizophrenia: when Turks do so, I am told, by immersing their imaginations in the history and spirit of the place, they feel most completely themselves.

I know of no other city that is so impregnated with a sense of fatefulness, and this is partly because few cities have been so important for so long. Constantine founded his capital, the New Rome, in AD 330, and there has not been a moment since when Istanbul was not conscious of its own mighty meaning. The successive dynasties that ruled the place competed with each other to proclaim its consequence. The Romans built their showy Hippodrome, adorning it with captured trophies and staging terrific chariot races beneath the golden horses of its tribune. The Greeks of Byzantium raised their marvellous cathedral, decorating it with precious frescoes and genuflecting in dazzling ritual before its jewelled reliquaries. The conquering Muslims of the Middle Ages commemorated themselves with mosques, schools and caravanserais across the city, each larger, more pious and more philanthropic than the last. The Ottomans built their vast Topkapi Palance, crammed with vulgar jewellery, where the ladies and eunuchs of the Seraglio gossiped life away in marble chambers, and the Sultans eyed their odalisques in exquisite pleasure kiosks above the sea. The mound of old Stamboul, the original Byzantium, is studded all over with monuments, so that every alleyway seems to lead to the courtyard of a stately mosque, a blackened obelisk or a triumphal column, a casket church of Byzantium or at least a magnificent city wall.

But in between them all, under the walls, behind the churches, like a hideous carpet spreads the squalor of the centuries. It is as though these famous buildings were built upon a foundation of undisturbed muck—as though every scrap of rubbish, every gob of spittle, every bucket-load of ordure, has been stamped into the very substance of the place, never to be cleaned or scraped. When it rains, which it often does, the lanes are soon mucky: but it is not just mud that cakes your shoes, not plain earth liquefied, but actually a glaucous composition of immemorial city excreta. The market streets of Istanbul are not exactly picturesque, if only because the citizenry is so drably dressed, in browns, greys and grubby blacks, but they are vividly suggestive of unbroken continuity. The dark cluttered mass of the covered bazaars—the clamour of the market men—the agonizing jams of trucks, cars, horses and carts in the backstreets—the clatter of looms in half-derelict tenements—scuttling dogs and scavenging cats—bent-backed porters carrying beds or crates or carcasses—the click-clack of the man selling plastic clothes pegs, the toot-toot of the man selling wooden whistles, the ting-ting of the water seller with his tin cups—listless detachment of coffee-shop men, oblivious over their cups and dominoes—stern attention of policemen strutting through the shops—the shouts of itinerant greengrocers—the blare of pop music from the record stores—the glowering stone walls, the high towers above—the tumultuous odours of spice, coffee, raw meat, gasoline, sweat, mud—the sheer swell and flow and muddle of humanity there, seething through that urban labyrinth, makes one feel that nobody has ever left Istanbul, that nothing has ever been discarded, that every century has simply added its shambled quota to the uncountable whole, and made these streets a perpetual exhibition of what Istanbul was, is and always will be.

Just as decomposing matter makes for fertile vegetation, so from the compost of Istanbul a timeless vigour emanates. Few cities move with such an intensity of effort, such straining virility. The generations of the dead are risen, to prod the living into life.

For yes, this is a vigour of the grave. These are bones rustling, and the restless ferry-boats of Istanbul are so many funeral craft, carrying their complements of dead men to and fro between the railway stations. Though Istanbul is home to some three million souls, though its suburbs stretch far along the Marmara shore, deep into Thrace, up the Bosporus almost to the Black Sea, though there are few towns on earth so agitated and congested, still it sometimes feels like a tomb-city.

Of all the great Turkish despots, only Kemal Ataturk, the latest, rejected Constantinople as his capital. It was Ataturk who renamed the city Istanbul, and he had no sympathy, it seems, for its sedimented pride—he visited the city reluctantly during his years in office, though he died there in 1938. He was a futurist, a reformer, a secularist, and old Byzantium must have seemed the very negation of his aspirations. To this day Istanbul has never really absorbed his visionary ideas, or become a natural part of the Turkey he created.

Of course it has lost much of the Oriental quaintness that the great man so resented. No longer do the gaily skirted peasants swirl into the covered markets: gone are the tumbled wooden houses of tradition, and only a few of the old Ottoman love nests along the Bosporus, those tottering clapboard mansions that the romantic travellers used to relish, still stand frail and reproachful among the apartment blocks. Ring roads and flyovers have cut their statutory swaths through the slums and city ramparts. The obligatory international hotels ornament the best sites. Here and there one sees blighted enclaves of contemporary planning, blown by litter, stuck all over with peeling posters, invested with car parks and sad gardens.

But it is not really a modern city at all, not modern by taste or instinct, and it seems to reject transplants from our century. In the Municipal Museum (housed in a former mosque in the shadow of the Emperor Valens' great aqueduct) there is dimly displayed an American plan for a new bridge over the

Golden Horn, with ceremonial approaches at either end. It is a lavish conception of spotless plazas and gigantic avenues, but it was doomed from the start, and survives only in an old brown frame upon a musty wall; even if it had been built, I do not doubt, long ago the mould of old Stamboul would have encroached upon its symmetries and rotted its high pretensions.

There can never be a fresh start in Istanbul. It is too late. Its successive pasts are ineradicable and inescapable. I always stay at the Pera Palas Hotel on the Galata hill, almost the last of the old-school grand hotels to survive the invasion of the multinationals—a haven of potted plants, iron-cage elevators, ample baths with eagle feet. It has been halfheartedly modernized once or twice, but like Istanbul itself, it really ignores improvements and is settled complacently into its own florid heritage. My bedroom this time was Number 205, overlooking the Golden Horn. It was clean, fresh and very comfortable—I love the hotel—but when, on my first morning, I lay flat on the floor to do my yoga, lo, from the deep recess beneath my double bed an authentic fragrance of the Ottomans reached me, dismissing the years and the vacuum cleaners alike: an antique smell of omelets and cigars, slightly sweetened with what I took to be attar of roses.

Something fibrous and stringy, like the inherited characteristics of a patrician clan, links the ages of Istanbul, and is as recognizable in its people today as a six-toed foot or albinism. For all its distracted air, in small matters at least Istanbul is a surprisingly reliable city. I never feel vulnerable to assault or robbery here, I seldom feel the need to check the bill, and even the most pestiferous of the local bravoes generally prove, if approached with sufficient firmness, dependable guides and advisers. *Yok* stands for rigidity, but for staunchness, too.

Istanbul has had to be staunch, to withstand the corrosions of time and retain its stature in the world. It has outlasted most of its rivals, after all, and generally wins its battles in the end. Scattered around Pera, the old foreigners' quarter of the city, are the former embassies of the powers, the nations of Europe that have periodically foreclosed Turkey as the bankrupt invalid of the Golden Horn. Nowadays, with the government in Ankara, they are mere consulates, but in their very postures you can still recognize the contempt with which their envoys and ambassadors, not so long ago, surveyed the pretensions of the Sublime Porte: the Russian embassy, like Tolstoy's estate behind its forecourt; the British a huge classical villa by the architect of the Houses of Parliament; the French with its private chapel in the garden; the Italian (once the Venetian) like a stately retreat upon the Brenta. They are still functioning, but they are half buried all the same in the debris of history, forlorn down messy cobbled alleyways or peering hangdog through their railings across the turmoil of the old Grand Rue.

Or take the Greek quarter across the Golden Horn. Here there stands the Patriarchate of the Greek Orthodox Church, the Vatican of Orthodox Christianity. Once it was an organization of immense power, attended by pilgrims and plenipotentiaries, surrounded by acolyte institutions, defying even the dominion of the Muslim caliphs down the road. Now it is pitifully diminished, an unobtrusive little enclave in a semi-slum, its ceremonial gateway symbolically painted black and welded shut forever: while on the hill behind it the huge Greek *lycée*, once aswarm with aspirants, now stands empty, shuttered and despised.

Istanbul outlives all its challengers, reduced of course in wordly influence since the days of the Ottoman Empire, but hardly at all in self-esteem. Those powers and principalities have risen and fallen, some humiliated, some exalted, but the matter of Istanbul outlasts them all. This is a survivor city, essentially aloof to victory or defeat. The nearest a foreign enemy has come to assaulting Istanbul in our century was in 1915, when the armies of the Western alliance in the Great War, landing on the Gallipoli Peninsula some 150 miles to the south, tried to march north to the city. Supported by the guns of the most powerful battle fleet ever seen in the Mediterranean, they threw half a million of the world's finest infantry ashore on Turkish soil and expected to be at the Golden Horn within the month.

Though Istanbul was rigidly blockaded, though British and Australian submarines roamed the Marmara and bombarded the roads to the city, though a warship was torpedoed within sight of the sultan's palace, though the rumble of the battle shivered the minarets on the heights of Stamboul—still the enemy armies never advanced more than five miles from their beachheads.

Istanbul had said *yok*.

In theory this is a secular city, just as Turkey is a secular state. Ataturk decreed it so. In practice the voice of the muezzin rings out across the city, electronically amplified nowadays, almost as insistently as it did in the days of the caliphs, when this was the formal capital of all Islam. Like everything else in Istanbul, the faith proves irrepressible, and it remains the most potent single element, I suppose, in the personality of the place. I went one day to the Blue Mosque at the time of Friday prayers and positioned myself inside its great doorway—discreetly I hoped—to watch the faithful at their devotions. Not for long. A young man of distinctly unecumenical aspect rose from the back row of worshippers and approached me darkly. 'Beat it,' he said, and without a moment's hesitation, beat it I did.

The muezzin voices are voices from the glorious past, never silenced, calling Istanbul always back again, home again to itself—back to the great days of the caliphs, the noble Ahmets and the munificent Mehmets, back to the times when the princes of this city could build incomparable monuments of belief and generosity, high on their seven hills above the sea. Nobody has built in Istanbul like that since the end of the caliphate and its empire, just as nobody has given Istanbul a faith or a pride to call its own. Even the name of the place has lost its majesty. 'Why did Constantinople get the works?' a popular song used to ask. 'That's nobody's business but the Turks'': but the new name lacks the grand hubris of the old, and sends a *frisson*, I am afraid, down almost nobody's spine.

So many a patriot of this city looks back to Islam. The mosques are busy, the fanatics are aflame, regressive religion is one of the fiercest political movements in Isanbul. Though it used to be postulated that Turkish Islam, like capitalism, would wither away in time, the average age of that Blue Mosque congregation looked strikingly young to me. And though the veil has been officially forbidden for half a century now, women are going to the university these days with black scarves drawn pointedly around their faces. The activist Muslims of Isanbul look outside their own country for inspiration—to Iran, to Pakistan, to the Arab states, where militant Islam is on the march or already in power: and when they take to the streets, as they recently did, or engage in student skirmishes, or burn cars, or break windows, the newspapers are unable to define this heady amalgam of nostalgia and zealotry, and cautiously describe them as Idealists.

On the other side, now as always, are the leftists, by which the press means the heterogeneous mass of liberals, anarchists, hooligans and real Communists, which roughly stands for change in an opposite direction. The longest graffito in the world is surely the one that somebody has painted along the whole expanse of the mole at the Kadiköy ferry station, containing in its message almost the entire idiom of the international Left, and leaving those with strong feelings about neo-Fascist hyenas with nothing much more to add. The leftists think of themselves as progressives, modernists, but they are really honouring a tradition older even than Islam: for long before the caliphate was invented, the city crowd was a force in Byzantium. In those days the rival factions of the Blues and the Greens, originally supporters of competing charioteers in the Hippodrome, were infinitely more riotous than any soccer crowd today, and the great circuit of the racetrack, around whose purlieus the back-pack nomads now drink their mint tea in The Pub or the Pudding Shop, was the supreme arena of anarchy, the place where the frustration of the people found its ferocious release in bloodshed and insurrection.

Even now, I think, the quality of mercy is fairly strained in Istanbul, and the threat of public violence is always present. It is not so long since the mob, in its inherited and ineradicable suspicion of Greece, burned down half the coverd bazaars of the city and destroyed everything Greek they could find. Step even now from a bus in Beyazit Square, on the Stamboul ridge, and you may find yourself looking straight down the gun barrel of a military patrol. Hang around long enough in Eminönü, by the waterfront, and you are sure to see somebody frog-marched off the scene by plainclothes toughs or clapped into handcuffs by the implacable military police.

But you feel these antagonisms, this touch of the sinister, only so to speak by osmosis. The Turks are a courteous people, very kind to harmless strangers, and the ruthless side of their nature is generally masked. For that matter, nearly everything in Istanbul is blurred by its own congealment and decay. Cairo, Calcutta, Istanbul—these are the three great cities of the world where you may observe the prophecies of the doomwatch specialists apparently coming true. Chaos has not arrived yet, but it feels imminent enough. The ferry steamers seem to swirl around in a perpetual state of near collision. There is hardly room on the sidewalks for the press of people. Ever and again the city traffic, balked by some unseen mishap far away along the system, comes helplessly to a halt. The festering rubbish dumps of Stamboul seem to heave with incipient disease.

It has not happened yet. The ferry-boats generally evade each other in the end. The traffic does move again. The plague rats have not yet emerged from their garbage. But the suggestion is always there, the shadow of breakdown and anarchy: incubating, one feels, in the day-to-day confusion.

* * *

The sense of foreboding that characterizes Istanbul has a half-illusory quality, and seems to bewilder its citizens as it does its visitors. This is a city of theatrical hazards. Fires and earthquakes have periodically ravaged it. Empires have risen and fallen within its boundaries. There is a humped island called Yassiada, ten or so miles from Istanbul in the Marmara, which was pointed out to me one day as the place where Prime Minister Menderes was imprisoned after a military coup in 1960. It looked a nice enough place to me: a companionable little island, not at all remote, which looked as though it might have some agreeable bathing beaches. And what became of Menderes? I ignorantly asked my companion as our ship sailed by. 'They killed him,' he replied.

Now *that* hardly seemed real, on a blue and sunny day, on the deck of a pleasure-steamer, on a trip around the islands. Half fictional, half fact, a nebulous sense of menace informs the conversations of Istanbul. The foreign businessman has chill presentiments as he leans with his gin and tonic over his balcony by the Bosporus, watching a Russian cruise-ship sliding by, cabin lights ablaze and hammer-and-sickle floodlit, towards Odessa and the Motherland. 'Something's going to happen. Something's going to crack . . .' The Turkish bank official, pausing didactically with your traveller's cheques beneath his thumb, attributes the malaise to strategy. 'Strategy is the curse of Istanbul—it's where we live; we can never be left in peace.' The army colonel, over a drink at the Hilton, talks apocalyptically through his moustache of conspiracies and conflicts. 'I'll tell you quite frankly—and the Americans know this well enough—the Greeks don't simply want Cyprus for themselves, they don't simply want to make the Aegean a Greek lake—*they want Istanbul itself!* They want to restore Byzantium!'

It is easy to feel perturbed in Istanbul. Every evening at the Pera Palas a string trio plays, attentively listened to by the German package tourists at their communal tables, and gives the place a comfortable, palm-court air. Two elderly gentlemen in gypsy outfits are on piano and accordion, and they are led by a romantic fiddler, adept at waltzes and polkas.

I was sitting there one evening when suddenly there burst into the room, driving the trio from its podium and severely disconcerting the *Hausfraus*, a team of ferocious Anatolian folk dancers, accompanied by a young man with a reedy trumpet and an apparently half-crazed drummer. The dancers were fairly crazed themselves. Apparently welded together into a multicoloured phalanx, they shrieked, they roared with laughter, they leaped, they whirled, they waved handkerchiefs—a performance of furious bravura, leaving us all breathless and aghast. They were like so many houris, come to dance over the corpses on a battlefield.

They withdrew as abruptly as they had arrived, and in the stunned hush that ensued I turned to the Americans at the next table. 'My God,' I said, 'I'm glad they're on our side!' But a knowing look crossed the man's face. 'Ah, but *are* they?' he replied.

You can never be quite sure, with the Turks. They are nobody's satellites, and they habitually leave the world guessing. This does not make for serenity, and Istanbul is not a blithe city. For foreigners it is a city, all too often, of homesickness and bafflement, for Turks a city where life gets tougher every day. I saw a protest demonstration one day clambering its way up the hill towards the Hippodrome, on the Stamboul ridge, and never did I see a demonstration so lacking in the fire of indignation. The hill is very steep there, and the cheerleaders, men and women in antiphony, found it hard to raise a response among their panting protégés: while flanking the procession on either side, guns across their bellies, helmets low over their foreheads, an escort of soldiers did their chesty best to keep up. An armoured car brought up the rear, flashing blue and white lights, but even it found the progress heavy going.

More telling still perhaps, one day I walked up a hill on the Pera side (every walk in Isanbul is up or down a hill) in the wake of a big brown bear, chained to the staff of a lanky man in black. It was a distinguished-looking bear, lean and handsome, but it walked through Istanbul in movements of infinite melancholy and weariness, as though the day, the walk up the hill, life itself would never end. I overtook it presently, and prodded by its master it stood on its hind legs for a moment to salute me as I passed: but it did so disdainfullly, I thought, and somewhat *grandly*.

Istanbul indeed is nothing if not grand. It may not be exuberant, it is seldom funny, its humour running characteristically to not very prurient posters and bawdy badinage. It is hardly uplifting: sometimes, when I take the old funicular from Galata hill to the Golden Horn, I feel that its carriages, sliding into their narrow black tunnels, are plunging me into perpetual night. It is never optimistic: one feels that dire things may happen at any moment, and all too often they do, arrests, accidents, collapses, unidentified gunshots and screaming sirens in the night being commonplaces of the city.

But grand, unquestionably. For all my unease in Istanbul, I greatly admire the place, and it is the grandeur that does it: not the grandeur of history or monument, but the grandeur of *yok*, the ornery strength and vigour that gives a living dignity to its affairs. There is one incomparable vantage from which to observe this ironic vitality—the deck of one of the restaurant boats which are moored beside the Galata Bridge; and there at a typical Istanbul lunchtime—greyish, that is, with a warm breeze off the Bosporus to flutter the canvases—I will end my essay.

The setting down there is terrific. The bulk of Stamboul rises magnificently behind our backs, the iron-brown Galata hill is stacked across the Golden Horn, and to the east the ships pass to and fro along the wide expanse of the Bosporus. Everything is a little hazed, though: not merely by the cloud of spiced smoke in which the restaurateur is cooking our fish, on the open quayside by the boat, but by a kind of permanent opacity of life and light along the Golden Horn, through which everything moves powerfully but inexactly.

Those inescapable ferry-boats, for instance, twist and scuttle in a dreamlike frenzy, and across the bridge the traffic seems to lurch without pattern or priority. Peddlers, defying the amassed tide of pedestrians like Californians wading into the surf, offer balloons, cutlery, incomprehensible household gadgets and sizzling corn on the cob. Military policemen saunter watchfully by, eyes darting right and left for deserters or unsoldierly conduct. From their boats below the quay smoke-shrouded fishermen hand up chunks of grilled fish to their customers above, who sprinkle rough salt upon them from pots tied to the railings and wander off munching into the crowd. Lines of indistinguishable youths hang over their fishing rods beneath the bridge, and sometimes clouds of pigeons, suddenly emerging from their roosts in the dusty façade of the mosque at the end of the bridge, swoop across the scene like huge grey raindrops.

It is a wonderfully animated scene, but animated it seems by habit: numbly animated, passively animated, like a huge mechanical theatre worked by the engines of history. Presently our food comes, with a chopped tomato salad on the side, a glass of beer and some fine rough Turkish bread. 'Oh,' we may perhaps murmur, in our foreign way, 'excuse me, but I wonder if we could possibly have some butter?' The waiter smiles, faintly but not unkindly. '*Yok*, he says, and leaves us to our victuals.

[1978]

ANGELA CARTER

(1940–1992)

Contemporary British writer Angela Carter produced a wealth of fiction imbued with fable, fantasy, and melodrama. Among her many works are *The Bloody Chamber and Other Stories* (1981) and *Nights at the Circus* (1984) in which she blurs distinctions between genres, settings, and states of consciousness. A great deal of travel literature straddles the realms of nonfiction and fiction, and in this tale, Angela Carter exploits the imaginative state of mind that travel can induce.

The selection that follows, "The Kiss," is from *Black Venus* (1985), one of her best-known books (published in the United States as *Saints and Strangers*). It begins like a travel sketch of the Central Asian city of Samarkand and spirals off into a speculative fancy about a dead conqueror's wife. The narrative suggests how the imagination of an observing traveler can be transported into a world of myth and history by the mere encounter with a landscape and culture. The spirit of place is so strong in Samarkand, and the sense of history so present in the atmosphere, that the story seems to arise simply and magically out of the narrator's presence in this remote land.

"The Kiss"

From *Black Venus*

The winters in Central Asia are piercing and bleak, while the sweating, foetid summers bring cholera, dysentery and mosquitoes, but, in April, the air caresses like the touch of the inner skin of the thigh and the scent of all the flowering trees douses this city's throat-catching whiff of cesspits.

Every city has its own internal logic. Imagine a city drawn in straightforward, geometric shapes with crayons from a child's colouring box, in ochre, in white, in pale terracotta. Low, blonde terraces of houses seem to rise out of the whitish, pinkish earth as if born from it, not built out of it. There is a faint, gritty dust over everything, like the dust those pastel crayons leave on your fingers.

Against these bleached pallors, the iridescent crusts of ceramic tiles that cover the ancient mausoleums ensorcellate the eye. The throbbing blue of Islam transforms itself to green while you look at it. Beneath a bulbous dome alternately lapis lazuli and veridian, the bones of Tamburlaine, the scourge of Asia, lie in a jade tomb. We are visiting an authentically fabulous city. We are in Samarkand.

The Revolution promised the Uzbek peasant women clothes of silk and on this promise, at least, did not welch. They wear tunics of flimsy satin, pink and yellow, red and white, black and white, red, green and white, in blotched stripes of brilliant colours that dazzle like an optical illusion, and they bedeck themselves with much jewellery made of red glass.

They always seem to be frowning because they paint a thick, black line straight across their foreheads that takes their eyebrows from one side of their faces to the other without a break. They rim their eyes with kohl. They look startling. They fasten their long hair in two or three dozen whirling plaits. Young girls wear little velvet caps embroidered with metallic thread and beadwork. Older women cover their heads with a couple of scarves of flower-printed wool, one bound tight over the forehead, the other hanging loosely on to the shoulders. Nobody has worn a veil for sixty years.

They walk as purposefully as if they did not live in an imaginary city. They do not know that they themselves and their turbaned, sheepskin jacketed, booted menfolk are creatures as extraordinary to the foreign eye as a unicorn. They exist, in all their glittering and innocent exoticism, in direct contradiction to history. They do not know what I know about them. They do not know that this city is not the entire world. All they know of the world is this city, beautiful as an illusion, where irises grow in the gutters. In the tea-house a green parrot nudges the bars of its wicker cage.

The market has a sharp, green smell. A girl with black-barred brows sprinkles water from a glass over radishes. In this early part of the year, you can buy only last summer's dried fruit—apricots, peaches, raisins—except for a few, precious, wrinkled pomegranates, stored in sawdust through the winter and now split open on the stall to show how a wet nest of garnets remains within. A local speciality of Samarkand is salted apricot kernels, more delicious, even, than pistachios.

An old women sells arum lilies. This morning, she came from the mountains, where wild tulips have put out flowers like blown bubbles of blood, and the wheedling turtle-doves are nesting among the rocks. This old woman dips bread into a cup of buttermilk for her lunch and eats slowly. When she has sold her lilies, she will go back to the place where they are growing.

She scarcely seems to inhabit time. Or, it is as if she were waiting for Scheherazade to perceive a final dawn had come and, the last tale of all concluded, fall silent. Then, the lily-seller might vanish.

A goat is nibbling wild jasmine among the ruins of the mosque that was built by the beautiful wife of Tamburlaine.

Tamburlaine's wife started to build this mosque for him as a surprise, while he was away at the wars, but when she got word of his imminent return, one arch still remained unfinished. She went directly to the architect and begged him to hurry but the architect told her that he would complete the work in time only if she gave him a kiss. One kiss, one single kiss.

Tamburlaine's wife was not only very beautiful and very virtuous but also very clever. She went to the market, bought a basket of eggs, boiled them hard and stained them a dozen different colours. She called the architect to the palace, showed him the basket and told him to choose any egg he liked and eat it. He took a red egg. What does it taste like? Like an egg. Eat another.

He took a green egg.

What does *that* taste like? Like the red egg. Try again.

He ate a purple egg.

One egg tastes just the same as any other egg, if they are fresh, he said.

There you are! she said. Each of these eggs looks different to the rest but they all taste the same. So you may kiss any one of my serving women that you like but you must leave me alone.

Very well, said the architect. But soon he came back to her and this time he was carrying a tray with three bowls on it, and you would have thought the bowls were all full of water.

Drink from each of these bowls, he said.

She took a drink from the first bowl, then from the second; but how she coughed and spluttered when she took a mouthful from the third bowl, because it contained, not water, but vodka.

This vodka and that water both look alike but each tastes quite different, he said. And it is the same with love.

Then Tamburlaine's wife kissed the architect on the mouth. He went back to the mosque and finished the arch the same day that victorious Tamburlaine rode into Samarkand with his army and banners and his cages full of captive kings. But when Tamburlaine went to visit his wife, she turned away from him because no woman will return to the harem after she has tasted vodka. Tamburlaine beat her with a knout until she told him she had kissed the architect and then he sent his executioners hotfoot to the mosque.

The executioners saw the architect standing on top of the arch and ran up the stairs with their knives drawn but when he heard them coming he grew wings and flew away to Persia.

This is a story in simple, geometric shapes and the bold colours of a child's box of crayons. This Tamburlaine's wife of the story would have painted a black stripe laterally across her forehead and done up her hair in a dozen, dozen tiny plaits, like any other Uzbek women. She would have bought red and white radishes from the market for her husband's dinner. After she ran away from him perhaps she made her living in the market. Perhaps she sold lilies there.

[1985]

APSLEY CHERRY-GARRARD

(1886–1959)

As a member of fellow Englishman Captain Robert F. Scott's last expedition to the Antarctic (1910–1913), Apsley Cherry-Garrard produced a book with a title as unforgettable as the author's name: *The Worst Journey in the World* (1922). His narrative dramatizes the physical and psychological challenges posed by the vast and hostile terrain of Antarctica. In the spirit of exploration and discovery, the men of the expedition took enormous risks.

In the passage that follows, the men face certain death by freezing after their tent blows away in a gale. Having come to the end of the earth, they huddle together, exposed to the elements and virtually imprisoned in a vast icy expanse. The author survived; however, the leader of the expedition, Scott, perished elsewhere in the Antarctic. (Scott's epitaph quotes lines from Tennyson's "Ulysses," a poem invoking the epic spirit of travel and adventure, which is found at the end of this anthology.)

From *The Worst Journey in the World*

I have heard tell of an English officer at the Dardanelles who was left, blinded, in No Man's Land betweeen the English and Turkish trenches. Moving only at night, and having no sense to tell him which were his own trenches, he was fired at by Turk and English alike as he groped his ghastly way to and from them. Thus he spent days and nights until, one night, he crawled towards the English trenches, to be fired at as usual. 'Oh God! what can I do!' someone heard him say, and he was brought in.

Such extremity of suffering cannot be measured: madness or death may give relief. But this I know: we on this journey were already beginning to think of death as a friend. As we groped our way back that night, sleepless, icy, and dog-tired in the dark and the wind and the drift, a crevasse seemed almost a friendly gift.

'Things must improve,' said Bill next day, 'I think we reached bed-rock last night.' We hadn't, by a long way.

It was like this.

We moved into the igloo for the first time, for we had to save oil by using our blubber stove if we were to have any left to travel home with, and we did not wish to cover our tent with the oily black filth which the use of blubber necessitates. The blizzard blew all night, and we were covered with drift which came in through hundreds of leaks: in this wind-swept place we had found no soft snow with which we could pack our hard snow blocks. As we flensed some rubber from one of our penguin skins the powdery drift covered every-thing we had.

Though uncomfortable this was nothing to worry about overmuch. Some of the drift which the blizzard was bringing would collect to leeward of our hut and the rocks below which it was built, and they could be used to make our hut more weather-proof. Then with great difficulty we got the blubber stove to start, and it spouted a blob of boiling oil into Bill's eye. For the rest of the night he lay, quite unable to stifle his groans, obviously in very great pain: he told us afterwards that he thought his eye was gone. We managed to cook a meal some-how, and Birdie got the stove going afterwards, but it was quite useless to try and warm the place. I got out and cut the green canvas outside the door, so as to get the roof cloth in under the stones, and then packed it down as well as I could with snow, and so blocked most of the drift coming in.

It is extraordinary how often angels and fools do the same thing in this life, and I have never been able to settle which we were on this journey. I never heard an angry word: once only (when this same day I could not pull Bill up the cliff out of the penguin rookery) I heard an impatient one: and these groans were the nearest approach to complaint. Most men would have howled. 'I think we reached bed-rock last night,' was stong language for Bill. 'I was incapacitated for a short time,' he says in his report to Scott. Endurance was tested on this journey under unique circumstances, and always these two men with all the burden of responsibility which did not fall upon myself, displayed that quality which is perhaps the only one which may be said with certainty to make for suc-cess, self-control.

We spent the next day—it was 21 July—in collecting every scrap of soft snow we could find and packing it into the crevasses between our hard snow blocks. It was a pitifully small amount but we could see no cracks when we had fin-ished. To counteract the lifting tendency the wind had on our roof we cut some great flat hard snow blocks and laid them on the canvas top to steady it against the sledge which formed the ridge support. We also pitched our tent outside the igloo door. Both tent and igloo were therefore eight or nine hundred feet up Terror: both were below an outcrop of rocks from which the mountain fell steeply to the Barrier behind us, and from this direction came the blizzards. In front of us the slope fell for a mile or more down to the ice-cliffs, so wind-swept that we had to wear crampons to walk upon it. Most of the tent was in the lee of the igloo, but the cap of it came over the igloo roof, while a segment of the tent itself jutted out beyond the igloo wall.

That night we took much of our gear into the tent and lighted the blubber stove. I always mistrusted that stove, and every moment I expected it to flare up and burn the tent. But the heat it gave, as it burned furiously, with the double lining of the tent to contain it, was considerable.

It did not matter, except for a routine which we never managed to keep, whether we started to thaw our way into our frozen sleeping-bags at 4 in the morning or 4 in the afternoon. I think we must have turned in during the afternoon of that Friday, leaving the cooker, our finnesko, a deal of our foot-gear, Bowers's bag of personal gear, and many other things in the tent. I expect we left the blubber stove there too, for it was quite useless at present to try and warm the igloo. The tent floor-cloth was under our sleeping-bags in the igloo.

'Things must improve,' said Bill. After all there was much for which to be thankful. I don't think anybody could have made a better igloo with the hard snow blocks and rocks which were all we had: we would get it air-tight by degrees. The blubber stove was working, and we had fuel for it: we had also found a way down to the penguins and had three complete, though frozen eggs: the two which had been in my mitts smashed when I fell about because I could not wear spectacles. Also the twilight given by the sun below the horizon at noon was getting longer.

But already we had been out twice as long in winter as the longest previous journeys in spring. The men who made those journeys had daylight where we had darkness, they had never had such low temperatures, generally nothing approaching them, and they had seldom worked in such difficult country. The nearest approach to healthy sleep we had had for nearly a month was when during blizzards the temperature allowed the warmth of our bodies to thaw some of the ice in our clothing and sleeping-bags into water. The wear and tear on our minds was very great. We were certainly weaker. We had a little more than a tin of oil to get back on, and we knew the conditions we had to face on that journey across the Barrier; even with fresh men and fresh gear it had been almost unendurable.

And so we spent half an hour or more getting into our bags. Cirrus cloud was moving across the face of the stars from the north, it looked rather hazy and thick to the south, but it is always difficult to judge weather in the dark. There was little wind and the temperature was in the minus twenties. We felt no particular uneasiness. Our tent was well dug in, and was also held down by rocks and the heavy tank off the sledge which were placed on the skirting as additional security. We felt that no power on earth could move the thick walls of our igloo, nor drag the canvas roof from the middle of the embankment into which it was packed and lashed.

'Things must improve,' said Bill.

I do not know what time it was when I woke up. It was calm, with that absolute silence which can be so soothing or so terrible as circumstances dictate. Then there came a sob of wind, and all was still again. Ten minutes and it was blowing as though the world was having a fit of hysterics. The earth was torn in pieces: the indescribable fury and roar of it all cannot be imagined.

'Bill, Bill, the tent has gone,' was the next I remember—from Bowers shouting at us again and again through the door. It is always these early morning shocks which hit one hardest: our slow minds suggested that this might mean a peculiarly lingering form of death. Journey after journey Birdie and I fought our way across the few yards which had separated the tent from the igloo door. I have never understood why so much of our gear which was in the tent remained, even in the lee of the igloo. The place where the tent had been was littered with gear, and when we came to reckon up afterwards we had everything except the bottom piece of the cooker, and the top of the outer cooker. We never saw these again. The most wonderful thing of all was that our finnesko were lying where they were left, which happened to be on the ground in the part of the tent which was under the lee of the igloo. Also Birdie's bag of personal gear was there, and a tin of sweets.

Birdie brought two tins of sweets away with him. One we had to celebrate our arrival at the Knoll: this was the second, of which we knew nothing, and which was for Bill's birthday, the next day. We started eating them on Saturday, however, and the tin came in useful to Bill afterwards.

To get that gear in we fought against solid walls of black snow which flowed past us and tried to hurl us down the slope. Once started nothing could have stopped us. I saw Birdie knocked over once, but he clawed his way back just in time. Having passed everything we could find in to Bill, we got back into the igloo, and started to collect things together, including our very dishevelled minds.

There was no doubt that we were in the devil of a mess, and it was not altogether our fault. We had had to put our igloo more or less where we could get rocks with which to build it. Very naturally we had given both our tent and igloo all the shelter we could from the full force of the wind, and now it seemed we were in danger not because they were in the wind, but because they were not sufficiently in it. The main force of the hurricane, deflected by the ridge behind, fled over our heads and appeared to form by suction a vacuum below. Our tent had either been sucked upwards into this, or had been blown away because some of it was in the wind while some of it was not. The roof of our igloo was being wrenched upwards and then dropped back with great crashes: the drift was spouting in, not it seemed because it was blown in from outside, but because it was sucked in from within: the lee, not the weather, wall was the worst. Already everything was six or eight inches under snow.

Very soon we began to be alarmed about the igloo. For some time the heavy snow blocks we had heaved up on to the canvas roof kept it weighted down. But it seemed that they were being gradually moved off by the hurricane. The tension became well-nigh unendurable: the waiting in all that welter of noise was maddening. Minute after minute, hour after hour—those snow blocks were off now anyway, and the roof was smashed up and down—no canvas ever made could stand it indefinitely.

We got a meal that Saturday morning, our last for a very long time as it happened. Oil being of such importance to us we tried to use the blubber stove, but after several preliminary spasms it came to pieces in our hands, some solder having melted; and a very good thing too, I thought, for it was more dangerous than useful. We finished cooking our meal on the primus. Two bits of the cooker having been blown away we had to balance it on the primus as best we could. We then settled that in view of the shortage of oil we would not have another meal for as long as possible. As a matter of fact God settled that for us.

We did all we could to stop up the places where the drift was coming in, plugging the holes with our socks, mitts and other clothing. But it was no real good. Our igloo was a vacuum which was filling itself up as soon as possible: and when snow was not coming in a fine black moraine dust took its place, covering us and everything. For twenty-four hours we waited for the roof to go: things were so bad now that we dare not unlash the door.

Many hours ago Bill had told us that if the roof went he considered that our best chance would be to roll over in our sleeping-bags until we were lying on the openings, and get frozen and drifted in.

Gradually the situation got more desperate. The distance between the taut-sucked canvas and the sledge on which it should have been resting became greater, and this must have been due to the stretching of the canvas itself and the loss of the snow blocks on the top: it was not drawing out of the walls. The crashes as it dropped and banged out again were louder. There was more snow coming through the walls, though all our loose mitts, socks and smaller clothing were stuffed into the worst places: our pyjama jackets were stuffed between the roof and the rocks over the door. The rocks were lifting and shaking here till we thought they would fall.

We talked by shouting, and long before this one of us proposed to try and get the Alpine rope lashed down over the roof from outside. But Bowers said it was an absolute impossibility in that wind. 'You could never ask men at sea to try such a thing,' he said. He was up and out of his bag continually, stopping up holes, pressing against bits of roof to try and prevent the flapping and so forth. He was magnificent.

And then it went.

Birdie was over by the door, where the canvas which was bent over the lintel board was working worse than anywhere else. Bill was practically out of his bag pressing against some part with a long stick of some kind. I don't know what I was doing but I was half out of and half in my bag.

The top of the door opened in little slits and that green Willesden canvas flapped into hundreds of little fragments in fewer seconds than it takes to read this. The uproar of it all was indescribable. Even above the savage thunder of that great wind on the mountain came the lash of the canvas as it was whipped to little tiny strips. The highest rocks which we had built into our walls fell upon us, and a sheet of drift came in.

Birdie dived for his sleeping-bag, and eventually got in, together with a terrible lot of drift. Bill also—but he was better off: I was already half into mine and all right, so I turned to help Bill. 'Get into your own,' he shouted, and when I continued to try and help him, he leaned over until his mouth was against my ear. '*Please*, Cherry,' he said, and his voice was terribly anxious. I know he felt responsible: feared it was he who had brought us to this ghastly end.

The next I knew was Bowers's head across Bill's body. 'We're all right,' he yelled, and we answered in the affirmative. Despite the fact that we knew we only said so because we knew we were all wrong, this statement was helpful. Then we turned our bags over as far as possible, so that the bottom of the bag was uppermost and the flaps were more or less beneath us. And we lay and thought, and sometimes we sang.

I suppose, wrote Wilson, we were all revolving plans to get back without a tent: and the one thing we had left was the floor-cloth upon which we were actually lying. Of course we could not speak at present, but later after the blizzard had stopped we discussed the possibility of digging a hole in the snow each night and covering it over with the floor-cloth. I do not think we had any idea that we could really get back in those temperatures in our present state of ice by such means, but no one ever hinted at such a thing. Birdie and Bill sang quite a lot of songs and hymns, snatches of which reached me every now and then, and I chimed in, somewhat feebly I suspect. Of course we were getting pretty badly drifted up. 'I was resolved to keep warm,' wrote Bowers, 'and beneath my debris covering I paddled my feet and sang all the songs and hymns I knew to pass the time. I could occasionally thump Bill, and as he still moved I knew he was alive all right—what a birthday for him!' Birdie was more drifted up than we, but at times we all had to hummock ourselves up to heave the snow off our bags. By opening the flaps of our bags we could get small pinches of soft drift which we pressed together and put into our mouths to melt. When our hands warmed up again we got some more; so we did not get very thirsty. A few ribbons of canvas still remained in the wall over our heads, and these produced volleys of cracks like pistol shots hour after hour. The canvas never drew out from the walls, not an inch. The wind made just the same noise as an express train running fast through a tunnel if you have both the windows down.

I can well believe that neither of my companions gave up hope for an instant. They must have been frightened, but they were never disturbed. As for me I never had any hope at all; and when the roof went I felt that this was the end. What else could I think? We had spent days in reaching this place through the darkness in cold such as had never been experienced by human beings. We had been out for four weeks under conditions in which no man had existed previously for more than a few days, if that. During this time we had seldom slept except from sheer physical exhaustion, as men sleep on the rack; and every minute of it we had been fighting for the bed-rock necessaries of bare existence, and always in the dark. We had kept ourselves going by enormous care of our feet and hands and bodies, by burning oil, and by having plenty of hot fatty food. Now we had no tent, one tin of oil left out of six, and only part of our cooker. When we were lucky and not too cold we could almost wring water from our clothes, and directly we got out of our sleeping-bags we were frozen into solid sheets of armoured ice. In cold temperatures with all the advantages of a tent over our heads we were already taking more than an hour of fierce struggling and cramp to get into our sleeping-bags—so frozen were they and so long did it take us to thaw our way in. No! Without the tent we were dead men.

And there seemed not one chance in a million that we should ever see our tent again. We were 900 feet up on the mountain side, and the wind blew about as hard as a wind can blow straight out to sea. First there was a steep slope, so hard that a pick made little impression upon it, so slippery that if you started down in finnesko you never could stop: this ended in a great ice-cliff some hundreds of feet high, and then came miles of pressure ridges, crevassed and tumbled, in which you might as well look for a daisy as a tent; and after that the open sea. The chances, however, were that the tent had just been taken up into the air and dropped somewhere in this sea well on the way to New Zealand. Obviously the tent was gone.

Face to face with real death one does not think of the things that torment the bad people in the tracts, and fill the good people with bliss. I might have speculated on my chances of going to Heaven; but candidly I did not care. I could not have wept if I had tried. I had no wish to review the evils of my past. But the past did seem to have been a bit wasted. The road to Hell may be paved with good intentions: the road to Heaven is paved with lost opportunities.

I wanted those years over again. What fun I would have with them: what glorious fun! It was a pity. Well has the Persian said that when we come to die we, remembering that God is merciful, will gnaw our elbows with remorse for thinking of the things we have not done for fear of the Day of Judgement.

And I wanted peaches and syrup—badly. We had them at the hut, sweeter and more luscious than you can imagine. And we have been without sugar for a month. Yes—especially the syrup.

Thus impiously I set out to die, making up my mind that I was not going to try and keep warm, that it might not take too long, and thinking I would try and get some morphia from the medical case if it got very bad. Not a bit heroic, and entirely true! Yes! comfortable, warm reader. Men do not fear death, they fear the pain of dying.

And then quite naturally and no doubt disappointingly to those who would like to read of my last agonies (for who would not give pleasure by his death?) I fell asleep. I expect the temperature was pretty high during this great blizzard, and anything near zero was very high to us. That and the snow which drifted over us made a pleasant wet kind of snipe marsh inside our sleeping-bags, and I am sure we all dozed a good bit. There was so much to worry about that there was not the least use in worrying: and we were so *very* tired. We were hungry, for the last meal we had had was in the morning of the day before, but hunger was not very pressing.

And so we lay, wet and quite fairly warm, hour after hour while the wind roared round us, blowing storm force continually and rising in the gusts to something indescribable. Storm force is force 11, and force 12 is the biggest wind which can be logged: Bowers logged it force 11, but he was always so afraid of overestimating that he was inclined to underrate. I think it was blowing a full hurricane. Sometimes awake, sometimes dozing, we had not a very uncomfort-able time so far as I can remember. I knew that parties which had come to Cape Crozier in the spring had experienced blizzards which lasted eight or ten days. But this did not worry us as much as I think it did Bill: I was numb. I vaguely called to mind that Peary had survived a blizzard in the open: but wasn't that in the summer?

It was in the early morning of Saturday (22 July) that we discovered the loss of the tent. Some time during that morning we had had our last meal. The roof went about noon on Sunday and we had had no meal in the inter-val because our supply of oil was so low; nor could we move out of our bags except as a last necessity. By Sunday night we had been without a meal for some thirty-six hours.

The rocks which fell upon us when the roof went did no damage, and though we could not get out of our bags to move them, we could fit ourselves into them without difficulty. More serious was the drift which began to pile up all round and over us. It helped to keep us warm of course, but at the same time in these comparatively high temperatures it saturated our bags even worse than they were before. If we did not find the tent (and its recovery would be a miracle) these bags and the floor-cloth of the tent on which we were lying were all we had in that fight back across the Barrier which could, I suppose, have only had one end.

Meanwhile we had to wait. It was nearly 70 miles home and it had taken us the best part of three weeks to come. In our less miserable moments we tried to think out ways of getting back, but I do not remember very much about that time. Sunday morning faded into Sunday afternoon,—into Sunday night,—into Monday morning. Till then the blizzard had raged with monstrous fury; the winds of the world were there, and they had all gone mad. We had bad winds at Cape Evans this year, and we had far worse the next winter when the open water was at our doors. But I have never heard or felt or seen a wind like this. I wondered why it did not carry away the earth.

In the early hours of Monday there was an occasional hint of a lull. Ordinarily in a big winter blizzard, when you have lived for several days and nights with that turmoil in your ears, the lulls are more trying than the noise: 'the feel of not to feel it'. I do not remember noticing that now. Seven or eight more hours passed, and though it was still blowing we could make ourselves heard to one another without great difficulty. It was two days and two nights since we had had a meal.

We decided to get out of our bags and make a search for the tent. We did so, bitterly cold and utterly miserable, though I do not think any of us showed it. In the darkness we could see very little, and no trace whatever of the tent. We returned against the wind, nursing our faces and hands, and settled that we must try and cook a meal somehow. We managed about the weirdest meal eaten north or south. We got the floor-cloth wedged under our bags, then got into our bags and drew the floor-cloth over our heads. Between us we got the primus alight somehow, and by hand we balanced the cooker on top of it, minus the two members which had been blown away. The flame flickered in the draughts. Very slowly the snow in the cooker melted, we threw in a plentiful supply of pemmican, and the smell of it was better than anything on earth. In time we got both tea and pemmican, which was full of hairs from our bags, penguin feathers, dirt and debris, but delicious. The blubber left in the cooker got burnt and gave the tea a burnt taste. None of us ever forgot that meal: I enjoyed it as much as such a meal could be enjoyed, and that burnt taste will always bring back the memory.

It was still dark and we lay down in our bags again, but soon a little glow of light began to come up, and we turned out to have a further search for the tent. Birdie went off before Bill and me. Clumsily I dragged my eider-down out of my bag on my feet, all sopping wet: it was impossible to get it back and I let it freeze: it was soon just like a rock. The sky to the south was as black and sinister as it could possibly be. It looked as though the blizzard would be on us again in a moment.

I followed Bill down the slope. We could find nothing. But, as we searched, we heard a shout somewhere below and to the right. We got on a slope, slipped, and went sliding down quite unable to stop ourselves, and came upon Birdie with the tent, the outer lining still on the bamboos. Our lives had been taken away and given back to us.

We were so thankful we said nothing.

[1922]

TIM CAHILL

(1944–)

Tim Cahill is an American travel writer and founding editor of *Outside* magazine. His books are distinguished by their sense of adventure and their dramatic titles: *Jaguars Ripped My Flesh* (1992), *Pecked to Death by Ducks* (1993), and *Pass the Butterworms, Please: Remote Journeys Oddly Rendered* (1997).

The essay that follows, "Jungles of the Mind," is from his first book, *A Wolverine Is Eating My Leg* (1989). In covering the mass suicide of a religious cult in Guyana led by Jim Jones, Cahill evokes the malevolent presence of the jungle in Joseph Conrad's *Heart of Darkness* (1899), a novel that sees the savagery of nature reflected in the human psyche. His account shows how fiction can shape a traveler's nonfiction narrative, and his essay is a fine example of the principle that Beldon C. Lane articulates in *Landscapes of the Sacred* (2002): "Landscape is first of all an effort of the imagination—a construed way of seeing the world. . . . The very choice and framing of the scene is itself a construction of the imagination."

"Jungles of the Mind"

From *A Wolverine Is Eating My Leg*

Joseph Conrad, in his brilliant evocations of the jungles of Africa and the Far East, used and perhaps overused the word *impenetrable*. In truth, those jungles, and the lowland jungles of Central and South America, only seem impenetrable from a road or river or trail or clearing. In those places where sunlight is allowed to reach the ground, a tangled wall erupts out of the earth, a dense green wall that protects the jungle from civilization and can easily be seen as a warning.

In the forest proper, under the endless, broad-leaved canopy, direct rays of the sun seldom reach the earth. What light there is seems tired, heavy, turgid—a flaccid twilight. The floor between the tree trunks is largely bare. But the jungle supports an abundance of life. The majority of invertebrate organisms in the Amazon basin have yet to be named, and generations' worth of botanical research has yet to be done. Above, arboreal frogs with adhesive pads on their feet creep over the dripping leaves. Hordes of bats pollinate the colorful flowers sprouting on tree trunks rather than attempt the tangle of greenery. Aquatic flatworms live in the perpetual moistness of the forest floor. There are tapirs and jaguars, spider and howler monkeys, amphibians, ants and anteaters. There are spiders that drop from the canopy above and eat birds, and there are more birds in the jungle than anywhere else on earth.

In the jungle rivers, one-hundred-pound rodents graze on reeds, and anacondas, those twenty- to thirty-foot-long green-and-white snakes, lie in wait for pigs and small deer that they will kill by constriction and eat whole. The jungle generates persistent reports of forty-foot anacondas, and one miner swears he's seen such a reptile, sunning itself on a riverbank, with the antlers of a deer protruding from its open mouth. "The snake was going to have to wait for the head to decompose before it could spit out those horns," the miner told me.

Despite the telling and retelling of such tales, despite the abundance of animal life—the shrieks and barks and howls one hears—it is the forest itself that captures the mind and sometimes ensnares the soul. "Contact with pure, unmitigated savagery," Conrad wrote, "with primitive nature and primitive man, brings sudden and profound trouble into the heart." For Conrad, civilization was not a matter of flush toilets and paved roads. In his jungle tales, good men, left in the isolation of the forest, became slave traders, murderers, less than men. The jungle provides "a suggestion of things vague, uncontrollable, and repulsive, whose discomposing intrusion excites the imagination and tries the civilized nerves of the foolish and the wise alike." I have felt these sensations, and have translated them as fear. Especially when lost in that troubling darkness, I have felt the sheer weight of indifferent animosity, of some vast, humid hatred.

In the jungle, a lost man feels driven by a desire to plunge ahead, while the hanging vines slap at his face and roots rise up to tangle his feet. Better to stop; sit, think. And that is when the green hostility begins to smother the soul. The mind's eye sees the forest as if it were a time-lapse film. Trees twist into grotesque shapes, the better to steal the sun. Parasites erupt out of healthy organisms. Creepers lash out to strangle lesser plants. Lianas—long, woody vines—drop from branches like thick ropes and root at the base of the host tree, choking off its life so that they themselves stand as a new tree with the dead one inside.

The jungle is moist and warm, and living things may grow and reproduce all year long. Competition comes not from the elements but from the volume of life. A lost man, sitting, thinking, perceives that every living thing longs for the death of every other living thing. He understands "the ever-ready suspicion of evil" Conrad wrote about, "the placid and impenetrable mass of an unjustifiable violence."

These thoughts took on a special clarity when, in the company of other reporters, I visited the necropolis of Jonestown, where the stench of decomposing bodies sent bile rising into my throat. I had already spent days talking with survivors, and I knew that Jim Jones had been deluded, probably addicted to drugs, and clinically paranoid even before he moved to the jungle. But the jungle tore at his mind and fed his paranoia: when the rains came early and the crops failed, it was because the CIA had seeded the clouds. In the jungle compound, from the wooden chair he called his throne, Jones passed on his paranoia to the people of Jonestown, for paranoia is a contagious disease. They saw soldiers in the bush beyond the clearing, and they could hear the growling of vehicles as these shadow forces massed for attack. It was a debilitating siege, and in the end, like the heroes of Masada, who killed themselves nearly two millenniums ago rather than surrender to the Romans, most of them committed suicide rather than submit to the shadow forces that lay in wait, out there in the jungle.

I'm not suggesting that the tragedy happened because Jonestown lay in the jungle. Still, it is impossible to conceive of a similar occurrence in Indianapolis or San Francisco. The madness, the *danse macabre* of suicide and murder, could have happened no place else but in the dark vastness of the jungle.

[2002]

COLIN THUBRON

(1939–)

British novelist and travel writer Colin Thubron has journeyed to many parts of the former Soviet Union and to China, and he remains fascinated by the peoples and cultures of the vast Central Asian steppes. His earlier travel books took him to Istanbul, Damascus, and Cyprus, and he returned to the Middle East for *Jerusalem* (1996). Thubron also explored the lands of the former Soviet Union for *The Lost Heart of Central Asia* (1984). In journeys to remote regions rarely visited by western travelers, he makes good use of his fluent Chinese and Russian to converse with the inhabitants and gain an appreciation of their lives and characters.

In the passage below, which concludes *In Siberia* (1999), he visits an abandoned prison camp from the Stalinist era. The hostile climate and treacherous political history of Siberia constitute a major theme throughout the book and particularly in these final scenes. In his encounters with two Russians, Fedor and Yuri, Thubron acknowledges the resilient spirits of people who have gamely endured terrible hardships.

From *In Siberia*

Perhaps because Fedor was a Russian Jew, he had grown obsessed by the labour camps. His apartment was full of political journals and old *samizdat*. His mirrors hung by string. The kitchen was littered with empty Moldovan wine bottles, and mountaineering and caving equipment blocked the hall. His beard, I think, had grown by default, and the study of persecution, or perhaps something else, touched him with melancholy.

It was he who knew that in this city whose darker past had been casually destroyed, one of the chief transit camps survived as the barracks of security police. 'They abandoned it five months ago. It'll probably be bulldozed soon. Everything gets bulldozed here. Now it's walled up of course.' His soft eyes assessed me. 'But I know a way in.'

So we returned to Transport Road where it dipped over a stream towards the northern mines. In a silent compound, ringed by cement walls and barbed wire, Fedor had found a crumbling hole. We squeezed through. On the far side, the snow showed no tracks. For a second we stood and stared, covered with cement dust. I wanted time to write down things, to remember. I was the first outsider to see this, he said, and would be the last. But we started furtively to run. Now when I scrutinise my dashed-off notes—their words jagged with cold—the place returns in violent snapshots.

I remember the canteen (we crawled in under barred windows) which prisoners had painted with naive scenes in pastel tints: a dream of rural peace. Its floor sagged in a storm of crashed timber.

I remember the dormitories, and the rooms where the prisoners (I imagined) had been issued their bombazine coats and wadded jackets.

Then I remember Fedor pointing to the three-storeyed block in front. Where a door opened on stone steps, he tugged from his satchel some waders and some helmets strapped with lights, and we lowered ourselves into a fetid darkness. Unfrozen water brimmed to our knees. Our words echoed and whispered. 'This was the punishment block.'

We waded down its passageways as down a sewer. I lost count of the iron doors awash with stench, the grilles giving on to blackness. Each dungeon was still fixed with twin wooden platforms bound in iron, and might have held forty prisoners. There were twenty such chambers in the basement alone. Their walls were sheathed in ice. Prisoners here, said Fedor (he had known one), used to press the bodies of the dead against the walls to insulate themselves from the cold. In the stone they had scratched weakly, illegibly, with their spoons. 'Ser . . . olenko . . . 1952 . . . Pant . . .' Our lights faded over them. In these hopeless caverns, he said, most people died. His friend had survived because he had been young.

'What had he done?' I asked.

'He didn't know,' Fedor said. 'He lost his memory.'

You lost your memory easily in Kolyma, Shalamov wrote. It was more expendable than lungs or hands. In fact you did not need it at all.

An hour before dawn I go back into the hills for the last time. A young geologist, Yuri, says he knows the track to Butugychag, and that his twin-axle van can reach there. But it is no place to linger. The native Evenk called it 'the Place where Reindeer Sicken', and their herdsmen sensed something was wrong there. Its earth is filled with radioactive uranium.

The moment we enter the mountains, the snow hits us in a blinding curtain. It swirls like ground-mist over the road, concealing crevices and black ice together, while our engine coughs and roars. Yuri goes quiet as the flakes thicken. The beam of our fog-lamp sucks them towards us down a funnel of silver light. Towards dawn we grind to a halt on a pass, while the blizzard tears the surface from the mountain above us in a howling dust. We wait as a wan morning breaks and Arctic hares shelter against our wheels.

Yuri just says: 'It'll pass.' He has a slow, open face. He never smiles. His yellow hair and moustache, and his lemon skin, are pure Russian. After a while he eases us down into a valley in the breaking dawn, while the falling snow thins and withdraws. Ahead we glimpse distant mountains, no longer rounded but fragile and one-dimensional, like the veins of giant leaves swept against the sky. Slag-heaps are hunched along the river, and sometimes a gold-panners' settlement starts up neat and white-walled, until we see its windows gaping. Beneath us the dead streams make translucent estuaries over the waste.

'This region's emptying. Its workers leave for Magadan.' Yuri is still employed, but there is no work for him, and his salary is ten months in arrears. He does not know what he will do. He is nearly thirty. 'And from Magadan the workers go west.'

Suddenly he tilts off the road on to a half-visible track. In front of us the falling snow sends wavering columns over the mountains. He says: 'This was the worst place, Butugychag. It didn't get worse than this. There were 25,000 prisoners working the mines, politicals and criminals togther. They didn't know about radiation. Even the guards didn't know.'

Already we are axle-deep in drifts, butting and plunging as if our chassis were elastic. The tracks of a hunter's Land Rover are filling with snow in front. 'If he can make it, so can we.' Once we crash through the ice of a stream, its released waters slapping at our doors, but we lumber out and up the far bank. 'That's what these machines are made for! Russian roads!'

For ten more miles we blunder in and out of drifts, over the half-wrecked bridges of the miners, along a sunken stream. A flurry of white ptarmigans gets up under our wheels, their black-tipped wings dipping like fighter-planes over the scrub. The tracks of the hunter's Land Rover disappear now, and soon we are climbing into a valley where even the larches thin away. Mountains circle and close it off, dropping their ridges in steep blades out of the white sky. As we go higher, the land becomes scarred and unnatural. The black embrasures of mineheads open in the summits, and cableways stagger high up across the snow-fields, then descend in a relay of broken gibbets to the valley floor. Under the mineheads the waste has tumbled down and powdered the slopes smooth. And the air around us has changed. The snow hangs in a luminous haze, filling the valley with its unearthly shining, and a smeared sun has risen.

To our right, behind a broken barbed-wire fence, the ruin of a three-storey factory rears white walls above the white stream. It was the flotation plant for uranium, Yuri says, dangerous to enter still, where a work-shift could be dead after a few months. He accelerates grimly, and the walls drop behind us. 'Even after they'd left, they died of it.'

A mile later the van flounders against impassable banks, and we walk up through a bright, cold silence. Sometimes the snow surges above our knees. Yuri tramps ahead, indifferent, with his hat tugged down to his neck. I follow in his footsteps, my heartbeat quickening, as if we are entering a cathedral or a morgue. Instead we reach a huddle of administrative buildings in yellow stone. They are all ruined, their roofs caved in, their doors unhinged or rotted away. The window-frames are snow-silvered rectangles of nothing. Steps lead up to a veranda and through a door to a 20-foot drop.

The poet Anatoly Zhigulin, who survived this camp in the 1950s, described brutal maimings, accidents, internecine murders, desperate strikes. A prisoner had no name, no self. He could be addressed only by his number. Some were in chains. They climbed four miles before they reached the mines; and from their camp on the far side of the mountain, a squad of women convicts trudged eight miles every day to carry home cold rations.

The iron frame of the camp gates stands redundant in the debris of its towers. Beneath the snow our feet snag on objects we only guess at, and drag up barbed wire. Rusted machinery pokes above the surface. Beyond, we stumble through the wrecks of barracks and prison cells. In the roofless rooms the guards' benches are still in place, with a range of hooks for their coats. The snow lies on their platform beds in hard, crystalline piles. A pair of boots is discarded by a stove. Everything emits a hand-to-mouth rusticity and squalor. Skeletal iron doors still swing on isolation cells a few feet square. The slots survive where the prisoners' gruel was pushed through, and the barred windows remain intact, and the stove in the guards' sauna.

The air seems thin. But Yuri's cheeks are pink and burnished. He is kicking the snow from around a grid of notched stumps to uncover wood foundations. 'That's where the tents were,' he says. 'That's where they slept.'

It was the same through much of Kolyma. The prisoners lived and died in tents. Despairingly they pressed insulating moss and peat between the twin layers of canvas, sprinkled them with sawdust, and stacked boards outside. Inside was a single cast-iron stove.

And now gently, insistently, the snow is falling. It drifts over the low stumps and covers the buildings with its pale indifference. It floats through the roofless passages, the guard chambers, the rooms of administration, of neglect, of boredom. It fills the valley with a sick translucence.

Yuri goes on kicking at the tent foundations, then looks up at me. 'You know, my grandfather was a village postman, who spent years in the camps for making a joke about Stalin.'

'A joke?'

'Yes. He was in charge of the village telephone, and one day he told somebody in passing: "By the way, Stalin's on the phone to you!" So he ended up in the camps for five years. My parents must have suffered for that.' He presses a wooden slat back with his boot. 'People grew up in their parents' silence.'

We climb to where he remembers the cemetery lay, but it is lost under snow. The opalescent light has intensified over the valley. Around us the trees and shrubs are laden and heavy, as if bearing white fruit. They shiver with tiny wagtails. I pick some dwarf-cedar needles, which prisoners used to boil in the futile hope of deflecting scurvy.

I say: 'Whatever it's like now, things are better than they were then.'

Yuri does not answer at first. Everything with him takes a long time. He has a slight stutter. He says: 'Those were religious times, in a way. People believed things.' He seems to envy that.

So suffering came down from the sky, as natural as rain or hail. There was no one to accuse. No one was near enough, embodied enough. Stalin's empire, like Hitler's Reich, was meant to last through all imaginable time. The past had been reorganised for ever, the future preordained.

I say, not knowing: 'You'll never go back to that.'

Yuri says: 'We're not the same as you in the West. Maybe we're more like you were centuries ago. We're late with our history here. With us, time still goes in circles.'

I don't want to hear this, not here in the heart of darkness. I want him to call this place an atrocious mystery. I want him not to understand it. With his blond moustache and Tartar cheekbones, I have cast him as the quintessential Russian, the litmus test for the future. The mountain air has gone to my head.

But his hand, which was tracing a circle, now tentatively lifts. 'Maybe we spiral a little,' he says, 'a little upwards.' He looks across to where the cableways limp in ghastly procession over the heights. 'I wish my grandfather had lived on. He loved a good joke, and people can joke about anything now. We've still got that. Jokes.'

I clasp his shoulder, but we are too fat in our quilted coats, and my hand slips from him. He smiles for the first time, on a mouthful of discoloured teeth, before turning back along the track.

And on that frozen hillside he starts to sing.

[1999]

MARY ROACH

(1959–)

Mary Roach is a magazine journalist and contributor to *Salon, Condé Nast Traveler,* and *Islands.* Travel can be a naturally comic subject, given its many possibilities for misadventure and misunderstanding. Roach has put her sense of humor to macabre use in another book, *Stiff: The Curious Life of Cadavers* (2003).

In "Monster in a *Ryokan*" (a *ryokan* is a traditional Japanese hotel), the comedy comes from the incongruous: the comparatively smaller scale of Japanese lodgings makes Roach (an American of average size) seem grotesquely large, and her difficulty in communicating with the Japanese only exaggerates her feelings. The essay illustrates how travelers can be confused—and inspired—by seemingly objective matters such as body size and room dimensions. All is relative; what is considered large in one culture may be small in another.

"Monster in a *Ryokan*"

A monster is a relative thing. In Godzilla's hometown, everyone was fifty feet tall and scaly. The sidewalks were wide enough that no one had to trample parked cars and knock over buildings. Only in Tokyo did Godzilla become a monster.

Likewise myself. In my own country, I am not thought of as brutish and rude—or anyway, no more so than the next slob. But in Japan, I am suddenly huge and clueless. I sprout extra limbs and make loud, unintelligible noises. In Japan, I am a monster.

I came to this conclusion following a recent stay at a *ryokan*, a traditional Japanese inn. It was raining the night I flew in to Tokyo, and the cab had dropped me at the wrong place. Having walked the remaining distance, stopping every few blocks to perform the quaint flailing pantomime of the lost foreigner, I was drenched and disheveled by the time I arrived at the right place.

I lumbered down the foot-path, crashing into bicycles and trampling tiny ornamental trees. As I opened the door, several of the staff could be seen fleeing from the room. Others crouched behind traditional Japanese furnishings, which, though pleasing to the eye, offer little in the way of protective cover.

"HRRARGGHH ARGGHH HAARGH RARRRRHSCHRVRANN." (Hello, I have a reservation.)

I lurched forward and stepped up to the reception window. The woman's face crumbled in distress. A large portion of this appeared to be directed at my feet. She pointed to a shelf of shoes and then she pointed to mine. The shoes on the shelf were dainty and immaculate. The shoes on my feet were wet and battered and huge.

I apologized for the size and condition of my footwear. This was not the problem. The problem was that I was wearing them *inside the ryokan.*

As an American, I was raised to believe that the simple act of passing one's soles across a nubbly plastic mat sporting a cute saying will somehow magically dislodge an accumulated eight hours of filth, muck, and germs. The Japanese do not share our faith in doormats. The Japanese remove their shoes at the door.

As a *ryokan* guest, you are expected to do the same. Inside the front door is a bench for you to sit on and take off your shoes. This is normally located directly across from the reception window, enabling the staff to tell at a glance that your socks a) don't match, b) need washing, and c) have little threadbare patches at the heels. You are then provided with a pair of Japanese slippers, which are open in the back so that the staff, over the course of your visit, can see that, indeed, all of your socks have threadbare heels.

The slippers, you soon learn, are special hallway slippers, not to be worn inside the rooms. In the rooms you wear only socks. That is, unless you are in the toilet room, in which case you exchange your special hallway slippers for special toilet slippers, which are never, under penalty of shame and humiliation, to be worn anywhere but the toilet.

I do not mean to imply that Japanese people are needlessly fastidious. I mean to imply that Americans are needlessly squalid—especially in hotels. In American hotels, the whole idea is to create as much of a mess as possible, as someone else will be cleaning it up. Do unto others as you figure they'd do unto you if you had a job cleaning hotel rooms.

Properly shod, I was shown to my room. It was approximately nine feet square and contained three or four pieces of traditional ankle-high furniture. To someone accustomed to the vast prairies and vistas of the American hotel room, this takes getting used to. In America, a single-occupancy room must contain a bed—heck, make it two!—large enough to accommodate lumberjacks and NBA centers lying spread-eagle in any direction. Though guests will be leaving their belongings strewn about the bed and floor, there must be a dresser, a desk, and a closet the size of Maine. There must be six bars of soap and a telephone in the bathroom. A *ryokan* room, on the other hand, serves the simple purpose for which it was designed: that is, to provide a neat, comfortable place to sleep for a few nights.

Though I appreciated the rational scale and modest aesthetics of my accommodations, I was nonetheless hopelessly disoriented. I kept running into walls and stumbling over traditional ankle-high furniture. Someone had spread bedding out all over the floor, which caused me to trip and smash headlong into a low-hanging lantern. Tea cups were capsized. Miniature dressers toppled and rolled. Soon the Japanese national guard would arrive with rifles and tranquilizer darts.

I tried to get a grip on myself. Thrashing violently in a small Japanese room is a dangerous proposition, as the walls are fashioned not from plaster, but from delicate sheets of waxy rice paper. It's like living inside a Dixie Cup. One false step and you come crashing through to the adjoining room, which in this case happened to be a carp pond, and god only knows what sort of slippers are required for that.

I decided to go soak in the tub. Like other large reptiles, I am plodding and ungainly on land, but surprisingly graceful underwater. I asked the staff for a robe and entered the steamy, tiled sanctum. To my great relief, the bath was already drawn and everything seemed self-explanatory.

Later, back in my room, I noticed a small booklet on the table. It was called *Information on How to Enjoy a Ryokan*—a "guide book" to "living, eating, and sleeping as the Japanese do." According to a section titled "Tips for Taking a Bath," I had committed no less than three ablutionary offenses. For starters, the bathtub is not for bathing, but for relaxing. To soap and rinse yourself inside the tub is an unthinkable act, akin to peeing in the pool or drinking milk straight from the carton. The cute plastic baskets are not floating soap dishes; they are for storing your clothes. The traditional Japanese robe closes left side over right, not right over left, and is called a *yukata*, not—as I had called it—a *yakuza*. (*Yakuza* are Japanese mafiosi, the guys who chop off their pinkies for dishonorable behavior, such as cowardice or soaping oneself in the tub.)

While I contemplated my sins, there was a knock (rustle? thwap?) on the wax paper. It was the proprietress, bearing a tray of tea. She seemed displeased. "I'm sorry about the soap," I blurted. "I didn't see the instruction book."

She smiled—the sort of bemused, resigned smile Fay Wray used to give King Kong after he tipped over the garage or stepped on the house pets. Without a word, she set down the tray and left.

Shortly thereafter, I noticed the toilet slippers on my feet. It was almost a relief. Every wrong thing that could be done had been done. I could only go uphill from here. I rested my huge wet head on my little prehensile arms and went to sleep.

[1999]

TODD MCEWEN

(1953–)

Todd McEwen's encounter with large American midwesterners and their gargantuan appetites makes him feel tiny. McEwen, a New Yorker, writes for *Granta* magazine and is the author of *Fisher's Hornpipe* (1983), *McX* (1990), and *Arithmetic* (1998).

Food is a preoccupation of travelers, and unusual cuisine is a frequent subject of travel writing. In the following selection, "They Tell Me You Are Big" McEwen uses exaggeration as a technique for humor to illustrate regional differences in perspectives on diet and size of portions. The essay points out that even in one's own country, a traveler can feel like a foreigner.

"They Tell Me You Are Big"

The technological parade of welcome: I was already dead with fatigue. Thank you for flying with us today, here is your ticket, change planes in Chicago, you'll have to change planes in Chicago, change in Chicago. They said it so often I began to get the idea I should change planes in Chicago. *Change planes*: the phrase began to lose any reference to travel; it acquired a dread phenomenological taint. But I did not change those sorts of planes in Chicago. Rather, in Chicago I *changed size*. For when I deplaned (more tech-talk) I walked into Big People Land.

I was obliged to go a short distance through a glass tube, the story of a life, from one gate to another. I then had an hour, a whole, giant hour to myself. In

Big People Land. And there they were. They were all about me: large surely-moving salesmen and mammoth middle managers, corn-fed beef-fed farm-bred monuments to metabolism. Flying from dairy states to beef capitals to commodities centres. From Fon-du-Lac to Dubuque, their huge briefcases *stuffed with meat*. Clinching beefy deals with muscular handshakes. Their faces were florid Mt Rushmores with aviator spectacles and sideburns uniformly metallic; their eyes, bovine, the size of Dutch plates, reflected their Low Country ancestries. Their hands were steam-shovels, their shoes big as our tiny neurotic New York family car. I'm not talking fat, although flesh is essential in Chicago. I'm talking big-boned, as the apologists say. I, a tiny under-nourished New York worrier, had been injected into the enlarged heart of America.

Airports like abattoirs are white. All this moving meat, these great bodies laughing, phoning, making valuable contacts, astonished me. I was overwhelmed by the size of everything and everybody, their *huge bigness!* I had to sit down. But where? Everything I sat in dwarfed, *engulfed* me. I was a baby opossum, writhing in a tablespoon in a Golden Nature Guide. I felt fear, tininess and hunger. I decided the only way to become as big as the Big People was to begin eating.

In the infinite coffee shop, my eyes struggled to take in the polyptych menu and its thousand offerings. Eggs with legs, friendly forks and spoons marched across it. GOOD MORNING! *Barnyard Suggestions* . . . What! I thought. Wanna meet this chicken in the hayloft in half an hour, fella? But these were not that kind of barnyard suggestion. Here in Big People Land, land-o-lotsa wholesomeness, they were suggesting I eat the following: (1) 3 strips of bacon, 2 pancakes, 2 eggs (any style), 2 sausages, juice, toast and coffee; (2) 6 strips of bacon, 5 pancakes, 4 eggs (any style), 3 sausages, juice, toast and coffee; or (3) 12 strips of bacon, 9 pancakes, 7 eggs (any style), 1 1/2 gallons of juice, 3 lbs of toast and a 'Bottomless Pit' (which I took to be a typographical error for 'Pot') of coffee. Thus emptying any barnyard I could imagine of all life. Again I was lost. I felt I was visiting Karnak. I pleaded for half an order of toast, eight pieces.

Outside the window, far away, Chicago was dawning. Obsidian towers, an art deco pipe-organ sprouting from the gold prairie, Lake Michigan still dark beyond. A brachycephalic woman was seated opposite me, biting big things. Her teeth were the size of horse teeth. She said we could see into the next state. She was eating such big things and so quickly a wind was blowing at our table. I turned from this and peered out through the clear air, into the next state. In the far distance I saw great shapes which I knew weren't mountains but my giant Midwestern relatives I am too small ever to visit.

Now I was filled with huge toast. I crawled, miniscule, back through the tubes to the gate. I bought a newspaper and my money looked puny and foreign in the vendor's big paw. In the chairs of Big People Land, my feet never touched the floor. I began to open the *Sun-Times*. But. It was big. Here it wasn't even Sunday and I was suddenly engaged in a desperate battle with what seemed to be a colossal duvet, a *mural* made of incredibly stiff paper. It unfolded and unfolded. It was a whale passing by, it covered me and all my possessions. It surged over the pillar ashtray and began to creep like fog over the gentleman next to me. Help I said. Scuse me, watch your paper there he said. *His tongue was the size of my dog.*

I was exhausted. I could do nothing but wait for my plane to be announced. I watched the Big People. What is it like to move about the world, to travel, free of the fears of the tiny: the fear of being crushed by all the big things Big People make and use? Not just newspapers and barnyard suggestions and airplanes but their Big Companies and their Eternal Truths and the endless statistics of baseball.

The airport was hugely hot with Big-People warmth. Warmth from the roaring heaters of their big roaring cars, from the blazing camp-fires of their substantial vacations. And I thought perhaps a few of these Big People were glowing not only from tremendous breakfasts and the excitement and reward of business but from their still-warm still-tousled beds of large love.

[1984]

AMITAV GHOSH

(1956–)

Amitav Ghosh is an anthropologist and novelist as well as a travel writer. He was born in Calcutta, India, and worked as a journalist there before studying at Oxford. Ghosh went to North Africa to learn Arabic and traveled in Morocco, Algeria, and Tunisia. His novels *Circle of Reason* (1985), *The Shadow Lines* (1988), *and Calcutta Chromosome* (1996) take place in India.

In An Antique Land (1992), excerpted below, is set in an Egypt village where Ghosh lived. The villagers' limited ideas about India make Ghosh appear especially foreign to them, but as "delegates from two superseded civilizations," they share certain perspectives on the West. He also learns that home and travel are not mutually exclusive concepts in the world of rural Egypt. The apparently provincial and settled villagers of the Nile delta have a tradition of travel and migration bound into their culture.

"The Imam and the Indian"

From *In an Antique Land*

I met the Imam of the village and Khamees the Rat at about the same time. I don't exactly remember now—it happened more than six years ago—but I think I met the Imam first.

But this is not quite accurate. I didn't really 'meet' the Imam: I inflicted myself upon him. Perhaps that explains what happened.

Still, there was nothing else I could have done. As the man who led the daily prayers in the mosque, he was a leading figure in the village, and since I, a foreigner, had come to live there, he may well for all I knew have been offended had I neglected to pay him a call. Besides, I wanted to meet him; I was intrigued by what I'd heard about him.

People didn't often talk about the Imam in the village, but when they did, they usually spoke of him somewhat dismissively but also a little wistfully, as they might of some old, half-forgotten thing, like the annual flooding of the Nile. Listening to my friends speak of him, I had an inkling, long before I actually met him, that he already belonged, in a way, to the village's past. I thought I knew this for certain when I heard that apart from being an Imam he was also, by profession, a barber and a healer. People said he knew a great deal about herbs and poultices and the old kind of medicine. This interested me. This was Tradition: I knew that in rural Egypt Imams and other religious figures are often by custom associated with those two professions.

The trouble was that these accomplishments bought the Imam very little credit in the village. The villagers didn't any longer want an Imam who was also a barber and a healer. The older people wanted someone who had studied at al-Azhar and could quote from Jamal ad-Din Afghani and Mohammad Abduh as fluently as he could from the Hadith, and the younger men wanted a fierce, black-bearded orator, someone whose voice would thunder from the mimbar and reveal to them their destiny. No one had time for old-fashioned Imams who made themselves ridiculous by boiling herbs and cutting hair.

Yet Ustad Ahmed, who taught in the village's secondary school and was as well-read a man as I have ever met, often said—and this was not something he said of many people—that the old Imam read a lot. A lot of what? Politics, theology, even popular science . . . that kind of thing.

This made me all the more determined to meet him, and one evening, a few months after I first came to the village, I found my way to his house. He lived in the centre of the village, on the edge of the dusty open square which had the mosque in its middle. This was the oldest part of the village: a maze of low mud huts huddled together like confectionery on a tray, each hut crowned with a billowing, tousled head of straw.

When I knocked on the door the Imam opened it himself. He was a big man, with very bright brown eyes, set deep in a wrinkled, weather-beaten face. Like the room behind him, he was distinctly untidy: his blue jallabeyya was mud-stained and unwashed and his turban had been knotted anyhow around his head. But his beard, short and white and neatly trimmed, was everything a barber's beard should be. Age had been harsh on his face, but there was a certain energy in the way he arched his shoulders, in the clarity of his eyes and in the way he fidgeted constantly, was never still: it was plain that he was a vigorous, restive kind of person.

'Welcome,' he said, courteous but unsmiling, and stood aside and waved me in. It was a long dark room, with sloping walls and a very low ceiling. There was a bed in it and a couple of mats but little else, apart from a few, scattered books: everything bore that dull patina of grime which speaks of years of neglect. Later, I learned that the Imam had divorced his first wife and his second had left him, so that now he lived quite alone and had his meals with his son's family who lived across the square.

'Welcome,' he said again, formally.

'Welcome to you,' I said, giving him the formal response, and then we began on the long, reassuring litany of Arabic phrases of greeting.

'How are you?'

'How are you?'

'You have brought blessings?'

'May God bless you.'

'Welcome.'

'Welcome to you.'

'You have brought light.'

'The light is yours.'

'How are you?'

'How are you?'

He was very polite, very proper. In a moment he produced a kerosene stove and began to brew tea. But even in the performance of that little ritual there was something about him that was guarded, watchful.

'You're the *doktor al-Hindi*,' he said to me at last, 'aren't you? The Indian doctor?'

I nodded, for that was the name the village had given me. Then I told him that I wanted to talk to him about the methods of his system of medicine.

He looked very surprised and for a while he was silent. Then he put his right hand to his heart and began again on the ritual of greetings and responses, but in a markedly different way this time; one that I had learnt to recognize as a means of changing the subject.

'Welcome.'

'Welcome to you.'

'You have brought light.'

'The light is yours.'

And so on.

At the end of it I repeated what I had said.

'Why do you want to hear about *my* herbs?' he retorted. 'Why don't you go back to your country and find out about your own?'

'I will,' I said. 'Soon. But right now . . . '

'No, no,' he said restlessly. 'Forget about all that; I'm trying to forget about it myself.'

And then I knew that he would never talk to me about his craft, not just because he had taken a dislike to me for some reason of his own, but because his medicines were as discredited in his own eyes as they were in his clients'; because he knew as well as anybody else that the people who came to him now did so only because of old habits; because he bitterly regretted his inherited association with these relics of the past.

'Instead,' he said, 'let me tell you about what I have been learning over the last few years. Then you can go back to your country and tell them all about it.'

He jumped up, his eyes shining, reached under his bed and brought out a glistening new biscuit tin.

'Here!' he said, opening it. 'Look!'

Inside the box was a hypodermic syringe and a couple of glass phials. This is what he had been learning, he told me: the art of mixing and giving injections. And there was a huge market for it too, in the village: everybody wanted injections, for coughs, colds, fevers, whatever. There was a good living in it. He wanted to demonstrate his skill to me right there, on my arm, and when I protested that I wasn't ill, that I didn't need an injection just then, he was offended. 'All right,' he said curtly, standing up. 'I have to go to the mosque right now. Perhaps we can talk about this some other day.'

That was the end of my interview. I walked with him to the mosque and there, with an air of calculated finality, he took my hand in his, gave it a perfunctory shake and vanished up the stairs.

Khamees the Rat I met one morning when I was walking through the rice fields that lay behind the village, watching people transplant their seedlings. Everybody I met was cheerful and busy and the flooded rice fields were sparkling in the clear sunlight. If I shut my ears to the language, I thought, and stretch the date palms a bit and give them a few coconuts, I could easily be back somewhere in Bengal.

I was a long way from the village and not quite sure of my bearings, when I spotted a group of people who had finished their work and were sitting on the path, passing around a hookah.

'*Ahlan!*' a man in a brown jallabeyya called out to me. 'Hullo! Aren't you the Indian *doktor?*'

'Yes,' I called back. 'And who're you?'

'He's a rat,' someone answered, raising a gale of laughter. 'Don't go any-where near him.'

'Tell me *ya doktor*,' the Rat said, 'if I get on to my donkey and ride steadily for thirty days will I make it to India?'

'No,' I said. 'You wouldn't make it in thirty months.'

'Thirty months!' he said. 'You must have come a long way.'

'Yes.'

'As for me,' he declared, 'I've never even been as far as Alexandria and if I can help it I never will.'

I laughed: it did not occur to me to believe him.

When I first came to that quiet corner of the Nile Delta I had expected to find on that most ancient and most settled of soils a settled and restful people. I couldn't have been more wrong.

The men of the village had all the busy restlessness of airline passengers in a transit lounge. Many of them had worked and travelled in the sheikhdoms of the Persian Gulf, others had been in Libya and Jordan and Syria, some had been to the Yemen as soldiers, others to Saudi Arabia as pilgrims, a few had vis-ited Europe: some of them had passports so thick they opened out like ink-blackened concertinas. And none of this was new: their grandparents and ancestors and relatives had travelled and migrated too, in much the same way as mine had, in the Indian subcontinent—because of wars, or for money and jobs, or perhaps simply because they got tired of living always in one place. You could read the history of this restlessness in the villagers' surnames: they had names which derived from cities in the Levant, from Turkey, from faraway towns in Nubia; it was as though people had drifted here from every corner of the Middle East. The wanderlust of its founders had been ploughed into the soil of the village: it seemed to me sometimes that every man in it was a trav-eller. Everyone, that is, except Khamees the Rat, and even his surname, as I dis-covered later, meant 'of Sudan'.

'Well, never mind *ya doktor*,' Khamees said to me now, 'since you're not going to make it back to your country by sundown anyway, why don't you come and sit with us for a while?'

He smiled and moved up to make room for me.

I liked him at once. He was about my age, in the early twenties, scrawny, with a thin, mobile face deeply scorched by the sun. He had that brightness of eye and the quick, slightly sardonic turn to his mouth that I associated with faces in the coffee-houses of universities in Delhi and Calcutta; he seemed to belong to a world of late-night rehearsals and black coffee and lecture rooms, even though, in fact, unlike most people in the village, he was completely illiterate. Later I learned that he was called the Rat—Khamees the Rat—because he was said to gnaw away at things with his tongue, like a rat did with its teeth. He laughed at everything, people said—at his father, the village's patron saint, the village elders, the Imam, everything.

That day he decided to laugh at me.

'All right *ya doktor*,' he said to me as soon as I had seated myself. 'Tell me, is it true what they say, that in your country you burn your dead?'

No sooner had he said it than the women of the group clasped their hands to their hearts and muttered in breathless horror: '*Haram! Haram!*'

My heart sank. This was a conversation I usually went through at least once a day and I was desperately tired of it. 'Yes,' I said, 'it's true; some people in my country burn their dead.'

'You mean,' said Khamees in mock horror, 'that you put them on heaps of wood and just light them up?'

'Yes,' I said, hoping that he would tire of this sport if I humoured him.

'Why?' he said. 'Is there a shortage of kindling in your country?'

'No,' I said helplessly, 'you don't understand.' Somewhere in the limitless riches of the Arabic language a word such as 'cremate' must exist, but if it does, I never succeeded in finding it. Instead, for lack of any other, I had to use the word 'burn'. That was unfortunate, for 'burn' was the word for what happened to wood and straw and the eternally damned.

Khamees the Rat turned to his spellbound listeners. 'I'll tell you why they do it,' he said. 'They do it so that their bodies can't be punished after the Day of Judgement.'

Everybody burst into wonderstruck laughter. 'Why, how clever,' cried one of the younger girls. 'What a good idea! We ought to start doing it ourselves. That way we can do exactly what we like and when we die and the Day of Judgement comes, there'll be nothing there to judge.'

Khamees had got his laugh. Now he gestured to them to be quiet again.

'All right then *ya doktor*,' he said. 'Tell me something else: is it true that you are a Magian? That in your country everybody worships cows? Is it true that the other day when you were walking through the fields you saw a man beating a cow and you were so upset that you burst into tears and ran back to your room?'

'No, it's not true,' I said, but without much hope: I had heard this story before and knew that there was nothing I could say which would effectively give it the lie. 'You're wrong. In my country people beat their cows all the time; I promise you.'

I could see that no one believed me.

'Everything's upside-down in their country,' said a dark, aquiline young woman who, I was told later, was Khamees's wife. 'Tell us *ya doktor*: in your country, do you have crops and fields and canals like we do?'

'Yes,' I said, 'we have crops and fields, but we don't always have canals. In come parts of my country they aren't needed because it rains all the year around.'

'Ya salám,' she cried, striking her forehead with the heel of her palm. 'Do you hear that, oh you people? Oh, the Protector, oh, the Lord! It rains all the year round in his country.'

She had gone pale with amazement. 'So tell us then,' she demanded, 'do you have night and day like we do?'

'Shut up woman,' said Khamees. 'Of course they don't. It's day all the time over there, didn't you know? They arranged it like that so that they wouldn't have to spend any money on lamps.'

We all laughed, and then someone pointed to a baby lying in the shade of a tree swaddled in a sheet of cloth. 'That's Khamees's baby,' I was told. 'He was born last month.'

'That's wonderful,' I said. 'Khamees must be very happy.'

Khamees gave a cry of delight. 'The Indian knows I'm happy because I've had a son,' he said to the others. 'He understands that people are happy when they have children: he's not as upside-down as we thought.'

He slapped me on the knee and lit up the hookah and from that moment we were friends.

One evening, perhaps a month or so after I first met Khamees, he and his brothers and I were walking back to the village from the fields when he spotted the old Imam sitting on the steps that led to the mosque.

'Listen,' he said to me, 'you know the old Imam, don't you? I saw you talking to him once.'

'Yes,' I said. 'I talked to him once.'

'My wife's ill,' Khamees said. 'I want the Imam to come to my house to give her an injection. He won't come if I ask him, he doesn't like me. You go and ask.'

'He doesn't like me either,' I said.

'Never mind,' Khamees insisted. 'He'll come if you ask him—he knows you're a foreigner. He'll listen to you.'

While Khamees waited on the edge of the square with his brothers I went across to the Imam. I could tell that he had seen me—and Khamees—from a long way off, that he knew I was crossing the square to talk to him. But he would not look in my direction. Instead, he pretended to be deep in conversation with a man who was sitting beside him, an elderly and pious shopkeeper whom I knew slightly.

When I reached them I said 'Good evening' very pointedly to the Imam. He could not ignore me any longer then, but his response was short and curt, and he turned back at once to resume his conversation.

The old shopkeeper was embarrassed now, for he was a courteous, gracious man in the way that seemed to come so naturally to the elders of the village. "Please sit down,' he said to me. 'Do sit. Shall we get you a chair?'

Then he turned to the Imam and said, slightly puzzled: 'You know the Indian *doktor*, don't you? He's come all the way from India to be a student at the University of Alexandria.'

'I know him,' said the Imam. 'He came around to ask me questions. But as for this student business, I don't know. What's *he* going to study? He doesn't even write in Arabic.'

'Well,' said the shopkeeper judiciously, 'that's true; but after all he writes his own languages and he knows English.'

'Oh those,' said the Imam. 'what's the use of *those* languages? They're the easiest languages in the world. Anyone can write those.'

He turned to face me for the first time. His eyes were very bright and his mouth was twitching with anger. 'Tell me,' he said, 'why do you worship cows?'

I was so taken aback that I began to stammer. The Imam ignored me. He turned to the old shopkeeper and said: 'That's what they do in his country—did you know?—they worship cows.'

He shot me a glance from the corner of his eyes. 'And shall I tell you what else they do?' he said to the shopkeeper.

He let the question hang for a moment. And then, very loudly, he hissed: 'They burn their dead.'

The shopkeeper recoiled as though he had been slapped. His hands flew to his mouth. 'Oh God!' he muttered. *'Ya Allah.'*

'That's what they do,' said the Imam. 'They burn their dead.'

Then suddenly he turned to me and said, very rapidly: 'Why do you allow it? Can't you see that it's a primitive and backward custom? Are you savages that you permit something like that? Look at you: you've had some kind of education; you should know better. How will your country ever progress if you carry on doing these things? You've even been to the West; you've seen how advanced they are. Now tell me: have you ever seen them burning their dead?'

The Imam was shouting now and a circle of young men and boys had gathered around us. Under the pressure of their interested eyes my tongue began to trip, even on syllables I thought I had mastered. I found myself growing angry—as much with my own incompetence as the Imam.

'Yes, they do burn their dead in the West,' I managed to say somehow. I raised my voice too now. 'They have special electric furnaces meant just for that.'

The Imam could see that he had stung me. He turned away and laughed. 'He's lying,' he said to the crowd. 'They don't burn their dead in the West. They're not an ignorant people. They're advanced, they're educated, they have science, they have guns and tanks and bombs.'

'We have them too!' I shouted back at him. I was as confused now as I was angry. 'In my country we have all those things too,' I said to the crowd. 'We have guns and tanks and bombs. And they're better than anything you have—we're way ahead of you.'

The Imam could no longer disguise his anger. 'I tell you, he's lying,' he said. 'Our guns and bombs are much better than theirs. Ours are second only to the West's.'

'It's you who's lying,' I said. 'You know nothing about this. Ours are much better. Why, in my country we've even had a nuclear explosion. You won't be able to match that in a hundred years.'

So there we were, the Imam and I, delegates from two superseded civilizations vying with each other to lay claim to the violence of the West.

At that moment, despite the vast gap that lay between us, we understood each other perfectly. We were both travelling, he and I: we were travelling in the West. The only difference was that I had actually been there, in person: I could have told him about the ancient English university I had won a scholarship to, about punk dons with safety pins in their mortar-boards, about superhighways and sex shops and Picasso. But none of it would have mattered. We would have known, both of us, that all that was mere fluff: at the bottom, for him as for me and millions and millions of people on the landmasses around us, the West meant only this—science and tanks and guns and bombs.

And we recognized too the inescapability of these things, their strength, their power—evident in nothing so much as this: that even for him, a man of God, and for me, a student of the 'humane' sciences, they had usurped the place of all other languages of argument. He knew, just as I did, that he could no longer say to me, as Ibn Battuta might have when he travelled to India in the fourteenth century: 'You should do this or that because it is right or good or because God wills it so.' He could not have said it because that language is dead: those things are no longer sayable; they sound absurd. Instead he had had, of necessity, to use that other language, so universal that it extended equally to him, an old-fashioned village Imam, and great leaders at SALT conferences: he had had to say to me: 'You ought not to do this because otherwise you will not have guns and tanks and bombs.'

Since he was a man of God his was the greater defeat.

For a moment then I was desperately envious. The Imam would not have said any of those things to me had I been a Westerner. He would not have dared. Whether I wanted it or not, I would have had around me the protective aura of an inherited expertise in the technology of violence. That aura would have surrounded me, I thought, with a sheet of clear glass, like a bullet-proof screen; or perhaps it would have worked as a talisman, like a press card, armed with which I could have gone off to what were said to be the most terrible places in the world that month, to gaze and wonder. And then perhaps I too would one day have had enough material for a book which would have had for its epigraph the line, *The horror! The horror!*–for the virtue of a sheet of glass is that it does not require one to look within.

But that still leaves Khamees the Rat waiting on the edge of the square.

In the end it was he and his brothers who led me away from the Imam. They took me home with them, and there, while Khamees's wife cooked dinner for us–she was not so ill after all–Khamees said to me: 'Do not be upset, *ya doktor*. Forget about all those guns and things. I'll tell you what: *I'll* come to visit you in your country, even though I've never been anywhere. I'll come all the way.'

He slipped a finger under his skull-cap and scratched his head, thinking hard.

Then he added: 'But if I die, you must bury me.'

[1986]

MIKE TIDWELL

(1962–)

Mike Tidwell worked as a Peace Corps volunteer in Zaire in the 1980s and now reports for the *Washington Post*. In *Amazon Stranger* (1996), Tidwell spent time in the rain forest of Ecuador with an American, a leader of a native Ecuadorian tribe who helped his people face down the petrochemical industry. *Bayou Farewell: The Rich Life and Tragic Death of Louisiana's Cajun Coast* (2003) combines travel writing and environmental criticism.

In *The Ponds of Kalambayi* (1990), excerpted here, Tidwell tells the story of his attempts to teach central African farmers how to raise fish and of his own education about communal sharing. The narrative is a good example of how living in a place, as opposed to merely traveling through it, helps the traveler become assimilated into the home culture, making him less a stranger and more a member of the community.

From *The Ponds of Kalambayi*

As I pressed on, determined to make fish culture work on this sinking island, I had more to worry about than just roads taking my life. People in villages across Kalambayi were trying to kill me too. They were feeding me too much. With little in the way of possessions, but driven by a congenital desire to share what they could, villagers gave me *fufu*–teeming, steaming metric tons of it.

Fufu, again, was the doughy white substance served at every meal. Women made it by pouring corn and manioc flour into boiling water, stirring the mixture with wooden spoons, then lumping the gummy results into calabash bowls where it assumed a size, shape and weight not unlike small bowling balls. It had little taste, but filled you up and that was its purpose: to compensate for the dishearteningly small servings of manioc leaves or dried fish that came with it. Kayemba Lenga told me a funny fable about how Kalambayan ancestors stole the recipe for *fufu* from mosquitoes long ago. Now, in protest, the bothersome insects buzz one's ears every night. Not being overly fond of *fufu*, nor the recurring malaria protesting mosquitoes had already given me, I asked Kayemba half-jokingly if it wasn't possible to give the recipe back.

But it wasn't possible. *Fufu* was as much a part of the landscape as the grass and rivers. In every village, around every corner, it was there, waiting for me, widening my waistline. Without exception, the villagers I visited each day insisted I have some before moving on. As in most traditional societies, the giving was ungrudging and automatic—born of kindness—and saying no simply was out of the question.

A fairly typical day:

I arrive at Bukasa's house at 8 a.m. and a bowl of *fufu* awaits me, releasing hot wisps into the morning air. "Come," he says. "Sit down. You need to eat before we go to the ponds." We eat and leave for work. At the ponds I meet Kayemba and Mulundu Ilunga who cheerfully drag me back to their houses for large, back-to-back servings. I thank them afterwards and leave for the next village, Bena Ngoyi. By the time I pull up to the huts it's 1 p.m.—lunchtime. Two more bowls of *fufu*. Sluggishly, my shirt buttons threatening to launch, I move on to Milamba for a quick look at a pond and a torturous sixth bowl. At the end of the day I'm transporting my bulk home under depressed tires when a man in Kalula flags me down. He want to discuss digging a pond. We sit and talk, and when I rise to leave he tells me to wait. I panic. "No seriously," I protest. "I'm not hungry. Really, no, please. Please don't." But he knows I'm just being polite. He has two wives and they both bring out *fufu*. I wash my hands. *Bon appetite*, he says.

This was something I hadn't counted on. I had expected a lot of challenges living in rural Africa, but being incapacitated by too much generosity, too much *fufu*, just wasn't one of them. And *fufu* wasn't the only thing weighing me down. Relentlessly, Kalambayans shared all their food, unloading on me whatever happened to be around when I rolled into view. They put oranges in my hands, peanuts in my pockets, stuffed sugarcane in my knapsack.

"It won't fit," I told Kayemba one day as he tried to tie an entire regime of bananas across my motorcycle handlebars. "I'll crash. Just give me five. 'That's enough."

"No, it's all right," he said. "I've got another regime in the house."

"I'll crash, Kayemba. Don't do it." I wasn't just being polite this time. He yielded and sulked for a moment until the absurdity of his attempt caught up with him and we both laughed so hard tears welled in our eyes.

It was truly overwhelming, all this giving. The Kalambayans were some of the poorest people anywhere in the world, and yet they were by far the most generous I had ever met. Indeed, each time I thought I had been offered everything they had to share, something new was laid at my feet.

Barely three months after I moved into the Lulenga cotton warehouse, the village chief, Mbaya Tshiongo, appeared at my door dressed in his threadbare trench coat and ripped tennis shoes. He was a meek, doddering septuagenarian with whom my previous contact had been limited to conversations in the market where I told him repeatedly that, yes, everything was fine and, no, I didn't need anything. Now he had come to my house with something more dramatic on his mind. Standing at his side were his four eligible daughters, shy and fresh as daisies.

"Michel," he began, leathery half-moons sagging under his eyes, "you live in my village and I am responsible for you. Take one of my daughters. You're alone. A wife will make your life better. Choose one and she will stay with you."

Half the people in the village were standing behind the chief waiting to see who I would choose. Flattered and panicked in equal measure, my chest thumping, I fumbled for a way out of this with minimal loss of face. I walked up to the chief, put my arm around his shoulders and quietly guided him inside, where I explained things: "I can't accept, chief. Really. They're beautiful women. But I'm fine by myself. I don't need a wife right now."

A cloud of perplexity crossed his face. He tried to reason with me. "But you *do* need a wife, Michel. Every man does. Look, I'll waive the dowry. You won't even have to pay me anything. Just take one." But I wouldn't budge. Standing to leave, the chief asked me to at least promise to let him know if I ever changed my mind. I said I would.

After the crowd dispersed and Chief Mbaya led his daughters, now wilted by rejection, back home, I was left alone in my house convinced there really were no limits to what these people would have me have. The intense desire to give moved me to admiration, especially because I knew villagers shared with each other with almost the same zeal they did with me, the visitor. It was a social habit lacking in my own culture and I was curious to know what it was, exactly, that produced it in Kalambayi.

Kazadi Manda, a lean, square-jawed fish farmer in Ntita Konyukua who had a mile-wide smile, provided part of the answer early one morning about a week later. We were sitting at his pond, tossing stones at toads and watching his tilapia eat a batch of papaya leaves spread across the liquid light of the pond's surface. His fish, like those of Chief Ilunga and the other new farmers, were coming along nicely, getting fat for the upcoming first harvests. After talking shop for a while, Kazadi and I turned our attention to other matters. I told him about Chief Mbaya coming to my house with his daughters.

"You're joking," he said. "He just walked up and said pick one and you refused?"

"Yes."

"But why? Why didn't you take one? It *is* a little strange that you live alone in that warehouse the way you do, don't you think? Nobody can understand it. Don't you want a wife?"

"Of course," I said. "Someday. If I can find the right person. But I barely knew these women."

"So?"

"I can't marry a woman just like that. I have to be in love first and she has to be in love with me. It takes time."

Kazadi didn't get it. The look of blank incomprehension on his face told me the relationship I was talking about didn't exist in his universe. He had no conception of the self, of the individual. Nor, by extension, did he fully understand the Western notion of romantic love between an individual man and woman.

"You don't get married for love," he told me. "You get married because you need a woman to cook your food and bear your children. Love is what you feel for your whole family. The happiness of your children and brothers and parents and grandparents—of all of them together—is what brings your own happiness. You can't get that by yourself or from a woman."

"So until I have a lot of children and a big group of relatives all around me I can never hope to be happy?" I said.

"That's right."

"Never?"

"Never."

Sitting at the pond, lisening to Kazadi pass on this truth with the conviction of an inspired cleric, I began to better understand the fabric of life in Kalambayi. The family was indeed paramount. Kazadi was wed to his relatives. And because each village was nothing but a collection of several extended families, and because it was often difficult, due to their size, to tell where one family began and another left off, this concern for the group was extended in large measure to include all members of the village and, ultimately, all people. Everyone treated everyone else more or less like a relative, whether he was or not. Everyone was taken care of, even Kalambayi's strange, white, American visitor—me.

Kazadi and I talked a while longer before spreading a final bundle of papaya leaves across the pond. When we finished he told me he wanted to harvest some peanuts from his field a short distance away. I didn't have to be in the next village for another hour, so I offered to help. He led the way up the valley.

It was a brilliant morning, warm and cloudless, with the sun poised low and the tawny hills around the valley almost cloth-like in their softness. A group of brown weaverbirds bobbed about a nearby tree. In the disance two women washed clothes in the drowsy sunlight, singing as they worked. Mornings like this served to remind me that it didn't rain every day in Kalambayi. It just seemed that way to me during my first few months because of all the destruction storms wrought. In truth, the sky was much more often blue than gray, and once I reached the villages and got off the roads, I usually enjoyed the fine weather and my new life working outdoors.

Kazadi and I moved through a stand of banana trees, then a cotton field, then a stretch of grass that left our pants wet with dew by the time we reached his small plot of peanuts. We walked to the distant-most corner of the field and went to work, pulling the plants from the ground with our hands. The soil was poor here, sandy as in most of Kalambayi, and the stems lifted easily. Working fifteen feet apart, we placed the plants in separate piles, first shaking dirt from the dangling shells. When each pile had roughly twenty plants, I figured we had about as many as Kazadi could carry comfortably back to his family. But he kept going. I did the same.

A moment later he finally stopped and tied the piles together in a large bundle. I went down to the spring to wash my hands. When I walked back up the hill to my motorcycle, the entire bundle of peanuts was tied, to my surprise, above the rear fender. Kazadi was hoeing in a field a little farther up. He stopped to wave goodbye. "They're raw," he said, pointing to the peanuts, "so boil them first and add a little salt before you eat them."

Curiously, this habit of giving in Kalambayi didn't rub off on me. Even as I watched, and was moved by, the sacrifices villagers like Kazadi made to keep me stocked with produce and filled with *fufu*, I didn't do the same. I didn't reciprocate. I accepted the food and other gifts when I could, but the idea of spreading around my own wealth in the same free and automatic manner didn't take hold. I hadn't been sent to Kalambayi to become like the people exactly. I taught fish culture. I shared an expertise. That was enough.

So on the off chance that I was hungry at the end of the day, I didn't eat in my yard like most people, inviting passers-by to join me. I took my tin of sardines and plate of fried rice and stayed inside behind a curtain pulled across the front door. I was glad to be alone and eating something other than *fufu*, glad to be listening to the BBC's "Globe Theatre" blessedly broadcast in English over my shortwave radio. If someone came while I was eating, a friend or fish farmer, I stood at the door and told him that, well, I was having dinner and could he please come back later. Lifelong experience at suburban dinner tables had taught me that mealtime visitors meant embarrassment. You made apologies and they went away or waited until you finished.

I didn't really care or really wasn't conscious of the fact that the villagers around me thought this habit was a little strange, a bit obscene, even for a visitor. Mbaya, my worker, didn't tell me. Nor did any of my neighbors. And no one said anything about the fact that I smoked whole cigarettes by myself, not passing a portion of each one to other men in my company as was the local habit. I just did these things. Just like I socked away money, saving as much of my living allowance as I could for the beer and *pommes frites* it would buy on my next trip to Mbuji Mayi.

To be sure, I had made a lot of changes since arriving—adapting to strange foods, learning to bathe in cold rivers, surrendering my native tongue for two years. But my attachment to the word "mine" was strong and stubborn. Whatever the villagers did, I had my things, I needed my things, and I didn't give them away. So much was this attitude a measure of who I was and the Western culture that produced me that during my early months it simply never occurred to me to try to change.

I suppose it's no wonder then that I treated Mutoba Muenyi the way I did. She was a beggar—a haggard, unkempt, insane beggar who roamed pretty much aimlessly through the villages of Kalambayi, sleeping in other people's huts or in cotton storage houses. Mbaya told me she was the daughter of a nearby village chief and had been made crazy years ago by the curse of a disgruntled husband.

I did my utmost to avoid Mutoba on those occasions she came to Lulenga and stood under the cluster of palm trees in the center of the village, babbling nonsense in her high-pitched voice while gesturing for food and money. I avoided her because I've never handled beggars well. They intimidate me. I had moved through the streets of enough American cities to know that the usual response when confronted by a bedraggled panhandler is to hang on to your money and keep walking.

So when I turned to answer a tap on my shoulder one afternoon in the Lulenga market and saw Mutoba—clothes unwashed, teeth rotten, arms motioning toward the avocados I was buying—I ignored her. When she followed me through the market, creating a scene, I told her to stop and quickly made my way home, embarrassed by her presence. A few weeks later she appeared again, this time planting herself at my door, asking for money. Again I shooed her away. It wasn't until our third encounter that things began to change. Mutoba involved me in a small nightmare. She made me pay, in a sense, for all my previous behavior.

It happened in Lulenga, early one morning in June. The village was silent and still in the predawn darkness, everyone asleep, when Mutoba crept to my house, pressed her face inches from my door and started singing loudly. Her harsh voice woke me like cymbals crashed above my bed. The song she sang was improvised, with lyrics telling how she was hungry and how I should give her something to eat.

Sleepy and annoyed, I lay in bed listening, cringing at the thought that half the village was doing the same thing. My clock said 5:45. "Ssssshhhhh," I hissed from my room, "be quiet. Go away. I don't have any food."

But the singing didn't stop. Not after five minutes. Not after ten. It went on and on, bludgeoning the morning quiet. Then something terrible happened. With mounting urgency, pushed on by the impurity of the local water, my body began signaling that it had something to contribute to the backyard outhouse—now. Cursing, I got up, grabbed my flashlight and began looking for the padlock to my door. Because the outhouse was around back, I would have to lock the front door on my way out, preventing Mutoba from entering while I was away. But suddenly there was a problem. I couldn't find my padlock. With my bowels approaching critical mass and Mutoba's hideous singing continuing outside, I searched everywhere, finding nothing. I had misplaced the lock.

There was nothing left to do but go outside. I opened the door. There she was. My flashlight revealed Mutoba's bare feet, her startled eyes. She didn't move. She just kept singing as I shut the door behind me. I dared not go to the outhouse now, leaving this crazy women unwatched by an unlocked door. I sprinted past her one hundred feet to the far end of the cotton warehouse. There, off to the side in a patch of knee-high grass next to a palm tree, I turned facing her and lowered myself to my haunches. All the while I kept my flashlight fixed warily on her at the doorstep. I squatted and Mutoba sang, each of us staring with equal shock at the spectacle before us.

And that's how most of the village found us. To my yard they came— mamas and papas and children rubbing sleep from their eyes. They filed out of their houses to see what all the commotion was about. A minute or so after the performance started, just as the rising sun was providing rosy light by which to see, there were several dozen thunderstruck people gathered along the edges of my yard, watching the mad showdown between crapping foreigner and crowing bag lady.

I was beside myself with humiliation and anger by the time I finished and stood. I walked straight to Mutoba. With the crowd looking on, I yelled at her to leave immediately. She, in turn, yelled back, calling me a *muena tshi-tua* over and over again. It was a name I had never heard before. After a moment, she finally left. The crowd, guffawing and embarrassed by all the ugliness, walked away.

About thirty minutes later, while I was sitting inside my house still trying to figure out what had just happened, Mbaya came by. He already had heard about the affair with Mutoba, but insisted I recount the story in full.

"You look a little ill," he said when I had finished.

"I feel ill."

Then I asked him a question: "What's a *muena tshitua*?" The words had stuck in my mind since Mutoba spoke them. "She called me a *muena tshitua*. What's that?"

Mbaya grew noticeably uncomfortable at this and heaved a forced laugh. "Oh it's nothing," he said. "You didn't know."

"Know what? What does it mean? What did she call me?"

Reluctantly, he told me. Mutoba had delivered one of the most serious charges one can make in Kalambayi. "A *muena tshitua*," he said, "is someone who doesn't share. She said you were stingy."

There was a brief pause after this, a few seconds when Mbaya avoided my eyes and I folded my arms. Hanging in the silence and permeating Mbaya's awkward manner seemed to be the suggestion that the *muena tshitua* label wasn't such a bad fit, that perhaps Mutoba was right.

"But how could I give her anything?" I asked him, breaking the silence. She had come at an outrageous hour, singing like a wild soul and wresting me from sleep, I said. Running her off was the only thing I could have done.

But even to myself my argument sounded a bit feeble. There were no mitigating circumstances to explain my other encounters with her, nor my conspicuously selfish behavior in general.

When I finished, Mbaya responded cautiously. Like most Kalambayans, he was often hesitant to openly criticize or correct. He softened what he was about to tell me by stressing that he thought I was basically a great guy and I shouldn't worry too much about what a deranged old woman told me. Then, delicately, he explained that I hadn't done the right thing that morning. It was all right to shoo Mutoba away, but the proper response was to give her a little food or whatever she needed first. That's what most people did.

He was right, of course. The same villagers who vigorously plied me with *fufu* and peanuts everywhere I went also took care of Mutoba. It wouldn't occur to them to do otherwise. She couldn't farm or provide for herself, so when her clothes became too torn, someone, somewhere, gave her new ones. When her filth became excessive, someone placed a piece of soap in her hand. And almost always, when mealtime came, someone gave her food. The sense of familiar generosity flowing through every village protected her.

But wrapped up in my own notions of privacy and propriety, trying to live in this culture without really being a part of it, I gave nothing to Mutoba. My problem, in a big sense, was greed. Not just greed toward the things I wanted to keep for myself, but toward this whole two-year trip abroad. I wanted to take as much from this African world as I could, to learn and experience, without surrendering any large part of myself, without making significant changes like replacing the faulty moral compass I had come with with one that made more sense in this poor setting. Clearly, this resistance was bound to fail me. I had no desire to "go native," to become like a typical villager in every way. But to have any meaningful experience here, to leave with true friends and true insights, I had to let go of some strong habits. I had to rip something out in order to add something new.

This wasn't the message Mbaya had in mind, really, when he tried to educate me on that strange morning Mutoba Muenyi came to my house, but it's the one that started to sink in. His message, though not in as many words, was more simple: "You've been here long enough, Michel. It's time you stopped being such an appalling tightwad."

[1990]

MALCOLM X AND ALEX HALEY

(1925–1965)

Malcolm X was one of America's most important black leaders during the civil rights movement of the 1960s. Born Malcolm Little, the son of a midwestern Baptist minister, he converted to Islam and became a member of the Black Muslims in 1953. Later he broke with the leader, Elijah Muhammad, and formed a rival organization that advocated active resistance to injustices against black people. In 1963, Malcolm X left the United States to travel to Mecca to perform the Hajj, the annual pilgrimage undertaken by Muslims as one of the five pillars of Islam. Malcolm X, accustomed only to the conflicts between black and white in his own country, was greatly impressed by the racial harmony he witnessed among the Muslim pilgrims, who came from many different countries and cultures.

The excerpt that follows is from *The Autobiography of Malcolm X* (1965) written with Alex Haley shortly before Malcolm X was assassinated. Religious pilgrimage is one of the oldest forms of travel; for all faiths, journeys to sacred places combine the pleasures and travails of travel with the promise of spiritual illumination. In this account of his pilgrimage, Malcolm X explains how the experience altered his views of race and his sense of himself as a Muslim.

"Mecca"

From *The Autobiography of Malcolm X*

The pilgrimaage to Mecca, known as Hajj, is a religious obligation that every orthodox Muslim fulfills, if humanly able, at least once in his or her lifetime.

The Holy Quran says it, "Pilgrimage to the Ka'ba is a duty men owe to God; those who are able, make the journey."

Allah said: "And proclaim the pilgrimage among men; they will come to you on foot and upon each lean camel, they will come from every deep ravine."

At one or another college or university, usually in the informal gatherings after I had spoken, perhaps a dozen generally white-complexioned people would come up to me, identifying themselves as Arabian, Middle Eastern or North African Muslims who happened to be visiting, studying, or living in the United States. They had said to me that, my white-indicting statements notwithstanding, they felt that I was sincere in considering myself a Muslim— and they felt that if I was exposed to what they always called "true Islam," I would "understand it, and embrace it." Automatically, as a follower of Elijah Muhammad, I had bridled whenever this was said.

But in the privacy of my own thoughts after several of these experiences, I did question myself: if one was sincere in professing a religion, why should he balk at broadening his knowledge of that religion? . . .

The literal meaning of Hajj in Arabic is to set out toward a definite objective. In Islamic law, it means to set out for Ka'ba, the Sacred House, and to fulfill the pilgrimage rites. The Cairo airport was where scores of Hajj groups were becoming *Muhrim*, pilgrims, upon entering the state of Ihram, the assumption of a spiritual and physical state of consecration. Upon advice, I arranged to leave in Cairo all of my luggage and four cameras, one a movie camera. I had bought in Cairo a small valise, just big enough to carry one suit, shirt, a pair of underwear sets and a pair of shoes into Arabia. Driving to the airport with our Hajj group, I began to get nervous, knowing that from there in, it was going to be watching others who knew what they were doing, and trying to do what they did.

Entering the state of Ihram, we took off our clothes and put on two white towels. One, the *Izar*, was folded around the loins. The other, the *Rida*, was thrown over the neck and shoulders, leaving the right shoulder and arm bare. A pair of simple sandals, the *na'l*, left the ankle-bones bare. Over the *Izar* waist-wrapper, a money belt was worn, and a bag, something like a woman's big hand-bag, with a long strap, was for carrying the passport and other valuable papers, such as the letter I had from Dr. Shawarbi.

Every one of the thousands at the airport, about to leave for Jedda, was dressed this way. You could be a king or a peasant and no one would know. Some powerful personages, who were discreetly pointed out to me, had on the same thing I had on. Once thus dressed, we all had begun intermittently calling out "*Labbayka! Labbayka!*" (Here I come, O Lord!) The airport sounded with the din of *Muhrim* expressing their intention to perform the journey of the Hajj.

Planeloads of pilgrims were taking off every few minutes, but the airport was jammed with more, and their friends and relatives waiting to see them off.

Those not going were asking others to pray for them at Mecca. We were on our plane, in the air, when I learned for the first time that with the crush, there was not supposed to have been space for me, but strings had been pulled, and someone had been put off because they didn't want to disappoint an American Muslim. I felt mingled emotions of regret that I had inconvenienced and discomfited whoever was bumped off the plane for me, and, with that, an utter humility and gratefulness that I had been paid such an honor and respect.

Packed in the plane were white, black, brown, red, and yellow people, blue eyes and blond hair, and my kinky red hair—all together, brothers! All honoring the same God Allah, all in turn giving equal honor to each other.

From some in our group, the word was spreading from seat to seat that I was a Muslim from America. Faces turned, smiling toward me in greeting. A box lunch was passed out and as we ate that, the word that a Muslim from America was aboard got up into the cockpit.

The captain of the plane came back to meet me. He was an Egyptian, his complexion was darker than mine; he could have walked in Harlem and no one would have given him a second glance. He was delighted to meet an American Muslim. When he invited me to visit the cockpit, I jumped at the chance.

The co-pilot was darker than he was. I can't tell you the feeling it gave me. I had never seen a black man flying a jet. That instrument panel: no one ever could know what all of those dials meant! Both of the pilots were smiling at me, treating me with the same honor and respect I had received ever since I left America. I stood there looking through the glass at the sky ahead of us. In America, I had ridden in more planes that probably any other Negro, and I never had been invited up into the cockpit. And there I was, with two Muslim seatmates, one from Egypt, the other from Arabia, all of us bound for Mecca, with me up in the pilots' cabin. Brother, I *knew* Allah was with me.

I got back to my seat. All of the way, about an hour's flight, we pilgrims were loudly crying out, "*Labbayka! Labbayka!*" The plane landed at Jedda. It's a seaport town on the Red Sea, the arrival or disembarkation point for all pilgrims who come to Arabia to go to Mecca. Mecca is about forty miles to the east, inland.

The Jedda airport seemed even more crowded than Cairo's had been. Our party became another shuffling unit in the shifting mass with every race on earth represented. Each party was making its way towad the long line waiting to go through Customs. Before reaching Customs, each Hajj party was assigned a *Mutawaf*, who would be responsible for transferring that party from Jedda to Mecca. Some pilgrims cried "*Labbayka!*" Others, sometimes large groups, were chanting in unison a prayer that I will translate, "I submit to no one but Thee, O Allah, I submit to no one but Thee. I submit to Thee because Thou hast no partner. All praise and blessings come from Thee, and Thou art alone in Thy kingdom." The essence of the prayer is the Oneness of God.

Only officials were not wearing the *Ihram* garb, or the white skull caps, long, white, nightshirt-looking gown and the little slippers of the *Mutawaf*, those who guided each pilgrim party, and their helpers. In Arabic an *mmmm* sound before a verb makes a verbal noun, so "*Mutawaf*" meant "the one who guides" the pilgrims on the "*Tawaf*," which is the circumambulation of the Ka'ba in Mecca.

I was nervous, shuffling in the center of our group in the line waiting to have our passports inspected. I had an apprehensive feeling. Look what I'm handing them. I'm in the Muslim world, right at The Fountain. I'm handing them the American passport which signifies the exact opposite of what Islam stands for.

The judge in our group sensed my strain. He patted my shoulder. Love, humility, and true brotherhood was almost a physical feeling wherever I turned. . . .

Nothing in either of my two careers as a black man in America had served to give me any idealistic tendencies. My instincts automatically examined the reasons, the motives, of anyone who did anything they didn't have to do for me. Always in my life, if it was any white person, I could see a selfish motive.

But there in that hotel that morning, a telephone call and a few hours away from the cot on the fourth-floor tier of the dormitory, was one of the few times I had been so awed that I was totally without resistance. That white man—at least he would have been considered "white" in America—related to Arabia's ruler, to whom he was a close advisor, truly an international man, with nothing in the world to gain, had given up his suite to me, for my transient comfort. He had *nothing* to gain. He didn't need me. He had everything. In fact, he had more to lose than gain. He had followed the American press about me. If he did that, he knew there was only stigma attached to me. I was supposed to have horns. I was a "racist." I was "anti-white"—and he from all appearances was white. I was supposed to be a criminal; not only that, but everyone was even accusing me of using his religion of Islam as a cloak for my criminal practices and philosophies. Even if he had had some motive to use me, he knew that I was separated from Elijah Muhammad and the Nation of Islam, my "power base," according to the press in America. The only organization that I had was just a few weeks old. I had no job. I had no money. Just to get over there, I had had to borrow money from my sister.

That morning was when I first began to reappraise the "white man." It was when I first began to perceive that "white man," as commonly used, means complexion only secondarily; primarily it described attitudes and actions. In America, "white man" meant specific attitudes and actions toward the black man, and toward all other non-white men. But in the Muslim world, I had seen that men with white complexions were more genuinely brotherly than anyone else had ever been.

That morning was the start of a radical alteration in my whole outlook about "white" men. . . .

Two young Arabs accompanied me to Mecca. A well-lighted, modern turnpike highway made the trip easy. Guards at intervals along the way took one look at the car, and the driver made a sign, and we were passed through, never even having to slow down. I was, all at once, thrilled, important, humble, and thankful.

Mecca, when we entered, seemed as ancient as time itself. Our car slowed through the winding streets, lined by shops on both sides and with buses, cars, and trucks, and tens of thousands of pilgrims from all over the earth were everywhere.

The car halted briefly at a place where a *Mutawaf* was waiting for me. He wore a white skullcap and long nightshirt garb that I had seen at the airport. He was a short, dark-skinned Arab, named Muhammad. He spoke no English whatever.

We parked near the Great Mosque. We performed our ablution and entered. Pilgrims seemed to be on top of each other, there were so many lying, sitting, sleeping, praying, walking.

My vocabulary cannot describe the new mosque that was being built around the Ka'ba. I was thrilled to realize that it was only one of the tremendous building tasks under the direction of young Dr. Azzam, who had just been my host. The Great Mosque of Mecca, when it is finished, will surpass the architectural beauty of India's Taj Mahal.

Carrying my sandals, I followed the *Mutawaf*. Then I saw the Ka'ba, a huge black stone house in the middle of the Great Mosque. It was being circumambulated by thousands upon thousands of praying pilgrims, both sexes, and every size, shape, color, and race in the world. I knew the prayer to be uttered when the pilgrim's eyes first perceive the Ka'ba. Translated, it is "O God, You are peace, and peace derives from You. So greet us, O Lord, with peace." Upon entering the Mosque, the pilgrim should try to kiss the Ka'ba if possible, but if the crowds prevent him getting that close, he touches it, and if the crowds prevent that, he raises his hand and cries out "Takbir!" ("God is great!") I could not get within yards. "Takbir!"

My feeling there in the House of God was a numbness. My *Mutawaf* led me in the crowd of praying, chanting pilgrims, moving seven times around the Ka'ba. Some were bent and wizened with age; it was a sight that stamped itself on the brain. I saw incapacitated pilgrims being carried by others. Faces were enraptured in their faith. The seventh time around, I prayed two *Rak'a*, prostrating myself, my head on the floor. The first prostration, I prayed the Quran verse "Say He is God, the one and only"; the second prostration: "Say O you who are unbelievers, I worship not that which you worship. . . ."

As I prostrated, the *Mutawaf* fended pilgrims off to keep me from being trampled.

The *Mutawaf* and I next drank water from the well of Zem Zem. Then we ran between the two hills, Safa and Marwa, where Hajar wandered over the same earth searching for water for her child Ishmael.

Three separate times, after that, I visited the Great Mosque and circumambulated the Ka'ba. The next day we set out after sunrise toward Mount Arafat, thousands of us, crying in unison: "Labbayka! Labbayka!" and "Allah Akbar!" Mecca is surrounded by the crudest-looking mountains I have ever seen; they seem to be made of the slag from a blast furnace. No vegetation is on them at all. Arriving about noon, we prayed and chanted from noon until sunset, and the *asr* (afternoon) and *Maghrib* (sunset) special prayers were performed.

Finally, we lifted our hands in prayer and thanksgiving, repeating Allah's words: "There is no God but Allah. He has no partner. His are authority and praise. Good emanates from Him, and He has power over all things."

Standing on Mount Arafat had concluded the essential rites of being a pilgrim to Mecca. No one who missed it could consider himself a pilgrim.

The *Ihram* had ended. We cast the traditional seven stones at the devil. Some had their hair and beards cut. I decided that I was going to let my beard remain. I wondered what my wife Betty, and our little daughters, were going to say when they saw me with a beard, when I got back to New York. New York seemed a million miles away. . . .

Here is what I wrote . . . from my heart:

"Never have I witnessed such sincere hospitality and the overwhelming spirit of true brotherhood as is practiced by people of all colors and races here in this Ancient Holy Land, the home of Abraham, Muhammad, and all the other prophets of the Holy Scriptures. For the past week, I have been utterly speechless and spellbound by the graciousness I see displayed all around me by people of *all colors.*

"I have been blessed to visit the Holy City of Mecca. I have made my seven circuits around the Ka'ba, led by a young *Mutawaf* named Muhammad. I drank water from the well of Zem Zem. I ran seven times back and forth between the hills of Mt. Al-Safa and Al-Marwah. I have prayed in the ancient city of Mina, and I have prayed on Mt. Arafat.

"There were tens of thousands of pilgrims, from all over the world. They were of all colors, from blue-eyed blonds to black-skinned Africans. But we were all participating in the same ritual, displaying a spirit of unity and brotherhood that my experiences in America had led me to believe never could exist between the white and the non-white.

"America needs to understand Islam, because this is the one religion that erases from its society the race problem. Throughout my travels in the Muslim world, I have met, talked to, and even eaten with people who in America would have been considered 'white'—but the 'white' attitude was removed from their minds by the religion of Islam. I have never before seen *sincere* and *true* brotherhood practiced by all colors together, irrespective of their color.

"You may be shocked by these words coming from me. But on this pilgrimage, what I have seen, and experienced, has forced me to *re-arrange* much of my thought-patterns previously held, and to *toss aside* some of my previous conclusions. This was not too difficult for me. Despite my firm convictions, I have been always a man who tries to face facts, and to accept the reality of life as new experience and new knowledge unfolds it. I have always kept an open mind, which is necessary to the flexibility that must go hand in hand with every form of intelligent search for truth.

"During the past eleven days here in the Muslim world, I have eaten from the same plate, drunk from the same glass, and slept in the same bed (or on the same rug)—while praying to the *same God*—with fellow Muslims, whose eyes were the bluest of blue, whose hair was the blondest of blond, and whose skin was the whitest of white. And in the *words* and in the *actions* and in the *deeds* of the 'white' Muslims, I felt the same sincerity that I felt among the black African Muslims of Nigeria, Sudan, and Ghana.

"We were *truly* all the same (brothers)—because their belief in one God had removed the 'white' from their *minds*, the 'white' from their *behavior*, and the 'white' from their *attitude*.

"I could see from this, that perhaps if white Americans could accept the Oneness of God, then perhaps, too, they could accept in *reality* the Oneness of Man—and cease to measure, and hinder, and harm others in terms of their 'differences' in color.

"With racism plaguing America like an incurable cancer, the so-called 'Christian' white American heart should be more receptive to a proven solution to such a destructive problem. Perhaps it could be in time to save America from imminent disaster—the same destruction brought upon Germany by racism that eventually destroyed the Germans themselves.

"Each hour here in the Holy Land enables me to have greater spiritual insights into what is happening in America between black and white. The American Negro never can be blamed for his racial animosities—he is only reacting to four hundred years of the conscious racism of the American whites. But as racism leads America up the suicide path, I do believe, from the experiences that I have had with them, that the whites of the younger generation, in the colleges and universities, will see the handwriting on the wall and many of them will turn to the *spiritual* path of *truth*—the *only* way left to America to ward off the disaster that racism inevitably must lead to. . . ."

The Pan American jet which took me home—it was Flight 115—landed at New York's Kennedy Air Terminal on May 21, at 4:25 in the afternoon. We passengers filed off the plane and toward Customs. When I saw the crowd of fifty or sixty reporters and photographers, I honestly wondered what celebrity I had been on the plane with.

But I was the "villain" they had come to meet.

In Harlem especially, and also in some other U.S. cities, the 1964 long, hot summer's predicted explosions had begun. Article after article in the white man's press had cast me as a symbol—if not a causative agent—of the "revolt" and of the "violence" of the American black man, wherever it had sprung up.

In the biggest press conference that I had ever experienced anywhere, the camera bulbs flashed, and the reporters fired questions.

"Mr. Malcolm X, what about those 'Blood Brothers,' reportedly affiliated with your organization, reportedly trained for violence, who have killed innocent white people?" . . . "Mr. Malcolm X, what about your comment that Negroes should form rifle clubs? . . ."

I answered the questions. I knew I was back in America again, hearing the subjective, scapegoat-seeking questions of the white man. New York white youth were killing victims; that was a "sociological" problem. But when black youth killed somebody, the power structure was looking to hang somebody. When black men had been lynched or otherwise murdered in cold blood, it was always said, "Things will get better." When whites had rifles in their homes, the constitution gave them the right to protect their home and themselves. But when black people even spoke of having rifles in their homes, that was "ominous."

I slipped in on the reporters something they hadn't been expecting. I said that the American black man needed to quit thinking what the white man had taught him—which was that the black man had no alternative except to beg for his so-called "civil rights." I said that the American black man needed to recognize that he had a strong, airtight case to take the United States before the United Nations on a formal accusation of "denial of human rights"—and that if Angola and South Africa were precedent cases, then there would be no easy way that the U.S. could escape being censured, right on its own home ground.

Just as I had known, the press wanted to get me off that subject. I was asked about my "Letter From Mecca"—I was all set with a speech regarding that:

"I hope that once and for all my Hajj to the Holy City of Mecca has established our Muslim Mosque's authentic religious affiliation with the 750 million Muslims of the orthodox Islamic World. And I *know* once and for all that the Black Africans look upon America's 22 million blacks as long-lost *brothers!* They *love* us! They *study* our struggle for freedom! They were so *happy* to hear how we are awakening from our long sleep—after so-called 'Christian' white America had taught us to be *ashamed* of our African brothers and homeland!

"Yes—I wrote a letter from Mecca. You're asking me 'Didn't you say that now you accept white men as brothers?' Well, my answer is that in the Muslim World, I saw, I felt, and I wrote home how my thinking was broadened!

Just as I wrote, I shared true, brotherly love with many white-complexioned Muslims who never gave a single thought to the race, or to the complexion, of another Muslim.

"My pilgrimage broadened my scope. It blessed me with a new insight. In two weeks in the Holy Land, I saw what I never had seen in thirty-nine years here in America. I saw all *races,* all *colors,*—blue-eyed blonds to black-skinned Africans—in *true* brotherhood! In unity! Living as one! Worshiping as one! No segregationists—no liberals; they would not have known how to interpret the meaning of those words.

"In the past, yes, I have made sweeping indictments of all white people. I never will be guilty of that again—as I know now that some white people *are* truly sincere, that some truly are capable of being brotherly toward a black man. The true Islam has shown me that a blanket indictment of all white people is as wrong as when whites make blanket indictments against blacks.

"Yes, I have been convinced that *some* American whites do want to help cure the rampant racism which is on the path to *destroying* this country!

"It was in the Holy World that my attitude was changed, by what I experienced there, and by what I witnessed there, in terms of brotherhood—not just brotherhood toward me, but brotherhood between all men, of all nationalities and complexions, who were there. And now that I am back in America, my attitude here concerning white people has to be governed by what my black brothers and I experience here, and what we witness here—in terms of brotherhood. The *problem* here in America is that we meet such a small minority of individual so-called 'good,' or 'brotherly' white people. Here in the United States, notwithstanding those few 'good' white people, it is the *collective* 150 million white people whom the *collective* 22 million black people have to deal with!

"Why, here in America, the seeds of racism are so deeply rooted in the white people collectively, their belief that they are 'superior' in some way is so deeply rooted, that these things are in the national white subconsciousness. Many whites are even actually unaware of their own racism, until they face some test, and then their racism emerges in one form or another.

"Listen! The white man's racism toward the black man here in America is what has got him in such trouble all over this world, with other non-white peoples. The white man can't separate himself from the stigma that he automatically feels about anyone, no matter who, who is not his color. And the non-white peoples of the world are sick of the condescending white man! That's why you've got all of this trouble in places like Viet Nam. Or right here in the Western Hemisphere—probably 100 million people of African descent are divided against each other, taught by the white man to hate and to mistrust each other. In the West Indies, Cuba, Brazil, Venezuela, all of South America, Central America! All of those lands are full of people with African blood! On the African continent, even, the white man has maneuvered to divide the black

African from the brown Arab, to divide the so-called 'Christian African' from the Muslim African. Can you imagine what can happen, what would certainly happen, if all of these African-heritage peoples ever *realize* their blood bonds, if they ever realize they all have a common goal—if they ever *unite?*"

The press was glad to get rid of me that day. I believe that the black brothers whom I had just recently left in Africa would have felt that I did the subject justice. Nearly through the night, my telephone at home kept ringing. My black brothers and sisters around New York and in some other cities were calling to congratulate me on what they had heard on the radio and television news broadcasts, and people, mostly white, were wanting to know if I would speak here or there.

The next day I was in my car driving along the freeway when at a red light another car pulled alongside. A white woman was driving and on the passenger's side, next to me, was a white man. "*Malcolm X!*" he called out—and when I looked, he stuck his hand out of his car, across at me, grinning. "Do you mind shaking hands with a white man?" Imagine that! Just as the traffic light turned green, I told him, "I don't mind shaking hands with human beings. Are you one?"

[1965]

Issues:
Tourism and Exile

INTRODUCTION

"The tourist is one of the best models available for modern man in general."

Dean MacCannell, *The Tourist: A New Theory of the Leisure Class*

"If true exile is a condition of terminal loss, why has it been transformed so easily into a potent, even enriching, motif of modern culture?"

Edward Said, "Reflections on Exile"

During the course of their journeys, travelers are often confronted by various issues of taste and judgment, extremes of wealth and poverty, conflicts between industrial development and the environment, and the painful inequities of history. At one end of the spectrum is the figure of the tourist, a member of the leisure class, who travels voluntarily to seek pleasure and entertainment. At the other end is the exile, who travels involuntarily, impelled by political conflict or natural catastrophe to leave home. The tourist is a figure of privilege, the exile a figure of misfortune. The tourist is often viewed as comic, the exile as tragic. Both figures, even though they represent quite opposite conditions of existence, have been used to symbolize modern man. For example, Dean MacCannell sees in the tourist a symbol of the consumer society, an agent of the commercialism, development, and exploitation that are exhausting the world's resources. Edward Said finds in the exile a representative for the masses of humanity who have been physically separated from homelands or spiritually separated from a community of beliefs and values that sustain peace of mind.

Many of the selections in this section discuss how the distinctions between travel and tourism provide an unending source of contention for critics of travel writing. Few people appreciate being labeled tourists; the term has embarrassing connotations. We speak of "travel writing" rather than "tourist writing." A phrase like "the literature of tourism" would suggest cruise advertisements, package tour publicity, slick brochures, the travel sections (not tourist sections) of newspapers, and glossy magazines like *The Condé Nast Traveler* or *Travel and Leisure. Travel*, with its literary heritage of ordeal, adventure, discovery, and illumination, is a much more flattering term to apply to one's activities than *tourism*.

Tourist implies an anti-heroic role in comparison to *traveler*. Often, the tourist is caricatured as a comic figure; the word connotes a sheep-like passivity and a childlike naïveté. Tourists usually travel in groups; they pay someone else to plan itineraries and make reservations for hotels and restaurants. They are led by guides who translate for them, simplify the mysteries of the foreign, and often feed them inaccurate information about sites and monuments. More than one critic has observed that part of the very identity of the tourist is an inherent self-ridicule.

In "The Semiotics of Tourism," Jonathan Culler argues that "Ferocious denigration of tourists is in part an attempt to convince oneself that one is not a tourist. The desire to distinguish between tourists and real travelers is a part of tourism—integral to it rather than outside it or beyond it." How much more flattering to the ego to consider oneself a traveler! Going it solo, deciphering maps, conversing with the locals in their own language, finding undiscovered places, reading deeply in the history and literature of the region, departing from the beaten path, having adventures, living on the cheap. Many contemporary travel writers find their inspiration in avoiding or mocking the banalities of tourism.

In fact, there are many forms of tourism, some quite physically or intellectually ambitious, like group treks, bicycle journeys, or study tours. Historically, tourists sought destinations that promised spiritual or cultural enlightenment— holy places, tombs of saints, churches, museums, and monuments. Tourism and pilgrimage have common origins as forms of group travel. In Europe, spas and mineral baths combined physical relief, healing, and entertainment. The sun-worshipping tourist is more a figure of the twentieth century. (The French Riviera was a winter resort until the 1930s, when patrons persuaded hotels to stay open for the summer.) Varieties of tourism multiplied as affluence and technology made any destination (like Antarctica) or leisure activity (even climbing Mt. Everest) possible.

Tourism can raise other, more serious questions than those of class, style, taste, and image. Tourism at its worst mirrors larger contemporary social problems and inequalities: the decline of quality and authenticity through commercialization and mass production, the destruction of the environment, the exploitation of poorer nations by richer ones. The pollution of the Mediterranean and the disfiguring of its coastline by huge, ugly apartments and hotels are generated by tourism. If mass tourism can contribute to the local economy, it can also cause destruction of wilderness and the habitats of wild animals. The invasion of aboriginal lands and the violation of cultural sanctity is a tourist problem. Forcing children and adolescents into prostitution to satisfy the appetites of visitors from wealthier countries is one of the darker sides of tourism.

Terrorism is often aimed at tourism; bloody headlines can force mass cancellations and stop the flow of revenue to tourist destinations. Terrorism, like war, constrains international travel and limits tourism. International travel has been undermined by the attacks on the World Trade Towers in New York on September 11, 2001, and the resulting wars in Afghanistan and Iraq. Social unrest and ethnic conflicts in other parts of the globe discourage travel. The kinds of social disorder that keep the tourist at home may at the same time create a different kind of traveler—the refugee and the exile.

While voluntary travel is a mark of good fortune in that it necessitates money and leisure, misfortune usually impels the involuntary traveler—the exile, the refugee, the homeless person, the tramp—to take to the road. The exile is frequently seen as a representative figure of modern man because the many political and social upheavals of the twentieth century have displaced masses of people, created vast numbers of refugees, and separated individuals from their families, cultures, and homelands.

On a more abstract level, intellectual and spiritual alienation, the loss of religious beliefs, and the feeling of loneliness and individual estrangement from social community often make modern writers and artists think of themselves as exiles. James Joyce, a major representative of literary modernism, left behind his native Ireland and lived abroad for most of his life. His motto for survival as an artist, expressed by one his characters in a famous phrase, "silence, exile, and cunning," draws on the metaphor of exile as a symbol of a spiritual condition.

The figure of the exile is often romanticized. Expatriates, people who choose to leave their own countries and live abroad while maintaining their original citizenship, constitute a kind of voluntary exile. Artists and writers sometimes choose this mode of existence to free themselves from the constraints of their own culture and celebrate their independence of spirit. One can be exiled in one's own country. In the era of the Great Depression in America, tramps and hoboes rode around the country illegally in freight trains; writers from later generations imitated this mode of travel for the risk and adventure that if offered. One of the most romanticized peoples for centuries have been the gypsies, nomadic cultures who make their homes on the road and excite both the fear and the imagination of settled peoples.

In the first group of selections below, tourism is the common concern. Paul Fussell defines and critiques tourism, contrasts it with exploration and travel, and explains the travel writer's dilemma in a world overrun with tourists. Mark Twain's humorous observations on his fellow cruise members show how the tourist was already a comic figure in the nineteenth century. P. J. O'Rourke updates Twain's perspective.

Then the readings shift to the viewpoint of native inhabitants as they look upon the tourists who descend on their homes. Robyn Davidson examines the effects of tourism on the landscapes and indigenous cultures of Australia. V. S. Naipaul and Jamaica Kincaid recall their memories of watching tourists disembark on the Caribbean islands that were their homes. Rudolfo Anaya and

Edward Abbey react to tourists in the American West, Anaya as a Chicano native of New Mexico and Abbey as a forest ranger watching his wilderness sanctuary invaded by campers and recreational vehicles. As travelers of color, James Baldwin and Caryl Phillips are more like exiles as they observe the curiosity and hostility they arouse among the inhabitants of white Europe.

Writers have sometimes joined the realm of the dispossessed in the spirit of exile in order to explore a literal sense of homelessness, to gain experience to write about travel as a state of physical and mental hardship as well as a release from the limitations of a comfortable, home-centered life. Jack London, who romanticized the freedom of the vagabond life, experienced poverty, sometimes by necessity, sometimes by choice. His narrative about venturing into urban slums provides a transition between tourism and the world of the poor. George Orwell followed London's example and joined the society of tramps in England of the 1920s. Chris McCandless, the "supertramp" whose story is told by Jon Krakauer, was inspired by the vagabond spirit of writer/travelers like Jack London. McCandless abandoned society for the wilderness, only to die in Alaska of starvation. In "The New Nomads," Eva Hoffman considers exile as a contemporary reality in light of the forced emigrations of political refugees in the twentieth century and her own experience as a Polish immigrant to Canada. Finally, Rebecca Solnit visits the gypsies of Ireland, called "Travellers," and considers the prejudices of settled society towards people who choose a transient life.

The readings of this section bring together three very different kinds of travelers: those who have the means and the freedom to travel for pleasure, education, and amusement; those who are forced by circumstance to leave their homes, usually against their wills; and those who choose to reject the comforts of a settled existence and live, as it were, on the road. In all of these selections, travel writing becomes a means of social criticism and commentary on cultural, morality, and human sensitivity.

Paul Fussell

(1924–)

In *Abroad: British Literary Traveling between the Wars* (1980), Paul Fussell observed that "Any adult recalling his childhood remembers moments when reading was revealed to be traveling." This book was one of the first contemporary analyses of travel writing as a genre, and it has influenced many subsequent studies of travel and literature. Fussell examines the literary qualities of travel writing by considering the work of English writers who left their country after World War I to escape the wartime ugliness and regimented routine.

In the chapter from *Abroad*, excerpted below, Fussell argues that in an age of mass tourism, true travel is no longer possible. In his view, tourism is a degraded, impure form of travel. This chapter brought rejoinders from readers, travelers, and writers who took issue with Fussell's argument that tourism had erased travel, or that the distinction is clear or even important. One thing is certain: Fussell inspired a debate about authenticity and taste, as well as the traveler's or tourist's very identity. *Abroad* is a kind of sequel to his previous work, *The Great War and Modern Memory* (1975), an analysis of the war's effect on literature, which won several prizes, including the National Book Award. Fussell is Professor Emeritus in the English Department at the University of Pennsylvania.

"From Exploration to Travel to Tourism"

From *Abroad: British Literary Traveling Between the Wars*

Two bits of data at the outset. When you entered Manhattan by the Lincoln Tunnel twenty years ago you saw from the high west bank of the Hudson a vision that lifted your heart and in some measure redeemed the potholes and noise and lunacy and violence of the city. You saw the magic row of transatlantic liners nuzzling the island, their classy, frivolous red and black and white and green uttering their critique of the utility beige-gray of the buildings. In the row might be the *Queen Mary* or the *Queen Elizabeth* or the *Mauretania*, the *United States* or the *America* or the *Independence*, the *Rafaello* or the *Michelangelo* or the *Liberté*. These were the last attendants of the age of travel, soon to fall victim to the jet plane and the cost of oil and the cost of skilled labor.

A second bit of data, this one rather nasty. An official of the Guyanese government was recently heard to say that Jonestown might be turned into a profitable tourist attraction, "on the order of Auschwitz or Dachau." The disappearance of the ships from the Hudson, like the remark from Guyana, helps define the advanced phase of the age of tourism.

The rudimentary phase began over a century ago, in England, because England was the first country to undergo industrialization and urbanization. The tediums of industrial work made "vacations" necessary, while the unwholesomeness of England's great soot-caked cities made any place abroad, by flagrant contrast, appear almost mystically salubrious, especially in an age of rampant tuberculosis. Contributing to the rise of tourism in the nineteenth century was the bourgeois vogue of romantic primitivism. From James "Ossian" Macpherson in the late eighteenth century to D. H. Lawrence in the early twentieth, intellectuals and others discovered special virtue in primitive peoples and places. Tourism is egalitarian or it is nothing, and its egalitarianism is another index of its origins in the nineteenth century. Whether in the Butlin's Camps of the British or the National Park campsites of America or Hitler's Strength-through-Joy cruises or the current Clubs Méditerranée, where nudity and pop-beads replace clothes and cash, it is difficult to be a snob and a tourist at the same time. By going primitive in groups one becomes "equal," playing out even in 1980 a fantasy devised well over a century ago, a fantasy implying that if simple is good, sincere is even better.

It was not always thus. Before tourism there was travel, and before travel there was exploration. Each is roughly assignable to its own age in modern history: exploration belongs to the Renaissance, travel to the bourgeois age, tourism to our proletarian moment. But there are obvious overlaps. What we recognize as tourism in its contemporary form was making inroads on travel as early as the mid-nineteenth century, when Thomas Cook got the bright idea of shipping sightseeing groups to the Continent, and though the Renaissance is over, there are still a few explorers. Tarzan's British father Lord Greystoke was exploring Africa in the twentieth century while tourists were being herded around the Place de l'Opéra.

And the terms *exploration, travel,* and *tourism* are slippery. In 1855 what we would call exploration is often called travel, as in Francis Galton's *The Art of Travel.* His title seems to promise advice about securing deckchairs in favorable locations and hints about tipping on shipboard, but his sub-title makes his intention clear: *Shifts and Contrivances Available in Wild Countries.* Galton's advice to "travelers" is very different from the matter in a Baedeker. Indeed, his book is virtually a survival manual, with instructions on blacksmithing, making your own black powder, descending cliffs with ropes, and defending a camp against natives: "Of all European inventions, nothing so impresses and terrifies savages as fireworks, especially rockets. . . . A rocket, judiciously sent up, is very likely to frighten off an intended attack and save bloodshed." On the other hand, the word *travel* in modern usage is equally misleading, as in phrases like *travel agency* and the *travel industry,* where what the words are disguising is *tourist agency* and the *tourist industry,* the idea of a *travel industry* constituting a palpable contradiction in terms, if we understand what real travel once was.

"Explorers," according to Hugh and Pauline Massingham, "are to the ordinary traveler what the Saint is to the average church congregation." The athletic, paramilitary activity of exploration ends in knighthoods for Sir Francis Drake and Sir Aurel Stein and Sir Edmund Hillary. No traveler, and certainly no tourist, is ever knighted for his performances, although the strains he may undergo can be as memorable as the explorer's. All three make journeys, but the explorer seeks the undiscovered, the traveler that which has been discovered by the mind working in history, the tourist that which has been discovered by entrepreneurship and prepared for him by the arts of mass publicity. The genuine traveler is, or used to be, in the middle between the two extremes. If the explorer moves toward the risks of the formless and the unknown, the tourist moves toward the security of pure cliché. It is between these two poles that the traveler mediates, retaining all he can of the excitement of the unpredictable attaching to exploration, and fusing that with the pleasure of "knowing where one is" belonging to tourism.

But travel is work. Etymologically a traveler is one who suffers *travail*, a word deriving in its turn from Latin *tripalium*, a torture instrument consisting of three stakes designed to rack the body. Before the development of tourism, travel was conceived to be like study, and its fruits were considered to be the adornment of the mind and the formation of the judgment. The traveler was a student of what he sought, and he was assisted by aids like the 34 volumes of the Medieval Town Series, now, significantly, out of print. One by-product of real travel was something that has virtually disappeared, the travel book as a record of an inquiry and a report of the effect of the inquiry on the mind and imagination of the traveler. Lawrence's Italian journeys, says Anthony Burgess, "by post-bus or cold late train or on foot are in that great laborious tradition which produced genuine travel books." And Paul Theroux, whose book *The Great Railway Bazaar* is one of the few travel books to emerge from our age of tourism, observes that "travel writing is a funny thing" because "the worst trips make the best reading, which is why Graham Greene's *The Lawless Roads* and Kinglake's *Eothen* are so superb." On the other hand, easy, passive travel results in books which offer "little more than chatting," or, like former British Prime Minister Edward Heath's *Travels*, "smug boasting." "Let the tourist be cushioned against misadventure," says Lawrence Durrell; "your true traveler will not feel that he has had his money's worth unless he brings back a few scars." (A personal note: although I have been both traveler and tourist, it was as a traveler, not a tourist, that I once watched my wallet and passport slither down a Turkish toilet at Bodrum, and it was the arm of a traveler that reached deep, deep in that cloaca to retrieve them.) If exploration promised adventures, travel was travel because it held out high hopes of misadventures.

From the outset mass tourism attracted the class-contempt of killjoys who conceived themselves independent travelers and thus superior by reason of intellect, education, curiosity, and spirit. In the mid-nineteenth century Charles Lever laments in *Blackwood's Magazine*:

> It seems that some enterprizing and unscrupulous man [he means Thomas Cook] has devised the project of conducting some forty or fifty persons . . . from London to Naples and back for a fixed sum. He contracts to carry them, feed them, and amuse them. . . . When I first read the scheme . . . I caught at the hope that the speculation would break down. I imagined that the characteristic independence of Englishmen would revolt against a plan that reduces the traveler to the level of his trunk and obliterates every trace and trait of the individual. I was all wrong. As I write, the cities of Italy are deluged with droves of these creatures.

Lever's word *droves* suggests sheep or cattle and reminds us how traditional in anti-tourist fulminations animal images are. (I have used *herded,* above.) "Of all noxious animals," says Francis Kilvert in the 1870's, "the most noxious is the tourist." And if not animals, insects. The Americans descending on Amalfi in the 1920's, according to Osbert Sitwell, resemble "a swarm of very noisy transatlantic locusts," and the tourists at Levanto in the 1930's, according to his sister Edith, are "the most awful people with legs like flies who come in to lunch in bathing costume—flies, centipedes."

I am assuming that travel is now impossible and that tourism is all we have left. Travel implies variety of means and independence of arrangements. The disappearance not just of the transatlantic lovelies but of virtually all passenger ships except cruise vessels (tourism with a vengeance) and the increasing difficulty of booking hotel space if one is not on a tour measure the plight of those who aspire still to travel in the old sense. Recently I planned a trip to the Orient and the South Pacific, hoping that in places so remote and, I dreamed, backward, something like travel might still just be possible. I saw myself lolling at the rail unshaven in a dirty white linen suit as the crummy little ship approached Bora Bora or Fiji in a damp heat which made one wonder whether death by yaws or dengue fever might be an attractive alternative. Too late for such daydreams. I found that just as I was inquiring, passenger ship travel in the Pacific disappeared, in April, 1978, to be precise. That month the ships of both the Matson and the Pacific Far East Lines were laid up for good, done in by the extortions of the oil-producing nations. In the same month even a small Chinese-owned "steam navigation company" running a regular service between Hong Kong and Singpore put away its toys. Formerly it had been possible to call at the remote island of Betio and Tarawa Atoll to pay respect to the ghosts of the United States and Japanese Marines, and an enterprising couple had built a small inn there. Now access to Betio and Tarawa is by air only and the plane flies on alternate Thursdays, which means you have to stay there two weeks if you go at all. No one will go there now. I did not go there but to the big places with big hotels and big airports served by big planes. I came to know what Frederic Harrison meant when he said, "We go abroad but we travel no longer." Only he wrote that in 1887. I suppose it's all a matter of degree. Perhaps the closest one could approach an experience of travel in the old sense today would be to drive in an aged automobile with doubtful tires through Roumania or Afghanistan without hotel reservations and to get by on terrible French.

One who has hotel reservations and speaks no French is a tourist. Anthropologists are fond of defining him, although in their earnestness they tend to miss his essence. Thus Valene L. Smith in *Hosts and Guests: The Anthropology of Tourism*: "A tourist is a temporarily leisured person who voluntarily visits a place away from home for the purpose of experiencing a change." But that pretty well defines a traveler too. What distinguishes the tourist is the motives, few of which are ever openly revealed: to raise social status at home and to allay social anxiety; to realize fantasies of erotic freedom; and most important, to derive secret pleasure from posing momentarily as a member of a social class superior to one's own, to play the role of a "shopper" and spender whose life becomes significant and exciting only when one is exercising power by choosing what to buy. Cant as the tourist may of the Taj Mahal and Mt. Etna at sunset, his real target today is the immense Ocean Terminal at Hong Kong, with its miles of identical horrible camera and tape-recorder shops. The fact that the tourist is best defined as a fantasist equipped temporarily with unaccustomed power is better known to the tourist industry than to anthropology. The resemblance between the tourist and the client of a massage parlor is closer than it would be polite to emphasize.

For tourist fantasies to bloom satisfactorily, certain conditions must be established. First, the tourist's mind must be entirely emptied so that a sort of hypnotism can occur. Unremitting Musak is a help here, and it is carefully provided in hotels, restaurants, elevators, tour buses, cable-cars, planes, and excursion boats. The tourist is assumed to know nothing, a tradition upheld by the American magazine *Travel* (note the bogus title), which is careful to specify that London is in England and Venice in Italy. If the tourist is granted a little awareness, it is always of the most retrograde kind, like the 30's belief, which he is assumed to hold, that "transportation," its varieties and promise, is itself an appropriate subject of high regard. (Think of the 1939 New York World's Fair, with its assumption that variety, celerity, and novelty in means of transport are inherently interesting: "Getting There Is Half the Fun.") A current day-tour out of Tokyo honors this convention. The ostensible object is to convey a group of tourists to a spot where they can wonder at the grandeurs of natural scenery. In pursuit of this end, they are first placed in a "streamlined" train whose speed of 130 miles per hour is frequently called to their attention. They are then transferred to an air-conditioned "coach" which whisks them to a boat, whence, after a ten-minute ride, they are ushered into a funicular to ascend a spooky gorge, after which, back to the bus, etc. The whole day's exercise is presented as a marvel of contrivance in which the sheer variety of the conveyances supplies a large part of the attraction. Hydrofoils are popular for similar reasons, certainly not for their efficiency. Of the four I've been on in the past few years, two have broken down spectacularly, one in Manila Bay almost sinking after encountering a submerged log at sophomoric high speed.

Tourist fantasies fructify best when tourists are set down not in places but in pseudo-places, passing through subordinate pseudo-places, like airports, on the way. Places are odd and call for interpretation. They are the venue of the traveler. Pseudo-places entice by their familiarity and call for instant recognition: "We have arrived." Kermanshah, in Iran, is a place; the Costa del Sol is a pseudo-place, or Tourist Bubble, as anthropologists call it. The Algarve, in southern Portugal, is a prime pseudo-place, created largely by Temple Fielding, the American author of *Fielding's Travel Guide to Europe*. That book, first published in 1948, was to tourism what Baedeker was to travel. It did not, says John McPhee, "tell people what to see. It told them . . . what to spend, and where." Bougainville is a place; the Polynesian Cultural Center, on Oahu, is a pseudo-place, but now Zermatt has been promoted to the status of its pre-eminent pseudo-place. Because it's a city that has been constructed for the purpose of being recognized as a familiar image, Washington is a classic pseudo-place, resembling Disneyland in that as in other respects. One striking post-Second War phenomenon has been the transformation of numerous former small countries into pseudo-places or tourist commonwealths, whose function is simply to entice tourists and sell them things. This has happened remarkably fast. As recently as 1930 Alec Waugh could report that Martinique had no tourists because there was no accommodation for them. Now, Martinique would seem to be about nothing but tourists, like Haiti, the Dominican Republic, Barbados, Bermuda, Hong Kong, Fiji, and the Greek Islands.

Today the tourist is readied for his ultimate encounter with placelessness by passing first through the uniform airport. Only forty years ago the world's airports exhibited distinctive characteristics betokening differences in national character and style. Being in one was not precisely like being in another. In Graham Greene's novel of 1935, *England Made Me*, the character Fred Hall, we are told, "knew the airports of Europe as well as he had once known the stations on the Brighton line—shabby Le Bourget; the great scarlet rectangle of the Tempelhof as one came in from London in the dark . . . ; the white sand blowing up round the shed at Tallinn; Riga, where the Berlin to Leningrad plane came down and bright pink mineral waters were sold in a tin-roofed shed." That sort of variety would be unthinkable now, when, as Bernard Bergonzi says, airport design has become a "ubiquitous international idiom."

Moving through the airport—or increasingly, being moved, on a literal endless belt—the tourist arrives at his next non-place, the airplane interior. The vapid non-allusive cheerfulness of its décor betrays its design and manufacture as Southern Californian. Locked in this flying cigar where distance is expressed in hours instead of miles or kilometers, the tourist is in touch only with the uniform furniture and fittings and experiences the environment through which the whole non-place is proceeding only as he is obliged to fasten or loosen his seat belt. Waugh was among the first to notice "the curious fact that airplanes have added nothing to our enjoyment of height. The human eye still receives the most intense images when the observer's feet are planted on the ground or on a building. The airplane belittles all it discloses." The calculated isolation from the actual which is tourism ("We fly you above the weather") is reflected as well in the design of the last of the serious passenger liners, the QEII. Here the designers carefully eliminated the promenade deck, formerly the place where you were vouchsafed some proximity to the ocean. Now, as John Malcolm Brinnin has said, "Travelers who love the sea, delight in studying its moods, and like to walk in the sight and smell of it, were left with almost no place to go." Except the bars and fruit-machines, doubtless the intention. As the ship has been obliged to compete in the illusion of placelessness with the airport and the jet, its interior design has given over its former ambitions of alluding to such identifiable places as country estates with fireplaces and libraries, urban tea-dance parlors, and elegant conservatories full of palms, ferns, and wicker, and instead has embraced the universal placeless style, eschewing organic materials like wood and real fabric in favor of spray-painted metal and dun plastic. I don't want to sound too gloomy, but there's a relation here with other "replacements" characterizing contemporary life: the replacement of coffee-cream by ivory-colored powder, for example, or of silk and wool by nylon; or glass by lucite, bookstores by "bookstores," eloquence by jargon, fish by fish-sticks, merit by publicity, motoring by driving, and travel by tourism. A corollary of that last replacement is that ships have been replaced by cruise ships, small moveable pseudo-places making an endless transit between larger fixed pseudo-places. But even a cruise ship is preferable to a plane. It is healthier because you can exercise on it, and it is more romantic because you can copulate on it.

Safe and efficient uniform international jet service began in earnest around 1957. That's an interesting moment in the history of human passivity. It's the approximate moment when radio narrative and drama, requiring the audience to do some of the work by suppplying the missing visual dimension by its own imagination, were replaced by television, which now does it all for the "viewer"—or stationary tourist, if you will. Supplying the missing dimension is exactly what real travel used to require, and it used to assume a large body of people willing to travail to earn illumination.

But ironically, the tourist is not without his own kinds of travails which the industry never prepares him for and which make tourism always something less than the ecstasy proposed. The sense that he is being swindled and patronized, or that important intelligence is being withheld from him, must trouble even the dimmest at one time or another. In addition to the incomprehensible but clearly crucial airport loudspeaker harangues, the tourist is faced by constant rhetorical and contractual challenges. He meets one the moment he accepts the standard airline baggage check and reads, "This is not the Luggage Ticket (Baggage Check) as described in Article 4 of the Warsaw Convention or the Warsaw Convention as amended by the Hague Protocol 1955." The question arises, if this baggage check is not that one, what is it? If it is not that Luggage Ticket (Baggage Check), how do you get the real one? And what does the real one say when you finally get it? Does it say, "This *is* the Luggage Ticket (Baggage Check) as described in, etc."? "On no account accept any substitute." Or "Persons accepting substitutes for the Luggage Ticket (Baggage Check) as described in Article 4 . . . will legally and morally have no recourse when their baggage is diverted (lost), and in addition will be liable to severe penalties, including immediate involuntary repatriation at their own expense."

Another cause of tourist travail is touts. The word *tout*, designating a man hounding a tourist to patronize a certain hotel or shop, dates approximately from Cook's first organized excursion to the Paris Exposition of 1855. Some tourist brochures will gingerly hint at such hazards as sharks, fetid water, and appalling food, but I've never seen one that prepared the tourist for the far greater threat of the tout.

Tour guides are touts by nature, required to lead tourists to shops where purchases result in commissions. In Kyoto recently a scholarly guide to the religious monuments, full of dignity and years, had to undergo the humiliation of finally conducting his group of tourists to a low ceramics shop. He almost wept. Tour guides are also by nature café touts: "Let's rest here a moment. I know you're tired. You can sit down and order coffee, beer, or soft drinks." And souvenir-shop touts: "This place has the best fly-whisks (postcards, scarabs, amber, coral, camera film, turquoise, pocket calculators) in town, and because you are with me you will not be cheated." All kinds of tourists are fair game for touts, but Americans seem their favorite targets, not just because of their careless ways with money and their instinctive generosity but also their non-European innocence about the viler dimensions of human nature and their desire to be liked, their impulse to say "Good morning" back instead of "Go away." It's a rare American who, asked "Where you from, Sir?" will venture "Screw you" instead of "Boise."

Touts make contemporary tourism a hell of importunity, and many of my memories of tourist trips reduce to memories of particular touts. There was the money-changing tout at Luxor so assiduous that I dared not leave the hotel for several days, and the gang of guide-touts outside Olaffson's Hotel, Port au Prince, who could be dealt with only by hiring one to fend off the others. There was the nice, friendly waiter at the best hotel in Colombo, Sri Lanka, whose kindly inquiries about one's plans cloaked his intention to make one lease his brother's car. There was the amiable student of English in Shiraz whose touching efforts at verbal self-improvement brought him gradually to the essential matter, the solicitation of a large gift. There was the sympathetic acquaintance in Srinigar whose free boat ride ended at his canalside carpet outlet. There was the civilized Assistant Manager of the Hotel Peninsula, Hong Kong, an establishment so pretentious that it picks up its clients at the airport in Rolls-Royces, who, repulsed at the desk, finally came up to my room to tout the hotel's tours. There were the well-got-up young men of Manila who struck up conversations, innocently expressing interest in your children and place of residence, and then gradually, and in their view subtly, began to beg. Rejected there, they then touted for shops. They then turned pimps, and, that failing, whores. The Philippines is a notable tout venue, like Turkey, Iran, Mexico, Egypt, and India. All are in the grip of a developing capitalism, halfway between the primitive and the overripe. In London there are no touts: it's easier there to make a living without the constant fear of humiliating rebuff. On the other hand, there are none in Papua New Guinea either. It is not yet sufficiently "developed," which means it doesn't yet have a sense of a richer outside world which can be tapped. In the same way, your real native of a truly primitive place doesn't steal from tourists. Not out of primitive virtue but out of ignorance: unlike a resident of, say, Naples, he doesn't know what incredible riches repose in tourists' luggage and handbags.

As I have said, it is hard to be a snob and a tourist at the same time. A way to combine both roles is to become an anti-tourist. Despite the suffering he undergoes, the anti-tourist is not to be confused with the traveler: his motive is not inquiry but self-protection and vanity. Dean MacCannell, author of the anthropological study *The Tourist*, remembers a resident of an island like Nantucket who remonstrated when, arriving, MacCannell offered to start the car before the ferry docked. "Only tourists do that," he was told. Abroad, the techniques practiced by anti-tourists anxious to assert their difference from all those tourists are more shifty. All involve attempts to merge into the surroundings, like speaking the language, even badly. Some dissimulations are merely mechanical, like a man's shifting his wedding ring from the left to the right hand. A useful trick is ostentatiously not carrying a camera. If asked about this deficiency by a camera-carrying tourist, one scores points by saying, "I never carry a camera. If I photograph things I find I don't really see them." Another device is staying in the most unlikely hotels, although this is risky, like the correlative technique of eschewing taxis in favor of local public transportation (the more complicated and confusing the better), which may end with the anti-tourist stranded miles out of town, cold and alone on the last tram of the night. Another risky technique is programmatically consuming the local food, no matter how nasty, and affecting to relish sheeps' eyes, fried cicadas, and shellfish taken locally, that is, from the sewagey little lagoon. Dressing with attention to local coloration used to be harder before jeans became the international costume of the pseudo-leisured.

But jeans are hard for those around sixty to get away with, and the anti-tourist must be careful to prevent betrayal by jackets, trousers, shoes, and even socks and neckties (if still worn) differing subtly from the local norms.

Sedulously avoiding the standard sights is probably the best method of disguising your touristhood. In London one avoids Westminster Abbey and heads instead for the Earl of Burlington's eighteenth-century villa at Chiswick. In Venice one must walk by circuitous smelly back passages far out of one's way to avoid being seen in the Piazza San Marco. In Athens, one disdains the Acropolis in favor of the eminence preferred by the locals, the Lycabettus. Each tourist center has its interdicted zone: in Rome you avoid the Spanish Steps and the Fontana di Trevi, in Paris the Deux Magots and the whole Boul' Mich area, in Nice the Promenade des Anglais, in Egypt Giza with its excessively popular pyramids and sphinx, in Hawaii Waikiki. Avoiding Waikiki brings up the whole question of why one's gone to Hawaii at all, but that's exactly the problem.

Driving on the Continent, it's essential to avoid outright giveaways like the French TT license plate. Better to drive a car registered in the country you're touring (the more suave rental agencies know this) if you can't find one from some unlikely place like Bulgaria or Syria. Plates entirely in Arabic are currently much favored by anti-tourists, and they have the additional advantage of frustrating policemen writing tickets for illegal parking.

Perhaps the most popular way for the anti-tourist to demarcate himself from the tourists, because he can have a drink while doing it, is for him to lounge—cameraless—at a café table and with palpable contempt scrutinize the passing sheep through half-closed lids, making all movements very slowly. Here the costume providing the least danger of exposure is jeans, a thick dark-colored turtleneck, and longish hair. Any conversational gambits favored by lonely tourists, like "Where are you from?" can be deflected by vagueness. Instead of answering Des Moines or Queens, you say, "I spend a lot of time abroad" or "That's really hard to say." If hard-pressed, you simply mutter "Je ne parle pas Anglais," look at your watch, and leave.

The anti-tourist's persuasion that he is really a traveler instead of a tourist is both a symptom and a cause of what the British journalist Alan Brien has designated *tourist angst,* defined as "a gnawing suspicion that after all . . . you are still a tourist like every other tourist." As a uniquely modern form of self-contempt, *tourist angst* often issues in bizarre emotional behavior, and it is surprising that it has not yet become a classic for psychiatric study. "A student of mine in Paris," writes MacCannell, "a young man from Iran dedicated to the [student] revolution, half stammering, half shouting, said to me, "Let's face it, we are all tourists!" Then, rising to his feet, his face contorted with . . . self-hatred, he concluded dramatically in a hiss: 'Even *I* am a tourist.' "

Tourist angst like this is distinctly a class signal. Only the upper elements of the middle classes suffer from it, and in summer especially it is endemic in places like Florence and Mikonos and Crete. It is rare in pseudo-places like Disneyland, where people have come just because other people have come. This is to say that the working class finds nothing shameful about tourism. It is the middle class that has read and heard just enough to sense that being a tourist is somehow offensive and scorned by an imagined upper class which it hopes to emulate and, if possible, be mistaken for. The irony is that extremes meet; the upper class, unruffled by contempt from any source, happily enrolls in Lindblad Tours or makes its way up the Nile in tight groups being lectured at by a tour guide artfully disguised as an Oxbridge archeologist. Sometimes the anti-tourist's rage to escape the appearance of tourism propels him around a mock-full-circle, back to a simulacrum of exploration. Hence the popularity of African safaris among the upper-middle class. One tourist agency now offers package exploristic expeditions to Everest and the Sahara, and to Sinai by camel caravan, "real expeditions for the serious traveler looking for more than an adventurous vacation." Something of the acute discomfort of exploration and the uncertainty of real travel can be recovered by accepting an invitation to "Traverse Spain's Sierra Nevada on horseback ($528.00).

But the anti-tourist deludes only himself. We are all tourists now, and there is no escape. Every year there are over two hundred million of us, and when we are jetted in all directions and lodged in our pseudo-places, we constitute four times the population of France. The decisions we imagine ourselves making are shaped by the Professor of Tourism at Michigan State University and by the "Travel Administrators" now being trained at the New School in New York and by the International Union of Official Travel Organizations, whose publications indicate what it has in mind for us: *Factors Determining Selection of Sites for Tourism Development*, for example, or *Potential International Supply of Tourism Resources*. Our freedom and mobility diminish at the same time their expansion is loudly proclaimed; while more choices appear to solicit us, fewer actually do. The ships will not come back to the Hudson, and some place in Guyana will doubtless be selected as a site for tourism development. The tourist is locked in, and as MacCannell has pointed out, as a type the tourist is "one of the best models of modern man-in-general."

[1980]

MARK TWAIN

(1835–1910)

Mark Twain grew up in the small town of Hannibal, Missouri, on the Mississippi River and realized his boyhood dream of becoming a riverboat pilot. After he succeeded in escaping Hannibal, Twain never stopped traveling. His knowledge of the Mississippi, gained from years of living and working on the river, enriched his novel, The Adventures of Huckleberry Finn (1885), as well as his memoir and travel book, Life on the Mississippi (1883). His earlier travel books include Roughing It (1872), a memoir of his days as a young journalist and fortune-seeker in the West.

The Innocents Abroad (1869) a book written about a trip to Europe and the Holy Land, has been called "the most popular American travel book." The group excursion to Europe, in the form of a cruise and guided tour of multiple countries, was a major kind of travel for well-to-do Americans in the latter half of the nineteenth century. Twain's book originated in a series of letters he wrote to a newspaper while he was traveling. In the letter below, one can see how the subject of tourism is already providing material for humor and satire.

"Return of the Holy Land Excursionists—the Story of the Cruise"

From The Innocents Abroad

To the Editor of the Herald:

The steamer Quaker City has accomplished at last her extraordinary voyage and returned to her old pier at the foot of Wall Street. The expedition was a success in some respects, in some it was not. Originally it was advertised as a "pleasure excursion." Well, perhaps, it was a pleasure excursion, but certainly it did not look like one; certainly it did not act like one. Any body's and every body's notion of a pleasure excursion is that the parties to it will of a necessity be young and giddy and somewhat boisterous. They will dance a good deal, sing a good deal, make love, but sermonize very little. Any body's and every body's notion of a well conducted funeral is that there must be a hearse and a corpse, and chief mourners and mourners by courtesy, many old people, much solemnity, no levity, and a prayer and sermon withal. Three-fourths of the Quaker City's passengers were between forty and seventy years of age! There was a picnic crowd for you! It may be supposed that the other fourth was composed of young girls. But it was not. It was chiefly composed of rusty old bachelors and a child of six years. Let us average the ages of the Quaker City's pilgrims and set the figure down as fifty years. Is any man insane enough to imagine that this picnic of patriarchs sang, made love, danced, laughed, told anecdotes, dealt in ungodly levity? In my experience they sinned little in these matters. No doubt it was presumed here at home that these frolicsome veterans laughed and sang and romped all day, and day after day, and kept up a noisy excitement from one end of the ship to the other; and that they played blind-man's buff or danced quadrilles and waltzes on moonlight evenings on the quarter-deck; and that at odd moments of unoccupied time they jotted a laconic item or two in the journals they opened on such an elaborate plan when they left home, and then skurried off to their whist and euchre labors under the cabin lamps. If these things were presumed, the presumption was at fault. The venerable excursionists were not gay and frisky. They played no blind-man's buff; they dealt not in whist; they shirked not the irksome journal, for alas! most of them were even writing books. They never romped, they talked but little, they never sang, save in the nightly prayer-meeting. The pleasure ship was a synagogue, and the pleasure trip was a funeral excursion without a corpse. (There is nothing exhilirating about a funeral excursion without a corpse.) A free, hearty laugh was a sound that was not heard oftener than once in seven days about those decks or in those cabins, and when it was heard it met with precious little sympathy. The excursionists danced, on three separate evenings, long, long ago, (it seems an age,) quadrilles, of a single set, made up of three ladies and five gentlemen, (the latter with handkerchiefs around their arms to signify their sex,) who timed their feet to the solemn wheezing of a melodeon; but even this melancholy orgie was voted to be sinful, and dancing was discontinued.

The pilgrims played dominoes when too much Josephus or Robinson's Holy Land Researches, or book-writing, made recreation necessary—for dominoes is about as mild and sinless a game as any in the world, perhaps, excepting always the ineffably insipid diversion they call croquet, which is a game where you don't pocket any balls and don't carom on any thing of any consequence, and when you are done nobody has to pay, and there are no refreshments to saw off, and, consequently, there isn't any satisfaction whatever about it—they played dominoes till they were rested, and then they blackguarded each other privately till prayer-time. When they were not seasick they were uncommonly prompt when the dinner-gong sounded. Such was our daily life on board the ship—solemnity, decorum, dinner, dominoes, devotions, slander. It was not lively enough for a pleasure trip; but if we had only had a corpse it would have made a noble funeral excursion. It is all over now; but when I look back the idea of these venerable fossils skipping forth on a six months' picnic, seems exquisitely refreshing. The advertised title of the expedition—"The Grand Holy Land Pleasure Excursion"—was a misnomer. "The Grand Holy Land Funeral Procession" would have been better—much better.

Wherever we went, in Europe, Asia, or Africa, we made a sensation, and, I suppose I may add, created a famine. None of us had ever been any where before; we all hailed from the interior; travel was a wild novelty to us, and we conducted ourselves in accordance with the natural instincts that were in us, and trammeled ourselves with no ceremonies, no conventionalities. We always took care to make it understood that we were Americans—Americans! When we found that a good many foreigners had hardly ever heard of America, and that a good many more knew it only as a barbarous province away off somewhere, that had lately been at war with somebody, we pitied the ignorance of the Old World, but abated no jot of our importance. Many and many a simple community in the Eastern hemisphere will remember for years the incursion of the strange horde in the year of our Lord 1867, that called themselves Americans, and seemed to imagine in some unaccountable way that they had a right to be proud of it. We generally created a famine, partly because the coffee on the Quaker City was unendurable, and sometimes the more substantial fare was not strictly first class; and partly because one naturally tires of sitting long at the same board and eating from the same dishes.

The people of those foreign countries are very, very ignorant. They looked curiously at the costumes we had brought from the wilds of America. They observed that we talked loudly at table sometimes. They noticed that we looked out for expenses, and got what we conveniently could out of a franc, and wondered where in the mischief we came from. In Paris they just simply opened their eyes and stared when we spoke to them in French! We never did succeed in making those idiots understand their own language. One of our passengers said to a shopkeeper, in reference to a proposed return to buy a pair of gloves, "*Along restay trankeel–may be ve coom Moonday;*" and would you believe it, that shopkeeper, a born Frenchman, had to ask what it was that had been said. Sometimes it seems to me, somehow, that there must be a difference between Parisian French and Quaker City French.

The people stared at us every where, and we stared at them. We generally made them feel rather small, too, before we got done with them, because we bore down on them with America's greatness until we crushed them. And yet we took kindly to the manners and customs, and especially to the fashions of the various people we visited. When we left the Azores, we wore awful capotes and used fine tooth combs—successfully. When we came back from Tangier, in Africa, we were topped with fezzes of the bloodiest hue, hung with tassels like an Indian's scalp-lock. In France and Spain we attracted some attention in these costumes. In Italy they naturally took us for distempered Garibaldians, and set a gunboat to look for any thing significant in our changes of uniform. We made Rome howl. We could have made any place howl when we had all our clothes on. We got no fresh raiment in Greece—they had but little there of any kind. But at Constantinople, how we turned out! Turbans, scimetars, fezzes, horse-pistols, tunics, sashes, baggy trowsers, yellow slippers—Oh, we were gorgeous! The illustrious dogs of Constantinople barked their under jaws off, and even then failed to do us justice. They are all dead by this time. They could not go through such a run of business as we gave them and survive.

And then we went to see the Emperor of Russia. We just called on him as comfortably as if we had known him a century or so, and when we had finished our visit we variegated ourselves with selections from Russian costumes and sailed away again more picturesque than ever. In Smyrna we picked up camel's hair shawls and other dressy things from Persia; but in Palestine–ah, in Palestine–our splendid career ended. They didn't wear any clothes there to speak of. We were satisfied, and stopped. We made no experiments. We did not try their costume. But we astonished the natives of that country. We astonished them with such eccentricities of dress as we could muster. We prowled through the Holy Land, from Cesarea Philippi to Jerusalem and the Dead Sea, a weird procession of pilgrims gotten up regardless of expense, solemn, gorgeous, green-spectacled, drowsing under blue umbrellas, and astride of a sorrier lot of horses, camels and asses than those that came out of Noah's ark, after eleven months of seasickness and short rations. If ever those children of Israel in Palestine forget when Gideon's Band went through there from America, they ought to be cursed once more and finished. It was the rarest spectacle that ever astounded mortal eyes, perhaps.

Well, we were at home in Palestine. It was easy to see that that was the grand feature of the expedition. We had cared nothing much about Europe. We galloped through the Louvre, the Pitti, the Ufizzi, the Vatican–all the galleries–and through the pictured and frescoed churches of Venice, Naples, and the cathedrals of Spain; some of us said that certain of the great works of the old masters were glorious creations of genius, (we found it out in the guide-book, though we got hold of the wrong picture sometimes,) and the others said they were disgraceful old daubs. We examined modern and ancient statuary with a critical eye in Florence, Rome, or any where we found it, and praised it if we saw fit, and if we didn't we said we preferred the wooden Indians in front of the cigar stores of America. But the Holy Land brought out all our enthusiasm. We fell into raptures by the barren shores of Galilee; we pondered at Tabor and at Nazareth; we exploded into poetry over the questionable loveliness of Esdraelon; we meditated at Jezreel and Samaria over the missionary zeal of Jehu; we rioted–fairly rioted among the holy places of Jerusalem; we bathed in Jordan and the Dead Sea, reckless whether our accident-insurance policies were extra-hazardous or not, and brought away so many jugs of precious water from both places that all the country from Jericho to the mountains of Moab will suffer from drouth this year, I think. Yet, the pilgrimage part of the excursion was its pet feature–there is no question about that. After dismal, smileless Palestine, beautiful Egypt had few charms for us. We merely glanced at it and were ready for home.

They wouldn't let us land at Malta–quarantine; they would not let us land in Sardinia; nor at Algiers, Africa; nor at Malaga, Spain, nor Cadiz, nor at the Madeira islands. So we got offended at all foreigners and turned our backs upon them and came home. I suppose we only stopped at the Bermudas because they were in the programme. We did not care any thing about any place at all. We wanted to go home. Homesickness was abroad in the ship—it was epidemic. If the authorities of New York had known how badly we had it, they would have quarantined us here.

The grand pilgrimage is over. Good-bye to it, and a pleasant memory to it, I am able to say in all kindness. I bear no malice, no ill-will toward any individual that was connected with it, either as passenger or officer. Things I did not like at all yesterday I like very well to-day, now that I am at home, and always hereafter I shall be able to poke fun at the whole gang if the spirit so moves me to do, without ever saying a malicious word. The expedition accomplished all that its programme promised that it should accomplish, and we ought to be satisfied with the management of the matter, certainly. Bye-bye!

[1869]

P. J. O'ROURKE

(1947–)

P. J. O'Rourke is an American political satirist, humorist, and frequent contributor to *Harper's*, *Atlantic Monthly*, and *Vanity Fair*. He is also a former editor of *National Lampoon* and currently on the staff of *Rolling Stone*. Among his books and collections of essays are *Parliament of Whores* (1992), *Give War a Chance* (1992), and *CEO of the Sofa* (2001).

O'Rourke's contemporary update of Mark Twain's critique of tourists in *The Innocents Abroad*, which appears below, was published in *Holidays in Hell* (1988), a collection of humorous pieces on travel. O'Rourke's attack on tourism employs the exaggeration and caricature typical of satire and finds fault with tourists for everything from their lack of education and imagination to their greedy consumerism.

"The Innocents Abroad, Updated"

From *Holidays in Hell*

On Saturday, June 8, 1867, the steamship *Quaker City* left New York harbor. On board was a group of Americans making the world's first package tour. Also on board was Mark Twain making the world's first fun of package tourism.

In its day *The Innocents Abroad* itinerary was considered exhaustive. It included Paris, Marseilles, the Rock of Gibraltar, Lake Como, some Alps, the

Czar, the pyramids and the Holy Land plus the glory that was Greece, the grandeur that was Rome and the pile of volcanic ash that was Pompeii.

When these prototypical tourists went home they could count themselves traveled. They had shivered with thoughts of lions in the Colosseum, "done" the Louvre, ogled Mont Blanc, stumbled through the ruins of the Parthenon by moonlight and pondered that eternal riddle—where'd its nose go?—of the Sphinx. They had seen the world.

But what if Mark Twain had to come back from the dead and escort 1980's tourists on a 1980's tour? Would it be the same? No. I'm afraid Mr. Twain would find there are worse things than innocents abroad in the world today.

In 1988 every country with a middle class to export has gotten into the traveling act. We Yanks, with our hula shirts and funny Kodaks, are no longer in the fore. The earth's travel destinations are jam-full of littering Venezuelans, peevish Swiss, smelly Norwegian backpackers yodeling in restaurant booths, Saudi Arabian businessmen getting their dresses caught in revolving doors and Bengali remittance men in their twenty-fifth year of graduate school pestering fat blonde Belgian *au pair* girls.

At least we American tourists understand English when it's spoken loudly and clearly enough. Australians don't. Once you've been on a plane full of drunken Australians doing wallaby imitations up and down the aisles, you'll never make fun of Americans visiting the Wailing Wall in short shorts again.

The Japanese don't wear short shorts (a good thing, considering their legs), but they do wear three-piece suits in the full range of tenement-hall paint colors, with fit to match. The trouser cuffs drag like bridal trains; the jacket collars have an ox yoke drape; and the vests leave six inches of polyester shirt snapping in the breeze. If the Japanese want to be taken seriously as world financial powers, they'd better quit using the same tailor as variety-show chimps.

The Japanese also travel in packs at a jog trot and get up at six A.M. and sing their company song under your hotel window. They are extraordinary shoplifters. They eschew the usual chothes and trinkets, but automobile plants, steel mills and electronics factories seem to be missing from everywhere they go. And Japs take snapshots of everything, not just everything famous but *everything*. Back in Tokyo there must be a billion color slides of street corners, turnpike off-ramps, pedestrian crosswalks, phone booths, fire hydrants, manhole covers and overhead electrical wires. What are the Japanese doing with these pictures? It's probably a question we should have asked before Pearl Harbor.

Worse than the Japanese, at least worse looking, are the Germans, especially at pool-side. The larger the German body, the smaller the German bathing suit and the louder the German voice issuing German demands and German orders to everybody who doesn't speak German. For this, and several other reasons, Germany is known as "the land where Israelis learned their manners."

And Germans in a pool cabana (or even Israelis at a discotheque) are nothing compared with French on a tropical shore. A middle-aged, heterosexual, college-educated male wearing a Mickey Mouse T-shirt and a string-bikini bottom and carrying a purse—what else could it be but a vacationing Frenchman? No tropical shore is too stupid for the French. They turn up on the coasts of Angola, Eritrea, Bangladesh and Sri Lanka. For one day they glory in *l'atmosphère très primitive* then spend two weeks in an ear-splitting snit because the natives won't make a *steak frite* out of the family water buffalo.

Also present in Angola, Eritrea and God-Knows-Where are the new breed of Yuppie "experience travelers." You'll be pinned down by mortar fire in the middle of a genocide atrocity in the Sudan, and right through it all come six law partners and their wives, in Banana Republic bush jackets, taking an inflatable raft trip down the White Nile and having an "experience."

Mortar fire is to be preferred, of course, to British sports fans. Has anyone checked the passenger list on *The Spirit of Free Enterprise?* Were there any Liverpool United supporters on board? That channel ferry may have been tipped over for fun. (Fortunately the Brits have to be back at their place of unemployment on Monday so they never get further than Spain.)

Then there are the involuntary tourists. Back in 1867, what with the suppression of the slave trade and all, they probably thought they'd conquered the involuntary tourism problem. Alas, no. Witness the African exchange students—miserable, cold, shivering, grumpy and selling cheap wrist watches from the top of cardboard boxes worldwide. (Moscow's Patrice Lumumba University has a particularly disgruntled bunch.) And the Pakistani family with twelve children who've been camped out in every airport on the globe since 1970—will somebody please do something for these people? Their toddler has got my copy of the *Asian Wall Street Journal*, and I won't be responsible if he tries to stuff it down the barrel of the El Al security guard's Uzi again.

Where will Mr. Clemens take these folks? What is the 1980's equivalent of the Grand Tour? What are the travel "musts" of today?

All the famous old monuments are still there, of course, but they're surrounded by scaffolds and green nets and signs saying, "Il pardonne la restoration bitte please." I don't know two people who've ever seen the same famous old monument. I've seen Big Ben. A friend of mine has seen half of the Sistine Chapel ceiling. No one has seen Notre Dame Cathedral for years. It's probably been sold to a shopping mall developer in Phoenix.

We've all, however, seen Dr. Meuller's Sex Shop in the Frankfurt airport. Dr. Meuller's has cozy booths where, for one deutsche mark a minute, we modern tourists can watch things hardly thought of in 1867. And there's nothing on the outside of the booths to indicate whether you're in there viewing basically healthy Swedish nude volleyball films or videos of naked Dobermans cavorting in food. Dr. Meuller's is also a reliable way to meet your boss, old Sunday School teacher or ex-wife's new husband, one of whom is always walking by when you emerge.

Dr. Meuller's is definitely a "must" of modern travel, as is the Frankfurt airport itself. If Christ came back tomorrow, He'd have to change planes in Frankfurt. Modern air travel means less time spent in transit. That time is now spent in transit lounges.

What else? There are "local points of interest" available until the real monuments are restored. These are small piles of stones about which someone will tell you extravagant lies for five dollars. ("And here, please, the Tomb of the Infant Jesus.") And there are the great mini-bars of Europe—three paper cartons of anise-flavored soda pop, two bottles of beer with suspended vegetable matter, a triangular candy bar made of chocolate-covered edelweiss and a pack of Marlboros manufactured locally under license. (N.B.: Open that split of Mumm's $\frac{1}{2}$-star in there, and $200 goes on your hotel bill faster than you can say "service non compris.")

In place of celebrated palaces, our era has celebrated parking spots, most of them in Rome. Romans will back a Fiat into the middle of your linguine al pesto is you're sitting too close to the restaurant window.

Instead of cathedrals, mosques and ancient temples, we have duty-free shops—at their best in Kuwait. I never knew there was so much stuff I didn't want. I assumed I wanted most stuff. But that was before I saw a $110,000 crêpe de chine Givenchy chador and a solid-gold camel saddle with twelve Rolex watches embedded in the seat.

The "sermons in stone" these days are all sung with cement. Cement is the granite, the marble, the porphyry of our time. Someday, no doubt, there will be "Elgin Cements" in the British Museum. Meanwhile, we tour the Warsaw Pact countries—cement everywhere, including, at the official level, quite a bit of cement in their heads.

Every modern tourist has seen *Mannix* dubbed in forty languages and the amazing watch adjustments of Newfoundland, Malaysia and Nepal (where time zones are, yes, half an hour off), and France in August when you can travel through the entire country without encountering a single pesky Frenchman or being bothered with anything that's open for business—though, somehow, the fresh dog crap is still a foot deep on the streets of Paris.

Astonishing toilets for humans are also a staple of up-to-date foreign adventure. Anyone who thinks international culture has become bland and uniform hasn't been to the bathroom, especially not in Yugoslavia where it's a hole in the floor with a scary old lady with a mop standing next to it. And, for astonishing toilet paper, there's India where there isn't any.

No present-day traveler, even an extra-odoriferous Central European one, can say he's done it all if he hasn't been on a smell tour of Asia. Maybe what seems pungent to the locals only becomes alarming when sniffed through a giant Western proboscis, but there are some odors in China that makes a visit to Bhopal seem like a picnic downwind from the Arpege factory. Hark to the cry of the tourist in the East: "Is it dead or is it dinner?"

Nothing beats the Orient for grand vistas, however, particularly of go-go girls. True, they can't Boogaloo and have no interest in learning. But Thai exotic dancers are the one people left who prefer American-made to Japanese. And they come and sit on your lap between sets, something the girls at the Crazy Horse never do. Now, where'd my wallet go?

Many contemporary tourist attractions are not located in one special place the way tourist attractions used to be. Now they pop up everywhere—that villainous cab driver with the all-consonant last name, for instance. He's waiting outside hotels from Sun City to the Seward Peninsula. He can't speak five languages and can't understand another ten. Hey! Hey! Hey, you! This isn't the way to the Frankfurt airport! Nein! Non! Nyet! Ixnay!

American embassies, too, are all over the map and always breathtaking. In the middle of London, on beautiful Grosvenor Square, there's one that looks like a bronzed Oldsmobile dashboard. And rising from the slums of Manila is another that resembles the Margarine of the Future Pavilion at the 1959 Brussels World Fair. I assume this is all the work of one architect, and I assume he's on drugs. Each American embassy comes with two permanent features—a giant anti-American demonstration and a giant line for American visas. Most demonstrators spend half their time burning Old Glory and the other half waiting for green cards.

Other ubiquitous spectacles of our time include various panics—AIDS, PLO terror and owning U.S. dollars predominate at the moment—and postcards of the Pope kissing the ground. There's little ground left unkissed by this pontiff, though he might think twice about kissing anything in some of the places he visits. (Stay away from Haiti, San Francisco and Mykonos, J.P., please.)

Then there's the squalor. This hasn't changed since 1867, but tourists once tried to avoid it. Now they seek it out. Modern tourists have to see the squalor so they can tell everyone back home how it changed their perspective on life. Describing squalor, if done with sufficient indignation, makes friends and relatives morally obligated to listen to our boring vacation stories. (Squalor conveniently available, at reasonable prices, in Latin America.)

No, the Grand Tour is no longer a stately procession of like-minded individuals through half a dozen of the world's major principalities. And it's probably just as well if Mark Twain doesn't come back from the dead. He'd have to lead a huge slew of multinational lunatics through hundreds of horrible countries with disgusting border formalities. And 1980's customs agents are the only thing worse than 1980's tourists. Damn it, give that back! You know perfectly well that it's legal to bring clean socks into Tanzania. Ow! Ouch! Where are you taking me!?

Of course you don't have to go to Africa to get that kind of treatment. You can have your possessions stolen right on the Piccadilly Line if you want. In fact, in 1987, you can experience most of the indignities and discomforts of travel in your own hometown, wherever you live. Americans flock in seething masses to any dim-wit local attraction—tall ships making a landing, short actors making a movie, Andrew Wyeth making a nude Helga fracas—just as if they were actually going somewhere. The briefest commuter flight is filled with businessmen dragging mountainous garment bags and whole computers on board. They are worst pests than mainland Chinese taking frigidaires home on the plane. And no modern business gal goes to lunch without a steamer trunk-size tote full of shoe changes, Sony Walkman tapes and tennis rackets. When she makes her way down a restaurant aisle, she'll crack the back of your head with this exactly the same way a Mexican will with a crate of chickens on a Yucatán bus ride.

The tourism ethic seems to have spread like one of the new sexual diseases. It now infects every aspect of daily life. People carry backpacks to work and out on dates. People dress like tourists at the office, the theater and church. People are as rude to their fellow countrymen as ever they are to foreigners.

Maybe the right thing to do is stay home in a comfy armchair and read about travel as it should be—in Samuel Clemens's *Huckleberry Finn*.

[1988]

ROBYN DAVIDSON

(1950–)

Robyn Davidson upholds the tradition of her fellow Australians as travelers. In her first book, *Tracks* (1980), she recounts her long trek across the vast and barren interior of Australia. She also traversed the deserts of Rajahstan in India with a nomadic group and wrote of her experience in *Desert Places* (1996), and she has edited *The Picador Book of Journeys* (2001).

Traveling Light (1989), from which the following essay, "Ayers Rock," is taken, is a collection of essays about still other travels in America and elsewhere. As a native Australian, Davidson understands the importance of Ayers Rock as a popular tourist destination and an emblem of the country, as well as a sacred site for Aboriginal people. The essay points out the conflicts between the enterprise of tourism and the value that the Aborigines place upon Ayers Rock. This kind of problem is repeated in encounters with tourists and indigenous peoples all over the world who need the tourist trade but are unwilling to see their lands and cultures damaged by hordes of visitors.

"Ayers Rock"

From *Traveling Light*

In the 'dead heart' of Australia, about two hundred miles southwest of Alice Springs, stands the most symbolically charged object in the country. Even city-dwellers, who have never visited it, will regard it as a quintessentially Australian monument. Europeans have been in this continent only two hundred years and anything that enhances a sense of national identity is clung to with desperate sentimentality.

The Pitjantjatjara Aborigines, to whom the object is profoundly significant, have been here for at least fifty thousand years. They believe their 'country'—a vast tract of desert spreading into three States—forms an axis about which the universe turns. Ethnocentricity perhaps, but when you gaze for the first time at Ayers Rock, floating like Leviathan in a sea of orange sand, it's easy to agree with them. It's like nothing else on earth.

It rises, isolated and improbable, over a thousand feet above the dunes. From a distance it is difficult to appreciate its size but, as you travel closer, its grandeur begins to penetrate your consciousness until, walking around the four-mile base, you are receiving a powerful dose of what Borges called 'the wonder distilled from elementary things'.

Ask geologists how it was formed, and they will tell you that unimaginable pressures transformed mud into stone dense enough to resist the processes of time which ground the surrounding land into grit. The Pitjantjatjara hold a different view.

In the beginning, before the world took on its present form, carpet-snake people journeyed from the east and settled at a sandhill containing Uluru waterhole. Meanwhile a party of venomous snake-men were creating havoc among all the other ancestral people. They came from the west and camped twenty miles from Uluru, where Katatjuta (a mass of mountainous pebbles), now exists. From there they set out across the plain to attack the harmless carpet-snake people.

What followed was a bloodbath to rival the Trojan wars. At the close of the creation period, or Dreamtime, Ayers Rock/Uluru rose up—a monolith bearing all the physical and metaphysical signs of that epic battle. A waterhole in the side of the Rock is the blood of a dying carpet-snake man; a fragment of

stone—the severed nose of a venomous snake warrior; a large cave—the mouth
of a woman weeping with grief for the loss of her son, and spitting 'arukwita'—
the spirit of disease and death—over her enemies. Some of these sites are so
sacred that only fully initiated Aborigines may go there.

Ayers Rock is particularly rich in Dreaming stories, being an intersection
of many different mythic odysseys. Wallaby people, spirit dingo, and willy-
wagtail woman all contributed to its topography. As every contemporary Pitjantjatjara is a direct descendant of one or another of the totemic heros he or
she is an integral part of the landscape created by that progenitor. Ancestor,
descendant, 'country', storyline and ritual art form an eternal continuum.

To traditional Aborigines then, the Western concept of owning country is
not so much ludicrous as obscene. This mutual incomprehension regarding the
meaning of land still forms the basis of cultural conflict. When Uluru National
Park was 'handed back' to the Pitjantjatjara under the Land Rights Act, that
conflict found an emotional focus.

I first visited the park over a decade ago. I had been walking for two weeks without seeing a soul. Up one sandhill, down another, and on either side of me an
infinity of dunes stretching away into blue. I was not looking forward to the
Rock, having overdosed on its shape on billboards advertising life insurance, on
postcards promoting the wonders of the Centre and on T-shirts sold in kitsch
shops in Alice Springs. But when I saw Uluru shimmering on the horizon, I
was spellbound. It was too ancient to be corruptible.

I spent a week there, exploring every cave, fold and gully of it. There were
three small motels at its base, a little shop, and some houses for the rangers.
Aborigines lived in their humpies just outside the settlement; tourists wandered into those camps taking photographs and being generally insensitive. I
spent a further week at Katatjuta before continuing west into blissful emptiness.

A few years later the Pitjantjatjara were granted freehold title to the park,
which they then leased back to the government. They had a say in its management, and they received a share of the financial benefits of tourism. The hand-
over ceremony was, apparently, very moving. White Australia had made a gesture towards acknowledging its genocidal past.

Three months ago a friend arrived in Alice Springs for a holiday. I had planned
to take her to some of the lesser-known beauty spots—not yet visually polluted
by rustic signs, garbage bins and tourist buses—but the greenhouse effect
wrecked my itinerary. Dry riverbeds had turned into torrents and all the roads
were cut. At least we could fly to the Rock. It would be covered in waterfalls—a
rare enough sight to make it appealing.

'I hope you don't mind roughing it,' I said, remembering the dilapidated
caravan I had stayed in last time. (Several years ago Yulara village was built

twenty miles north of Ayers Rock, to house the tourists and take the ecological pressure off the Rock and the social pressure off the Aborigines who still lived at its base. I imagined a conglomerate of prefab buildings and porta-loos—hardly romantic, but adequate.)

A decade is a long time to live without experiencing the sandhill country of Central Australia. When I got off the plane I decided to give in to nostalgia and pantheism and walk the five miles to Yulara. My friend climbed into the bus, along with all the American, Japanese and German tourists wearing funny hats.

Oh, the unearthly beauty of the dunes. They were the colour of conch shells, of rosebuds. Thanks to the rain, there were explosions of colour everywhere—purple parakeelya, bright yellow grevillea, blue shrubs sprouting scarlet flowers, silky orange trunks of desert poplars, and, furring the ridges of the dunes, pincushions of pale green spinifex. I struggled to the top of a sandhill and there it was, bruise-coloured, striped by waterfalls, and capped with grey mist. The rain came down in buckets but what did it matter? I was strolling through an infinite garden, I was there and I was happy . . . Until I turned a corner and saw Yulara. This was no village, this was a *town*. An architect-designed town with Sheraton hotels, a mock Greek amphitheatre and tourist-trap boutiques. 'My God,' said my friend, when I found her huddled in the motel-style room complete with television and microwave, 'this place is a space bubble. If you step outside the force-field you fall into the void.'

When the shock had worn off we covered ourselves in green plastic garbage bags and scuttled across to the tourist information office. The vision that greeted us was straight out of Baudrillard—a large group of people absorbed in watching a video of the very landscape they could see perfectly well through the wrap-around windows. We hired a car and drove straight to the Rock.

As it swelled in front of us the 'oos' and 'aas' from the passenger seat turned into awed whispers and then silence. The 'skin' of the Rock was changing from steel grey to purple to shiny red. We drove right round it, past all the new carparks and rustic signs, one of which invited us to the sunset viewing point—a sandhill from which tourists are instructed to point their cameras at the Rock. Why this particular sandhill in an ocean of sandhills? No one knows. But the tourists obediently line up along it by the hundred, snapping away. It is a remarkable and dispiriting sight.

Having completed our circumnavigation, we parked the car, took off our shoes, tied on our plastic bags, and stepped out into the freezing wind. The path took us around the western face, past the white line painted up the side of the Rock. A sign informed us that the 'climbing line' was closed due to slippery conditions. Tourists were ignoring the warning by the dozen and oblivious to the little iron plaques commemorating the deaths of several climbers who had turned into pancakes on the sand below. By the time I had walked a mile I was so numb with cold that I took off all my clothes and plunged into one of the new waterholes beneath a thundering cascade that came down at us from the gods. The water was pure as crystal and so deep in places it was blueish black. We struggled through the needles of rain until we came to another sign notifying the public that this small fenced-off area was a sacred site and must not be visited. A group of tourists was reading it, one of them then crossed the fence and headed off for the cave. I called him back and explained in my most polite voice that the Rock belonged, morally and legally, to Aboriginal people and that he was their guest and that he was about to break their law and as he could explore every part of the rock except two or three tiny sections why did he feel the need to trespass. He told me to fuck off.

We spent the remaining two days in the space bubble, eating and reading books.

Tourism is not the benign industry governments would have us believe. Unless it is rigorously controlled, it can fundamentally alter the natural environment and adversely affect the host culture tourists wish to experience. In the Northern Territory the people most affected by tourism are the Aborigines, yet they are the least likely to receive its financial benefits.

The custodians of Ayers Rock are lucky in many respects. They have the power to veto the use of Uluru. (Recently they turned away a musician who offered enormous amounts of money to make a video on top of it—a new definition of 'rock clip'.) Even so, many of them are abandoning it for more private settlements out in the desert. They don't mind people visiting their country, but do not like being on display or being opted into a tourist industry in order to please a government that is still antagonistic to Aboriginal control of land. They worry about and feel responsible for the climbers who fall to their deaths, and they are powerless against the trespassers who blunder about in fertility caves ignorant of the deep distress this causes.

It may eventually come about that the very element which attracts so many visitors to Uluru—Aboriginal culture—is swamped by a kind of tourist imperialism.

Which isn't to say that one should not visit this 'wonder of the world', only that history is full of uncomfortable ironies.

[1993]

V. S. NAIPAUL

(1932–)

V. S. Naipaul left his home on the Caribbean island of Trinidad to attend Oxford University. His many travel books and novels mirror the places he has visited and lived, and his characters often dwell in an atmosphere of exile, alienation, and rootlessness. In his travel book on the Caribbean, *The Middle Passage* (1962), he recalls reading as a child to escape the confines of Trinidad. His early works, *The Mystic Masseur* (1957), *Miguel Street* (1959), and *A House for Mr. Biswas* (1961) are comic in tone; however, after he visited India, the land of his ancestors, the tone of his writing became more somber. His first travel book about the Indian subcontinent, *An Area of Darkness* (1964), emphasized the poverty, corruption, and chaos of the country. His many subsequent travel books on India and the Islamic world continued in a critical vein. Naipaul's fiction is generally about expatriates in third-world countries or immigrants coping with life in England. In the mid-1960s, he taught and traveled in East Africa. Naipaul has also written about race and culture in the American South (*A Turn in the South*, 1989). In 2001, Naipaul was awarded the Nobel Prize for literature.

This selection from *A Way in the World* (1994) shows a rather appreciative view of tourists from the viewpoint of an islander as the visitors descended on Trinidad and brought him a sense of the world outside his small country.

"Passenger: A Figure from the Thirties"

From *A Way in the World*

I used to feel—in the way of childhood, not putting words to feelings—that the light and the heat had burnt away the history of the place. I distrusted the ideas of glamour that were given us by postcards and postage stamps (ideas repeated by our local artists): certain bays and beaches, the Pitch Lake, certain flowering trees, certain buildings, our mixed population.

Many years later I thought that that feeling of the void had to do with my temperament, the temperament of a child of a recent Asian-Indian immigrant community in a mixed population: the child looked back and found no family past, found a blank. But I feel again now that I was responding to something that was missing, something that had been rooted out.

Like people of small or far-off communities, we liked the idea of being visited. And though I distrusted tourist-board ideas of glamour, I feel that without these ideas (if only as things to reject or react against), without the witness of our visitors, we would have been floating people, like the aborigines first come upon below Point Galera, living instinctive, unobserved lives.

I suppose visitors, tourists, began to come in number when steam replaced sail. The tourists at the turn of the century didn't come for the sun. They came for the sights; they protected themselves against the sun. With Edwardian layers of clothes, and with hats and umbrellas and parasols, they came to look at the diggings for the Panama Canal; they walked on the hard surface of the Pitch Lake; they looked at cocoa pods and coconuts growing on trees (crops requiring abundant plantation labour).

They also came for the history. They wanted to be in the waters of the great naval battles of the eighteenth century, when the powers of Europe fought over these small, rich sugar islands of the Caribbean. After the First World War, that idea of glory vanished. The naval battles and the once great names of the eighteenth-century admirals were forgotten. The tourists came for the sun, to get away from winter and the Depression; they came to be in places that were unspoilt, places that time had passed by, places, it might be said, that had never been discovered. So history was set on its head; the islands were refashioned.

Every year the cruise ships brought one or two writers who were keeping journals and taking photographs for their "travel books." These books, though descended in form from Victorian travel journals, were not like the books of Trollope or Charles Kingsley or Froude of fifty or sixty years before. There were no imperial "problems" now about the islands and the Spanish Main: no Victorian gloom about labour shortages after the abolition of slavery, about neglected or disaffected colonies, the rivalry of other powers, no nerves about an empire shrinking.

These cruise books, though very much about travel in the colonies, were about a part of the world that had, as it were, been cleansed of its past. The grainy photographs of, say, the fortifications of Cartagena in Colombia were photographs of an antiquity, something dimly connected with gold and galleons and the Spanish. The ruins of the black Emperor Christophe's Citadelle in Haiti were like an Egyptian mystery. This world was dead and safe.

These cruise books resembled one another. They couldn't have made much money for anybody, and I suppose they were a product of the Depression, written by hard-pressed men for public-library readers who dreamed of doing a cruise themselves one day in warm waters somewhere. Though this particular travel form required the writer to be always present, and knowledgeable, and busy, the books they wrote were curiously impersonal. That might have been because the writers had to get in everything earlier writers had got in; and also, I feel, because the writers of these travel books were really acting, acting being writers, acting being travellers, and, especially, acting being travellers in the colonies.

The Trinidad chapter of such a book would begin with an account of docking in the morning. It would speak of the mixed population in the streets. One writer might observe African people walking about and eating bananas; another would notice East Indian women with their jewellery and Indian costumes. There might be a visit to the Angostura Bitters factory; the Pitch Lake and the oilfields; a bay; a visit to a calypso tent or, if it wasn't the calypso season, a visit to a yard connected with one of the ecstatic local African sects, Shango or the Shouters.

There would be a well-connected local guide in the background. He had acted as guide for other writers and knew the Trinidad drill. Apart from him—and he would be white or mulatto and slightly aloof—the local people were far away, figures in the background. Of these people anything could be said. The Africans who had been seen eating bananas by one writer might, by another writer, be put into two-toned shoes. They might be put into new and squeaky two-toned shoes; and the writer might go on to say that Africans were so fond of squeaky shoes that they took brand-new shoes to shoemakers and asked them to "put in a squeak." As for the Indians of the countryside, they were a people apart; very little was known about their language or religion; and it was felt by the writer and his guide that this kind of knowledge didn't matter.

These books didn't cause offence. Very few local people read them. Some of the more extravagant things—like the squeaks in the two-toned shoes—chimed in with the local African sense of humour, the calypso fantasy. And then—hard to imagine now—local people lived with the idea of disregard. You could train yourself to read through this disregard in books and find things that were useful to you.

A book about Trinidaad in the early 1930s had the pidgin or creole title of *If Crab No Walk*. It was by Owen Rutter, a name which has no other association for me. In his book Owen Rutter wrote this sentence: "The trains are all right, but the buses are a joke." My father hung a whole article for a local magazine on these words of Owen Rutter's. This would have been not long after I was born. Some years later—still a child—I came upon the magazine in my father's desk. I was entranced by the article, with its comic drawings and its examples of the wit and nonsense destination-rhymes of local bus conductors. I looked at this article many times; I suppose it was one of the things that helped to give me an idea of where I was. Without the Rutter book my father might not have seen that the local buses were something he could write about. So there is a kind of chain.

I am not sure, but I believe it was words of Owen Rutter's again that a local literary magazine put below a photograph of a Trinidad beach: "The desolate splendour of a palm-fringed beach at sunset." That was set next to a photograph of a sunset sky with some words from Keats below it: "While barrèd clouds bloom the soft-dying day." Beaches and sunsets were beautiful, of course; but those words of Keats (though they didn't match the photograph, and were mysterious) and Rutter's foreign witness were like an extra blessing.

We were not alone in this need for foreign witness. Even someone like Francis Parkman, with all his Boston security, when he was on the Oregon Trail in the 1840s, felt on occasion, in the splendour of the American wilderness, that in order to show himself equal to a particular scene he had to make some comparison to Italian painting, which at that time he would have known only in imperfect reproductions.

Perhaps there is no pure or primal gift of vision. Perhaps vision can only be tutored, and depends on an ability to compare one thing with another. Columbus saw a fifteenth-century galley where I, standing on the other side, saw a tumble of black rocks with trees that I would not have been able to recognize in another setting. Not many hours after seeing that galley, he was sailing close to the southern coast of the island, and he saw aboriginal village gardens as fair as those of Valencia in the spring. It was a comparison he had made more than once before, about islands far to the north, which are physically quite different. But it was the only way he had of describing vegetation he hadn't seen before, and it is all that we have of the first sighting of the untouched aboriginal island.

Centuries on, we needed our visitors to give us some idea of where and what we were. We couldn't have done it ourselves. We needed foreign witness. But disregard came with this witness. And that was like a second setting of history on its head. Because in this traveller's view—this distant view of people eating bananas and wearing squeaky shoes, this view of a smallness that a cruise passenger could take in in a morning or a day—we, who had come in a variety of ways from many continents, were made to stand in for the aborigines and were held responsible for the nullity which had been created long before we had been transported to it.

[1994]

JAMAICA KINCAID

(1949–)

Jamaica Kincaid is from the Caribbean island of Antigua. To pursue her education as a writer, Kincaid left Antigua in her teens and went to the United States. Eventually she became a contributor to *The New Yorker* magazine and also published fiction drawn from her Caribbean experience. Among her works are *Annie John* (1985), set in Antigua, and *Lucy* (1990), about a young woman from the Caribbean who comes to work in America. Kincaid has also written profiles of family members who stayed on Antigua: *Autobiography of My Mother* (1996) and *My Brother* (1997).

The following selection, "The Ugly Tourist," comes from *A Small Place* (1988), which Kincaid wrote after returning to Antigua for a visit. By writing in the second person, she gives the impression of being inside the mind of an introspective tourist as seen by a perceptive and highly critical islander. Her essay takes up the issue of economic disparity between poor native and wealthy tourist; she challenges readers (as tourists) to see themselves as exploitive and insensitive.

"The Ugly Tourist"

From *A Small Place*

The thing you have always suspected about yourself the minute you become a tourist is true: A tourist is an ugly human being. You are not an ugly person all the time; you are not an ugly person ordinarily; you are not an ugly person day to day. From day to day, you are a nice person. From day to day, all the people who are supposed to love you on the whole do. From day to day, as you walk down a busy street in the large and modern and prosperous city in which you work and live, dismayed, puzzled (a cliché, but only a cliché can explain you) at how alone you feel in this crowd, how awful it is to go unnoticed, how awful it is to go unloved, even as you are surrounded by more people than you could possibly get to know in a lifetime that lasted for millennia, and then out of the corner of your eye you see someone looking at you and absolute pleasure is written all over that person's face, and then you realise that you are not as revolting a presence as you think you are (for that look just told you so). And so, ordinarily, you are a nice person, an attractive person, a person capable of drawing to yourself the affection of other people (people just like you), a person at home in your own skin (sort of; I mean, in a way; I mean, your dismay and puzzlement are natural to you, because people like you just seem to be like that, and so many of the things people like you you find admirable about yourselves—the things you think about, the things you think really define you—seem rooted in these feelings): a person at home in your own house (and all its nice house things), with its nice back yard (and its nice backyard things), at home on your street, your church, in community activities, your job, at home with your family, your relatives, your friends—you are a whole person. But one day, when you are sitting somewhere, alone in that crowd, and that awful feeling of displacedness comes over you, and really, as an ordinary person you are not well equipped to look too far inward and set yourself aright, because being ordinary is already so taxing, and being ordinary takes all you have out of you, and though the words "I must get away" do not actually pass across your lips, you make a leap from being that nice blob just sitting like a boob in your amniotic sac of the modern experience to being a person visiting heaps of death and ruin and feeling alive and inspired at the sight of it; to being a person lying on some faraway beach, your stilled body stinking and glistening in the sand, looking like something first forgotten, then remembered, then not important enough to go back for; to being a person marvelling at the harmony (ordinarily, what you would say is the backwardness) and the union these other people (and they are other people) have with nature. And you look at the things they can do with a piece of ordinary cloth, the things they fashion out of cheap, vulgarly colored (to you) twine, the way they squat down over a hole they have made in the ground, the hole itself is something to marvel at, and since you are being an ugly person this ugly but joyful thought will swell inside you; their ancestors were not clever in the way yours were and not ruthless in the way yours were, for then would it not be you who would be in harmony with nature and backwards in that charming way? An ugly thing, that is what you are when you become a tourist, an ugly, empty thing, a stupid thing, a piece of rubbish pausing here and there to gaze at this and taste that, and it will never occur to you that the people who inhabit the place in which you have just passed cannot stand you, that behind their closed doors they laugh at your strangeness (you do not look the way they look); the physical sight of you does not please them; you have bad manners (it is their custom to eat their food with their hands); you try eating their way, you look silly; you try eating the way you always eat, you look silly; they do not like the way you speak (you have an accent); they collapse helpless from laughter, mimicking the way they imagine you must look as you carry out some everyday bodily function. They do not like you. *They do not like me!* That thought never actually occurs to you. Still, you feel a little uneasy. Still, you feel a little foolish. Still, you feel a little out of place. But the banality of your own life is very real to you; it drove you to this extreme, spending your days and your nights in the company of people who despise you, people you do not like really, people you would not want to have as your actual neighbour. And so you must devote yourself to puzzling out how much of what you are told is really, really true (Is ground-up bottle glass in peanut sauce really a delicacy around here, or will it do just what you think ground-up bottle glass will do? Is this rare, multicoloured, snout-mouthed fish really an aphrodisiac, or will it cause you to fall asleep permanently?). Oh, the hard work all of this is, and is it any wonder, then, that on your return home you feel the need of a long rest, so that you can recover from your life as a tourist?

That the native does not like the tourist is not hard to explain. For every native of every place is a potential tourist, and every tourist is a native of somewhere. Every native everywhere lives a life of overwhelming and crushing banalty and boredom and desperation and depression, and every deed, good and bad, is an attempt to forget this. Every native would like to find a way out, every native would like a rest, every native would like a tour. But some natives—most natives in the world—cannot go anywhere. They are too poor. They are too poor to go anywhere. They are too poor to escape the reality of their lives; and they are too poor to live properly in the place where they live, which is the very place you, the tourist, want to go—so when the natives see you, the tourist, they envy you, they envy your abiltiy to leave your banality and boredom, they envy your ability to turn their own banality and boredom into a source of pleasure for yourself.

[1988]

RUDOLFO ANAYA

(1937–)

Rudolfo Anaya was one of seven children in a family of New Mexico ranchers and farmers. He started writing while attending the University of New Mexico, where he later taught. Like most of his fiction, his first novel, *Bless Me Ultima* (1972), is set in the southwest. In addition to numerous novels, among them *Tortuga* (1988), *Albuquerque* (1992), and *Zia Summer* (1995), Anaya has edited works on Chicano literature and culture and written a travel book, *A Chicano in China* (1986).

In the essay that follows, Anaya takes a more tolerant view toward the tourist, and he places tourism in the context of immigration and land use. To illustrate his argument that travel can quickly reverse the position of native and tourist, Anaya changes roles when he journeys to the Mediterranean, home of his Spanish ancestors.

"Why I Love Tourists: Confessions of a Dharma Bum"

I was born on the eastern llano of New Mexico—at just the right moment, so my mother said—a tourist from the great beyond. Just another guest on Earth looking for his dharma nature. I discovered the core of my nature in the people of my region. But we also discover elements of our essential nature by traveling to other places, by meeting other people. To tour is to move beyond one's circle. So we're all tourists on Earth, we go from here to there if only to just have a look.

But tourists and natives often clash, perhaps because the tourist cannot love the place as much as the native. We learn to love the land that nurtures us. We, the natives, become possessive about "our place." Westerners especially feel a great love toward this land that stretches north and south along the spine of the Rocky Mountains. I believe this sense of possessiveness about "our land" means we, the denizens of the West, are turning inward. We now truly understand that "there's no where else to go," so we had better take care of what's left.

The open spaces of the West once allowed for great mobility, and so the nature of those who came here was more ample, more extroverted. Today the real and the mythic frontier has disappeared, so we seem to be growing more introverted. Maybe we just want to be left alone.

Change and the progress of technology are bothering us. Next to Alburquerque where I live, a city has been built around the Intel Corporation; the subdivisions spread across sand hills where once only coyotes and jackrabbits roamed. Along the Rio Grande valley subdivisions cover farming land. We know what overdevelopment of the land can do. We know we're running out of water, out of space, out of clean air to breathe

Westerners seem bound by one desire: to keep the land the way it was. Now the megacities are crowding us in. More and more people seem to be touring our turf. Are all those tourists looking for a place to settle? That's what bothers us. There are just too many tourists discovering and rediscovering the West. The tourist has become the "other" to the westerner. I hear my New Mexican paisanos say: "Take their money but let them go back where they came from. Please don't let them settle here."

Tourism is a very important segment of the western economy. Tourists bring bucks to grease Las Vegas, Disneyland, L.A., Seattle, and San Francisco, bucks to oceanside resorts and Rocky Mountain ski slopes, bucks for boating and hunting and fishing. Tourism has become the west's clean industry. But deep inside we, the natives, know it's got its inherent problems.

Tourism affects our lives, we believe, because it affects not only the topography; it also affects the sacred. We believe there is a spirit in the land; we know we cannot trample the flesh of the Earth and not affect its soul. Earth and spirit of the place go hand in hand. The transcendent has blessed this land and we don't want it ruined, we don't want it destroyed. We have a covenant with the land, we have become the keepers of the land. No wonder so many dharma bums—those looking for their essential relationship to the Earth—have crossed the West's rugged terrain, looking for a home, not just a home with a majestic view, but a home rooted to a landscape that allows the true nature of the person to develop.

We have all been tourists at one time or another. We have traveled to distant places to entertain and rest the body, and also to enlighten the spirit. The two are intertwined. We go looking for that revelation on the face of the Earth that speaks to the soul.

There are sensitive tourists, dharma bums who care about illuminating their nature and who appreciate the region and people they experience on their journey. There are some who respect the place and allow themselves to be changed by the people and region they visit. They return from the journey fulfilled, more aware of other cultures.

Then there are those who breeze through the place, accepting nothing of the local culture, learning little, complaining constantly, and leaving in their wake a kind of displacement. The natives take their money and are thankful when they're gone. Those travelers return home to complain about the food, the natives, and about the different lifestyles they encountered. They should never have left home. They did not travel to illuminate the spirit.

The land draws tourists to the West. They come to see the majestic mountains, arid deserts, the Pacific Ocean. Some come to experience our diverse cultural groups. Others come only to visit the cultural artifacts of the west: Las Vegas, Disneyland, L.A., Silicon Valley, Hoover Dam. Those who experience only the artifacts miss the spirit we natives find imbued in the landscape. Those who deal *only* in artifacts miss the history and culture of the West's traditional communities. And so tourists also symbolize the tension between tradition and change, a change that in some places carries the weight of impending doom.

Have the traditionalists grown tired of sharing the spirit of the West? Are we tired of those who come and trample our sacred land? And is the West really one unified region? When we speak of tourism are we only talking about people visiting here from outside the West, or do we also speak of internal tourism? From Montana to New Mexico, we hear complaints about tourists from outside the region. But in New Mexico, for example, we also complain about the Texans as tourists. Today I hear complaints about the nouveau riche Califonians. Even Oregonians shrink from California tourists: "Please don't let them settle here," they whisper to each other.

The West was never one homogenous region; it is not only the land of the pioneers and the cowboy of the western movies. The West is a grouping of micro-regions and cultural groups. Even the grandeur of the Rocky Mountains can't unify us, because there are too many different landscapes in the West, too many different indigenous histories. My home, the northern Rio Grande, is such a micro-region, with its unique history and people. It is—and here I show my indigenous bias—one of the most interesting multicultural areas of the West.

The Spanish/Mexicano side of my ancestors were tourists who journeyed to this region in the late sixteenth century. Imagine the Pueblo Indians seeing the Spanish colonists coming up the Rio Grande in 1598. I'm sure they shook their heads and said, "There goes the neighborhood." In many ways *it did go.* If anyone has suffered from tourists, it is the Native American communities.

But the tourists kept coming into the land of the pueblos. The first entradas were from south to north as Spanish-speakers expanded north. In the nineteenth century the east to west migrations began. In a scene from my novel *Shaman Winter*, I describe Kearny marching into New Mexico with the Army of the West in 1846. The Mexicanos in the crowd yell: "Why don't you go back where you came from!" "Go home gringos!" "Hope they keep going right on to California." "We ought to pass a Spanish Only law if they stay."

Of course those "tourists" didn't go home. And they changed the West forever. Each group introduced a new overlay of culture. Each brought a new set of stories, their own history and mythology to the West. Now the balance of what the land can hold has reached a critical point. Maybe we're uncertain about tourists because they represent the unknown. If the tourist decides to return to settle—and history teaches us that's the pattern—each one is a potential threat to the land, each one represents one more house to be built, more desert to be plowed up, more water consumed. They represent development in a fragile land already overdeveloped.

It's not just the growth in numbers we fear. We are convinced that outsiders know nothing of the nature of our relationship to the earth. This relationship defines our nature. I feel connected to la tierra de Nuevo México. This earth is all I know, it nourishes my soul, my humanity. The gods live in the Earth, the sky, the clouds.

Growing up in eastern New Mexico, I felt the Ilano speak to me. The Ilano as brother, father, mother. Constant breezes caressed me, sang to me, whispered legends, stirred my memory. The Pecos River engulfed me with its bosque of alamos, river willows, Russian olives, thick brush. It sang a song of memory as it flowed south to empty into the Rio Grande, from there into the Gulf of Mexico. Tuly, time and the river sang in my heart.

This early attachment and sensibility to the land became love, love for the place and the people. The people molded me. The Hispano/Mexicanos of the Ilano were cattlemen and sheepmen who taught me a way of relating to the earth. The farmers from the Pecos River Valley initiated me into another relationship with nature; they planted my roots in that earth as they planted seeds. I saw the people struggle to make a living, I heard the stories they told. History and traditions were passed down, and everything related to the place and the people. Some of the teaching was unspoken; it was there in the silence of the Ilano, the faces of the people.

People told stories, joys and tragedies carried in the breezes, so I, too, became a storyteller. Listening to the people's story and then retelling the story relates one to the place. Will tourists who visit our land pause long enough to listen to our stories? The bones buried in the earth tell the story. Who will listen?

This spiritual connection to the land seems to describe the westerner. Even in the harshest weather and the longest drought, we stand in awe of the earth. Awe describes our relationship to the land. Perhaps tourists are simply people who don't stand still long enough to feel the immediacy of awe. They don't understand the intimacy of relationships woven into the people of the land.

As a child I felt this awe on the Ilano, along the river, on those hills which shaped my childhood. So the Earth for me has a particular feel, it is the New Mexican landscape, the Ilano and Pecos River of childhood, the Rio Grande and Sangre de Cristo Mountains of my later life, the desert which is always at the edge.

Still, we must be kind to tourists. It's part of our heritage to be kind to strangers. And we have all been tourists at one time or another. I, too, have been a tourist, a seeker who wanted to explore beyond the limits of my immediate environment.

One description of the Anglo-American culture has been its mobility. Anglo-Americans, we are told, are a restless lot. They couldn't just stay over there in the thirteen colonies, no, they had to go West. They love to quote the oft-repeated "Go west, young man, go west." So much a part of the history and mythology of this country is known from that western movement. Land, they smelled land, and gold and beaver pelts and gas and oil, all of which drew them west. So, Anglos are natural-born tourists. Now they've even been to the moon. Maybe some people just take to touring better than others. Or perhaps there are times when mass migrations take place; need and adventure move entire populations.

The Indohispanos of New Mexico have ancient roots in the land. Our European ancestors settled in the Hispano homeland along the northern Rio Grande in 1598. Remember those Espanioles coming up the Rio Grande? They took to the land, became as indigenous and settled as their vecinos in the pueblos. Wars, adventure, and extreme economic necessity have taken them beyond the homeland's frontier.

In this region Hispanics also claim tourist heroes. Cabeza de Vaca comes to mind. Shipwrecked on the coast of Texas, he set out on an odyssey that lasted seven or eight years. He is the Odysseus of the Southwest. Never mind that he was lost. Perhaps to be "lost" as a tourist is essential. Only thus can you enter fully into the place and the people. He was the first European tourist in Texas. Can you imagine the awe he experienced?

And he turned out to be a typical tourist. He went back to Mexico and spread the word. "Texas was great," Cabeza de Vaca told the viceroy in Mexico City. "The streets are paved with gold. There are pueblos four or five stories high. And a strange animal called a buffalo roams the plains by the millions."

Other Spanish explorers quickly followed Cabeza de Vaca. Coronado came north. A tourist looking for gold and the fabled cities of Cibola. He found only Indian pueblos, the original natives living in houses made of adobes. Accommodations in Native America weren't the best in the sixteenth century, so the Spanish tourists returned home, discouraged they hadn't found cities with streets paved with gold.

But the Spaniards were consumate note-takers. They mapped the land, described it and the natives, and they sent letters to their neighbors back in Mexico. "You've got to see this place. La Nueva México is virgin land. Very little traffic, and the native arts and crafts are out of this world. I brought a clay pot for dos reales. I can sell it in Spain for twice that. In a few years the place will be spoiled. Come see it before it's gone."

Gone? That's what we fear. What if the spirit that attracted us here in the first place leaves?

Tourists do spoil things. The minute tourists discover a new place, they also bring their garbage with them. Some set up businesses to ship the clay pots back home, organizing the natives in ways the natives never wanted to be organized. Tourism leads to strange kinds of enterprises, some good, some not very humanistic.

But I didn't learn about tourism in the West by reading the Spanish explorer's notes. In my childhood we weren't taught the history of our land as it occurred from the colonizations that came to el norte from the south. We were only taught the history of the pioneers, the western movement. How many times did little Chicanitos in school have to sing "Oh My Darling Clementine?"

The first tourists I encountered were in Santa Rosa, New Mexico, my home town. On highway 66, right after World War II. It was the best of times, it was the worst of times. People were moving west, tourists in search of California. I remember one particular afternoon at a gas station where we went to fill our bike tires after goathead punctures. A car stopped. Dad, mom, son, and daughter. Blonde, blue-eyed gringos from the east. They usually didn't pay attention to the brown Mexicanitos gathered at the gas station. But this Ozzie and Harriet Nelson family did. They talked briefly to me.

"Where you from?" Ozzie asked.
"Here," I said.
"Just here?" he said, looking around.
"Yes." I had never considered anyplace other than just here.
Here was home.
He wasn't too interested. "Oh," he said and went off to kick his car's tires.
"Where are *you* from?" I asked Harriet.
"Back east."
"Where are you going?" I asked.
"We're tourists," she answered. "We're going to California."

Heading west on highway 66, into the setting sun.

Imagine, I thought to myself. A family can travel to California as tourists. Just to go look. Look at what? The Pacific Ocean. I knew it from the maps at school. I knew then I wanted to be a tourist.

I ran home and told my mother. "Mama, I want to be a tourist."

Her mouth dropped. She stopped rolling tortillas and made the sign of the cross over me. "Where did you get that idea?" I told her about the family I had just met.

"No, mijito," she said. "Only the Americanos can be tourists. Now go help Ultima with her herbs and get those crazy ideas out of your mind."

I went away saddened. Why was it a crazy idea to be a tourist? Was my mother telling me to beware of touristss?

"Why is it only the Americanos get to be tourists?" I asked Ultima. She knew the answer to almost any question that had to do with healing and sickness of the soul, but I could see that tourists puzzled her.

"They have cameras, they take pictures," she finally answered.

"What's wrong with that?"

"The spirit of who we are cannot be captured in the picture," she said. "When you go to a different place you can know it by taking a picture, or you can let the place seep into your blood. A real turista is one who allows the spirit of that place to enter."

She looked across the hills of the llano, then turned her gaze to the river. "The river is like a turista. The water moves, but yet the river remains constant. So to travel also means to go within. This place, or any place, can change you. You discover pieces of yourself when you go beyond your boundaries. Or you can stay in one place and learn the true nature of your soul."

I knew Ultima had never been a tourist. She only knew the few villages around Santa Rosa. But she was far wiser than anyone I knew. She had traveled within, and so she knew herself. She knew the land and its people.

Still I questioned her. "My tio Benito and his family are tourists, aren't they? They're always going to Colorado or Texas."

Again she shook her head. "They go to work in the beet fields of Colorado and to pick cotton in Texas. Poor people who go to work aren't turistas."

So, tourists didn't go to work. They just went to look, and maybe take pictures. What a life. I knew I *really* wanted to be tourist.

"Who knows," Utima said, "maybe someday you will travel beyond this river valley. You may even go to China."

China, I thought. On the round world globe at school it was directly across from Santa Rosa. One day I dug a hole in the schoolyard. "You better watch out, Rudy," the girls warned me. "You could fall through to China." They ran away laughing.

For a class project I wrote away to cruise lines and did a report on cruise ships. They circled the globe. They went to Greece. Spain. Italy. They went to the Mediterranean world. Maybe someday I will take a ship on the Mediterranean, I thought.

For another project I made a sculpture of clay. The pyramids of Giza and the Sphinx. Set on a plaster board with sand for the desert and twigs for palm trees. It was real to me. I got an A.

"What do you want to be when you grow up?" the teacher asked.

"I want to be a tourist," I said.

"Esta loco," the kids whispered.

Yes, to dream of travel in that time and place was to be a little crazy. I settled for books to bring distant places to me.

But I did go to China. In 1984 my wife and I and a small group of colleagues traveled through China. I saw wonders my ancestors of the Pecos River could only imagine. Bejing, Xian, the Yangtze River, the Great Wall. I got so much into the place and the people at one point I felt transformed into a Chinese man. That's the kind of transformation the sensitive tourist looks for, becoming one with the place and people. If only for a short while. I have never written travel journals, but I did write one about China. *A Chicano in China.*

The memory of who I am stretches beyond the here and now. It resides in the archetypes, a biologic stream that is a strand into the past, to distant places and people. We sense the truth of images in stories and myths. And so we set out to test the memory. Was I related to China and its people? Was the Chinese dragon the Quetzalcoatl of the Aztecs? Was the god of nature, the golden carp which I described in *Bless Me, Ultima,* related to the golden carp that thrive in Chinese lakes? Was the bronze turtle resting at temple entrances related to the boy called Tortuga in my novel by that name?

We travel to seek connections. What are the tourists who come west seeking? Is our job to take their money and be done with them, or should we educate them? Should they read our books and history before applying for visas to our sacred land?

Later in life I did cruise on the Mediterranean, from the Greek Isles through the Bosporus into magical Constantinople. From Spain—where I practiced my New Mexican Spanish in many a tapas bar—to Italy down to Israel and into Eygpt. Cruising the Nile, like a lowrider on Saturday night, I was transported into a past so deep and meaningful, I became Egyptian. I cut my hair like an Egyptian, wore the long robe, prayed at the temples, and entered into the worship. A tourist must also be a pilgrim.

I didn't participate in any revolutions like Lawrence of Arabia. I was a tourist. I knew my role and my parameters. But even as tourists we can enter the history of the place. I would go back to the Nile at the drop of a tortilla. Now I consider my Rio Grande a sister of the Nile. Long ago Mediterranean people, my ancestors, came to Rio Grande, bringing their dreams. I am part of that dream that infused the land. I am part of all the dreams that have settled here.

How do we teach these connections to tourists that visit our Rio Grande, or the Colorado River, or the Columbia? There are relationships of rivers. Those from the east bring knowledge of their Mississippi, their Ohio, their Hudson. They bring a knowledge of their place and history. How we connect to each other may show us how we can save the West, and save the world.

Still we fear that tourism has become just one more consumer item on the supermarket shelf. Tourists who come only to consume and don't connect their history to ours leave us empty.

Is there an answer to this topic of tourism in the West? The issue is complex. My tio Benito and his family, who as I mentioned earlier went as workers to Texas and Colorado, weren't considered tourists, and yet they gave their work and sweat to the land. But they remained invisible. They worked the earth of the West, like prior groups have worked the western land, but they remained invisible.

The Mexicano workers who right now are constructing the history of the West through their work in the fields are not considered tourists. And yet they are lending their language, their music, and their food to enrich our region. The Pacific Rim has been connected to Asia for a long time, and that relationship continues to thrive in our time. The West now speaks, Japanese, Chinese, and Korean.

Maybe the West is going through a new era. We are a vast and exciting region where new migrations of people are creating an exciting multicultural world, one that has very little in common with the older, conservative myth of the West. Perhaps the idea of the West as the promised land isn't dead; a new infusion of cultures continues even as postmodern technology changes our landscape once again.

I am fascinated with the migrations of people. I have tried to emphasize this by saying some of those past migrations to the West were tourists. I don't mean to be flippant. We know most often it is necessity that moves groups of people. But migrations are a normal course of human events. Today, as in the past, it isn't only curiosity and available leisure time that creates the tourist. When people have to feed their families they will migrate.

Our challenge is to be sensitive to those who migrate across the land. A lot of mistakes were made in the past by those too arrogant to appreciate the native ways. Clashes between the cultural groups of the West exploded into atrocities. That, too, is part of our history. To not repeat that waste is the challenge. The answer lies in how we educate ourselves and those tourists exploring our region. In this effort major attention has to be paid to the migrant workers, those who put sweat and labor into the land but may not have the leisure time we normally associate with tourists. In many ways they know our region better than most of us, and many are settling into the land.

In Spanish we have a saying: Respeto al ajeno. Respect the other person's property, respect the foreigner. As we respect places and people in our travels, we expect to be respected by those who travel through our land. Respect can be taught. After all, we are on Earth "only for a while" as the Aztec poet said. We are all dharma bums learning our true nature from the many communities of the West. Let us respect each other in the process.

[2001]

EDWARD ABBEY

(1927–1989)

Edward Abbey, a persistent and tireless critic of American environmental policies, left his native New Jersey as a young man and traveled west, riding the rails and hitchhiking. The canyon country in Utah appealed so strongly to him that he settled there and went to to work for the U.S. Forest Service at Arches National Monument. He expressed his love of the wilderness and his alarm at seeing it abused by tourists and whittled away by developers. Abbey argued eloquently for wilderness preservation in a number of books and essays, among them *Slickrock: Endangered Canyons of the Southwest* (1971), *Journey Home: Some Words in Defense of the American West* (1977), and *Voices Crying in the Wilderness* (1990). One of his many novels, *The Monkey Wrench Gang* (1975), is about environmental vigilantes who attacked symbols of industrial development in the wilderness and sabotaged power plants.

The following excerpts from *Desert Solitaire* (1968), one of his first books, shows him as a hermit in spirit, savoring the wilderness and decrying its invasion by motorized vehicles. Abbey's work exemplifies how travel writing and nature writing are close in spirit.

From *Desert Solitaire*

What are the Arches? From my place in front of the housetrailer I can see several of the hundred or more of them which have been discovered in the park. These are natural arches, holes in the rock, windows in stone, no two alike, as varied in form as in dimension. They range in size from holes just big enough to walk through to openings large enough to contain the dome of the Capitol building in Washington, D.C. Some resemble jug handles or flying buttresses, others natural bridges but with this technical distinction: a natural bridge spans a watercourse—a natural arch does not. The arches were formed through hundreds of thousands of years by the weathering of the huge sandstone walls, or fins, in which they are found. Not the work of a cosmic hand, nor sculptured by sand-bearing winds, as many people prefer to believe, the arches came into being and continue to come into being through the modest wedging action of rainwater, melting snow, frost, and ice, aided by gravity. In color they shade from off-white through buff, pink, brown and red, tones which also change with the time of day and the moods of the light, the weather, the sky.

Standing there, gaping at this monstrous and inhuman spectacle of rock and cloud and sky and space, I feel a ridiculous greed and possessiveness come over me. I want to know it all, possess it all, embrace the entire scene intimately, deeply, totally, as a man desires a beautiful woman. An insane wish? Perhaps not—at least there's nothing else, no one human, to dispute possession with me.

The snow-covered ground glimmers with a dull blue light, reflecting the sky and the approaching sunrise. Leading away from me the narrow dirt road, an alluring and primitive track into nowhere, meanders down the slope and toward the heart of the labyrinth of naked stone. Near the first group of arches, looming over a bend in the road, is a balanced rock about fifty feet high, mounted on a pedestal of equal height; it looks like the head from Easter Island, a stone god or a petrified ogre.

Like a god, like an ogre? The personification of the natural is exactly the tendency I wish to suppress in myself, to eliminate for good. I am here not only to evade for a while the clamor and filth and confusion of the cultural apparatus but also to confront, immediately and directly if it's possible, the bare bones of existence, the elemental and fundamental, the bedrock which sustains us. I want to be able to look at and into a juniper tree, a piece of quartz, a vulture, a spider, and see it as it is in itself, devoid of all humanly ascribed qualities, anti-Kantian, even the categories of scientific description. To meet God or Medusa face to face, even if it means risking everything human in myself. I dream of a hard and brutal mysticism in which the naked self merges with a non-human world and yet somehow survives still intact, individual, separate. Paradox and bedrock.

Well—the sun will be up in a few minutes and I haven't even begun to make coffee. I take more baggage from my pickup, the grub box and cooking gear, go back in the trailer and start breakfast. Simply breathing, in a place like this, arouses the appetite. The orange juice is frozen, the milk slushy with ice. Still chilly enough inside the trailer to turn my breath to vapor. When the first rays of the sun strike the cliffs I fill a mug with steaming coffee and sit in the door-way facing the sunrise, hungry for the warmth.

Suddenly it comes, the flaming globe, blazing on the pinnacles and minarets and balanced rocks, on the canyon walls and through the windows in the sandstone fins. We greet each other, sun and I, across the black void of ninety-three million miles. The snow glitters between us, acres of diamonds almost painful to look at. Within an hour all the snow exposed to the sunlight will be gone and the rock will be damp and steaming. Within minutes, even as I watch, melting snow begins to drip from the branches of a juniper nearby; drops of water streak slowly down the side of the trailerhouse.

I am not alone after all. Three ravens are wheeling near the balanced rock, squawking at each other and at the dawn. I'm sure they're as delighted by the return of the sun as I am and I wish I knew the language. I'd sooner exchange ideas with the birds on earth than learn to carry on intergalactic communications with some obscure race of humanoids on a satellite planet from the world of Betelgeuse. First things first. The ravens cry out in husky voices, blue-black wings flapping against the golden sky. Over my shoulder comes the sizzle and smell of frying bacon.

That's the way it was this morning. . . .

The ease and relative freedom of this lively job at Arches follow from the comparative absence of the motorized tourists, who stay away by the millions. And they stay away because of the unpaved entrance road, the unflushable toilets in the campgrounds, and the fact that most of them have never even heard of Arches National Monument. (Could there be a more genuine testimonial to its beauty and integrity?) All this must change.

I'd been warned. On the very first day Merle and Floyd had mentioned something about developments, improvements, a sinister Master Plan. Thinking that *they* were the dreamers, I paid little heed and had soon forgotten the whole ridiculous business. But only a few days ago something happened which shook me out of my pleasant apathy.

I was sitting out back on my 33,000-acre terrace, shoeless and shirtless, scratching my toes in the sand and sipping on a tall iced drink, watching the flow of evening over the desert. Prime time: the sun very low in the west, the birds coming back to life, the shadows rolling for miles over rock and sand to the very base of the brilliant mountains. I had a small fire going near the table—not for heat or light but for the fragrance of the juniper and the ritual appeal of the clear flames. For symbolic reasons. For ceremony. When I heard a faint sound over my shoulder I looked and saw a file of deer watching from fifty yards away, three does and a velvet-horned buck, all dark against the sundown sky. They began to move. I whistled and they stopped again, staring at me. "Come on over," I said, "have a drink." They declined, moving off with casual, unhurried grace, quiet as phantoms, and disappeared beyond the rise. Smiling, thoroughly at peace, I turned back to my drink, the little fire, the subtle transformations of the immense landscape before me. On the program: rise of the full moon.

It was then I heard the discordant note, the snarling whine of a jeep in low range and four-wheel-drive, coming from an unexpected direction, from the vicinity of the old foot and horse trail that leads from Balanced Rock down toward Courthouse Wash and on to park headquarters near Moab. The jeep came in sight from beyond some bluffs, turned onto the dirt road, and came up the hill toward the entrance station. Now operating a motor vehicle of any kind on the trails of a national park is strictly forbidden, a nasty bureaucratic regulation which I heartily support. My bosom swelled with the righteous indignation of a cop: by God, I thought, I'm going to write these sons of bitches a ticket. I put down the drink and strode to the housetrailer to get my badge.

Long before I could find the shirt with the badge on it, however, or the ticket book, or my shoes or my park ranger hat, the jeep turned in at my driveway and came right up to the door of the trailer. It was a gray jeep with a U.S. Government decal on the side—Bureau of Public Roads—and covered with dust. Two empty water bags flapped at the bumper. Inside were three sunburned men in twill britches and engineering boots, and a pile of equipment: transit case, tripod, survey rod, bundles of wooden stakes. (*Oh no!*) The men got out, dripping with dust, and the driver grinned at me, pointing to his parched open mouth and making horrible gasping noises deep in his throat.

"Okay," I said, "come on in."

It was even hotter inside the trailer than outside but I opened the refrigerator and left it open and took out a pitcher filled with ice cubes and water. As they passed the pitcher back and forth I got the full and terrible story, confirming the worst of my fears. They were a survey crew, laying out a new road into the Arches.

And when would the road be built? Nobody knew for sure; perhaps in a couple of years, depending on when the Park Service would be able to get the money. The new road—to be paved, of course—would cost somewhere between half a million and one million dollars, depending on the bids, or more than fifty thousand dollars per linear mile. At least enough to pay the salaries of ten park rangers for ten years. Too much money, I suggested—they'll never go for it back in Washington.

The three men thought that was pretty funny. Don't worry, they said, this road will be built. I'm worried, I said. Look, the party chief explained, you *need* this road. He was a pleasant-mannered, soft-spoken civil engineer with an unquestioning dedication to his work. A very dangerous man. Who *needs* it? I said; we get very few tourists in this park. That's why you need it, the engineer explained patiently; look, he said, when this road is built you'll get ten, twenty, thirty times as many tourists in here as you get now. His men nodded in solemn agreement, and he stared at me intently, waiting to see what possible answer I could have to that.

"Have some more water," I said. I had an answer all right but I was saving it for later. I knew that I was dealing with a madman.

As I type these words, several years after the little episode of the gray jeep and the thirsty engineers, all that was foretold has come to pass. Arches National Monument has been developed. The Master Plan has been fulfilled. Where once a few adventurous people came on weekends to camp for a night or two and enjoy a taste of the primitive and remote, you will now find serpentine streams of baroque automobiles pouring in and out, all through the spring and summer, in numbers that would have seemed fantastic when I worked there: from 3,000 to 30,000 to 300,000 per year, the "visitation," as they call it, mounts ever upward. The little campgrounds where I used to putter around reading three-day-old newspapers full of lies and watermelon seeds have now been consolidated into one master campground that looks, during the busy season, like a suburban village: elaborate housetrailers of quilted aluminum crowd upon gigantic camper-trucks of Fiberglas and molded plastic; through their windows you will see the blue glow of television and hear the studio laughter of Los Angeles; knobby-kneed oldsters in plain Bermudas buzz up and down the quaintly curving asphalt road on motorbikes; quarrels break out between campsite neighbors while others gather around their burning charcoal briquettes (ground campfires no longer permitted—not enough wood) to compare electric toothbrushes. The Comfort Stations are there, too, all lit up with electricity, fully equipped inside, though the generator breaks down now and then and the lights go out, or the sewage backs up in the plumbing system (drain fields were laid out in sand over a solid bed of sandstone), and the water supply sometimes fails, since the 3000-foot well can only produce about 5gpm—not always enough to meet the demand. Down at the beginning of the new road, at park headquarters, is the new entrance station and visitor center, where admission fees are collected and where the rangers are going quietly nuts answering the same three basic questions five hundred times a day: (1) Where's the john? (2) How long's it take to see this place? (3) Where's the Coke machine?

Progress has come at last to the Arches, after a million years of neglect. Industrial Tourism has arrived.

[1968]

JAMES BALDWIN

(1924–1987)

James Baldwin became a traveler when he realized that segregation and racial hatred made it impossible for him to continue life in the United States. He went to France in the late 1940s and spent the next 10 years of his life as an expatriate. One of nine children, Baldwin grew up in Harlem. His stepfather was a preacher, and Baldwin in his youth discovered a talent for the pulpit. As a Holy Roller preacher at the Fireside Pentecostal Church, he attracted larger congregations than his stepfather for several years until he lost his faith. His own writing retains the influence of religious oratory and witness. His first novel, *Go Tell It on the Mountain* (1953), was drawn from his years in Harlem. *Giovanni's Room* (1956), a novel about expatriatism and homosexuality, was also published while Baldwin remained abroad. He returned to the United States to take part in the civil rights movement, but after the assassination of Dr. Martin Luther King in 1967, Baldwin left the country again and lived abroad for the rest of his life.

The essay that follows, "Stranger in the Village," is from *Notes of a Native Son* (1953). It reverses the roles of white explorer and African native. As a traveler, Baldwin enters the "white wilderness" of the small mountain village in Switzerland where many of the Swiss have never seen a typewriter. His essay widens from a traveler's impressions to an argument about race relations in America; he expands metaphorically on his position as stranger and concludes that black people are no longer strangers in western civilization. "The world is white no longer, and it will never be white again."

"Stranger in the Village"

From *Notes of a Native Son*

From all available evidence no black man had ever set foot in this tiny Swiss village before I came. I was told before arriving that I would probably be a "sight" for the village; I took this to mean that people of my complexion were rarely seen in Switzerland, and also that city people are always something of a "sight" outside of the city. It did not occur to me—possibly because I am an American—that there could be people anywhere who had never seen a Negro.

It is a fact that cannot be explained on the basis of the inaccessibility of the village. The village is very high, but it is only four hours from Milan and three hours from Lausanne. It is true that it is virtually unknown. Few people making plans for a holiday would elect to come here. On the other hand, the villagers are able, presumably, to come and go as they please—which they do: to another town at the foot of the mountain, with a population of approximately five thousand, the nearest place to see a movie or go to the bank. In the village there is no movie house, no bank, no library, no theater; very few radios, one jeep, one station wagon; and at the moment, one typewriter, mine, an invention which the woman next door to me here had never seen. There are about six hundred people living here, all Catholic—I conclude this from the fact that the Catholic church is open all year round, whereas the Protestant chapel, set off on a hill a little removed from the village, is open only in the summertime when the tourists arrive. There are four or five hotels, all closed now, and four or five *bistros*, of which, however, only two do any business during the winter. These two do not do a great deal, for life in the village seems to end around nine or ten o'clock. There are a few stores, butcher, baker, *épicerie*, a hardware store, and a money-changer—who cannot change travelers' checks, but must send them down to the bank, an operation which takes two or three days. There is something called the *Ballet Haus*, closed in the winter and used for God knows what, certainly not ballet, during the summer. There seems to be only one schoolhouse in the village, and this for the quite young children; I suppose this to mean that their older brothers and sisters at some point descend from these mountains in order to complete their education—possibly, again, to the town just below. The landscape is absolutely forbidding, mountains towering on all four sides, ice and snow as far as the eye can reach. In this white wilderness, men and women and children move all day, carrying washing, wood buckets of milk or water, sometimes skiing on Sunday afternoons. All week long boys and young men are to be seen shoveling snow off the rooftops, or dragging wood down from the forest in sleds.

The village's only real attraction, which explains the tourist season, is the hot spring water. A disquietingly high proportion of these tourists are cripples, or semi-cripples, who come year after year—from other parts of Switzerland, usually—to take the waters. This lends the village, at the height of the season, a rather terrifying air of sanctity, as though it were a lesser Lourdes. There is often something beautiful, there is always something awful, in the spectacle of a person who has lost one of his faculties, a faculty he never questioned until it was gone, and who struggles to recover it. Yet people remain people, on crutches or indeed on deathbeds; and wherever I passed, the first summer I was here, among the native villagers or among the lame, a wind passed with me—of astonishment, curiosity, amusement, and outrage. That first summer I stayed two weeks and never intended to return. But I did return in the winter, to work; the village offers, obviously, no distractions whatever and has the further advantage of being extremely cheap. Now it is winter again, a year later, and I am here again. Everyone in the village knows my name, though they scarcely ever use it, knows that I come from America—though, this, apparently, they will never really believe: black men come from Africa—and everyone knows that I am the friend of the son of a woman who was born here, and that I am staying in their chalet. But I remain as much a stranger today as I was the first day I arrived, and the children shout *Neger! Neger!* as I walk along the streets.

It must be admitted that in the beginning I was far too shocked to have any real reaction. In so far as I reacted at all, I reacted by trying to be pleasant—it being a great part of the American Negro's education (long before he goes to school) that he must make people "like" him. This smile-and-the-world-smiles-with-you routine worked about as well in this situation as it had in the situation for which it was designed, which is to say that it did not work at all. No one, after all, can be liked whose human weight and complexity cannot be, or has not been, admitted. My smile was simply another unheard-of phenomen which allowed them to see my teeth—they did not, really, see my smile and I began to think that, should I take to snarling, no one would notice any difference. All of the physical characteristics of the Negro which had caused me, in America, a very different and almost forgotten pain were nothing less than miraculous—or infernal—in the eyes of the village people. Some thought my hair was the color of tar, that it had the texture of wire, or the texture of cotton. It was jocularly suggested that I might let it all grow long and make myself a winter coat. If I sat in the sun for more than five minutes some daring creature was certain to come along and gingerly put his fingers on my hair, as though he were afraid of an electric shock, or put his hand on my hand, astonished that the color did not rub off. In all of this, in which it must be conceded there was the charm of genuine wonder and in which there were certainly no element of intentional unkindness, there was yet no suggestion that I was human: I was simply a living wonder.

I knew that they did not mean to be unkind, and I know it now; it is necessary, nevertheless, for me to repeat this to myself each time that I walk out of the chalet. The childen who shout *Neger!* have no way of knowing the echoes this sound raises in me. They are brimming with good humor and the more daring swell with pride when I stop to speak with them. Just the same, there are days when I cannot pause and smile, when I have no heart to play with them; when, indeed, I mutter sourly to myself, exactly as I muttered on the streets of a city these children have never seen, when I was no bigger than these children are now: *Your* mother *was a nigger.* Joyce is right about history being a nightmare—but it may be the nightmare from which no one *can* awaken. People are trapped in history and history is trapped in them.

There is a custom in the village—I am told it is repeated in many villages—of "buying" African natives for the purpose of converting them to Christianity. There stands in the church all year round a small box with a slot for money, decorated with a black figurine, and into this box the villagers drop their francs. During the *carnaval* which precedes Lent, two village children have their faces blackened—out of which bloodless darkness their blue eyes shine like ice—and fantastic horsehair wigs are placed on their blond heads; thus disguised, they solicit among the villagers for money for the missionaries in Africa. Between the box in the church and the blackened children, the village "bought" last year six or eight African natives. This was reported to me with pride by the wife of one of the *bistro* owners and I was careful to express astonishment and pleasure at the solicitude shown by the village for the souls of black folks. The *bistro* owner's wife beamed with a pleasure far more genuine than my own and seemed to feel that I might now breathe more easily concerning the souls of at least six of my kinsmen.

I tried not to think of these so lately baptized kinsmen, of the price paid for them, or the peculiar price they themselves would pay, and said nothing about my father, who having taken his own conversion too literally never, at bottom, forgave the white world (which he described as heathen) for having saddled him with a Christ in whom, to judge at least from their treatment of him, they themselves no longer believed. I thought of white men arriving for the first time in an African village, strangers there, as I am a stranger here, and tried to imagine the astounded populace touching their hair and marveling at the color of their skin. But there is a great difference between being the first white man to be seen by Africans and being the first black man to be seen by whites. The white man takes the astonishment as tribute, for he arrives to conquer and to convert the natives, whose inferiority in rela-tion to himself is not even to be questioned; whereas I, without a thought of conquest, find myself among a people whose culture controls me, has even, in a sense, created me, people who have cost me more in anguish and rage than they will ever know, who yet do not even know of my existence. The astonishment with which I might have greeted them, should they have stumbled into my African village a few hundred years ago, might have rejoiced their hearts. But the astonishment with which they greet me today can only poison mine.

And this is so despite everything I may do to feel differently, despite my friendly conversations with the bistro owner's wife, despite their three-year-old son who has at last become my friend, despite the *saluts* and *bonsoirs* which I exchange with people as I walk, despite the fact that I know that no individual can be taken to task for what history is doing, or has done. I say that the cul-ture of these people controls me—but they can scarcely be held responsible for European culture. America comes out of Europe, but these people have never seen America, nor have most of them seen more of Europe than the hamlet at the foot of their mountain. Yet they move with an authority which I shall never have; and they regard me, quite rightly, not only as a stranger in their village but as a suspect latecomer, bearing no credentials, to everything they have—however unconsciously—inherited.

For this village, even were it incomparably more remote and incredibly more primitive, is the West, the West onto which I have been so strangely grafted. These people cannot be, from the point of view of power, strangers anywhere in the world; they have made the modern world, in effect, even if they do not know it. The most illiterate among them is related, in a way that I am not, to Dante, Shakespeare, Michelangelo, Aeschylus, Da Vinci, Rembrandt, and Racine; the cathedral at Chartres says something to them which it cannot say to me, as indeed would New York's Empire State Building, should anyone here ever see it. Out of their hymns and dances come Beethoven and Bach. Go back a few centuries and they are in their full glory—but I am in Africa, watching the conquerors arrive.

The rage of the disesteemed is personally fruitless, but it is also absolutely inevitable; this rage, so generally discounted, so little understood even among the people whose daily bread it is, is one of the things that makes history. Rage can only with difficulty, and never entirely, be brought under the domination of the intelligence and is therefore not susceptible to any arguments whatever. This is a fact which ordinary representives of the *Herrenvolk*, having never felt this rage and being unable to imagine, quite fail to understand. Also, rage cannot be hidden, it can only be dissembled. This dissembling deludes the thoughtless, and strengthens rage and adds, to rage, contempt. There are, no doubt, as many ways of coping with the resulting complex of tensions as there are black men in the world, but no black man can hope ever to be entirely liberated from this internal warfare—rage, dissembling, and contempt having inevitably accompanied his first realization of the power of white men. What is crucial here is that, since white men represent in the black man's world so heavy a weight, white men have for black men a reality which is far from being reciprocal; and hence all black men have toward all white men an attitude which is designed, really, either to rob the white man of the jewel of his naïveté, or else to make it cost him dear.

The black man insists, by whatever means he finds at his disposal, that the white man cease to regard him as an exotic rarity and recognize him as a human being. This is a very charged and difficult moment, for there is a great deal of will power involved in the white man's naïveté. Most people are not naturally reflective any more than they are naturally malicious, and the white man prefers to keep the black man at a certain human remove because it is easier for him thus to preserve his simplicity and avoid being called to account for crimes committed by his forefathers, or his neighbors. He is inescapably aware, nevertheless, that he is in a better position in the world than black men are, nor can he quite put to death the suspicion that he is hated by black men therefore. He does not wish to be hated, neither does he wish to change places, and at this point in his uneasiness he can scarcely avoid having recourse to those legends which white men have created about black men, the most usual effect of which is that the white man finds himself enmeshed, so to speak, in his own language which describes hell, as well as the attributes which lead one to hell, as being as black as night.

Every legend, moreover, contains its residuum of truth, and the root function of language is to control the universe by describing it. It is of quite considerable significance that black men remain, in the imagination, and in overwhelming numbers in fact, beyond the disciplines of salvation; and this despite the fact that the West has been "buying" African natives for centuries. There is, I should hazard, an instantaneous necessity to be divorced from this so visibly unsaved stranger, in whose heart, moreover, one cannot guess what dreams of vengeance are being nourished; and, at the same time, there are few things on earth more attractaive than the idea of the unspeakable liberty which is allowed the unredeemed. When, beneath the black mask, a human being begins to make himself felt one cannot escape a certain awful wonder as to what kind of human being it is. What one's imagination makes of other people is dictated, of course, by the laws of one's own personality and it is one of the ironies of black-white relations that, by means of what the white man imagines the black man to be, the black man is enabled to know who the white man is.

I have said, for example, that I am as much a stranger in this village today as I was the first summer I arrived, but this is not quite true. The villagers wonder less about the texture of my hair than they did then, and wonder rather more about me. And the fact that their wonder now exists on another level is reflected in their atitudes and in their eyes. There are the children who make those delightful, hilarious, sometimes astonishingly grave overtures of friendship in the unpredictable fashion of children; other children, having been taught that the devil is a black man, scream in genuine anguish as I approach. Some of the older women never pass without a friendly greeting, never pass, indeed, if it seems that they will be able to engage me in conversation; other women look down or look away or rather contemptuously smirk. Some of the men drink with me and suggest that I learn how to ski—partly, I gather, because they cannot imagine what I would look like on skis—and want to know if I am married, and ask questions about my *métier*. But some of the men have accused *le sale nègre*—behind my back—of stealing wood and there is already in the eyes of some of them that peculiar, intent, paranoaic malevolence which one sometimes surprises in the eyes of American white men when, out walking with their Sunday girl, they see a Negro male approach.

There is a dreadful abyss between the streets of this village and the streets of the city in which I was born, between the children who shout *Neger!* today and those who shouted *Nigger!* yesterday—the abyss is experience, the American experience. The syllable hurled behind me today expresses, above all, wonder: I am a stranger here. But I am not a stranger in America and the same syllable rising on the American air expresses the war my presence has occasioned in the American soul.

For this village brings home to me this fact: that there was a day, and not really a very distant day, when Americans were scarcely Americans at all but discontented Europeans, facing a great unconquered continent and strolling, say, into a marketplace and seeing black men for the first time. The shock this spectacle afforded is suggested, surely, by the promptness with which they decided that these black men were not really men but cattle. It is true that the necessity on the part of the settlers of the New World of reconciling their moral assumption with the fact—and the necessity—of slavery enhanced immensely the charm of this idea, and it is also true that this idea expresses, with a truly American bluntness, the attitude which to varying extents all masters have had toward all slaves.

But between all former slaves and slave-owners and the drama which begins for Americans over three hundred yeaars ago at Jamestown, there are at least two differences to be observed. The American Negro slave could not suppose, for one thing, as slaves in past epochs had supposed and often done, that he would ever be able to wrest the power from his master's hands. This was a supposition which the modern era, which was to bring about such vast changes in the aims and dimensions of power, put to death; it only begins in unprecedented fashion, and with dreadful implications, to be resurrected today. But even had this supposition persisted with undiminished force, the American Negro slave could not have used it to lend his condition dignity, for the reason that this supposition rests on another: that the slave in exile yet remains related to his past, has some means—if only in memory—of revering and sustaining the forms of his former life, is able, in short, to maintain his identity.

This was not the case with the American Negro slave. He is unique among the black men of the world in that his past was taken from him, almost literally, at one blow. One wonders what on earth the first slave found to say to the first dark child he bore. I am told that there are Haitians able to trace their ancestry back to African kings, but any American negro wishing to go back so far will find his journey through time abruptly arrested by the signature on the bill of sale which served as the entrance paper for his ancestor. At the time—to say nothing of the circumstances—of the enslavement of the captive black man who was to become the American Negro, there was not the remotest possibility that he would ever take power from his master's hands. There was no reason to suppose that his situation would ever change, nor was there, shortly, anything to indicate that his situation had ever been different. It was his necessity, in the words of E. Franklin Frazier, to find a "motive for living under American culture or die." The identity of the American Negro comes out of this extreme situation, and the evolution of this identity was a source of the most intolerable anxiety in the minds and the lives of his masters.

For the history of the American Negro is unique also in this: that the question of his humanity, and of his rights therefore as a human being, became a burning one for several generations of Americans, so burning a question that it ultimately became one of those used to divide the nation. It is out of this argument that the venom of the epithet *Nigger!* is derived. It is an argument which Europe has never had, and hence Europe quite sincerely fails to understand how or why the argument arose in the first place, why its effects are frequently disastrous and always so unpredictable, why it refuses until today to be entirely settled. Europe's black possessions remained—and do remain—in Europe's colonies, at which remove they represented no threat whatever to European identity. If they posed any problem at all for the European conscience it was a problem which remained comfortingly abstract: in effect, the black man, as a *man* did not exist for Europe. But in America, even as a slave, he was an inescapable part of the general social fabric and no American could escape having an attitude toward him. Americans attempt until today to make an abstraction of the Negro, but the very nature of these abstractions reveals the tremendous effects the presence of the Negro has had on the American character.

When one considers the history of the Negro in America it is of the greatest importance to recognize that the moral beliefs of a person, or a people, are never really as tenuous as life—which is not moral—very often causes them to appear; these create for them a frame of reference and a necessary hope, the hope being that when life has done its worst they will be enabled to rise above themselves and to triumph over life. Life would scarcely be bearable if this hope did not exist. Again, even when the worst has been said, to betray a belief is not by any means to have put oneself beyond its power; the betrayal of a belief is not the same thing as ceasing to believe. If this were not so there would be no moral standards in the world at all. Yet one must also recognize that morality is based on ideas and that all ideas are dangerous—dangerous because ideas can only lead to action and where the action leads no man can say. And dangerous in this respect: that confronted with the impossibility of remaining faithful to one's beliefs, and the equal impossibility of becoming free of them, one can be driven to the most inhuman excesses. The ideas on which American beliefs are based are not, though Americans often seem to think so, ideas which originated in America. They came out of Europe. And the establishment of democracy on the American continent was scarcely as radical a break with the past as was the necessity, which Americans faced, of broadening this concept to include black men.

This was, literally, a hard necessity. It was impossible, for one thing, for Americans to abandon their beliefs, not only because these beliefs alone seemed able to justify the sacrifices they had endured and the blood that they had spilled, but also because these beliefs afforded them their only bulwark against a moral chaos as absolute as the physical chaos of the continent it was their destiny to conquer. But in the situation in which Americans found themselves, these beliefs threatened an idea which, whether or not one likes to think so, is the very warp and woof of the heritage of the West, the idea of white supremacy.

Americans have made themselves notorious by the shrillness and the brutality with which they have insisted on this idea; but they did not invent it; and it has escaped the world's notice that those very excesses of which Americans have been guilty imply a certain, unprecedented uneasiness over the idea's life and power, if not, indeed, the idea's validity. The idea of white supremacy rests simply on the fact that white men are the creators of civilization (the present civilization, which is the only one that matters; all previous civilizations are simply "contributions" to our own) and are therefore civilization's guardians and defenders. Thus it was impossible for Americans to accept the black man as one of themselves, for to do so was to jeopardize their status as white men. But not so to accept him was to deny his human reality, his human weight and complexity, and the strain of denying the overwhelmingly undeniable forced Americans into rationalizations so fantastic that they approached the pathological.

At the root of the American Negro problem is the necessity of the American white man to find a way of living with the Negro in order to be able to live with himself. And the history of this problem can be reduced to the means used by Americans—lynch law and law, segregation and legal acceptance, terrorization and concession—either to come to terms with this necessity, or to find a way around it, or (most usually) to find a way of doing both these things at once. The resulting spectacle, at once foolish and dreadful, led someone to make the quite accurate observation that "the Negro-in-America is a form of insanity which overtakes white men."

In this long battle, a battle by no means finished, the unforeseeable effects of which will be felt by many future generations, the white man's motive was the protection of his identity; the black man was motivated by the need to establish an identity. And despite the terrorization which the Negro in America endured and endures sporadically until today, despite the cruel and totally inescapable ambivalence of his status in his country, the battle for his identity has long ago been won. He is not a visitor to the West, but a citizen there, an American; as American as the Americans who despise him, the Americans who fear him, the Americans who love him—the Americans who became less than themselves, or rose to be greater than themselves by virtue of the fact that the challenge he represented was inescapable. He is perhaps the only black man in the world whose relationship to white men is more terrible, more subtle, and more meaningful than the relationship of bitter possessed to uncertain possessors. His survival depended, and his development depends, on his ability to turn his peculiar status in the Western world to his own advantage and, it may be, to the very great advantage of that world. It remains for him to fashion out of his experience that which will give him sustenance, and a voice.

The cathedral at Chartres, I have said, says something to the people of this village which it cannot say to me; but it is important to understand that this cathedral says something to me which it cannot say to them. Perhaps they are struck by the power of the spires, the glory of the windows; but they have known God, after all, longer than I have known him, and in a different way, and I am terrified by the slippery bottomless well to be found in the crypt, down which heretics were hurled to death, and by the obscene, inescapable gargoyles jutting out of the stone and seeming to say that God and the devil can never be divorced. I doubt that the villagers think of the devil when they face a cathedral because they have never been identified with the devil. But I must acccept the status which myth, if nothing else, gives me in the West before I can hope to change the myth.

Yet, if the American Negro has arrived at his identity by virtue of the absoluteness of his estrangement from his past, American white men still nourish the illusion that there is some means of recovering the European innocence, of returning to a state in which black men do not exist. This is one of the greatest errors Americans can make. The identity they fought so hard to protect has, by virtue of that battle, undergone a change: Americans are as unlike any other white people in the world as it is possible to be. I do not think, for example, that it is too much to suggest that the American vision of the world—which allows so little reality, generally speaking, for any of the darker forces in human life, which tends until today to paint moral issues in glaring black and white—owes a great deal to the battle waged by Americans to maintain between themselves and black men a human separation which could not be bridged. It is only now beginning to be borne in on us—very faintly, it must be admitted, very slowly, and very much against our will—that this vision of the world is dangerously inaccurate, and perfectly useless. For it protects our moral high-mindedness at the terrible expense of weakening our grasp of reality. People who shut their eyes to reality simply invite their own destruction, and anyone who insists on remaining in a state of innocence long after that innocence is dead turns himself into a monster.

The time has come to realize that the interracial drama acted out on the American continent has not only created a new black man, it has created a new white man, too. No road whatever will lead Americans back to the simplicity of this European village where white men still have the luxury of looking on me as a stranger. I am not, really, a stranger any longer for any American alive. One of the things that distinguishes Americans from other people is that no other people has ever been so deeply involved in the lives of black men, and vice versa. This fact faced, with all its implications, it can be seen that the history of the American Negro problem is not merely shameful, it is also something of an achievement. For even when the worst has been said, it must also be added that the perpetual challenge posed by this problem was always, somehow, perpetually met. It is precisely this black-white experience which may prove of indispensable value to us in the world we face today. This world is white no longer, and it will never be white again.

[1953]

CARYL PHILLIPS

(1958–)

Caryl Phillips was raised in England by parents who emigrated from St. Kitts in the West Indies and was educated at Oxford. His writing reflects the major themes and issues in countries that were formerly parts of European empires: racial conflict, contested histories of slavery and domination, and questions of identity and social justice. Much of his fiction draws upon the complicated experiences of travel in the postcolonial world: immigration, exile, and return. His first novel, *Final Passage* (1985), concerns the difficulties of West Indians who settle in England. *A State of Independence* (1986) is about the challenge of returning to the Caribbean and trying to be at home.

In the essay below, "In the Falling Snow," taken from *The European Tribe* (1987), Phillips finds that his black skin elicits suspicion and hostility from the Norwegians. He picks Norway as his destination because he wants to see, as he explains, "how many of 'their' ideas about me, if any, I subconsciously believed."

"In the falling snow"

From *The European Tribe*

In the falling snow
A laughing boy holds out his palms
Until they are white.

Richard Wright

By the time I reached Oslo's Fornebu airport I was tiring badly. I had spent the greater part of a year travelling, but I consoled myself with the thought that at least I would not have to endure the drudgery of a long queue at passport control. I had treated myself to Club class, and assumed therefore that I would disembark before most passengers. Ahead of me were two young American businessmen. They were swiftly processed with a smile. I stepped forward and presented myself. With one hand resting on my unopened passport, the customs officer fired a barrage of questions at me. How much money did I have? Where was I going to stay? Did I have a return ticket? Had I been to Norway before? Was I here on businesss? I threw down my return ticket and stared at her, my body barely able to contain my rage. 'Stand to one side,' she said. I stood to one side and watched as she dealt with each passenger in turn. There were no questions asked of them.

When everyone had gone through, she picked up my passport and ticket, and then left her counter. Five minutes later she reappeared in the company of a male officer. 'How much money do you have?' he asked. I don't know. 'How much money is in your bank account?' Which bank account? I asked. 'Do you have any credit cards?' Yes. He nodded as though disappointed. 'Please wait here.' They both disappeared. On their return they found me looking down at the space between my feet, afraid of what I might say if I caught their eyes. 'You can proceed now.' I did not move. 'Go on, you can proceed through customs control.' I looked up and took both my passport and my ticket from the man. The sentence began from the soles of my feet and travelled right up through my body. 'You pair of fucking ignorant bastards.' 'Come with me, sir.' I was instructed to reclaim my luggage, which were the only two pieces left on the revolving belt. In gaoler-like silence, they frogmarched me into the customs hall where I was searched. A middle-aged English woman who had witnessed the episode turned upon my escorts. 'You should be ashamed,' she said. At least it was clear to somebody else what was happening. The scene could not be dismissed as paranoia, or as a result of my having a 'chip on my shoulder'.

They ushered me into the chief's office. I stood and listened as the pair of them explained, in Norwegian, to the chief the reason for my presence. As they spoke all three of them kept glancing in my direction. Eventually, the case for the prosecution came to an end. The chief put down a sheaf of papers and came over to face me. 'You must behave like a gentleman,' he told me. 'This', I assured him, 'is how gentlemen behave when they meet arseholes.' He asked me if I found it culturally difficult to deal with a woman customs officer. I burst out laughing. He suggestd that I 'leave now'. Leave for where? 'Oslo, or wherever you will be staying.' I picked up my luggage, but had one final question for him. I asked if his staff would be treating Desmond Tutu, who was due to collect his Nobel Peace Prize in a week's time, in the same manner. 'You may leave now.'

Any ideas I had of a free and easy Scandinavia had already been destroyed. Like her neighbours Denmark and Sweden, Norway is now having to come to terms with people of different cultural backgrounds, and inevitably this is producing an unpleasant backlash. Out of a population of 4 million, Norway has

80,000 immigrants, 63,000 of whom are from Europe or the United States. This leaves 16,000 non-whites, mainly originating from Pakistan and the Middle East. The non-whites constitute only 0.35 per cent of the population, yet a recent poll in the daily newspaper *Aftenposten* showed that 87 per cent of Norwegians did not want any more immigrant workers to enter the country; 33 per cent preferred not to see immigrant workers in the street; 52 per cent wanted them to abandon their cultural traditions and adjust to Norwegian life; and 94 per cent of them said they would not welcome an immigrant into their homes.

Norwegian resentment revolves around the usual fears of immigrant hygiene, unemployment, sexual fears, and displeasure at having to finance the social welfare support system that maintains some immigrants but far more Norwegians. Unfortunately, a similar bitterness exists in both Sweden and Denmark, where acts of racist violence are becoming more commonplace. Norwegian magazines, like *Innvandrer Informasjon*, which seek to promote racial harmony by featuring articles illustrated with pictures of Africans in scandinavian clogs, are no substitute for political will. It would appear that Ibsen's century-old observation (in *Ghosts*, 1881) of his fellow countrymen still holds true: 'It isn't just what we have inherited from our father and mother that walks in us. It is all kinds of old and obsolete beliefs. They are not alive in us; but they remain in us none the less, and we can never rid ourselves of them.'

In a way, I came to Norway to test my own sense of negritude. To see how many of 'their' ideas about me, if any, I subconsciously believed. Under a volley of stares it is only natural to want eventually to recoil and retreat. In a masochistic fashion, I was testing their hostility. True, it is possible to feel this anywhere, but in Paris or New York, in London or Geneva, there is always likely to be another black person around the corner or across the road. Strength through unity in numbers is an essential factor in maintaining a sense of sanity as a black person in Europe. But, I asked myself, what happens 300 miles inside the Arctic Circle in mid-December, with nothing but reindeer and Lapps for many miles in any direction? I knew they would stare, for it is unlikely that many of them would have ever seen a black person before. Only then would I find out how much power, if any, was stored away in the historical battery that feeds my own sense of identity.

From the beginning my 'experiment' went crucially wrong. I flew to Tromsö, a town about 200 miles inside the Arctic Circle where I hired a car. It began to snow quite heavily so I checked into a hotel, then decided to find a nightclub. The first person I met in the club was a Trinidadian woman. I had foolishly underestimated the extent of the Caribbean diaspora. She was as shocked as I was, and anxious to strike up a conversation. I soon discovered that she was thirty-one, had three boys aged nine, eleven and fourteen, whose father was a Norwegian from whom she was now separated. She had met him in San Fernando, Trinidad when he was sailing through the Caribbean. Her move to Norway had caused a permanent breach with her parents and her life here with him had recently fallen apart. She was drunk, and oblivious to the leering contempt with which other men in the club watched her. Then she remembered her children. They did not like her to go out at nights, so she urged me to speak to them on the telephone. My voice would prove that she had met a West Indian and justify her neglect.

Her phone call was brief, and she returned to confess that she was anxious to leave her children and have some fun on her own. When the eldest boy reached sixteen she would be free. 'I'm still good-looking, aren't I?' she asked. 'I still can have a life of my own, but you know, I love Tromsö more than any-where. I hate Trinidad.' She paused. 'But I have my own life now.' I asked her what she liked about Tromsö. 'The nature,' was her reply. I began to feel for the three boys waiting at home. Like a potter's wheel that has suddenly been jammed to a halt, West Indians have been flung out into history and tried to make good wherever they have landed. She was the saddest case I had come across. Defying everything that I know about the caring attitude of Caribbean women to motherhood, she was lost and ailing. As I made ready to leave the club she took my arm. Did I want to meet her children? They might be asleep if we stayed and had another drink or two, and that way I would be able to meet them in the morning. I suggested that she ask somebody else and left.

The next day I drove for hours. The snow lay thick, the landscape a chilled whitewashed canvas with no human beings, just a metal forest of rickety trees, and an odd mirror-glass lake breaking the monotony. Fifty miles north-east of Tromsö I stopped for petrol in a small town. It was mid-afternoon and pitch black. The ninety minutes of winter daylight had long since passed. Turning to face me, the woman attendant dropped the petrol pump in shock. Did she imagine that I was going to molest her? I picked up the pump and gave it back to her. She made some gesture to indicate that her hands were greasy. I smiled. From the car cassette player I hear Bob Marley singing 'Redemption Song': 'Emancipate yourself from mental slavery' did not refer to black people.

I arrived back in Oslo the day Bishop Desmond Tutu received his Nobel Peace Prize. On the television he talked about the need for moral action by the West with regard to South Africa, stating that a concerted and unified eco-nomic and political embargo was essential. He made the demand in the knowl-edge that the vested economic interests of the West would make such action unlikely. Norway trades openly and extensively with South Africa. Their lack of moral fortitude, and that of the rest of Western Europe, will inevitably help contribute to a bloody and protracted finale to this current chapter of South African history. Norway's presentation of a Peace Prize to Bishop Tutu seemed curious. Pontius Pilate washing his hands?

The following day I attended a 'Desmond Tutu Celebration' in Oslo's 'Peo-ple's Hall'. Organized by the Norwegian Trade Union movment, the festivities were attended by representatives from the church and state, the laureate and his family. Again he spoke passionately on the need for 'economic pressure' and, naturally enough, he received a standing ovation. There then followed a series of performances that included a Norwegian 'punk' band, a black American singer who delivered a barely recognizable version of Stevie Wonder's 'I Just Called To Say I Love You', and a Scandinavian poet. Just when the evening seemed lost, seven blonde-haired Swedish schoolchilden strode on to the stage and proceeded to clap hands and, without accompaniment, sing a medly of African folk songs. Bishop Tutu and his family rushed to join them on stage. The spontaneity and vigour of their performance warmed an otherwise frosty evening. In this unexpected scene, there was, at last, hope.

After the celebrations I found myself sharing a table in an Oslo late bar with a drunk Norwegian. He complained to me that his fiancée had recently 'run off' to do Third World aid work in Kenya, and was now refusing to come back. In a lilting and desperate voice, he asked me how black and white can grow to understand each other. I could only tell him the truth; in many ways, we already did but that a touch of mutual respect always helped. We shook hands on it. My ten minutes of solitary peace were soon disturbed by a drunk Eritrean 'brother', who informed me that I must not stay in Europe too long as I would just get old and be pointed out as 'an old nigger'. He suggested that I go back to where I came from He was 'studying' in Norway. I asked him how long he had been here. 'Fourteen years,' but he was quick to explain that he had only stayed for so long because he knew how to deal with the white man. An hour later I watched as they carried him out. He was unconscious before his drunken body reached Norway's sub-zero streets.

[1987]

EVA HOFFMAN

(1945–)

Eva Hoffman emigrated from Poland to Canada with her family, who had survived the Holocaust. She has written about her life as an immigrant in *Lost in Translation: A Life in a New Language* (1990). For her next book, *Exit into History: A Journey through the New Eastern Europe* (1993), she traveled back to Poland to revisit her past and observe changes brought by the fall of the Soviet Union.

In the selection that follows, from an essay, "The New Nomads," Hoffman reconsiders the meanings of exile and home in light of the persecution, displacement, and population shifts during and after World War

II. Historically, nomads have been members of traditional cultures that traveled with the seasons. Their homes are, in effect, set patterns of travel rather than fixed places. In her essay, Hoffman applies the term *nomads* to the involuntary travelers of the twentieth century, the exiles and refugees uprooted and displaced by social conflict.

From "The New Nomads"

"Therefore the Lord God sent him forth from the garden of Eden, to till the ground from whence he was taken. So he drove out the man; and he placed at the east of the garden of Eden Cherubims, and a flaming sword which turned every way, to keep the way of the tree of life." Thus Genesis, on humankind's first exiles. Since then, is there anyone who does not—in some way, on some level—feel that they are in exile? We feel ejected from our first homes and landscapes, from childhood, from our first family romance, from our authentic self. We feel there is an ideal sense of belonging, of community, of attunement with others and at-homeness with ourselves, that keeps eluding us. The tree of life is barred to us by a flaming sword, turning this way and that to confound us and make the task of approaching it harder.

On one level, exile is a universal experience. But, of course, exile also refers to a specific social and political condition—although even in that sense, it was never a unitary category, and we tend to compress too many situations under its heading. The different circumstances surrounding individual migration, and the wider political or cultural contexts within which it takes place, can have enormous practical and psychic repercussions, reflected in the various words we use for those who leave one country for another. There are refugees, émigrés, emigrants, and expatriates, designations that point to distinct kinds of social, but also internal, experience. It matters enormously, for starters, whether you choose to leave or are forced to; it matters also whether you're coming to a new land unprotected and unprovided for or whether you can expect, or transport, some kind of safety net. When my family came from Poland to Canada, we were immigrants, a term that has connotations of class—lower than émigrés, higher perhaps than refugees—and degree of choice—more than is given to refugees, less than to expatriates.

Historically, too, the symbolic meaning and therefore the experience of exile has changed. In medieval Europe, exile was the worst punishment that could be inflicted. This was because one's identity was defined by one's role and place in society; to lose that was to lose a large portion of one's self. After being banished from Florence, Dante lived less than a hundred miles from his city-state—and yet he felt that his expulsion was a kind of psychic and social death, and his dream was either of return or of revenge (which he certainly executed very effectively in the *Inferno*). Real life, for Dante, was in Florence; it could not exist fully anywhere else. Joseph Conrad's father wrote to his infant son, who had been born during a time when Poland was erased from the map, "Tell yourself that you are without land, without love, without Fatherland, without humanity—as long as Poland, our Mother, is enslaved." In other words, for a patriot of an occupied nation, it was possible to feel radically exiled within that country, as long as it did not possess the crucial aspect of national sovereignty.

All of these forms of exile implied a highly charged concept of home—although that home was not necessarily coeval with one's birthplace. For the medieval clerics and church functionaries who traveled from monastery to monastery, the center of gravity was the city that housed the papal seat. The Jews have had the most prolonged historical experience of collective exile; but they survived their Diaspora—in the sense of preserving and maintaining their identity—by nurturing a powerful idea of home. That home existed on two levels: there were the real communities that Jews inhabited in various countries; but on the symbolic and perhaps the more important plane, home consisted of the entity "Israel," which increasingly became less a geographic and more a spiritual territory, with Jerusalem at its heart. While living in dispersion, Jews oriented themselves toward this imaginative center of the world, from which they derived their essential identity.

In our own century, the two great totalitarianisms, Nazi and Soviet, produced the most potent forms of exile, although the Soviet expulsions proved more permanent. The refugees from Nazi Germany, with their bright galaxy of artists and intellectuals—Hannah Arendt, Bertolt Brecht, Theodor Adorno, Herbert Marcuse, and others—were pushed from their country by a vile regime, but once the war was over, they could go back, and some chose to do so. The exiles from Eastern Europe—Vladimir Nabokov, Czeslaw Milosz, Milan Kundera, Joseph Brodsky, and others—thought that their banishment was for life, though history reversed it for some of them in the end.

But in recent years, in Europe most markedly, great tectonic shifts in the political and social landscape have taken place, which I think are affecting the very notion of exile—and of home. For what is happening today is that cross-cultural movement has become the norm rather than the exception, which in turn means that leaving one's native country is simply not as dramatic or traumatic as it used to be. The ease of travel and communication, combined with the loosening of borders following the changes of 1989, give rise to endless crisscrossing streams of wanderers and guest workers, nomadic adventurers and international drifters. Many are driven by harsh circumstance, but the element of voluntarism, of choice, is there for most. The people who leave the former Soviet Union nowadays are likely to be economic migrants or mafia tax dodgers buying up elegant real estate in London rather than dissidents expelled by ruthless state power. In one Bengali village, for example, there is a tradition of long seasonal migration, or sojourning. Many of the village's men leave for several years or even decades, but always with the intention of returning. These are hardly privileged émigrés or expatriates, but neither are they powerless victims of globalization. Instead, they are people with agency and intentionality, playing the system. Smart young men choose different countries for the timely economic advantages they offer—better wages, better interest rates. Almost all go back, a bit richer and a bit more important in the eyes of their fellow villagers. Theirs are migrations divested of tragedy if not of adversity.

Of course, there are still parts of the world, South America or Southeast Asia, where political dissidents are expelled by demagogic dictatorships and cannot return while those dictatorships endure. There are still refugees from Bosnia whose return is barred by the sword of violence. I do not mean to underestimate for a moment their hardships, but I would think that even in their case, the vastly increased mobility and communicative possibilities of our world change the premises of their banishment: friends can visit or phone; they know that if the govenment of their country changes—and political arrangements, along with everything else, have become susceptible to quicker change—they can go back, or travel back and forth.

The *Herald Tribune* recently characterized the increasing numbers of American expatriates in Europe: "They are the Americans abroad, and their number is soaring in a time when travel is unblinkingly routine, communications easy and instant, and telecommuting a serious option. They are abroad in a world where they can watch the Super Bowl live from a Moscow sports bar or send an e-mail from an Internet cafe in Prague."

Well, exactly. We all recognize these basic features of our new, fast-changing social landscape. Whether we have left or not, we know how easy it is to leave. We know that we live in a global village, although the village is very virtual indeed—a village dependent not on locality or the soil but on what some theorists call deterritorialization—that is, the detachment of knowledge, action, information, and identity from specific place or physical source. We have become less space-bound, if not yet free of time.

Simultaneously there has grown up a vast body of commentary and theory that is rethinking and revising the concept of exile and the related contrapuntal concept of home. The basic revision has been to attach a positive sign to exile and the cluster of mental and emotional experiences associated with it. Exile used to be thought of as a difficult condition. It involves dislocation, disorientation, self-division. But today, at least within the framework of postmodern theory, we have come to value exactly those qualities of experience that exile demands—uncertainty, displacement, the fragmented identity. Within this conceptual framework, exile becomes, well, sexy, glamorous, interesting. Nomadism and diasporism have become fashionable terms in intellectual discourse. What is at stake is not only, or not even primarily, actual exile but our preferred psychic positioning, so to speak, how we situate ourselves in the world. And these days we think the exilic position has precisely the virtues of instability, marginality, absence, and outsiderness. This privileging of exile compresses two things: first, a real description of our world, which indeed has become more decentered, fragmented, and unstable, and second, an approbation of these qualities, which is more problematic, because it underestimates the sheer human cost of actual exile as well as some of its psychic implications, and perhaps even lessons.

My emigration took place during the Cold War, though not in the worst Stalinist years. My parents chose to leave, though that choice was so overdetermined that it could hardly have been called "free." But I happened to be a young and unwilling emigrant, yanked from my childhood, which I had believed to be happy. Therefore, I felt the loss of my first homeland acutely, fueled by the sense (the certain knowledge, it seemed then) that this departure was irrevocable. Poland was abruptly sundered from me by an unbridgeable gap; it was suddenly elsewhere, unreachable, on the other side, and I felt, indeed, as if I were being taken out of life itself.

This kind of abrupt rupture breeds its own set of symptoms and syndromes. It is, first of all, a powerful narrative shaper; it creates chiaroscuro contrasts, a stark sense of biographical drama. The stories that emerged from the Cold War are legion, but one certain outcome of exile that takes place in a bipolar world is the creation of a bipolar personal world. Spatially, the world becomes riven into two parts, divided by an uncrossable barrier. Temporally, the past is all of a sudden on one side of a divide, the present on the other.

Flash-forward to 1994, and a rather ordinary trip I took to Kraków that year with an English friend. The Westernization of my native town was everywhere evident. Where previously there had been no market, there was now commerce. Where before there was the great Eastern European nada, now there were boutiques, Krups coffee machines, Armani suits. It was perhaps the presence of my Western friend, who kept saying that Kraków looked like any small European city with a well-preserved historical center, that made me realize palpably what I had known in principle: that the differences between East and West were blurring pretty completely and that simultaneously the various divisions and oppositions I had set up in my inner landscape were shifting and blurring, too. When I came upon a lone shopwindow featuring a display familiar from the days of yore—a dry loaf of bread, an apple, and a desultory can of Coke—I pointed it out to my friend excitedly. Look! This was how it used to be! But this was not the way things were now. The dusty little vitrine was a trace, a remaining mark of a world that, for all its misery, had the appeal of familiarity and, most saliently, of clarity. Now I would have to live in a world in which the bipolar structure was gone, in which everything is intermingled and no site is more privileged—either in its deprivation or in its pleasures—than anywhere else. I would have to change my narrative.

At this vanishing of contrasts I confess that I felt not only relief but regret. It was a regret, undoubtedly perverse, for the waning of clarity. But I also felt the loss of the very sense of loss I had experienced on my emigration. For the paroxysm I experienced on leaving Poland was, for all the pain, an index of the significance I attached to what I left behind.

Still, what had I mourned in 1959? What was it that stood for home? Though I was too young to know it, the fervor of my feelings was produced by the Cold War. And yet my response had nothing of geopolitics about it. As a bare adolescent, I was too politically innocent to be a budding nationalist; in any case, as a daughter of Jewish parents recently transplanted from the Ukraine and not fully engaged in the body politic, I was in a poor position to become a patriot. So it was not the nation I felt exiled from, not Conrad's father's Poland; my homeland was made of something much earlier, more primary than ideology. Landscapes, certainly, and cityscapes, a sense of place. I was lucky enough to grow up in a city that really is quite enchanting and that escaped the ravages of the war. There was the webwork of friendships and other relationships, for example with my teachers. But there were also elements less palpable that nevertheless constituted my psychic home.

For the great first lessons of my uprooting were in the normous importance of language and of culture. My first recognition, as I was prized out of familiar speech and social environment, was that these entities are not luxuries or even external necessities but the medium in which we live, the stuff of which we are made. In other words, they constitute us in a way of which we perhaps remain unconscious if we stay safely ensconced within one culture.

For a while, like so many emigrants, I was in effect without language, and from the bleakness of that condition, I understood how much our inner existence, our sense of self, depends on having a living speech within us. To lose an internal language is to subside into an inarticulate darkness in which we become alien to ourselves; to lose the ability to describe the world is to render that world a bit less vivid, a bit less lucid. And yet the richness of articulation gives the hues of subtlety and nuance to our perceptions and thought. To me, one of the most moving passages in Nabokov's writing is his invocation of Russian at the end of *Lolita*. There he summons not only the melodiousness or euphony of Russian sounds, compelling though these may be, but the depth and wholeness with which the original language exists within us. It is that relationship to language, rather than any more superficial mastery, that is so difficult to duplicate in languages one learns subsequently.

In more religious times, certain languages were considered sacred; that is, they were thought, in the words of a wonderful social historian, Benedict Anderson, to have "ontological reality inseparable from a single system of representation." Arabic, for example, was considered to be the only language in which the Koran could be written; the sacred texts could not be translated into any other language. So with Latin for the medieval Catholic church and Hebrew for Orthodox Jews. Some premodern people today still have the sense that their language is the true language, that it corresponds to reality in a way other languages don't. And it may be that one's first language has, for the child, this aura of sacrality. Because we learn it unconsciously, at the same time as we are learning the world, the words in one's first language seem to be equivalent to the things they name. They seem to express us and the world directly. When we learn a language in adulthood, we know that the words in it "stand for" the things they describe; that the signs on the page are only signs—arbitrary, replaceable by others. It takes time before a new language begins to inhabit us deeply, to enter the fabric of the psyche and express who we are.

As with language, so with culture: what the period of first, radical dislocation brought home was how much we are creatures of culture, how much we are constructed and shaped by it—and how much incoherence we risk if we fall out of its matrix. We know that cultures differ in customs, food, religions, social arrangements. What takes longer to understand is that each culture has subliminal values, predispositions, and beliefs that inform our most intimate assumptions and perceptions, our sense of beauty, for example, or of acceptable distances between people or notions of pleasure and pain. On that fundamental level, a culture does not exist independently of us but within us. It is inscribed in the psyche, and it gives form and focus to our mental and emotional lives. We could hardly acquire a human identity outside it, just as we could hardly think or perceive outside language. In a way, we are nothing more—or less—than an encoded memory of our heritage.

It is because these things go so deep, because they are not only passed on to us but *are* us, that one's original home is a potent structure and force and that being uprooted from it is so painful. Real dislocation, the loss of all familiar external and internal parameters, is not glamorous, and it is not cool. It is a matter not of willful psychic positioning but of an upheaval in the deep material of the self.

[1997]

JACK LONDON

(1876–1916)

Jack London grew up poor in California and became an inveterate traveler, a romantic who championed the working class. While still a teenager, he joined a march of the unemployed across the country to Washington, but he dropped out in Missouri and rode the rails as a hobo until the 1896 gold rush in the Klondike lured him to Alaska. London drew on his experiences there for his most popular book, *The Call of the Wild* (1903). Subsequent travels took him to Asia to cover the Russo-Japanese War, then to the South Seas in a ship he had built, and finally to Mexico to report on the revolution. London's *The Road* (1907), in which he gives detailed instructions on how to hop a freight and survive as a hobo, inspired many subsequent accounts of the vagabond life, including Jack Kerouac's *On the Road*.

In "The Descent," taken from *The People of the Abyss* (1903), he treats his journey into the London slums ironically as a kind of travel, even consulting the leading tour agency of the time, Thomas Cook and Son.

"The Descent"

From *The People of the Abyss*

"But you can't do it, you know," friends said, to whom I applied for assistance in the matter of sinking myself down into the East End of London. "You had better see the police for a guide," they added, on second thought, painfully endeavoring to adjust themselves to the psychological processes of a madman who had come to them with better credentials than brains.

"But I don't want to see the police," I protested. "What I wish to do, is to go down into the East End and see things for myself. I wish to know how those people are living there, and why they are living there, and what they are living for. In short, I am going to live there myself."

"You don't want to live down there!" everybody said, with disapprobation writ large upon their faces. "Why, it is said there are places where a man's life isn't worth tu'pence."

"The very places I wish to see," I broke in.

"But you can't, you know," was the unfailing rejoinder.

"Which is not what I came to see you about," I answered brusquely, somewhat nettled by their incomprehension. "I am a stranger here, and I want you to tell me what you know of the East End, in order that I may have something to start on."

"But we know nothing of the East End. It is over there, somewhere." And they waved their hands vaguely in the direction where the sun on rare occasions may be seen to rise.

"Then I shall go to Cook's," I announced.

"Oh, yes," they said, with relief. "Cook's will be sure to know."

But O Cook, O Thomas Cook & Son, pathfinders and trail-clearers, living signposts to all the world and bestowers of first aid to bewildered travellers—unhesitatingly and instantly, with ease and celerity, could you send me to Darkest Africa or Innermost Thibet, but to the East End of London, barely a stone's throw distant from Ludgate Circus, you know not the way!

"You can't do it, you know," said the human emporium of routes and fares at Cook's Cheapside branch. "It is so—ahem—so unusual."

"Consult the police," he concluded authoritatively, when I persisted. "We are not accustomed to taking travellers to the East End; we receive no call to take them there, and we know nothing whatsoever about the place at all."

"Never mind that," I interposed, to save myself from being swept out of the office by his flood of negations. "Here's something you can do for me. I wish you to understand in advance what I intend doing, so that in case of trouble you may be able to identify me."

"Ah, I see; should you be murdered, we would be in position to identify the corpse."

He said it so cheerfully and cold-bloodedly that on the instant I saw my stark and mutilated cadaver stretched upon a slab where cool waters trickle ceaselessly, and him I saw bending over and sadly and patiently identifying it as the body of the insane American who would see the East End.

"No, no," I answered; "merely to identify me in case I get into a scrape with the 'bobbies.' " This last I said with a thrill; truly, I was gripping hold of the vernacular.

"That," he said, "is a matter for the consideration of the Chief Office.

"It is so unprecedented, you know," he added apologetically.

The man at the Chief Office hemmed and hawed. "We make it a rule," he explained, "to give no information concerning our clients."

"But in this case," I urged, "it is the client who requests you to give the information concerning himself."

Again he hemmed and hawed.

"Of course," I hastily anticipated, "I know it is unprecedented, but—"

"As I was about to remark," he went on steadily, "it is unprecedented, and I don't think we can do anything for you."

However, I departed with the address of a detective who lived in the East End, and took my way to the American consul-general. And here, at last, I found a man with whom I could 'do business.' There was no hemming and hawing, no lifted brows, open incredulity, or blank amazement. In one minute I explained myself and my project, which he accepted as a matter of course. In the second minute he asked my age, height, and weight, and looked me over. And in the third minute, as we shook hands at parting, he said: "All right, Jack. I'll remember you and keep track."

I breathed a sigh of relief. Having built my ships behind me, I was now free to plunge into that human wilderness of which nobody seemed to know anything. But at once I encountered a new difficulty in the shape of my cabby, a gray-whiskered and eminently decorous personage, who had imperturbably driven me for several hours about the 'City.'

"Drive me down to the East End," I ordered, taking my seat.

"Where, sir?" he demanded with frank surprise.

"To the East End, anywhere. Go on."

The hansom pursued an aimless way for several minutes, then came to a puzzled stop. The aperture above my head was uncovered, and the cabman peered down perplexidly at me.

"I say," he said, "wot plyce yer wanter go?"

"East End," I repeated. "Nowhere in particular. Just drive me around, anywhere."

"But wot's the haddress, sir?"

"See here!" I thundered. "Drive me down to the East End, and at once!"

It was evident that he did not understand, but he withdrew his head and grumblingly started his horse.

Nowhere in the streets of London may one escape the sight of abject poverty, while five minutes' walk from almost any point will bring one to a slum; but the region my hansom was now penetrating was one of unending slum. The streets were filled with a new and different race of people, short of stature, and of wretched or beer-sodden appearance. We rolled along through miles of bricks and squalor, and from each cross street and alley flashed long vistas of bricks and misery. Here and there lurched a drunken man or woman, and the air was obscene with sounds of jangling and squabbling. At a market, tottery old men and women were searching in the garbage thrown in the mud for rotten potatoes, beans, and vegetables, while little children clustered like flies around a festering mass of fruit, thrusting their arms to the shoulders into the liquid corruption, and drawing forth morsels, but partially decayed, which they devoured on the spot.

Not a hansom did I meet with in all my drive, while mine was like an apparition from another and better world, the way the children ran after it and alongside. And as far as I could see were the solid walls of brick, the slimy pavements, and the screaming streets; and for the first time in my life the fear of the crowd smote me. It was like the fear of the sea; and the miserable multitudes, street upon street, seemed so many waves of a vast and malodorous sea, lapping about me and threatening to well up and over me.

"Stepney, sir; Stepney Station," the cabby called down.

I looked about. It was really a railroad station, and he had driven desperately to it as the one familiar spot he had ever heard of in all that wilderness.

"Well?" I said.

He spluttered unintelligibly, shook his head, and looked very miserable. "I'm a strynger 'ere," he managed to articulate. "An' if yer don't want Stepney Station, I'm blessed if I know wotcher do want."

"I'll tell you what I want," I said. "You drive along and keep your eye out for a shop where old clothes are sold. Now, when you see such a shop, drive right on till you turn the corner, then stop and let me out."

I could see that he was growing dubious of his fare, but not long afterward he pulled up to the curb and informed me that an old clothes shop was to be found a bit of the way back.

"Won'tcher py me?" he pleaded. "There's seven an' six owin' me."

"Yes," I laughed, "and it would be the last I'd see of you."

"Lord lumme, but it'll be the last I see of you if yer don't py me," he retorted.

But a crowd of ragged onlookers had already gathered around the cab, and I laughed again and walked back to the old clothes shop.

Here the chief difficulty was in making the shop-man understand that I really and truly wanted old clothes.But after fruitless attempts to press upon me new and impossible coats and trousers, he began to bring to light heaps of old ones, looking mysterous the while and hinting darkly. This he did with the pal-pable intention of letting me know that he had 'piped my lay,' in order to bull-dose me, through fear of exposure, into paying heavily for my purchases. A man in trouble, or a high-class criminal from across the water, was what he took my measue for—in either case, a person anxious to avoid the police.

But I disputed with him over the outrageous difference between prices and values, till I quite disabused him of the notion, and he settled down to drive a hard bargain with a hard customer. In the end I selected a pair of stout though well-worn trousers, a frayed jackeet with one remaining button, a pair of bro-gans which had plainly seen service where coal was shovelled, a thin leather belt, and a very dirty cloth cap. My underclothing and socks, however, were new and warm, but of the sort that any American waif, down in his luck, could acquire in the ordinary course of events.

"I must sy yer a sharp 'un," he said, with counterfeit admiration, as I handed over the ten shillings finally agreed upon for the outfit. "Blimey, if you ain't ben up an' down Petticut Lane afore now. Yer trouseys is wuth five bob to hany man, an' a docker 'ud give two an' six for the shoes, to sy nothin' of the coat an' cap an' new stoker's singlet an' hother things."

"How much will you give me for them?" I demanded suddenly. "I paid you ten bob for the lot, and I'll sell them back to you, right now, for eight. Come, it's a go!"

But he grinned and shook his head, and though I had made a good bar-gain, I was unpleasanatly aware that he had made a better one.

I found the cabby and a policeman with their heads together, but the lat-ter, after looking me over sharply and particularly scrutinizing the bundle under my arm, turned away and left the cabby to wax mutinous by himself. And not a step would he budge till I paid him the seven shillings and sixpence owing him. Whereupon he was willing to drive me to the ends of the earth, apologizing profusely for his insistence, and explaining that one ran across queer customers in London Town.

But he drove me only to Highbury Vale, in North London, where my luggage was waiting for me. Here, next day, I took off my shoes (not without regret for their lightness and comfort), and my soft, gray travelling suit, and, in fact, all my clothing; and proceeded to array myself in the clothes of the other and unimaginable men, who must have been indeed unfortunate to have had to part with such rags for the pitiable sums obtainable from a dealer.

Inside my stoker's singlet, in the armpit, I sewed a gold sovereign (an emergency sum certainly of modest proportions); and inside my stoker's singlet I put myself. And then I sat down and moralized upon the fair years and fat, which had made my skin soft and brought the nerves close to the surface; for the singlet was rough and raspy as a hair shirt, and I am confident that the most rigorous of ascetics suffer no more than did I in the ensuing twenty-four hours.

The remainder of my costume was fairly easy to put on, though the brogans, or brogues, were quite a problem. As stiff and hard as if made of wood, it was only after a prolonged pounding of the uppers with my fists that I was able to get my feet into them at all. Then, with a few shillings, a knife, a handkerchief, and some brown papers and flake tobacco stowed away in my pockets, I thumped down the stairs and said good-by to my foreboding friends. As I passed out the door, the 'help,' a comely, middle-aged woman, could not conquer a grin that twisted her lips and separated them till the throat, out of involuntary sympathy, made the uncouth animal noises we are wont to designate as 'laughter.'

No sooner was I out on the streets than I was impressed by the difference in status effected by my clothes. All servility vanished from the demeanor of the common people with whom I came in contact. Presto! in the twinkling of an eye, so to say, I had become one of them. My frayed and out-at-elbows jacket was the badge and advertisement of my class, which was their class. It made me of like kind, and in place of the fawning and too-respectful attention I had hitherto received, I now shared with them a comradeship. The man in corduroy and dirty neckerchief no longer addressed me as 'sir' or 'governor.' It was 'mate,' now—and a fine and hearty word, with a tingle to it, and a warmth and gladness, which the other term does not possess. Governor! It smacks of mastery, and power, and high authority—the tribute of the man who is under to the man on top, delivered in the hope that he will let up a bit and ease his weight. Which is another way of saying that it is an appeal for alms.

[1903]

GEORGE ORWELL

(1903–1950)

George Orwell, born in India as Eric Blair, the son of a British civil servant, took a pen name in his attempt to escape a middle-class identity and write about the life of the poor. Orwell attended Eton, the exclusive British prep school, on scholarship, but he went to India as an imperial policeman rather than continue his education at university. He soon grew to hate the injustices of imperialism, left India, and returned to England to become a writer. Orwell documented the poverty of workers in the industrial midlands of England (*The Road to Wigan Pier*, 1937). *Homage to Catalonia* (1938), an account of fighting in the Spanish Civil War, came about when Orwell journeyed to Spain as a reporter and was inspired to join the anti-Fascist cause as a combatant. His anti-totalitarian fable *Animal Farm* (1945) and novel *1984* (1948) gained him international fame.

The essay that follows is from *Down and Out in Paris and London* (1933) about Orwell's own experience of poverty as a low-paid restaurant worker in France and a tramp in England. Orwell subjects himself to the difficulties of tramping in order to write authoritatively about the ordeals to which the British government subjected the homeless, and he examines the hostility which settled members of society felt towards transients.

From *Down and Out in Paris and London*

To sell my clothes I went down into Lambeth, where the people are poor and there are a lot of rag shops. At the first shop I tried the proprietor was polite but unhelpful; at the second he was rude; at the third he was stone deaf, or pretended to be so. The fourth shopman was a large blond young man, very pink all over, like a slice of ham. He looked at the clothes I was wearing and felt them disparagingly between thumb and finger.

"Poor stuff," he said, "very poor stuff, that is." (It was quite a good suit.) "What yer want for 'em?"

I explained that I wanted some older clothes and as much money as he could spare. He thought for a moment, then collected some dirty-looking rags and threw then on to the counter. "What about the money?" I said, hoping for a pound. He pursed his lips, then produced a *shilling* and laid it beside the clothes. I did not argue—I was going to argue, but as I opened my mouth he reached out as though to take up the shilling again; I saw that I was helpless. He let me change in a small room behind the shop.

The clothes were a coat, once dark brown, a pair of black dungaree trousers, a scarf and a cloth cap; I had kept my own shirt, socks and boots, and I had a comb and razor in my pocket. It gives one a very strange feeling to be wearing such clothes. I had worn bad enough things before, but nothing at all like these; they were not merely dirty and shapeless, they had—how is one to express it?—a gracelessness, a patina of antique filth, quite different from mere shabbiness. They were the sort of clothes you see on a bootlace seller, or a tramp. An hour later, in Lambeth, I saw a hang-dog man, obviously a tramp, coming towards me, and when I looked again it was myself, reflected in a shop window. The dirt was plastering my face already. Dirt is a great respecter of persons; it lets you alone when you are well dessed, but as soon as your collar is gone it flies towards you from all directions.

I stayed in the streets till late at night, keeping on the move all the time. Dressed as I was, I was half afraid that the police might arrest me as a vagabond, and I dared not speak to anyone, imagining that they must notice a disparity between my acccent and my clothes. (Later I discovered that this never happened.) My new clothes had put me instantly into a new world. Everyone's demeanour seemed to have changed abruptly. I helped a hawker pick up a barrow that he had upset. "Thanks, mate," he said with a grin. No one had called me mate before in my life—it was the clothes that had done it. For the first time I noticed, too, how the attitude of women varies with a man's clothes. When a badly dressed man passes them they shudder away from him with a quite frank movement of disgust, as though he were a dead cat. Clothes are powerful things. Dressed in a tramp's clothes it is very difficult, at any rate for the first day, not to feel that you are genuinely degraded. You might feel the same shame, irrational but very real, your first night in prison. . . .

I want to set down some general remarks about tramps. When one comes to think of it, tramps are a queer product and worth thinking over. It is queer that a tribe of men, tens of thousands in number, should be marching up and down England like so many Wandering Jews. But though the case obviously wants considering, one cannot even start to consider it until one has got rid of certain prejudices. These prejudices are rooted in the idea that every tramp, *ipso facto*, is a blackguard. In childhood we have been taught that tramps are blackguards, and consequently there exists in our minds a sort of ideal or typical tramp—a repulsive, rather dangerous creature, who would die rather than work or wash, and wants nothing but to beg, drink and rob hen-houses. This tramp-monster is no truer to life than the sinister Chinaman of the magazine stories, but he is very hard to get rid of. The very word "tramp" evokes his image. And the belief in him obscures the real questions of vagrancy.

To take a fundamental question about vagrancy: Why do tramps exist at all? It is a curious thing, but very few people know what makes a tramp take to the road. And, because of the belief in the tramp-monster, the most fantastic reasons are suggested. It is said, for instance, that tramps tramp to avoid work, to beg more easily, to seek opportunities for crime, even—least probable of reasons—because they like tramping. I have even read in a book of criminology that the tramp is an atavism, a throw-back to the nomadic stage of humanity. And meanwhile the quite obvious cause of vagrancy is staring one in the face. Of course a tramp is not a nomadic atavism—one might as well say that a commercial traveller is an atavism. A tramp tramps, not because he likes it, but for the same reason as a car keeps to the left; because there happens to be a law compelling him to do so. A destitute man, if he is not supported by the parish, can only get relief at the casual wards, and as each casual ward will only admit him for one night, he is automatically kept moving. He is a vagrant because, in the state of the law, it is that or starve. But people have been brought up to believe in the tramp-monster, and so they prefer to think that there must be some more or less villainous motive for tramping.

As a matter of fact, very little of the tramp-monster will survive inquiry. Take the generally accepted idea that tramps are dangerous characters. Quite apart from experience, one can say *a priori* that very few tramps are dangerous, because if they were dangerous they would be treated accordingly. A casual ward will often admit a hundred tramps in one night, and these are handled by a staff of at most three porters. A hundred ruffians could not be controlled by three unarmed men. Indeed, when one sees how tramps let themselves be bullied by the workhouse officials, it is obvious that they are the most docile, broken-spirited creatures imaginable. Or take the idea that all tramps are drunkards—an idea ridiculous on the face of it. No doubt many tramps would drink if they got the chance, but in the nature of things they cannot get the chance. At this moment a pale watery stuff called beer is sevenpence a pint in England. To be drunk on it would cost at least half a crown, and a man who can command half a crown at all often is not a tramp. The idea that tramps are impudent social parasites ("sturdy beggars") is not absolutely unfounded, but it is only true in a few per cent of the cases. Deliberate, cynical parasitism, such as one reads of in Jack London's books on American tramping, is not in the English character. The English are a conscience-ridden race, with a strong sense of the sinfulness of poverty. One cannot imagine the average Englishman deliberately turning parasite, and this national character does not necessarily change because a man is thrown out of work. Indeed, if one remembers that a tramp is only an Englishman out of work, forced by law to live as a vagabond, then the tramp-monster vanishes. I am not saying, of course, that most tramps are ideal characters; I am only saying that they are ordinary human beings, and that if they are worse than other people it is the result and not the cause of their way of life.

It follows that the "Serve them damned well right" attitude that is normally taken towards tramps is no fairer than it would be towards cripples or invalids.

When one has realised that, one begins to put oneself in a tramp's place and understand what his life is like. It is an extraordinarily futile, acutely unpleasant life. I have described the casual ward—the routine of a tramp's day—but there are three especial evils that need insisting upon. The first is hunger, which is the almost general fate of tramps. The casual ward gives them a ration which is probably not even meant to be sufficient, and anything beyond this must be got by begging—that is, by breaking the law. The result is that nearly every tramp is rotted by malnutrition; for proof of which one need only look at the men lining up outside any casual ward. The second great evil of a tramp's life—it seems much smaller at first sight, but it is a good second—is that he is entirely cut off from contact with women. This point needs elaborating.

Tramps are cut off from women, in the first place, because there are very few women at their level of society. One might imagine that among destitute people the sexes would be as equally balanced as elsewhere. But it is not so; in fact, one can almost say that below a certain level society is entirely male. The following figures, published by the L.C.C. from a night census taken on February 13th, 1931, will show the relative numbers of destitute men and destitute women:

Spending the night in the streets, 60 men, 18 women.[1]
In shelters and homes not licensed as common lodging-houses, 1,057 men,
    137 women.
In the crypt of St. Martin's-in-the-Fields Church, 88 men, 12 women.
In L.C.C. casual wards and hostels, 674 men, 15 women.

It will be seen from these figures that at the charity level men outnumber women by something like ten to one. The cause is presumably that unemployment affects women less than men; also that any presentable woman can, in the last resort, attach herself to some man. The result, for a tramp, is that he is condemned to perpetual celibacy. For of course it goes without saying that if a tramp finds no women at his own level, those above—even a very little above—are as far out of his reach as the moon. The reasons are not worth discussing, but there is no doubt that women never, or hardly ever, condescend to men who are much poorer than themselves. A tramp, therefore, is a celibate from the moment when he takes to the road. He is absolutely without hope of getting a wife, a mistress, or any kind of woman except—very rarely, when he can raise a few shillings—a prostitute.

It is obvious what the results of this must be: homosexuality, for instance, and occasional rape cases. But deeper than these there is the degradation worked in man who knows that he is not even considered fit for marriage. The sexual impulse, not to put it any higher, is a fundamental impulse, and starva-

---

[1]This must be an underestimate. Still, the proportions probably hold good.

tion of it can be almost as demoralising as physical hunger. The evil of poverty is not so much that it makes a man suffer as that it rots him physically and spiritually. And there can be no dobut that sexual starvation contributes to this rotting process. Cut off from the whole race of women, a tramp feels himself degraded to the rank of a cripple or a lunatic. No humiliation could do more damage to a man's self-respect.

The other great evil of a tramp's life is enforced idleness. By our vagrancy laws things are so arranged that when he is not walking the road he is sitting in a cell; or, in the intervals, lying on the ground waiting for the casual ward to open. It is obvious that this is a dismal, demoralising way of life, especially for an uneducated man.

Besides these one could enumerate scores of minor evils—to name only one, discomfort, which is inseparable from life on the road; it is worth remembering that the average tramp has no clothes but what he stands up in, wears boots that are ill-fitting, and does not sit in a chair for months togther. But the important point is that a tramp's sufferings are entirely useless. He lives a fantastically disagreeable life, and lives it to no purpose whatever. One could not, in fact invent a more futile routine than walking from prison to prison, spending perhaps eighteen hours a day in the cell and on the road. There must be at the least several tens of thousands of tramps in England. Each day they expend innumerable foot-pounds of energy—enough to plough thousands of acres, build miles of road, put up dozens of houses—in mere, useless walking. Each day they waste between them possibly ten years of time in staring at cell walls. They cost the country at least a pound a week a man, and give nothing in return for it. They go round and round, on an endless boring game of general post, which is of no use, and is not even meant to be of any use to any person whatever. The law keeps this process going, and we have got so accustomed to it that we are not surprised. But it is very silly.

Granting the futility of a tramp's life, the question is whether anything could be done to improve it. Obviously it would be possible, for instance, to make the casual wards a little more habitable, and this is actually being done in some cases. During the last year some of the casual wards have been improved—beyond recognition, if the accounts are true—and there is talk of doing the same to all of them. But this does not go to the heart of the problem. The problem is how to turn the tramp from a bored, half alive vagrant into a self-respecting human being. A mere increase of comfort cannot do this. Even if the casual wards became positively luxurious (they never will)[1] a tramp's life would still be wasted. He would still be a pauper, cut off from marriage and home life, and a dead loss to the community.

---

[1]In fairness it must be added that a few of the casual wards have been improved recently, at least from the point of view of sleeping accommodation. But most of them are the same as ever, and there has been no real improvement in the food.

What is needed is to depauperise him, and this can only be done by finding him work—not work for the sake of working, but work of which he can enjoy the benefit. At present, in the great majority of casual wards, tramps do no work whatever. At one time they were made to break stones for their food, but this was stopped when they had broken enough stone for years ahead and put the stonebreakers out of work. Nowadays they are kept idle, because there is seemingly nothing for them to do. Yet there is a fairly obvious way of making them useful, namely this: Each workhouse could run a small farm, or at least a kitchen garden, and every able-bodied tramp who presented himself could be made to do a sound day's work. The produce of the farm or garden could be used for feeding the tramps, and at the worst it would be better than the filthy diet of bread and margarine and tea. Of course, the casual wards could never be quite self-supporting, but they could go a long way towards it, and the rates would probably benefit in the long run. It must be remembered that under the present system tramps are as dead a loss to the country as they could possibly be, for they do not only do no work, but they live on a diet that is bound to undermine their health; the system, therefore, loses lives as well as money. A scheme which fed them decently, and made them produce at least a part of their own food, would be worth trying.

[1933]

JON KRAKAUER

(1954–)

Jon Krakauer first reported in *Outdoor* magazine on Chris McCandless, a graduate of Emory University who starved to death while on a personal odyssey in the Alaskan wilderness. The story generated so much attention and so many additional questions that Krakauer did further research for a book, *Into the Wild* (1995), about Chris's life and death. The author puts McCandless into a tradition of Americans who have sought escape and purity in the wilderness. With a detective's instinct and thoroughness, Krakauer pieces together the story of Chris's motives and his journey from interviews, diary entries, annotated books, and photos. Krakauer has also written on mountain climbers in *Eiger Dreams* (1997); another book, *Into Thin Air* (1998) chronicles a disastrous expedition he accompanied to Mount Everest.

In the selection that follows, taken from *Into the Wild*, Krakauer focuses on Chris McCandless at the heart of his quest, living alone in the wild. McCandless exemplifies the traveler at an extreme, romanticizing the primitive, rejecting life in settled society, and trying to subsist by hunting and gathering food.

"The Alaska Interior"

From *Into the Wild*

I wished to acquire the simplicity, native feelings, and virtues of savage life; to divest myself of the factitious habits, prejudices and imperfections of civiliza-tion; . . . and to find, amidst the solitude and grandeur of the western wilds, more correct views of human nature and of the true interests of man. The sea-son of snows was preferred, that I might experience the pleasure of suffering, and the novelty of danger.

> Estwick Evans,
> A Pedestrious Tour, of Four Thousand Miles,
> Through the Western States and Territories,
> During the Winter and Spring of 1818

Wilderness appealed to those bored or disgusted with man and his works. It not only offered an escape from society but also was an ideal stage for the roman-tic individual to exercise the cult that he frequently made of his own soul. The solitude and total freedom of the wilderness created a perfect setting for either melancholy or exultation.

> Roderick Nash,
> Wilderness and the American Mind

On April 15, 1992, Chris McCandless departed Carthage, South Dakota, in the cab of a Mack truck hauling a load of sunflower seeds: His "great Alaskan odyssey" was under way. Three days later he crossed the Canadian border at Roosville, British Columbia, and thumbed north through Skookumchuck and Radium Junction, Lake Louise and Jasper, Prince George and Dawson Creek—where, in the town center, he took a snapshot of the signpost marking the official start of the Alaska Highway. MILE "0," the sign reads, FAIRBANKS 1,523 MILES.

Hitchhiking tends to be difficult on the Alaska Highway. It's not unusual, on the outskirts of Dawson Creek, to see a dozen or more doleful-looking men and women standing along the shoulder with extended thumbs. Some of them may wait a week or more between rides. But McCandless experienced no such delay. On April 21, just six days out of Carthage, he arrived at Liard River Hot-springs, at the threshold of the Yukon Territory.

There is a public campground at Liard River, from which a boardwalk leads half a mile across a marsh to a series of natural thermal pools. It is the most popular way-stop on the Alaska Highway, and McCandless decided to pause there for a soak in the soothing waters. When he finished bathing and attempted to catch another ride north, however, he discovered that his luck had changed. Nobody would pick him up. Two days after arriving, he was still at Liard River, impatiently going nowhere.

At six-thirty on a brisk Thursday morning, the ground still frozen hard, Gaylord Stuckey walked out on the boardwalk to the largest of the pools, expecting to have the place to himself. He was surprised, therefore, to find someone already in the steaming water, a young man who introduced himself as Alex.

Stuckey—bald and cheerful, a ham-faced sixty-three-year old Hoosier—was en route from Indiana to Alaska to deliver a new motor home to a Fairbanks RV dealer, a part-time line of work in which he'd dabbled since retiring after forty years in the restaurant business. When he told McCandless his destination, the boy exclaimed, "Hey, that's where I'm going, too! But I've been stuck here for a couple of days now, trying to get a lift. You mind if I ride with you?"

"Oh, jiminy," Stuckey replied. "I'd love to, son, but I can't. The company I work for has a strict rule against picking up hitchhikers. It could get me canned." As he chatted with McCandless through the sulfurous mist, though, Stuckey began to reconsider: "Alex was clean-shaven and had short hair, and I could tell by the language he used that he was a real sharp fella. He wasn't what you'd call a typical hitchhiker. I'm usually leery of 'em. I figure there's probably something wrong with a guy if he can't even afford a bus ticket. So anyway, after about half an hour I said, 'I tell you what, Alex: Liard is a thousand miles from Fairbanks. I'll take you five hunded miles, as far as Whitehorse; you'll be able to get a ride the rest of the way from there.'"

A day and a half later, however, when they arrived in Whitehorse—the capital of the Yukon Territory and the largest, most cosmopolitan town on the Alaska Highway—Stuckey had come to enjoy McCandless's company so much that he changed his mind and agreed to drive the boy the entire distance. "Alex didn't come out and say too much at first," Stuckey reports. "But it's a long, slow drive. We spent a total of three days together on those washboard roads, and by the end he kind of let his guard down. I tell you what: He was a dandy kid. Real courteous, and he didn't cuss or use a lot of that there slang. You could tell he came from a nice family, Mostly he talked about his sister. He didn't get along with his folks too good, I guess. Told me his dad was a genius, a NASA rocket scientist, but he'd been a bigamist at one time—and that kind of went against Alex's grain. Said he hadn't seen his parents in a couple of years, since his college graduation."

McCandless was candid with Stuckey about his intent to spend the summer alone in the bush, living off the land. "He said it was something he'd wanted to do since he was little," says Stuckey. "Said he didn't want to see a single person, no airplanes, no sign of civilization. He wanted to prove to himself that he could make it on his own, without anybody else's help."

Stuckey and McCandless arrived in Fairbanks on the afternoon of April 25. The older man took the boy to a grocery store, where he bought a big bag of rice, "and then Alex said he wanted to go out to the university to study up on what kind of plants he could eat. Berries and things like that. I told him, 'Alex, you're too early. There's still two foot, three foot of snow on the ground. There's nothing growing yet.' But his mind was pretty well made up. He was champing at the bid to get out there and start hiking." Stuckey drove to the University of Alaska campus, on the west end of Fairbanks, and dropped McCandless off at 5:30 P.M.

"Before I let him out," Stuckey says, "I told him, 'Alex, I've driven you a thousand miles. I've fed you and fed you for three straight days. The least you can do is send me a letter when you get back from Alaska.' And he promised he would.

"I also begged and pleaded with him to call his parents. I can't imagine anything worse than having a son out there and not knowing where he's at for years and years, not knowing whether he's living or dead. 'Here's my credit card number,' I told him. '*Please* call them!' But all he said was 'Maybe I will and maybe I won't.' After he left, I thought, 'Oh, why didn't I get his parents' phone number and call them myself?' But everything just kind of happened so quick."

After dropping McCandless at the university, Stuckey drove into town to deliver the RV to the appointed dealer, only to be told that the person responsible for checking in new vehicles had already gone home for the day and wouldn't be back until Monday morning, leaving Stuckey with two days to kill in Fairbanks before he could fly home to Indiana. On Sunday morning, with time on his hands, he returned to the campus. "I hoped to find Alex and spend another day with him, take him sightseeing or something. I looked for a couple of hours, drove all over the place, but didn't see hide or hair of him. He was already gone."

After taking his leave of Stuckey on Saturday evening, McCandless spent two days and three nights in the vicinity of Fairbanks, mostly at the university. In the campus book store, tucked away on the bottom shelf of the Alaska section, he came across a scholarly, exhaustively researched field guide to the region's edible plants, *Tanaina Plantlore/Dena'ina K'et'una: An Ethnobotany of the Dena'ina Indians of Southcentral Alaska* by Prisilla Russell Kari. From a postcard rack near the cash register, he picked out two cards of a polar bear, on which he sent his final messages to Wayne Westerberg and Jan Burres from the university post office.

Perusing the classified ads, McCandless found a used gun to buy, a semiautomatic .22-caliber Remington with a 4-x-20 scope and a plastic stock. A model called the Nylon 66, no longer in production, it was a favorite of Alaska trappers because of its light weight and reliability. He closed the deal in a parking lot, probably paying about $125 for the weapon, and then purchased four one-hunded-round boxes of hollow-point long-rifle shells from a nearby gun shop.

At the conclusion of his preparations in Fairbanks, McCandless loaded up his pack and started hiking west from the university. Leaving the campus, he walked past the Geophysical Institute, a tall glass-and-concrete building capped with a large satellite dish. The dish, one of the most distinctive landmarks on the Fairbanks skyline, had been erected to collect data from satellites equipped with synthetic aperture radar of Walt McCandless's design. Walt had in fact visited Fairbanks during the start-up of the receiving station and had written some of the software crucial to its opeation. If the Geophysical Institute prompted Chris to think of his father as he tramped by, the boy left no record of it.

Four miles west of town, in the evening's deepening chill, McCandless pitched his tent on a patch of hard-frozen ground surrounded by birch trrees, not far from the crest of a bluff overlooking Gold Hill Gas & Liquor. Fifty yards from his camp was the terraced road cut of the George Parks Highway, the road that would take him to the Stampede Trail. He woke early on the morning of April 28, walked down to the highway in the predawn gloaming, and was pleasantly surprised when the first vehicle to come along pulled over to give him a lift. It was a gray Ford pickup with a bumper sticker on the back that declared, I FISH THEREFORE I AM. PETERSBURG, ALASKA. The driver of the truck, an electrician on his way to Anchorage, wasn't much older than McCandless. He said his name was Jim Gallien.

Three hours later Gallien turned his truck west off the highway and drove as far as he could down an unplowed side road. When he dropped McCandless off on the Stampede Trail, the temperature was in the low thirties—it would drop into the low teens at night—and a foot and a half of crusty spring snow covered the ground. The boy could hardly contain his excitement. He was, at long last, about to be alone in the vast Alaska wilds.

As he trudged expectantly down the trail in a fake-fur parka, his rifle slung over one shoulder, the only food McCandless carried was a ten-pound bag of long-grained rice—and the two sandwiches and a bag of corn chips that Gallien had contributed. A year earlier he'd subsisted for more than a month beside the Gulf of California on five pounds of rice and a bounty of fish caught with a cheap rod and reel, an experience that made him confident he could harvest enough food to survive an extended stay in the Alaska wilderness, too.

The heaviest item in McCandless's half-full backpack was his library: nine or ten paperbound books, most of which had been given to him by Jan Burres in Niland. Among these volumes were titles by Thoreau and Tolstoy and Gogol, but McCandless was no literary snob: He simply carried what he thought he might enjoy reading, including mass-market books by Michael Crichton, Robert Pirsig, and Louis L'Amour. Having neglected to pack writing paper, he began a laconic journal on some blank pages in the back of *Tanaina Plantlore*.

The Healy terminus of the Stampede Trail is traveled by a handful of dog mushers, ski tourers, and snow-machine enthusiasts during the winter months, but only until the frozen rivers begin to break up, in late March or early April. By the time McCandless headed into the bush, there was open water flowing on most of the larger streams, and nobody had been very far down the trail for two or three weeks; only the faint remnants of a packed snow-machine track remained for him to follow.

McCandless reached the Teklanika River his second day out. Although the banks were lined with a jagged shelf of frozen overflow, no ice bridges spanned the channel of open water, so he was forced to wade. There had been a big thaw in early April, and breakup had come early in 1992, but the weather had turned cold again, so the river's volume was quite low when McCandless crossed—probably thigh-deep at most—allowing him to splash to the other side without difficulty. He never suspected that in so doing, he was crossing his Rubicon. To McCandless's inexperienced eye, there was nothing to suggest that two months hence, as the glaciers and snowfields at the Teklanika's headwater thawed in the summer heat, its discharge would multiply nine or ten times in volume, transforming the river into a deep, violent torrent that bore no resemblance to the gentle brook he'd blithely waded across in April.

From his journal we know that on April 29, McCandless fell through the ice somewhere. It probably happened as he traversed a series of melting beaver ponds just beyond the Teklanika's western bank, but there is nothing to indicate that he suffered any harm in the mishap. A day later, as the trail crested a ridge, he got his first glimpse of Mt. McKinley's high, blinding-white bulwarks, and a day after that, May 1, some twenty miles down the trail from where he was dropped by Gallien, he stumbled upon the old bus beside the Sushana River. It was outfitted with a bunk and a barrel stove, and previous visitors had left the improvised shelter stocked with matches, bug dope, and other essentials. "Magic Bus Day," he wrote in his journal. He decided to lay over for a while in the vehicle and take advantage of its crude comforts.

He was elated to be there. Inside the bus, on a sheet of weathered plywood spanning a broken window, McCandless scrawled an exultant declaration of independence:

TWO YEARS HE WALKS THE EARTH. NO PHONE, NO POOL, NO PETS, NO CIGARETTES. ULTI-MATE FREEDOM. AN EXTREMIST. AN AESTHETIC VOYAGER WHOSE HOME IS THE ROAD. ESCAPED FROM ATLANTA. THOU SHALT NOT RETURN, 'CAUSE "THE WEST IS THE BEST." AND NOW AFTER TWO RAMBLING YEARS COMES THE FINAL AND GREATEST ADVENTURE. THE CLI-MACTIC BATTLE TO KILL THE FALSE BEING WITHIN AND VICTORIOUSLY CONCLUDE THE SPIR-ITUAL PILGRIMAGE. TEN DAYS AND NIGHTS OF FREIGHT TRAINS AND HITCHHIKING BRING HIM TO THE GREAT WHITE NORTH. NO LONGER TO BE POISONED BY CIVILIZATION HE FLEES, AND WALKS ALONE UPON THE LAND TO BECOME LOST IN THE WILD.

ALEXANDER SUPERTRAMP
MAY 1992

Reality, however, was quick to intrude on McCandless's reverie. He had difficulty killing game, and the daily journal entries during his first week in the bush include "Weakness," "Snowed in," and "Disaster." He saw but did not shoot a grizzly on May 2, shot at but missed some ducks on May 4, and finally killed and ate a spruce grouse on May 5; but he didn't shoot anything else until May 9, when he bagged a single small squirrel, by which point he'd written "4th day famine" in the journal.

But soon thereafter his fortunes took a sharp turn for the better. By mid-May the sun was circling high in the heavens, flooding the taiga with light. The sun dipped below the northern horizon for fewer than four hours out of every twenty-four, and at midnight the sky was still bright enough to read by. Everywhere but on the north-facing slopes and in the shadowy ravines, the snowpack had melted down to bare ground, exposing the previous season's rose hips and lingonberries, which McCandless gathered and ate in great quantity.

He also became much more successful at hunting game and for the next six weeks feasted regularly on squirrel, spruce grouse, duck, goose, and porcupine. On May 22, a crown fell off one of his molars, but the event didn't seem to dampen his spirits much, because the following day he scrambled up the nameless, humplike, three-thousand-foot butte that rises directly north of the bus, giving him a view of the whole icy sweep of the Alaska Range and mile after mile of uninhabited country. His journal entry for the day is characteristically terse but unmistakably joyous: "CLIMB MOUNTAIN!"

McCandless had told Gallien that he intended to remain on the move during his stay in the bush. "I'm just going to take off and keep walking west," he'd said. "I might walk all the way to the Bering Sea." On May 5, after pausing for four days at the bus, he resumed his perambulation. From the snapshots recovered with his Minolta, it appears that McCandless lost (or intentionally left) the by now indistinct Stampede Trail and headed west and north through the hills above the Sushana River, hunting game as he went.

It was slow going. In order to feed himself, he had to devote a large part of each day to stalking animals. Moreover, as the ground thawed, his route turned into a gauntlet of boggy muskeg and impenetrable alder, and McCandless belatedly came to appreciate one of the fundamental (if counterintuitive) axioms of the North: winter, not summer, is the preferred season for traveling overland through the bush.

Faced with the obvious folly of his original ambition, to walk five hundred miles to tidewater, he reconsidered his plans. On May 19, having traveled no farther west than the Toklat River—less than fifteen miles beyond the bus—he turned around. A week later he was back at the derelict vehicle, apparently without regret. He'd decided that the Sushana drainage was plenty wild to suit his purposes and that Fairbanks bus 142 would make a fine base camp for the remainder of the summer.

Ironically, the wilderness surrounding the bus—the patch of overgrown country where McCandless was determined "to become lost in the wild"— scarcely qualifies as wilderness by Alaska standards. Less than thirty miles to the east is a major thoroughfare, the George Parks Highway. Just sixteen miles to the north, beyond an escarpment of the Outer Range, hundreds of tourists rumble daily into Denali Park over a road patrolled by the National Park Service. And unbeknownst to the Aesthetic Voyager, scattered within a six-mile radius of the bus are four cabins (although none happened to be occupied during the summer of 1992).

But despite the relative proximity of the bus to civilization, for all practical purposes McCandless was cut off from the rest of the world. He spent nearly four months in the bush all told, and during that period he didn't encounter another living soul. In the end the Sushana River site was sufficiently remote to cost him his life.

In the last week of May, after moving his few possessions into the bus, McCandless wrote a list of housekeeping chores on a parchmentlike strip of birch bark: collect and store ice from the river for refrigerating meat, cover the vehicle's missing windows with plastic, lay in a supply of firewood, clean the accumulation of old ash from the stove. And under the heading "<u>LONG TERM</u>" he drew up a list of more ambitious tasks: map the area, improvise a bathtub, collect skins and feathers to sew into clothing, construct a bridge across a nearby creek, repair mess kit, blaze a network of hunting trails.

The diary entries following his return to the bus catalog a bounty of wild meat. May 28: "Gourmet Duck!" June 1 "5 Squirrel." June 2: 'Porcupine, Ptarmigan, 4 Squirrel, Grey Bird." June 3: "Another Porcupine! 4 Squirrel, 2 Grey Bird, Ash Bird." June 4: "A THIRD PORCUPINE! Squirrel, Grey Bird." On June 5, he shot a Canada goose as big as a Christmas turkey. Then, on June 9, he bagged the biggest prize of all: "<u>MOOSE!</u>" he recorded in the journal. Overjoyed, the proud hunter took a photograph of himself kneeling over his trophy, rifle thrust triumphantly overhead, his features distorted in a rictus of ecstasy and amazement, like some unemployed janitor who'd gone to Reno and won a million-dollar jackpot.

Although McCandless was enough of a realist to know that hunting game was an unavoidable component of living off the land, he had always been ambivalent about killing animals. That ambivalence turned to remorse soon after he shot the moose. It was relatively small, weighing perhaps six hundred or seven hundred pounds, but it nevertheless amounted to a huge quantity of meat. Believing that it was morally indefensible to waste any part of an animal that has been shot for food, McCandless spent six days toiling to preserve what he had killed before it spoiled. He butchered the carcass under a thick cloud of flies and mosquitoes, boiled the organs into a stew, and then laboriously excavated a burrow in the face of the rocky stream bank directly below the bus, in which he tried to cure, by smoking, the immense slabs of purple flesh.

Alaskan hunters know that the easiest way to preserve meat in the bush is to slice it into thin strips and then air-dry it on a makeshift rack. But McCandless, in his naïveté, relied on the advice of hunters he'd consulted in South Dakota, who advised him to smoke his meat, not an easy task under the circumstances. "Butchering extremely difficult," he wrote in the journal on June 10. "Fly and mosquito hordes. Remove intestines, liver, kidneys, one lung, steaks. Get hindquarters and leg to stream."

June 11: "Remove heart and other lung. Two front legs and head. Get rest to stream. Haul near cave. Try to protect with smoker."

June 12: "Remove half rib-cage and steaks. Can only work nights. Keep smokers going."

June 13: "Get remainder of rib-cage, shoulder and neck to cave. Start smoking."

June 14: "Maggots already! Smoking appears ineffective. Don't know, looks like disaster. I now wish I had never shot the moose. One of the greatest tragedies of my life."

At that point he gave up on preserving the bulk of the meat and abandoned the carcass to the wolves. Although he castigated himself severely for this waste of a life he'd taken, a day later McCandless appeared to regain some perspective, for his journal notes, "henceforth will learn to accept my errors, however great they be."

Shortly after the moose episode McCandless began to read Thoreau's *Walden*. In the chapter titled "Higher Laws," in which Thoreau ruminates on the morality of eating, McCandless highlighted, "when I had caught and cleaned and cooked and eaten my fish, they seemed not to have fed me essentially. It was insignificant and unnecessary, and cost more than it came to."

"THE MOOSE,' McCandless wrote in the margin. And in the same passage he marked,

The repugnance to animal food is not the effect of experience, but is an instinct. It appeared more beautiful to live low and fare hard in many respects; and though I never did so, I went far enough to please my imagination. I believe that every man who has ever been earnest to preserve his higher or poetic faculties in the best condition has been particularly inclined to abstain from animal food, and from much food of any kind. . . .

It is hard to provide and cook so simple and clean a diet as will not offend the imagination; but this, I think, is to be fed when we feed the body; they should both sit down at the same table. Yet perhaps this may be done. The fruits eaten temperately need not make us ashamed of our appetites, nor interrupt the worthiest pursuits. But put an extra condiment into your dish, and it will poison you.

"YES," wrote McCandless and, two pages later, "<u>Consciousness</u> of food. Eat and cook with <u>concentration</u>. . . . Holy Food." On the back pages of the book that served as his journal, he declared:

> *I am reborn. This is my dawn. <u>Real</u> life has just begun.*
>
> <u>*Deliberate Living:*</u> *Conscious attention to the basics of life, and a constant attention to your immediate environment and its concerns, example→ A job, a task, a book; anything requiring efficient concentration (Circumstance has no value. It is how one <u>relates</u> to a situation that has value. All true meaning resides in the personal relationship to a phenomenon, what it means to you).*
>
> *The Great Holiness of* **FOOD**, *the Vital Heat.*
>
> <u>*Positivism,*</u> *the Insurpassable Joy of the Life Aesthetic.*
>
> *Absolute Truth and Honesty.*
>
> *Reality.*
>
> *Independence.*
>
> *Finality–Stability–Consistency.*

As McCandless gradually stopped rebuking himself for the waste of the moose, the contentment that began in mid-May resumed and seemed to continue through early July. Then, in the midst of this idyll, came the first of two pivotal setbacks.

Satisfied, apparently, with what he had learned during his two months of solitary life in the wild, McCandless decided to return to civilization: It was time to bring his "final and greatest adventure" to a close and get himself back to the world of men and women, where he could chug a beer; talk philosophy, enthrall strangers with tales of what he'd done. He seemed to have moved beyond his need to assert so adamantly his autonomy, his need to separate himself from his parents. Maybe he was prepared to forgive their imperfections; maybe he was even prepared to forgive some of his own. McCandless seemed ready, perhaps, to go home.

Or maybe not; we can do no more than speculate about what he intended to do after he walked out of the bush. There is no question, however, that he intended to walk out.

Writing on a piece of birch bark, he made a list of things to do before he departed: "Patch Jeans, Shave!, Organize pack. . . ." Shortly thereafter he propped his Minolta on an empty oil drum and took a snapshot of himself brandishing a yellow disposable razor and grinning at the camera, clean-shaven, with new patches cut from an army blanket stitched onto the knees of his filthy jeans. He looks healthy but alarmingly gaunt. Already his cheeks are sunken. The tendons in his neck stand out like taut cables.

On July 2, McCandless finished reading Tolstoy's "Family Happiness," having marked several passaages that moved him:

He was right in saying that the only certain happiness in life is to live for others. . . .

I have lived through much, and now I think I have found what is needed for happiness. A quiet secluded life in the country, with the possibility of being useful to people to whom it is easy to do good, and who are not accustomed to have it done to them; then work which one hopes may be of some use; then rest, nature, books, music, love for one's neighbor—such is my idea of happiness. And then, on top of all that, you for a mate, and children, perhaps—what more can the heart of a man desire?

Then, on July 3, he shouldered his backpack and began the twenty-mile hike to the improved road. Two days later, halfway there, he arrived in heavy rain at the beaver ponds that blocked access to the west bank of the Teklanika River. In April they'd been frozen over and hadn't presented an obstacle. Now he must have been alarmed to find a three-acre lake covering the trail. To avoid having to wade through the murky chest-deep water, he scrambled up a steep hillside, bypassed the ponds of the north, and then dropped back down to the river at the mouth of the gorge.

When he'd first crossed the river, sixty-seven days earlier in the freezing temperatures of April, it had been an icy but gentle knee-deep creek, and he'd simply strolled across it. On July 5, however, the Teklanika was at full flood, swollen with rain and snowmelt from glaciers high in the Alaska Range, running cold and fast.

If he could reach the far shore, the remainder of the hike to the highway would be easy, but to get there he would have to negotiate a channel some one hundred feet wide. The water, opaque with glacial sediment and only a few degrees warmer than the ice it had so recently been, was the color of wet concrete. Too deep to wade, it rumbled like a freight train. The powerful current would quickly knock him off his feet and carry him away.

McCandless was a weak swimmer and had confessed to several people that he was in fact afraid of the water. Attempting to swim the numbingly cold torrent or even to paddle some sort of improvised raft across seemed too risky to consider. Just downstream from where the trail met the river, the Teklanika erupted into a chaos of boiling whitewater as it accelerated through the narrow gorge. Long before he could swim or paddle to the far shore, he'd be pulled into these rapids and drowned.

In his journal he now wrote, "Disaster. . . . Rained in. River look impossible. Lonely, scared." He concluded, correctly, that he would probably be swept to his death if he attempted to cross the Teklanika at that place, in those conditions. It would be suicidal; it was simply not an option.

If McCandless had walked a mile or so upstream, he would have discovered that the river broadened into a maze of braided channels. If he'd scouted carefully, by trial and error he might have found a place where these braids were only chest-deep. As strong as the current was running, it would have certainly knocked him off his feet, but by dog-paddling and hopping along the bottom as he drifted downstream, he could conceivably have made it across before being carried into the gorge or succumbing to hypothermia.

But it would still have been a very risky proposition, and at that point McCandless had no reason to take such a risk. He'd been fending for himself quite nicely in the country. He probably understood that if he was patient and waited, the river would eventually drop to a level where it cxould be safely forded. After weighing his options, therefore, he settled on the most prudent course. He turned around and began walking to the west, back toward the bus, back into the fickle heart of the bush.

[1995]

REBECCA SOLNIT

(1961–)

British writer Rebecca Solnit has studied travel extensively from very different critical perspectives. *Wanderlust* (2000) is a cultural history of walking; *Savage Dreams: A Journey into the Hidden Wars of the American West* (1994) combines travel with documentary journalism. *As Eve Said to the Serpent* (2001) examines how gender affects the representation of landscape.

In *A Book of Migrations: Some Passages in Ireland* (1997), which is excerpted below, Solnit journeys around Ireland and hears repeatedly about the "Travellers," itinerant people who have a history of controversy among the Irish, just as gypsies everywhere have stirred the imaginations and the moral disapproval of settled societies. Like settled people in any country, the Irish generally look more favorably upon tourists with money to spend than upon modern nomads like gypsies.

"Travellers"

From A Book of Migrations: Some Passages in Ireland

I couldn't tell when my ride was supposed to come to an end. I had been keeping an eye on a young woman with heavy gold hoops in her ears I thought might be a Traveller, but she got off before we came to anything that looked like a prison, and so I asked the bus driver where Wheatfields Prison was. When he found out I was looking for the Clondalkin Traveller site at the walls of the prison his middleaged face hitherto as bland as a sofa cushion bunched up in fury. "Why are you interested in *them?*" he demanded, and I said noncommittal things. His rage increased and he said that they had killed the son of his friend "and the boy was just going on fifteen, he was a lovely lad. And they sat outside the courthouse laughing and drinking. Him as did it got only nine months but the boy's gone forever. As far as I'm concerned, they're the scum of the earth." All of them, I asked, and he said yes. I asked him if he'd ever spoken to any of them, and he said he didn't need to, and why was I going to? I'd been invited to visit, I said, and thought I'd see for myself. Not for nothing was I raised by a fair-housing activist, and I threw in a few platitudes about not judging a whole population by the actions of an individual.

Hate had entered my holiday, along with nomads. My travels up the west coast of Ireland had come to an end with a question about Travellers, a question only Dublin seemed capable of answering, and Dublin had answered it with a swarm of facts, a few encounters, and an invitation to visit a Traveller family. We had come to the end of the line on this bus route from downtown Dublin, and the bus driver insisted that I stand up and hold onto the pole next to his seat so he could give me a private tour of the suburban tragedy he was so bitter about. With an angry sweep of the arm he showed me the bare earth rectangle full of bare new blocks of houses where his friend lived. And as he turned around on his route on this muggy afternoon, he showed me the cemetery where the boy was buried and the camp where the killer—an inadvertent killer by means of drunk driving—lived; I wondered if the driver had done his time in Wheatfields Prison so that the whole story was all at the end of this bus line.

The bus driver also wanted to show me where they—some Travellers, but to him all Travellers—had broken into a waterpipe, "and if you or I did it we'd be punished for it." He seemed as furious that they weren't paying for the water as that his friend's son had died. We passed a wide lawn with a row of little concrete plugs along its perimeter to prevent any Travellers from pulling over to camp and, on the other side of the road, a pipe pointing straight up and trickling water and an encampment of a few trailers with debris scattered around them. If this is what freeloading looked like, it didn't look very luxurious. He finally let me go on a nondescript road with directions to walk down it until I saw the prison—and the admonition, Be careful, it's a mugger's paradise. With its weedy bulldozer heaps and brand new rows of identical houses, it looked more like the road to nowhere, and I set off down it with my offering of peaches and cherries weighing heavier and heavier on this hot June day.

All along my meander up the west coast the people I met had been murmuring stray facts and opinions about Travellers, as Ireland's indigenous nomadic people are currently called. A woman who apparently lived in a trailer herself, outside one of the hostels in Bantry, had told me that they were grand people if you got to know them, though few enough did. While I was walking with the giantess in Ennis a sandyhaired boy of nine or ten had begged change from us and acknowledged he was a Traveller when I gave him a coin, but he was too cringing to tell me more. When the man who drove me to Galway had exhausted the subject of stone walls I'd asked him about Travellers. He told me a story about how Galway is divided into four quadrants, and each quadrant had been shirking responsibility for building a halting site for Travellers for so long that the bishop of Galway had offered the land next to his palace. I had seen Travellers' big black and white carthorses grazing by the dump near Portumna and a long row of trailers on the narrow shoulder of the road back to Galway. Sister Kathleen had said her family always had a load of turf or a can of milk for the Travellers who came by the farm when she was a girl and they were called Tinkers. Bride in Westport had amplified that, saying the primitiveness of the Travellers' lifestyle was only contextual and recent; she herself had grown up in a farmhouse without running water, and they got along well with the Travellers who came along then. Later on, Lee in Ballydehob wrote me a letter about encountering a Travelling man who was standing up in his cart and driving his team of heavy horses at a full gallop, with a gleam of joy and sense of power in his face, and their eyes met in a moment of camaraderie and recognition. Hated, isolated, and sometimes admired, but why? . . .

All over Europe, similar versions of the conflict between nomads and the sedentary majority are taking place, and though nomad sympathizers and supporters exist, they are themselves often a minority. Nomads are literally unsettling for sedentary populations, or at least those intent on ethnic nationalism. They move through the continuous landscape of roads rather than within the closed loop of borders, stitching the distances together with their circuits. If nomads are indigenous they disturb the idea of a homogeneous folk with roots in the native soil; if they're not, they're considered invaders—and in many places, several centuries of residence haven't qualified Gypsies as natives in the eyes of their neighbors and sometimes their governments. "Their very existence constituted dissidence," Jean-Pierre Liégeois says of Gypsies, and death, imprisonment, expulsion, enslavement, and forced settlement are among the punishments that have been meted out for nomadism in Europe.

* * *

. . . no one knows exactly at what point Travellers emerged from the rest of Irish society. The term *Traveller* itself has been accepted in the last few decades as the

Travellers' own more civil alternative to *Tinker*, a word which like *Negro* has become derogatory, and to *itinerant*, with its social-worker overtones. Too, Travelling, as it is sometimes capitalized, is foundational to the group's distinct identity, unlike the fading craft of tinsmithing or tinkering. Those who consider nomadism a deviant or dissolute way of life often suggest that Travellers are nothing more than refugees from the economic crises of the potato Famine and perhaps of Cromwell, people who took to the road as beggars and don't know how to get off the road. The idea that it is a very recent way of life or not a way of life, a culture, at all, that it is only a crisis condition of marginal and subnormal people, accords well with the idea that Travelling is a problem to which integration into sedentary life is the solution. A group of Travellers emigrated to the United States during the Famine and remains a distinct group in Georgia, retaining some of the nomadism, language, and other ethnic hallmarks, making it clear that the culture or ethnicity was fully developed a century and a half ago.

Travellers themselves sometimes tell a story akin to that of the Wandering Jew, in which they are the descendants of the metalworker who made the nails for the Crucifixion and for that deed were sentenced to wander the earth until the end of time. In her study of Travellers, Artelia Court proposes possible links to the outcasts and wandering craftspeople of pre-Christian Celtic society in Ireland. External evidence suggests that some version of the Travellers existed as far back as the twelfth century, when references to "tinklers" and "tynkers" appear; an English law against "wandering Irish" was passed in 1243. Travellers have a language or dialect of their own called *cant*, *shelta*, or *gammon*, which scrambles words of Irish and English derivation, and one of the strongest arguments for the ancientness of the culture is that their word for priest, *cuinne*, is an old term for druids, otherwise known only from ancient manuscripts. Other linguistic elements suggest roots before the twelfth century. But all the evidence is slight: there are clearly wandering craftspeople and beggars and references that mingle Gypsies and Tinkers from the sixteenth century onward, but there are few details. Tinkers are not Gypsies; they are as fair-skinned and Catholic as anyone in Ireland, and it has been proposed that though Gypsies spread all the way from their origins in India to England, they never reached Ireland because their commercial-nomad niche was already filled by Tinkers. At the turn of the twentieth century, Synge wrote of Tinkers along with all other denizens of the road, but the distinctions are blurred. It seems as though so many groups were wandering the roads for so many reasons that Travellers didn't stand out very dramatically, until everyone else stopped moving.

It is now a matter of debate whether they constitute a distinct ethnic group. Some Travellers seem to want the legal protection and cultural recognition such an identity would confer; others, to think that such status would further alienate them from the mainstream of Irish life. In their report on the ethnic issue, the National Federation of the Irish Travelling People declared, "In their deep religious feeling, generosity and attachment to the family, Travellers have clung to aspects of Irish life to a far greater extent than the settled community." Much of what the sedentary Irish say about the Travellers is what the English and Anglo-Americans once said about the Irish: they drink, they brawl, they have too many children and too little work ethic, they're improvident, dirty, and lawless. The very terms in which the sedentary speak suggest that the Travellers have preservd the tribal and not yet European culture of an earlier Ireland.

Kerby Miller, in his history of Irish emigration to North America, writes about the ways in which the Catholic Irish were at odds with the industrial and Protestant-dominated societies they found themselves in: they "seemed so premodern that to bourgeois observers from business-minded cultures, the native Irish often appeared 'feckless,' 'childlike' and 'irresponsible'. . . . The shrewdest recognized that ancient communal values and work habits persisted despite commercialization. . . . In adddition, the Catholic lower classes seemed to lack bourgeois concepts of time and deferred gratification. . . ." Court writes of the "antiquated traditions and artifacts that had vanished elsewhere but which Ireland possessed in abundance" after the Second World War, adding, "And even among these countrymen the Tinkers were conspicuous for remaining doggedly true to themselves." "We are Irish," insisted placards at some Travellers' rights demonstrations in the 1980s, since their differences from the mainstream were regarded as alien rather than anachronistic. It may be that the Travellers stand out for not having changed enough in a society that has transformed itself radically in the last several decades.

Though possessing ancient origins may, for the sedentary scholars of Travellers, confer greater legitimacy on them, it is apparently of less interest to the subjects themselves. The authenticity of origins, the historical basis for identity, may not be their method. That notion more than almost anything convinced me that they did constitute a distinct culture or subculture in this history-haunted place. The anthropologist Sinéad Ní Shuinear writes, "Some nomadic peoples—the Jews of the Old Testament spring immediately to mind—cultivate both literacy and historical memory. Others, even without literacy, enshrine genealogy and significant events into formal litanies to be memorised and passed on verbatim by specialists. But others still—and this includes most commercial nomadic groups—treat the past itself as a sort of baggage which would tie them down in the present. Instead, they cultivate an intense present-time orientation, living in a perpetual now, deriving their sense of identity not from taproots deep into the past, but from vast networks of living kin. The essence of Gypsy and Traveller culture is its fluidity. Gypsies and Travellers everywhere are supremely indifferent to their own origins." She cites the Italian anthropologist, Leonardo Piasere, who "argues that Gypsies and Travellers are not ignorant illiterates, but have very deliberately rejected literacy, knowing that it would solidify the past, thus imposing a baggage of precedent curtailing flexibility in the present." Like the Western Shoshone and other nomads, Travellers traditionally destroy all the belongings of a person who has died, a process that tends to rule out heirlooms and vast accumulation, a means of keeping its practitioners even materially in the present.

The French theorists and nomad enthusiasts Deleuze and Guattari declare that the hierarchical model of the tree has dominated too much of Western thought and offer in its place the rhizome, the loosely structured, horizontally spreading root system of plants such as strawberries; Ní Shuinear's proposal that Travellers are organized socially and imaginatively around contemporary networks rather than historical taproots echoes their metaphor. The intimation of such a radically divergent sense of time, space, and society electrified me, but other information and conversation tempered my romanticism. The enormous contemporary enthusiasm for nomads—the romanticism that has brought into being so many boutiques, tattoo parlors, artists' projects, pseudoethnic recordings, and books with "nomad" in their names—is premised on the dubious idea that nomads embody on a mass scale the freedom of the solitary traveler, the romantic figure silhouetted against an exotic landscape like the individualist tree. For those of us who are largely sedentary, travel is a way out of the world that surrounds us, but nomads rarely if ever leave their world: it moves with them. The Traveller activist Michael McDonagh explains that "for Travellers, the physical fact of moving is just one aspect of a nomadic mind-set that permeates every aspect of our lives. Nomadism entails a way of looking at the world, a different way of perceiving things, a different attitude to accommodation, to work, and life in general. Just as settled people remain settled people even when they travel, Travellers remain Travellers even when they are not travelling."

The spatial freedom that might otherwise dissolve their society and identity altogether as it does for us temporarily, as respite, vacation, and escape, is counterbalanced by a greater rigidity of social structure. Architecture and geography hold our lives in place—identities built into the layout of the house, the status of the address, and the routine of the day—but custom alone must hold theirs in lieu of place and therefore must surround them as surely and solidly as a locale. The nomad's fluidity of time and space and work and property all occur within a stubbornly conservative culture perpetuated in tightly knit families. Likewise extreme feats of travel have little to do with nomads. It is exhilarating that individuals should walk the length of a continent or carry a sixty-pound pack over the remote mountains, but such feats are for solitary adventurers in their prime, not for groups for whom travel is a permanent condition including all the goods and generations, and certainly not for commercial nomads like the Travellers and Gypsies who earn their living from interactions with the sedentary community. Still, one romantic attribute remains, that of movement itself, of the constantly shifting scene, the unpredictable life lived closer to the bone of those in motion, uninsulated by the buildings and goods and familiarity of settled life: that is a romanticism Travellers and sedentary people seem to share.

Travellers have traditionally been self-employed or temporarily employed, surviving on a plethora of skills and talents, and often shifting roles and images to accord with the work—abjection for begging, an air of responsibility for contract labor. Indeed much of what seems to be considered Traveller and Gypsy dishonesty is the art of saying what works and pleases in wildly varying and often hostile circumstances. Taking permanent jobs conflicts with the fluid autonomy of their identity, argue some of the sociologists of Travelling. They may be the last people in the industrialized world to have collectively escaped wage labor, escaped selling their time and setting their lives to someone else's schedule, but the price of their social redemption seems to be the surrender of the fluidity of their labor, spatial, and temporal structures via the taking of jobs. By many accounts and oral histories, Travellers who get ahead often take it as an opportunity to take time off or travel, disregarding the longterm security to which the wage earner aspires. Freya Stark, the travel writer who spent years among the pastoralist nomads of the Muslim world, writes, "The life of insecurity is the nomad's achievement. He does not try, like our building world, to believe in a stability which is non-existent; and in his constant movement with the seasons, in the lightness of his hold, puts something right, about which we are constantly wrong. His is in fact the reality, to which the most solid of our structures are illusion; and the ramshackle tents in their crooked gaiety, with cooking pots propped up before them and animals about, show what a current flows round all the stone erections of the ages."

In the picture most accounts paint, Travellers throughout the first half of the twentieth century continued their professions of tinsmithing (from which the term *tinker* comes—the tinkers or tinsmiths made many of the milking cans, buckets, pots, and pans farm families used), horsetraining and trading, begging, fortunetelling, selling balladsheets, handicrafts, and other small items, and working as migrant agricultural and manual labor, encountering hostility and some brutality but at levels that allowed them to continue to be nomadic. They Travelled mostly on backroads and consorted mostly with rural people—one Traveller term for the sedentary is *country people*—though they found work in English cities and the outskirts of Irish towns from time to time. They were appreciated for their skills, wares, and the news and novelty they brought to isolated communities. They were disliked for begging, for sometimes sneaking their horses into farmers' fields and crops to graze, for the dishonesty with which nomads often deal with sedentary people, for theft and suspected theft, and maybe for being an unfamiliar intrusion into familiar landscapes. It isn't clear when they began using barreltop wagons, but they seem to have pitched roadside tents made of hazel branches and some kind of tarp beforehand. Anyone who has encountered the wet Irish land and sky can appreciate how strong the nomadic impulse must be to survive in those circumstances (partially settled Travellers now often say they yearn to roam in the summertime, when the weather is fine).

In the 1950s and 1960s horsedrawn wagons began to be replaced by cars pulling trailers, and horses are now kept more for pleasure than for use (though tourists can rent facsimiles of the wagons, complete with horse, and play Gypsy on the backroads; I had seen such a rental site in Westport). It may have been cars and the concomitant shrinkage of distance and access to manufactured goods that doomed their symbiosis with the countryside; it is often said that plastic did in their way of life. Handmade tinware was replaced by mass-manufactured goods, and as distances shrank and cars replaced horses Travellers' functions as pedlars and horsetraders also eroded. Roadsides were relandscaped to make roadside camping difficult or impossible across the country, unregulated space dried up, and they began to stay longer wherever they were, however unwelcome, since finding another halting site would be hard. Ironically, hostility seems to make them stay rather than go. There are regulations that halting sites and housing must be built for them, but many projects have been delayed by opposition and many that do exist are inadequate or inappropriate in their design. In the 1970s a Traveller told an oral historian, "For a woman a house is a grand thing for her to put the children in. But for a man a house is only a payment of rents. . . . Lots of travellers have houses in the winter and they leaves them lonely when they take to the roads in the summer. It's only a bother having the house and it's not healthy to be shut inside them four walls with no trees in sight and only the windys to keep you half breathing. No, I'd sleep in a stables before I'd sleep in a house. . . ."

Travellers now appear to be something of a displaced population, in flight from the destruction of rural life as much as any farm people, but they are seen less as refugees than intruders wherever they go. Many have ended up on the periphery of towns and cities, and some have gone to England. The programs of forcing them to settle into fixed houses are over, but the elimination of the necessary sites and circumstances for Travelling continues, as do some voluntary housing programs. Though Travellers are central to the scrap metal and car parts industries in Ireland, and a few Travelling families have become wealthy antique dealers (and, because of their wealth, are seldom counted as Travellers), a high pecentage are on the dole. In a country with more than 20 percent unemployment overall and intense exclusion of Travellers from all institutions, welfare dependency is not surprising. But in addition to the suspicion nomads and minorities usually attract, the Travellers are now hated with the peculiar fury taxpayers reserve for those they consider freeloaders.

Most recently the authorities have become better at navigating a middle ground, of providing housing adapted to the needs and customs of these increasingly immobilized nomads. In such a housing complex did Cathleen McDonagh and her family live, up against the walls of Wheatfield Prison. I recognized it from the Travellers' parish worker's description: a double row of diminutive houses with wide driveways, arranged in two lines flanking a central green, with a high gray prison wall behind looking like the back of a stage set. When I reached the grass a group of little boys ran up to greet me and inspect me. They were tough, scruffy, but polite, and I could tell I wouldn't get far without their cooperation. So I told the one who seemed to be the leader, a stout, chestnut-haired boy of about ten in an undershirt, who I was looking for. She's my cousin, he said, and began to lead me to her trailer. The boys asked if I was a social worker, and I told them that I was a writer from America. I knew that would keep them busy for a while and it did; they too had to know who I'd back in the World Cup. A middleaged man came up to us, another inspector; I introduced myself and we shook hands. It was John McDonagh, Cathleen's father, a powerful-looking, big-bellied man whose mild face gave him a horse's air of harmless power. Cathleen, he told me, was in her sister's house, and so we doubled back the way the boys had led me, and he took me into a kitchen with a plump woman—the sister—washing lettuce, a child in a high chair and another one roaming around the tiny room, and Cathleen sitting and talking. She showed me around the tidy house, which was bigger than it looked from outside, showed me her nieces sitting on the edge of their bed knitting and looking very diligent for girls of twelve or so, and took me into the parlor. I perched among the fat lace pillows on the sofa, facing the corner cabinet of richly colored dishes, the mantelpiece's two plates depicting a horse fair, and my hostess.

In her cut-off jeans and black t-shirt, she looked much much more at ease than in the long patterned skirt in the Dublin office. I had met her at the Travellers' Parish, where she was studying to advance her education beyond the primary-school level where she had left off, and to gain the skills to become a Travellers' rights advocate. She was a bigboned, broadshouldered woman of my own age—early thirties—with high cheekbones and powerful pale blue eyes beneath her thick brown hair. In the parlor, amid the lace and china, she continued to talk of prejduce in the low, flat voice she'd used before, a voice that sounded both cowed and resistant. She spoke in examples rather than abstractions. She spoke of how every Traveller is held accountable for the acts of any one of them. Of how when Travellers misbehave, they tend to do so in public—almost every aspect of their lives is much more visible, outdoors and by the roadside—

and thus gain an exaggerated reputation for drinking and brawling. Of how they don't want special treatment, only the rights of the rest of the citizenry: access to the same education, entry to the same places, housing or at least halting sites. She told me about last Christmas when her brother came over from England. It's customary, she said, to do a good deal of celebrating around Christmas, and so she spent all she had on a disco outfit. But when they got to the club in Dundalk, they were told they would have to wait because there were too many already inside. But there were people all around them pouring in. Apartheid Irish style. You get very guarded after experiences like that, which is why Travellers might not be easy to get to know. People think they're rich because of their vans and jewelry, but they buy the vans on credit and need them for their work, just as settled people do their houses, and the jewelry is akin to savings. All her own jewelry, she told me, was gifts—the three gold bangles from her parents, the big gold hoop earrings from her brother in England. She frequently ended he sentences Please God, to indicate that her desire or ambition was tempered by God's approval, and her religion was an important part of her life.

The ice broken or at least a little thawed, we went into her trailer—her parents, she said, had allowed her to remain unmarried, and she had a trailer of her own—and she began to have real conversation with me in a different, more natural voice. Her brother and other men kept dropping by to say hello and inspect me, and I met her younger brother William and inspected the dagger tattooed on his forearm in return. The trailer, the kind that hitches to the back of a car, was the size of a small room, and everything in it was neatly arranged, the bed folded back into a couch. The clock she had broken that morning, however, was lying on a counter all in pieces. She had beautiful dishes arrayed on narrow shelves above the windows and two books on another counter: Bruce Chatwin's *The Songlines* and Peter Matthiessen's *Indian Country*.

It turned out she was interested in Native Americans and identified with them, with better grounds than most who do. She had acutely picked out their nomadism as one of the reasons why Euro-Americans considered them barbaric and one of the grounds for persecuting them. Civilizing Indians usually entailed transforming them from nomads into agriculturalists, tied to the success or failure of individual labor on a small piece of land. The sedentary toil of agriculture was usually considered inseparable from or foundational for culture itself by the nineteenth-century Americans who made Indian policy; what they would think of the present's postagricultural societies is hard to imagine. Turning Native American nomads into agriculturalists largely failed, but it did succeed in justifying a drastically reduced land base for them and thereby freeing up much of their land for others. My hostess also pointed out that what the Jews and Gypsies killed in the Nazi holocaust had in common was nomadism, and I was glad I'd introduced myself as a Jew and might thereby be considered an honorary nomad. (I had somewhere around Galway stopped telling people of my mixed ancestry, because it was clear I wasn't Irish in the way the Irish were, because trying to explain that being mixed didn't mean being nothing was getting tiresome, and because declaring Jewishness dried up any further questions. I thought I'd probably only really ever feel Irish Catholic if I went to Israel.)

Each door Cathleen led me through seemed to take me into a more personal sphere; we had moved from the formal interview on her sister's sofa to the conversation in her trailer to the festive visit in her parents' trailer next door. I seemed to have been accepted, at least as a guest. In her parents' trailer Cathleen laid out thinly cut fresh bread, cold meats, and tomatoes and began to make cup after cup of strong tea for us all, washing the cups thoroughly between each round. Her parents' trailer was airy and comfortable, a spotless salon of windows, couches, kitchenette, and a central table. What do you call them, they asked me, and I said, Trailers. They looked satisfied and said that Travellers too called them trailers; only country people called them caravans. And they asked me about American rest stops; they had heard wondrous stories that the US government built them copiously along the highways and anyone was allowed to halt at them unharassed.

My own country took on new enchantment for me as I told them of the western American infrastructure of rest stops and camp grounds and trailer parks and interstate highways. Of the quite respectable middle-class retirees who sold their houses and took to the road in trailers, migrating like birds alone and in flocks, south in the winter and anywhere in the summer. Of how much of the populace was, if not nomadic, at least restless and rootless, moving on an average of once every five and a half years. Of states where the majority of homes seemed to be prefab trailers that could be trucked to the next loction. Of how many fine gradations there are between the absolutely fixed and the fluid in the US, rather than Ireland's stark gap. Of my own adventures in my pickup truck with the shell on the back, traveling around the West, living out of the truck for weeks on end sometimes, traveling sometimes with my younger brother in his pickup when we went to political actions together. As I spoke of days of driving five hundred miles or so alone, of driving a hundred miles down Nevada's secondary highways without seeing another soul, I became homesick for my own roadscapes. Any doubts I'd had about disconnectedness, rootlessness, and fossil fuel economies were bowled over by our collective evocation of the lure of the open road.

I swapped my tales with road stories of theirs, mostly of Mrs. McDonagh's. Mrs. McDonagh, Cathleen's mother, impressed me as a remarkable woman. Stout and weathered, with her shapeless dress and her graybrown hair pulled back casually, she had made no efforts at beautification but she radiated a calm joy in her expressions and her sweetvoiced stories. Though one might expect a nomad to flicker like a flame, she gave instead the impression of enormous earthy solidity and complete participation in the present. Life seemed to delight her. She told me they could see the mountains from where they were, the Dublin mountains. That her mother was from County Meath, and there was always a town you'd go back to. That home was where your people were buried. And one of the great pleasures of travel was going back to a place in which a significant passage of your life had occurred, revisiting expriences inextricably linked to a distinct locale (unlike, she implied, the sedentary, whose different dramas may all occur on the same thereby unevocative home front). She grew up in the wattle tents—the tents made of tarps and hazel wands—and there would be a big tent with a fire to cook on and sing around. There was a wagon to sleep in (though she didn't make it clear if it was always there along with the wattle tents). She hadn't learned to read or write, which was inconvenient, because you had to ask people to help with your letters, so they always knew your business. When a white moth came and fluttered between us on the couch where we sat, she said, A little moth. That means a letter's coming.

Now it was ten years since they had Travelled, she said, but they went off all the time in vans. And she spoke of their journeys. She had wanted to emigrate to Australia once in the 1960s when visas and jobs were easy to come by, but at the last minute her husband had backed out. He was a less enthusiastic adventurer. She wanted someday to see Russia and Germany, and they had gone on pilgrimages to Knock in Ireland and Lourdes in France. She deplored the long hours of waiting and the poor organization at Lourdes, but they had gone there all along the backroads of France, and the French people they met had been so friendly—a report which was itself testimony to their talent for travel. They were very devout; Cathleen had told me of a pilgrimage to Saintes-Maries-de-la-Mer near Arles in southern France, a place of great Gypsy pilgrimage as well. When her mother recited the places she'd like to go, Cathleen added, Please God, Jerusalem. "Narrow and wide," concluded my notes. "Muslim. Freedom. Change," and I never could make sense of them. Darkness had fallen while we had been swapping stories, and darkness fell very late that time of year. They sent for William, and he drove me back to central Dublin in his van, fast, as I swayed between him and his sister around the bends in the roads.

[1997]

IV

Home:
Memory and Return

INTRODUCTION

"We shall not cease from exploration
And the end of all our exploring
Will be to arrive where we started
And know the place for the first time."

"Little Gidding," from *The Four Quartets*, T. S. Eliot

"Home is a notion that only nations of the homeless fully appreciate and only the uprooted comprehend."

Wallace Stegner, *Angle of Repose*

In Eliot's oft-quoted lines above, the metaphor of life as a spiritual journey of exploration comes full circle. In actual travel, home is the point of departure, and it is usually where the journey ends. The end—not only the conclusion but also the purpose of the journey—is revealed in a deeper understanding of home and its relation to the traveler. Home becomes a source of meaning and a symbol of fulfillment, a site that can be fully understood only after one has left it and later returned. In other words, the knowledge of self that arises from the experience of travel may be realized when travelers return home, wherever that may be, and reflect differently and more deeply on the meaning of home for them. For example, the kind of illumination that Malcolm X attains in his pilgrimage to Mecca (Part II) is only fully apparent to him after he is back in the United States.

If one has been forced from home by some external cause—war, political oppression, poverty, natural catastrophe—the meaning and value of home becomes sharper and more poignant. As the quotation above from Wallace Stegner makes clear, the meaning of home is clearest to those who have been denied a home. The modern French writer Simone Weil expressed a similar but more general view about home: "To be rooted is perhaps the most important and least recognized need of the human soul."

Travel may itself be a need for the human soul, but it also clarifies to the traveler the need for roots—for rest, a sense of belonging, a state of peace and fulfillment. The selections in this section consider home from many perspectives: those of the adult remembering childhood homes, transients who can only dream of owning a home, the homeowner who prefers rootedness to wandering, the student coming home from college, the immigrant going back to a childhood or an ancestral home, the epic wanderer at the end of his journey.

The first selections center on physical and material places that have served as homes. Margaret Atwood looks back on the variety of homes she knew and relates ideas of home to being a child, being female, and being Canadian. Lars Eighner recalls a temporary "home" he fashioned as a homeless person. Vikram Seth distills the transient's longing for a home into a short poem. From his home in Indiana, Scott Sanders argues the virtues of establishing roots and staying put. John Daniels takes an opposing point of view: travel keeps one from becoming dull, narrow, and provincial. For Chang Rae Lee, the memory of the home which he left to attend boarding school centers on the kitchen and his mother's cooking.

Adopting new homes through living abroad or immigration separates the writer from the memories of childhood or the traditions of ancestors. After several years as an expatriate in England, Bill Bryson looks anew at his native Iowa with both condescension and nostalgia. Maya Angelou goes back to the continent from which her ancestors were taken in slavery, and Andrew Pham returns to the country from which his family fled after the Vietnam War.

Germaine Greer argues that home cannot be recovered and that exile is perpetual, since "our earthly condition is a journey away from home." Pico Iyer, who has adopted Japan as a home, finds that he will always be considered an alien there despite his Asian roots. In a more abstract manner, Annie Dillard extends the spirit of exile and wandering to a larger sense of humans in the universe. The poems by Alfred, Lord Tennyson and Constantine Cafavy express very different responses to home as the ultimate destination of the journey. Tennyson's *Ulysses* finds home to be dull and sets forth again on the seas; Cafavy views home as the motive for the journey, the destination that is important only because it draws the traveler through the journey to return.

In these variations on the theme of home, the traveler is not always transformed by the journey (as mythic travelers usually are), but at least is made more aware of truths about the nature of home. The new realizations about home are also realizations about the self that has been formed by home. The separation from home caused by travel—separation from one's culture, one's habits of thinking, the patterns of one's life—illuminates those elements of the self more clearly when the traveler returns.

Margaret Atwood

(1939–)

Margaret Atwood is one of Canada's foremost poets, critics, novelists, and feminists. She has woven travel motifs into many of her novels. The woods and lakes of eastern Canada become psychic symbols in *Surfacing* (1972), a story of a woman's search for her father and her return to home, nature, and ultimately a primitive state in the wilderness. Among her many novels is *Bodily Harm* (1982), in which a woman escapes to a Caribbean island after staging death by drowning. Atwood has also written extensively on Canadian literature and culture from her viewpoint as one who strongly identifies with Canada as home.

In the essay below, Atwood recalls, in a childhood marked by continual uprooting and traveling, how her various homes all give meaning to the word *home*.

"Approximate Homes"

I. Down Home

Down home, they would say, although what they meant was north on the map. I used to wonder—why was home always down? Nobody ever said *up home*. But now I know: home is down the way memory is down, and hidden springs of water. Derelict cities, abandoned bones, lost keys.

Home is buried. You have to dig for it.

2. The Home for Incurable Children

In one of my phases of being a child, which took place in Toronto at the end of the forties, there was a building called The Home for Incurable Children.

We make fun of our predecessors for their euphemisms, but in fact these were mostly for sex. In other matters they were blunt in their labelling to the point of crudeness. Thus we once had The Provincial Lunatic Asylum: no beating about the bush there. And orphans were put into orphanages. Everything in its place.

The Home for Incurable Children was made of brownish-red brick, and was grim. There was the sign with its name in big black letters, right on the lawn. There on the lawn, too, in summer, were the incurable children, dressed usually in white, sitting usually in chairs, wan and set apart—a warning to us other children. If we became for some reason incurable, would we too be put in there? And where were the mummies and daddies?

These childen, we were told in sad adult voices, would never grow up. We did not confuse this state with what we knew about Peter Pan. In fact, The Home for Incurable Children made growing up seem a more desirable thing than perhaps it was, and we became very anxious to do it.

Once I'd managed to escape from childhood as far as high school, The Home for Incurable Children still obsessed me. It was the name: I could see it contained a swarm of meanings. Did "incurable children" mean those who could not be cured of being children? Was it childhood itself that was the disease? And "home"—why call it a home, when everyone knew it wasn't a real home at all, but, like "homes for the elderly," the exact opposite? If such places really were homes, what a sinister and quicksand twist it gave the word!

A home wasn't where the heart was, but where it wasn't. It was where you were stuck when nobody wanted you. *Home* was the name for longing.

3. A House Is Not a Home

It was little girls who taught me the game called "playing house." It was never called "playing home." The real-estate ads always say "home," not "house," but little girls are the reverse. For them, the house comes first.

My brother was no good at this game. His idea of the thing was a sand house, or better still a fortress, which we would then drop rocks on. Occasionally he would go so far as to play Baby to my doting Mother, but only in order to scream and demand things. I quickly saw that with him I was better off as part of a bombing squadron.

The little girls however knew houses backwards and forwards. The cupboards will be here, this will be the table, these are the beds; here is where we do the ironing, this is the stove, over there can be the sink. Such talk would go on for some time. Then, finally, everything would be in order; and then what?

It was the *and then what* I had trouble with. The other little girls would solve the problem by serving a meal or having someone fall ill, but these were not enough for me; because after the meal must come the washing of the dishes, and then another meal, and after the illness must come a cure; and after the cure, then another meal or another illness, and then what?

Playing house, so comforting for other little girls, caused a great deal more anxiety for me than it was worth, faced with those dolly teacups, those plates made of leaves, that cutlery of twigs, those relentless cupboards, tables, and beds, in endless variations and proliferations but always essentially the same—how much more desirable it seemed to reduce them to rubble with a few well-placed sticks of dynamite.

At least it would be an end. At least, then, you would know.

4. Home Free

Long ago, before television and the fears of their parents had drawn them indoors, children used to stay out after supper. In the late-spring evenings, humid and dense and smelling of lilacs and mowed lawns, they would play in groups and gangs and mobs, in the streets and in and out of their yards, and in vacant lots and on beaches—long, intricate, exciting, tedious, and inexplicable games.

Here is one we played. It was called "Kick the Can." You needed a can—a tomato juice can, big size, was about right. It had to be large enough to make a clanging noise when kicked. A home space would be marked out, drawn with a stick in the dirt; the can would be placed on its frontier. An It was chosen, who had to guard both home space and can. The other children would run tantalizingly near; if tagged they were caught, and imprisoned in the home, where they had to stay, held by invisible walls, sneering and jumping up and down and licking the blood from their scraped elbows. But if a free child could run close enough to kick the can, there would be a general escape.

When almost all had been caught and were locked into home, the It could go further afield in search of prey; but if the last remaining free one could sneak into the home space untagged, and yell *Home free!*, the power of the It was shattered and all enchantments broken, and the game was over.

The home space—how odd it was! A precious thing, to be guarded; also a dungeon. You didn't want to be kept in it against your will, yet it was bliss to enter it when forbidden, sliding in, skidding in, throwing yourself in, and shrieking at the top of your lungs: *Home free!* What a relief, what a triumph! And what a triumph also to kick the tomato juice can, so that everyone could run away from home. Well, it was more or less how we felt about our real homes: ours to claim when we wanted them, ours to be trapped in, ours to escape from.

I may have got the rules wrong though; I may have mixed them up with some other game. It was quite a long time ago now.

5. The Consumer's Gas "Miss Future Homemaker Contest"

The fifties was the age of contests: contests for teenaged girls. I once met someone who had been Miss Wool, and who'd had to wear an itchy wardrobe and carry around a live lamb, which peed on her. A friend of mine was once Miss Vodka, which was more dangerous as it involved a clutch of middle-aged men who'd been testing the product. She leapt from a moving convertible, and quit.

The Consumers' Gas "Miss Future Homemaker Contest" was less hazardous. It was held during the Home Show. You had to iron a shirt with a gas iron, cook a dinner on a gas stove, and do a third thing involving gas, which I have repressed. Myself and my partner—was it you, Sally?—were chosen as the entrants from our high school Home Economics class. In this cass we were learning to be homemakers, or else—like our teacher, who was a Miss and whose hobby was skiing—we were learning to teach other girls to be them.

By the year of the contest we were quite advanced. We'd progressed from sewing aprons to sewing whole outfits, with box pleats and interfacing and dressmaker buttonholes; we'd gone from applesauce to balanced meals with each food group represented. I do not jeer at such knowledge. I shudder to think how many young girls now are hurled into life without it, and are forced to read magazines. The making of a choux paste is a skill I retain, though seldom use. They were not called choux then, however, but cream puffs. As I said, it was the fifties.

For the Miss Future Homemaker Contest, Sally and I dressed neatly and wore aprons; homemakers were supposed to be very clean and efficient. The menu for the dinner was pre-set: meat loaf, frozen peas, baked potatoes. There was a time limit—how fast you could get the shirt wrinkle-free and slide the meat loaf out of the oven. (This aspect of it I found hilarious. The husband marches in from the office, left right left right. Off with the old wrinkly shirt, on with the newly pressed one, and Hup! over to the table. Whomp! goes the meat loaf onto his plate! Blop! goes the baked potato! Pitter-patter go the peas! And now, for the third thing involving gas. . . .)

Sally and I were speedy, but we didn't win, although we each received a charm bracelet with little golden bells on it. Perhaps the judges detected my lack of sincerity; but did they really think that I thought that this rushing about in aprons with gas appliances had anything to do with real life? Not mine, that was for sure; I wasn't going to end up making any homes! Not me.

I did make some, though. Several of them. I once knitted a whole bedspread, if you can believe it. I once put up two dozen jars of mustard pickle. I once baked bread.

6. Home Land

I don't have a home town, but I have a home land. A chunk of pink granite sticking out of the ground, a kettle bog, a horizon line of ragged black spruce. ah! there you are! Home!

I'm most at home in an airplane, a thousand feet up, skimming over the taiga at one remove. Lake, lake, lake, swamp, sprinkle of low hills, twist of river; ice creeping out from the shores. It has to be big, though; rocky, sparse, a place you could find yourself lost in easy as pie, and walk around in circles and die of exposure. Me too, you understand; when it comes to home, I'm no expert.

Out the window, way down there: desolation, instant panic, slow starvation. With a view like that you can feel comfortable.

7. No Home Town

Between 1936 and 1948 my parents moved twenty times. Sometimes between two fixed points—to a city in the late fall, to the forest in the early spring; sometimes it was from one city to another. My mother and father were from Nova Scotia, and that was *home* to them. But it wasn't where I was. So where was I?

Here and there, but never both at once. Home was not a place but a trajectory; it was the dotted line that marked our trail. It would appear out of boxes and suitcases, be packed away, appear again in a different form, in a different room, after a long and uncomfortable journey, hundreds of miles in the back of a car stuffed full of bundles and packages, then on the bottom of a canoe with the rain dribbling down your neck or on a sleigh drawn by horses over the creaking ice. You couldn't count on home. You couldn't count on it to stay put.

What has become of them, those provisional homes—the second-floor apartment in Ottawa with its long dark hallways, and the French Canadian and the English Canadian who lived below, and were always squabbling, and were married to each other? Or the drafty mansion in Sault Ste. Marie, which was falling apart and stood in a field of cabbages, with the hole in the ceiling through which we dropped crayons onto the stove to melt in puddles of smelly colour? Or the one house that was torn down, or the other one that burned down; or the tent whose roof you weren't supposed to touch for fear of leaks? That tent had no floor, and the mice always got in; they knew a good home when they saw it.

We're almost home now, they would say, in the middle of the rainstorm or the middle of the night, whichever was darker, and that was always the best part of home: the moment before lamplight. Home was somethng that was constantly being approached but could never be reached, because we'd left it days ago, we'd locked the door and hidden the key, and it was already behind us. It's not only that you can't go home again, you can never get there in the first place.

Here we are—home at last! they would say; though home had no location, only a direction: *homeward.* And yet we went on—we go on—believing we are there.

[1997]

LARS EIGHNER

(1948–)

Lars Eighner attended the University of Texas and now lives in Austin as a freelance writer. He has published *Gay Cosmos* (1995) and a novel, *Pawn to Queen Four* (1995), set in Texas. For three years, homeless and accom-

panied by his dog, he survived on the streets and highways of the Southwest. He became adept at living off garbage thrown into dumpsters. One
of his dumpster discoveries was a computer, on which he wrote *Travels with
Lizbeth* (1993), an account of those homeless years.

The following passage, "In the Bamboo," taken from *Travels with Lizbeth*, recalls a makeshift camp formerly inhabited by a friend. The place
evokes Eighner's childhood reading of a travel classic and provides, for a
short time, a few of the comforts of home. His experience illustrates how
the rootlessness of transient life gives even a temporary refuge the welcome
qualities of home.

"In the Bamboo"

From *Travels with Lizbeth*

Lizbeth and I went first to the stand of bamboo where we had slept before we
left Austin. It was still there. Just as I had been told at Ramblin' Red's, the project to remove the brush and the homeless the brush concealed had not
reached the bamboo. I surveyed it as I had not before.

I discovered Tim had camped in it, for I had told him while he was in jail
of the places I had found to sleep. Evidently when he had been released from
jail he had worked at a fast-food restaurant until he got the money for his bus
ticket to L.A. His uniforms were among the things he had left at the camp. He
had packed up everything in plastic garbage bags, but the growing bamboo had
pierced the bags and everything had been ruined by mildew, including his
expensive motorcycle leathers.

As he had taunted me that he would force me to return to Austin, he had
said he would give me the bicycle he had stashed there. He planned to be a star
in Hollywood and would never want the bicycle again. I found a bicycle in the
bamboo and I supposed it was the one he meant.

There were several well-marked trails and old camps in the bamboo. I left the
old camps intact and contributed Tim's gear to one of them, for I meant for them
to be decoys. I carved a nine-by-four-foot room out of the wall of bamboo and was
pleased to discover that the entrance was invisible from even a few feet away.

By all rights I should have felt perfectly hopeless. The trip to Hollywood
was a better chance than I could expect to have ever again. But as a boy I had
read *The Swiss Family Robinson* over and over—I loved the idea of it so. Putting
the camp together in the bamboo was just such an enterprise. I found shower
curtains and learned to layer them to keep the rain off our heads. I rigged several of them on bamboo poles so they could be lowered down the bamboo

walls; I was planning against the winter winds, although it was July. I camouflaged the shower curtains overhead to prevent their being seen by aircraft.

I installed cushions and a foam mattress on them. I put in makeshift bookshelves. I found some large fresh dry cells and wired them to a radio so I did not have to change the batteries every hour as I listened to the news. When I satisfied myself that light in my camp would not call attention to us at night, I discovered how to make lamps that would burn on cooking oil, a commodity that was always available in abundance in the Dumpsters.

In spite of the obvious trails, it was very rare that anyone else entered the bamboo at all. I could see no reason I might not bathe in the bamboo, and I set out vessels to catch rainwater for this purpose. I always had some little project. I had come to believe that Lizbeth and I would die homeless. And that seemed to me too bad. But then, why shouldn't I try to make us as comfortable as I could, wherever I could? I had put us to considerable discomfort several times in my attempts to struggle against homelessness. For a time I would just accept it and make the best of it.

Of course this was a policy easier to effect while we were out of public view in the bamboo than it would have been if we were still sleeping in the open in Adams Park.

The first month in the bamboo was an adventure and a vacation. Curious as it sounds, I needed a vacation. I had worked very hard in Hollywood, and one of the principal problems of self-employment is that after eight hours or ten or twelve, no boss comes by to say that you might as well knock off for the day. We went around in the coolness of the morning to the Dumpsters and returned to the bamboo to eat—although because of the rats, raccoons, and possums I was careful never to bring food into our sleeping quarters. I puttered around camp, installing whatever improvement I had thought of, and in the heat of the day we lay in comfort and I read. I wrote long letters and began to make a few sketches, which have become the present book. I could read at night by the light of my improvised lamp. And if I read too late and overslept the next morning, I had nothing to fear.

This was as good as homeless life gets, and that could not last.

[1993]

VIKRAM SETH

(1952–)

Vikram Seth is a poet and novelist as well as the author of a travel book, *From Heaven's Lake: Travels through Sinkiang and Tibet* (1983). Born in Calcutta and educated at Oxford and Stanford Universities, Seth set his novel, *A Suitable Boy* (1993), in India; it follows the lives of Hindu and Muslim families. A novel in verse, *The Golden Gate* (1986), is about expatriate Indian communities in San Francisco. Seth's numerous volumes of poetry show Chinese influences and in their subjects and motifs reflect his wide experience in travel.

The selection that follows, "Homeless," is a simple and poignant expression of a desire for the continuity and comforting material reality of home. The transient's yearning for the peace of a home is at the opposite end of the spectrum from the home dweller's restless yearning to travel.

"Homeless"

I envy those
Who have a house of their own,
Who can say their feet
Rest on what is theirs alone,
Who do not live on sufferance   5
In strangers' shells,
As my family has all our life,
And as I probably will.

A place on the earth, untenured,
Soil, grass, brick, air;   10
To know I will never have to move:
To review the seasons from one lair.
When night comes, to lie down in peace;
To know that I may die as I have slept;
That things will not revert to a strangers' hand; 15
That those I love may keep what I have kept.

[1995]

SCOTT RUSSELL SANDERS

(1945–)

Born, raised, and still living in Ohio, Scott Russell Sanders often writes about what seems to be the very opposite of the desire to travel—the need to be fixed in the realities of home as place and physical structure. Nevertheless, he identifies the journey as the larger metaphor for human existence, of which home is a part. His meditations on home "are bound together by the ancient plot of a journey in the wilderness in search of vision." This journey comes both from the example of his ancestors, the American pioneers who went into the wilderness to make homes, and from the universal human desire to fit into some larger whole, to find "our place in the web of things." The restlessness and constant movement of Americans troubles Sanders: "A vagabond wind has been blowing here for a long while. . . ."

Staying Put: Making a Home in a Restless World (1993), which is excerpted below, focuses on the human instinct to be grounded in one place rather than the instinct to travel. For Sanders—a literary descendant of Henry David Thoreau—writing about home, however, shares one characteristic with writing about travel: both celebrate our material and spiritual connection to the natural world.

From *Staying Put: Making a Home in a Restless World*

Because so few of us build our own homes, we forget that our dwellings, like our bodies, are made from the earth. The first humans who settled in this part of the country fashioned their huts from bark, their tepees from tanned hides draped over poles. They warmed themselves at fires of buffalo chips and brush. How could they forget that they had wrapped themselves in the land? When white pioneers came to this region, a family would sometimes camp inside a hollow sycamore while they built a log cabin; so when at length they moved into the cabin, they merely exchanged life inside a single tree for life inside a stack of them. The bark on the walls and the clay in the chinks and the fieldstone in the chimney reminded them whence their shelter had come. Our technology has changed, but not our ultimate source. Even the newest ticky-tacky box in the suburbs, even the glitziest high tech mansion, even an aluminum trailer is only a nest in disguise.

Nature does not halt at the property line, but runs right through our yard and walls and bones. Possums and raccoons browse among kitchen scraps in the compost bin. Moss grows on the shady side of the roof, mildew in the bathtub, mold in the fridge. Roots from our front yard elm invade the drains. Mice invade the cupboards. (The best bait, we've found, is peanut butter.) Male woodpeckers, advertising for mates, rap on the cedar siding of the porch. Wrens nest in our kitchen exhaust fan, the racket of their hungry chicks spicing up our meals. Blue jays clack noisily in the gutters, turning over leaves in a search for bugs. Thousands of maples sprout from those gutters each spring.. Water finds its way into the basement year round. For all our efforts to seal the joints, rain and snowmelt still treat the basement like any other hole in the ground.

When we bought the house, it was covered with English ivy. "That's got to come off," Ruth said. "Think of all the spiders breeding outside Eva's window!"

Under assault from crowbar, shears, and wire brush, the ivy came off. But there has been no perceptible decline in the spider population, indoors or out. Clean a corner, and by the time you've put away the broom, new threads are gleaming. The spiders thrive because they have plenty of game to snare. Poison has discouraged the termites, but carpenter ants still look upon the house as a convenient heap of dead wood. (When Eva first heard us talk about carpenter ants, she imagined they would be dressed as her daddy was on weekends, with sweatband across the forehead, tool belt around the waist, and dangling hammer on the hip.) Summer and fall, we play host to crickets, grasshoppers, moths, flies, mosquitoes, and frogs, along with no-see-ums too obscure to name.

Piled up foursquare and plumb, the house is not only composed from the land but is itself a part of the landscape. Weather buffets it, wind sifts through. Leaves collect on the roof, hemlock needles gather on the sills, ice and thaw nudge the foundation, seeds lodge in every crack. Like anything born, it is mortal. If you doubt that, drive the back roads of the Ohio Valley and look at the forsaken farms. Abandon a house, even a brick one such as ours, and it will soon be reclaimed by forest. Left to itself, the land says bloodroot, chickadee, beech. Our shelter is on loan; it needs perpetual care.

The word *house* derives from an Indo-European root meaning to cover or conceal. I hear in that etymology furtive, queasy undertones. Conceal from what? From storms? beasts? enemies? from the eye of God? *Home* comes from a different root meaning "the place where one lies." That sounds less fearful to me. A weak, slow, clawless animal, without fur or fangs, can risk lying down and closing its eyes only where it feels utterly secure. Since the universe is going to kill us, in the short run or the long, no wonder we crave a place to lie in safety, a place to conceive our young and raise them, a place to shut our eyes without shivering or dread.

Married seven years already at the time we bought our house, I forgot to carry Ruth over the threshold, but I did carry Eva, and when newborn Jesse came home from the hospital, I carried him as well. Whatever else crossing the threshold might symbolize—about property or patriarchy—it should mean that you have entered a place of refuge. Not a perfect refuge, for there is no such thing: disease can steal in, so can poison or thugs, hunger and pain. If the people who cross the threshold are bent or cruel, the rooms will fill with misery. No locks will keep armies out, no roof will hold against a tornado. No, not perfectly safe, yet home is where we go to hide from harm, or, having been hurt, to lick our wounds.

At 1113 East Wylie, we have no shrine in the yard, no hex sign on the gable, no horseshoe nailed over the door. But I sympathize with those who mark their houses with talismans to ward off evil. Our neighbors across the street have a small box mounted on their doorpost, a mezuza, which contains a slip of paper bearing words from Deuteronomy (6: 4–5): "Hear, O Israel: the Lord our God is one Lord; and you shall love the Lord your God with all your heart, and with all your soul, and with all your might." The words announce their faith, honor their God, and turn away the wicked. Each family, in its own manner, inscribes a visible or invisible message on its doorway, a message contrary to the one that Dante found over the gateway to Hell. Take hope, we say, rest easy, ye who enter here.

However leaky or firm, whether tar paper or brick, the shell of a house gives only shelter; a home gives sanctuary. Perhaps the most familiar definition of *home* in the American language comes from Robert Frost's "The Death of the Hired Man," in lines spoken by a Yankee farmer:

> *"Home is the place where, when you have to go there,*
> *They have to take you in."*

Less familiar is the wife's reply:

> *"I should have called it*
> *Something you somehow haven't to deserve."*

The husband's remark is pure Yankee, grudging and grim. I side with the wife. Home is not where you *have* to go but where you *want* to go; nor is it a place where you are sullenly admitted, but rather where you are welcomed—by the people, the walls, the tiles on the floor, the flowers beside the door, the play of light, the very grass.

While I work on these pages, tucking in lines to make them tight, our newspapaer carries an article with a grisly headline: HOMELESS WOMAN CRUSHED WITH TRASH. No one knows the woman's name, only that she crawled into a dumpster to sleep, was loaded into a truck, was compressed with the trash, and arrived dead at the incinerator. She wore white tennis shoes, gray sweatpants, red windbreaker, and, on her left hand, "a silver Indian Thunderbird ring." Nearby residents had seen her climb into the dumpster, and later they heard the truck begin to grind, but they did not warn the driver soon enough, and so the woman died. Being homeless meant that she had already been discarded by family, neighbors, and community, and now she was gathered with the trash.

This happened in Indianapolis, just up the road from my snug house. I read the article twice; I read it a dozen times. I pinned the clipping to the wall beside my desk, and I keep returning to it as to a sore.

It *is* a sore, an affront, an outrage that thousands upon thousands of people in our country have nowhere to live. Like anyone who walks the streets of America, I grieve over the bodies wrapped in newspapers or huddled in cardboard boxes, the sleepers curled on steam grates, the futureless faces. This is cause for shame and remedy, not only because the homeless suffer, but because they have no place to lay their heads in safety, no one except dutiful strangers to welcome them. Thank god for dutiful strangers; yet they can never take the place of friends. The more deeply I feel my own connection to home, the more acutely I feel the hurt of those who belong to no place and no one.

The longing for a safe place to lie down echoes through our holy songs and scriptures. Abused and scorned, we look over Jordan, and what do we see? A band of angels coming for to carry us home. If earth has no room for us, we are promised, then heaven will. The string of assurances in the Twenty-third Psalm ends with the most comforting one of all:

> *Surely goodness and mercy shall follow me*
> *all the days of my life;*
> *and I shall dwell in the house of the Lord*
> *for ever.*

If we are ever going to dwell in the house of the Lord, I believe, we do so now. If any house is divinely made, it is this one here, this great whirling mansion of planets and stars.

Each constellation of the zodiac is said to live in its own house, Leo and Libra and Aquarius, and so on through all the twelve that ride the merry-go-round of our year. I do not believe that our future is written in the sky. And yet there is some truth in sketching houses around the stars. Viewed from chancy earth, they appear to be stay-at-homes, abiding in place from generation to generation, secure beyond our imagining. And if the constellations belong in their houses so beautifully and faithfully, then so might we.

In baseball, home plate is where you begin your journey and also your destination. You venture out onto the bases, to first and second and third, always striving to return to the spot from which you began. There is danger on the basepath—pick-offs, rundowns, force-outs, double plays—and safety only back at home. I am not saying, as a true fan would, that baseball is the key to life; rather, life is the key to baseball. We play or watch this game because it draws pictures of our desires.

The homing pigeon is not merely able to find the roost from astounding distances; the pigeon *seeks* its home. I am a homing man. Away on solo trips, I am never quite whole. I miss family, of course, and neighbors and friends; but I also miss the house, which is planted in the yard, which is embraced by a city, which is cradled in familiar woods and fields, which gather snow and rain for the Ohio River. The house has worked on me as steadily as I have worked on the house. I carry slivers of wood under my fingernails, dust from demolition in the corners of my eyes, aches from hammering and heaving in all my joints.

During my lifetime the labels *homemaker* and *housewife* have come to seem belittling, as though a woman who wears them lacks the gumption to be anything else. A similar devaluation hit the word *homely* itself, which originally meant plain, simple, durable, worthy of use in the home, and gradually came to mean drab, graceless, ugly. Men can now be called househusbands, but the male variant, like the female, is used apologetically, as though qualified by the word *only*.

In a recent letter, a friend wrote me, "I'm still just a househusband; but I'm looking for work." I'd be surprised if there wasn't plenty of work to do in his own house. It's a rare home that couldn't do with more care. Wendell Berry warns us about that need in his poem "The Design of a House":

> *Except in idea, perfection is as wild*
> *as light; there is no hand laid on it.*
> *But the house is a shambles*
> *unless the vision of its perfection*
> *   upholds it like stone.*

Our rooms will only be as generous and nurturing as the spirit we invest in them. The Bible gives us the same warning, more sternly: Unless God builds the house, it will not stand. The one I live in has been standing for just over sixty years, a mere eyeblink, not long enough to prove there was divinity in the mortar. I do know, however, that mortar and nails alone would not have held the house together even for sixty years. It has also needed the work of many hands, the wishes of many hearts, vision upon vision, through a succession of families.

Real estate ads offer houses for sale, not homes. A house is a garment, easily put off or on, casually bought and sold; a home is skin. Merely change houses and you will be disoriented; change homes and you bleed. When the shell you live in has taken on the savor of your love, when your dwelling has become a taproot, then your house is a home.

[1993]

JOHN DANIEL

(1948–)

John Daniel, a poet, outdoorsman, and resident of Washington State, has written *Winter Creek: One Writer's Natural* History (2002), *The Trail Home: Nature, Imagination, and the American West* (1992), and *Common Ground: Poems* (1988).

"A Word in Favor of Rootlessness," featured below, could be read as a defense of traveling as opposed to staying put. Daniel fears that stability and security, becoming settled in one place, may deaden the spirit. He wonders whether the American tendency to take to the road may have more beneficial than harmful effects by renewing people's vitality and energy. In support of his argument, he cites examples from popular music, Native American mythology, and writers like John Muir and Edward Abbey, who integrate travel with writing about nature and the environment.

"A Word in Favor of Rootlessness"

I am one of the converted when it comes to the cultural and economic necessity of finding place. Our rootlessness—our refusal to accept the discipline of living as responsive and responsible members of neighborhoods, communities, landscapes, and ecosystems—is perhaps our most serious and widespread disease. The history of our country, and especially of the American West, is in great part a record of damage done by generations of boomers, both individual and corporate, who have wrested from the land all that a place could give and continually moved on to take from another place. Boomers such as Wallace Stegner's father, who, as we see him in *The Big Rock Candy Mountain,* "wanted to make a killing and end up on Easy Street." Like many Americans, he was obsessed by the fruit of Tantalus: "Why remain in one dull plot of Earth when Heaven was reachable, was touchable, was just over there?"

We don't stand much chance of perpetuating ourselves as a culture, or of restoring and sustaining the health of our land, unless we can outgrow our boomer adolescence and mature into stickers, or nesters—human beings willing to take on the obligations of living in communities rooted in place, conserving nature as we conserve ourselves. And maybe, slowly, we are headed in that direction. The powers and virtues of place are celebrated in a growing body of literature and discussed in conferences across the country. Bioregionalism, small-scale organic farming, urban food co-ops, and other manifestations of the spirit of place seem to be burgeoning, or at least coming along.

That is all to the good. But as we settle into our home places and local communities and bioregional niches, as we become the responsible economic and ecologic citizens we ought to be, I worry a little. I worry, for one thing, that we will settle in place so pervasively that no unsettled places will remain. But I worry about us settlers, too. I feel at least a tinge of concern that we might allow our shared beliefs and practices to harden into orthodoxy, and that the bath water of irresponsibility we are ready to toss out the home door might contain a lively baby or two. These fears may turn out to be groundless, like most of my insomniac broodings. But they are on my mind, so indulge me, if you will, as I address some of the less salutary aspects of living in place and some of the joys and perhaps necessary virtues of rootlessness.

No power of place is more elemental or influential than climate, and I feel compelled at the outset to report that we who live in the wet regions of the Northwest suffer immensely from our climate. Melville's Ishmael experienced a damp, drizzly November in his soul, but only now and again. For us it is eternally so, or it feels like eternity. From October well into June we slouch in our mossy-roofed houses listening to the incessant patter of rain, dark thoughts slowly forming in the dull cloud chambers of our minds. It's been days, weeks, *years*, we believe, since a neighbor knocked or a letter arrived from friend or agent or editor. Those who live where sun and breezes play, engaged in their smiling businesses, have long forgotten us, if they ever cared for us at all. Rain drips from the eaves like poison into our souls. We sit. We sleep. We check the mail.

What but climate could it be that so rots the fiber of the Northwestern psyche? Or if not climate itself, then an epiphenomenon of climate—perhaps the spores of an undiscovered fungus floating out of those decadent forests we environmentalists are so bent on saving. Oh, we try to improve ourselves. We join support groups and twelve-step programs, we drink gallons of cappuccino and café latte, we bathe our pallid bodies in the radiance of full-spectrum light machines. These measures keep us from dissolving outright into the sodden air, and when spring arrives we bestir ourselves outdoors, blinking against the occasional cruel sun and the lurid displays of rhododendrons. By summer we have cured sufficiently to sally forth to the mountains and the coast, where we linger in sunglasses and try to pass for normal.

But it is place we're talking about, the powers of place. As I write this, my thoughts are perhaps unduly influenced by the fact that my right ear has swollen to the size and complexion of a rutabaga. I was working behind the cabin this afternoon, cutting up madrone and Douglas fir slash with the chain saw, when I evidently stepped too close to a yellow jacket nest. I injured none of their tribe, to my knowledge, but one of them sorely injured me. Those good and industrious citizens take place pretty seriously. I started to get out the .22

and shoot every one of them, but thought better of it and drank a tumbler of bourbon instead.

And now, a bit later, a spectacle outside my window only confirms my bitter state of mind. The place in question is the hummingbird feeder, and the chief influence of that place is to inspire in hummingbirds a fiercely intense desire to impale one another on their needlelike beaks. Surely they expend more energy blustering in their buzzy way than they can possibly derive from the feeder. This behavior is not simply a consequence of feeding Kool-Aid to already over-amped birds—they try to kill each other over natural flower patches too. Nor can it be explained as the typically mindless and violent behavior of the male sex in general. Both sexes are represented in the fray, and females predominate. It is merely a demonstration of over-identification with place. Humans do it too. Look at Yosemite Valley on the Fourth of July. Look at any empty parking space in San Francisco. Look at Jerusalem.

When human beings settle in a place for the long run, it may be that good things occur overall. There are dangers, though. Stickers run the substantial risk of becoming sticks-in-the-mud. Consider my own state of Oregon, which was settled by farmers from the Midwest and upper South who had one epic move in them, across the Oregon Trail, and having found paradise resolved not to stir again until the millennium. The more scintillating sorts—writers, murderers, prostitutes, lawyers, other riffraff—tended toward Seattle or San Francisco. And so it happens that we Oregonians harbor behind our bland and aggreable demeanor a serious streak of moralism and conformism. We have some pretty strict notions about the way people should live. It was we who started the nationwide spate of legal attacks on gay and lesbian rights, and it is we who annually rank among the top five states in citizen challenges to morally subversive library books, books such as *Huckleberry Finn, The Catcher in the Rye,* and *The Color Purple.*

This pernicious characteristic is strongest, along with some of our best characteristics, where communities are strongest and people live closest to the land—in the small towns. When my girlfriend and I lived in Klamath Falls in the early 1970s, we were frequently accosted by Mrs. Grandquist, our elderly neighbor across the road. She was pointedly eager to lend us a lawn mower, and when she offered it she had the unnerving habit of staring at my hair. Our phone was just inside the front door, and sometimes as we arrived home it rang before we were entirely *through* the door. "You left your lights on," Mrs. Grandquist would say. Or, "You ought to shut your windows when you go out. We've got burglars, you know." Not in that block of Denver Avenue, we didn't. Mrs. Grandquist and other watchful citizens with time on their hands may have kept insurance rates down, but the pressure of all those eyes and inquiring minds was at times intensely uncomfortable. Small towns are hard places in which to be different. Those yellow jackets are wary, and they can sting.

Customs of land use can become as ossified and difficult to budge as social customs. The Amish, among other long-established rural peoples, practice a good and responsible farming economy. But long-term association with a place no more *guarantees* good stewardship than a long-term marriage guarantees a loving and responsible relationship. As Aldo Leopold noted with pain, there are farmers who habitually abuse their land and cannot easily be induced to do otherwise. Thoreau saw the same thing in Concord—landspeople who, though they must have known their places intimately, misstreated them continually. They whipped the dog every day because the dog was no good, and because that's the way dogs had always been dealt with.

As for us of the green persuasions, settled or on the loose, we too are prone—perhaps more prone than most—to orthodoxy and intolerance. We tend to be overstocked in piety and self-righteousness, deficient in a sense of humor about our values and our causes. Here in the Northwest, where debate in the last decade has focused on logging issues, it's instructive to compare bumper stickers. Ours say, sanctimoniously, "Stumps Don't Lie" or "Love Your Mother." Those who disagree with us, on the other hand, sport sayings such as "Hug a Logger—You'll Never Go Back to Trees," or "Earth First! (We'll Log the Other Planets Later)."

I don't mean to minimize the clear truth that ecological blindness and mis-conduct are epidemic in our land. I only mean to suggest that rigid ecological correctness may not be the most helpful treatment. All of us, in any place or community or movement, tend to become insiders; we all need the stranger, the outside, to shake our perspective and keep us honest. Prominent among Edward Abbey's many virtues was his way of puncturing environmentalist pieties (along with every other brand of piety he encountered). What's more, the outsider can sometimes see landscape with a certain clarity unavailable to the longtime resident. It was as a relative newcomer to the Southwest that Abbey took the notes that would become his best book, in which he imagined the canyon country of the Colorado Plateau more deeply than anyone had imagined it before or has imagined it since. His spirit was stirred and his vision sharpened by his outsider's passion. I don't know that he could have written *Desert Solitaire* if he had been raised in Moab or Mexican Hat.

Unlike Thoreau, who was born to his place, or Wendell Berry, who returned to the place he was born to, Edward Abbey came to his place from afar and took hold. More of a lifelong wanderer was John Muir, who we chiefly identify with the Sierra Nevada but who explored and sojourned in and wrote of a multitude of places, from the Gulf of Mexico to the Gulf of Alaska. I think Muir needed continually to see new landscapes and life forms in order to keep his ardent mind ignited. Motion for him was not a pathol-ogy but a devotion, an essential joy, a continuous discovery of place and self. Marriage to place is something we need to realize in our culture, but not all of us are the marrying kind. The least happy period of Muir's life was his tenure as a settled fruit farmer in Martinez, California. He was more given to the exhilarated attention and fervent exploration of *wooing*, more given to rapture than to extended fidelity. "Rapture" is related etymologically to "rape," but unlike the boomer, who rapes a place, the authentic wooer allows the place to enrapture him.

Wooing ofen leads to marriage, of course, but not always. Is a life of wooing place after place less responsible than a life of settled wedlock? It may be less sustainable, but the degree of its responsibility depends on the quality of the wooing. John Muir subjected himself utterly to the places he sought out. He walked from Wisconsin to the Gulf Coast, climbed a tree in a Sierra windstorm, survived a subzero night on the summit of Mount Shasta by scalding himself in a sulfurous volcanic vent. There was nothing macho about it—he loved where he happened to be and refused to miss one lick of it. In his wandering, day to day and minute to minute, he was more placed than most of us ever will be, in a lifetime at home or a life on the move. Rootedness was not his genius and not his need. As the followers of the Grateful Dead like to remind us, quoting J. R. R. Tolkien, "Not all who wander are lost."

Muir's devoted adventuring, of course, was something very different from the random restlessness of many in our culture today. Recently I sat through a dinner party during which the guests, most of them thirty-something, compared notes all evening about their travels through Asia. They were experts on border crossings, train transport, currency exchange, and even local art objects, but nothing I heard that evening indicated an influence of land or native peoples on the traveler's soul. They were travel technicians. Many backpackers are the same, passing through wilderness places encapsulated in maps and objectives and high-tech gear. There is a pathology there, a serious one. It infects all of us to one degree or another. We have not yet arrived where we believe—and our color slides show—we have already been.

But if shifting around disconnected from land and community is our national disease, I would argue, perversely perhaps, or perhaps just homeopathically, that it is also an element of our national health. Hank Williams and others in our folk and country traditions stir something in many of us when they sing the delights of the open road, of rambling on the loose by foot or thumb or boxcar through the American countryside. Williams's "Ramblin' Man" believes that God intended him for a life of discovery beyond the horizons. Is this mere immaturity? Irresponsibility? An inability to relate to people or place? Maybe. But maybe also renewal, vitality, a growing of the soul. It makes me very happy to drive the highways and back roads of the West, exchanging talk with people who live where I don't, pulling off somewhere, anywhere, to sleep in the truck and wake to a place I've never seen. I can't defend the cost of that travel in fossil fuel consumption and air befoulment—Williams's rambler at least took the fuel-efficient train—but I do know that it satisfies me as a man and a writer.

Such pleasure in movement—the joy of hitting the trail on a brisk morning, of watching from a train the towns and fields pass by, of riding a skateboard or hang glider or even a 747—must come from a deep and ancient source. All of us are descended from peoples whose way was to roam with the seasons, follwing game herds and the succession of edible plants, responding to weather and natural calamities and the shifting field of relations with their own kind. And those peoples came, far deeper in the past, from creatures not yet human who crawled and leapt and swung through the crowns of trees for millions of years, evolving prehinsile hands and color binocular vision as a consequence, then took to the ground and learned to walk upright and wandered out of Africa (or so it now seems) across the continents of Earth. Along the way we have lost much of the sensory acuity our saga evoked in us, our ability to smell danger or read a landscape or notice nuances of weather, but the old knowing still stirs an alertness, an air of anticipation, when we set out on our various journeys.

Native cultural traditions reflect the value of the traveler's knowing. In Native American stories of the Northwest, I notice tht Coyote doesn't seem to have a home. Or if he does, he's never there. "Coyote was traveling upriver," the stories begin. "Coyote came over Neahkanie Mountain," "Coyote was going there. . . ." the stories take place in the early time when the order of the world was still in flux. Coyote, the placeless one, helps people and animals find their proper places. You wouldn't want to base a code of ethics on his character, which is unreliable and frequently ignoble, but he is the agent who introduces human beings to their roles and responsibilities in life. Coyote is the necessary inseminator. (Sometimes literally.) He is the shifty and shiftless traveler who fertilizes the locally rooted bloomings of the world.

Maybe Coyote moves among us as the stranger, often odd or disagreeable, sometimes dangerous, who brings reports from far places. Maybe that stranger is one of the carriers of our wildness, one of the mutant genes that keep our evolution fresh and thriving. It is for that stranger, says Elie Weisel, that an extra place is set at the Seder table. The voyager might arrive, the one who finds his home in the homes of others. He might tell a story, a story no one in the family or local community is capable of telling, and childen might hear that story and imagine their lives in a new way.

It could be Hank Williams who stops in, and he'll sing to you half the night (and maybe yours will be the family he needs, and he won't die of whiskey and barbiturates in the back seat of a car). Or Huck Finn might be your stranger, on the run from "sivilization," dressed as a girl and telling stupendous lies. It could be Jack Keouac and Neal Cassady, on the road with their Beat buddies, hopped-up on speed, and they never *will* stop talking. It might be Gerry Nana-push, the Chippewa power man Louise Erdrich has given us, escaped from jail still again to slip through the mists and snows with his ancient powers. Or it might be Billy Parham or John Grady Cole, Cormac McCarthy's boy drifters. They'll want water for their horses, they'll be ready to eat, and if you're wise you'll feed them. They won't talk much themselves, but you might find yourself telling them the crucial story of your life.

Or yours could be the house where Odysseus calls, a still youngish man returning from war, passionate for his family and the flocks and vineyards of home. Just as likely, though, he could be an old man when he stands in your door. No one's quite sure what became of Odysseus. Homer tells us that he made it to Ithaca and set things in order, but the story leaves off there. Some say he resumed his settled life, living out his days as a placed and prosperous landsman. But others say that after all his adventures he couldn't live his old life again. Alfred, Lord Tennyson writes that he shipped out from Ithaca with his trusted crew. Maybe so. Or maybe the poet got it only half right. Maybe Penelope, island bound for all those years, was stir crazy herself. Maybe they left Telemachus the ranch and set out westward across the sea, two gray spirits "yearning in desire / To follow knowledge like a sinking star, / Beyond the utmost bound of human thought."

[1995]

CHANG-RAE LEE

(1963–)

Chang-Rae Lee came to the United States from South Korea with his parents when he was three. His father practiced psychiatry in suburban New York, and Lee graduated from Yale and earned an M.F.A. at the University of Oregon. His first novel, *Native Speaker* (1995), won the Hemingway Foundation/PEN Award. In 1999, he published a second novel, *A Gesture Life*, about the cultural conflicts and war memories of a Japanese-American of Korean descent.

In "Coming Home Again," which follows, Lee returns to the house where he grew up as his mother is dying. Lee's essay represents the first real travel that many children or adolescents undergo—the trip away from home to boarding school or college. This experience has distanced Lee from home. The central room in his home—the kitchen—and the central memory of his childhood—his mother's cooking—come together in this essay. The smells, textures, and tastes of food become the symbol of home and of Korean culture and parental sacrifice, all rendered poignant by the distance he has traveled away from them.

"Coming Home Again"

When my mother began using the electronic pump that fed her liquids and medication, we moved her to the family room. The bedroom she shared with my father was upstairs, and it was impossible to carry the machine up and down all day and night. The pump itself was attached to a metal stand on casters, and she pulled it along wherever she went. From anywhere in the house, you could hear the sound of the wheels clicking out a steady time over the grout lines of the slate-tiled foyer, her main thoroughfare to the bathroom and the kitchen. Sometimes you would hear her halt after only a few steps, to catch her breath or steady her balance, and whatever you were doing was instantly suspended by a pall of silence.

I was usually in the kitchen, preparing lunch or dinner, poised over the butcher block with her favorite chef's knife in my hand and her old yellow apron slung around my neck. I'd be breathless in the sudden quiet, and, having ceased my mincing and chopping, would stare blankly at the brushed sheen of the blade. Eventually, she would clear her throat or call out to say she was fine, then begin to move again, starting her rhythmic *ka-jug*; and only then could I go on with my cooking, the world of our house turning once more, wheeling through the black.

I wasn't cooking for my mother but for the rest of us. When she first moved downstairs she was still eating, though scantily, more just to taste what we were having than from any genuine desire for food. The point was simply to sit together at the kitchen table and array ourseves like a family again. My mother would gently set herself down in her customary chair near the stove. I sat across from her, my father and sister to my left and right, and crammed in the center was all the food I had made—a spicy codfish stew, say, or a casserole of gingery beef, dishes that in my youth she had prepared for us a hundred times.

It had been ten years since we'd all lived together in the house, which at fifteen I had left to attend boarding school in New Hampshire. My mother would sometimes point this out, by speaking of our present time as being "just like before Exeter," which surprised me, given how proud she always was that I was a graduate of the school.

My going to such a place was part of my mother's not so secret plan to change my character, which she worried was becoming too much like hers. I was clever and able enough, but without outside pressure I was readily given to sloth and vanity. The famous school—which none of us knew the first thing about—would prove my mettle. She was right, of course, and while I was there I would falter more than a few times, academically and otherwise. But I never thought that my leaving home then would ever be a problem for her, a private quarrel she would have even as her life waned.

Now her house was full again. My sister had just resigned from her job in New York City, and my father, who typically saw his psychiatric patients until eight or nine in the evening, was appearing in the driveway at four-thirty. I had been living at home for nearly a year and was in the final push of work on what would prove a dismal failure of a novel. When I wasn't struggling over my prose, I kept occupied with the things she usually did—the daily errands, the grocery shopping, the vacuuming and the cleaning, and, of course, all the cooking.

When I was six or seven years old, I used to watch my mother as she prepared our favorite meals. It was one of my daily pleasures. She shooed me away in the beginning, telling me that the kitchen wasn't my place, and adding, in her half-proud, half-deprecating way, that her kind of work would only serve to weaken me. "Go out and play with your friends," she'd snap in Korean, "or better yet, do your reading and homework." She knew that I had already done both, and that as the evening approached there was no place to go save her small and tidy kitchen, from which the clatter of her mixing bowls and pans would ring through the house.

I would enter the kitchen quietly and stand beside her, my chin lodging upon the point of her hip. Peering through the crook of her arm, I beheld the movements of her hands. For *kalbi*, she would take up a butchered short rib in her narrow hand, the flinty bone shaped like a section of an airplane wing and deeply embedded in gristle and flesh, and with the point of her knife cut so that the bone fell away, though not completely, leaving it connected to the meat by the barest opaque layer of tendon. Then she methodically butterflied the flesh, cutting and unfolding, repeating the action until the meat lay out on her board, glistening and ready for seasoning. She scored it diagonally, then sifted sugar into the crevices with her pinched fingers, gently rubbing in the crystals. The sugar would tenderize as well as sweeten the meat. She did this with each rib, and then set them all aside in a large shallow bowl. She minced a half-dozen cloves of garlic, a stub of ginger-root, sliced up a few scallions, and spread it all over the meat. She wiped her hands and took out a bottle of sesame oil, and, after pausing for a moment, streamed the dark oil in two swift circles around the bowl. After adding a few splashes of soy sauce, she thrust her hands in and kneaded the flesh, careful not to dislodge the bones. I asked her why it mattered that they remain connected. "The meat needs the bone nearby," she said, "to borrow its richness." She wiped her hands clean of the marinade, except for her little finger, which she would flick with her tongue from time to time, because she knew that the flavor of a good dish developed not at once but in stages.

Whenever I cook, I find myself working just as she would, readying the ingredients—a mash of garlic, a julienne of red peppers, fantails of shrimp—and piling them in little mounds about the cutting surface. My mother never left me any recipes, but this is how I learned to make her food, each dish coming not from a list or a card but from the aromatic spread of a board.

I've always thought it was particularly cruel that the cancer was in her stomach, and that for a long time at the end she couldn't eat. The last meal I made for her was on New Year's Eve, 1990. My sister suggested that instead of a rib roast or a bird, or the usual overflow of Korean food, we make all sorts of finger dishes that our mother might fancy and pick at.

We set the meal out on the glass coffee table in the family room. I prepared a tray of smoked-salmon canapés, fried some Korean bean cakes, and made a few other dishes I thought she might enjoy. My sister supervised me, arranging the platters, and then with some pomp carried each dish in to our parents. Finally, I brought out a bottle of champagne in a bucket of ice. My mother had moved to the sofa and was sitting up, surveying the low table. "It looks pretty nice," she said. "I think I'm feeling hungry."

This made us all feel good, especially me, for I couldn't remember the last time she had felt any hunger or had eaten something I cooked. We began to eat. My mother picked up a piece of salmon toast and took a tiny corner in her mouth. She rolled it around for a moment and then pushed it out with the tip of her tongue, letting it fall back onto her plate. She swallowed hard, as if to quell a gag, then glanced up to see if we had noticed. Of course we all had. She attempted a bean cake, some cheese, and then a slice of fruit, but nothing was any use.

She nodded at me anyway, and said, "Oh, it's very good." But I was already feeling lost and I put down my plate abruptly, nearly shattering it on the thick glass. There was an ugly pause before my father asked me in a weary, gentle voice if anything was wrong, and I answered that it was nothing, it was the last night of a long year, and we were together, and I was simply relieved. At midnight, I poured out glasses of champagne, even one for my mother, who took a deep sip. Her manner grew playful and light, and I helped her shuffle to her mattress, and she lay down in the place where in a brief week she was dead.

My mother could whip up most anything, but during our first years of living in this country we ate only Korean foods. At my harangue-like behest, my mother set herself to learning how to cook exotic American dishes. Luckily, a kind neighbor, Mrs. Churchill, a tall, florid young woman with flaxen hair, taught my mother her most trusted recipes. Mrs. Churchill's two young sons, palish, weepy boys with identical crew cuts, always accompanied her, and though I liked them well enough, I would slip away from them after a few minutes, for I knew that the real action would be in the kitchen, where their mother was playing guide. Mrs. Churchill hailed from the state of Maine, where the finest Swedish meatballs and tuna casserole and angel food cake in America are made. She readily demonstrated certain techniques—how to layer wet sheets of pasta for a lasagna or whisk up a simple roux, for example. She often brought gift shoeboxes containing curious ingredients like dried oregano, instant yeast, and cream of mushroom soup. The two women, though at ease and jolly with each other, had difficulty communicating, and this was made worse by the often confusing teminology of Western cuisine ("corned beef," "deviled eggs"). Although I was just learning the language myself, I'd gladly play the interlocutor, jumping back and forth between their places at the counter, dipping my fingers into whatever sauce lay about.

I was an insistent child, and, being my mother's firstborn, much too prized. My mother could say no to me, and did often enough, but anyone who knew us—particularly my father and sister—could tell how much the denying pained her. And if I was overconscious of her indulgence even then, and suffered the rushing pangs of guilt that she could inflict upon me with the slightest wounded turn of her lip, I was too happily obtuse and venal to let her cease. She reminded me daily that I was her sole son, her reason for living, and that if she were to lose me, in either body or spirit, she wished that God would mercifully smite her, strike her down like a weak branch.

In the traditional fashion, she was the house accountant, the maid, the launderer, the disciplinarian, the driver, the secretary, and, of course, the cook. She was also my first basketball coach. In South Korea, where girls' high school basketball is a popular spectator sport, she had been a star, the point guard for the national high school team that once won the all-Asia championships. I learned this one Saturday during the summer, when I asked my father if he would go down to the schoolyard and shoot some baskets with me. I had just finished the fifth grade, and wanted desperately to make the middle school team the coming fall. He called for my mother and sister to come along. When we arrived, my sister immediately ran off to the swings, and I recall being annoyed that my mother wasn't following her. I dribbled clumsily around the key, on the verge of losing control of the ball, and flung a flat shot that caromed wildly off the rim. The ball bounced to my father, who took a few not so graceful dribbles and made an easy layup. He dribbled out and then drove to the hoop for a layup on the other side. He rebounded his shot and passed the ball to my mother, who had been watching us from the foul line. She turned from the basket and began heading the other way.

"*Um-mah*," I cried at her, my exasperation already bubbling over, "the basket's over *here*!"

After a few steps she turned around, and from where the professional three-point line must be now, she effortlessly flipped the ball up in a two-handed set shot, its flight truer and higher than I'd witnessed from any boy or man. The ball arced cleanly into the hoop, stiffly popping the chain-link net. All afternoon, she rained in shot after shot, as my father and I scrambled after her.

When we got home from the playground, my mother showed me the photograph album of her team's championship run. For years I kept it in my room, on the same shelf that housed the scrapbooks I made of basketball stars, with magazine clippings of slick players like Bubbles Hawkins and Pistol Pete and George (the Iceman) Gervin.

It puzzled me how much she considered her own history to be immaterial, and if she never patently diminished herself, she was able to finesse a kind of self-removal by speaking of my father whenever she could. She zealously recounted his excellence as a student in medical school and reminded me, each night before I started my homework, of how hard he drove himself in his work to make a life for us. She said that because of his Asian face and imperfect English, he was "working two times the American doctors." I knew that she was building him up, buttressing him with both genuine admiration and her own brand of anxious braggadocio, and that her overarching concern was that I might fail to see him as she wished me to—in the most dawning light, his pose steadfast and solitary.

In the year before I left for Exeter, I became weary of the oft-repeated accounts of my father's success. I was a teenager, and so ever inclined to be dismissive and bitter toward anything that had to do with family and home. Often enough, my mother was the object of my derision. Suddenly, her life seemed so small to me. She was there, and sometiems, I thought, *always* there, as if she were confined to the four walls of our house. I would even complain about her cooking. Mostly, though, I was getting more and more impatient with the difficulty she encountered in doing everyday things. I was afraid for her. One day, we got into a terrible argument when she asked me to call the bank, to question a discrepancy she had discovered in the monthly statement. I asked her why she couldn't call herself. I was stupid and brutal, and I knew exactly how to wound her.

"Whom do I talk to?" she said. She would mostly speak to me in Korean, and I would answer in English.

"The bank manager, who else?"

"What do I say?"

"Whatever you want to say."

"Don't speak to me like that!" she cried.

"It's just that you should be able to do it yourself," I said.

"You know how I feel about this!"

"Well, maybe then you should consider it *practice*," I answered lightly, using the Korean word to make sure she understood.

Her face blanched, and her neck suddenly became rigid, as if I were throttling her. She nearly struck me right then, but instead she bit her lip and ran upstairs. I followed her, pleading for forgiveness at her door. But it was the one time in our life that I couldn't convince her, melt her resolve with the blandishments of a spoiled son.

When my mother was feeling strong enough, or was in particulaly good spirits, she would roll her machine into the kitchen and sit at the table and watch me work. She wore pajamas day and night, mostly old pairs of mine.

She said, "I can't tell, what are you making?"

"*Mahn-doo* filling."

"You didn't salt the cabbage and squash."

"Was I supposed to?"

"Of course. Look, it's too wet. Now the skins will get soggy before you can fry them."

"What should I do?"

"It's too late. Maybe it'll be OK if you work quickly. Why didn't you ask me?"

"You were finally sleeping."

"You should have woken me."

"No way."

She sighed, as deeply as her weary lungs would allow.

"I don't know how you were going to make it without me."

"I don't know, either. I'll remember the salt next time."

"You better. And not too much."

We often talked like this, our tone decidedly matter-of-fact, chin up, just this side of being able to bear it. Once, while inspecting a potato fritter batter I was making, she asked me if she had ever done anything that I wished she hadn't done. I thought for a moment, and told her no. In the next breath, she wondered aloud if it was right of her to have let me go to Exeter, to live away from the house while I was so young. She tested the batter's thickness with her finger and called for more flour. Then she asked if, given a choice, I would go to Exeter again.

I wasn't sure what she was getting at, and I told her that I couldn't be certain, but probably yes, I would. She snorted at this and said it was my leaving home that had once so troubled our relationship. "Remember how I had so much difficulty talking to you? Remember?"

She believed back then that I had found her more and more ignorant each time I came home. She said she never blamed me, for this was the way she knew it would be with my wonderful new education. Nothing I could say seemed to quell the notion. But I knew that the problem wasn't simply the *education*; the first time I saw her again after starting school, barely six weeks later, when she and my father visited me on Parents Day, she had already grown nervous and distant. After the usual campus events, we had gone to the motel where they were staying in a nearby town and sat on the beds in our room. She seemed to sneak looks at me, as though I might discover a horrible new truth if our eyes should meet.

My own secret feeling was that I had missed my parents greatly, my mother especially, and much more than I had anticipated. I couldn't tell them that these first weeks were a mere blur to me, that I felt completely overwhelmed by all the studies and my much brighter friends and the thousand irritating details of living alone, and that I had really learned nothing, save perhaps how to put on a necktie while sprinting to class. I felt as if I had plunged too deep into the world, which, to my great horror, was much larger than I had ever imagined.

I welcomed the lull of the motel room. My father and I had nearly dozed off when my mother jumped up excitedly, murmured how stupid she was, and hurried to the closet by the door. She pulled out our old metal cooler and dragged it between the beds. She lifted the top and began unpacking plastic containers, and I thought she would never stop. One after the other they came out, each with a dish that traveled well—a salted stewed meat, rolls of Korean-style sushi. I opened a container of radish kimchi and suddenly the room bloomed with its odor, and I reeled in the very peculiar sensation (which perhaps only true kimchi lovers know) of simultaneously drooling and gagging as I breathed it all in. For the next few minutes, they watched me eat. I'm not certain that I was even hungry. But after weeks of pork parmigiana and chicken patties and wax beans, I suddenly realized that I had lost all the savor in my life. And it seemed I couldn't get enough of it back. I ate and I ate, so much and so fast that I actually went to the bathroom and vomited. I came out dizzy and sated with the phantom warmth of my binge.

And beneath the face of her worry, I thought, my mother was smiling.

From that day, my mother prepared a certain meal to welcome me home. It was always the same. Even as I rode the school's shuttle bus from Exeter to Logan airport, I could already see the exact arrangement of my mother's table.

I knew that we would eat in the kitchen, the table brimming with plates. There was the *kalbi* of course, broiled or grilled depending on the season. Leaf lettuce, to wrap the meat with. Bowls of garlicky clam broth with miso and tofu and fresh spinach. Shavings of cod dusted in flour and then dipped in egg wash and fried. Glass noodles with onions and shiitake. Scallion-and-hot-pepper pancakes. Chilled steamed shrimp. Seasoned salads of bean sprouts, spinach, and white radish. Crispy squares of seaweed. Steamed rice with barley and red beans. Homemade kimchi. It was all there—the old flavors I knew, the beautiful salt, the sweet, the excellent taste.

After the meal, my father and I talked about school, but I could never say enough for it to make any sense. My father would often recall his high school principal, who had gone to England to study the methods and traditions of the public schools, and regaled students with stories of the great Eton man. My mother sat with us, paring fruit, not saying a word but taking everything in. When it was time to go to bed, my father said good night first. I usually watched television until the early morning. My mother would sit with me for an hour or two, perhaps until she was accustomed to me again, and only then would she kiss me and head upstairs to sleep.

During the following days, it was always the cooking that started our conversations. She'd hold an inquest over the cold leftovers we ate at lunch, discussing each dish in terms of its balance of flavors or what might have been prepared differently. But mostly I begged her to leave the dishes alone. I wish I had paid more attention. After her death, when my father and I were the only ones left in the house, drifting through the rooms like ghosts, I sometimes tried to make that meal for him. Though it was too much for two, I made each dish anyway, taking as much care as I could. But nothing turned out quite right—not the color, not the smell. At the table, neither of us said much of anything. And we had to eat the food for days.

I remember washing rice in the kitchen one day and my mother's saying in English, from her usual seat, "I made a big mistake."

"About Exeter?"

"Yes. I made a big mistake. You should be with us for that time. I should never let you go there."

"So why did you?" I said.

"Because I didn't know I was going to die."

I let her words pass. For the first time in her life, she was letting herself speak her full mind, so what else could I do?

"But you know what?" she spoke up. "It was better for you. If you stayed home, you would not like me so much now."

I suggested that maybe I would like her even more.

She shook her head. "Impossible."

Sometimes I still think about what she said, about having made a mistake. I would have left home for college, that was never in doubt, but those years I was away at boarding school grew more precious to her as her illness progressed. After many months of exhaustion and pain and the haze of the drugs, I thought that her mind was beginning to fade, for more and more it seemed that she was seeing me again as her fifteen-year-old boy, the one she had dropped off in New Hampshire on a cloudy September afternoon.

I remember the first person I met, another new student, named Zack, who walked to the welcome picnic with me. I had planned to eat with my parents— my mother had brought a coolerful of food even that first day—but I learned of the cookout and told her that I should probably go. I wanted to go, of course. I was excited, and no doubt fearful and nervous, and I must have thought I was only thinking ahead. She agreed wholeheartedly, saying I certainly should. I walked them to the car, and perhaps I hugged them, before saying goodbye. One day, after she died, my father told me what happened on the long drive home to Syracuse.

He was driving the car, looking straight ahead. Traffic was light on the Massachusetts Turnpike, and the sky was nearly dark. They had driven for more than two hours and had not yet spoken a word. He then heard a strange sound from her, a kind of muffled chewing noise, as if something inside her were grinding its way out.

"So, what's the matter?" he said, trying to keep an edge to his voice.

She looked at him with her ashen face and she burst into tears. He began to cry himself, and pulled the car over onto the narrow shoulder of the turn-pike, where they stayed for the next half hour or so, the blank-faced cars dron-ing by them in the cold, onrushing night.

Every once in a while, when I think of her, I'm driving alone somewhere on the highway. In the twilight, I see their car off to the side, a blue Olds coupe with a landau top, and as I pass them by I look back in the mirror and I see them again, the two figures huddling together in the front seat. Are they sleep-ing? Or kissing? Are they all right?

[1996]

BILL BRYSON

(1951–)

Bill Bryson writes of travel as if it were situation comedy. He exploits the humorous potential of travel, the misconceptions and mishaps. *Neither Here Nor There* (1992), a series of quick takes on a tour of European coun-tries from Norway to the Mediterranean, dreives its humor from the incongruities of innocence and cynicism. *Notes from a Small Island* (1995) comes from Bryson's many years of living in England. Two of his Ameri-can books are *Lost Continent: Travels in Small-Town America* (1989) and *A Walk in the Woods: Rediscovering America on the Appalachian Trail* (1998). In the latter, a humorous account of hiking, he does some serious walking in the wilderness with a companion who is in even worse shape than Bryson himself. Bryson returned to America after living abroad for a number of years and published his impressions in *I'm a Stranger Here Myself: Notes on Returning to the U.S. after 20 Years Away* (1999).

In this excerpt from the essay "Fat Girls in Des Moines," home appears first as a place to escape, and Bryson writes satirically of the provincialism of his native Iowa. But as he becomes nostalgic remembering childhood vacations, his feelings about home change, and he ends on a note of homesickness and a resolve to go back. The essay combines both the desire to escape from home and, after an interval of travel, the desire to recover it through memory.

From *Fat Girls in Des Moines*

I come from Des Moines. Somebody had to. When you come from Des Moines you either accept the fact without question and settle down with a local girl named Bobbi and get a job at the Firestone Factory and live there forever and ever, or you spend your adolescence moaning at length about what a dump it is and how you can't wait to get out, and then you settle down with a local girl named Bobbi and get a job at the Firestone Factory and live there forever and ever.

Hardly anyone leaves. This is because Des Moines is the most powerful hypnotic known to man. Outside town there is a big sign that says: WELCOME TO DES MOINES. THIS IS WHAT DEATH IS LIKE. There isn't really. I just made that up. But the place does get a grip on you. People who have nothing to do with Des Moines drive in off the interstate, looking for gas or hamburgers, and stay forever. There's a New Jersey couple up the street from my parents' house whom you see wandering around from time to time looking faintly puzzled but strangely serene. Everybody in Des Moines is strangely serene.

The only person I ever knew in Des Moines who wasn't serene was Mr. Piper. Mr. Piper was my parents' neighbour, a leering, cherry-faced idiot who was forever getting drunk and crashing his car into telephone poles. Everywhere you went you encountered telephone poles and road signs leaning dangerously in testimony to Mr. Piper's driving habits. He distributed them all over the west side of town rather in the way dogs mark trees. Mr. Piper was the nearest possible human equivalent to Fred Flintstone, but less charming. He was a Shriner and a Republican—a Nixon Republican—and he appeared to feel that he had a mission in life to spread offence. His favourite pastime, apart from getting drunk and crashing his car, was to get drunk and insult the neighbours, particularly us because we were Democrats, though he was prepared to insult Republicans when we weren't available.

Eventually, I grew up and moved to England. This irritated Mr. Piper almost beyond measure. It was worse than being a Democrat. Whenever I was in town, Mr. Piper would come over and chide me. 'I don't know what you're doing over there with all those Limeys,' he would say. 'They're not clean people.'

'Mr. Piper, you don't know what you're talking about,' I would reply in my affected British accent. 'You are a cretin.' You could talk like that to Mr. Piper because (one) he *was* a cretin and (two) he never listened to anything that was said to him.

'Bobbi and I went over to London two years ago and our hotel room didn't even have a *bathroom* in it,' Mr. Piper would go on. 'If you wanted to take a leak in the middle of the night you had to walk about a mile down the hallway. That isn't a clean way to live.'

'Mr. Piper, the English are paragons of cleanliness. It is a well-known fact that they use more soap per capita than anyone else in Europe.'

Mr. Piper would snort derisively at this. 'That doesn't mean diddly-squat, boy, just because they're cleaner than a bunch of Krauts and Eye-ties. My God, a *dog's* cleaner than a bunch of Krauts and Eye-ties. And I'll tell you something else: if his Daddy hadn't bought Illinois for him, John F. Kennedy would never have been elected President.'

I had lived around Mr. Piper long enough not to be thrown by this abrupt change of tack. The theft of the 1960 presidential election was a long-standing pliant of his, one that he brought into the conversation every ten or twelve minutes regardless of the prevailing drift of the discussion. In 1963, during Kennedy's funeral, someone in the Waveland Tap punched Mr. Piper in the nose for making that remark. Mr. Piper was so furious that he went straight out and crashed his car into a telephone pole. Mr. Piper is dead now, which is of course one thing that Des Moines prepares you for.

When I was growing up I used to think that the best thing about coming from Des Moines was that it meant you didn't come from anywhere else in Iowa. By Iowa standards, Des Moines is a Mecca of cosmopolitanism, a dynamic hub of wealth and education, where people wear three-piece suits and dark socks, often simultaneously. During the annual state high school basketball tournament, when the hayseeds from out in the state would flood into the city for a week, we used to accost them downtown and snidely offer to show them how to ride an escalator or negotiate a revolving door. This wasn't always so far from reality. My friend Stan, when he was about sixteen, had to go and stay with his cousin in some remote, dusty hamlet called Dog Water or Dunceville or some such improbable spot—the kind of place where if a dog gets run over by a truck everybody goes out to have a look at it. By the second week, delirious with boredom, Stan insisted that he and his cousin drive the fifty miles into the county town, Hooterville, and find something to do. They went bowling at an alley with warped lanes and chipped balls and afterwards had a chocolate soda and looked at a *Playboy* in a drugstore, and on the way home the cousin sighed with immense satisfaction and said, 'Gee thanks, Stan. That was the best time I ever had in my whole life!' It's true.

I had to drive to Minneapolis once, and I went on a back road just to see the country. But there was nothing to see. It's just flat and hot, and full of corn and soybeans and hogs. I remembr one long, shimmering stretch where I could see a couple of miles down the highway and there was a brown dot beside the road. As I got closer I saw it was a man sitting on a box by his front yard in some six-house town with a name like Spiggot or Urinal, watching my approach with inordinate interest. He watched me zip past and in the rear-view mirror I could see him still watching me going on down the road until at last I disappeared into a heat haze. The whole thing must have taken about five minutes. I wouldn't be surprised if even now he thinks of me from time to time.

He was wearing a baseball cap. You can always spot an Iowa man because he is wearing a baseball cap advertising John Deere or a feed company, and because the back of his neck has been lasered into deep crevasses by years of driving a John Deere tractor back and forth in a blazing sun. (This does not do his mind a whole lot of good either.) His other distinguishing feature is that he looks ridiculous when he takes off his shirt because his neck and arms are chocolate brown and his torso is as white as a sow's belly. In Iowa it is called a farmer's tan and it is, I believe, a badge of distinction.

Iowa woman are almost always sensationally overweight—you see them at Merle Hay Mall in Des Moines on Saturdays, clammy and meaty in their shorts and halter-tops, looking a little like elephants dressed in children's clothes, yelling at their kids, calling names like Dwayne and Shauna. Jack Kerouac, of all people, thought that Iowa women were the prettiest in the country, but I don't think he ever went to Merle Hay Mall on a Saturday. I will say this, however—and it's a strange, strange thing—the teenaged daughters of these fat women are always utterly delectable, as soft and gloriously rounded and naturally fresh-smelling as a basket of fruit. I don't know what it is that happens to them, but it must be awful to marry one of these nubile cuties knowing that there is a time bomb ticking away in her that will at some unknown date make her bloat out into something huge and grotesque, presumably all of a sudden and without much notice, like a self-inflating raft from which the stopper has been abruptly jerked.

Even so, I don't think I would have stayed in Iowa. I never really felt at home there, even when I was small. In about 1957, my grandparents gave me a Viewmaster for my birthday and a packet of discs with the title 'Iowa—Our Glorious State'. I can remember thinking, even then, that the selection of glories was a trifle on the thin side. With no natural features of note, no national parks or battlefields or famous birthplaces, the Viewmaster people had to stretch their creative 3D talents to the full. Putting the Viewmaster to your eyes and clicking the white handle gave you, as I recall, a shot of Herbert Hoover's birthplace, impressively three-dimensional, followed by Iowa's other great treasure, the Little Brown Church in the Vale (which inspired the song whose tune nobody ever quite knows), the highway bridge over the

Mississippi River at Davenport (all the cars seemed to be hurrying towards Illinois), a field of waving corn, the bridge over the Missouri River at Council Bluffs and the Little Brown Church in the Vale again, taken from another angle. I can remember thinking even then that there must be more to life than that.

Then one grey Sunday afternoon when I was about ten I was watching TV and there was a documentary on about movie-making in Europe. One clip showed Anthony Perkins walking along some venerable old city street at dusk. I don't remember now if it was Rome or Paris, but the street was cobbled and shiny with rain and Perkins was hunched deep in a trench coat and I thought: 'Hey, *c'est moi!*' I began to read—no, I began to consume—*National Geographics*, with their pictures of flowing Lapps and mist-shrouded castles and ancient cities of infinite charm. From that moment, I wanted to be a European boy. I wanted to live in an apartment on a tree-lined street across from a park in the heart of a city, and from my bedroom window look out on a vista of hills and roof-tops. I wanted to ride trams and understand strange languages. I wanted friends named Werner and Marco who wore short pants and played soccer in the street and owned toys made of wood. I cannot for the life of me think why. I wanted my mother to send me out to buy three-foot-long loaves of bread from an aromatic shop with a wooden pretzel hung above the entrance. I wanted to step outside my front door and *be* somewhere.

As soon as I was old enough I left. I left Des Moines and Iowa and the United States and the War in Vietnam and Watergate, and settled across the world. And now when I come home it is to a foreign country, full of serial murderers and sports teams in the wrong towns (the Indianapolis Colts? the Toronto Blue Jays?) and a personable old fart who is President. My mother knew that personable old fart when he was a sportscaster called Dutch Reagan at WHO Radio in Des Moines. 'He was just a nice, friendly kind of dopey guy,' my mother says.

Which, come to that, is a pretty fair description of most Iowans. Don't get me wrong. I am not for a moment suggesting that Iowans are mentally deficient. They are a decidedly intelligent and sensible people who, despite their natural conservatism, have always been prepared to elect a conscientious, clear-thinking liberal in preference to some cretinous conservative. (This used to drive Mr. Piper practically insane.) And Iowans, I am proud to tell you, have the highest literacy rate in the nation: 99.5 per cent of grown-ups there can read. When I say they are kind of dopey, I mean that they are trusting and amiable and open. They are a tad slow, certainly—when you tell an Iowan a joke, you can see a kind of race going on between his brain and his expression—but it's not because they're incapable of high-speed mental activity, it's only that there's not much call for it. Their wits are dulled by simple, wholesome faith in God and the soil and their fellow man.

Above all, Iowans are friendly. You go into a strange diner in the South and everything goes quiet, and you realize all the other customers are looking at you as if they are sizing up the risk involved in murdering you for your wallet and leaving your body in a shallow grave somewhere out in the swamps. In Iowa you are the centre of attention, the most interesting thing to hit town since a tornado carried off old Frank Sprinkel and his tractor last May. Everybody you meet acts like he would gladly give you his last beer and let you sleep with his sister. Everyone is strangely serene.

The last time I was home, I went to Kresge's downtown and bought a bunch of postcards to send back to England. I bought the most ridiculous ones I could find—a sunset over a feedlot, a picture of farmers bravely grasping a moving staircase beside the caption: 'We rode the escalator at Merle Hay Mall!'—that sort of thing. They were so uniformly absurd that when I took them up to the check-out, I felt embarrassed by them, as if I were buying dirty magazines and hoped somehow to convey the impression that they weren't really for me. But the check-out lady regarded each of them with great interest and deliberation—just like they always do with dirty magazines, come to that.

When she looked up at me she was almost misty-eyed. She wore butterfly eyeglasses and a beehive hairdo. 'Those are real nice,' she said. 'You know, honey, I've bin in a lot of states and seen a lot of places, but I can tell you that this is just about the purtiest one I ever saw.' She really said 'purtiest'. She really meant it. The poor woman was in a state of terminal hypnosis. I glanced at the cards and to my surprise I suddenly saw what she meant. I couldn't help but agree with her. They were purty. Together, we made a little pool of silent admiration. For one giddy, careless moment, I was almost serene myself.

My father liked Iowa. He lived his whole life in the state, and indeed is even now working his way through eternity there, in Glenview Cemetery in Des Moines. But every year he became seized with a quietly maniacal urge to get out of the state and go on vacation. Every summer, without a whole lot of notice, he would load the car to groaning, hurry us into it, take off for some distant point, return to get his wallet after having driven almost to the next state, and take off again for some distant point. Every year it was the same. Every year it was awful.

The big killer was the tedium. Iowa is in the middle of the biggest plain this side of Jupiter. Climb on to a roof-top almost anywhere in the state and you are confronted with a featureless sweep of corn as far as the eye can see. It is 1,000 miles from the sea in any direction, 600 miles from the nearest mountain, 400 miles from skyscrapers and muggers and things of interest, 300 miles from people who do not habitually stick a finger in their ear and swivel it around as a preliminary to answering any question addressed to them by a stranger. To reach anywhere of even passing interest from Des

Moines by car requires a journey that in other countries would be considered epic. It means days and days of unrelenting tedium, in a baking steel capsule on a ribbon of highway.

In my memory, our vacations were always taken in a big blue Rambler station wagon. It was a cruddy car—my dad always bought cruddy cars, until he got to the male menopause and started buying zippy red convertibles—but it had the great virtue of space. My sister and I in the back were yards away from my parents in front, in effect in another room. We quickly discovered during illicit forays into the picnic hamper that if you stuck a bunch of Ohio Blue tip matches into an apple or hard-boiled egg, so that it resembled a porcupine, and casually dropped it out the back window, it was like a bomb. It would explode with a small bang and a surprisingly big flash of blue flame, causing cars following behind to veer in an amusing fashion.

My dad, miles away up front, never knew what was going on or could understand why all day long cars would zoom up alongside him with the driver gesticulating furiously, before tearing off into the distance. 'What was that all about?' he would say to my mother in a wounded tone.

'I don't know, dear,' my mother would say mildly. My mother only ever said two things. She said: 'I don't know, dear.' And she said: 'Can I get you a sandwich, honey?' Occasionally on our trips she would volunteer other bits of information like 'Should that dashboard light be glowing like that, dear?' or 'I think you hit that dog/man/blind person back there, honey,' but mostly she kept quiet. This was because on vacations my father was a man obsessed. His principal obsession was trying to economize. He always took us to the crummiest hotels and motor lodges—the sort of places where there were never any coat hangers because they had all been used by abortionists. And at the roadside eating houses, you always knew, with a sense of doom, that at some point before finishing you were going to discover someone else's congealed egg yolk lurking somewhere on your plate or plugged between the tines of your fork. This, of course, meant cooties and a long, painful death.

But even that was a relative treat. Usually we were forced to picnic by the side of the road. My father had an instinct for picking bad picnic sites—on the apron of a busy truck stop or in a little park that turned out to be in the heart of some seriously deprived ghetto so that groups of Negro children would come and stand silently by our table and watch us eating white people's foods like Hostess Cupcakes and crinkle-cut potato chips—and it always became incredibly windy the moment we stopped so that my mother spent the whole of lunchtime chasing paper plates over an area of about an acre.

In 1957 my father invested $19.98 in a gas stove that took an hour to assemble and was so wildly temperamental that we children were always ordered to stand well back when it was being lit. This always proved unnecessary, however, because the stove would flicker to life for only a few seconds before spluttering out, and my father would spend many hours turning it this way and that to keep it out of the wind, simultaneously addressing it in a low, agitated tone normally associated with the chronically insane. All the while my sister and I would implore him to take us some place with air-conditioning and linen tablecloths and ice cubes clinking in glasses of clear water. 'Dad,' we would beg, 'you're a successful man. You make a good living. Take us to a Howard Johnson's.' But he wouldn't have it. He was a child of the Depression and where capital outlays were involved he always wore the haunted look of a fugitive who has just heard bloodhounds in the distance.

Eventually, with the sun low in the sky, he would hand us hamburgers that were cold and raw and smelled of butane. We would take one bite and refuse to eat any more. So my father would lose his temper and throw everything into the car and drive us at high speed to some roadside diner where a sweaty man with a floppy hat would sling hash while grease fires danced on his grill. And afterwards, in a silent car filled with bitterness and unquenched basic needs, we would mistakenly turn off the main highway and get lost and end up in some no-hope town with a name like Draino, Indiana, or Tapwater, Missouri, and get a room in the only hotel in town, the sort of rundown place where if you wanted to watch TV it meant you had to sit in the lobby and share a cracked leatherette sofa with an old man with big sweat circles under his arms. The old man would almost certainly have only one leg and probably one other truly arresting deficiency, like no nose or a caved-in forehead, which meant that although you were sincerely intent on watching *Laramie* or *Our Miss Brooks*, you found your gaze being drawn, ineluctably and sneakily, to the amazing eaten-away body sitting beside you. You couldn't help yourself. Occasionally the man would turn out to have no tongue, in which case he would try to engage you in a lively conversation.

On another continent, 4,000 miles away, I am quietly seized with that nostalgia that overcomes you when you have reached the middle of your life and your father has recently died and it dawns on you that when he went he took a part of you with him. I want to go back to the magic places of my youth—to Mackinac Island, Estes Park, Gettysburg—and see if they were as good as I remember them. I want to hear the long, low sound of a Rock Island locomotive calling across a still night, and the clack of it receding into the distance. I want to see lightning bugs, and hear cicadas shrilling, and be inescapably immersed in that hot, crazy-making August weather that makes your underwear scoot up every crack and fissure and cling to you like latex, and drives mild-mannered men to pull out handguns in bars and light up the night with gunfire. I want to look for Ne-Hi Pop and Burma Shave signs and go to a ball game and sit at a marble-topped soda fountain and drive through the kind of small town that Deanna Durbin and Mickey Rooney used to live in in the movies. It's time to go home.

[1988]

MAYA ANGELOU

(1928–)

Memoirist, poet, screenwriter, civil rights leader, actress, dancer, and singer, Maya Angelou is one of the most celebrated figures of her generation. At President Clinton's inauguration in 1993, Angelou was invited to read a poem she had composed for the occasion. Her first book, the memoir *I Know Why the Caged Bird Sings* (1970), which moves from childhood in her native Alabama to a troubled adolescence, remains her best-known work, but her autobiography continues in multiple volumes.

    All God's Children Need Traveling Shoes (1986), excerpted below, covers her life in the 1960s, when she lived in Egypt and later Ghana, where her son was attending university. Angelou's return to Africa, the land of her ancestors, represents a particular kind of American journey. Her account offers yet another perspective on home, a place of one's origins and the collective home of one's people.

From *All God's Children Need Traveling Shoes*

Each morning Ghana's seven-and-one-half million people seemed to crowd at once into the capital city where the broad avenues as well as the unpaved rutted lanes became gorgeous with moving pageantry: bicycles, battered lorries, hand carts, American and European cars, chauffeur-driven limousines. People on foot struggled for right-of-way, white-collar workers wearing white knee-high socks brushed against market women balancing large baskets on their heads as they proudly swung their wide hips. Children, bright faces shining with palm oil, picked openings in the throng, and pretty young women in western clothes affected not to notice the attention they caused as they laughed together talking in the musical Twi language. Old men sat or stooped beside the road smoking homemade pipes and looking wise as old men have done eternally.

    The too sweet aromas of flowers, the odors of freshly fried fish and stench from open sewers hung in my clothes and lay on my skin. Car horns blew, drums thumped. Loud radio music and the muddle of many languages shouted or murmured. I needed country quiet.

The Fiat was dependable, and I had a long weekend, money in my purse, and a working command of Fanti, so I decided to travel into the bush. I bought roasted plaintain stuffed with boiled peanuts, a quart of Club beer and headed my little car west. The stretch was a highway from Accra to Cape Coast, filled with trucks and private cars passing from lane to lane with abandon. People hung out of windows of the crowded mammie lorries, and I could hear singing and shouting when the drivers careened those antique vehicles up and down hills as if each was a little train out to prove it could.

I stopped in Cape Coast only for gas. Although many Black Americans had headed for the town as soon as they touched ground in Ghana, I successfully avoided it for a year. Cape Coast Castle and the nearby Elmina Castle had been holding forts for captured slaves. The captives had been imprisoned in dungeons beneath the massive buildings and friends of mine who had felt called upon to make the trek reported that they felt the thick stone walls still echoed with old cries.

The palm tree–lined streets and fine white stone buildings did not tempt me to remain any longer than necessary. Once out of the town and again onto the tarred roads, I knew I had not made a clean escape. Despite my hurry, history had invaded my litle car. Pangs of self-pity and a sorrow for my unknown relatives suffused me. Tears made the highway waver, and were salty on my tongue.

What did they think and feel, my grandfathers, caught on those green Savannahs, under the baobab trees? How long did their families search for them? Did the dungeon wall feel chilly and its slickness strange to my grandmothers who were used to the rush of air against bamboo huts and the sound of birds rattling their grass roofs?

I had to pull off the road. Just passing near Cape Coast Castle had plunged me back into the eternal melodrama.

There would be no purging, I knew, unless I asked all the questions. Only then would the spirits understand that I was feeding them. It was a crumb, but it was all I had.

I allowed the shapes to come to my imagination: children passed tied together by ropes and chains, tears abashed, stumbling in dull exhaustion, then women, hair uncombed, bodies gritted with sand, and sagging in defeat. Men, muscles without memory, minds dimmed, plodding, leaving bloodied footprints in the dirt. The quiet was awful. None of them cried, or yelled, or bellowed. No moans came from them. They lived in a mute territory, dead to feeling and protest. These were the legions, sold by sisters, stolen by brothers, bought by strangers, enslaved by the greedy and betrayed by history.

For a long time, I sat as in an open-air auditorium watching a troop of tragic players enter and exit the stage.

The visions faded as my tears ceased. Light returned and I started the car, turned off the main road, and headed for the interior. Using rutted track roads, and lanes a little larger than foot paths, I found the River Pra. The black water moving quietly, ringed with the tall trees, seemed enchanted. A fear of snakes kept me in the car, but I parked and watched the bright sun turn the water surface into a rippling cloth of lamé. I passed through villages which were little more than collections of thatch huts with goats and small children wandering in the lanes. The noise of my car brought smiling adults out to wave at me.

In the late afternoon, I reached the thriving town that was my destination. A student whom I had met at Legon had spoken to me often of the gold-mining area, of Dunkwa, his birthplace. His reports had so glowed with the town's virtues, and I had chosen that spot for my first journey.

My skin color, features and the Ghana cloth I wore made me look like any young Ghanaian woman. I could pass if I didn't talk too much.

As usual, in the towns of Ghana, the streets were filled with vendors selling their wares of tinned pat milk, hot spicy Killi Willis (fried, ripe plaintain chips), Pond's Cold Cream and anti-mosquito incense rings. Farmers were returning home, children returning from school. Young boys grinned at mincing girls and always there were the market women, huge and impervious. I searched for a hotel sign in vain and as the day lengthened, I started to worry. I didn't have enough gas to get to Koforidua, a large town northeast of Dunkwa, where there would certainly be hotels, and I didn't have the address of my student's family. I parked the car a little out of the town center and stopped a woman carrying a bucket of water on her head and a baby on her back.

"Good day." I spoke in Fanati, and she responded. I continued, "I beg you. I am a stranger looking for a place to stay."

She repeated, "Stranger?" and laughed. "You are a stranger? No. No."

To many Africans only Whites could be strangers. All Africans belonged somewhere, to some clan. All Akan-speaking people belong to one of eight blood lines (Abosua) and one of eight spirit lines (Ntoro).

I said, "I am not from here."

For a second fear darted in her eyes. There was the possibility that I was a witch or some unhappy ghost from the country of the dead. I quickly said, "I am from Accra." She gave me a good smile. "Oh, one Accra. Without a home." She laughed. The Fanti word *Nkran*, for which the capitol was named, means the large ant that builds ten-foot-high domes of red clay and lives with millions of other ants.

"Come with me." She turned quickly, steadying the bucket on her head and led me between two corrugated tin shacks. The baby bounced and slept on her back, secured by the large piece of cloth strapped around her body. We passed a compound where women were pounding the dinner foo foo in wooden bowls.

The woman shouted, "Look what I have found. One Nkran has no place to sleep tonight." The women laughed and asked, "One Nkran? I don't believe it."

"Are you taking it to the old man?"

"Of course."

"Sleep well, alone, Nkran, if you can." My guide stopped before a small house. She put the water on the ground and told me to wait while she entered the house. She returned immediately followed by a man who rubbed his eyes as if he had just been awakened.

He walked close and peered hard at my face. "This is the Nkran?" The woman was adjusting the bucket on her head.

"Yes, Uncle. I have brought her." She looked at me, "Good-bye, Nkran. Sleep in peace. Uncle, I am going." The man said, "Go and come, child," and resumed studying my face. "You are not Ga." He was reading my features.

A few small childen had collected around his knees. They could barely hold back their giggles as he interrogated me.

"Aflao?"

I said, "No."

"Brong-ahafo?"

I said, "No. I am——." I meant to tell him the truth, but he said, "Don't tell me. I will soon know." He continued staring at me. "Speak more. I will know from your Fanti."

"Well, I have come from Accra and I need to rent a room for the night. I told that woman that I was a stranger . . ."

He laughed. "And you are. Now, I know. You are Bambara from Liberia. It is clear you are Bambara." He laughed again. "I always can tell. I am not easily fooled." He shook my hand. "Yes, we will find you a place for the night. Come." He touched a boy at his right. "Find Patience Aduah, and bring her to me."

The children laughed and all ran away as the man led me into the house. He pointed me to a seat in the neat little parlor and shouted, "Foriwa, we have a guest. Bring beer." A small Black women with an imperial air entered the room. Her knowing face told me that she had witnessed the scene in her front yard.

She spoke to her husband. "And, Kobina, did you find who the stranger was?" She walked to me. I stood and shook her hand. "Welcome, stranger." We both laughed. "Now don't tell me, Kobina, I have ears, also. Sit down, Sister, beer is coming. Let me hear you speak."

We sat facing each other while her husband stood over us smiling. "You, Foriwa, you will never get it."

I told her my story, adding a few more words I had recently learned. She laughed grandly. "She is Bambara. I could have told you when Abaa first brought her. See how tall she is? See her head? See her color? Men, huh. They only look at a woman's shape."

Two childen brought beer and glasses to the man who poured and handed the glasses around. "Sister, I am Kobina Artey; this is my wife Foriwa and some of my children."

I introduced myself, but because they had taken such relish in detecting my tribal origin I couldn't tell them that they were wrong. Or, less admirably, at that moment I didn't want to remember that I was an American. For the first time since my arrival, I was very nearly home. Not a Ghanaian, but at least accepted as an African. The sensation was worth a lie.

Voices came to the house from the yard.

"Brother Kobina," "Uncle," "Auntie."

Foriwa opened the door to a group of people who entered speaking fast and looking at me.

"So this is the Bambara woman? The stranger?" They looked me over and talked with my hosts. I understood some of their conversation. They said that I was nice looking and old enough to have a little wisdom. They announced that my car was parked a few blocks away. Kobina told them that I would spend the night with the newlyweds, Patience and Kwame Duodu. Yes, they could see clearly that I was a Bambara.

"Give us the keys to your car, Sister; someone will bring your bag."

I gave up the keys and all resistance. I was either at home with friends, or I would die wishing that to be so.

Later, Patience, her husband, Kwame, and I sat out in the yard around a cooking fire near to their thatched house which was much smaller than the Artey bungalow. They explained that Kobina Artey was not a chief, but a member of the village council, and all small matters in that area of Dunkwa were taken to him. As Patience stirred the stew in the pot, which was balanced over the fire, children and women appeared sporadically out of the darkness carrying covered plates. Each time Patience thanked the bearers and directed them to the house, I felt the distance narrow between my past and present.

In the United States, during segregation, Black American travelers, unable to stay in hotels restricted to White patrons, stopped at churches and told the Black ministers or deacons of their predicaments. Church officials would select a home and then inform the unexpecting hosts of the decision. There was never a protest, but the new hosts relied on the generosity of their neighbors to help feed and even entertain their guests. After the travelers were settled, surreptitious knocks would sound on the back door.

In Stamps, Arkansas, I heard so often, "Sister Henderson, I know you've got guests. Here's a pan of biscuits."

"Sister Henderson, Mama sent a half a cake for your visitors."

"Sister Henderson, I made a lot of macaroni and cheese. Maybe this will help with your visitors."

My grandmother would whisper her thanks and finally when the family and guests sat down at the table, the offerings were so different and plentiful it appeared that days had been spent preparing the meal.

Patience invited me inside, and when I saw the table I was confirmed in my earlier impression. Ground nut stew, garden egg stew, hot pepper soup, kenke, kotomre, fried plantain, dukuno, shrimp, fish cakes, and more, all crowded together on variously patterned plates.

In Arkansas, the guests would never suggest, although they knew better, that the host had not prepared every scrap of food, especially for them.

I said to Patience, "Oh, Sister, you went to such trouble."

She laughed, "It is nothing, Sister. We don't want our Bambara relative to think herself a stranger anymore. Come, let us wash and eat."

After dinner I followed Patience to the outdoor toilet, then they gave me a cot in a very small room.

In the morning I wrapped my cloth under my arms, sarong fashion, and walked with Patience to the bath house. We joined about twenty women in a walled enclosure that had no ceiling. The greetings were loud and cheerful as we soaped ourselves and poured buckets of water over our shoulders.

Patience introduced me. "This is our Bambara sister."

"She's a tall one all right. Welcome, Sister."

"I like her color."

"How many children, Sister?" The woman was looking at my breasts.

I apologized, "I only have one."

"One?"

"One?"

"One!" Shouts reverberated over the splashing water. I said, "One, but I'm trying."

They laughed. "Try hard, sister. Keep trying."

We ate leftovers from the last night feast and I said a sad good-bye to my hosts. The children walked me back to my car with the oldest boy carrying my bag. I couldn't offer money to my hosts, Arkansas had taught me that, but I gave change to the children. They bobbed and jumped and grinned.

"Good-bye, Bambara Auntie."

"Go and come, Auntie."

"Go and come."

I drove into Cape Coast before I thought of the gruesome castle and out of its environs before the ghosts of slavery caught me. Perhaps their attempts had been half-hearted. After all, in Dunkwa, although I let a lie speak for me, I had proved that one of their descendants, at least one, could just briefly return to Africa, and that despite cruel betrayals, bitter ocean voyages and hurtful centuries, we were still recognizable.

[1986]

ANDREW X. PHAM

(1967–)

Andrew X. Pham fled Vietnam with his family several years after the fall of Saigon in 1975. Like many Vietnamese, they escaped in overcrowded boats and had to be rescued on the high seas. They eventually made their way to California, where Pham was educated. Against the wishes of his father, he quit his job as an engineer and went on a bicycling odyssey in a journey of self-discovery. He eventually flew to Vietnam, where he visited his birthplace and biked north to Hanoi and back to Saigon. *Catfish and Mandala: A Two-Wheeled Voyage through the Landscape and Memory of Vietnam* (1999) tells the story of his trip.

"Viet-Kieu," a chapter from that book, is the name that Vietnamese call their countrymen who have emigrated and taken citizenship elsewhere. The episode excerpted below comes near the end of the journey and centers on Pham's conflicting sense of his Vietnamese and American identities. It offers yet another version of the journey back to an earlier home and a very contemporary version of the return of an American immigrant to the land of his ancestors.

"Viet-Kieu"

From *Catfish and Mandala*

The closer I come to Nha Trang the more frequently I see group tours busing to local points of interest. The locals are familiar with the tourist traffic and don't shout "*Oy! Oy!*" at foreigners. The main road loops around a mountain and enters the outskirts of the city from the south side. There is a shortcut, some high school kids point out to me, up the mountain and along the cliff. It's a good sporting ride, they say. I'm about to bag 120 miles today and have no wish to climb a mountain. I come into the city the easy way.

Although the outlying area is a mirror image of all the other dusty little towns, the city center is far more developed than anything I've seen. I limp the battered bike through town, heading toward the water where the locals have told me there is lodging. Shady lanes unroll between banks of sprawling buildings set back behind brick fences. There's a nice flavor here predating the Liberation of '75. I was just a kid then, but I remembr Mom being very hip with her bell-bottoms and buggy sunglasses. She must have wasted scores of film rolls in Nha Trang, her favorite city. The breeze is fresh, sweet, not salty like Phan

Thiet. Out on the beachfront boulevard, I am suddenly in Waikiki! Someone has ripped it out of Hawaii and dropped it in downtown Nha Trang. A colossal skeleton of the Outrigger Hotel is being framed on the beach practically in the surf line. Tall, gleaming towers of glass and steel are already taking residence a stone's throw from the water. The sandy stretch of beach is jammed with fancy restaurants, bars hopping with modern rock, jazz, and Vietnamese pop. Aromas of grilled food turn heads and sharpen appetites. Along the avenue, fat Europeans and Australians pad about in thong bikinis, sheer sarongs, and Lycra shorts, dropping wads of dollars for seashells, corals, lacquered jewelry boxes, and bad paintings, loot, mementos, evidence.

I take the cheapest room available to a Viet-kieu at a government-run hotel (for some reason, Danes and Germans get lower rates), jump through a cold shower, then get back on my bike to head to the Vietnamese part of Nha Trang, where the food is cheaper and better. I am ravenous. Diarrhea be damned. Tonight I'm going to eat anything I want. After nearly three months of sporadic intestinal troubles, I'm still hoping that my sysem will acclimatize. I'm Vietnamese after all, and these microorganisms once thrived in my gut as thoroughly as in any Vietnamese here.

I eat dinner at an alley diner, nine tables crammed between two buildings lit with a couple of bare light bulbs. The family running the place says they are happy to have me, although they generally don't like foreigners. Eat too little, drink too little, but talk too much, they complain. Foreigners like to sit and sit and talk. Vietnamese eat and get out. Lounging is done in coffeehouses and beer halls. No problem. I prove to them I'm Vietnamese. I down two large bottles of Chinese beer and gorge myself on a monstrous meal of grilled meat served with a soy-and-pork-fat gravy, wrapping the meat in rice paper, cucumber, mint, pickled daikon, sour carrot, fresh basil, lettuce, chili pepper, cilantro, and rice vermicelli. Then I clear out quickly. I go to a hotel to check on a friend who might be in town. As a tour gudie, he is a regular at the hotel. The concierge confirms that my friend Cuong and his tour are in town. I leave him a note and wait for him at an ice-cream parlor down the street

"Hello! Andrew!"

"Cuong!"

I met him a few weeks after I arrived in Saigon. We bummed around the city several times with his girlfriends. I like him. We both agreed to check on each other when in Nha Trang or Vung Tau, both major cities on his itinerary.

He skips across the street, penny-loafing around the dog shit as he dodges motorbikes. Cuong doesn't wear sandals. No more. Not ever again. He told me. You can tell a Vietnamese by the way he wears his sandals. Is the stem firmly held between the toes? Or does the ball of the heel drag beyond the sandal? Do the sandals flap like loose tongues when he walks? Does he know there is mud between his toes? All this from a man who—in his own words—"dribbled away *[his]* youth as a roadside petro-boy selling gasoline out of glass bottles, wiping down motor-bikes, hustling for dimes, and playing barefoot soccer in the dirt."

He smoothes his shirt, fingers the ironed pleats of his gray slacks, straightens his pin-striped blue tie with red polka dots. Then, grinning, he steps closer and pumps my hand enthusiastically. "Calvin," he corrects me. "I'm sticking with your suggestion: Calvin. It's easier for the foreigners to pronounce." I'd come up with the name at his request. He wanted something that started with a "C" and was short and sharp and American.

"You made it! You're not hurt? No?" he says, patting me on the arm and looking me over. "A little thinner and darker, yes. Incredible. You biked all that way? Yes, yes, of course you did."

"You got my message?"

"Of course. May I join you?" he queries, forever the Vietnamese gentleman. I fill him in on all that happened since I last saw him nearly two months ago. When a waitress brings him his chilled Coke—no ice, just like the way foreigners drink their soda—he thanks her. She looks at him, a little startled to hear a Vietnamese man uttering platitudes like Westerners. Calvin has picked up the habit because he finds it more genteel and civilized.

I first made his acquaintance at a sidewalk café. He took me for a Japanese and wanted to practice his English. When I told him I was a Vietnamese from California, he was very uncomfortable using the term Viet-kieu, explaining that people said it with too many connotations. Sometimes, it was just a word, other times an insult or a term of segregation. *"Vietnamese are Vietnamese if they believe they are,"* he had said by way of explanation, and I liked him on the instant.

By Saigon standards, Calvin is a yuppie who came into his own by the most romantic way possible—by the compulsion of a promise made to his mother on her deathbed. One afternoon, when we were touring the outer districts of Saigon on his motorbike, Calvin pointed to a pack of greyhound-lean young men, shirtless, volleying a plastic bird back and forth with their feet. *"That was me. That's how I was until I was twenty-two. Can you believe it? I threw away all my young years, working odd jobs and messing around. I just didn't care."* His mother bequeathed him, her only child, a small sum, which he spent on English classes, not bothering to finish up high school. With what little remained, he bribed his way into a job as a hotel bellhop and worked his way up. He entered a special school for tour guides. After three years of intense training, he makes four hundred dollars a month plus two hundred in tips. Now, twenty-nine, single, and rich even by Saigon standards, he fares better than college grads who are blessed if they can command two hundred dollars a month. His biggest regret: *"I wish my mother could see me now."*

Calvin sips his Coke and plucks a pack of Marlboros from his shirt pocket, the American cigarette one of his main props for marking himself one of the upwardly mobile. "I'm down to half a pack a day," he mumbles apologetically, offering me a smoke. I decline. He puts his cigarette down saying: "Dirty, dirty Vietnamese habit." Calvin keeps a list of "dirty Vietnamese habits" and steels himself against them.

I tell him that Americans used to call cigarettes "white slavers." He considers that for a moment then smirks. *"That has a double meaning for us, doesn't it."* He counts the cigarettes remaining in the pack. *"Last one today,"* he announces. He seems to want my approval so I nod. Vindicated, he ignites the last of his daily nicotine allowance. He sighs the smoke downwind. *"Tell me. Tell me everything about your trip."*

As I recount the events since I last saw him, Calvin grows increasingly excited, digging me more for the details of Vietnam than for the actual mechanics of bike touring. How did the police treat you? Hanoi people are more formal than Southerners, aren't they? You think Uncle Ho's body is a hoax? What's the countryside like? Is it pretty like the Southern country? He flames another cigarette and orders us a round of beer. By our third round, he has chain-smoked into a second pack of Marlboros.

Late in the night, when I am sapped of tales from the road, Calvin, who is beer-fogged, leans back in his chair and asks, *"America is like a dream, isn't it?"*

After all I've seen, I agree. *"Sure."*

We contemplate the beer in our glasses. I ask him, *"Do you want to go there?"* I don't know why I ask him this. Maybe, believing that he is my equivalent in Vietnam, I want him to say he really loves the country and that it is magical, wonderful in ways I have yet to imagine. More powerful, more potent than the West.

Calvin sounds annoyed. *"Of course, Who wouldn't?"* He pauses, taking long, pensive drags on his cigarette. *"But perhaps only to visit. To see, understand–no?"*

"Why?"

"Simple. Here . . . here, I am a king." He leans over the table, shaking the cigarette at me. *"In America you, I mean all you Viet-kieu, are guests. And guests don't have the same rights as hosts."* He sits back, legs crossed at the knees, and throws a proprietary arm over the city. *"At least, here, I am king. I belong. I am better than most Vietnamese."*

"No, we're not guests. We're citizens. Permanent. Ideally we are all equal. Equal rights," I insert lamely, the words, recalled from elementary school history lessons, sounding hollow.

"Right, but do you FEEL like an American? Do you?"

Yes! Yes! Yes, I do. I really do, I want to shout it in his face. Already, the urge leaves a bad taste in my mouth. *"Sometimes, I do. Sometimes, I feel like I am a real American."*

I wish I could tell him. I don't mind forgetting who I am, but I know he wouldn't understand. I don't mind being looked at or treated just like another American, a white American. No, I don't mind at all. I want it. I like it. Yet every so often when I become really good at tricking myself, there is always that inevitable slap that shocks me out of my shell and prompts me to reassess everything.

How could I tell him my shame? How could I tell him about the drive-bys where some red-faced white would stick his head out of his truck, giving me the finger and screaming, "Go home, Chink!" Could I tell him it chilled me to wonder what would happen if my protagonist knew I was Vietnamese? What if his father had died in Vietnam? What if he was a Vietnam vet? Could I tell Calvin about the time my Vietnamese friends and I dined in a posh restaurant in Laguna Beach in Southern California? A white man at the next table, glaring at us, grumbled to his wife, "They took over Santa Ana. And now they're here. This whole state is going to hell." They was us Vietnamese. Santa Ana was now America's Little Saigon.

Could I tell Calvin I was initiated into the American heaven during my first week Stateside by eight black kids who pulverized me in the restroom, calling me Viet Cong? No. I grew up fighting blacks, whites, and Chicanos. The whites beat up the blacks. The blacks beat up the Chicanos. And everybody beat up the Chinaman whether or not he was really an ethnic Chinese. These new Vietnamese kids were easy pickings, small, bookish, passive, and not fluent in English.

So, we congregate in Little Saigons, we hide out in Chinatowns and Japantowns, blending in. We huddle together, surrounding ourselves with the material wealth of America, and wave our star-spangled banners, shouting: "We're Americans. We love America."

I cannot bring myself to confront my antagonists. Cannot always claim my rights as a nauralized citizen. Cannot, for the same reason, resist the veterans' pleas for money outside grocery stores. Cannot armor myself against the pangs of guilt at every homeless man wearing army fatigues. Sown deep in me is a seed of discomfort. Maybe shame. I see that we Vietnamese Americans don't talk about our history. Although we often pretend to be modest and humble as we preen our successful immigrant stories, we rarely admit even to ourselves the circumstances and the cost of our being here. We elude it all like a petty theft committed ages ago. When convenient, we take it as restitution for what happened to Vietnam.

Calvin senses my discomfort. It is his talent, a marked skill of his trade. He looks away, reaching for yet another cigarette to cover the silence I opened. He asks me the one question that Vietnamese throughout Vietnam have tried to broach obliquely: *Do they look down on Vietnamese in America? Do they hate you?*"

I don't want to dwell on that. Vietnamese believe that white Americans are to Viet-kieu as Viet-Kieu are to Vietnamese, each one a level above the next, respectively. And, somehow, this shames me, maybe because I cannot convince myself that it is entirely true or false. I divert the thrust and ask him, "*You are*

Westernized. You know how different foreigeners are from Vietnamese. How do you feel showing them around the country?"

"I like the work. Many of them are very nice. Curious about our culture. I like the Australians most. Rowdy and lots of trouble, but they respect Vietnamese."

"But don't you see the reactions on their faces when they see our squalor? Don't you hear the things they say about us? Don't tell me you've never heard it."

He looks uncomfortable, drawing deep from his nicotine stick, sighing the smoke to the stars. Then to his credit and my everlasting respect for him, he says quietly, facing the sky, "I do. I can't help it but I do. I take them out on the Saigon streets, you know, the poor parts because they ask me. They want pictures. I see them flinch at the beggars, the poverty of Vietnamese. The chicken-shacks we live in."

A wordless lull falls betwen us. We're both drunk. I am irritated at having to delve into a subject I avoid, and feeling mean-spirited I have goaded him onto equally disconcerting ground.

"It's very hard being a tour guide. Sometimes I feel like a pimp." He switches into his tour-guide English: "Here, look at this, sir. Yes, ma'am, these are the average Vietnamese. Yes, they are poor. Yes, sir. Here is our national monument. Very big. Very important to Vietnamese. You impressed? No, not so big?" He shrugs, saying, "I know they've got bigger monuments in their countries. Older, more important. What do our little things mean to them?"

The silence tells me we are moving too far into no-man's-land. One more cigarette. More beer. Tusking the smoke out of his nostrils, he seems to brace himself, gathering force like a wave, building before cresting white. As his beliefs come barreling out, I know the crushing impact of his words will stay with me, for in them I catch a glimpse of myself and of the true Cuong, the Cuong that came before and is deeper than the suave Calvin facing me. "Vietnamese aren't ashamed of our own poverty. We're not ashamed of squatting in mud huts and sleeping on rags. There is no shame in being poor. We were born into it just as Westerners are born white. The Westerners are white as we are yellow. There is already a difference between us. Our poverty is minor in the chasm that already exists. A small detail. The real damning thing is the fact that there are Viet-kieu, our own brothers, skin of our skin, blood of our blood, who look better than us, more civilized, more educated, more wealthy, more genteel. Viet-kieu look kingly next to the average Vietnamese. Look at you, look at me. You're wearing old jeans and I'm wearing a suit, but it's obvious who . . . who is superior. Can't you see? We look like monkeys because you make us look like monkeys just by your existence."

"Is this truly how Vietnamese see us Viet-kieu?"

"Some call you the lost brothers. Look at you. Living in America has lightened your skin, made you forget your language. You have tasted Western women and you're probably not as attracted to Vietnamese women anymore. You eat nutritious Western food and you are bigger and stronger than us. You know better than to smoke and drink like Vietnamese. You know exercise is good so you don't waste your time sitting in cafés and smoking your hard-earned money away. *Someday, your blood will mix so well with Western blood that there will be no difference between you and them. You are already lost to us.*"

I listen with dismay as his observations fall on me like a sentence, but I can tell in the back of his mind he is saying: And I want to be more like you because that's where the future is. He must suspect I am doubting what he has told me the first time our paths crossed: "*Vietnamese are Vietnamese if they believe they are.*"

[1999]

GERMAINE GREER

(1939–)

Germaine Greer, one of the founding figures of contemporary feminism, was born in Australia but has residences in England and Italy and has lived in the United States and Asia. *The Female Eunuch*, which she published in 1970, became a central work for the feminist movement. *The Obstacle Race* (1979), *The Politics of Human Fertility* (1984), *and The Change: Women, Aging, and Menopause* (1991) continued her research and polemical writing on women's roles and identities.

The essay below, written for a collection of essays on the subject of exile, is a concise meditation on the uncertainties of home as a concept and as a reality in modern history. Exile, rather than rootedness, she argues, "is the human condition."

"The Adopted Home Is Never Home"

There is an expression in English 'to make one's home' somewhere. I may be said to have made my home in England, but the English actually deny the right of the individual to make her home where she pleases. 'Do I detect an accent?' asks the optician/taxi-driver/door-to-door salesman. 'South Africa? New Zealand? Whereabouts in Australia? How long've you been over here?' I too detect an accent, an accent of smug ignorance and confident superiority. By ferreting out my accent my interlocutor reminds himself that greatly to his credit he is an Englishman, 'echt Englisch'.

I could answer that my ancestors came over with William the Conqueror. Instead, sullenly, I reply '1964' nearly 30 years ago, and I have been paying taxes ever since. Do I regard Australia as home? Yeah, I guess I do but then, like many a child sleeping in a shop doorway, I regard the happiest day of my life as the day I ran away from home. It was a long day, because I didn't stop running till I fetched up in Europe. My ancestors were born in Lincolnshire, Ulster, Eire, the Ticino and Schleswig-Holstein. I have more right to live in any of those places than I do in Australia.

Australia is, was, and ever shall be someone else's country. The British delusion that they discovered it and claimed it for the British Empire has always depended upon a nonsensical description of the continent as *Terra nullius*, empty land, theirs for the planting of a piece of coloured cloth on a stick. The empire builders knew there were people in Australia; the definition of the country as *Terra nullius* relied upon the denial of human status to those people. The British people who were sent to make their homes there were also denied human status, being criminals.

They were greatly outnumbered by the people who were forced by poverty and oppression to make the unrepeatable journey half-way round the world, many of whom died or faced greater hardship in Australia than they would have had to endure in the old country. Whether convicts, indentured servants, soldiers, agricultural labourers or mineworkers, once they were dumped in someone else's country they had no option but to make a go of it, which meant not only that they had to defend a spurious claim to the land at the expense of its real owners but that they had to carry the guilt. For the vast majority there was never the option of going home. The Australian classic novel, *The Fortunes of Richard Mahony*, has for its hero the man who tried to go home. It traces the erosion of his personality by the gradual realistion that he is permanently exiled.

Colonialism is a continuing disaster founded on a mistake. The explosion of the European people that eclipsed and displaced the African nations and imposed a long agony on the indigenous peoples of the Americas cannot be undone. Europeans may die out in Europe because of their extreme reluctance to breed in any numbers, and their genetic presence in other countries will gradually be diluted, but the disrupted populations will never be able to reclaim a homeland so fundamentally changed as to be no longer home.

Just so, the migrant's adopted home is never home but the migrant is too changed to be welcome in her old country. Only in dreams will she see the skies of home. The ache of exile cannot be assuaged by travelling anywhere, least of all by retracing old steps looking for houses that have been bulldozed and land-scapes that have disappeared under urban sprawl and motorway.

Home is the one place that you can keep strangers out of: home, like the Englishman's castle, cannot be penetrated by outsiders. Because the ideology of home justifies chauvinism and racism, it is as well that there is in creation no such place. The only unchanging place where we really will belong and all will be satisfied is heaven, and heaven cannot be brought about on earth. Failure to recognise the fact that earthly home is a fiction has given us the anguish of

Palestine and the internecine raging of the Balkans. The ideology of home primes the bombs of the PPK and the IRA; The rest of us can face the fact that our earthly journey is a journey away from home. Exile being the human condition, no government subsidy can provide the chariot that will carry us home.

[1993]

Pico Iyer

(1957–)

Pico Iyer is a writer with a truly international—rather than national—identity. The son of Indian parents, he moved to America from England; he has lived in several countries and traveled in many more. He is the author of seven books, including *Video Night in Katmandu: and Other Reports from the Not-So-Far East* (1989) and *Falling off the Map: Some Lonely Places of the World* (1993). After taking up residence in Japan, Iyer wrote *The Lady and the Monk: Four Seasons in Kyoto* (1991), an expatriate's commentary on Japanese culture.

In *Global Soul: Jet Lag, Shopping Malls, and the Search for Home* (2000), excerpted below, Iyer's combination of Asian and Western qualities excites the curiosity and suspicion of the Japanese immigration authorities so routinely that he ironically views the interrogation center as a kind of "home," symbolic of his status in a monocultural country. For Iyer, the very question "What is home?" has multiple answers.

"The Alien Home"

From *Global Soul*

I am reminded of how little I belong here—how alien I am to Japan's image of itself—each time I return to the place I like to treat as home. At the Immigration desk, the authorities generally scrutinize my passport with a discernible sense of alarm: a foreigner who neither lives nor works here, yet seems to spend most of his time here; an alien who's clearly of Asian ancestry, yet brandishes a British passport; a postmodern riddle who seems to fit into none of the approved categories.

After I've been reluctantly waved on to the customs hall, I collect my bag and park my cart in a line of obviously law-abiding Japanese tourists returning from their holidays in California. When it's my turn to be questioned, I am confronted with a customs officer who is, for some reason, always very young and uncommonly fresh-faced. He (or sometimes she) goes through the standard list of queries: where have I come from? How long will I stay? What am I doing here? Then, abruptly, he asks, "You have marijuana, heroin, LSD, cocaine?" No, I say, I don't. "You have ever had marijuana, heroin, LSD, cocaine?" he goes on, waving, now, a laminated picture of these forbidden substances. No, I say, not always able to keep a straight face. "Porno video?" No.

"Please open your bag."

At this, he pores carefully over all my belongings—the stacks of faded notes in a hand even I can't read; the scattered bottles of hotel shampoo, which have already begun to leak and deface everything in their vicinity; the Olympic pins I'm bringing for my girlfriend's children, and the elaborate set of inhalers I need to protect myself from Japan's allergy-producing cedar trees.

Then, almost inevitably, he comes upon a tiny red tablet of Sudafed antiallergy medicine. Gravely, he mutters something to a colleague. Whispers are exchanged. Then, nervously, they radio a superior, and, with brusque politeness, I am led away, by at least two officers, to a distant room. My guards look anxious and unhappy, as if they recall that the only time Paul McCartney was separated from Linda was as the result of a Japanese customs check.

In the back-room interrogation center, my home from home, I know the drill by heart, having visited so often, and proceed to take off my clothes, till I am down to my underpants. Meanwhile, as many as seven uniformed officials gingerly go through my possessions, surveying every last bottle of leaked shampoo, every last sticky Mento in my coat pocket, even the temple charm in my wallet. My shoes are shaken out, my toothbrush holder is fearfully inspected, a stick of incense is held up as if it contained cannabis

Then I am subjected to a barrage of questions. Why do I carry over-the-counter allergy pills that contain a stimulant as proscribed as LSD or cocaine? What prompted me to bring antihistamines into a peace-loving island? Will I formally consent to hand over my drugs to the Japanese authorities, and authorize a confiscation of my tablets, while signing a confession?

I am more than happy to do all of that, sometimes saying so in such amiable gibberish that the officials, fingers sticky with shampoo, tell me, "Okay, okay. You'd better leave before you miss the last train." But my answers only compound their dissatisfaction. "Where were you born?" One asks me, while another tests my case for false bottoms. "England," I say, as they scrutinize a Hideo Nomo telephone card. "No, where were you really born?" "Oxford, England," I say, "as it says on my passport." "What are you doing here?" I show them my *Time* business-card, my Time Inc. photo ID, even my name in a copy of *Time* magazine. I show them a whole book I wrote on Japan, interviews I've conducted in Japanese magazines, notes on Japanese topics I'm working up. Unhappy with this, they try a spot quiz. "Who is Masako-san? What is the importance of Kyoto? Where are you really from?"

Sometimes, sensibly enough, I have made sure that not a single antihistamine tablet could be found within a hundred-yard radius of my person. But, really, that's beside the point, since it's not my allergies that trouble them. Once, I was strip-searched for making a phone call from the customs hall, once for going to the men's room. Once, I was taken aside because my overcoat was "*abunomaru*" (I was flying to the Himalayas), and once I was even stopped as I was going out of the country ("Why is your photo so creased?" "Because so many Japanese officials have pored over it"), and the British embassy was hastily faxed on a Sunday night to authorize my departure.

What concerns the Japanese, obviously, is just that I'm a Global Soul, a full-time citizen of nowhere, and, more specifically, one who looks like exactly the kind of person who threatens to destroy their civic harmony. During the Gulf War, I was routinely treated as if I were Saddam Husssein's favorite brother; at other times, I have been detained on the grounds of resembling an Iranian (41,000 of whom have stolen into Japan and live illegally, in tent cities in Tokyo parks, or nine to a shabby guest-house room, undermining the local economy with fake telephone cards). The rest of the time, I am suspected of being what I am—an ill-dressed, dark, and apparently shiftless Indian without a fixed address.

The newly mobile world and its porous borders are a particular challenge to a uniculture like Japan, which depends for its presumed survival upon its firm distinctions and clear boundaries, its maintenance of a civil uniformity in which everyone knows everyone else, and how to work with them. And it's not always easy for me to explain that it's precisely that ability to draw strict lines around itself—to sustain an unbending sense of within and without—that draws me to Japan. In the postmodern world, to invert Robert Frost, home is the place where, when you have to go there, they don't have to take you in.

[2000]

Annie Dillard

(1945–)

Annie Dillard observes of the natural world closely and philosophically, in the manner of Thoreau. The prose of her many books and essays is distinguished by a lyrical, poetic style. *Pilgrim at Tinker Creek* (1974) is composed largely of musings inspired by the country around Roanoke Valley,

Virginia, where she lived. Among Dillard's other works are a book on writing as a vocation (*The Writing Life*, 1989) and her memoir of growing up in Pittsburgh, Pennsylvania (*An American Girlhood*, 1987).

"Sojourner," which follows, is taken from a collection of essays on travel and place, *Teaching a Stone to Talk* (1982). It begins with the image of the mangrove tree which can form small islands and exist as a kind of traveling plant. The mangrove becomes a symbol of man as nomad and exile—the "sojourner" of the title. Dillard's imaginative linking of tree, man, and the planet earth itself as wanderers takes the idea of travel to a high level of abstraction and questions the very possibility of home as permanent and fixed in a universe of constant motion and change.

"Sojourner"

From *Teaching a Stone to Talk*

If survival is an art, then mangroves are artists of the beautiful: not only that they exist at all—smooth-barked, glossy-leaved, thickets of lapped mystery—but that they can and do exist as floating islands, as trees upright and loose, alive and homeless on the water.

I have seen mangroves, always on tropical ocean shores, in Florida and in the Galápagos. There is the red mangrove, the yellow, the button, and the black. They are all short, messy trees, waxy-leaved, laced all over with aerial roots, woody arching buttresses, and weird leathery berry pods. All this angles from a black muck soil, a black muck matted like a mud-sopped rag, a muck without any other plants, shaded, cold to the touch, tracked at the water's edge by herons and nosed by sharks.

It is these shoreline trees which, by a fairly common accident, can become floating islands. A hurricane flood or a riptide can wrest a tree from the shore, or from the mouth of a tidal river, and hurl it into the ocean. It floats. It is a mangrove island, blown.

There are floating islands on the planet; it amazes me. Credulous Pliny describd some islands thought to be mangrove islands floating on a river. The people called these river islands *the dancers*, "because in any consort of musicians singing, they stir and move at the stroke of the feet, keeping time and measure."

Trees floating on rivers are less amazing than trees floating on the poisonous sea. A tree cannot live in salt. Mangrove trees exude salt from their leaves; you can see it, even on shoreline black mangroves, as a thin white crust. Lick a leaf and your tongue curls and coils; your mouth's a heap of salt.

Nor can a tree live without soil. A hurricane-born mangrove island may bring its own soil to the sea. But other mangrove trees make their own soil—and their own islands—from scratch. These are the ones which interest me. The seeds germinate in the fruit on the tree. The germinated embryo can drop anywhere—say, onto a dab of floating muck. The heavy root end sinks; a leafy plumule unfurls. The tiny seedling, afloat, is on its way. Soon aerial roots shooting out in all directions trap debris. The sapling's networks twine, the interstices narrow, and water calms in the lee. Bacteria thrive on organic broth; amphipods swarm. These creatures grow and die at the trees' wet feet. The soil thickens, accumulating rainwater, leaf rot, seashells, and guano; the island spreads.

More seeds and more muck yield more trees on the new island. A society grows, interlocked in a tangle of dependencies. The island rocks less in the swells. Fish throng to the backwaters stilled in snarled roots. Soon, Asian mudskippers—little four-inch fish—clamber up the mangrove roots into the air and peer about from periscope eyes on stalks, like snails. Oysters clamp to submersed roots, as do starfish, dog whelk, and the creatures that lie among tangled kelp. Shrimp seek shelter there, limpets a holdfast, pelagic birds a rest.

And the mangrove island wanders on, afloat and adrift. It walks teetering and wanton before the wind. Its fate and direction are random. It may bob across an ocean and catch on another mainland's shores. It may starve or dry while it is still a sapling. It may topple in a storm, or pitchpole. By the rarest of chances, it may stave into another mangrove island in a crash of clacking roots, and mesh. What it is most likely to do is drift anywhere in the alien ocean, feeding on death and growing, netting a makeshift soil as it goes, shrimp in its toes and terns in its hair.

We could do worse.

I alternate between thinking of the planet as home—dear and familiar stone hearth and garden—and as a hard land of exile in which we are all sojourners. Today I favor the latter view. The word "sojourner" occurs often in the English Old Testament. It invokes a nomadic people's sense of vagrancy, a praying people's knowledge of estrangement, a thinking people's intuition of sharp loss: "For we are strangers before thee, and sojourners, as were all our fathers: our days on the earth are as a shadow, and there is none abiding."

We don't know where we belong, but in times of sorrow it doesn't seem to be here, here with these silly pansies and witless mountains, here with sponges and hard-eyed birds. In times of sorrow the innocence of the other creatures—from whom and with whom we evolved—seems a mockery. Their ways are not our ways. We seem set among them as among lifelike props for a tragedy—or a broad lampoon—on a thrust rock stage.

It doesn't seem to be here that we belong, here where space is curved, the earth is round, we're all going to die, and it seems as wise to stay in bed as budge. It is strange here, not quite warm enough, or too warm, too leafy, or inedible, or windy, or dead. It is not, frankly, the sort of home for people one would have thought of—although I lack the fancy to imagine another.

The planet itself is a sojourner in airless space, a wet ball flung across nowhere. The few objects in the universe scatter. The coherence of matter dwindles and crumbles toward stillness. I have read, and repeated, that our solar system as a whole is careering through space toward a point east of Hercules. How I wonder: what could that possibly mean, east of Hercules? Isn't space curved: When we get "there," how will our course change, and why? Will we slide down the universe's inside arc like mud slung at a wall? Or what sort of welcoming shore is this east of Hercules? Surely we don't anchor there, and disembark, and sweep into dinner with our host. Does someone cry, "Last stop, last stop"? At any rate, east of Hercules, like east of Eden, isn't a place to call home. It is a course without direction; it is "out." And we are cast.

These are enervating thoughts, the thoughts of despair. They crowd back, unbidden, when human life as it unrolls goes ill, when we lose control of our lives or the illusion of control, and it seems that we are not moving toward any end but merely blown. Our life seems cursed to be a wiggle merely, and a wandering without end. Even nature is hostile and poisonous, as though it were impossible for our vulnerability to survive on these acrid stones.

Whether these thoughts are true or not I find less interesting than the possibilities for beauty they may hold. We are down here in time, where beauty grows. Even if things are as bad as they could posssibly be, and as meaningless, then matters of truth are themselves indifferent; we may as well please our sensibilities and, with as much spirit as we can muster, go out with a buck and wing.

The planet is less like an enclosed spaceship—spaceship earth—than it is like an exposed mangrove island beautiful and loose. We the people started small and have since accumulated a great and solacing muck of soil, of human culture. We are rooted in it; we are bearing it with us across nowhere. The word "nowhere" is our cue: the consort of musicians strikes up, and we in the chorus stir and move and start twirling our hats. A mangrove island turns drift to dance. It creates its own soil as it goes, rocking over the salt sea at random, rocking day and night and round the sun, rocking round the sun and out toward east of Hercules.

[1982]

ALFRED, LORD TENNYSON

(1809–1892)

Alfred, Lord Tennyson was a dominant literary figure during the reign of Queen Victoria (1837–1901). He often drew from myth and folklore his poetry. *Idylls of the King* (1859) is a poetic retelling of the stories of King Arthur and the Roundtable. *In Memoriam* (1850) arose from his grief over the death of a friend, Arthur Hallam.

"Ulysses," which follows, was written in the same period as *In Memoriam*. It draws on perhaps the most seminal work of travel literature in western culture, the journey home from the Trojan War chronicled in Homer's epic poem, *The Odyssey*. Ulysses (the Roman name for Odysseus, the hero of the epic) is pictured after he has returned home and the epic tale is done. Only domestic peace, old age, and death await him, and he is restless. Ulysses vows to set sail again. Travel becomes the symbol of the eternally questing human spirit, the life of action, the indomitable will "To strive, to seek, to find, and not to yield."

"Ulysses"

It little profits that an idle king,
By this still hearth, among these barren crags,
Matched with an agéd wife, I mete and dole
Unequal laws unto a savage race,
That hoard, and sleep, and feed, and know not me.   5
I cannot rest from travel; I will drain
Life to the lees. All times I have enjoyed
Greatly, have suffered greatly, both with those
That love me, and alone; on shore, and when
Through scudding drifts the rainy Hyades   10
Vexed the dim sea. I am become a name;
For always roaming with a hungry heart
Much have I seen and known—cities of men
And manners, climates, councils, governments,
Myself not least, but honored of them all—   15
And drunk delight of battle with my peers,
Far on the ringing plains of windy Troy.
I am a part of all that I have met;

Yet all experience is an arch wherethrough
Gleams that untraveled world whose margin fades   20
For ever and for ever when I move.
How dull it is to pause, to make an end.
To rust unburnished, not to shine in use!
As though to breathe were life! Life piled on life
Were all too little, and of one to me   25
Little remains; but every hour is saved
From that eternal silence, something more,
A bringer of new things; and vile it were
For some three suns to store and hoard myself,
And this gray spirit yearning in desire   30
To follow knowledge like a sinking star,
Beyond the utmost bound of human thought.
        This is my son, mine own Telemachus,
To whom I leave the scepter and the isle,—
Well-loved of me, discerning to fulfill   35
This labor, by slow prudence to make mild
A rugged people, and through soft degrees
Subdue them to the useful and the good.
Most blameless is he, centered in the sphere
Of common duties, decent not to fail   40
In offices of tenderness, and pay
Meet adoration to my household gods,
When I am gone. He works his work, I mine.
        There lies the port; the vessel puffs her sail;
There gloom the dark, broad seas. My mariners,   45
Souls that have toiled, and wrought, and thought with me,—
That ever with a frolic welcome took
The thunder and the sunshine, and opposed
Free hearts, free foreheads—you and I are old;
Old age hath yet his honor and his toil.   50
Death closes all; but something ere the end,
Some work of noble note, may yet be done,
Not unbecoming men that strove with Gods.
The lights begin to twinkle from the rocks;
The long day wanes; the slow moon climbs; the deep   55
Moans round with many voices. Come, friends,
'Tis not too late to seek a newer world.
Push off, and sitting well in order smite
The sounding furrows; for my purpose holds
To sail beyond the sunset, and the baths   60

Of all the western stars, until I die.
It may be that the gulfs will wash us down;
It may be we shall touch the Happy Isles,
And see the great Achilles, whom we knew.
Though much is taken, much abides; and though   65
We are not now that strength which in old days
Moved earth and heaven, that which we are, we are,—
One equal temper of heroic hearts,
Made weak by time and fate, but strong in will
To strive, to seek, to find, and not to yield.   70

[1860]

CONSTANTINE CAFAVY

(1863–1933)

Constantine Cafavy lived most of his life in Alexandria, Egypt. He wrote
of classical and mythological themes, reflecting the heritage of the Hel-
lenistic and Greco-Roman periods in ancient civilization. Though he did
not publish his poems, his work became popular with English readers
through translations in the 1950s. The most recent version of his work is
Before Time Could Change Them: The Complete Poems of Constantine Cafavy,
translated and edited by Theoharis C. Theoharis (2001).

The poem that follows, "Ithaca," evokes the ancient Greek city of
Ithaca that was home to Odysseus and the final destination in his epic
journey. As a metaphor for home, Ithaca also becomes a symbol of the
very origin and purpose of life's journey. In the poem, Ithaca as home is
less important as a destination than as a motivation for the journey.
Implicit in the poem is the notion that the rich experience of the journey
is of greater value than reaching its end.

"Ithaca"

As you set out toward Ithaca,
hope the way is long,
full of reversals, full of knowing.
Laistrygonians and Cyclops,
angry Poseidon you should not fear,   5

never will you find such things on your way
if your thought stays lofty, if refined
emotion touches your spirit and your body.
Laistrygonians and Cyclops,
savage Poseidon you will not meet,   10
if you do not carry them with you in your soul,
if your soul does not raise them up before you.

Hope the way is long.
May there be many summer mornings when,
with what pleasure, with what joy,   15
you shall enter first-seen harbors;
may you stop at Phoenician bazaars
and acquire the fine things sold there,
nacre and coral, amber and ebony,
and sensual perfumes, every kind there is,   20
as much as you can abundant sensual perfumes;
may you go to many Egyptian cities
to learn and learn again from those educated.

Keep Ithaca always in your mind.
Arriving there is what has been ordained for you.   25
But do not hurry the journey at all.
Better if it lasts many years;
and you dock an old man on the island,
rich with all that you've gained on the way,
not expecting Ithaca to give you wealth.   30
Ithaca gave you the beautiful journey.
Without her you would not have set out.
She has nothing more to give you.

And if you find her poor, Ithaca has not fooled you.
Having become so wise, with so much experience,   35
you will have understood, by then, what these Ithacas mean.

[From *Poems, 1900–1915*]

APPENDIX

TRAVEL AND FILM

As a supplement to the medium of print, film provides a sensual and dramatic dimension, a more immediate experience of travel. There are two main categories of movies related to travel: documentaries or travelogues, non-fictional in nature (often shown on television or as an accompaniment to a lecture by a traveler); and feature films, usually fictional in nature, in which travel or a journey is an essential part of the structure and story. Often these films are adapted from book versions.

What follows is a list of web sites for travelogues and documentaries, as well as a list of feature films, arranged alphabetically, each with a brief comment. Web sites often list travelogues by country and producer and offer full descriptions of the films and information on how to obtain them. Feature films don't usually advertise themselves as travelogues, but many movie genres may be inherently about travel—films on such subjects as adventure, sea voyages, searches and quests, chases and pursuits, international spying, war, escape, emigration, exile, and journeys home, to name a few. For the most part, I've omitted science fiction and time-travel movies, a related genre. Readers are welcome to suggest additions to either list by e-mailing me at despey@english.upenn.edu.

The web sites on travelogues and documentaries listed below have been chosen for their thoroughness of documentation and their links to related sites. Usually they include detailed descriptions of the films, photos, and even film clips, as well as information about purchase price, rentals, or lecture bookings. Often there are links to other travel web sites, with information about transportation, accommodation, sightseeing, and so on. Travelogues frequently have close ties to the travel business.

Web Sites for Travel Documentaries

There are many ways to search online for travel documentaries. One of the easiest ways to get an extensive alphabetical list is to search Google for "Travel Documentaries." Below are a number of web sites with listings for travel documentaries in DVD or VHS format.

www.discovery.com. Links to Travel Channel and daily television schedule.

www.lynximages.com/exotictravel.htm. List of PBS Travel and Nature films.

www.maps2anywhere.com/. (Click on "Travel Videos DVD.") An extensive listing of travel videos, arranged geographically and also by producers—Lonely Planet, National Geographic, Globe Trekker, Rand McNally, and so on.)

www.pbs.org/life/life_travel.html. Alphabetical listing of travel programs and destinations. Alternately, go to **www.pbs.org** and search "video index" and then "travel" for a longer but less organized list of links.

www.ricksteves.com/home.htm. Home page for Rick Steves—tourist guide, travel entrepreneur, and producer of a PBS series of travelogues.

www.shopbps.org/seeAll/index.jsp. Click on "Travel." Alphabetical index of PBS Travel Movies and Videos.

www.trailwoodfilms.com. Home page of Trailwood Films and Media, with list of travel, adventure, and wildlife documentaries.

test.travelchannel.co.uk/schedules.asp. Home page of the United Kingdom Travel Channel, with links to Europe, Africa, and Middle East.

www.travelfilms.org. Home page of the Travel Adventure Cinema Society with profiles of travel lecturers, their travelogues, and sites of travel film producers.

www.travelvideostore.com. Website with large selection of travel videos, with links to geographical destinations and specialized kinds of travel.

www.worldtravelfilms.com/videos.htm. List of travel films, arranged alphabetically by country or region, with description as well as rental and booking information.

dir.yahoo.com/Entertainment/Television_Shows/Recreation_and_Sports/Travel. A variety of links to travel sites, travel programs on television, and individual writers and producers like Michael Palin and Bill Bryson.

Feature Films Related to Travel

The feature films below are chosen especially for their relevance to the themes and issues of the anthology. The very question of why a feature film could be considered a travel film can lead to a useful discussion of the nature of travel, film, and representation. Foreign films, for example (films set in a country or region that is foreign to the viewer), are—in effect—travel experiences for the viewer. A foreign film can transport the viewer in spirit to the location and the culture of the region where the film is set. Watching a foreign film can be a kind of armchair travel and can strongly influence the viewer's assumptions and opinions about a particular country. One of the best databases for foreign films, indexed by country, genre, and languages, is www.foreignfilms.com/.

Of course, the very word "foreign" is relative. For example, much of the world outside the United States gets its impressions of this country from American films that give a limited (and frequently stereotyped) view. By the same token, films made in other countries or American films set in foreign countries can strongly influence, and often distort, an American audience's impressions of those countries. Any film represents the viewpoints and cultural perspectives of its writers, actors, and producers.

The Roman numerals at the end of each item in the list of feature films below suggest what sections in the anthology are especially related to the themes and issues in the films.

Adventure of Robinson Crusoe (1952). Best film version of the Defoe classic and archetypal travel narrative about shipwreck and desert island. Directed by Luis Bunuel.

Other versions are *Mr. Robinson Crusoe* (1932) with Douglas Fairbanks, and *Robinson Crusoe* (1998) with Pierce Brosnan. (I, II)

Adventures of Huckleberry Finn (1960). One of the best film versions of Mark Twain's novel. The other is a 1985 production of the novel for PBS. (I, II)

The African Queen (1951). A movie version of the C. S. Forester novel, in which Katherine Hepburn and Humphrey Bogart travel downriver in East Africa in World War I to combat the Germans. (II)

Amelia Earhart: The Final Flight (1994). Diane Keaton stars as the famous female aviator of the 1930s. (II)

Ariel (1988). A Finnish film about the cross-country journey of an unemployed mine worker. (III)

Around the World in 80 Days (1956). Film version of the Jules Verne novel, directed by Mike Todd. (II)

The Big Sky (1952). The Howard Hawks adaptation of the novel by A. B. Guthrie, Jr., about an expedition up the Missouri River. (II)

Black Like Me (1964). James Whitmore stars as a white man who colors his skin to pass for black and travels in the South. After the book by reporter John Howard Griffin. (III)

The Border (1982). Story concerns relations between illegal Mexican aliens and U.S. border patrolmen. With Jack Nicholson and Harvey Keitel. (III)

Bound for Glory (1976). The vagabond life of American folksinger Woody Guthrie. (III)

The Bounty (1984). Most recent version of well-known tale of nineteenth-century voyage and mutiny, with Mel Gibson and Anthony Hopkins. Earlier versions are *Mutiny on the Bounty* (1935) starring Charles Laughton, and *Mutiny on the Bounty* (1962) with Trevor Howard and Marlon Brando. (I)

Bread and Chocolate (1978). Italian film about travails of migrant workers in Switzerland. (III)

Call of the Wild (1972). After Jack London's book of the same title, about adventure, romance, and sled dogs in Alaska. Also remade several times for television. (III)

Captains Courageous (1937). Film version of Rudyard Kipling's novel of a boy's initiation into life of the sea, starring Spencer Tracy, Lionel Barrymore, and Mickey Rooney. (I)

Cold Mountain (2003). A Civil War odyssey, influenced by Homer's epic, about a veteran's desertion and return home, with Jude Law and Nicole Kidman in lead roles. After the novel by Charles Frazier. (IV)

Coming Home (1978). One of the first films about Vietnam War veterans' difficulties readjusting to the U.S., with Jane Fond and Jon Voight. (III, IV)

The Crimson Pirate (1952). One of the best of the pirate sagas, as Burt Lancaster sails the Mediterranean. (I)

Crocodile Dundee (1986). Australian hunter guides American reporter around the outback, then travels to New York. (II)

Death in Venice (1971). Film version of Thomas Mann's novella about fatal infatuation of aging artist on holiday. (III)

The Defiant Ones (1958). Sidney Poitier and Tony Curtis as two escaped convicts on the road, chained to each other. (III)

Deliverance (1972). Adaptation of James Dickey's novel about four men's terrifying canoe trip down a Georgia river. (III)

Dirty Pretty Things (2002). Harrowing contemporary tale of exiles and illegal immigrants in London. (III)

Dodsworth (1936). Adaptation of Sinclair Lewis's novel in which an American businessman faces changes on a European trip. (III)

Down to the Sea in Ships (1949). Richard Widmark and Dean Stockwell in saga of young man's rite of passage on a whaling ship. (I, II)

East-West (1999). Love of country lures Russian émigré back to disillusioning homeland. (IV)

Easy Rider (1969). Counter-cultural road saga of two motorcyclists on cross-country trip, with Peter Fonda, Dennis Hopper, and Jack Nicholson. (III)

Eboli (1979). A writer's exile in a small Italian village during the years of fascism, after *Christ Stopped at Eboli*, by Carlo Levi. (III)

The Emerald Forest (1985). American engineer searches the jungle for son kidnapped by an Amazon tribe. (III)

The Emigrants (1971). Max von Sydow and Liv Ullman in a tale of Swedish farm family who emigrate to America in the nineteenth century. (III, IV)

Emperor of the North (1973). Hobos and company police ride the rails and battle in the Northwest. Starring Lee Marvin and Ernest Borgnine. (III)

Enchanted April (1991). Mediterranean transforms English housewives (and their spouses) who vacation in Italy. (II)

The Endless Summer (1966). Documentary about surfers traveling the world in search of the best waves. *The Endless Summer II* (1994) renews the search. (II)

The English Patient (1996). Adaptation of novel set in World War II by Michael Ondaatje, with desert romance, plane crash, and evacuation to Italy. (II)

Far and Away (1992). Tom Cruise and Nicole Kidman as Irish immigrants who sail for America and go west. (II, III)

Far Horizons (1952). Fictional version of Lewis and Clark expedition. (II)

A Far Off Place (1993). Bushman guide leads city dwellers across the Australian outback, with criminals in pursuit. (II, III)

Fast Charlie, the Moonbeam Rider (1993). Cross-country motorcycle race, set in World War I era. (II)

The Fast Runner (2002). Epic journey of young Inuit man across the wilderness of northern Canada, based on a folk tale. (II, IV)

From Mao to Mozart: Isaac Stern in China (1980). Award-winning documentary about violinist's visit to China. (II)

Get on the Bus (1996). Spike Lee's fictional account of men on the way from Los Angeles to Washington as part of the Million Man March. (III)

The Gods Must Be Crazy (1981). Comedy about cultural conflicts between bushmen and whites in South Africa. Followed by *The Gods Must Be Crazy II* (1989). (III)

The Grapes of Wrath (1940). Film version of John Steinbeck's novel about migrants on the road from Oklahoma to California during the Depression. (III)

Grass (1925). Early documentary about Iranian nomads moving with their herds across forbidding terrain. (III, IV)

Green Mansions (1959). Romantic escape to Eden-like South America, after the novel by W. H. Hudson. (I)

Greystoke, Legend of Tarzan, Lord of the Apes (1984). One of the better of many versions and episodes of the Tarzan saga, after the book by Edgar Rice Burroughs. (I)

Harry and Tonto (1974). Art Carney as an old man who travels with his cat across America. (I, II,)

Hawaii (1966). Movie version of James Michener's novel about the history of missionaries in the Hawiian Islands. (III)

Heart of Darkness (1994). This version exemplifies how difficult it is to transform Joseph Conrad's classic novel into a movie. (II, III)

Hearts of Darkness: A Filmmaker's Apocalpyse (1991). Francis Ford Coppola's documentary about the monumental difficulties in making the movie *Apocalypse Now* (1979), the Vietnam War saga inspired by Conrad's novel. (II, III)

A High Wind in Jamaica (1965). Abandoned on a pirate vessel, children revert to their primitive natures. (I, II, III)

Homeward Bound: The Incredible Journey (1993). Pets (with human qualities) undertake amazing trek to rejoin family which has become separated from them. A remake of *The Incredible Journey* (1963). (IV)

If It's Tuesday, This Must Be Belgium (1969). Comedy about the dizzy itinerary of American tourists in Europe. (III)

The Inn of the Sixth Happiness (1958). Ingrid Bergman struggles to become a missionary in China. (II)

Journey of Hope (1990). The story of a Turkish family who set out for Switzerland in search of a better life. (III)

Journey through Rosebud (1972). Documentary about problems of Native Americans on South Dakota reservation. (III, IV)

Kandahar (2001). A journalist returns to her birthplace in Afghanistan. (IV)

The Killing Fields (1984). Account of one Cambodian's journey of survival though chaos of the Cambodian revolution and genocide, based on the memoir by *New York Times* journalist Sidney Schanberg. (III)

King of the Gypsies (1978). Follows the fortunes of three generations of gypsies in New York, after the book by Peter Maas. (III, IV)

King Solomon's Mines (1985). Film adaptation of H. Rider Haggard's adventure novel set in southern Africa. There are also two earlier versions from 1937 and 1950. (I)

Kings of the Road (1976). The final film in a trilogy by German director Wim Wenders about a film worker traveling along the border between East and West Germany. (III)

K–2 (1992). Film version of play by Patrick Myers, about an attempt to climb the fabled mountain in the Himalayas. (II)

Lawrence of Arabia (1962). David Lean's film about the British adventurer in the Middle East, based on T. E. Lawrence's *Seven Pillars of Wisdom*, starring Peter O'Toole. (II, III)

Lolita (1962). Film adaptation of the novel by Vladimir Nabokov, much of which takes place on the road and in motels. Remade in 1997. (III)

The Long Way Home (1997). Documentary about Jewish prisoners freed from concentration camps, seeking a homeland. (III, IV)

Lord Jim (1965). Film of Joseph Conrad's novel set in Southeast Asia, starring Peter O'Toole as the title character. (II, III)

Lord of the Flies (1963). Movie version of William Golding's novel about a group of boys who become savage after a plane crash strands them on an island. (I, III)

Lost Horizon (1937). Story of the fabled Shangri-La, the remote Himalayan world of James Hilton's novel, starring Ronald Colman and Jane Wyman. Remade in 1973. (I)

Mad Max (1979). One of a series of three movies about a post-apocalyptic road culture, starring Mel Gibson. The others are *Road Warrior* (1981) and *Mad Max Beyond Thunderdome* (1985). (III)

The Man Who Would Be King (1975). Sean Connery and Michael Caine as imperial entrepreneurs in John Huston's movie based on the story by Rudyard Kipling. (I, II)

Map of the Human Heart (1993). Tale of an Inuit boy who is taken from the Canadian wilderness to modern civilization. (III, IV)

Mediterraneo (1991). Italian film about soldiers stranded on a Greek Island during World War II and pacified, like the Lotos Eaters of *The Odyssey*. (I, II)

Midnight Cowboy (1969). Tenderfoot Jon Voight comes from the back country to hustle in New York City, then meets derelict (Dustin Hoffman), and they head for the Florida sun. (III)

The Mission (1986). Robert De Niro and Jeremy Irons as Jesuit missionaries in the jungles of eighteenth-century Brazil. (II, III)

Moby Dick (1956). Remake of 1930 version of Herman Melville's novel, with Gergory Peck as Captain Ahab. (I, III)

Molokai: The Story of Father Damien (1999). Story of the famed religious minister to a colony of lepers in the Hawaiian Islands. (III, IV)

The Moon and Sixpence (1942). Adapted from Somerset Maugham's novel about the life of the painter Paul Gauguin and his escape to Tahiti. (I, II)

Moscow on the Hudson (1984). Robin Williams as a Russian defector, trying to cope in the U.S. (III)

The Mosquito Coast (1986). Harrison Ford in the film of Paul Theroux's novel about a disgruntled inventor who takes his family to seek the good life in the jungles of Central America. (II, III)

Mountains of the Moon (1990). The story of Sir Richard Burton's nineteenth-century search for the source of the Nile River, after the biographical novel, *Burton and Speke*, by William Harrison. (II)

Mr. Hobbs Takes a Vacation (1962). Dated comedy about mishaps on family vacation, with James Stewart and Maureen O'Hara. (III)

Mr. Hulot's Holiday (1953). Jacques Tati in a humorous French classic about an eccentric vacationer at a seaside resort. (III)

My Father's Glory (1990). A boy's memories of a vacation in Provence, based on the memoirs of Maurice Pagnol. The companion film is *My Mother's Castle* (1990). (I, II)

Nanook of the North (1922). Groundbreaking ethnographic documentary about the life of the Eskimos. (IV)

National Lampoon's Vacation (1983). The first of several films that exploit the farcical potential of Chevy Chase and family vacations. Others are *National Lampoon's European Vacation* (1985) and *National Lampoon's Christmas Vacation* (1989). (III)

Never on Sunday (1960). Merlina Mercouri stars in this film about a Greek prostitute and a vacationing intellectual. It gave a great boost to Greek tourism. (II, III)

Night of the Hunter (1955). An evil Robert Mitchum pursues homeless children. (III)

The Night of the Iguana (1964). Richard Burton and Elizabeth Taylor star in this film version of a Tennessee Williams play about expatriates in Mexico. Filmed in Puerto Vallarta, it put the town on the map as a popular tourist destination. (III)

Not One Less (1999). Chinese film about a young girl, a substitute teacher for village school, who journeys to the city to find a runaway pupil. (II, III)

Not Quite Paradise (1986). International volunteers struggle with life and romance on an Israeli kibbutz. (II, III)

Nowhere in Africa (2001). A Jewish family struggles on a farm in Kenya after fleeing Germany in 1938. (III, IV)

O Brother Where Art Thou? (2000). Convicts break out of jail and make their way home with the help of music in a comedy containing numerous references to Homer's *Odyssey*. (I,II)

The Old Man and the Sea (1958). Film version of Ernest Hemingway's parable of an old Cuban fisherman battling the elements. Spencer Tracy starred in the original, Anthony Quinn in 1990 remake for television. (I)

On Any Sunday (1971). Documentary on motorcyling, with Steve McQueen, by the producer of *The Endless Summer*. Sequel is *On Any Sunday Revisited* (2000). (II)

Once in Paris (1978). Screenwriter goes to Paris to write, falls in love. (III)

Oscar and Lucinda (1997). Clergyman Ralph Fiennes and heiress Cate Blanchett gamble on transporting a glass and iron church over sea and land to wilderness. After the novel by Peter Carey. (II)

Outback (1971). Schoolteacher unhinged by encounter with the inhabitants of rural Australia. (III)

Out of Africa (1985). Robert Redford and Meryl Streep as lovers in film version of Karen Blixen's story about life on an African farm in colonial times. (IV)

Papillon (1973). Steve McQueen and Dustin Hoffman in an odyssey of escape from the notorious French prison on Devil's Island. (II, III)

Paris Blues (1961). Paul Newman and Sidney Poitier romance tourists while working as expatriate musicians in the Latin Quarter of Paris. (III)

Passage to India (1984). David Lean's film of E. M. Forster's novel about relations between English and Indians in the waning days of empire. (II, III)

Pathfinder (1988). A Norwegian film set in Finland, adapted from a Lapp folktale about a local boy who pretends to guide a group of criminals. (I, II)

Peking Opera Blues (1986). Chinese adventure film, set in 1913, about revolutionary guerillas. (II)

Powow Highway (1989). Native American road film about a Cheyenne on a pilgrimage to New Mexico with an Indian activist. (II, III)

Priest of Love (1981). A biographical narrative about perpetual traveler D. H. Lawrence and his last years in Central America and the Mediterranean. (I, II)

The Quiet Man (1952). Irish-American favorite. Yank John Wayne goes back to live in his native Ireland and becomes entangled in local marriage customs. (IV)

Rabbit-Proof Fence (2002). Three Aboriginal girls escape from a boarding school and travel 1,500 miles over Australian outback to return home. (IV)

Rain Man (1988). Tom Cruise returns home to father's funeral, then embarks on cross-country road trip with his autistic brother (Dustin Hoffman). (II, IV)

The Road Home (1999). Chinese film about businessman who returns to his native village and remembers his father's own arrival in village as schoolteacher. (IV)

Road Trip (2000). Comedy about college student who makes emergency journey to Texas to recover incriminating videotape. (II)

A Room with a View (1985). Adapted from E. M. Forster's novel about a young woman's awakening to love and sexuality on a trip to Florence, starring Helena Bonham Carter, Daniel Day Lewis, and Julian Sands. (II, IV)

The Royal Hunt of the Sun (1969). Film version of Peter Shaffer's play about the Spanish explorer Pizarro and the search for treasure in South America. (I, III)

The Sand Pebbles (1966). American gunboat runs river blockade in China to rescue missionaries during civil war in 1926. With Steve McQueen, Richard Crenna, and Candice Bergen. (II)

Sayonara (1957). From James Michener's novel about an American pilot who falls in love with a Japanese, starring Marlon Brando. (II)

Scarecrow (1973). A road film with Gene Hackman and Al Pacino as drifters who end up in Detroit. (II, III)

Scott of the Antarctic (1948). John Mills as the determined British explorer intent on reaching the South Pole. (II)

The Sea Gypsies (1978). Family adventure about sailing around the world and surviving shipwreck in Alaska. (II)

Seven Years in Tibet (1997). Brad Pitt as an Austrian mountain climber who meets the Dalai Lama and finds peace in Tibet. (II)

Shackleton (2002). Kenneth Branagh as Ernest Shackleton, leader of the 1914 expedition to the South Pole. There is also a NOVA documentary about the expedition made for PBS, *Shackleton's Voyage of Endurance* (2002). (II)

She (1935). Film version of H. Rider Haggard's adventure novel seeking mythical woman who has the power of eternal life. Remade in 1965 and 1985. (II)

The Sheltering Sky (1990). John Malkovich and Debra Winger take a nightmare journey into the Sahara in this film of the novel by Paul Bowles. (III)

Ship of Fools (1965). After Katherine Ann Porter's novel about an assorted cast of sordid shipboard characters. (III)

Siddhartha (1973). From Herman Hesse's novel about the journey and enlightenment of the Buddha. (II)

The Spirit of St. Louis (1957). James Stewart as Charles Lindbergh, making the first solo flight across the Atlantic. (II)

Stanley and Livingstone (1939). Spencer Tracy as Henry Stanley, searching in Africa for the vanished missionary, David Livingstone. (II)

Stealing Beauty (1996). An American girl comes of age during a summer in Tuscany. (II, III)

Strangers (1953). Ingrid Bergman and George Sanders as a couple who try to reconcile on a trip through Italy. (II)

Sullivan's Travels (1942). A movie director tries poverty and street life in an effort to make a film about real life. (III)

The Sun Also Rises (1957). American tourists and expatriates in Paris and Spain, drinking in cafes, romancing, and following the bullfights. From Ernest Hemingway's novel. Stars Robert Taylor, Ava Gardner, and Mel Ferrer. (III)

Swiss Family Robinson (1940). A family goes off to a desert island in this tale inspired by Robinson Crusoe. Remade in 1960. (I, II)

Tabu—A Story of the South Seas (1931). A combination of documentary, ethnography, and narrative about a Tahitian pearl fisherman. (II)

The Talented Mr. Ripley (1999). Travel provides the structure for this tale of tourism, impersonation, and murder, starring Matt Damon, after the novel by Patricia Highsmith. Other versions are *Purple Noon* (1960) with Alan Delon, *The American Friend* (1977) with Dennis Hopper, and *Ripley's Game* (2002) starring John Malkovich. (II, III)

Thelma and Louise (1991). Susan Sarandon and Geena Davis as fugitives in what becomes a women's road movie. (III)

Those Magnificent Men in Their Flying Machines (1965). London-to-Paris airplane race in the early days of aviation. (II)

Three Coins in the Fountain (1954). American women tourists in Rome find romance. (III)

The Three Musketeers (1939). Alexandre Dumas's picaresque adventure novel becomes a kind of eighteenth-century French road movie in film version. Remade many times—in 1948, 1974, and 1993. (II)

Time of the Gypsies (1989). A Yugoslav film, made in the Gypsy language of Romany, about a young gypsy's coming of age. (II, III)

Titanic (1953). The most famous tourist disaster, in the heyday of ocean liners. Starring Barbara Stanwyck and Richard Basehart. Remade in 1958 as documentary-style *A Night to Remember*, and again in 1997, with Kate Winslett and Leonard DiCaprio. (III)

Toby Tyler, or Ten Weeks with the Circus (1960). One of the most famous runaway stories, the child as traveler. (I, II)

Tom Jones (1963). Henry Fielding's picaresque novel, memorably filmed with Albert Finney and Diana York. (II)

Travels with my Aunt (1972). From Graham Greene's book about being taken all around Europe by a crazy aunt. (II)

Treasure Island (1934). First film version of Robert Louis Stevenson's adventure novel of desert islands and buried treasure. Remade in 1950 and 1972. (I, II)

The Treasure of the Sierra Madre (1948). Humphrey Bogart in John Huston's version of the B. Traven novel about the odyssey of three greedy prospectors. (II)

The Trip to Bountiful (1985). Geraldine Page as unhappy widow who leaves son's family and makes a journey to her childhood home. (IV)

The Tuttles of Tahiti (1942). Charles Laughton as father who takes family to the Eden of Tahiti. (II)

20,000 Leagues Under the Sea (1954). The best film adaptation from among Jules Vernes's many travel fantasies. (I)

Two for the Road (1967). Albert Finney and Audrey Hepburn as a couple whose marriage is reviewed in three intersecting stories about their trips to France at various times in their life. (II, III)

2001: A Space Odyssey (1968). Space travel as conceived in Arthur C. Clarke's novel, *The Sentinel*. A sequel, *2010*, appeared in 1984. (I, II)

Ulysses (1954). Kirk Douglas in an Italian film that follows the travels of Homer's epic adventurer. (I)

Under the Volcano (1984). Albert Finney as the alcoholic consul in Malcolm Lowry's expatriate novel set in Mexico. (III)

Vagabond (1985). Powerful French film about a drifter and the lives she affects. (III)

Voyage of the Damned (1976). A ship of German Jewish refugees turned back at Havana, based on a historical event. Starring Max von Sydow and Orson Welles. (III)

Voyage to the Beginning of the World (1997). Portuguese road movie about old film director, played by Marcello Mastroianni, who revisits scenes from his past. (IV)

Voyager (1991). Movie version of Max Frisch's novel *Homo Faber*, about an American drifter who relives his student days and journeys to Greece with a young woman. (III)

The Wages of Fear (1952). Yves Montand in adventure film about fugitive truck drivers making long hauls of nitroglycerin in South America. Remade as *The Sorcerers* in 1967. (II)

Walkabout (1971). A young Australian Aborigine undergoing his rite of passage by traveling alone in the outback encounters and guides two abandoned suburban children. (II, IV)

Welcome in Vienna (1986). Two Austrian Jewish refugees who have fled to America return to their homeland as soldiers near the end of World War II. The third in Alex Corti's film trilogy, which includes *God Doesn't Believe in Us Anymore* and *Santa Fe.* (III)

Welcome to Sarajevo (1997). Documentary about journalists covering the Bosnian War, concerned for orphans and refugees. (III)

Westward the Women (1951). A wagon train full of women journeys west to seek husbands on the frontier. (II)

When the Cat's Away (1996). A young French woman returning from holidays journeys through Paris in search of her lost cat. (II, IV)

Where Angels Fear to Tread (1991). Helen Mirren as widow who travels in Italy, marries an Italian, and loses her British reserve. From the novel by E. M. Forster. (II)

White Hunter, Black Heart (1990). Clint Eastwood as John Huston in Africa directing the movie *The African Queen.* Based on novel by Peter Viertel about his experiences on the original film crew. (II)

White Mischief (1988). The sordid lives of British expatriates in Kenya during the waning days of empire, after the book by James Fox. (III)

The Wind and the Lion (1975). Sean Connery as the Moroccan sheik Raisuli who kidnaps an American woman and provokes international incident. (II)

The Wizard of Oz (1939). The archetypal child's fantasy road movie, based on the novel by L. Frank Baum. (I)

Woody Guthrie: Hard Travelin' (1984). Documentary about the legendary vagabond American folk singer. (II, III)

World Traveler (2002). A man walks out on his family and tries to sort out his life by taking to the road. (I, II)

The Year of Living Dangerously (1983). Mel Gibson and Sigourney Weaver as expatriates in Sukarno's Indonesia during the failed Communist uprising and the repression. (II)

Y Tu Mama Tambien (2001). Two spoiled Mexican youths on a rite-of-passage road trip with a dying woman. (II)

Zorba the Greek (1964). Anthony Quinn as the earthy Greek peasant who guides a young Alan Bates in his venture on the island of Crete. After the novel by Nikos Kazantzakis. Even more than *Never on Sunday*, it popularized Greece and the Aegean Isles as tourist destinations. (II)

CREDITS

INDEX OF
AUTHORS AND TITLES